1,014 GRE*

Practice Questions

The Princeton Review

1,014 GRE*

Practice Questions

Neill Seltzer and the
Staff of The Princeton Review

PrincetonReview.com

Random House, Inc. New York

The Princeton Review, Inc.
2315 Broadway
New York, NY 10024
E-mail: editorialsupport@review.com

ISBN: 978-0-375-42901-9
ISSN: 1943-4855

Editors: Laura Braswell and Rebecca Lessem
Production Editor: Emma Parker
Production Coordinator: Mary Kinzel
Illustrations by: The Production Department
of The Princeton Review

Printed in the United States of America.

10   9   8   7   6   5   4   3   2   1

John Katzman, Founder
Michael J. Perik, President, CEO
Stephen Richards, COO, CFO
John Marshall, President, Test Preparation Services
Rob Franek, VP, Test Prep Books, Publisher

Editorial
Seamus Mullarkey, Associate Publisher
Laura Braswell, Senior Editor
Rebecca Lessem, Senior Editor
Selena Coppock, Editor
Heather Brady, Editor

Production Services
Scott Harris, Executive Director, Production Services
Kim Howie, Senior Graphic Designer

Production Editorial
Meave Shelton, Production Editor
Emma Parker, Production Editor

Research & Development
Christy Jehn, Managing Editor
Ed Carroll, Agent for National Content Directors
Liz Rutzel, Project Editor

Random House Publishing Team
Tom Russell, Publisher
Nicole Benhabib, Publishing Manager
Ellen L. Reed, Production Manager
Alison Stoltzfus, Associate Managing Editor

Acknowledgments

The following people deserve thanks for their help with this book: Lauren Akamine, Jonathan Arak, Forrest Bankston, Maralyssa Bann, Laura Braswell, Adam Cadre, Ed Carroll, Vanessa Coggshall, Joe Consiglio, Cynthia Cowan, Adam Davis, Cathy Evans, John Fulmer, Peter Hanink, Christopher Hinkle, Dara Hogue, Karen Hoover, Kim Howie, Jary Juliano, Kimberly Kendal, John Kim, Stephen Klosterman, Anna Konstantatos, Rebecca Lessem, Sionainn Marcoux, Joan Martin, Melanie Martin, John Massari, Mike Matera, Lisa Mayo, Seamus Mullarkey, Aaron Murray, Andrew Nynka, Abolaji Ogunshola, Jerome O'Neill, Emma Parker, Emillie Parrish, Adam Perry, Doug Pierce, Nicole-Henriett Pirnie, Krista Prouty, Debbi Reynolds, Lisa Rothstein, Liz Rutzel, Meave Shelton, David Stoll, Phil Thomas, Scott Thompson, Kerry Thornton, Shawn Waugh, David Weiskopf, Jonathan Weitzell, Sarah Woodruff, and David Zharkovsky.

A special thanks to Neill Seltzer for conceptualizing this book from start to finish, and to Graham Sultan for helping those conceptions become a reality.

A very special thanks to Adam Robinson, who conceived of and perfected the Joe Bloggs approach to standardized tests and many of the other successful techniques used by The Princeton Review.

Contents

Introduction

SO YOU'VE DECIDED TO GO TO GRAD SCHOOL...

Much like the SAT that you probably took to get into college, the GRE, or the Graduate Record Exam as it is officially known, is required for admission to many graduate programs. GRE test takers include future engineers, historians, philosophers, psychologists, nurses; even veterinarians. In short, the GRE is used by almost all graduate programs except medical school, law school, and business school. It may seem odd that a student who is applying for an advanced degree in architecture must take the same exam that a student applying for a degree in comparative literature does. In many respects, it is. The GRE, like the SAT, purports to test aptitude instead of specific knowledge of a subject. Depending on what grad school program you are going to, you might also have to take a GRE subject exam.

Some programs simply have a minimum combined score that all applicants must achieve. Others, such as creative writing programs, care far more about the Verbal score than they do about the Math. One would think that engineering programs would care more about the Math score (and some do), but most engineering applicants score in the very highest percentiles on the GRE quantitative section. Therefore Verbal scores, not Math scores, become more effective when comparing one candidate to another.

If you are frustrated that the skills you need for the GRE bear little resemblance to the subjects you will be studying in grad school, remember three things:

1. The GRE is not a content test. It does not test a body of knowledge, such as U.S. History or French. It is designed to test a very specific way of thinking.
2. Taking the GRE is a skill, and like any other skill, it can be learned. That is what this book and *Cracking the GRE* are all about. With diligence and practice, you can learn everything you need to know for the GRE in a surprisingly short period of time.
3. The GRE is only one factor of many that will be considered for admission, and it is often the easiest to change.

HOW MUCH DOES THE GRE MATTER?

The simple answer is: It depends. Some programs consider the GRE very important, and others view it as more of a formality. Because the GRE is used for such a wide range of graduate studies, the relative weight given to it will vary from field to field and from school to school. A master's program in English Literature will not evaluate the GRE the same way that a Ph.D. program in physics will, but it's hard to predict what the exact differences will be. A physics department may care more about the Math score than the Verbal score, but given that nearly all of its applicants will have high Math scores, a strong Verbal score might make you stand out and help you gain admission.

How schools weigh the scores will differ not only from school to school but also from student to student. Schools may use GRE scores to validate the verbal abilities of international students who wrote fantastic essays. They may also be used in lieu of work experience for applicants who are only a year or two out of undergrad, or as a more recent snapshot for adult students returning to school after a decade or so. Mostly they are there so that schools have an apples-to-apples comparison of applicants with wildly divergent college, work, and life experiences. Also, most applicants are pretty qualified, so GRE scores are often an easy way to narrow down the pool.

How your program uses your scores will determine quite a bit about how you prepare for the test.

The best way to find out how your GRE score will be weighted is to contact the programs that you're thinking about applying to and ask them. Speak directly with someone in your prospective graduate department. Contrary to what many people think, grad schools are usually quite willing to tell you how they evaluate the GRE and other aspects of your application, and they might just give you an idea of what they're looking for.

In any case, remember that the GRE is only one part of an application to grad school. Many other factors are considered, such as:

- undergraduate transcripts (i.e., your GPA, relevant courses, and the quality of the school you attended)
- work experience
- any research or work you've done in that academic field
- subject GREs (for certain programs)
- essays (Personal Statements or other essays)
- recommendations
- interviews

The GRE can be a significant part of your graduate school application (which is why you bought this book), but it certainly isn't the only part.

Don't worry about getting a good or bad GRE score. There is only the score you have and the score you need to get to go where you want to go. The gap between the two represents the amount of work you will have to do in the meantime. If you need an additional 50 points, that shouldn't be too difficult to achieve. Polish up on your vocabulary, master the pacing of the exam, take some practice tests, and you should do fine. If you need another 100 points, that will take some more work. You'll need to learn more vocabulary, identify and address your weaknesses on the quantitative section, and continue to practice. If you can push yourself to do that on your own, then this book and access to a few practice tests should be all you need. If you need more than 100 points, or if you aren't likely to put in the time on your own, you will need a course or a tutor. It all starts with the research. Once you know the score you have and the score you need, you will know how much time you need to put in to prepare for the real test.

THE TEST—OVERVIEW

There are four primary sections on the GRE: Analytical Writing, Verbal, Quantitative, and "Pretest." The Pretest is typically a third experimental, unscored quantitative or Verbal section masquerading as a scored one. Here is the breakdown:

Section	Number of Questions	Time
Analytical Writing	1 Issue task	45 min.
	1 Argument task	30 min.
Verbal	30	30 min.
Quantitative	28	45 min.
Experimental	Varies	Varies

The total testing time is approximately 3 hours and 15 minutes, but the whole experience will take about 4 hours. When you are taking practice tests, make sure to complete all sections—even the essays—because stamina is an issue. Knowing how your brain works after two to three hours of intense concentration is big part of being prepared.

When You Get There

The testing centers can be intimidating places. You will be asked to show ID when you come in. You will be issued a locker where you can store your belongings, because you cannot bring anything with you into the test center. Then you will be asked to fill out a questionnaire and a legal disclaimer stating that you are who you say you are and that your reasons for taking the test are on the up and up; no taking it just for fun! The test centers cater to people taking a wide variety of tests, which means that you will be sitting in a very plain waiting room with a bunch of other fidgety, stressed-out people until you are called to the testing room.

In the testing room you will be issued a cubicle with a computer, six sheets of scratch paper, two pencils, and a set of headphones that you can use to block out noise. In the beginning of the test you will be given a tutorial on how to work the computer (scrolling, clicking with the mouse, accepting answers, etc). If you have taken a few practice tests, you'll already know what to do. Save yourself time and skip the section.

The Test Itself

The first section is the 45-minute Analysis of an Issue essay. You will be given a choice between two issue topics. The clock starts as soon as the two topics appear on screen. A complete list of the issue topics can be found on the ETS website under GRE—General Test—Test Preparation—Sample Questions. The test has a basic word processing function that will allow you to cut, paste, erase, and scroll. It does not have a spell check, but spelling is not scored on the GRE, so don't worry about it.

The second section is the 30-minute Analysis of an Argument essay. You get only one Argument, so you don't get to choose. A complete list of potential arguments can be found on the ETS website in the place mentioned above. You will be offered an optional 10-minute break after you complete your second essay. Take as much time as you need to refresh yourself, but the more time you take, the longer you'll be stuck in your cubicle. Technically, you are not allowed to use your scratch paper during untimed sections, but this is not always enforced, so you can start setting up your scratch paper if you want. (More on this later.)

After the essays, most students will have three multiple-choice sections with one minute between each section. You cannot skip questions or go back to a question once you have entered and accepted an answer.

All three sections will look like typical Verbal or Math sections, but only two of the three will count. The experimental section may be either Math or Verbal and may come first, second, or third. Occasionally ETS will identify the experimental section if it steps too far outside of the standard format so as to not confuse those who are taking the test. For the most part, the experimental section is used to gather data on new questions so that they can be added to the general pool of scored questions.

There may also be an optional Research section. If present, it will come after the multiple choice sections. ETS will attempt to bribe you with a chance at winning a small scholarship ($500) toward your grad school tuition. Unless you are a particularly generous soul, don't bother.

SCORING

After you have taken the scored portion of the exam, you will be given the opportunity to cancel your scores. Unless you passed out mid-section, left five to ten questions blank, or started hallucinating while on the clock, there is not much to be gained from canceling your scores. Your test fee is non-refundable. If you cancel, you will never know how you did. Your record will reflect that you took the test on this day, but that you cancelled your scores. You should find out how the program you want to attend will deal with multiple scores. Unless you have a compelling reason to believe that your scores were a disaster, accept them.

Once you accept your scores, you will see your Math and Verbal scores only. Writing scores and percentiles will come about ten days later in the mail. You must turn in your scratch paper and collect your ID on your way out.

Some schools look only at the most recent scores, while others combine scores, but most prefer to accept the highest. The CAT (Computer Adaptive Test) is not like any other test most students have taken. People don't often do their best the first time they take it. They tend to do better the second time, even if it is only a week or two later, because they are more comfortable and more relaxed. Practice tests can make a world of difference.

In addition to the dubious honor of contributing to ETS's research and development, your registration fee also buys you score reporting for up to four schools. This will be the last section of your test. Later, if you wish to have scores sent to schools, ETS will charge you approximately $15 per school. Some students are reluctant to send scores to first-choice schools before knowing their scores. Send the scores anyway. If you are planning to apply to a particular school, that school will see all of your prior scores, even if you take the test five times. If you don't apply, they'll put the scores in a file, and after a year or two, they'll throw them away. If you happen to know the school and department code for the schools of your choice, this part will go a bit faster. If not, no problem, you will have to negotiate a series of drop-down menus by state, school, and department.

Taking the GRE is a long and grueling process. The more you have prepared, the less stressed you will feel on test day. Every Math or Verbal concept that you might see on the test is contained in this book. For the well prepared student, there should be no surprises on test day. You should know precisely what your target score is and how to achieve it.

What Does a GRE Score Look Like?

You will receive separate Verbal and Quantitative scores. They are reported on a scale from 200 to 800, and they can rise or fall by multiples of ten. The third digit is thus always a zero—you can't receive a score of 409 or 715 on a section of the GRE. Your Analytical Writing section will be listed separately, and it is scored on a scale of 0–6 in half-point increments.

Here's a look at the percentile rankings of different GRE scores. Percentile rankings tell you what percent of test takers scored beneath a given score. For example, a 620 in Verbal corresponds to the 88th percentile; this means that 88 percent of test takers scored *below* 620 on the Verbal section.

Score	Math Percentile	Verbal Percentile	Score	Math Percentile	Verbal Percentile
800	94	99	500	26	60
780	89	99	480	23	54
760	85	99	460	20	48
740	80	99	440	17	43
720	75	98	420	14	37
700	70	97	400	12	31
680	66	95	380	10	25
660	61	93	360	8	20
640	57	91	340	6	15
620	52	88	320	5	10
600	47	85	300	3	5
580	42	81	280	2	3
560	38	76	260	2	1
540	34	70	240	1	1
520	30	65	220	1	

OTHER RESOURCES

In addition to this book, you have some other worthwhile resources to consider.

Princeton Review.com contains one full-length free CAT test and a free online course demo. It also contains e-mail tips for test takers and Word du Jour to help with your vocabulary.

Cracking the GRE—While this book is primarily about providing additional practice items for each subject, *Cracking the GRE* is like a full course in your hands. It contains all of the strategies, tips, and advice that have the made The Princeton Review the best standardized test preparation company in the world.

GRE Verbal Workout—*Verbal Workout for the GRE* gives you everything you need to tackle the Verbal portion of the GRE test. It includes hundreds of practice exercises to sharpen your skills.

Word Smart for the GRE—This book highlights defines and breaks down the words that are most frequently tested on the exam. There are also quizzes and secondary definitions to help you avoid test tricks and traps.

HOW TO USE THIS BOOK

This book is about building good test-taking habits, not about finding answers.

Over four hours of testing, your brain will get tired, and you will begin to do things by habit without thinking about them actively. If your habits are good, they will help carry you even when your brain starts to check out. If you have not taken the time to create good test-taking habits, you will just get sloppy, and sloppiness will kill your score.

The creation of habits requires repetition, and that's where this book comes in. Practice your approach to different question types. Then, time and large score fluctuations will cease to be an issue. There will be no such thing as having a good or bad test day. You will be in control, and you will have your scores right where you want them.

1. Take the Assessment

Start by taking the Math and Verbal assessment tests provided at the beginning of the book. Check your scores and find your areas of weakness. Pick two or three areas to focus on. The number of questions in a drill represents the frequency with which the question type shows up on most CAT exams. Start with the high frequency topics and focus on those first.

2. Learn Our Strategies

Each question type begins with a brief synopsis of the basic approach. Read these sections carefully. These approaches have been tried, tested, and refined by hundreds of test takers over the years. They are here because they work and represent good habits. How does the approach described by the book differ from your own? Can yours be improved? Some of the new techniques may feel awkward at first, but they're there because they work.

3. Practice Our Strategies

Start working on the drills in this book. Use your scratch paper, stick to your approach, and drill until it becomes habit. By the time you are done, every time a question of that type pops up, your hand and your mind will know instinctively what to do, no matter how tired you get. This is a powerful tool.

What You Won't Find in This Book

If you are just starting your GRE prep, need more than 50–60 points, or don't yet have an approach, this book is not the place to start. This book is not for teaching. It is a workbook for practice and drilling. *Cracking the GRE* describes the test and the techniques in much more depth. It breaks down the approach to each question in a step-by-step manner with plenty of examples. *Cracking the GRE* is where you go to learn *how* to take the test; this book is where you go to *practice* taking it.

STRATEGIES

Now that you know a little about the test and the book, let's review a few quick strategies.

Pacing

Here's how it works. When you sit down at the computer, your potential score could be anything between 200 (the lowest) and 800 (the highest). The computer doesn't know your potential, so it throws an average question at you. If you get it right, it assumes that you must be an above-average test taker. Therefore, it automatically assigns you a harder question. At the same time, it narrows down your potential scoring range, because now it has some data. You can no longer get a 200, but an 800 is still in range. By answering the first question correctly, you have just bumped yourself into a higher scoring bracket.

If you answer the second question correctly, the process continues. In fact, every time you answer a question, correctly or incorrectly, the computer adjusts its assumptions and assigns you another question, so it can gather more data. The additional data allows it to narrow your potential scoring range. By the time you get to the end of the test, the computer has lots of data (all cross-referenced with that of other test takers), and your potential scoring range, at this point, is quite narrow. By the time you get to the end of the test, the computer is just fine-tuning; a correct or incorrect answer won't have all that much impact.

While the actual algorithms used in scoring the test can get quite complicated, there is really only one central fact that you should take away from this description of the test. Questions at the beginning of the test have an enormous impact on your score, while questions at the end have very little. Strategically, this means that you need to go as slowly as necessary to ensure that you get the first ten to twelve questions correct. If that means that you run out of time at the tail end, so be it. Speed kills on the GRE. **In the first half of the test, accuracy is everything.**

Of course there are a few caveats to this system. If you got a question right, then a question wrong, then one right, then one wrong, and so on for a stretch of six questions in the middle of the test, the questions would cancel each other out, and your score would not change significantly. If you got those same three questions wrong in a row, however, you would have sent your score into a negative trend, thereby negatively impacting your final score. If you guess on one question, pay particular attention to the next one.

The last wrinkle to this system is that leaving blanks at the end of the test counts against you more than wrong answers do. When you are down to your last three minutes, stop trying to solve problems. Simply eliminate one or two obvious wrong answers per question and guess. If time gets really tight and you still have questions left, pick one letter and use it as your answer for all remaining questions, so that you have responded to every item before time runs out.

Summary:

- The first ten questions are all about accuracy. Work slowly and carefully. Accuracy is more important than time.
- If you know you guessed on the prior question, pay particularly close attention to the next one.
- If you are running out of time, select one letter for all remaining items rather than leave questions blank.

HOW TO USE SCRATCH PAPER

After pacing, the next important skill on the GRE is the use of your scratch paper. On a paper and pencil test, you can solve problems right on the page. On the GRE CAT, you don't have that luxury.

Proper use of scratch paper ensures that techniques are happening and happening correctly. It can help you deal with a question that you might not otherwise know how to approach, protect against careless errors, have a remarkable effect on efficiency, and relieve an enormous amount of the mental stress that occurs during testing.

On the Verbal section, the scratch paper has two primary functions: It allows you to park your thinking on the page and to keep track of which answer choices are still in and which are out. Quickly evaluate each answer choice with a check for one that could work, an X for one that will not, an M or horizontal squiggle for a maybe, and a question mark for one you do not know.

By parking your thinking on the page you create clarity and organization, both of which lead to less stress, less mental effort, and ultimately less mental fatigue. Students who do the work in their heads will spend 20 percent of their time just looking at the screen, keeping track of what is in or out.

On the Math section, there are a few question types that provoke very specific set-ups on your scratch paper. Keep your page organized with space on one side for the question set-up and space on the other side for calculations. Once you see the question type, make your set ups and start filling in information. When you have completed a question, draw a horizontal line across the page and start the next one in a clean space. Now you have organized your thinking and approach and set yourself up to succeed on the problem. This is stress-free living on the GRE CAT. It all starts with the scratch paper.

On the Verbal, use your scratch paper as a place to park your thinking. Once you have evaluated each answer choice, select from the ones that remain and move on.

Learn the set-ups for each question type. Do your work on the page. If you get off track, you will be able to find out why and where.

On the Verbal, do not be afraid to use the maybe sign. Before you spend ten minutes scratching your head trying to assess a difficult answer choice, give it the maybe. You can always spend more time on an answer choice IF you have to, but you never want to spend more time than you have to.

POE (PROCESS OF ELIMINATION)

POE means finding (and eliminating) all the wrong answers you can. Eliminating one or two obviously incorrect answers can increase your chances of choosing the correct answer. Eliminate three incorrect choices, and you have a fifty-fifty chance of earning points by guessing! You have to answer each question to get to the next one, and if you have to guess, why not improve your odds?

Verbal Strategies

There are four types of questions in the Verbal portion of the test. They are Analogies, Antonyms, Reading Comprehension, and Sentence Completions. You will have 30 minutes to answer 30 questions. Within the first ten problems, you are guaranteed to see at least a couple of each question type.

The Verbal portion of the GRE is one giant vocabulary test. The more words you know, the better you will do. Learning giant lists of vocabulary words is an inefficient process, because only a tiny portion of those words will actually show up on the test. Learning new words, however, is never bad and is one of the few aspects of this process that has lasting value. The five hundred words in this book have been selected for the frequency with which they appear on the GRE. Of the five hundred words you will learn, four might appear on the test you take. Because they are difficult words, however, they are likely to show up on questions where knowing them is the difference between getting that question right or wrong.

No one knows all of the words on the GRE. That means Process of Elimination is critical. This is where scratch paper comes in handy. Use your techniques to give each word a check, a squiggle, an x, or a question mark, and then move on. Use scratch paper for your POE work. If your hand is moving, you are actively assessing and eliminating answer choices; you are parking that thinking on the page.

On average, you have one minute per question. A Reading Comprehension question, however, may take two, three, or even four minutes. One way to improve your score is to get good at Analogies, Sentence Completions, and Antonyms, so that you have plenty of time left to devote to Reading Comprehension.

With good technique, none of the Sentence Completions, analogies, or antonyms should take more than 30–40 seconds. The drilling ensures that you are getting the maximum number of points that your vocabulary will allow and that you are doing the problems in the most efficient way possible. Once this is done you can relax and spend plenty of time on Reading Comprehension, where speed can lead to the greatest number of mistakes.

Math Strategies

In the Math portion of the test, you will have 45 minutes to answer 28 questions. Math questions come in four basic formats: Charts, Problem Solving, Quantitative Comparisons, and Numeric Entry.

- Charts are just that: They give information in charts, graphs, or tables and ask for information (often percentages). Just as you do on Reading Comprehension, you will have a split screen and multiple questions (usually two or three) that refer to the same set of charts.
- Problem Solving questions resemble the standard five-answer multiple choice questions that you might remember from the SAT.
- Quantitative Comparisons—also known as Quant Comps—give information in two columns. You are asked to identify if one quantity is bigger, if both quantities are always the same, or if there is not enough information to determine which column is bigger. These have only four answer choices.
- Numeric Entry questions are new to the GRE, and they are not multiple choice. The concepts are the same as elsewhere on the test, but you must supply your own answer.

Here is a brief description of some general techniques that apply to the Math section as a whole. Techniques that relate to specific question types will be discussed at the top of each drill. These are brief descriptions, so for a more in depth look at the techniques and practice problems, use *Cracking the GRE*.

Calculating

In general, ETS is not interested in testing your ability to do lots of calculations. Therefore, if you find yourself doing extensive calculations on a particular question, you are probably off track. Often you can calculate your way to the correct answer if necessary, but usually there is a better way. Your success depends upon how quickly and readily you can spot the opportunities for shortcuts and eliminate wrong answers.

Reading

In many ways, the Math portion of the test is as much a test of reading as the Verbal portion. When you see a large block of text, break it down into bite-sized pieces and solve the problem one step at a time. Skipping or combining steps leads to trouble. Use your pencil to follow along with the text on the screen as you're reading. Reading too quickly leads to careless errors, which will hurt your score.

Ballparking

Ballparking is the use of approximation to more easily spot the wrong answers. First, you can Ballpark by rounding off the numbers to make a calculation simpler. This saves time and reduces the chances for careless error. In order to Ballpark, you need to understand what the question is asking. Make sure to park your thinking and your Ballparked answers on paper.

Ballparking is also a valuable way to check your work, because it helps you eliminate answers that don't make sense. The correct answer to a question which asks for the number of students in a class will not contain a fraction. (ETS won't generally chop a student in half.) A question in which a person bicycles uphill one way and downhill on the way home will not involve a distance greater than the distance a person could or would bike to work in a day. Ballparking won't necessarily eliminate four out of five wrong answers (although it could), but it will eliminate a few incorrect answers, and it will tell you whether the answer you came up with actually makes sense.

Let's try some examples.

Four containers of flour are on the table: The first contains $\frac{1}{3}$ of a pound, the second contains $\frac{1}{6}$ of a pound, the third contains $\frac{1}{9}$ of a pound, and the fourth contains $\frac{1}{18}$ of a pound. If each container can hold one pound of flour, how many additional pounds of flour are required to fill all four containers?

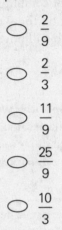

○ $\frac{2}{9}$

○ $\frac{2}{3}$

○ $\frac{11}{9}$

○ $\frac{25}{9}$

○ $\frac{10}{3}$

The question is asking for how many pounds of flour are required to fill the four containers. The first container requires $\frac{2}{3}$ of a pound more flour, the second $\frac{5}{6}$, the third $\frac{8}{9}$, and the fourth $\frac{17}{18}$. Simplify the calculation by rounding off the fractions. The fractions $\frac{5}{6}, \frac{8}{9}$, and $\frac{17}{18}$ are all very close to one, so round those up and your calculation becomes $\frac{2}{3} + 1 + 1 + 1$. Thus, the answer will about 3.5. The only answer that is even close is choice (E).

Paul drives from his apartment to his parents' house and back. On the trip to his parents' house, he travels at an average speed of 60 miles per hour. On the return trip, Paul drives at an average speed of 80 miles per hour. Which of the following is the closest approximation of Paul's average speed, in miles per hour, for the round trip?

- ○ 60.0
- ○ 68.6
- ○ 70.0
- ○ 71.4
- ○ 80.0

Combine elimination of trap answers with Ballparking. Eliminate choice (C) as a trap answer because it's too obvious. Now use Ballparking to eliminate some more answer choices. You know that the average speed should be somewhere near 70 mph even though that's not exactly the answer. That helps you eliminate choices (A) and (E) because you are looking for the average. Now think about the time spent on each leg of the trip. Going to his parents' house, Paul spends more time driving at 60 mph than at 80 mph. Thus, the overall average speed will be weighted on the side of 60; the answer is 68.6. If you have to make a guess, at the very least, you have a 50/50 shot on a tough question.

1. Double-check before you choose an answer that was "too easy" on a difficult question.

2. When you get stuck on a tough question, eliminate the predictable trap answers before you guess.

Now that you have the basic strategies, let's move on to the drills so you can put them to use!

Drills

Diagnostic Test

MATH DRILL

$$y \neq 0$$

Column A	Column B
$175y^2$	$-\dfrac{y^2}{7}$

○ The quantity in Column A is greater.
○ The quantity in Column B is greater.
○ The two quantities are equal.
○ The relationship cannot be determined
   from the information given.

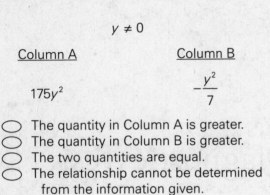

Column A	Column B
$\sqrt{8}$	The length of line segment *PR*

○ The quantity in Column A is greater.
○ The quantity in Column B is greater.
○ The two quantities are equal.
○ The relationship cannot be determined
   from the information given.

The "hash" of a three-digit integer with three
distinct integers is defined as the result of
interchanging its units and hundreds digits.
The absolute value of the difference between
a three-digit integer and its hash must be
divisible by

○ 9
○ 7
○ 5
○ 4
○ 2

Column A	Column B
$35{,}043 \times 25{,}430$	$35{,}430 \times 25{,}043$

○ The quantity in Column A is greater.
○ The quantity in Column B is greater.
○ The two quantities are equal.
○ The relationship cannot be determined
   from the information given.

$$a = (17)^4$$

Column A	Column B
1	The units digits of *a*

○ The quantity in Column A is greater.
○ The quantity in Column B is greater.
○ The two quantities are equal.
○ The relationship cannot be determined
   from the information given.

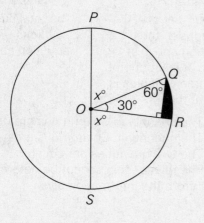

In the circle with center O above, $PS = 8$. If $x = 75$, then what is the perimeter of the shaded region?

○ $6 - 2\sqrt{3}$

○ $\dfrac{2\pi}{3}$

○ $\dfrac{2\pi}{3} + 8$

○ $\dfrac{2\pi}{3} - 2\sqrt{3} + 6$

○ $\dfrac{2\pi}{3} + 2\sqrt{3} + 6$

x and y are positive numbers.

Column A	Column B
$\sqrt{x} - \sqrt{y}$	$\sqrt{x - 2\sqrt{xy} + y}$

○ The quantity in Column A is greater.
○ The quantity in Column B is greater.
○ The two quantities are equal.
○ The relationship cannot be determined from the information given.

The positive sequence $s_1, s_2, s_3 \dots s_n \dots$ is defined by $s_n = s_{n-1} + 5$ for $n \geq 2$. If $s_1 = 7$, then the nth term in the sequence is

○ $5n - 5$
○ $5n - 2$
○ $5n$
○ $5n + 2$
○ $5n + 7$

Column A	Column B
The least prime factor of 7^2	The least prime factor of 2^7

○ The quantity in Column A is greater.
○ The quantity in Column B is greater.
○ The two quantities are equal.
○ The relationship cannot be determined from the information given.

The average (arithmetic mean) of a, b, c, and d is 7.

Column A	Column B
15	The average (arithmetic mean) of $4a - 5c$, $b - 24$, $8c - a$, and $3d + 2b$

○ The quantity in Column A is greater.
○ The quantity in Column B is greater.
○ The two quantities are equal.
○ The relationship cannot be determined from the information given.

In the figure above, the width of the larger square is equal to the diagonal (not shown) of the smaller square.

Column A	Column B
The area of the smaller square	The area of the shaded region

○ The quantity in Column A is greater.
○ The quantity in Column B is greater.
○ The two quantities are equal.
○ The relationship cannot be determined from the information given.

If $x = 3^2$, then what is the value of x^x ?

○ 3^4
○ 3^8
○ 3^9
○ 3^{12}
○ 3^{18}

x, y, and z are positive integers such that $x + y + z = 10$.

Column A	Column B
The number of solutions of the equation above in which at least one of the three variables is greater than 3	The total number of solutions of the equation above

○ The quantity in Column A is greater.
○ The quantity in Column B is greater.
○ The two quantities are equal.
○ The relationship cannot be determined from the information given.

Questions 14–15 refer to the following graphs.

INCOME OF CLUB *G* BY SOURCE IN 2002
(total income = $17,000,000)

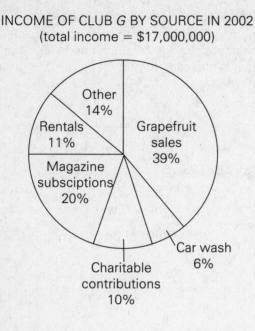

MEMBERSHIP OF CLUB *G*, 1995–2003

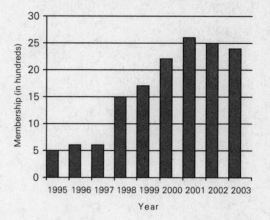

What was the approximate average (arithmetic mean) membership for the years 1997 through 2001, inclusive?

◯ 600
◯ 1,300
◯ 1,500
◯ 1,700
◯ 2,500

If income from grapefruit sales decreased 45 percent from 2002 to 2003, then which of the following represents income from grapefruit sales in 2003 ?

◯ $\dfrac{0.39}{0.45}\left(\$17,000,000\right)$

◯ $\dfrac{0.39}{1.55}\left(\$17,000,000\right)$

◯ $\dfrac{0.39}{0.55}\left(\$17,000,000\right)$

◯ $\left(1.45\right)\left(0.39\right)\left(\$17,000,000\right)$

◯ $\left(0.55\right)\left(0.39\right)\left(\$17,000,000\right)$

$$11 < y < 17$$

Column A	Column B
$\dfrac{y + 17}{y}$	$\dfrac{y + 11}{11}$

○ The quantity in Column A is greater.
○ The quantity in Column B is greater.
○ The two quantities are equal.
○ The relationship cannot be determined from the information given.

Column A	Column B
1.07	$\dfrac{1}{1 - 0.07}$

○ The quantity in Column A is greater.
○ The quantity in Column B is greater.
○ The two quantities are equal.
○ The relationship cannot be determined from the information given.

To fill a larger concert hall, a madrigal singing group consisting of sopranos, altos, and basses, in a 5:7:3 ratio, needs 40 singers. What is the least number of basses the group will need?

If $mx + qy - nx - py = 0$, $p - q = 2$, and $\dfrac{y}{x} = -\dfrac{1}{3}$, then which of the following is true?

○ $n - m = \dfrac{2}{3}$

○ $n - m = -\dfrac{2}{3}$

○ $m + n = \dfrac{2}{3}$

○ $m + n = \dfrac{3}{2}$

○ $m + n = -\dfrac{3}{2}$

Questions 20–21 refer to the following graphs.

SENIOR MANAGEMENT OF COMPANY Y

Average Salaries of Senior Managers at Company Y

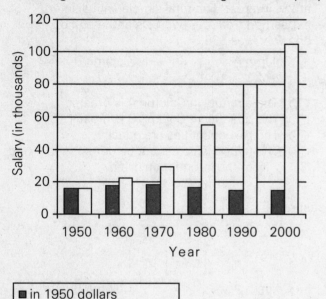

■ in 1950 dollars
□ in actual-year dollars

Number of Senior Managers at Company Y

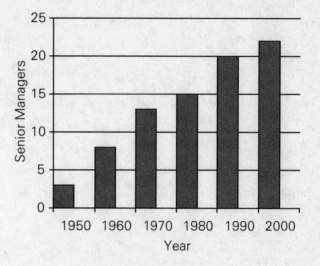

If from 1980 to 2007, the number of senior managers increased by 60 percent, then what was the increase in the number of senior managers from 2000 through 2007, inclusive?

- ⬭ 2
- ⬭ 4
- ⬭ 6
- ⬭ 9
- ⬭ 12

Which of the following can be inferred from the data?

I. From 1990 to 2000, the average salary, in 1950 dollars, increased by more than 10%.
II. In 1960, there were fewer than 5 senior managers.
III. For the decades shown, the number of senior managers increased by the greatest percentage between 1980 and 1990.

- ⬭ None
- ⬭ I only
- ⬭ II only
- ⬭ II and III only
- ⬭ I, II, and III

The volume of a cube with edge of length 2 is how many times the volume of a cube with edge of length $\sqrt{2}$?

○ $\sqrt{2}$

○   2

○ $2\sqrt{2}$

○   4

○   8

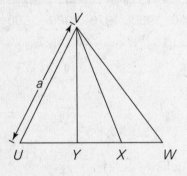

In equilateral triangle UVW, Y is the midpoint of line segment UW and X is the midpoint of line segment YW.

Column A	Column B
$\dfrac{7}{4}a$	The perimeter of $\triangle VXY$

○   The quantity in Column A is greater.
○   The quantity in Column B is greater.
○   The two quantities are equal.
○   The relationship cannot be determined from the information given.

Mr. Sjogren deposited a total of $2,000 in two different CDs. He deposited x dollars in one CD at 1% interest and y dollars in another CD at 2% interest. The total simple annual interest earned from the two CDs at the end of one year was $25.

Column A	Column B
x	y

○   The quantity in Column A is greater.
○   The quantity in Column B is greater.
○   The two quantities are equal.
○   The relationship cannot be determined from the information given.

$$|x-y| = |x-z| - |y-z|$$

Column A	Column B
$|x|$	$|y|$

○   The quantity in Column A is greater.
○   The quantity in Column B is greater.
○   The two quantities are equal.
○   The relationship cannot be determined from the information given.

Rachel and Rob live 190 miles apart. They both drive in a straight line toward each other to meet for tea. If Rachel drives at 50 mph and Rob drives at 70 mph, then how many miles apart will they be exactly 45 minutes before they meet?

- ○ 50
- ○ 60
- ○ 70
- ○ 90
- ○ 100

BILLIE'S TIME SHEET FOR JULY 2

Time in:	8:57 in the morning
Time out:	5:16 in the afternoon
Time spent stacking shelves:	80% of total time spent at work.

According to the time sheet above, Billie spent approximately how many hours stacking shelves on July 2 ?

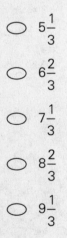

- ○ $5\frac{1}{3}$
- ○ $6\frac{2}{3}$
- ○ $7\frac{1}{3}$
- ○ $8\frac{2}{3}$
- ○ $9\frac{1}{3}$

What is the probability that the sum of two different single-digit prime numbers will NOT be prime?

- ○ 0
- ○ $\frac{1}{2}$
- ○ $\frac{2}{3}$
- ○ $\frac{5}{6}$
- ○ 1

VERBAL DRILL

British modernists used the literary tropes of fragmentation and failure to explore the impending ------ of British colonialism; through their literature, the modernists illustrated the imminent ------ of the Empire.

- ⬭ avarice. .destruction
- ⬭ demise. .sunset
- ⬭ envy. .eclipse
- ⬭ castigation. .rise
- ⬭ dissolution. .wealth

PIQUE:

- ⬭ aggrieve
- ⬭ dulcify
- ⬭ shirk
- ⬭ aggrandize
- ⬭ rouse

INSENSIBLE:

- ⬭ pragmatic
- ⬭ cogent
- ⬭ insensate
- ⬭ rational
- ⬭ cognizant

LUMINOUS:

- ⬭ stentorian
- ⬭ incandescent
- ⬭ mellifluous
- ⬭ stygian
- ⬭ innocuous

SINGULARITY:

- ⬭ hilarity
- ⬭ ordinariness
- ⬭ plurality
- ⬭ celerity
- ⬭ opprobrium

AUSTERE:

- ⬭ spartan
- ⬭ ticklish
- ⬭ unadventurous
- ⬭ plumed
- ⬭ fiendish

EQUIVOCATION : HEDGE::

- ◯ valedictory : greet
- ◯ affidavit : swear
- ◯ peroration : summarize
- ◯ homily : praise
- ◯ exhortation : dismiss

MISCREANT : BASE::

- ◯ harridan : charming
- ◯ magistrate : lax
- ◯ adjudicator : dismissive
- ◯ regent : stately
- ◯ tyro : green

PENURIOUS:

- ◯ repentant
- ◯ harmless
- ◯ wealthy
- ◯ penal
- ◯ parsimonious

Although one would think it impossible to design ------ definition for such a subjective conceipt, the French have defined the worlds greatest cuisine as that which does the most with the least, using their innumberable varieties of cheese as verifiable proof.

- ◯ an endemic
- ◯ a metaphysical
- ◯ a theoretical
- ◯ an ephemeral
- ◯ an empirical

QUARRY : HUNT::

- ◯ terminus : voyage
- ◯ guerdon : repetition
- ◯ accolade : campaign
- ◯ epitome : culture
- ◯ anomaly : puzzle

The development of hydrogen-powered cars will always be ------ by the physical fact that, although hydrogen contains more energy per gallon than does gasoline, it is much less dense than gasoline, and thus carries less energy per pound, making it ------ for any vehicle to carry enough hydrogen on board for long trips.

- ◯ assisted. .easy
- ◯ inhibited. .convenient
- ◯ enhanced. .austere
- ◯ hindered. .exacting
- ◯ parodied. .unrealistic

Questions 13–14 refer to the following passage.

Critics of Mark Twain's novel, *Huckleberry Finn*, view the protagonist's proclamation "All right then I will go to hell" in chapter 31 as the story's climax. Twain's novel lent itself to such radical interpretations because it was the first major American work to depart from traditional European novelistic structures, thus providing critics with an unfamiliar framework. The remaining twelve chapters act as a counterpoint, commenting on, if not reversing, the first part where a morality play receives greater confirmation. Huck's journey down the Mississippi represents a rite of passage, in which the character's personal notions of right and wrong comes into constant conflict with his socially constructed conscience by the various people and situations the protagonist encounters.

The novel's cyclical structure encourages critics to see the novel's disparate parts as interlinked; the novel begins and ends with the boys playing games. Granted, this need not argue to an authorial awareness of novelistic construction; however, it does facilitate attempts to view the novel as a unified whole. Nevertheless, any interpretation that seeks to unite the last few chapters with the remaining book is bound to be somewhat unconvincing. This is not because such an interpretation is unnecessarily rigid, but because *Huckleberry Finn* encompasses individual scenes of the protagonist's self-recognition that resist inclusion into an all-encompassing interpretation. In this respect, the protagonist can best be likened to the Greek tragic figure, Oedipus.

The author most probably mentions the "novel's cyclical structure" in order to

- ⟶ demonstrate that Twain was keenly aware of novelistic construction
- ⟶ show that the remaining twelve chapters have little connection to the rest of the novel
- ⟶ support the critic's position that Twain was unaware of novelistic construction
- ⟶ provide support for a particular critical interpretation of Twain's work
- ⟶ argue that Twain's protagonist has much in common with Oedipus

Which of the following best expresses the main idea of the passage?

- ⟶ In order to understand Twain's novel, critics must compare its protagonist to Oedipus
- ⟶ Twain's novel contains some chapters that resist easy inclusion into a unified interpretation.
- ⟶ The unconventional structure of *Huckleberry Finn* indicates a lack of authorial awareness.
- ⟶ Twain's novel was the first major American novel to discard traditional European structures.
- ⟶ The protagonist of *Huckleberry Finn* is considered a modern day Oedipus by critics.

ASPERITY:

- ⬭ visual expression
- ⬭ partition
- ⬭ contretemps
- ⬭ hallucinatory experience
- ⬭ empressement

IMPECCABLE : REPROACH::

- ⬭ implacable : stoicism
- ⬭ interminable : sojourn
- ⬭ impotent : puissance
- ⬭ indeterminate : certitude
- ⬭ impenetrable : quagmire

DEMIT : ABDICATE::

- ⬭ enter : disembark
- ⬭ approve : ratify
- ⬭ maintain : supply
- ⬭ unfetter : liberate
- ⬭ receive : rescind

The prosecutor failed to make a ------ argument; despite a surfeit of ------ to bolster his claims, he left the jury little choice but to acquit the defendant.

- ⬭ meticulous. .consternation
- ⬭ condescending. .refutation
- ⬭ dubious. .peroration
- ⬭ trenchant. .sanctimony
- ⬭ cogent. .substantiation

MERCENARY : SOLDIER::

- ⬭ amanuensis : stenographer
- ⬭ soubrette : maid
- ⬭ botanist : researcher
- ⬭ academician : professor
- ⬭ culinarian : cook

Dr. Hanash would never entirely abjure the often ------ article; despite its many detractors, the work ------ polemic discourse for years after its publication and remains pervasive in the literature today.

- ⬭ spurned. .forestalled
- ⬭ praised. .fomented
- ⬭ cited. .solidified
- ⬭ traduced. .engendered
- ⬭ evidenced. .produced

Comparative historian Marc Ferro claims that the largest discrepancy in knowledge between what academic historians and what the average citizen knows about history is found in the United States. How has this situation come about? Certainly the problem does not lie with the secondary literature. Whereas in the past, American historians were handicapped by secondary literature that was clearly biased towards a European viewpoint, since the civil rights movement of the 1950s and 60s, the secondary literature in American history has become far more comprehensive. And it cannot be simply a matter of space constraints; the average high school history textbook is well over a thousand pages in length.

One theory holds that American history textbooks are simply the socializing instruments of a controlling elite. The stratification of American society is preserved, according to this theory, by the creation of what Marx termed "false consciousness." The theory holds that the way people think about their society and their history is crucial to maintaining the status quo. If the power elites come to believe that their success is the deserved product of their hard work and ingenuity, then there will be no desire to change the system. Similarly, if the lower classes are taught that their plight is solely due to their failings, they will be more likely to accept their fate and less likely to rise up in revolution. Griffin and Marciano contend that history textbooks promote nothing more than hegemony.

Many educational theorists share this viewpoint, which in their discipline is often known as critical theory. Proponents of this view, including Kozol, Friere, and Giroux, argue that the dominant classes would never create or foster an educational system that taught subordinate classes how to critically evaluate society and the injustices it contains. As long as schools serve to transmit culture, the power elite will never allow any real reform in the system.

It is all too easy to blame citizens' poor understanding of American history on some shadowy coterie of cultural aristocracy. But critical theory and other theories that lay the blame for American ignorance of history on the doorstep of the elites cannot explain their own success. Is it not a paradox that critical theory scholarship dominates its field? If the titans of society had

as much power as the critical theorists contend, they would surely censor or marginalize the works of social scientists in this field. Furthermore, graduates of "elite" preparatory schools are exposed to alternative interpretations of history, subversive teachers, and unfiltered primary source materials more frequently than are students at public institutions. This would seem to indicate that the powerbrokers have little control over what happens at their very own schools, let alone far flung rural schools or schools deep in urban territory. The real culprit may be something not as insidious as a vast upper class conspiracy, but more along the lines of pernicious forces working at a highly local level. Almost half of the states have textbook adoption boards consisting of members of the community. These boards review and recommend what books are taught in neighborhood schools. And because textbook publishers are first and foremost seeking to maximize profit, it is these local boards that they must appease.

According to the passage, proponents of critical theory believe which of the following?

I. The creation of a false consciousness is necessary to preserve the stratification of American society.

II. It is not in the interests of the powerful classes of society to engender critical reflection among the majority of citizens.

III. Members of the upper classes may be freely taught alternative interpretations of history, but not members of the subordinate classes.

- ⬭ I only
- ⬭ II only
- ⬭ I and II only
- ⬭ II and III only
- ⬭ I, II, and III

It can be inferred from the passage that
- ◯ Marx was an early proponent of critical theory
- ◯ textbooks are not solely designed as teaching instruments
- ◯ the secondary literature on American history is no longer biased
- ◯ textbook publishers do not take the views of the power elite into account
- ◯ under the current system, real education reform is impossible

The author of the passage suggests that critical theory
- ◯ is simply another means by which the power elite preserves the stratification of American society
- ◯ does not contain any of the same biases which have appeared in the secondary literature prior to the civil rights movement
- ◯ is the predominant theoretical framework used by historians to explain the discrepancies in the historical knowledge of the average citizen
- ◯ is not unique in its attempts to attribute Americans' poor knowledge of history to the machinations of a particular class of individuals
- ◯ is unable to explain how the power elites in society are able to create a false consciousness among the citizens

The passages indicate that Griffin and Marciano
- ◯ are among the leading critical theorists
- ◯ believe that the lower classes may revolt
- ◯ see textbooks as tools of domination
- ◯ hold many of the same views as Kozol, Friere, and Giroux
- ◯ believe textbook publishers should not make profit a priority

LUCULENT:
- ◯ comprehensible
- ◯ recondite
- ◯ illegible
- ◯ meretricious
- ◯ intelligent

Questions 26–27 refer to the following passage.

One of the most noxious wind-borne allergens is ragweed (Ambrosia), as evidenced by an estimated 30 million sufferers in the U.S. alone and a societal cost of over $3 billion. Each plant is able to produce more than a billion grains of pollen over the course of a season, and the plant is the prime cause of most cases of hay fever in North America. Although the plant produces more pollen in wet years, humidity rates above seventy percent tend to depress the spread of pollen by causing the grains to clump.

Ragweed spreads rapidly by colonizing recently disturbed soil, such as that engendered by roads, subdivisions, and cultivation and has adapted to a multitude of climatic conditions, including desert and high mountain areas. Complete elimination is virtually impossible. Physical removal is undone by even one seed or one bit of root left behind. Ragweed regenerates in about two weeks from only a half-inch of stem, usually with additional branching and flowering, so mowing can actually be counterproductive. Ragweed is susceptible to only the most aggressive herbicides, and because ragweed tends to cover large areas, control would mean widespread use of highly toxic chemicals. Control by natural predators? No known mammal browses on ragweed. Some species of *Lepidoptera* (butterflies, skippers, and moths) larvae feed on ragweed, but this arena of control is not well funded, and consequently not well-researched. Given the health issues and costs occasioned by ragweed, government funding for natural control research is warranted.

Which of the following can be inferred about the spread of ragweed pollen?

○ Allergies caused by the spread of ragweed pollen cost the U.S. more to treat than any other type of allergy.

○ Some ragweed plants produce fewer grains of pollen when exposed to certain highly toxic herbicides.

○ Ragweed plants adapted to desert and mountain climes tend to spread fewer grains of pollen than do plants in other locations.

○ The clumping of pollen grains caused by high humidity levels affects the ability of the wind to carry the grains.

○ The spread of ragweed pollen is the cause of all cases of hay fever in the United States.

The author most probably mentions some species of *Lepidoptera* in order to

○ detail a species that may be more effective at controlling ragweed than are the most aggressive herbicides

○ suggest a potential research avenue to the problem of controlling ragweed that is at present poorly explored

○ discuss a type of mammal that feeds on ragweed plants and may be successful at controlling the spread of ragweed

○ plead with the government to spend more money and put more research efforts into finding a natural control for ragweed

○ argue that complete elimination of the ragweed plant will only be possible if the government funds research into natural controls of ragweed

COUNTENANCE:

○ innervate
○ sanction
○ inveigh
○ tolerate
○ interdict

COZEN : DUPE::

○ navigate : martyr
○ ensconce : mercenary
○ panegyrize : narcissist
○ inflame : alchemist
○ contemn : churl

Bolstered in part by the ------ economy, the "decluttering" movement has expanded its following to include those initiates who have ------ purged existences in order to prioritize their financial, as well as emotional, necessities.

○ floundering. .rejected
○ robust. .attempted
○ flagging. .embraced
○ steady. .maintained
○ rising. .endorsed

ANSWERS

Math Drill

1. A
2. B
3. A
4. A
5. C
6. D
7. C
8. D
9. A
10. C
11. C
12. E
13. C
14. E
15. D
16. D
17. B
18. 9
19. A
20. A
21. A
22. C
23. B
24. A
25. D
26. D
27. B
28. C

Verbal Drill

1. B
2. B
3. E
4. D
5. B
6. D
7. B
8. E
9. C
10. E
11. A
12. D
13. D
14. B
15. E
16. D
17. B
18. E
19. A
20. D
21. C
22. B
23. D
24. C
25. B
26. D
27. B
28. E
29. E
30. C

EXPLANATIONS

Math Drill

1. **A** Since y^2 is always positive, Column A is positive and Column B is negative. The answer is choice (A). You can prove this by Plugging In several different values for y.

2. **B** Straight angle PSR measures 180 degrees, so angle QSR must be 90 degrees, and angle SQR must be 45 degrees. So triangle QSR is a 45-45-90 triangle. Dividing QR by $\sqrt{2}$ gives you the lengths of QS and SR, that is, $\dfrac{2}{\sqrt{2}}$. Angle QPS measures 30°, so triangle PQS is a 30-60-90 triangle, and you can find PS by multiplying QS by $\sqrt{3}$, which gives you $\sqrt{6}$. Add the lengths of SR and PS to find the length of PR, which is $\sqrt{2} + \sqrt{6}$. But $\sqrt{2} + \sqrt{6} \neq \sqrt{8}$. Rather, simplify $\sqrt{8}$ to $2\sqrt{2} = \sqrt{2} + \sqrt{2}$. Compare this to Column B, and realize that you can ignore a $\sqrt{2}$ in each column. $\sqrt{6}$ is greater than $\sqrt{2}$, so Column B is greater.

3. **A** Plug In a three-digit integer, such as 341. Swapping the 1 and the 3 gives you 143. Subtracting 143 from 341 gives you 198 (which is already positive, so its absolute value is also 198). 198 is not divisible by 7, 5, or 4, so eliminate choices (B),(C), and (D). Plug In another number, such as 546. Its hash is 645. Subtracting 546 from 645 gives you 99, which is not divisible by 2, so eliminate choice (E). Even if the hundreds digit or the units digit are zero, the difference between a three-digit integer and its hash is still divisible by 9. The answer is choice (A).

4. **A** Before you start multiplying these huge numbers, realize that no GRE question requires a great deal of arithmetic. Notice that the three digits after the thousands place have merely been swapped to form Column B from Column A. So, represent Column A as (35K + 43)(25K + 430) and Column B as (35K + 430)(25K + 43) (K is short for 1,000). In FOILing these, you'll see that the result from multiplying the First expressions together is (35K)(25K) in both Columns. Similarly, the result from multiplying the Last expressions is (43)(430) in both Columns. So these expressions can be ignored in comparing the two Columns. All that remains is the Outer terms added to the Inner terms. In Column A, this is (35K)(430) + (43)(25K), and in Column B, this is (35K)(43) + (25K)(430). If you factor out 43 from each Column, you obtain 43(350K + 25K) and 43(35K + 250K), or 43(375K) and 43(285K) for Columns A and B, respectively. Column A is larger.

5. **C** You don't need actually to calculate the value of a, just the value of the units digit. 17^2 has a units digit of 9 because 7^2 is 49. Squaring 17^2 gives you 17^4, whose last digit is therefore the last digit in 9^2, that is, 1. Hence, both Columns are equal, and the answer is choice (C).

6. D If $x = 75$, both angles marked x add up to 150 degrees, so the remaining angle in the semicircle (angle QOR) must measure 30 degrees. PS is a diameter, so the circumference of the circle must be $\pi d = 8\pi$. The length of arc QR must represent the same fraction of the circumference as central angle QOR does of 360 degrees: $\dfrac{30°}{360°} = \dfrac{\text{length of } \overset{\frown}{QR}}{8\pi}$, so the length of arc QR is $\dfrac{2\pi}{3}$. The diameter of the circle is 8, so radii OQ and OR have length 4. The triangle inside sector QOR is a 30-60-90 triangle because angle QOR measures 30 degrees and you are shown a right angle. The remaining angle must be 60 degrees to add up to 180. So, the leg of the triangle across from the 30 degree angle will be half of OQ, which is 2, and the other leg that forms part of radius OR will have length $2\sqrt{3}$. So, the remainder of radius OR must have length $4 - 2\sqrt{3}$. Adding the three edge lengths of the shaded region gives you $\dfrac{2\pi}{3} + 2 + \left(4 - 2\sqrt{3}\right) = \dfrac{2\pi}{3} - 2\sqrt{3} + 6$; the answer is choice (D).

7. C Column B contains a common quadratic pattern. Factor the right-hand side

$\sqrt{x - 2\sqrt{xy} + y} = \sqrt{\left(\sqrt{x} - \sqrt{y}\right)^2} = \sqrt{x} - \sqrt{y}$. Both Columns are equal, so the answer is choice (C).

8. D Plug In 2 for n to find the second term in the sequence: $s_n = s_{n-1} + 5$ so $s_2 = s_{2-1} + 5 = s_1 + 5 = 12$, your target number. Now Plug In 2 into the answer choices for n to see which equals 12. Only choice (D) works.

9. A The Columns are already represented as the product of prime factors: $7^2 = (7)(7)$, so the least prime factor of Column A is its only prime factor, 7. Similarly, $2^7 = (2)(2)(2)(2)(2)(2)(2)$, so Column B is 2. Be careful! Remember that you are being asked to determine the *greater* of these two Columns. The answer is choice (A).

10. C To find the average of a list of numbers, add them up and divide by the number of elements in the list. You are told that $\dfrac{a+b+c+d}{4} = 7$, so $a + b + c + d = 28$. You can substitute this into the simplified form of Column B as follows: $\dfrac{(4a - 5c) + (b - 24) + (8c - a) + (3d + 2b)}{4} = \dfrac{3a + 3b + 3c + 3d - 24}{4} = \dfrac{3(a+b+c+d) - 24}{4} = \dfrac{3(28) - 24}{4} = \dfrac{60}{4} = 15$. Both Columns are equal, so the answer is choice (C). Alternatively, you can Plug In values for a, b, c, and d. The easiest way to make their average equal 7 is to Plug In 7 for all four values.

11. **C** Plug In an easy number for the width of the smaller square, such as 3. So the area of the smaller square is $s^2 = 3^2 = 9$. Drawing in the diagonal of a square forms two 45-45-90 triangles, so the diagonal (the hypotenuse of either triangle) has length $3\sqrt{2}$. You are told that this is the width of the larger square, so the area of the larger square is $s^2 = \left(3\sqrt{2}\right)^2 = 18$. The area of the shaded region is the result when the area of the smaller square is subtracted from that of the larger: $18 - 9 = 9$. Thus, both Columns are equal, and the answer is choice (C).

12. **E** First, evaluate x: $x = 3^2 = 9$. Notice that the answers are presented as powers of 3, not a list of actual numbers. So $x^x = (3^2)^9 = 3^{18}$, and the answer is choice (E).

13. **C** Be systematic. Start generating solutions (x, y, z) by making x and y as small as possible, so that z will be as large as possible: (1, 1, 8). Now increase x and y one unit at a time to try to make z decrease to 3: (2, 2, 6) and (3, 3, 4) are the next solutions you can generate. At this point, if you increase either x or y by 1, z becomes 3, but the variable you increased becomes greater than 3: (3, 4, 3), or (4, 3, 3). No matter what you do, one of the variables will be greater than 3. Thus, all solutions include a variable greater than 3, and the answer is choice (C).

14. **E** The question asks for the amount of a 45% decrease on the current grapefruit sales. Try setting up your actual equation before doing any calculations. The current amount of grapefruit sales is .39 (17M). 45% of that number is (.45) (.39) (17M). Because it's a decrease, we have to subtract 45% from the current total, or [.39 (17M)]−[(.45) (.39) (17M)]. Notice that you have the same terms on both sides of the minus sign. This means that we can factor these terms out, like this: (.39) (17M) (1−.45). Now take a look at the answer choices. Choice E fits the bill with (.55) (.39) (17M).

15. **D** To find the average membership, add up the total membership and divide by the number of years. Ignoring the hundreds in the second chart, the average should be: $\dfrac{6+15+17+22+26}{5} = \dfrac{86}{5} = 17.2$. The vertical axis indicates numbers in hundreds, so multiply by 100 to get 17,200; the answer is choice (D).

16. **D** First, simplify the expression in each Column by splitting up the fraction. Thus, Column A becomes $1+\dfrac{17}{y}$ and Column B becomes $\dfrac{y}{11}+1$. Both Columns contain 1, so it can be eliminated from the comparison. Now Plug In 12 for y: Column A becomes $\dfrac{17}{12}=1\dfrac{5}{12}$, and Column B becomes $\dfrac{12}{11}=1\dfrac{1}{11}$. Column A is larger, so eliminate choices (B) and (C). Now Plug In 16 for y: Column A becomes $\dfrac{17}{16}=1\dfrac{1}{16}$, and Column B becomes $\dfrac{16}{11}=1\dfrac{5}{11}$. Column B is larger, so eliminate choice (A); the answer is choice (D).

17. **B** First, simplify the expression in each Column by turning it into a fraction. Thus, Column A

becomes $1\frac{7}{100}$ and Column B becomes $\frac{1}{0.93} = \frac{1}{\frac{93}{100}} = \frac{100}{93} = 1\frac{7}{93}$. Both Columns contain 1, so it

can be eliminated from the comparison. 7 divided by 93 will be larger than 7 divided by 100; the

latter is divided into more pieces, so each piece will be smaller. Therefore, the answer is choice (B).

18. **9** With a ratio of 5:7:3, the total number of singers must be at least 15. If you double the number, and keep the ratio, there would be 30 singers. To have at least 40 singers with the same ratio, the actual total would be 45, or 3 times 15, which means there are three times the number of basses (3) in the ratio, or 9.

19. **A** Notice that the question gives you information about p and q, and the answer choices refer to m and n. Therefore, you need to isolate those from the variables x and y by factoring. Regrouping the first given equation gives you $(m - n)x + (q - p)y = 0$. Because $p - q = -(q - p)$, the second given equation tells you that $q - p = -2$. Cross-multiplying the third given equation yields $x = -3y$. Substituting the last two results into the regrouped first equation yields $(m - n)(-3y) + (-2)y = 0$. Moving the second expression to the other side of the equation yields $(m - n)(-3y) = 2y$. Inspecting this equation tells you that $(m - n)(-3) = 2$, so $m - n = -\frac{2}{3}$. Because $m - n = -(n - m)$, you know that $n - m = \frac{2}{3}$, and the answer is choice (A).

20. **A** The number of senior managers in 1980 was 15. To find 60 percent of this, multiply $\frac{60}{100}(15) = \frac{3}{5}(15) = 9$. So in 2007, there were 15 + 9 = 24 senior managers. In 2000, there were 22, so the increase from 2000 to 2007 was 2; the answer is choice (A).

21. **A** In the first bar graph, the average salary, *in 1950 dollars*, actually appears to have slightly decreased from 1990 to 2000, so statement I is false. Eliminate choices (B) and (E). In the second bar graph, there were 8 senior managers in 1960, so statement II is also false. Eliminate choices (C) and (D); the answer is choice (A).

22. **C** The volume of the larger cube is $s^3 = 2^3 = 8$ and the volume of the smaller cube is $s^3 = \left(\sqrt{2}\right)^3 = 2\sqrt{2}$.

Dividing the larger by the smaller yields $\frac{8}{2\sqrt{2}} = \frac{4}{\sqrt{2}} = \frac{4\sqrt{2}}{2} = 2\sqrt{2}$, and the answer is choice (C).

23. B Because VY bisects UW, it is an altitude—this is true in any triangle that is at least isosceles. So $\angle VYW$ measures 90 degrees. In an equilateral triangle, all three angles measure 60 degrees. So $\angle YVW$ measures 30 degrees, and $\triangle VYW$ is a 30-60-90 triangle. Plug In an easy number for a, such as 4. All three sides have length 4, and because you are given that Y and X are the midpoints of UW and YW, respectively, you can conclude that $YW = 2$, and $YX = 1$. Using YW as the side opposite the 30 degree angle in the 30-60-90 triangle, multiply by $\sqrt{3}$ to get $2\sqrt{3}$, the length of VY. Now use the Pythagorean theorem to find the final side of $\triangle VXY : (1)^2 - (2\sqrt{3})^2 = (VX)^2; VX = \sqrt{13}$. So the perimeter of $\triangle VXY$ is $1+2\sqrt{3}+\sqrt{13} \approx 1+2(1.7)+\sqrt{13}=4.4+\sqrt{13}$. $\sqrt{9}=3$ and $\sqrt{16}=4$, so $\sqrt{13}$ must be bigger than 3, and Column B is therefore larger than 7.4. Plugging In 4 for a in Column A gives you 7, so Column B is larger.

24. A If x and y were equal, then $1,000 would be invested at each rate, earning $10 at 1% and $20 at 2%, for a total of $30. The CDs earned only $25, so more must have been invested at the lower rate; the answer is choice (A).

25. D You can define $|a - b|$ as "the distance from a to b on a number line." Thus, the given equation becomes "the distance from x to y is the distance from x to z minus the distance from y to z." You can draw this on a number line two different ways:

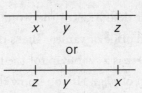

You are asked to compare $|x| = x - 0$ to $|y| = |y - 0|$, which can be translated as "the distance from x to 0" and "the distance from y to 0". You only know that y is between x and z, and you are given no information about whether the points are on the positive or negative half of the number line, so you cannot determine which is closer to 0, so the answer is choice (D).

26. D Together, Rachel and Rob cover 120 of the 190 miles in one hour. This means that they cover $\frac{3}{4}$ that distance in $\frac{3}{4}$ that time, that is, 90 miles in any 45 minute period. So, 45 minutes before they meet, they are 90 miles apart, and the answer is choice (D). If you picked choice (E), you found how far they had traveled 45 minutes before they met, rather than how far they had left to travel.

27. **B** First, figure out how many hours Billie worked. From 9 a.m. to 5 p.m. is 8 hours. She started work 3 minutes before 9 a.m. and finished at 16 minutes after 5p.m., for a total of 19 more minutes, which is close to 20 minutes, or $\frac{1}{3}$ of an hour. So Billie worked approximately $8\frac{1}{3}$ hours. To take 80 percent of this, multiply by $\frac{80}{100} = \frac{4}{5}$. So she spent $\left(\frac{4}{5}\right)\left(8\frac{1}{3}\right) = \left(\frac{4}{5}\right)\left(\frac{25}{3}\right) = \frac{100}{15} = 6\frac{2}{3}$ hours; the answer is choice (B).

28. **C** The single-digit primes are 2, 3, 5, and 7. Be systematic in listing the results. Start with 2, adding it to the other numbers, then move to 3, and so forth: 2 + 3 = 5; 2 + 5 = 7; 2 + 7 = 9; 3 + 5 = 8; 3 + 7 = 10; 5 + 7 = 12. Out of these six results, 5 and 7 are prime, but the other four results are not, so the probability you seek is $\frac{4}{6} = \frac{2}{3}$, and the answer is choice (C).

Verbal Drill

1. **B** This sentence employs parallel structure, and the semicolon trigger tells you that both blanks will go in the same direction. You can recycle *fragmentation* for the first blank and *failure* for the second blank; POE all answers except choice (B).

2. **B** Although the most familiar definition of the word *pique* is to excite interest or curiosity, the primary definition is to wound pride or vanity. That's the definition being tested here, so the opposite is to soothe or please. *Aggrieve* is a synonym for the meaning tested here, and *rouse* is a synonym of the more familiar definition of *pique*. If you know that *pique* is negative, then you know you need a positive word. *Aggrieve* is negative, so eliminate choice (A). *Dulcify* means to mollify, which is a pretty good match, so the best answer is choice (B).

3. **E** *Insensible* means unconscious or unaware, so the opposite is aware. *Insensate* is a synonym. *Pragmatic* and *rational* are traps, because if you think that *insensible* means not sensible, you are looking for an answer like sensible. If you're not sure what *insensible* means, you can still eliminate choice (C); it has the same prefix as *insensible*, so it's not likely to be its opposite. *Cognizant* means aware, so the best answer is choice (E).

4. **D** *Luminous* means emitting light, so the opposite is characterized by darkness. *Incandescent* is a synonym. If you're not sure what *luminous* means, you may be able to guess its meaning using roots. *Lum* means light, so the correct answer must have something to do with darkness. *Stygian* means dark or gloomy, so the best answer is choice (D).

5. **B**   *Singularity* is unusualness or exceptionalness, so the opposite is normality. *Singularity* contains the word singular, so *plurality* is a trap. Depending on the context, *singularity* is either positive or neutral, so you can eliminate solely positive words. *Hilarity* and *celerity* are positive; eliminate choices (A) and (D). *Ordinariness* means normality, so the best answer is choice (B).

6. **D**   *Austere* means bare or unadorned, so the opposite is adorned. *Spartan* is a synonym. *Austere* is negative, so you're looking for an answer that's positive. *Spartan, unadventurous,* and *fiendish* are negative and *ticklish* is neutral; eliminate choices (A), (B), (C), and (E). *Plumed* means adorned, so the best answer is choice (D).

7. **B**   *Equivocation* is speech used to *hedge* one's point or to avoid getting pinned down. Note the secondary meaning of *hedge* here; you can see that it is a verb by comparing it to the other right-side words. A *valedictory* (think of the valedictorian at a graduation) is someone who says goodbye, not someone whose purpose is to *greet* the audience. An *affidavit* is speech used to *swear* that a statement is true, so keep choice (B). A *peroration* does not *summarize*; in fact, a *peroration* is a very long speech. (The prefix *per-* can mean through or thoroughly, so *peroration* is an oration which is very thorough and lengthy.) A *homily* is a sermon which gives a moral lesson, but it may or may not *praise* someone. Finally, an *exhortation* is speech used to encourage an audience, not *dismiss* it, leaving you with choice (B) for the answer.

8. **E**   A *miscreant* is a person with a *base* or villainous nature. Note the secondary meaning of *base* here, which you can see is an adjective by glancing at the other right-side words. Is a *harridan* a *charming* person? Actually, no—a *harridan* is a scolding, shrewish woman. Is a *magistrate*, or a legal administrator, a *lax* person? Not necessarily. An *adjudicator* is someone who judges a situation, but is not necessarily *dismissive*. A *regent* is someone who helps rule, but a *regent* is not necessarily *stately*. Finally, a *tyro* is a beginner, or someone who is *green*, leaving you choice (E) for the answer.

9. **C**   Although the primary definition of *penurious* is stingy, it can also mean poor. That's the definition being tested here, so the opposite is rich. *Parsimonious* is a synonym for the primary definition. If you know that *penurious* is negative, you know you need a positive word. *Penal* and *parsimonious* are clearly negative, so eliminate choices (D) and (E). *Wealthy* means rich, so the best answer is choice (C).

10. **E**   The sentence starts with a different direction trigger: *Although.* In this case the sentence is looking for something which is the opposite of *subjective.* A good word for the blank, therefore, would be *objective.* This is supported by the notion that the definition must be verifiable. *Empirical* means *provable* and is therefore the best synonym. The answer is choice (E).

11.   A   A *quarry* is the goal of a *hunt*; for example, a *quarry* could be a buck or a fox. The choices use some hard vocabulary, so try to eliminate choices with words you know based on this relationship. For example, is an *accolade*, or statement of praise, the goal of a *campaign*? Not necessarily. Is an *epitome* the goal of a *culture*? No, so eliminate that choice as well. Is an *anomaly* the goal of a *puzzle*? No. You are left with two difficult choices. A *terminus* is the endpoint, or goal, of a *voyage*. A *guerdon* is a reward, which is not the goal of a *repetition*, leaving you with choice (A) for the answer.

12.   D   The trigger *although* introduces two conflicting aspects of hydrogen-powered cars. The first clue states that *hydrogen contains more energy per gallon than does gasoline*, which is a good thing. The trigger indicates a change of direction, so a good word for the first blank is challenged. Start with the first half of the answers and look for a word that means challenged. Use POE to eliminate choices (A), (C), and (E). The second blank continues in the same direction as the first, based on the second trigger, *thus*, so a good word for that blank is unlikely. That means you can eliminate choice (B), because *convenient* does not match unlikely. Choice (D) is the best match.

13.   D   According to the author, *The novel's cyclical structure encourages critics to see the novel's disparate parts as interlinked…however, it does facilitate attempts to view the novel as a unified whole.* Thus, the cyclical structure supports a critical interpretation of the novel. Choice (D) best summarizes this idea.

14.   B   In the first paragraph, the author states, *The remaining twelve chapters act as a counterpoint, commenting on—if not reversing,—the first part where a morality play receives greater confirmation.* According to the second paragraph of the passage, *Huckleberry Finn encompasses individual scenes of the protagonist's self-recognition*, that resist inclusion into an all-encompassing interpretation. Throughout the passage, the author shows that the novel has certain elements that do not fit nicely into a unified vision of the book. Choice (B) is the best restatement of the information given in the passage.

15.   E   *Asperity* means harshness in tone or manner, so the opposite is friendliness or warmth. If you know that *asperity* is negative, you know you need a positive answer. *Visual expression* and *partition* are neutral, and *contretemps* is negative; eliminate choices (A), (B), and (C). You can also eliminate choice (D), because, like *visual expression*, it has no opposite. *Empressement* means extreme cordiality, so the best answer is choice (E).

16.   D   Someone who is *impeccable* is faultless, or not deserving of *reproach*. There is some tough vocabulary in the answer choices. Start by trying to eliminate based on vocabulary you know. For example, an *implacable* person is beyond pleasing, not undeserving of *stoicism*. Something *interminable* is endless, but not undeserving of a *sojourn*, or a brief stay. Someone *impotent* lacks *puissance*, but is not undeserving of it. Something *indeterminate* is not deserving of *certitude* because it is not certain; hold on to that choice. A *quagmire* may be *impenetrable*, but something *impenetrable* is not unworthy of a *quagmire*, leaving you with choice (D) as the best answer.

17. **B** To *abdicate* is to formally *demit*—or give up—a position. If you weren't sure about the meanings of those words, or about what kind of relationship they had, you could still try to eliminate by working backwards. *Enter* is the reverse of *disembark*. Do *demit* and *abdicate* seem similar or different? If you know that they are similar words, you can eliminate choice (A) by using this side-of-the-fence approach. To *ratify* something is to formally *approve* it, which does match the stem-pair relationship, if you were able to recognize it. Even if you did not know that relationship yet, keep choice (B) because it does at least have a defining relationship. *Maintain* and *supply* do not have a defining relationship (you could maintain something by supplying it, but this is a stretch, not a definition), so eliminate choice (C). To *unfetter* someone is to *liberate* them, so keep choice (D) for now. *Receive* and *rescind* have no relationship, eliminating choice (E). Comparing your final options—choice (B) and choice (D)—the aspect of formality makes choice (B) the better match and the best answer.

18. **E** If the jury acquitted the defendant, or let him off the hook, the prosecutor could not have done a very good job. Therefore, you know that he failed to make a good argument, despite the fact that he had a lot of something to bolster his claims. What would bolster, or help, his claims? Some great evidence would definitely help him, so use evidence for the second blank. Working from the first blank first, you can see that *condescending* and *dubious* do not match the word you filled in, good. *Meticulous*, *trenchant*, and *cogent* all could refer to good arguments, so keep those choices for now. Look at the second blank options; *consternation* and *sanctimony* do not match evidence. *Substantiation* is a good match, so select choice (E).

19. **A** A *mercenary* is a hired *soldier*. Looking at your choices, an *amanuensis* is a hired *stenographer*. *Soubrette* is a fancy word for *maid*, but it doesn't mean a hired maid. *Botanist* and *researcher* do not have a defining relationship. *Academician* is a fancy word for *professor*, and a *culinarian* is a fancy word for *cook*, but neither pair matches the stem pair relationship, leaving you with choice (A) for the answer.

20. **D** The article is described in turns as having *detractors* and as a *fixture* in the literature. There is more than one trigger in the sentence, so be sure to keep track of which clues are relevant to which blank. If you start with the first blank, and know the meanings of *abjure* and *detractor*, you might infer that the article was often criticized. You can immediately eliminate choice (B). *Cited* and *evidenced* are distracting choices. They are associated with research and publication, but it is unlikely that someone would regret writing a frequently cited work. The second blank is neutral, but knowing that *polemic discourse* followed *for years after its publication*, you should look for a word that means encouraged. *Forestalled* is opposite in meaning to encouraged, therefore you can eliminate choice (B). Choice (D) is the best match here.

21.   **C**   In order to answer this question, you must understand what critical theory is. The third paragraph mentions critical theory directly, and states that its proponents believe *the dominant classes would never create or foster an educational system that taught subordinate classes how to critically evaluate society and the injustices it contains.* This most closely matches statement II. Eliminate choice (A). The second paragraph is also important because the author states that critical theorists share the views of the theorists mentioned in the second paragraph. These theorists hold that *the stratification of American society is preserved...by the creation of what Marx termed false consciousness...The theory holds that the way people think about their society and their history is crucial to maintaining the status quo.* This matches statement I. Eliminate choices (B) and (D). The third choice is incorrect. The author mentions this point in the critique of critical theory in the final paragraph. Choice (C) is the best answer.

22.   **B**   Choice (B) is supported by the final lines of the passage, which indicate that textbook publishers are *first and foremost* seeking to maximize profit. Thus, textbooks are not just teaching instruments, but money makers. Choice (A) is not supported by the passage. The theorists use Marx's term, but that doesn't mean he was a member of the school. Choice (C) is wrong; the passage simply says the literature is *more comprehensive.* That's not the same as saying it is no longer biased. Choice (D) is not supported by the passage. Although the author rejects the idea that the power elites are in control of textbooks, it may still be true that publishers take their views into account. Choice (E) is put forth by the critical theorists, but it is not necessarily true.

23.   **D**   In the final paragraph, the author states, *but critical theory and other theories that lay the blame for American ignorance of history on the doorstep of the elites cannot explain their own success.* Thus, there must be other theories similar to critical theory and critical theory is not unique, which supports choice (D). There is no information to support either choice (A) or (B). Choice (C) is wrong because critical theory is used by educational theorists, not historians. Choice (E) is not supported by the passage.

24.   **C**   The passage's discussion of Griffin and Marciano is limited to a single sentence: *Griffin and Marciano contend that history textbooks promote nothing more than hegemony.* The choice that most closely matches this sentence is choice (C). The other choices are not mentioned in conjunction with Griffin and Marciano.

25.   **B**   *Luculent* means clear or easy to understand, so the opposite is difficult to understand. *Comprehensible* is a synonym. *Illegible* is a trap because *luculent* refers to difficulty in understanding concepts or meanings, not words that aren't written clearly. If you know that *luculent* is positive, you know you need a negative word. *Comprehensible* and *intelligent* are positive; eliminate choices (A) and (E). *Recondite* means difficult to understand, so the best answer is choice (B).

26. **D** The first paragraph states that ragweed is one of the most noxious *wind-borne allergens*. Later, the paragraph states that *humidity rates above seventy percent tend to depress the spread of pollen by causing the grains to clump*. If the pollen is borne by the wind and its spread is depressed by clumping, the clumping must have some negative affect on the wind's ability to carry the pollen. The passage doesn't mention the cost of treating other allergies, so choice (A) is wrong. Nothing supports choice (B). The passage doesn't compare the rates of production of plants in different climates, so choice (C) cannot be inferred. Choice (E) goes too far; the passage states that ragweed pollen is the cause of *most cases* not all as the choice states.

27. **B** The answer to this question lies in the line, *Some species of Lepidoptera (butterflies, skippers, and moths) larvae feed on ragweed, but this arena of control is not well funded, and consequently not well-researched.* The author mentions the species to indicate that there may be a potential answer to the problem of controlling ragweed, but this answer has not been fully explored. This most closely matches choice (B). Choice (A) is wrong because the author doesn't make a comparison between the methods of control. Choice (C) is wrong because the species discussed are not mammals. The author does suggest the government explore natural remedies, but choice (D) doesn't properly answer the question. The mention of *some species of Lepidoptera* is not used to *plead with the government*. Choice (E) is incorrect because earlier in the passage the author indicates that complete elimination of the ragweed is unlikely.

28. **E** The primary meaning of *countenance* is face or visage, but when used as a verb it means to tolerate or approve. That's the definition being tested here, so the opposite is to denounce or forbid. If you know that *innervate* is a medical word that relates to nerves, you can eliminate choice (A)—otherwise, hold on to it. *Sanction* and *tolerate* are both synonyms for *countenance*. Even if you weren't sure what countenance meant, two answers with the same meaning can't both be correct, so eliminate choices (B) and (D). To *inveigh* against something means to speak against it, but it's not quite strong enough. *Interdict* means to prohibit or forbid, which is closer to what we need, making the best answer choice (E).

29. **E** This is definitely a difficult question, starting with hard vocabulary in the stem pair. A *dupe* is someone who is easy to *cozen*, or trick. If you don't know these words, try working backwards and see if any pairs do not have defining relationships. Do *navigate* and *martyr* have a defining relationship? No, so eliminate choice (A). Similarly, *ensconce* and *mercenary* have no real connection. A *narcissist* is someone who is likes to *panegyrize*, or bestow praises upon, him or herself. Could a *dupe* be someone who likes to *cozen* him or herself? Maybe—keep choice (C). *Inflame* and *alchemist* do not have a defining relationship. A *churl* is a rude and boorish person, who would be easy *to contemn*. A *dupe* is someone who is easy to *cozen*, or fool, so choice (E) is a good match for the stem-pair relationship. That makes more sense than choice (C) does, making choice (E) the best answer. Remember, don't be afraid to choose words you don't really know if the rest definitely don't work.

30.   **C**   Start with one blank at a time. Don't be immediately drawn in by *bolstered* in the first blank, as there really is not enough information to describe the economy. If you move to the second blank, the clue *initiates* may signify that new followers have begun *simplified existence*. You should then be able to eliminate choice (A). *Maintained* doesn't quite mean "begin," but hold onto it for the moment. Turning back to the first blank, you know that new followers have joined the movement *in order to prioritize financial necessities*, thus you might infer that the economy is bad. Now eliminate answers (B), (D), and (E). Choice (C) is the best match here.

Verbal

Analogies

ANALOGIES

On analogy questions you are given two words, in all caps. These are your stem words. You have to identify the relationship between the two stem words and find the pair of words in the answer choices that has the same relationship. Each question contains twelve separate words, some of which you'll know and some of which you won't, and six different relationships. To think your way through one of these questions is difficult and requires lots of mental effort. Fortunately, a good approach will maximize your chances of getting any one question right, minimize the possibility for careless errors, and make the whole process efficient and relatively straight forward.

Step 1: Make a defining sentence

If you know the stem words, the first step is to make a sentence that defines one of the words in terms of the other. You can try to describe the relationship in your head, but a good sentence will pinpoint that relationship much more quickly and reliably and will give you a template into which you can insert the answer pairs. A good sentence will be short, will start with one word (it doesn't matter which) and end with the other, and, above all, will be definitional. In fact, a very easy way to make a sentence is to cover up one word and to define the other, using the second word in the process. If you use the word "means" in the middle, that's even better.

Here are some examples.

> EDUCATION : IGNORANCE
>
> *Ignorance* means without *education*.

> SODA : BEVERAGE
>
> *Soda* is a type of *beverage*.

> ADHESIVE : BOND
>
> An *adhesive* is something used to *bond*.

What NOT to do.

> CONCIERGE : HOTEL
>
> A *hotel* has a *concierge*.

Yes, a *hotel* does in fact have a *concierge*, but a *hotel* also has rooms, a front desk, and perhaps mints on the pillow—but the sentence doesn't tell us anything about the relationship between the two.

SCRAWL : WRITE

To *write* a letter, some people *scrawl*.

Yes, but what kind of writing is meant? Also, don't add in concepts, such as a letter, that aren't an inherent part of the definition. To *scrawl* means to *write* poorly—a much better sentence.

AMPLIFY : VOLUME

Amplification means increasing the *volume*.

Using the given part of speech is a crucial tool for making effective sentences. The part of speech of a word will remain consistent through all answer choices and should never change; some words have an entirely different meaning in other parts of speech.

Recycled Relationships

There is a small set of relationships that ETS likes to use over and over again. Keep an eye out for them!

Type of	LIMERICK : VERSE :: termite : insect
Used to	AX : CHOP :: needle : knit
Characteristic of	KNOWLEDGE : EXPERT :: doubt : skeptic
Degree	FEAR : TERROR :: anger : rage
Without	FLAWLESS : BLEMISH :: apathetic : emotion

Step 2: Apply your defining sentence to all five answer choices

Once you have created a good sentence, plug each pair of words in the answer choices into the same sentence.

Here is an example.

AQUARIUM : FISH

○ nest : birds
○ meadow : cows
○ gaggle : geese
○ corral : horses
○ water : lily

Sentence:	An AQUARIUM is a place to house FISH.
Answer choice (A):	A nest is a place to house birds. Does it make sense? No. Cross it off on your scratch paper.
Answer choice (B):	A meadow is a place to house cows. Does it make sense? Hmm. A meadow doesn't really house cows but they do sometimes live there. Don't spend ten minutes thinking about it, give it the maybe and move on.
Answer choice (C):	A gaggle is a place to house geese. No, keep it literal, a gaggle is a group of geese, not a place to house geese. Get rid of it.
Answer choice (D):	A corral is a place to house horses. Yes, give it a check mark.
Answer choice (E):	Water is a place to house lilies. Could you have lilies on land? Not sure? Give it a maybe.

Step 3: When in doubt, be more specific

If you know all of the words, and your sentence does not eliminate four out of five answer choices, go back and make your sentence more specific.

If you know all the words and your sentence does not eliminate four out of five answer choices, go back and make a more specific sentence.

Sentence:	An AQUARIUM is a container used to house FISH.
Answer choice (B):	A meadow is a container used to house cows. No, cross it off.
Answer choice (D):	A corral is a container used to house horses. Sure. Don't over think it, just keep it in.
Answer choice (E):	Water is a container used to house lilies. No. Cross it off.

Step

4

Step 4: Work backwards

If you don't know one of the stem words well enough to make a defining sentence out of it, the process remains essentially the same, except upside down. You skip directly to the answer choices and make a sentence out of each of them in turn, and then apply it to the stem pair to see whether it makes sense. If you can't make a good sentence out of an answer choice, it may be because there is no good relationship. In that case, you can cross it off.

COMPULSIVE : ????

◯ bellicose : passive
◯ miserly : thrifty
◯ excited : scurrilous
◯ inevitable : flagrant
◯ hostile : affable

Answer choice (A)   Bellicose means not passive. Does compulsive mean
                       not -------- ? Maybe. You don't have to know what
                       the word is, just that there could be a sensible word
                       that would fit this definition. The first answer choice
                       seems viable. Keep it.

Answer choice (B)   *Miserly* means overly *thrifty*. Does compulsive mean
                       overly something? Maybe. That answer sounds good,
                       so give it a check.

Answer choice (C)   The words *excited* and *scurrilous* have no definitional
                       relationship. If you looked one up in the dictionary,
                       you wouldn't see the other. Cross this pair off.

Answer choice (D)   The same applies to *inevitable* and *flagrant*. Cross it
                       off.

Answer choice (E)   Hostile means not *affable*. Does compulsive mean
                       not ------- ? Maybe. It works, but this pair of words
                       has the same relationship as choice (A). If one were
                       correct, the other would have to be correct as well.
                       Cross them both off.

On your scratch paper you should be left with only one answer, choice (B). You just got to the correct answer without ever knowing one of the two stem words. That's powerful.

For more practice and a more in-depth look at The Princeton Review Analogy techniques, check out our student-friendly guidebook, *Cracking the GRE.*

ANALOGIES: DRILL 1

STUDY : LEARN ::
- ⬭ hunt : gather
- ⬭ search: find
- ⬭ permeate : penetrate
- ⬭ work : raise
- ⬭ agree : maintain

SUFFOCATE : OXYGEN ::
- ⬭ steal : money
- ⬭ ionize : water
- ⬭ imprison : freedom
- ⬭ inhibit : drive
- ⬭ build : supplies

SOLILOQUY : PLAY ::
- ⬭ stanza : sonnet
- ⬭ piano : concerto
- ⬭ aria : opera
- ⬭ duet : ballet
- ⬭ overture : musical

COWARD : BRAVE ::
- ⬭ martyr : religious
- ⬭ agnostic : uncertain
- ⬭ hero : vanquished
- ⬭ traitor : amicable
- ⬭ philanthropist : stingy

EVAPORATE : VAPOR ::
- ⬭ season : salt
- ⬭ rust : copper
- ⬭ centrifuge : fluid
- ⬭ petrify : stone
- ⬭ incinerate : inferno

MINUTIAE : DETAILS ::
- ⬭ queries : rejoinders
- ⬭ quibbles : complaints
- ⬭ particles : materials
- ⬭ approximations : estimations
- ⬭ cells : organisms

DIDACTIC : INSTRUCT ::
- ⬭ dynamic : energize
- ⬭ rhetorical : narrate
- ⬭ comical : amuse
- ⬭ imperative : obey
- ⬭ pedantic : insist

RECLUSE : WITHDRAWN ::
- ⬭ pacifist : belligerent
- ⬭ procrastinator : unattainable
- ⬭ isolationist : malicious
- ⬭ miser : despondent
- ⬭ bigot : prejudiced

FOOLPROOF : FAIL ::
- ⬭ immortal : die
- ⬭ taut : snap
- ⬭ translucent : shine
- ⬭ viscous : solidify
- ⬭ volatile : detonate

INSOMNIA : SLEEP ::
- ⬭ hyperactivity : fidget
- ⬭ dyslexia : read
- ⬭ malnutrition : eat
- ⬭ paranoia : imagine
- ⬭ hemophilia : bleed

AUDACIOUS : TREPIDATION ::
- ◯ laconic : verbosity
- ◯ sordid : aspiration
- ◯ obstinate : intransigence
- ◯ sardonic : subordination
- ◯ cursory : accretion

GARRULOUS : TALKATIVE ::
- ◯ cantankerous : affable
- ◯ prudent : irresolute
- ◯ suspicious : fallacious
- ◯ cloying : sweet
- ◯ obtuse : abstruse

FURTIVE : STEALTH ::
- ◯ dissolute : contrition
- ◯ loquacious : astuteness
- ◯ whimsical : fancy
- ◯ arduous : fortitude
- ◯ pontifical : veneration

MERCURIAL : MOOD ::
- ◯ paranoid : mistrust
- ◯ fickle : affection
- ◯ ebullient : geniality
- ◯ dynamic : delirium
- ◯ bellicose : anarchy

DISABUSE : ERROR ::
- ◯ maintain : dereliction
- ◯ vilify : reputation
- ◯ deride : paucity
- ◯ discern : discrimination
- ◯ rehabilitate : dependence

FEARLESS : DAUNT ::
- ◯ lugubrious : contain
- ◯ serene : placate
- ◯ vivacious : befriend
- ◯ avaricious : induce
- ◯ impassive : perturb

COMPLIANT : SERVILE ::
- ◯ credulous : gullible
- ◯ arduous : futile
- ◯ cowering : fawning
- ◯ pleasant : effortless
- ◯ adventurous : audacious

QUERULOUS : CARP ::
- ◯ profligate : squander
- ◯ arrogant : fawn
- ◯ perfidious : safeguard
- ◯ culpable : deride
- ◯ laconic : ramble

URBANE : GAUCHERIE ::
- ◯ confident : coterie
- ◯ fearful : devastation
- ◯ guileless : chicanery
- ◯ diffident : magnanimity
- ◯ conniving : imposture

PLUTOCRACY : AFFLUENCE ::
- ◯ oligarchy : dissent
- ◯ patriarchy : androcentricity
- ◯ hegemony : geography
- ◯ republic : discourse
- ◯ anarchy : jurisprudence

ANALOGIES: DRILL 2

ANIMAL : DOG ::
- ⬭ blanket : sheet
- ⬭ team : sport
- ⬭ minnow : fish
- ⬭ finger : hand
- ⬭ music : jazz

NICOTINE : TOBACCO ::
- ⬭ enamel : tooth
- ⬭ vitamin: spinach
- ⬭ caffeine : coffee
- ⬭ carbohydrate : bread
- ⬭ tomato : ketchup

MUTED : COLOR ::
- ⬭ arcane : speech
- ⬭ cacophonous : sound
- ⬭ cubist : construction
- ⬭ insipid : flavor
- ⬭ cloying : sentiment

UNTENABLE : DEFENDED ::
- ⬭ arduous : executed
- ⬭ ephemeral : perpetuated
- ⬭ caustic : eroded
- ⬭ viscous : solidified
- ⬭ inimical : desiccated

PRATE : SPEAK ::
- ⬭ demean : laud
- ⬭ cajole : inveigle
- ⬭ pause : loiter
- ⬭ gaze : inspect
- ⬭ meander : walk

OBTUSENESS : INTELLIGENCE ::
- ⬭ skepticism : doubt
- ⬭ gregariousness : apathy
- ⬭ condolence : sympathy
- ⬭ callousness : sensitivity
- ⬭ acuteness : perception

FANATICISM : ENTHUSIASM ::
- ⬭ abhorrence : repugnance
- ⬭ authority : cooperation
- ⬭ zealousness : chastity
- ⬭ reticence : extroversion
- ⬭ pedantry : athleticism

PERTURB : PLACIDITY ::
- ⬭ excite : unrest
- ⬭ vex : personality
- ⬭ dam : flow
- ⬭ thrust : protrusion
- ⬭ mold : plasticity

COLOSSUS : FIGURINE ::
- ⬭ porcelain : miniature
- ⬭ epic : poem
- ⬭ gladiator : arena
- ⬭ grandiloquence : loquacity
- ⬭ eagle : hawk

DISGUISE : RECOGNITION ::
- ⬭ inure: hardship
- ⬭ stupefy : befuddlement
- ⬭ elude : escape
- ⬭ guard : incursion
- ⬭ camouflage : covering

CAESURA : VERSE ::

○ inoculation : immunity
○ dormancy : volcano
○ intermittence : signal
○ abeyance : action
○ stagnancy : hyperactivity

DISABUSE : DECEPTION ::

○ rebuke : disapproval
○ manumit : bondage
○ inveigle : treachery
○ preen : superciliousness
○ neglect : enervation

COGENCY : UNCONVINCING ::

○ education : erudite
○ cognizance : aware
○ salience : inconspicuous
○ memorization : understanding
○ instruction : ample

BENEDICTION : BLESSING ::

○ abhorrence : eulogy
○ celebration : antipathy
○ valentine : amorousness
○ anathema : condemnation
○ encomium : education

EXOSKELETON : INSECT ::

○ fungi : mushroom
○ wolverine : pelt
○ epidermis : human
○ human : bone
○ thorax : hornet

PEDIGREE : ANCESTORS ::

○ medicine : history
○ transcript : grades
○ filigree : mothers
○ actions : memory
○ venom : hate

COMPENDIUM : SUCCINCT ::

○ neophyte : extensive
○ extrapolation : concise
○ abridgement : spacious
○ expansion : accretive
○ reliability : literal

MERCENARY : LUCRE ::

○ guerilla : subterfuge
○ operative : employment
○ highwayman : spoils
○ harlequin : romance
○ lollygag : existentialism

CACOPHONY : AUDITORY ::

○ dissonance : oratory
○ stridence : behavioral
○ stench : olfactory
○ rancor : cerebral
○ stimulus : digital

IMPRECATION : INJURIOUS ::

○ prediction : harmonious
○ hygiene : salubrious
○ anathema : wholesome
○ hex : opaque
○ boon : propitious

ANALOGIES: DRILL 3

TRANQUILIZER : CALM ::
- ⬭ quietus : sedate
- ⬭ antihistamine : sneeze
- ⬭ medication : ail
- ⬭ shot : cry
- ⬭ stimulant : excite

BLACKSMITH : IRON ::
- ⬭ cobbler : leather
- ⬭ clay : sculptor
- ⬭ hammer : nail
- ⬭ clothes : designer
- ⬭ horseshoe : anvil

DELAY : FILIBUSTER ::
- ⬭ anger : criticism
- ⬭ authorize : influence
- ⬭ dilate : reduction
- ⬭ probe : inquisition
- ⬭ brush : palette

TALISMAN : MAGICAL ::
- ⬭ amulet : circular
- ⬭ novel : suspenseful
- ⬭ medium : communicative
- ⬭ malediction : evil
- ⬭ magician : hirsute

ANIMATE : BIOLOGY ::
- ⬭ porcine : swine
- ⬭ aqueous : ichthyology
- ⬭ aquatic : entomology
- ⬭ ephemeral : arachnid
- ⬭ avian : ornithology

FRENZY : SEDATE ::
- ⬭ delirium : mad
- ⬭ agitation : cheerful
- ⬭ uniqueness : mundane
- ⬭ stoicism : still
- ⬭ simplicity : clear

SOLILOQUY : SINGLETON ::
- ⬭ epilogue : thespian
- ⬭ monologue : playwright
- ⬭ multitude : ensemble
- ⬭ duet : dyad
- ⬭ choreography : company

STRATAGEM : DECEIVE ::
- ⬭ maneuver : find
- ⬭ gambit : lose
- ⬭ ambuscade : surprise
- ⬭ gambol : attack
- ⬭ rumpus : faint

SUBPOENA : WITNESS ::
- ⬭ indict : criminal
- ⬭ conjure : spirit
- ⬭ perjure : attorney
- ⬭ query : supplicant
- ⬭ trace : waif

ASTROLOGY : ASTRONOMY ::
- ⬭ economics : ethics
- ⬭ phrenology : psychology
- ⬭ biology : neurology
- ⬭ sociology : chronology
- ⬭ massage : therapy

MALAPROPISM : VERBAL ::
- ◯ tic : facial
- ◯ miscalculation : mathematical
- ◯ mumble : aural
- ◯ hypothesis : theoretical
- ◯ etiquette : social

LUBRICATE : ABRASION ::
- ◯ aerate : ventilation
- ◯ adulterate : impurities
- ◯ decant : spoilage
- ◯ synthesize : replication
- ◯ hydrate : desiccation

PLUCK : QUIT ::
- ◯ bravado : swagger
- ◯ gall : ail
- ◯ gravitas : amuse
- ◯ hubris : importune
- ◯ vim : expire

PARENTHESIS : EXPLANATION ::
- ◯ footnote : citation
- ◯ sidebar : summary
- ◯ ampersand : conjugation
- ◯ paragraph : thesis
- ◯ prelude : ultimatum

DART : PROJECTILE ::
- ◯ bow : arrow
- ◯ tug : ship
- ◯ dirigible : balloon
- ◯ shiv : knife
- ◯ jalopy : transport

APOSTATE : RELIGION ::
- ◯ iconoclast : apostasy
- ◯ pacifist : violence
- ◯ recluse : society
- ◯ heretic : doctrine
- ◯ sycophant : subordination

INSIPID : STIMULATION ::
- ◯ pallid : chroma
- ◯ trivial : detail
- ◯ hirsute : fervor
- ◯ robust : vigor
- ◯ moribund : proximity

STREAM : EDDY ::
- ◯ report : error
- ◯ ocean : tide
- ◯ flock : rogue
- ◯ trend : anomaly
- ◯ field : canal

AMORPHOUS : CONTOUR ::
- ◯ taut : tension
- ◯ limpid : opacity
- ◯ malleable : plasticity
- ◯ prosaic : poetry
- ◯ quotidian : repetition

PATRIOTIC : CHAUVINISTIC ::
- ◯ pedagogical : instructive
- ◯ omnipotent : ubiquitous
- ◯ voracious : ravenous
- ◯ competent : adept
- ◯ steadfast : obdurate

ANALOGIES: DRILL 4

BOUQUET : FLOWERS ::
- ○ canton : geese
- ○ bark : trees
- ○ fog : precipitation
- ○ cairn : stones
- ○ pool : water

PEDIATRICS : CHILDREN ::
- ○ toxicology : poison
- ○ genealogy : heredity
- ○ optometry : eyes
- ○ anesthesiology : surgery
- ○ zoology : animals

DECIBEL : SOUND ::
- ○ pint : milk
- ○ gram : ounce
- ○ volume : amplitude
- ○ fathom : depth
- ○ calorie : light

SYNONYMOUS : MEANING ::
- ○ harmonious : melody
- ○ amorphous : shape
- ○ dissenting : belief
- ○ contiguous : shape
- ○ identical : appearance

PIRATE : TAKE ::
- ○ swindle : dupe
- ○ counterfeit : print
- ○ plunder : swoop
- ○ surrender : expunge
- ○ plagiarize : cheat

COLLUSION : CONSPIRATORS ::
- ○ sophistry : pundits
- ○ naivety : ingénue
- ○ delusion : prophets
- ○ intuition : animals
- ○ deception : brigands

DIVERT : SHUNT ::
- ○ exit : enter
- ○ review : correct
- ○ shun : ostracize
- ○ quiet : close
- ○ circulate : disseminate

EQUIVOCATE : COMMITMENT ::
- ○ elucidate : proposal
- ○ ruminate : theory
- ○ dither : decision
- ○ excoriate : critique
- ○ mollify : appeasement

CENSORSHIP : INFORMATION ::
- ○ austerity : moderation
- ○ survey : demographic
- ○ purification : dross
- ○ deforestation : desertification
- ○ globalization : communication

SPEAK : RETICENT ::
- ○ wait : keen
- ○ evade : furtive
- ○ chastise : laudable
- ○ fight : bellicose
- ○ grow : petulant

ENDEMIC : REGION ::
- ⃝ emblematic : nation
- ⃝ innate : organism
- ⃝ mutant : genome
- ⃝ inchoate : idea
- ⃝ divergent : standard

ARMADA : VEHICLE ::
- ⃝ cordite : explosive
- ⃝ army : general
- ⃝ navy : army
- ⃝ swarm : bee
- ⃝ phalanx : formation

PECCADILLO : SIN ::
- ⃝ penance : forgiveness
- ⃝ exaltation : delectation
- ⃝ hoard : accumulation
- ⃝ hubris : pride
- ⃝ bagatelle : composition

ATTENTIVE : OFFICIOUS ::
- ⃝ magisterial : authoritative
- ⃝ impromptu : spontaneous
- ⃝ risible : ribald
- ⃝ timorous : craven
- ⃝ pecuniary : usurious

FRESCO : WALL ::
- ⃝ fountain : courtyard
- ⃝ parquetry : floor
- ⃝ thatch : roof
- ⃝ statuary : passage
- ⃝ gargoyle : church

PERFUNCTORY : ENTHUSIASM ::
- ⃝ insolent : veneration
- ⃝ phlegmatic : composure
- ⃝ quixotic : refulgence
- ⃝ sedulous : assiduity
- ⃝ effusive : encomium

ADULT : CHILD ::
- ⃝ horse : mare
- ⃝ sheep : ram
- ⃝ chicken : capon
- ⃝ cow : veal
- ⃝ dog : whelp

BLANDISHMENT : COAX ::
- ⃝ alloy : debase
- ⃝ egress : enter
- ⃝ guffaw : regale
- ⃝ abscission : detach
- ⃝ torque : rotate

RING : ARENA ::
- ⃝ mendicant : liar
- ⃝ equipoise: fairness
- ⃝ buckler : shield
- ⃝ frieze: painting
- ⃝ rebus : symbol

SHARD : POTTERY ::
- ⃝ cinder : coal
- ⃝ flange : wheel
- ⃝ viand : food
- ⃝ ream : paper
- ⃝ crumb : bread

ANALOGIES: DRILL 5

SCALPEL : SURGEON ::
- ⬭ laser : agronomist
- ⬭ violin : composer
- ⬭ art : philistine
- ⬭ lathe : carpenter
- ⬭ ruler : teacher

ENVELOPE : LETTER ::
- ⬭ womb : fetus
- ⬭ package : ribbon
- ⬭ recipe : ingredient
- ⬭ house : furnace
- ⬭ case : animal

BARRAGE : EXPLOSIVE ::
- ⬭ symphony : sound
- ⬭ deluge : water
- ⬭ grenade : bomb
- ⬭ trench : soldier
- ⬭ abstract : painting

PANEGYRIC : EULOGIZE ::
- ⬭ ode : criticize
- ⬭ lampoon : satirize
- ⬭ tirade : entertain
- ⬭ diatribe : extirpate
- ⬭ homily : sanctify

WARY : GULLED ::
- ⬭ loquacious : befriended
- ⬭ taciturn : goaded
- ⬭ passionate : moved
- ⬭ tenacious : deterred
- ⬭ inured : placated

WARDROBE : CLOTHES ::
- ⬭ stove : crockery
- ⬭ bookcase : books
- ⬭ crowd : people
- ⬭ zoo : animals
- ⬭ chair : cushion

ANECDOTE : STORY ::
- ⬭ chapter : novel
- ⬭ skit : play
- ⬭ epic : poem
- ⬭ mobile : sculpture
- ⬭ melody : song

ALLERGY : REACTION ::
- ⬭ rash : body
- ⬭ malady : ailment
- ⬭ antihistamine : symptoms
- ⬭ grimace : expression
- ⬭ chortle : feedback

FANATICAL : ENTHUSIASTIC ::
- ⬭ pedantic : educated
- ⬭ flamboyant : stylish
- ⬭ cautious : circumspect
- ⬭ pious : virtuous
- ⬭ idolatrous : devoted

HOAX : HOODWINK ::
- ⬭ ruse : enchant
- ⬭ morass : expedite
- ⬭ stratagem : malign
- ⬭ encomium : praise
- ⬭ banter : solidify

INVINCIBLE : SUBJUGATED ::

- ◯ improvident : dismissed
- ◯ unmeasurable : gauged
- ◯ haughty : beseeched
- ◯ melded : bifurcated
- ◯ costly : discounted

GRIEF : KEEN ::

- ◯ glee : chortle
- ◯ jejune : blanch
- ◯ elongated : yawn
- ◯ genteel : fumble
- ◯ ingenuous : deceive

BUTTRESS : INSTABILITY ::

- ◯ carapace : defense
- ◯ portal : accessibility
- ◯ endowment : security
- ◯ soporific : vigilance
- ◯ pontoon : flotation

SKIRMISH : BATTLE ::

- ◯ revolt : sanguine
- ◯ campaign : pyrrhic
- ◯ spat : argument
- ◯ coup : abrupt
- ◯ siege : monolithic

FILIGREE : ORNAMENT ::

- ◯ flambeau : douse
- ◯ tapestry: weave
- ◯ filament : tangle
- ◯ ewer : gauge
- ◯ piton : moor

DOGGEREL : VERSE ::

- ◯ pulp : magazine
- ◯ cameo : heirloom
- ◯ concerto : quartet
- ◯ cubism : perspective
- ◯ haiku : ode

STYGIAN : DARK ::

- ◯ sidereal : bright
- ◯ innocuous : fatal
- ◯ churlish : impolite
- ◯ unfathomable : trenchant
- ◯ stealthy : contemporaneous

EVANESCENT : DISAPPEAR ::

- ◯ immutable : change
- ◯ quiescent : still
- ◯ tempting : snare
- ◯ prolific : write
- ◯ munificent : give

SUITCASE : LUGGAGE ::

- ◯ penguin : amphibian
- ◯ summit : range
- ◯ bank : river
- ◯ hat : millinery
- ◯ soloist : troupe

MALADROIT : SKILL ::

- ◯ charitable : benevolence
- ◯ exigent : urgency
- ◯ incisive : insolence
- ◯ tenebrous : light
- ◯ articulate : verbosity

ANALOGIES: DRILL 6

RUFFLE : GARMENT ::
- ○ shade : window
- ○ hanging : wall
- ○ handle : briefcase
- ○ pavement : street
- ○ lace : shoe

EMIGRATE : EXILE ::
- ○ enlist : conscript
- ○ ban : bar
- ○ acclimate : welcome
- ○ flee : sprint
- ○ plant : cultivate

ANTIDOTE : POISON ::
- ○ emetic : nausea
- ○ prognosis : treatment
- ○ sedative : relaxation
- ○ antiseptic : infection
- ○ antihistamine : respiration

PEST : IRKSOME ::
- ○ surgeon : talented
- ○ tyro : inexperienced
- ○ concierge : polite
- ○ champion : indecisive
- ○ director : boastful

AMPLIFY : VOLUME ::
- ○ grow : width
- ○ augment : size
- ○ relax : tension
- ○ climb : rung
- ○ glide : updraft

CENTRIFUGE : SEPARATE ::
- ○ odometer : calculate
- ○ lumber : saw
- ○ levee : flood
- ○ sieve : sift
- ○ barometer : forecast

INDELIBILITY : ERASURE ::
- ○ incorrigibility : reform
- ○ exegesis : analysis
- ○ immorality : paternoster
- ○ ineffability : trust
- ○ incorruptibility : odor

EXPIATE : GUILT ::
- ○ appease : forgiveness
- ○ boast : reputation
- ○ angle : compliment
- ○ buff : roughness
- ○ flatter : favor

INFILTRATE : ENTER ::
- ○ thwart : prevent
- ○ accuse : confront
- ○ avoid : elude
- ○ eavesdrop : hear
- ○ blame : censure

PARQUET : WOOD ::
- ○ macramé : beads
- ○ bouquet : corsage
- ○ decoupage : covering
- ○ carpet : slate
- ○ patchwork : cloth

HEMORRHAGE : BLEEDING ::
- ◯ somnolent : strengthen
- ◯ myopia : vision
- ◯ palpitation : heartbeat
- ◯ nausea : tension
- ◯ fracture : splinting

IRASCIBLE : TEMPER ::
- ◯ peckish : hunger
- ◯ astute : mind
- ◯ viscous : fluidity
- ◯ bellicose : rage
- ◯ extravagant : spending

CREDULOUS : DUPE ::
- ◯ archaic : hag
- ◯ craven : coward
- ◯ sagacious : hermit
- ◯ pedantic : teacher
- ◯ virtuous : viceroy

MELODRAMA : EXAGGERATED ::
- ◯ fallacy : erroneous
- ◯ tragedy : comedic
- ◯ novelty : substantial
- ◯ serendipity : intentional
- ◯ primogeniture : just

INTERESTED : AGOG ::
- ◯ guileless : trusting
- ◯ neat : fastidious
- ◯ dogmatic : canonical
- ◯ mesmerized : curious
- ◯ adulterated : pure

SELFLESSNESS : ALTRUIST ::
- ◯ benevolence : monarch
- ◯ heterodoxy : schismatic
- ◯ belligerence : provocateur
- ◯ flippancy : braggart
- ◯ verbosity : raconteur

USURY : INTEREST ::
- ◯ prodigality : spending
- ◯ hubris : courage
- ◯ wistfulness : nostalgia
- ◯ parthenogenesis : conception
- ◯ husbandry : agriculture

HEDONIST : PLEASURE ::
- ◯ ecclesiastic : homiletics
- ◯ sybarite : teetotalism
- ◯ votary : religion
- ◯ misanthrope : humankind
- ◯ boor : effrontery

QUAIL : COURAGE ::
- ◯ pine : vigor
- ◯ expurgate : obscenity
- ◯ aggrandize : intensity
- ◯ stanch : flow
- ◯ remonstrate : unfairness

LUMBER : GRACE ::
- ◯ belie : impression
- ◯ intimate : secret
- ◯ list : lean
- ◯ saunter : speed
- ◯ sap : vitality

ANALOGIES: DRILL 7

PERIMETER : SQUARE ::
- ⬭ circumference : circle
- ⬭ volume : cube
- ⬭ angle : tangent
- ⬭ degree : radian
- ⬭ parallelogram : rectangle

Question 2 of 20

DETOXIFY : POISON ::
- ⬭ parch : moisture
- ⬭ clarify : evidence
- ⬭ soak : liquid
- ⬭ melt : solid
- ⬭ outfit : clothing

Question 3 of 20

CAUSTIC : EAT AWAY ::
- ⬭ acridness : embitter
- ⬭ magnanimity : succor
- ⬭ ennui : jade
- ⬭ leaven : rise
- ⬭ cacophony : gall

Question 4 of 20

DERMATOLOGIST : SKIN ::
- ⬭ orthopedist : feet
- ⬭ psychologist : dreams
- ⬭ pediatrician : kidneys
- ⬭ periodontist : gums
- ⬭ cardiologist : arteries

Question 5 of 20

PLUMMET : FALL ::
- ⬭ bifurcate : repel
- ⬭ perambulate : walk
- ⬭ flush : redden
- ⬭ abscond : depart
- ⬭ whirl : spin

Question 6 of 20

HEAT : CALORIE ::
- ⬭ altimeter : elevation
- ⬭ energy : joule
- ⬭ gas : combustion
- ⬭ electricity : circuit
- ⬭ turbine : fluid

Question 7 of 20

PRESCIENCE : FUTURE ::
- ⬭ adumbration : antecedent
- ⬭ truculence : sentiment
- ⬭ equivocation : ambiguity
- ⬭ connoisseur : discrimination
- ⬭ omniscience : everything

Question 8 of 20

SUSPICIOUS : PARANOID ::
- ⬭ pious : heretical
- ⬭ egotistical : jealous
- ⬭ thrifty : miserly
- ⬭ obstinate : stubborn
- ⬭ derision : angry

Question 9 of 20

ASSERT : BELABOR ::
- ⬭ attack : fulminate
- ⬭ descant : comment
- ⬭ sway : waver
- ⬭ annoy : prattle
- ⬭ scold : harangue

Question 10 of 20

DIALECTIC : REASONING ::
- ⬭ canon : religion
- ⬭ hubris : presumption
- ⬭ rhetoric : credibility
- ⬭ pedagogy : intelligence
- ⬭ convention : practice

ADULTERATE : PURITY ::
○ enervate : emotion
○ damp : intensity
○ moralize : probity
○ ameliorate : tolerable
○ slake : hunger

ACCELERATE : TEMPO ::
○ inhibit : outburst
○ extrapolate : quality
○ disseminate : concentration
○ amplify : volume
○ exacerbate : prowess

PARRY : BLOW ::
○ dam : flow
○ demur : opponent
○ arrest : attention
○ divulge : query
○ spar : kick

JUGGERNAUT : CRUSH ::
○ libertine : revolt
○ rebus : defy
○ virago : nag
○ muse : flatter
○ leviathan : demolish

TRANSGRESSION : MORALITY ::
○ approbation : approval
○ faux pas : etiquette
○ court-martial : military
○ pilferage : culpability
○ tirade : impropriety

GOURMAND : FOOD ::
○ maverick : group
○ epicure : wine
○ pedant : learning
○ neophyte : convert
○ sybarite : luxury

STRIATE : RIDGES ::
○ bedecked : bangles
○ crafted : imperfections
○ hermetic : illustrations
○ amplified : improvements
○ piebald : patches

TURRET : TOWER ::
○ lancet : amphibian
○ hamlet : municipality
○ spinet : loom
○ pamphlet : propaganda
○ doublet : duplicate

BALLAST : STABILITY ::
○ fulcrum : balance
○ monocle : vision
○ sextant : altitude
○ fuel : energy
○ odometer : mileage

INVEIGH : ATTACK ::
○ flog : punish
○ calumniate : accuse
○ beatify : gladden
○ panegyrize : praise
○ asseverate : denounce

ANSWERS

Drill 1
1. B
2. C
3. C
4. E
5. D
6. B
7. C
8. E
9. A
10. B
11. A
12. D
13. C
14. B
15. E
16. E
17. A
18. A
19. C
20. B

Drill 3
1. E
2. A
3. D
4. D
5. E
6. C
7. D
8. C
9. B
10. B
11. B
12. E
13. C
14. A
15. D
16. B
17. A
18. D
19. B
20. E

Drill 2
1. E
2. C
3. D
4. B
5. E
6. D
7. A
8. C
9. B
10. D
11. D
12. B
13. C
14. D
15. C
16. B
17. D
18. C
19. C
20. B

Drill 4
1. D
2. C
3. D
4. E
5. B
6. B
7. C
8. C
9. C
10. A
11. B
12. D
13. E
14. D
15. B
16. A
17. E
18. A
19. C
20. E

Drill 5

1. D
2. A
3. B
4. B
5. D
6. B
7. B
8. D
9. E
10. D
11. B
12. A
13. D
14. C
15. E
16. A
17. C
18. E
19. D
20. D

Drill 6

1. B
2. A
3. D
4. B
5. B
6. D
7. A
8. D
9. D
10. E
11. A
12. B
13. B
14. A
15. B
16. B
17. A
18. C
19. A
20. D

Drill 7

1. A
2. A
3. D
4. D
5. E
6. B
7. E
8. C
9. E
10. A
11. B
12. D
13. A
14. C
15. B
16. E
17. E
18. B
19. D
20. D

EXPLANATIONS

Drill 1

1. **B** Make a defining sentence: A person will *study* in order to *learn*. The best answer is choice (B) because a person will *search* in order to *find*. Choices (A), (D), and (E) do not have defining relationships. Choice (C) is tempting, but to *permeate* is to *penetrate* completely. It is not necessarily true that to *study* is to *learn* completely, as one can study something difficult and not learn it.

2. **C** Make a defining sentence: To *suffocate* is to deny *oxygen*. The best answer is choice (C) because *imprison* means to deny *freedom*. Choices (A), (B), and (E) do not have defining relationships. Choice (D) has a relationship but it is different from the stem pair: To *inhibit* is to stop a person's *drive*.

3. **C** Make a defining sentence: A *soliloquy* is performed by one person in a *play*. The best answer is choice (C) because an *aria* is performed by one person in an *opera*. If you don't know one of the words in the stem pair, work backwards with the words you do know, use word roots, and POE. Remember that "*sol-*" means *one*. A *concerto* is a musical piece that can use a variety of instruments, not just a *piano*, so choice (B) does not have a defining relationship. A *duet* involves two people, not one, eliminating choice (D). A *stanza* is a section of a *sonnet* (among other forms), and an *overture* is the beginning of a *musical* (among other works), so these choices do not fit into the original sentence.

4. **E** Make a defining sentence using the "characteristic of" option from "recycled relationships": Being *brave* is not characteristic of a *coward*. The best answer is choice (E) because being *stingy* is not characteristic of a *philanthropist*. Not every *martyr* is motivated by being *religious*, so choice (A) does not have a defining relationship. Being *uncertain* is characteristic of an *agnostic*, so choice (B) is the opposite relationship from the one in the stem pair. A *hero* does get beaten sometimes, and being a *traitor* doesn't necessarily mean that one is not *amicable*, so choices (C) and (D) do not have defining relationships.

5. **D** Make a defining sentence: To *evaporate* is to turn into *vapor*. The best answer is choice (D) because to *petrify* is to turn into *stone*. Choice (B) does not have a defining relationship at all, and it should be eliminated. *Salt* is used to *season*, and an *inferno* is a thing that *incinerates*, so choices (A) and (E) do not have the same relationship as the stem pair. To *centrifuge* is to separate parts of a *fluid*, so choice (C) also has the wrong relationship.

6. **B** Make a defining sentence: *minutiae* are very small *details*. The best answer is choice (B) because *quibbles* are very small *complaints*. If you don't know one of the words in the stem pair, try working backwards and using word roots and POE. Remember that "*min-*" means small. Choice (A) does not have a defining relationship and should be eliminated. Choices (C) and (E) have "part of" relationships, and *minutiae* are not parts of details. The words *approximation* and *estimation* are too similar; synonyms are tempting common traps, so eliminate choice (D).

7. C   Make a defining sentence: Something *didactic* is intended to *instruct*. The best answer is choice (C) because something *comical* is intended to *amuse*. If you don't know one of the words in the stem pair, try working backwards and using POE. Choices (B) and (E) do not have defining relationships, so they should be eliminated. When something is *imperative*, the intent is that it should be obeyed, not that it will itself *obey*, so choice (D) does not have the same relationship as the stem pair. Something *dynamic* is used to *energize*, so choice (A) also contains a relationship slightly different from the stem pair.

8. E   Make a defining sentence using a recycled relationship: Being *withdrawn* is characteristic of a *recluse*. The best answer is choice (E) because being *prejudiced* is characteristic of a *bigot*. A *pacifist* is a person who is *not belligerent*, so choice (A) has the opposite relationship. A *miser* is not necessarily *despondent*: He may be happy in his penny-pinching. Choices (B) and (C) do not have defining relationships.

9. A   Make a defining sentence: Something *foolproof* cannot *fail*. The best answer is choice (A) because something *immortal* cannot *die*. Choices (B) and (C) have associations but not defining relationships. Something that is *viscous* is not currently solidified, but that doesn't mean that it cannot *solidify*, so choice (D) doesn't have a defining relationship either. Something that is *volatile* is quite likely to *detonate*, so choice (E) has the opposite relationship from the stem pair.

10. B   Make a defining sentence: Someone with *insomnia* finds it difficult to *sleep*. The best answer is choice (B) because someone with *dyslexia* finds it difficult to *read*. If you don't know one of the words in the stem pair, or you just can't make a good defining sentence, try working backwards and using POE. Someone with *hyperactivity* is known to *fidget*, and someone with *paranoia* is known to *imagine*. Besides going in the opposite direction, choices (A) and (D) have the same defining sentence, so eliminate them. In choice (C), someone with *malnutrition* hasn't had enough to *eat*. This answer is a close second, but *insomnia* is about the difficulty of getting to *sleep*, not the dire result of not sleeping. Thus choice (B) is better. For someone with *hemophilia*, it is dangerous to *bleed*. It makes no sense that for someone with *insomnia*, it is dangerous to *sleep*, so eliminate choice (E).

11. A   Make a defining sentence using a recycled relationship: To be *audacious* is to lack *trepidation*. The best answer is choice (A) because to be *laconic* is to lack *verbosity*. If you don't know one of the words in the stem pair, try working backwards and using POE. Choices (B), (D), and (E) do not have defining relationships, so they should be eliminated. *Intransigence* is characteristic of one who is *obstinate*, so choice (C) has a relationship that is opposite to the one in the stem pair.

12. D   Make a defining sentence: To be *garrulous* is to be excessively *talkative*. The best answer is choice (D) because to be *cloying* is to be excessively *sweet*. If you don't know one of the words in the stem pair, use POE. To be *cantankerous* is to be excessively non-*affable*, so choice (A) has the opposite relationship from the one in the stem pair. Choices (B), (C), and (E) do not have defining relationships and should be eliminated.

13.   C   Make a defining sentence: To be *furtive* is to act with *stealth*. The best answer is choice (C) because to be *whimsical* is to act with *fancy*. If you don't know one of the words in the stem pair, or you just can't make a good defining sentence, try working backwards and using POE. Choices (A), (B), and (E) do not have defining relationships and should be eliminated. Something *arduous* may require *fortitude*, but this is not the definition, so eliminate choice (D).

14.   B   Make a defining sentence: Someone *mercurial* has changing *moods*. The best answer is choice (B) because someone *fickle* has changing *affections*. If you don't know one of the words in the stem pair, try working backwards and using POE. Choices (C), (D), and (E) do not have defining relationships, so they can be eliminated. Someone *paranoid* simpy has *mistrust*, not changing *mistrust*. It does not make sense that to be *mercurial* is to have *mood*, so eliminate choice (A).

15.   E   Make a defining sentence: To *disabuse* is to bring an end to a person's *error*. The best answer is choice (E) because to *rehabilitate* is to bring an end to a person's *dependence*. If you don't know one of the words in the stem pair, or you just can't make a good defining sentence, try working backwards and using POE. Choices (A) and (C) do not have defining relationships. To *vilify* is to hurt a person's *reputation*. It makes no sense to say that to *disabuse* is to hurt a person's *error*, so eliminate choice (B). To *discern* is to make a *discrimination*. It could make sense to say that to *disabuse* is to make an *error*, so try using roots and sides of the fence to pick between choices (D) and (E). The root "*dis-*" means "away from," so going away from abuse sounds like getting rid of error. The words in choice (D) are on the same side, and those in choice (E) are on opposite sides, so choice (E) is more likely to be the credited response.

16.   E   Make a defining sentence: One cannot *daunt* someone who is *fearless*. The best answer is choice (E) because one cannot *perturb* someone who is *impassive*. If you don't know one of the words in the stem pair, or you just can't make a good defining sentence, use POE. Choices (A), (C), and (D) do not have defining relationships, so they should be eliminated. One who is *serene* may be easy to *placate*, but the definitional relationship is weak because *placate* suggests that the serene person has been angry; plus, the direction is opposite. Eliminate choice (B).

17.   A   Make a defining sentence: Someone *servile* is overly *compliant*. The best answer is choice (A) because someone *gullible* is overly *credulous*. If you don't know one of the words in the stem pair, or you just can't make a good defining sentence, try working backwards. Choices (B), (C), and (D) have associations but not defining relationships, so they should be eliminated. Choice (E) may be tempting, but *audacious* is too close in meaning to *adventurous*, and there is no negative connotation in *audacious*, as there is in *servile*.

18.   A   Make a defining sentence: A *querulous* person is one who *carps*. The best answer is choice (A) because a *profligate* person is one who *squanders*. If you don't know one of the words in the stem pair, use POE. An *arrogant* person will not *fawn*, a *perfidious* person will not *safeguard*, and a *laconic* person will not *ramble*. Because all three sentences go the opposite direction from the stem pair, answer choices (B), (C), and (E) may be eliminated. Choice (D) contains an association but not a defining relationship, so this choice may also be eliminated.

19.   C   Make a defining sentence: An *urbane* person acts without *gaucherie*. The best answer is choice (C) because a *guileless* person acts without *chicanery*. If you don't know one of the words in the stem pair, or you just can't make a good defining sentence, try working backwards. Choices (A), (B), and (D) do not contain defining relationships, so they can be eliminated. A *conniving* person acts with *imposture*. Because choices (C) and (E) go in opposite directions from each other, your best strategy would be just to pick one and move on if you don't know the meaning of one of the words in the stem pair. If you dig a little deeper in comparing choices (C) and (E), you will observe that *conniving* involves conspiracy, while *imposture* is simple deception, which one can practice alone, while the words in choice (C) are inherently related.

20.   B   Make a defining sentence: A *plutocracy* is a government in which power derives from *affluence*. The best answer is choice (B) because a *patriarchy* is a government in which power derives from *androcentricity*. If you don't know one of the words in the stem pair, try working backwards and using word roots and POE. Remember that "*-cracy*" means "government." Similarly, *androcentricity* can be broken down into roots: "*andro-*" means "man," and "*-centr-*" means center. Choices (A) and (D) do not have defining relationships, so they should be eliminated. *Anarchy* is characterized by the absence of *jurisprudence*; it seems unlikely that a government would be characterized by an absence of *affluence*, so you can eliminate choice (E). *Hegemony* has no relationship with *geography*. Guess between choices (B) and (C) if you don't know the words. To be very precise, every government derives power from someplace—religion, the people, or, in the present case, wealth—but *hegemony* is about the degree of power, not the source.

Drill 2

1.   E   Keep your defining sentence simple by using a recycled relationship: A *dog* is a type of *animal*. The best answer is choice (E) because *jazz* is a type of *music*. Choice (A) does not have a defining relationship because it is only an association, so eliminate it. In choice (B), a *team* is a group of people who play a *sport*—not the relationship you're looking for. Choice (D) has a "part of" relationship, which is different from the stem pair. Choice (C) reverses the order of the relationship; a fish is not a type of minnow but *vice versa*.

2.   C   Make a defining sentence: *Nicotine* is a drug found in *tobacco*. The best answer is choice (C) because *caffeine* is a drug found in *coffee*. The other answer choices also have "found in" relationships, but only choice (C) is about a drug.

3.   D   Make a defining sentence using a recycled relationship: *Muted* means having very little *color*. The best answer is choice (D) because *insipid* means having very little *flavor*. Choices (A) and (C) do not have defining relationships, so eliminate them. *Cacophonous* means having discordant *sound*, so choice (B) has a different relationship from the stem pair. *Cloying* means having excessive *sentiment*, so choice (E) has an opposite relationship from the stem pair.

4. **B** Make a defining sentence: Something *untenable* cannot be *defended*. The best answer is choice (B): Something *ephemeral* cannot be *perpetuated*. Something *arduous* is *executed* with great difficulty, but it can be *executed*, so eliminate choice (A). *Caustic* and *eroded* are on the same side of the fence, but we are looking for a pair on different sides of the fence, so eliminate choice (C). Something *viscous* is not currently *solidified*, but that doesn't mean that it couldn't become *solidified*, so cross off choice (D). *Inimical* and *desiccated* have no relationship, so eliminate choice (E).

5. **E** Make a defining sentence: To *prate* is to *speak* without purpose. The best answer is choice (E) because to *meander* is to *walk* without purpose. All the other choices have connections but not the ones you want. To *demean* means the opposite of *laud*. To *loiter* means to *pause* for a long time. *Cajole* and *inveigle*, as well as *gaze* and *inspect*, are too close in meaning; the credited response will not be a synonym.

6. **D** Make a defining sentence using a recycled relationship: *Obtuseness* is a lack of *intelligence*. The best answer is choice (D) because *callousness* is a lack of *sensitivity*. Choice (B) does not have a defining relationship, so eliminate it. Choices (A) and (C) express similar, "characterized by" relationships, so you can eliminate both of them. In addition, they both go in the opposite direction from the stem pair. Choice (E) has a "high degree of" relationship, not a "lack of" relationship.

7. **E** Make a defining sentence: *Fanaticism* is an extreme form of *enthusiasm*. The best answer is choice (B) because *abhorrence* is an extreme form of *repugnance.*. Choices (B), (C), and (E) do not have defining relationships, so eliminate them. One who has *reticence* lacks *extroversion*, so choice (D) has an opposite relationship from the stem pair.

8. **C** Make a defining sentence: To *perturb* is to interrupt the *placidity* of something. The best answer is choice (C) because to *dam* is to interrupt the *flow* of something. If you're unsure of the meaning of *placidity,* use word associations. *Placid* signifies "calm" or "peaceful," and "placate" means "soothe or appease." *Perturb*, meanwhile, sounds like "disturb," to which it is nearly identical in meaning. Choice (B) does not have a defining relationship, so you can eliminate it. To *excite* is to cause *unrest*, and to *thrust* is to cause *protrusion*. Choices (A) and (D) have similar relationships, so eliminate both of them. Plus, the relationships go in the opposite direction from the stem pair. *Plasticity* means the quality of being easy to *mold*, so choice (E) isn't the relationship you're looking for.

9. **B** Make a defining sentence: A *colossus* is an extremely large *figurine*. The best answer is choice (B) because an *epic* is an extremely large *poem*. If you don't know one of the words in the stem pair, work backwards and use word roots and POE. You might notice that *colossus* sounds like "colossal," so it might be something big. *Eagle* and *hawk* are different species of birds, so eliminate choice (E). Choice (A) is merely an association, so it can also be eliminated. A *gladiator* fights in an *arena*, and because nothing is likely to fight in a *figurine*, you should feel safe eliminating choice (C). *Grandiloquence* and *loquacity* are both undesirable qualities in a speaker, but the first is about pomposity, and the second is about length, so eliminate choice (D).

10. **D** Make a defining sentence: To *disguise* is intended to prevent *recognition*. The best answer is choice (D) because to *guard* is intended to prevent *incursion*. To *inure* is to become accustomed to *hardship,* to *stupefy* is to cause *befuddlement,* and to *camouflage* is to use a concealing *covering,* so choices (A), (B), and (E) have different relationships from the stem pair. Choice (C) contains two synonyms, a known trap, so it can be eliminated.

11. **D** If you know the meaning of the words, you can make a defining sentence: *Caesura* is a pause or break in the *verse*. The best answer is choice (D) because *abeyance* is a pause in the *action*. If you don't know one of the words in the stem pair, or you just can't make a good defining sentence, work backwards and use POE. Choice (C) does not have a defining relationship, so you can eliminate it. *Dormancy* is a period of inactivity in a *volcano;* it seems unlikely that there would be a period of inactivity in a *response,* so eliminate choice (B). *Stagnancy* is the opposite of *hyperactivity;* antonyms are unlikely to be the credited response, so eliminate choice (E). *Inoculation* is the process of strengthening *immunity,* so choices (A) and (D) both have good relationships. Guess from these two choices if you don't know the meaning of *latency.*

12. **B** Make a defining sentence: To *disabuse* is to free someone from *deception*. The best answer is choice (B) because to *manumit* is to free someone from *bondage*. There is some difficult vocabulary here, but if you focus on the "*dis-*" (meaning "away from"), you can infer that the word must signify something close to "lack of abuse," suggesting that its meaning is on the other side of the fence from *deception*. The words in choices (A) and (D) go in the same direction, and choices (C) and (E) don't have defining relationships. Choice (B) is the only choice left.

13. **C** Make a defining sentence: *Cogency* means a condition exactly the opposite of *unconvincing*. The best answer is choice (C) because *salience* means a condition that is opposite of *inconspicuous*. If you have a vague idea of what *cogency* means but aren't entirely sure of the definition, start by seeing whether the word is positive or negative. *Cogency* is positive, while *unconvincing* is negative. The stem words are on opposite sides of the fence, so eliminate choices (A) and (B), which contain words on the same side of the fence. Choices (D) and (E) do not have defining relationships, so eliminate them as well.

14. **D** Make a defining sentence: *Benediction* is a religious *blessing*. The best answer is choice (D), because *anathema* is a religious *condemnation*. Even if you don't know the exact definition of *benediction,* you might recognize it as a positive word, making the stem words go the same way. Choice (B) doesn't work, because *celebration* is positive while *antipathy* is negative. People say positive things in a *eulogy,* while *abhorrence* is definitely negative, thus eliminating choice (A) for the same reason. Choice (E) does not have a defining relationship. A *valentine* expresses *amorousness,* so choice (C) sounds similar to choice (D), and you need to look for some kind of difference between the two. Do you think a *benediction* is more likely to be a thing, like a *valentine,* or an act, like *censure*? If you're still not sure, make a guess and move on.

15.   C   Make a defining sentence: An *exoskeleton* provides external protection for an *insect*. The best answer is choice (C) because the *epidermis* provides external protection for a *human*. Choice (A) has a "type of" relationship, which doesn't match the stem pair. Choice (B) seems intriguing, but goes in the opposite direction of the stem pair. Choice (D) also goes in the opposite direction and switches the relationship from external to internal. The *thorax* is a part of the body of a *hornet*, so eliminate choice (E).

16.   B   Make a defining sentence: A *pedigree* is a list of someone's *ancestors*. The best answer is choice (B) because a *transcript* is a list of someone's *grades*. Where have you heard the stem words before? Most people know pedigree in terms of purebred dogs; a pedigree tells you who a dog's parents and grandparents were. Choices (A), (C), and (D) do not have defining relationships. Work backwards to eliminate choice (E): *Venom* is an expression of *hate*, but it's not very likely that a *pedigree* is an expression of *ancestors*.

17.   D   Make a defining sentence: A *compendium* is characterized by being *succinct*. The best answer is choice (D) because an *expansion* is characterized by being *accretive*. If you are unsure of the meanings, work backwards and use POE. Choice (E) does not have a defining relationship, so eliminate it. Choice (B) seems that it could have a relationship: An *extrapolation* might be *concise*, but it also might not be; it's weak at best. A *neophyte* lacks *extensive* experience, quite the contrary to the relationship in the stem words; look at the roots—"*neo-*" means new. Could something new be characterized as *extensive*? Probably not, so eliminate choice (A). An *abridgement* makes a work shorter, but not in terms of space, so choice (C) does not have a defining relationship. Also *abridgement* looks suspiciously similar to *succinct*; maybe there's a trap here.

18.   C   Make a defining sentence: A *mercenary* works for *lucre*. The best answer is choice (C) because a *highwayman* works for *spoils*. If you aren't sure of the meanings, use word association and POE. *Lucre* sounds like "lucrative," which means something profitable. A *guerilla* may use *subterfuge* but does not work for *subterfuge*, so eliminate choice (A). Choices (B), (D), and (E) do not have defining relationships, so eliminate them. Choice (D) is an example of a common association; watch out for these.

19.   C   Make a defining sentence: A *cacophony* is unpleasant to the *auditory* sense. The best answer is choice (C) because a *stench* is unpleasant to the *olfactory* sense. If you are unsure of the words, try to use word association. *Cacophony* contains the stem "*phon-*," like phonetic or phone. These words have to do with sound, as does the word *auditory*. Choices (A), (D), and (E) do not have defining relationships, so eliminate them. *Stridence* is an unpleasant *behavioral* quality, but because there is no *behavioral* sense, choice (C) is a better match.

20. **B**   Make a defining sentence: An *imprecation* is meant to be *injurious*. The best answer is choice (B) because *hygiene* is meant to be *salubrious*. *Imprecation* and *injurious* are both negative words, so you want an answer choice that has both words on the same side of the fence. If you aren't sure what *salubrious* means, use word association: Some people say "*Salut*" at a meal, and "salutations" are positive greetings. Thus *hygiene* and *salubrious* are both positive. Choices (A), (C), and (D) don't have defining relationships, so eliminate them. In choice (E), a *boon* is meant to be *propitious,* but a *boon* is a result, not an action.

Drill 3

1. **E**   Make a defining sentence: A *tranquilizer* is used to *calm*. The best answer is choice (E) because a *stimulant* is used to *excite*. Choices (B) and (C) have other relationships: An *antihistamine* is given to help a person not *sneeze*, and *medication* is given to help a person not *ail*. Choice (D) does not have a defining relationship, so eliminate it. Choice (A) might look appealing because of the association with "quiet," but *quietus* actually means "death" and thus has no relationship to *sedate*.

2. **A**   Make a defining sentence: A *blacksmith* is a person who works with *iron*. The best answer is choice (A) because a *cobbler* is a person who works with *leather*. Choices (B) and (D) seem appealing at first glance, but they reverse the left-right order. A *horseshoe* isn't a person who works with an *anvil*; a *horseshoe* gets hammered on an *anvil*, so eliminate choice (E). A person works with both *hammer* and *nail*; they do not work with each other, so eliminate choice (C).

3. **D**   Make a defining sentence: A *filibuster* is used to *delay*. The best answer is choice (D) because *inquisition* is used to *probe*. Choice (A) might seem appealing, but is a *criticism* used to *anger*? People might become angry if they are criticized, but that is not by definition the intention of criticism. The relationship in choice (B) is weak: One might use *influence* to *authorize* but maybe not. *Reduction* is not used to *dilate*, but quite the contrary, so eliminate choice (C). *Brush* and *palette* have an association but no defining relationship, thus choice (E) can also be eliminated.

4. **D**   Make a defining sentence: A *talisman* is meant to cause something *magical*. The best answer is choice (D) because a *malediction* is meant to cause something *evil*. If you don't know *malediction*, remember that the root "*mal-*" means "bad." Choices (A), (B), (C), and (E) all have weak relationships: Some *amulets* are *circular*, but not all; some *mediums* are *communicative,* but not all; *some novels* are suspenseful, but not all, and while some *magicians* may be *hirsute* (hairy), this is not a defining characteristic. Note also in choice (A) that *amulet* is a synonym for *talisman*; could this be a trap answer?

5. **E** Make a defining sentence: *Biology* is the study of things *animate*. The best answer is choice (E) because *ornithology* is the study of things *avian*. If you're not a scientist, you may need to make heavy use of POE here. Choice (D) has no defining relationship, so eliminate it. Choice (A) has closely related words, but *swine* is not the study of anything. *Ichthyology* is the study of fish, while *aqueous* means "containing or dissolved in water." Thus choice (B) is incorrect. *Entomology* is the study of insects, not things *aquatic*. Just guess if you don't know these technical words.

6. **C** Make a defining sentence: *Frenzy* is characterized by not being *sedate*. The best answer is choice (C) because *uniqueness* is characterized by not being *mundane*. Choices (A) and (D) have the opposite relationship from the stem words, so eliminate them. Choice (E) contains words that could be related, but the relationship is weak—and even so, the words have the opposite relationship. It's not necessarily true that one who is *agitated* is not also *cheerful*, so choice (B) does not have a defining relationship.

7. **D** Make a defining sentence: A *soliloquy* is a performance by a *singleton*. The best answer is choice (D) because a *duet* is a performance by a *dyad*. Choice (C) clearly does not have this relationship. The remaining answer choices all may sound appealing, but be picky! Is an *epilogue* a performance by a *thespian*? It could be, but an epilogue could also appear at the end of a book. The same goes for choices (B) and (E); the relationship could hold true, but it isn't defining.

8. **C** Make a defining sentence: A *stratagem* is used to *deceive*. The best answer is choice (C) because an *ambuscade* is used to *surprise*. If you aren't sure of the words, use POE. Choices (A), (D), and (E) do not have defining relationships, so eliminate them. One can *lose* a *gambit,* but one might also win a *gambit*, so there's no defining relationship in choice (B) either. You might notice that *ambuscade* sounds like "ambush"—turns out, they're synonyms.

9. **B** Make a defining sentence: To *subpoena* means to summon a *witness*. The best answer is choice (B) because to *conjure* means to summon a *spirit*. Choice (A) is incorrect because to *indict* means to formally charge, not summon, a *criminal*. The words in choices (C), (D), and (E) don't have defining relationships.

10. **B** Make a defining sentence: *Astrology* is a less scientific version of *astronomy*. The best answer is choice (B) because *phrenology* is a less scientific version of *psychology*. Choices (A) and (D) don't have defining relationships. Although *neurology* might be thought of as a sub-sub-branch of *biology*, and *massage* can be a type of *therapy*, they're not by definition less scientific versions, so eliminate choices (C) and (E).

11. **B** Make a defining sentence: A *malapropism* is a type of *verbal* mistake. The best answer is choice (B) because a *miscalculation* is a type of *mathematical* mistake. Choice (A) may sound tempting, but a *tic* is an involuntary *facial* spasm, not a mistake. Choices (C) and (D) don't have defining relationships. The words *hypothesis* and *theoretical* have some connection but not of the mistake variety. Choice (E) is incorrect because *etiquette* describes proper *social* behavior, not a *social* mistake.

12. **E**   Make a defining sentence: You *lubricate* to avoid *abrasion*. The best answer is choice (E) because you *hydrate* to avoid *desiccation*. Choices (A) and (B) have the opposite relationship from the stem pair because you *aerate* to create *ventilation*, not avoid it, and to *adulterate* means to add *impurities*. The words in choices (C) and (D) don't have defining relationships. To *decant* means to pour, so there is no relation to *spoilage*, and to *synthesize* means to create a man-made version, which does not have to involve *replication*.

13. **C**   Make a defining sentence: To have *pluck* means one is unlikely to *quit*. The best answer is choice (C) because to have *gravitas* means one is unlikely to *amuse*. Remember to check for secondary meanings when you see familiar words in unfamiliar pairs. If you don't know one of the words in the stem pair or just can't make a good defining sentence, try working backwards. To *swagger* is to show *bravado*. Could to *quit* mean to show *pluck*? If you don't know what *pluck* means, maybe. Choices (B) and (D) do not have defining relationships. Choice (E) has, at best, a weak relationship, leaving you with choices (A) and (C). *Gravitas* sounds like "gravity," so maybe it has something to do with heaviness, putting it on the opposite side of the fence from *amuse*. Try to guess whether you think *pluck* and *quit* are on the same side, making choice (A) your selection, or on opposite sides, suggesting choice (C).

14. **A**   Make a defining sentence: A *parenthesis* is a place to put an *explanation*. The best answer is choice (A) because a *footnote* is a place to put a *citation*. Choices (D) and (E) don't have defining relationships, so eliminate them. Although you can put a *summary* in a *sidebar*, that's not the defined purpose of a *sidebar*, so eliminate choice (B). In choice (C), an *ampersand* is a type of punctuation that substitutes for a particular *conjunction*; it's not a place. Eliminate it.

15. **D**   Make a defining sentence: A *dart* is a thin, lightweight *projectile*. The best answer is choice (D) because a *shiv* is a thin, lightweight type of *knife*. Choice (A) is incorrect because the words have a "used to" relationship. Choice (C) has a "type of" relationship, but a *dirigible* is a very large type of *balloon*, not a lightweight version. Choice (B) is just plain "type of." A *jalopy* is an old type of *transport*, but choice (E) isn't the best relationship, either.

16. **B**   Make a defining sentence: An *apostate* is someone who forsakes *religion*. The best answer is choice (B) because a *pacifist* is someone who disapproves of *violence*. Choice (A) is incorrect because the words do not have a defining relationship; an *iconoclast* may attack religion, while *apostasy* involves simple abandoning it. Although a *recluse* might disapprove of *society,* he also might not, which means that choice (C) does not have a defining relationship. A *heretic* is someone who defies orthodox *doctrine*. Although defiance might imply some level of disapproval, that's not part of the definition. The words in choice (E) have the opposite relationship from the stem pair because a *sycophant* is someone who accepts *subordination*.

17. A   Make a defining sentence: *Insipid* means not characterized by *stimulation*. This is a "lack of" relationship. The best answer is choice (A) because *pallid* means not characterized by *chroma*. If you don't know one of the words in the stem pair or just can't make a good defining sentence, try working backwards. As for choices (B) and (C), there's no defining relationship between *trivial* and *detail* or *hirsute* and *fervor*, though if you're not sure what *hirsute* means, you don't want to eliminate it. *Robust* means full of *vigor*. Could a word mean full of *stimulation*? Sure—you'd have to keep this one. *Moribund* and *proximity* don't have a defining relationship. So you are down to choices (A) and (D). *Chroma* sounds like "chrome," which is pretty bright stuff, and *pallid* sounds like "pale," so these two words are probably on opposite sides of the fence. You need to decide whether you think *insipid* is on the same or the opposite side of the fence from *stimulation*.

18. D   Make a defining sentence: An *eddy* is a disturbance or atypical spot in a *stream*. The best answer is choice (D) because an *anomaly* is a disturbance or atypical spot in a *trend*. If you don't know one of the words in the stem pair or just can't make a good defining sentence, try working backwards. Choice (A) is incorrect because an *error* can occur anywhere, not just in a *report*, so these two words don't have a defining relationship. The *tide* is the back-and-forth pattern of water flow in the *ocean*. Could an *eddy* be the back-and-forth pattern of water flow in a *stream*? Maybe, so keep choice (B) if you're not sure. *Rogue* and *flock* don't have a defining relationship; neither do *canal* and *field*, eliminating choices (C) and (E). Picking between choices (B) and (D) requires a guess as to whether you think an *eddy* is more likely to be a repeating, regular ebb and flow or a discontinuity in flow.

19. B   Make a defining sentence: *Amorphous* means without *contour*. This is a classic "without" recycled relationship. The best answer is choice (B) because *limpid* means without *opacity*. If you don't know the words in the stem pair, work backwards and use POE. Choice (E) has no defining relationship, so eliminate it. Something *taut* is characterized by *tension*, and something *malleable* is characterized by *plasticity,* so choices (A) and (C) have the opposite relationship from the stem pair. The origin of *prosaic* is "prose," and it can mean ordinary, dull, straightforward—i.e., not *poetry* —so there is a relationship, but choice (D) is about literature; choice (B) is about physical things, like the stem pair.

20. E   Make a defining sentence: *Chauvinistic* is a negative and extreme version of *patriotic*. The best answer is choice (E) because *obdurate* is a negative and extreme version of *steadfast*. If you don't know one of the words in the stem pair, or you just can't make a good defining sentence, try working backwards. In choice (A), something *pedagogical* is designed to be *instructive*, and *patriotic* wasn't really designed to be anything. In choice (B), *omnipotent* and *ubiquitous* are completely unrelated. *Voracious* and *ravenous* are synonyms, which are common traps, so eliminate choice (C). *Adept* means highly *competent*. It's possible to be highly patriotic, so choice (D) seems plausible. However, because *chauvinism* has a negative connotation, choice (E) is the better guess.

Drill 4

1. **D**   Make a defining sentence: A *bouquet* is a collection of *flowers*. The best answer is choice (D) because a *cairn* is a collection of *stones*. A *flock* could be considered a collection of *geese*, so keep it for now. *Bark* is a covering for *trees*, so choice (B) doesn't have the same relationship as the stem pair. *Fog* and *precipitation* have a loose association, but no defining relationship, and a *pool* is a *collection* of water in a sense, but not of discrete items as in a *bouquet*. Thus, choices (C) and (E) are wrong. To compare choices (A) and (D), make a more specific sentence. The biggest difference is that a *flock* is a voluntary collection of *geese*, while both a *bouquet* and a *cairn* are man-made. Thus the relationship in choice (D) is closer.

2. **C**   Make a defining sentence: *Pediatrics* is the field of medicine that treats *children*. The best answer is choice (C) because *optometry* is the field of medicine that treats *eyes*. Choices (A), (B), and (E) do not contain fields of medicine. Choice (D) is incorrect because *anesthesiology* is often used during *surgery* but is not used to treat *surgery*.

3. **D**   Make a defining sentence: A *decibel* is a unit used to measure *sound*. The best answer is choice (D) because a *fathom* is a unit used to measure *depth*. Choice (A) is incorrect because, although a *pint* can be used to measure *milk*, this is not a defining relationship. The words in choices (B) and (C) don't have defining relationships. Choice (E) is incorrect because a *calorie* is used to measure heat, not *light*.

4. **E**   Make a defining sentence: *Synonymous* means having the same *meaning*. The best answer is choice (E) because *identical* means having the same *appearance*. Choice (A) is incorrect because *harmonious* means having a pleasant *melody*, not an identical one. Choice (B) has a "without" recycled relationship. The words in choices (C) and (D) do not have defining relationships.

5. **B**   Make a defining sentence with the stem pair: To *pirate* means to *take* without payment or proper authority. The best answer is choice (B) because to *counterfeit* means to *print* without proper authority. If you don't know one of the words in the stem pair or just can't make a good defining sentence, try working backwards and use POE. Choices (C) and (D) don't have defining relationships, so eliminate them. To *swindle* is the same as to *dupe*. Could *pirate* and *take* be synonyms? No, synonym relationships are a known trap, and *pirate* has a negative connotation, unlike *take*. Choice (A) is out. To *plagiarize* means to *cheat* by copying. Could *pirate* mean to *take* by copying? Not very likely, so eliminate choice (E).

6. **B**   Make a defining sentence: *Collusion* is characteristic of *conspirators*. The best answer is choice (B) because *naivety* is characteristic of an *ingénue*. The words in choices (A), (C), (D), and (E) do not have defining relationships.

7.   C   Make a defining sentence with the stem pair: To *shunt* is to *divert* in a rough or strong way. The best answer is choice (C) because to *shun* is to *ostracize* in a rough or strong way. The words in choice (A) are antonyms. Choice (B) is wrong because you might *review* in order to *correct*, but this is a weak relationship. *Quiet* has no relationship to *close*, and *disseminate* and *circulate* are also synonyms, a known trap; in addition, there is no connotation of harshness. Eliminate choices (D) and (E).

8.   C   Make a defining sentence: To *equivocate* means to avoid making a *commitment*. The best answer is choice (C) because to *dither* mean to avoid making a *decision*. The words in choices (A) and (B) do not have defining relationships. Choice (D) has an incorrect "degree of" relationship, and choice (E) has an incorrect "used to" relationship.

9.   C   Make a defining sentence: *Censorship* is designed to remove *information*. The best answer is choice (C) because *purification* is designed to remove *dross*. Choices (A) and (B) are not about removing anything. Choices (D) and (E) have relationships that are weak, at best.

10.   A   Make a defining sentence: Someone *reticent* doesn't want to *speak*. The best answer is choice (A) because someone *keen* doesn't want to *wait*. If you don't know one of the words in the stem pair, or you just can't make a good defining sentence, try working backwards or using sides of the fence. *Speak* and *reticent* are on different sides of the fence. Choices (B) and (D) both have words that are on the same side of the fence. *Petulant* has no relationship to *grow*, and the relationship in choice (E) is not definitional. Choice (C) does have words on different sides of the fence, but the relationship is not the same as the stem pair: Someone *laudable* does not deserve to be *chastised*. The person who is *laudable* is the receiver, not the actor.

11.   B   Make a defining sentence: *Endemic* means naturally occurring in a *region*. The best answer is choice (B) because *innate* means naturally occurring in an *organism*. If you don't know one of the words in the stem pair, or you just can't make a good defining sentence, work backwards and use POE. Choice (A) does not have a defining relationship, so eliminate it. *Mutant* means differing from the standard *genome*. Could something differ from the standard *region*? Not likely, so eliminate choice (C). *Inchoate* could refer to a newly forming *idea*, but since other things can be newly forming, too, the relationship is a little dubious. Could something refer to a newly forming *region*? Maybe—hold on to choice (D). *Divergent* means differing from the *standard*, making choice (E) pretty similar to choice (C). It doesn't make any more sense, so eliminate it. Between choices (B) and (D), choice (B) sounds more likely.

12. **D** Make a defining sentence: An *armada* is a large, coherent group of *vehicles*. The best answer is choice (D) because a *swarm* is a large, coherent group of *bees*. If you don't know one of the words in the stem pair, or you just can't make a good defining sentence, try working backwards. Choice (C) has no defining relationship, so eliminate it. A *cordite* is a type of *explosives*. Could an *armada* be an intense deployment *of vehicles*? Maybe—keep choice (A). A *general* leads an *army*. Could a *vehicle* lead an *armada?* That doesn't really make much sense—eliminate choice (B). A *phalanx* is a dense *formation* of people, for example soldiers. Could an *armada* be a dense *vehicle* of people? Pretty weird; elminate choice (E). Between choices (A) and (D), the fact that a *barrage* has an extreme aspect to it, while a *swarm* is simply a collection, should lead you to choice (D) as the most straightforward guess.

13. **E** Make a defining sentence: A *peccadillo* is a minor *sin*. The best answer is choice (E) because a *bagatelle* is a minor *composition*. If you had trouble defining the words or making a sentence, try working backwards. Choice (B) has no defining relationship, so eliminate it. *Penance* is part of seeking *forgiveness*, but it doesn't make sense that there would be a word about seeking *sin*, so eliminate choice (A). A *hoard* is a very large *accumulation*, just as *hubris* is very large *pride*. Choices (C) and (D) can't both be right, so they must both be wrong.

14. **D** Make a defining sentence: *Officious* is a high and negative degree of *attentive*. The best answer is choice (D) because *craven* is a high and negative degree of *timorous*. *Authoritative* isn't a high degree of *magisterial*; they can be used synonymously, so eliminate choice (A). *Impromptu* and *spontaneous* are nearly exact synonyms, so there's no degree relationship in choice (B) either. You might notice that *pecuniary* and *usurious* both have to do with money, but the two words have no definitional relationship to each other, eliminating choice (E). Things that are *risible* and *ribald* are humorous in different ways, but there's no degree relationship in choice (C).

15. **B** Make a defining sentence: *Fresco* is a decoration put on a *wall*. The best answer is choice (B) because *parquetry* is a decoration put on a *floor*. If you don't know the exact relationship, use process of elimination. Choices (A), (D), and (E) do not have defining relationships. *Thatch* is put on a *roof* but protection, not decoration, eliminating choice (C).

16. **A** Make a defining sentence: *Perfunctory* means without *enthusiasm*. The best answer is choice (A) because *insolent* means without *veneration*. Choices (B) and (C) do not have defining relationships. Something done in a *sedulous* manner is done with *assiduity*, not without it, so eliminate choice (D). *Effusive* and *encomium* are both words with positive connotations, but they have no defining relationship to one another, eliminating choice (E).

17. **E** Make a defining sentence with the stem pair: An *adult* is a grown-up *child*. The best answer is choice (E): a *dog* is a grown-up *whelp*. If you're not a serious animal lover, you may need to use POE here. A *mare* is a female *horse*, and a *ram* is a male *sheep*, so choices (A) and (B) don't fit into the defining sentence. A *capon* is a neutered *chicken*, so choice (C) doesn't work either. Be careful about choice (D). *Veal* is a term applied to young *cow* but only when the *cow* is being eaten as food, so you can eliminate choice (D).

18. **A** Make a defining sentence using a recycled relationship: A *blandishment* is used to *coax*. The best answer is choice (A) because an *alloy* is used to *debase*. An *egress* is used to exit, not to *enter*, eliminating choice (B). A *guffaw* is the result of being regaled, not something used to *regale*, so eliminate choice (C). Choice (D) is wrong because *abscission* is the act of detaching; it is not used to *detach*. Choice (E) is wrong because, while *torque* is a force that produces rotation; it is not applied intentionally in order to *rotate*.

19. **C** Make a defining sentence: A *ring* is a type of *arena*. The problem is that a *mendicant* is a type of *liar*, a *buckler* is a type of *shield*, and a *frieze* is a type of *painting*. Specfically a *ring* is a type of *arena* for contest or combat. A *buckler* is a type of *shield* for combat. The correct answer is choice (C).

20. **E** Make a defining sentence: A *shard* is a broken piece of *pottery*. The best answer is choice (E) because a *crumb* is a broken piece of *bread*. A *cinder* is the residue of *coal*, not a piece of *coal*, so eliminate choice (A). A *flange* holds wheels together; it is not a piece of *wheel*. *Viand* is a formal word for *food*, so choice (C) is also missing the relationship we want. A *ream* is a specific quantity of *paper*, not a piece of *paper*, eliminating choice (D).

Drill 5

1. **D** Make a defining sentence: A *scalpel* is a tool used by a *surgeon*. The best answer is choice (D): a *lathe* is a tool used by a *carpenter*. Choice (B) and (E) show no defining relationship. An *agronomist* is involved in farming, not *lasers*, so choice (A) doesn't make sense. *Art* is not a tool, eliminating choice (C).

2. **A** Make a defining sentence: An *envelope* is designed to contain a *letter*. The best answer is choice (A) because a *womb* is designed to contain a *fetus*. Choices (B), (D), and (E) do not have defining relationships. Choice (C) is tricky, because it could fit into your sentence, but a *recipe* does not contain an *ingredient* in the same physical way.

3. **B** If you know both words in the stem pair, make a defining sentence: A *barrage* is an overwhelming onrush of *explosives*. The best answer is choice (B) because a *deluge* is an overwhelming onrush of *water,* as in a flood or downpour. Work backwards if you don't know *barrage*. Choice (C) does not have a defining relationship and can be eliminated. A *cacophony* is a collection of discordant *sounds*, but not necessarily a huge number of them at one time. Could a *barrage* be a collection of discordant *explosives*? Choice (A) is unlikely. A *trench* is a place where *soldiers* protect themselves. Could a *barrage* be a place where *explosives* protect themselves? Eliminate choice (D). Choice (E) is not very appealing because, though some *paintings* are *abstract*, this relationship is fairly weak.

4. **B**   Make a defining sentence: A *panegyric* is a written or spoken creation used to *eulogize*. The best answer is choice (B) because a *lampoon* is a written or spoken creation used to *satirize*. If you don't know one of the words in the stem pair, or you just can't make a good defining sentence, try working backwards. Choice (A) can't be right because an *ode* is used to praise, not *criticize*. A *tirade* is an angry speech; it might be used to *entertain* in some rare circumstances, but choice (C) does not contain a defining relationship. Be careful about choice (E): A *homily* is a religious speech, and to *sanctify* is a religious action, but they can't be used to define each other. In choice (D), a *diatribe* is an angry speech, which would not normally be used to *extirpate* (destroy totally). This leaves you with choice (B). If you don't know the word *lampoon*, you might be able to associate it with humor magazines or comedic films that contain *lampoon* in their titles.

5. **D**   Make a defining sentence: Someone *wary* is not easily *gulled*. The best answer is choice (D): Someone *tenacious* is not easily *deterred*. Work backwards if you don't know *gulled*. *Loquacious* means talkative, which has nothing to do with *befriended*, so there is no defining relationship in choice (A). *Taciturn* means quiet, and to *goad* means to prod, so choice (B) doesn't have a defining relationship either. One who is *passionate* is easily *moved*. Could one who is *wary* be easily affected in some way? Hard to imagine, so choice (C) is unlikely. The words in choice (E) both have to do with being calm, but *inured* means one has become accustomed to something bad, while *placated* means someone has been calmed by another person—not a definitional relationship.

6. **B**   This question tests a secondary meaning of *wardrobe*: A *wardrobe* is a place to keep *clothes*. The best answer is choice (B): A *bookcase* is a place to keep *books*. *Stove* and *crockery* are both used in a kitchen, but they have no relationship to each other, so eliminate choice (A). A *crowd* is a large group of *people*, so choice (C) doesn't fit into your sentence. A *cushion* goes on a *chair*, so choice (E) isn't the same relationship either. In choice (D), a *zoo* is a place to keep *animals*, but a*nimals* are kept forcibly in a *zoo*. *Clothes* can't be forced to do anything.

7. **B**   Make a defining sentence: An *anecdote* is a short type of *story*. The best answer is choice (B) because a *skit* is a short type of *play*. A *chapter* is a part of a *novel*, so choice (A) doesn't fit into your sentence. An *epic* is a long *poem*, so choice (C) is the opposite of what you're looking for. Choice (D) doesn't work either because a *mobile* is a type of *sculpture*, but it is not a short version. A *melody* is one characteristic of a *song*, so choice (E) doesn't have the type of relationship in the stem pair.

8. **D**   Make a defining sentence: An *allergy* is a type of negative *reaction*. The best answer is choice (D) because a *grimace* is a type of negative *expression*. A *rash* is negative, but it is not itself a *body*, eliminating choice (A). *Malady* and *ailment* are both negative words, and in fact are synonyms, definitely eliminating choice (B). An *antihistamine* relieves *symptoms*, so choice (C) doesn't have the relationship you're looking for. Also be careful about the possible lure of trying to tie *allergy* to *antihistamine*. Finally, a *chortle* is not necessarily any type of *feedback*, eliminating choice (E).

9. **E** Make a defining sentence: *Fanatical* means excessively *enthusiastic*. The best answer is choice (E) because *idolatrous* means excessively *devoted*. Choices (A) and (D) have strong associations, but they do not have defining relationships. *Flamboyant* means excessively showy, but not necessarily excessively *stylish*, eliminating choice (B). Choice (C) is a trap, because *circumspect* and *cautious* are synonyms.

10. **D** Make a defining sentence using a recycled relationship: A *hoax* is used to *hoodwink* someone. The best answer is choice (D) because an *encomium* is used to *praise* someone. None of the word pairs in the other four choices have any relationship to each other; even if you don't know the word *encomium*, you might be able to get the answer by POE.

11. **B** Make a defining sentence: *Invincible* means unable to be *subjugated*. The best answer is choice (B) because *unmeasurable* means unable to be *gauged*. Choice (A) does not have a defining relationship, so eliminate it. Someone *haughty* may or may not be able to be *beseeched*, so eliminate choice (C). Likewise, something *melded* may or may not be able to be *bifurcated*, so eliminate choice (D). Finally, something *costly* may or may not be *discounted*, eliminating choice (E).

12. **A** Make a defining sentence: *Keen* means to express *grief*. (Note that the test writers are using a secondary meaning of *keen* here. Looking down the right-side words, you can see that *keen* must be a verb, since the other right-hand words are verbs). The best answer is choice (A) because *recoil* is what someone does in a *ghastly* situation. If you aren't sure about the words in the stem pair, work backwards and use POE. The words in choice (B) have no relationship, but if you don't know *jejune* either, don't eliminate it right away. Choice (C) does not have a defining relationship, so eliminate it. A *genteel* person attempts not to *fumble*. Could a *dolorous* person attempt not to *keen*? Maybe, so hold on to choice (D). An *ingenuous* person does not *deceive*. Could a *dolorous* person not *keen*? Again, maybe, so you are left with choices (A), (D), and (E), and possibly choice (B). The strongest of these is choice (A), which has a same-side-of-the-fence connection, and choice (D), which has words on opposites sides. Maybe you can get a gut feeling about the stem words, but if not, make a guess.

13. **D** Make a defining sentence: A *buttress* works against *instability*. The best answer is choice (D) because a *soporific* works against *vigilance*. All of the other answer choices have a same-side-of-the-fence relationship. A *carapace* provides *defense*, and a *portal* provides *accessibility*. Likewise, an *endowment* can provide *security*, although this relationship is not as strong. Finally, a *pontoon* provides *flotation*.

14. **C** Make a defining sentence: A *skirmish* is a brief *battle*. The best answer is choice (C) because a *spat* is a brief *argument*. If you don't know one of the words in the stem pair, or you just can't make a good defining sentence, use POE. Choice (A) doesn't work because a *revolt* could be *sanguine*, but not necessarily. Similarly in choice (B), a *campaign* may or may not be *pyrrhic*. A *coup* is an *abrupt* event, which goes opposite of the relationship in the stem pair, eliminating choice (D). Finally, there is no relationship in choice (E).

15. E Make a defining sentence: *Filigree* is used to *ornament* something. The best answer is choice (E) because a *piton* is used to *moor* something. If you don't know one of the words in the stem pair, or you just can't make a good defining sentence, work backwards and use POE. One might *douse* a *flambeau* or *tangle* a *filament,* but these are not defining relationships, so eliminate choices (A) and (C). For the same reason, eliminate choice (D). You could *weave* a *tapestry*, but can you *ornament* a *filigree*? If you're not sure, guess between choices (B) and (E).

16. A Make a defining sentence: *Doggerel* is a crude type of *verse*. The best answer is choice (A) because *pulp* is a crude type of *magazine*. If you don't know one of the words in the stem pair, or if you just can't make a good defining sentence, use POE. A *cameo* may be an *heirloom,* but that's not a defining relationship, so eliminate choice (B). Likewise, *concerto* and *quartet* do not have a defining relationship, so eliminate choice (C). *Cubism* is interesting in its use of *perspective*, but choice (D) also does not have a defining relationship. *Haiku* and *ode* are both types of poems, but they don't relate to each other, eliminating choice (E).

17. C If you know the stem words, first try to make a defining sentence using a recycled relationship: *Stygian* is an exceptionally unpleasant degree of *dark*. The best answer is choice (C) because *churlish* is an exceptionally unpleasant degree of *impolite* . If you don't know one of the stem words, or you just can't make a good sentence, work backwards and use POE. Choices (A), (D), and (E) do not have defining relationships, so eliminate them if you know the words. In choice (B), something *innocuous* is certainly not *fatal,* although this relationship is a bit of a stretch as a definition. Could *stygian* mean not *dark*? Perhaps, although true antonyms are extremely rare in the analogies; with two adjectives, one is virtually always in a degree or connotative relationship to the other.

18. E Make a defining sentence: *Evanescent* means tending to *disappear*. The best answer is choice (E) because *munificent* means tending to *give*. If you don't know one of the stem words, or you just can't make a good defining sentence, work backwards and use POE. Choices (C) and (D) don't have defining relationships, so eliminate them. *Immutable* means not able to *change*. Could *evanescent* mean not able to disappear? Maybe—hold on to it. *Quiescent* means quiet or still, so to *still* is to make something *quiescent*. To *disappear* isn't an action done to something else, so eliminate choice (B). Guess between choices (A) and (E) if you don't know the words; try to use sides of the fence if you can.

19. D Make a defining sentence: A *suitcase* is a type of *luggage*. The best answer is choice (D) because a *hat* is a type of *millinery*. Choices (B) and (E) don't have defining relationships, so eliminate them. Choice (A) has no relationship. A *bank* is next to a *river*, so choice (C) doesn't match the relationship in the stem pair.

20. **D** Make a defining sentence: *Maladroit* means lacking in *skill*. The best answer is choice (D) because *tenebrous* means lacking in *light*. If you don't know one of the stem words, or you just can't make a good defining sentence, try using sides of the fence. As a root, "*mal-*" means bad. *Skill* is good, so you need words that are on opposite sides of the fence. The words in choices (A) and (B) have defining relationships but are on the same side of the fence, so eliminate them. Choices (C) and (E) don't have defining relationships, so you can eliminate them also.

Drill 6

1. **B** Make a defining sentence: A *ruffle* is a decoration for a *garment*. The best answer is choice (B) because a *hanging* is a decoration for a *wall*. Choices (C), (D), and (E) have good definitional relationships but do not involve decorations. A *shade* is sometimes used for decoration but also has another purpose, meaning choice (A) is not the best fit.

2. **A** Make a defining sentence: To *emigrate* is to take an action that would entail being *exiled* if done by force. The best answer is choice (A) because to *enlist* is to take an action that would entail being *conscripted* if done by force. Choices (C) and (D) do not have defining relationships and can be eliminated. To *ban* is to *bar* someone else, eliminating choice (B). The words in choice (E) do not refer to people, so it can be eliminated, too.

3. **D** Make a defining sentence: An *antidote* cancels the effect of *poison*. The best answer is choice (D) because an *antiseptic* cancels the effects of *infection*. An *emetic* may help you deal with *nausea* but doesn't necessarily eliminate it. The *prognosis* describes the likely result of *treatment*. Is an *antidote* the likely result of *poison*? Nope, the root "anti-" suggests "against," so eliminate it. A *sedative* is used to induce *relaxation*. Does an *antidote* induce *poison*? Nope, so eliminate it. An *antihistamine* helps improve *respiration*. Does an *antidote* help improve *poison*? No again.

4. **B** Make a defining sentence using a recycled relationship: A *pest* is characterized as being *irksome*. The best answer is choice (B) because a *tyro* is characterized as being *inexperienced*. None of the remaining choices have defining relationships, so you could arrive at the credited response purely through POE.

5. **B** Make a defining sentence: To *amplify* means to increase in *volume*. The best answer is choice (B) because to *augment* means to increase in *size*. The words in choice (A) do not have a defining relationship, so eliminate it. To *relax* is to decrease *tension*, not increase, so eliminate choice (C). To *climb* might be to move up a *rung*, but the relationship is not definitional. Eliminate choice (D). To *glide* requires the use of an *updraft*, but does not involve increasing an *updraft*, so eliminate choice (E).

6. **D** Make a defining sentence: A *centrifuge* is used to *separate*. The best answer is choice (D) because a *sieve* is used to *sift*. If you don't know one of the words in the stem pair, or you just can't make a good defining sentence, work backwards and use POE. Choices (A) and (E) do not have defining relationships, so eliminate them. You use a *saw* to cut *lumber*, but the second words are all verbs, so *saw* is a verb, too. To *saw* is just to cut using a saw and isn't automatically linked to *lumber*. Eliminate choice (B). A *levee* is designed to prevent a *flood*, but *flood* needs to be a verb, too. You could say that to *flood* is to go over the *levee*, although this attempt is a stretch as a definition. Furthermore, could to *separate* mean to go over the *centrifuge*? Nope—to *separate* doesn't mean to go over anything. Eliminate choice (C).

7. **A** Make a defining sentence: *Indelibility* prevents *erasure*. The best answer is choice (A) because *incorrigibility* prevents *reform*. Choices (D) and (E) don't have defining relationships, so eliminate it. *Exegesis* and *analysis* are synonyms; this relationship is different from the stem pair, so eliminate choice (B). Remember also that synonyms are common traps. *Immorality* has only a tangential relationship to *paternoster* so eliminate choice (C).

8. **D** Make a defining sentence: You *expiate* in order to remove *guilt*. The best answer is choice (D) because you *buff* in order to remove *roughness*. If you don't know the words, or you just can't make a good sentence, work backwards and use POE. The words in choices (A) and (C) have some associations but no defining relationship, so eliminate them. You *boast* in order to inflate your *reputation*. Could *expiate* be something you do in order to inflate your *guilt*? That possibility doesn't really make sense because most of us don't seek to increase guilt. Eliminate choice (B). In choice (E), someone will *flatter* in order to win *favor*. Do we try to win *guilt*? No, so eliminate that one, too.

9. **D** Make a defining sentence: To *infiltrate* means to use stealth in order to *enter*. The best answer is choice (D) because to *eavesdrop* means to use stealth in order to *hear*. *Thwart* is synonymous with *prevent*. *Infiltrate* and *enter* are not exactly the same, and the relationship of two verbs will almost always be one in which one word is a degree or specific version of the other, not true synonyms, so eliminate choice (A). Choice (B) is out because you can *accuse* without having to *confront*, so these words do not have a defining relationship. *Avoid* and *elude* may be tempting, but the second word is a specific version of the first, rather than vice versa, as in the stem words. Eliminate choice (C). To *censure* is a high degree of to *blame* and thus has a different relationship from the stem pair. So choice (E) can be eliminated as well.

10. **E** Make a defining sentence: *Parquet* means a pattern made of *wood*. The best answer is choice (E) because *patchwork* means a pattern made of *cloth*. If you don't know the words, or you just can't make a good sentence, work backwards and use POE. Choices (B) and (D) do not have defining relationships, so eliminate them. *Macramé* often incorporates *beads* but is actually made with cords, so choice (A) does not have a defining relationship either. *Decoupage* decorates a surface, so it is used as *covering*. Could *parquet* be used as *wood*? Definitely not, so eliminate choice (C).

11.   A   Make a defining sentence: *Hemorrhage* is excessive or profuse *bleeding*. The best answer is choice (A) because *somnolent* is excessive *sleepiness*. Choice (D) has no defining relationship, so eliminate it. Watch out for some of the trap answers, though, such as choices (B) and (C): *myopia* is bad *vision*, not excessive *vision*, and a *palpitation* is an irregular, not an excessive, *heartbeat*. Choice (E) has the wrong relationship because *splinting* is a way to treat a *fracture*.

12.   B   Make a defining sentence: Someone *irascible* is characterized by a quick, sharp *temper*. The best answer is choice (B) because someone *peekish* is characterized by a quick, sharp *hunger*. The words in choice (A) have no defining relationship, so eliminate it. *Viscous* means lacking *fluidity*, and *extravagant* means excessive *spending*, so choices (C) and (E) don't have the same relationship as the stem pair. Eliminate choice (D) because someone *bellicose* may be characterized by *rage*, but *rage* is not necessary as a part of the definition nor must it be quick and sharp.

13.   B   Make a defining sentence using a recycled relationship: A *dupe* is characterized as being *credulous*. The best answer is choice (B) because a *coward* is characterized as being *craven*. Even if you're not sure what *craven* means, none of the other choices have defining relationships, so you can eliminate all of them.

14.   A   Make a defining sentence using a recycled relationship: A *melodrama* is characterized as being *exaggerated*. The best answer is choice (A) because a *fallacy* is characterized as being *erroneous*. The words in choices (B), (C), and (E) do not have defining relationships, so eliminate them. *Serendipity* is characterized as not being *intentional*. This relationship is opposite from the stem pair, so eliminate choice (D).

15.   B   Make a defining sentence using a recycled relationship: Someone *agog* is extremely *interested*. The best answer is choice (B) because someone *fastidious* is extremely *neat*. If you don't know one of the stem words, or you just can't make a good defining sentence, work backwards and use POE. The words in choices (A) and (C) have associations but not defining relationships, so eliminate them. *Mesmerized* is a greater degree of *curious*. Could *interested* be a greater degree of *agog*? No, because *interested* is a fairly neutral word; eliminate choice (D). *Adulterated* and *pure* in choice (E) are antonyms. Could *interested* be the opposite of *agog*? Yes, if you don't know the meaning, but antonyms are more likely to be a trap than to be the credited response.

16.   B   Make a defining sentence using a recycled relationship: *Selflessness* is characteristic of an *altruist*. The best answer is choice (B) because *heterodoxy* is characteristic of a *schismatic*. Even if you're not sure what some of these words mean, you can still arrive at the credited response by using POE. None of the other choices contain defining relationships.

17.   A   Make a defining sentence: *Usury* is excessive *interest*. The best answer is choice (A) because *prodigality* is excessive *spending*. If you don't know one of the stem words, or you just can't make a good defining sentence, work backwards and use POE. The words in choice (B) do not have a defining relationship, so eliminate it. *Wistfulness* is a common characteristic of *nostalgia*. Could *usury* be a characteristic of *inter est*? Possibly, so keep choice (C). *Parthenogenesis* is a type of *conception*. If *parthenogenesis* is not familiar, you could look at the roots: "Genesis" has to do with origins or birth, and you might remember that the Parthenon is a temple to the virgin goddess Athena. Maybe *usury* could be a type of *interest*, so hold on to choice (D). *Husbandry* is a synonym for *agriculture*. Synonyms are a known trap, so choice (E) is extremely unlikely. You are left with choices (A) and (D). Tough one! Both "degree of" and "type of" are recycled relationships, so just make a guess and move on.

18.   C   Make a defining sentence: A *hedonist* is one whose life is devoted to *pleasure*. The best answer is choice (C) because a *votary* is one whose life is devoted to *religion*. In fact, the word "devoted" shares a root with *votary*. Choice (E) does not contain a defining relationship, so eliminate it. Could an *ecclesiastic* be one whose life is devoted to *homiletics*? Possibly, if you don't know one of the words, so keep choice (A). A *sybarite* would definitely not be devoted to *teetotlalism,* and because *hedonist* and *sybarite* are synonyms, choice (B) may be a trap. A *misanthrope* is one who dislikes *humankind*. Could there be a word that means one who dislikes *pleasure*? That idea seems unlikely, so eliminate choice (D). If your vocabulary isn't up to the task, just guess between choices (A) and (C) and move on.

19.   A   Make a defining sentence: Looking down the left side of the answers reveals that *quail* is a verb, so use the secondary definition, to *quail* is to lose *courage*. The best answer is choice (A): to *pine* is to lose *vigor*. *Expurgate* means to remove *obscenity*, so choice (B) is not quite correct. *Aggrandize* means to increase in *intensity* rather than to decrease, so eliminate choice (C). To *stanch* means to stop the *flow* of fluid, so choice (D) does not quite match. There is no relationship between *remonstrate* and *unfairness*, so eliminate choice (E).

20.   D   Make a defining sentence: A secondary meaning of *lumber* is to walk without *grace*. The best answer is choice (D) because to *saunter* is to walk without *speed*. To *belie* means to give a false *impression*, so choice (A) does not contain the correct relationship. There is no defining relationship between *intimate* and *secret*, so eliminate choice (B). Eliminate choice (C) because the definition goes in the opposite direction from the stem pair: using a secondary definition, to *list* is characterized by a *lean*. To *sap* means to lessen in *vitality,* so choice (E) is incorrect also.

Drill 7

1. A   Make a defining sentence: *Perimeter* is the distance around a *square*. The best answer is choice (A) because *circumference* is the distance around a *circle*. The *volume* of a *cube* is the amount of space it occupies, not the distance around it, and any solid figure, not just a cube, has volume, so choice (B) does not contain a defining relationship. Choice (C) does not show a defining relationship either. A *degree* is not the distance around a *radian*, so eliminate choice (D). A *rectangle* is a type of *parallelogram*, so eliminate choice (E).

2. A   Make a defining sentence: To *detoxify* is to remove *poison*. The best answer is choice (A) because to *parch* is to remove *moisture*. There is no defining relationship between *clarify* and *evidence*, so eliminate choice (B). Neither choices (D) nor (E) contain words that have a relationship meaning "to remove." To *soak* means to fill with *liquid*, so the relationship in choice (C) is the opposite of the one in the stem pair.

3. D   Make a defining sentence: A *caustic* is a substance that will *eat away* another substance. The best answer is choice (D) because *leaven* is a substance that will *alter* another substance. The words in choices (B) and (E) do not have defining relationships, so eliminate them. To *embitter* means to cause *acridness*, and to *jade* means to cause *ennui*, but *acridness* and *ennui* are the results of the actions of their respective verbs, not the causes, as in the stem pair. Eliminate choices (A) and (C).

4. D   Make a defining sentence: A *dermatologist* is one whose specialty is *skin*. The best answer is choice (D) because a *periodontist* is one whose specialty is *gums*. Choices (A), (B), and (C) do not show a defining relationship. A cardiologist specializes in the study of the heart rather than the study of arteries, so eliminate choice (E).

5. E   Make a defining sentence: To *plummet* means to *fall* rapidly. The best answer is choice (E) because to *whirl* means to *spin* rapidly. There is no relationship between the words in choice (A). *Perambulate* and *walk* are synonyms, a known trap, so the words in choice (B) do not contain the correct relationship. *Flush* and *redden* can also be synonyms, so eliminate choice (C). *Abscond* means to *depart* stealthily, so eliminate choice (D).

6. B   Make a defining sentence: A *calorie* is a unit used to measure *heat*. The best answer is choice (B) because a *joule* is a unit used to measure *energy*. An *altimeter* is a tool, not a unit, used to measure *elevation*, so choice (A) doesn't fit. *Gas* and *combustion* lack a defining relationship, so eliminate choice (C). *Electricity* follows a *circuit* but is not measured by it, so eliminate choice (D). A *turbine* is a device powered by a *fluid*, so choice (E) doesn't fit our sentence either.

7. **E**   Make a defining sentence: *Prescience* means knowledge of the *future*. The best answer is choice (E) because *omniscience* means knowledge of *everything*. If you don't know the words, roots are very helpful here: "*science*" is about knowing, and "*omni-*" means "all." There is no relationship between *adumbration* and *antecedent*, so eliminate choice (A). *Truculence* means a fierce, aggressive *sentiment*, so eliminate choice (B). *Equivocation* is the intentional use of *ambiguity* in language, so eliminate choice (C). A *connoisseur* has knowledge, or *discrimination*, in a particular field, but not knowledge of *discrimination*, so eliminate choice (D).

8. **C**   Make a defining sentence: *Paranoid* means overly *suspicious*. The best answer is choice (C) because *miserly* means overly *thrifty*. *Heretical* and *pious* are antonyms, so choice (A) is not a good fit. Choice (B) does not show a defining relationship. *Stubborn* is an exact synonym for *obstinate*, as opposed to being overly *obstinate*, so eliminate choice (D). The words in choice (E) do not have a defining relationship, so choice (E) is incorrect.

9. **E**   Make a defining sentence: To *belabor* means to *assert* excessively. The best answer is choice (E) because to *harangue* means to *scold* excessively. To *fulminate* means to *attack* loudly or vehemently, not necessarily excessively, so eliminate choice (A). To *descant* is to *comment* at length, but the left-right order here is reversed, so eliminate choice (B). To *sway* means to cause someone else to *waver*, so the words in choice (C) do not contain the correct relationship. *Annoy* and *prattle* have no defining relationship, so eliminate choice (D).

10. **A**   Make a defining sentence: *Dialectic* is the system of principles of *reasoning*. The best answer is choice (A) because a *canon* is the system of principles of a *religion*. *Hubris* means arrogant *presumption*, not a system of principles, so eliminate choice (B). Neither choices (C) nor (D) contain words with defining relationships. A *convention* is a generally accepted *practice*, so choice (E) doesn't quite fit.

11. **B**   Make a defining sentence: To *adulterate* means to take away *purity*. The best answer is choice (B) because to *damp* means to take away *intensity*. The words *enervate* and *emotion* do not have a defining relationship, so eliminate choice (A). In choice (C), to *moralize* means to insist on *probity*, a relation that goes the opposite direction from the stem pair. *Ameliorate* means to make more *tolerable*, so choice (D) is not a good fit. Choice (E) is close, but *slake* means to quench *thirst*, not hunger.

12. **D**   Make a defining sentence: To *accelerate* means to increase *tempo*. The best answer is choice (D) because to *amplify* means to increase *volume*. Choices (B), (C), and (E) do not contain words with defining relationships, so eliminate them. To *inhibit* means to suppress something, though not necessarily an *outburst*, and choice (A) also goes the opposite direction from the stem pair.

13. **A**   Make a defining sentence: To *parry* is to block a *blow*. The best answer is choice (A) because to *dam* is to block a *flow*. If you don't know one of the words in the stem pair, or you just can't make a good defining sentence, use POE. None of the other choices have defining relationships, so they can all be eliminated.

14. **C** Make a defining sentence: What a *juggernaut* does is *crush*. The best answer is choice (C) because what a *virago* does is *nag*. If you don't know one of the words in the stem pair, or you just can't make a good defining sentence, use POE. None of the other choices have defining relationships, so eliminate them.

15. **B** Make a defining sentence: A *transgression* is an act that violates the standards of *morality*. The best answer is choice (B) because a *faux pas* is an act that violates the standards of *etiquette*. *Approbation* is an expression of *approval*, so eliminate choice (A). A *court-martial* is a *military* trial, not an act that violates the standards of the *military*, so choice (C) doesn't fit. Choices (D) and (E) do not contain words with defining relationships.

16. **E** Make a defining sentence: A *gourmand* is one who is overly fond of *food*. The best answer is choice (E) because a *sybarite* is one who is overly fond of *luxury*. A *maverick* is one who does not follow the *group*, so eliminate choice (A). In choice (B), an *epicure* appreciates fine *wine*, but there is no connotation of excess. A *pedant* is one who makes an excessive display of *learning* but isn't necessarily fond of it, so choice (C) does not fit. One meaning of *neophyte* is one who is a new *convert*, but this relationship is not the one you need, so eliminate choice (D).

17. **E** Make a defining sentence: Something *striate* is marked with *ridges*. The best answer is choice (E) because something *piebald* is marked with *patches*. Even if you're not sure of some of the words, you can arrive at the credited response through POE. None of the other choices contain defining relationships.

18. **B** Make a defining sentence: A *turret* is a small *tower*. The best answer is choice (B) because a *hamlet* is a small *municipality*. Even if you're not sure of some of the words, you can arrive at the credited response through POE. None of the other choices contain defining relationships. Choice (D) may be tempting, but *propaganda* may be disseminated in many ways, not just in a *pamphlet*.

19. **D** Make a defining relationship: *Ballast* is something that provides *stability*. The best answer is choice (D) because *fuel* is something that provides *energy*. A *fulcrum* helps to provide *balance*, but it does not provide *balance* in itself, eliminating choice (A). A *monocle* enhances *vision*, but does not provide it, eliminating choice (B). A *sextant* measures star positions, and an *odometer* measures *mileage*, so eliminate choices (C) and (E).

20. **D** Make a defining sentence: To *inveigh* means to *attack* verbally. The best answer is choice (D) because to *panegyrize* means to *praise* verbally. To *flog* means to *punish* physically, not verbally, so eliminate choice (A). To *calumniate* means to *accuse* falsely, so choice (B) can't be the credited response. *Beatify* means to *gladden* extremely, in fact to a state of bliss, and because there's no sense of something verbal, choice (C) doesn't fit. The words in choice (E) do not have a defining relationship.

Sentence Completions

SENTENCE COMPLETIONS

Every Sentence Completion question is like a mini reading comprehension passage. It will have characters, a speaker, and a main idea. Aside from vocabulary, the key to nailing these questions is grasping the main idea, and, also like reading comprehension, having a clear idea of what you're looking for before you get to the answer choices.

Here is an example you will never see.

> The home team's supporters were ------ before the
> start of the final game.
> ○ rancorous
> ○ intrepid
> ○ reverent
> ○ ebullient
> ○ irascible

Could the team's supporters be *rancorous*? Could they be *intrepid*? How about *reverent*, *ebullient*, or *irascible*? Most people plug all of the answer choices into the sentence to see which one sounds the best. This approach gives ETS five chances to lead you astray, and they'll use all five. All answer choices will fit grammatically into the blank, and quite a few of them will make a degree of sense. When you plug answer choices into the sentence to see which ones sound right, you are playing right into the test makers' hands. **The answer choices are very carefully selected and tested for the sole purpose of misleading test takers.** Don't let them mislead you.

CHOOSE YOUR OWN WORD

The alternative is to fill in the blank with your own word or phrase. When you do this, a few good things happen. First, it forces you to actively engage with the story being told by the sentence. There is no autopilot when you are completing the sentence yourself. Second, it protects you from manipulation in the form of the answer choices. Armed with your own word for the blank, you can quickly and efficiently work through the answer choices looking for ones that closely match your own word and avoiding ones that will change the meaning of the sentence.

GET A CLUE

To fill in the blank you need only to find the story or the clue that is in every sentence. The clue is the part of the sentence that tells you what goes in the blank. It is like an arrow that points to one answer choice and one answer choice only. Every sentence has a clue. The previous example, which you would never see, would look like this on the real test.

> The home team's supporters, feeling a joyous confidence in the dominance of their team, were ------ before the start of the final game.

The first version tells you that the fans were feeling something before the start of the game, but there is no indication of what that something might be. Were they nervous? confident? Angry? Happy? There is no way to tell because there is no clue. In the second version, you are told that they are happy and confident because their team is dominant. This is the clue. **To fill in the blank, often the easiest and most accurate thing to do is to simply recycle the clue.** In this case you would say that the fans were *joyous* and *confident* before the start of the game. Now you know precisely what that blank requires, and, when you get to the answer choices, you are looking for words that mean the same thing as or are similar to *joyous* and *confident*. The word or phrase you come up with for the blank acts as a filter. A well chosen word/phrase will allow only one answer choice to pass through, the correct one.

WHAT TO SCRIBBLE

As on the rest of the verbal test, scratch paper allows for an efficient two-pass approach through the answer choices. The question is not Right or Wrong, it is Maybe or Gone. Take the first word, *rancorous*. Perhaps you don't know exactly what it means, but you know it is a negative word. You are looking for positive words, so eliminate it. The second word is *intrepid*. It's positive; you might know that it means something like confident. Don't spend time figuring out if it is the right answer or not, just give it the Maybe mark on your scratch paper and move on. The next word is *reverent*. Does it mean joyous and confident? No, cross it off. If you don't know ebullient, it must stay in. If you have studied your vocabulary list, you will know that *irascible* means irritable. That is neither *joyous* nor *confident*, so you can cross it off.

Now according to your scratch paper you have a Maybe that kind of works, and a word you've never seen before. At the tail end of the test, pick one and move on. In the first ten, take a second look at the words and see if you can tease out some more information. Do you know the root? Have you seen it in context? If you don't know *intrepid*, perhaps you do know trepidation, meaning fearful. In-trepid, therefore means not fearful. You may also have heard it in context as a name for a battleship or to describe explorers. That may cover confident, but 'not fearful' is not the same thing as *joyous*. It does not match the words you picked, so choose the one remaining answer choice, *ebullient*, which is correct because it actually means joyously unrestrained.

TRIGGERS

Some sentences contain triggers. Triggers tell you whether the word in the blank will be the same as the clue or the opposite. ETS loves triggers, so start paying attention to them when you see them both on the Sentence Completion questions and on the Reading Comprehension questions.

Here is a list of common triggers.

therefore	but
and	although
because	despite
since	however
;	nonetheless
:	whereas

Here is an example.

> Although at first glance the two incidents appear
> ------ to the Smithfield intersection, they are, upon
> examination, strong evidence of a connection
> between the height of the corn at the corner and
> the accidents that occurred farther down the road.

The word in the blank describes the relationship between the incidents and the intersection. The second part of the sentence tells you that the incidents are evidence of *a connection* between the two. *A connection* is your clue, but the sentence starts with the different direction trigger, *although*. You're going to fill in the blank, therefore, with the opposite of your clue, or something along the lines of not connected or unconnected. When you go to the answer choices, you can forget all about the sentence and simply look for words that mean the same thing as or are similar to unconnected.

STRATEGY SUMMARY

- **Read the sentence.** Mouth the sentences to yourself and track words with a pencil. Remember that good readers often skip words knowing that they will pick up meaning in context. This will get you into trouble when you have no context to rely on.
- **Fill in the blank.** Identify clues and triggers and come up with your own word or phrase for the blank.
- **Process of Elimination (POE).** Eliminate answer choices that don't match yours. Make sure that you are keeping track of your work on your scratch paper.
- **Guess from the remaining.** On the front half, use roots and context to make as educated a guess as possible. If you are running short on time, a 50/50 shot is a victory. Guess and move on to the next question.

This whole process shouldn't take more than 30–45 seconds.

TWO-BLANK SENTENCES

When you get to two-blank sentences, the process remains the same, you just do it for one blank at a time. Scratch paper really comes in handy here. There is only one minor difference: on a one blank sentence; you eliminate any answer choice that does not match yours. On a two-blank sentence, if a word could work, you must keep it in. ETS will occasionally create an answer choice that contains the perfect word—the one you yourself came up with—for one blank and a word you've never seen, but which is wrong for the other blank. This will be a very tempting answer choice, especially if your only other alternative is an answer choice with two words that work, but not perfectly.

Here's an example.

> Methods that are ------- for displaying quantitative data are more likely to produce precise, credible, and truthful findings, whereas the simplified methods found on most standard desktop applications can be vague, -------, or downright misleading.
>
> ○ reductive. .profligate
> ○ superior. .implausible
> ○ colorful. .authentic
> ○ nuanced. .faithful
> ○ runic. .unsubstantiated

Start with the second blank. Your clues are *credible* with *whereas* as a different direction trigger, and *misleading* with *or downright* as a same direction, but amplifying trigger. You need something that means *not credible* or a bit less harsh than *misleading*. To make your life easier, jot down not credible and almost misleading on your scratch paper and start working through the answer choices. Does *profligate* mean not credible or almost misleading? If you're not sure, keep it in. Does *implausible* mean not credible? Yes, give it a check mark. Does *authentic* mean not credible or almost misleading? No, it means the opposite, so cross off the whole answer choice and do the same for *faithful*. *Unsubstantiated* could work, so give that a check mark as well.

Now when you go to the answer choices, you need only look at the first, second, and fifth answer choices, but first you need to choose your own word or phrase for the blank. The story being told in the sentence is all about methods for displaying information. The second set of methods is simplified and not so good, the first set, however, must be not simplified and better. Use those as your words for the blank.

Does *reductive* mean not simplified? Not sure? Keep it in and give it the question mark. Does *superior* mean better or not simplified? It could, give it a check mark. Does *runic* mean better or not simplified? Not sure? Keep it in.

Your scratch paper, at this point, should look like this.

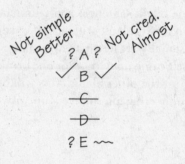

How much more information do you need? You have an answer choice that works for both blanks. Choose it and move on.

For more practice and a more in-depth look at The Princeton Review sentence completion techniques, check out our student-friendly guidebook, *Cracking the GRE*.

SENTENCE COMPLETIONS: DRILL 1

Just as different people can have very different personalities, so too can pets—even those of the same species and breed possess varied ------.

- ◯ initiations
- ◯ implementations
- ◯ characteristics
- ◯ rationalizations
- ◯ temperaments

Although Woodrow Wilson had long ------ entering the United States in World War I, the Germans' resumption of unrestricted submarine warfare in 1917 provided the ------ for his change in position.

- ◯ championed. .excuse
- ◯ opposed. .catalyst
- ◯ debated. .anachronism
- ◯ resisted. .mitigation
- ◯ imagined. .deterrent

During the peace talks, the skilled diplomat did not underestimate the importance of language; she ------ planned and considered each word she ------.

- ◯ meticulously. .articulated
- ◯ indifferently. .translated
- ◯ mindlessly. .uttered
- ◯ carelessly. .penned
- ◯ painstakingly. .invoked

If one were asked who transmitted the first radio broadcast of the human voice, one might guess the ------ inventor Guglielmo Marconi, but in fact the feat was accomplished by the much less well-known Reginald Fessenden.

- ◯ infamous
- ◯ renowned
- ◯ contingent
- ◯ cogent
- ◯ insistent

The difference in economic terms between a bond and a note is still observed by the United States Treasury, but in other markets the _____(i)_____ the two terms have become unimportant and the two words are used _____(ii)_____.

Blank (i)	Blank (ii)
distinction between	statistically
similarity of	interchangeably
usefulness of	differentially

Now known as Administrative Professionals' Day, Secretaries' Day was created in 1952 by Harry F. Klemfuss, a public relations professional who ------ the value and significance of administrative assistants in order to attract more women to the profession.

- ◯ proscribed
- ◯ touted
- ◯ refuted
- ◯ undermined
- ◯ admonished

When editing manuscripts, literary scholars and historians must remain acutely aware of textual ——; the differences among the extant editions of the same work—resulting from printer errors, editing demands, or constant revisions—often make it difficult for scholars to publish truly —— texts.

- ◯ anomalies. .cosmetic
- ◯ parodies. .innovative
- ◯ irregularities. .original
- ◯ conformities. .realistic
- ◯ congruities. .accurate

With a similar contrast between a partly cloudy sky and a dark street, the cover of the recent rock CD —— a famous surrealist painting from the early 1900s.

- ◯ admires
- ◯ obfuscates
- ◯ evokes
- ◯ disenchants
- ◯ sanctions

Although John F. Kennedy was known for his carefree flag football games, Gerald Ford should be —— as our football president: He turned down offers to play for two National Football League teams in order to pursue a career in public service.

- ◯ relegated
- ◯ abrogated
- ◯ annulled
- ◯ criticized
- ◯ apotheosized

Though many —— endlessly praised his work, Dan often wished for some honest criticism.

- ◯ sycophants
- ◯ pedants
- ◯ benefactors
- ◯ adversaries
- ◯ mavericks

Although they are —— today, objects from Germany's Bauhaus School of design—including buildings, furniture, and house wares—were not —— during the years when the school was active.

- ◯ exonerated. .maintained
- ◯ unwieldy. .adorned
- ◯ slandered. .honored
- ◯ abhorred. .desired
- ◯ prized. .coveted

The mathematics necessary to describe Einstein's Relativity Theory is surprisingly ——, even though the theory requires an understanding of —— ideas like the curvature of space and the interrelatedness of time and the speed of light.

- ◯ elementary. .abstruse
- ◯ difficult. .complex
- ◯ simple. .obtuse
- ◯ involved. .poignant
- ◯ guileless. .straightforward

Although considerable _____(i)_____ resources had already been expended on the new drug, development had to be halted due to adverse effects during human testing; once hailed as a kind of _____(ii)_____ that could be used to treat numerous physical and mental ailments, the drug will likely be remembered only as a financial albatross that bankrupted its developers.

Blank (i)	Blank (ii)
assiduous	sinecure
pecuniary	mendicant
wholesome	panacea

Sheila would often ------ about her boyfriend's habits, but everyone could tell that her seemingly bitter complaints were mostly facetious.

- ⬭ waffle
- ⬭ rail
- ⬭ dissemble
- ⬭ grieve
- ⬭ mince

Although the defendant's plea for ------ was supported even by his victims—who thought that the accused had been punished enough—the judge refused to ------ such supplications and imposed a more severe penalty than anyone had requested.

- ⬭ approbation. .compromise
- ⬭ clemency. .countenance
- ⬭ enervation. .bestow
- ⬭ lenience. .hinder
- ⬭ delay. .aggrandize

SENTENCE COMPLETIONS: DRILL 2

Carey and Skylar's constant bickering dismayed their mother, who had grown weary of their ——.

- ◯ squabbles
- ◯ laudations
- ◯ affectations
- ◯ procrastinations
- ◯ humor

The Mayor was so —— by the long trial that, despite his eventual acquittal, he admitted his failing health and declined to run for re-election.

- ◯ distraught
- ◯ exonerated
- ◯ inspired
- ◯ debilitated
- ◯ vindicated

Many television viewers associate the obscure holiday of Festivus with its depiction in a popular situation comedy, and thus believe it to be ——; one of the sitcom's writers, however, had long —— Festivus, a tradition based on a celebration dating back thousands of years.

- ◯ deceptive. .ridiculed
- ◯ fictitious. .observed
- ◯ fabricated. .forgotten
- ◯ hackneyed. .belied
- ◯ archaic. .pilloried

While any bird egg will suffice for the tradition of egg decorating, those with —— shells are preferred, so as to prevent breaking when their contents are hollowed.

- ◯ tenuous
- ◯ pristine
- ◯ permeable
- ◯ resilient
- ◯ obtuse

A former aficionado, Nicholas —— his interest in motorcycles after a dangerous accident —— him from further riding.

- ◯ abjured. .dissuaded
- ◯ redoubled. .cautioned
- ◯ denied. .emboldened
- ◯ diverted. .encouraged
- ◯ developed. .prevented

The New Woman author's willingness to publicly —— the prevailing Victorian ideals made her an easy target for censure and condemnation in late-Victorian Britain, as those whose values were based on conventional wisdom found the author's radical ideas to be ——.

- ◯ bolster. .indecorous
- ◯ flout. .repugnant
- ◯ support. .laudatory
- ◯ divulge. .scandalous
- ◯ rebuff. .titillating

The Roman Empire's military and political ------ was often challenged by the smaller, but ambitious Persians, who for centuries fought wars intended to usurp Rome's dominion.

- ○ heterodoxy
- ○ methodology
- ○ hegemony
- ○ impotence
- ○ timorousness

Although video games are often thought of as ------ entertainment, many manufacturers of such products view their creations as legitimate, ------ endeavors, commensurate with respected works of literature or film.

- ○ tawdry. .aesthetic
- ○ jocular. .lucrative
- ○ necessary. .pugnacious
- ○ garish. .wry
- ○ specialized. .imaginative

The sophists were widely known in ancient Greece for their ability to craft stories and persuade listeners using only the beauty of the language bereft of facts or evidence; thus, Plato ------ the sophists as adept speakers who abused their powers of persuasion by using ------ to sway their followers.

- ○ bemoaned. .insightfulness
- ○ trumpeted. .eloquence
- ○ vilified. .naiveté
- ○ excoriated. .chicanery
- ○ commended. .verisimilitude

Although Father's Day, first celebrated in 1908, is now an honored tradition in the United States, it did not always enjoy such _____(i)_____ ; rather, unofficial _____(ii)_____ from prominent figures such as Woodrow Wilson and William Jennings Bryan were required before Americans embraced the holiday.

Blank (i)	Blank (ii)
decorum	opprobrium
ennui	accolades
esteem	hyperbole

Although cod stocks in the North Atlantic are starting to ------ after past decades of overfishing, marine biologists ------ that a return to the fishing practices of the past might still cause the rapid extinction of these populations.

- ○ replenish. .extol
- ○ flourish. .laud
- ○ rebound. .admonish
- ○ dwindle. .remit
- ○ atrophy. .obfuscate

Unlike some former alumni who had been asked to address the school, Jason was ------ to address such a large audience and, thus, showed no signs of ------.

- ○ eager. .aggression
- ○ late. .warmth
- ○ loathe. .trepidation
- ○ prepared. .disquiet
- ○ not keen. .bombast

When the mother _____(i)_____ the disruptive child, she did not expect his siblings to encourage malevolent behavior; rather, she anticipated that the children would mock and _____(ii)_____ their troublesome brother and through this punishment, he would refrain from harassing others.

Blank (i)	Blank (ii)
touted	deride
calumniated	laud
pilloried	renege

Many city-dwellers have a ------ of knowledge about their food sources: indeed, a number of people have never even seen a live chicken or cow.

- ○ pith
- ○ dross
- ○ surfeit
- ○ dirge
- ○ dearth

Most fans dismissed the press release detailing the comedian's ill health as a hoax, as she had frequently ------ her audience by feigning a physical ailment as part of her stage routine.

- ○ reconnoitered
- ○ hoodwinked
- ○ lambasted
- ○ vitiated
- ○ derided

SENTENCE COMPLETIONS: DRILL 3

An aloe plant may be an excellent choice for those who are interested in gardening but keep busy schedules; aloes easily ------ without frequent watering or careful maintenance.

- ○ facilitate
- ○ ingest
- ○ consume
- ○ flourish
- ○ advance

Although Blanche thought that her short stories on the modern family were unique and engaging, reviewers deemed them ------ and ------.

- ○ mundane. .lackluster
- ○ unusual. .irrelevant
- ○ commonplace. .convoluted
- ○ excessive. .obtuse
- ○ matchless. .intriguing

The artist, who specialized in ------ scenes, eagerly sat down to paint his favorite landscape—a peaceful pasture filled with hills and valleys.

- ○ halcyon
- ○ perennial
- ○ bucolic
- ○ eclectic
- ○ quiescent

The group of ------ horticulturists agreed that they had never before seen such a ------ example of Tasmanian flora, although any professional botanist could have easily discerned that the plant was a fake.

- ○ illustrious. .authentic
- ○ famous. .rare
- ○ neophyte. .archetypal
- ○ eager. .counterfeit
- ○ novice. .redolent

The administration had nothing but contempt for the ultimate Frisbee team and frequently spoke ------ of it.

- ○ didactically
- ○ affably
- ○ jocularly
- ○ morosely
- ○ disdainfully

Some consider "Hallmark Holiday" a disparaging term, because the moniker ------ that the holiday exists mainly for ------ purposes, rather than for significant religious ones.

- ○ belies. .paltry
- ○ pretends. .dramatic
- ○ insinuates. .picayune
- ○ insists. .transcendent
- ○ implies. .profane

Lindsay, cognizant of the effects of second-hand smoke but hesitant to inconvenience her guests, ------, as she was unsure whether to ask people to smoke outside during the party.

○ dissembled
○ vacillated
○ equivocated
○ disparaged
○ concurred

As she considered the many avenues of study open to her, the doctoral candidate's ideas for her dissertation remained ------; she had the outline of an intriguing proposal, but a ------ methodology continued to elude her.

○ inchoate. .comprehensive
○ extemporaneous. .intractable
○ didactic. .indefatigable
○ tentative. .grandiloquent
○ ingenious. .fulsome

While some academics applaud the modern-ist movement in many universities to treat history and fiction as inherently related fields, there remains a vocal group of traditional his-torians and literary critics who _____(i)_____ such a _____(ii)_____ world-view and insist that the _____(iii)_____ nature of the two disci-plines must be inviolate.

Blank (i)	Blank (ii)	Blank (iii)
venerate	dogmatic	separate
deride	axiomatic	logical
celebrate	heretical	intertwined

Huckleberry Finn was one of the first major American novels to be written in a ------ style, using the voice of the common person describing everyday events.

○ erudite
○ reticent
○ urbane
○ quotidian
○ quixotic

The American love affair with the game of poker is no ------ infatuation, having persisted, albeit ------, for more than a century and a half.

○ inveterate. .casually
○ neoteric. .intermittently
○ nascent. .consistently
○ imminent. .clandestinely
○ archaic. .infrequently

While diligence and ------ will serve a person well, anyone who has achieved success in this unpredictable world should ------ the role of luck, no matter how hard she may have worked.

○ industry. .diminish
○ perseverance. .condemn
○ creativity. .grant
○ assiduity. .concede
○ perspicacity. .court

With his relentless energy but equally diminutive attention span, Garlin _____(i)_____ his talents on several potentially exciting but uncompleted projects, much to the dismay of his friends who, while venerating his enthusiasm, ____(ii)____ his unfocused nature.

Blank (i)	Blank (ii)
squandered	impugned
evinced	parried
burnished	defalcated

The origins of La Tomatina, an annual Spanish event in which participants hurl overripe tomatoes at one another for up to two hours, are ------, with possible theories including a friendly food fight and a volley aimed at a bad musician.

- ◯ esoteric
- ◯ ephemeral
- ◯ apposite
- ◯ enigmatic
- ◯ ubiquitous

The ------ group in the adjoining room made it difficult for students taking the mid-term examination to concentrate.

- ◯ obstreperous
- ◯ quiescent
- ◯ rapacious
- ◯ enervated
- ◯ antagonistic

SENTENCE COMPLETIONS: DRILL 4

Susan ——— the theater; she bought tickets for all the shows put on by the local drama group.

- ○ abhorred
- ○ cherished
- ○ owned
- ○ loathed
- ○ managed

The consistently reliable reception in Sweden has helped to spur a large ——— of cell phone sales, such that the nearly ——— devices can be seen in even the unlikliest of places.

- ○ proliferation. .ubiquitous
- ○ reduction. .scarce
- ○ flattening. .pedestrian
- ○ dwindling. .omnipresent
- ○ explosion. .meager

Currently a ——— in philately, Roger decided to pursue his new hobby because he had already become an expert numismatist.

- ○ dilettante
- ○ philanderer
- ○ mentor
- ○ specialist
- ○ eccentric

Every artist takes ——— approach when starting a canvas; some paint swiftly, fueled by their fervent inspiration, while others paint ———, carefully considering every brush stroke.

- ○ a reflective. .audaciously
- ○ an idiosyncratic. .meticulously
- ○ an archetypal. .timorously
- ○ a quotidian. .particularly
- ○ a unique. .expeditiously

Prior to taking on the new invader, the defending army had engaged in arduous combat; it is likely that the ——— resulting from waging two battles in two days played a part in its subsequent defeat.

- ○ bellicosity
- ○ pugnacity
- ○ pacification
- ○ enervation
- ○ aggravation

His financial ——— would have earned Martin nothing but accolades from his peers, were it not for his alleged involvement with a ——— investment firm earlier in his career.

- ○ acumen. .stellar
- ○ shrewdness. .bankrupt
- ○ sophistry. .creative
- ○ wizardry. .novice
- ○ limitations .discreditable

Despite his own preference for more ------ and literal subjects, the French writer Molière was widely known for his biting comic ------ plays that were usually performed right after longer, more dramatic productions.

- ○ maudlin. .parodies
- ○ cheerful. .sermons
- ○ whimsical. .burlesques
- ○ morose. .satires
- ○ subtle. .soliloquies

Ironically, the myth of Martin Van Buren's ------ was due largely to circumstances that had little to do with Van Buren himself; in reality, of all the U.S. presidents since Andrew Jackson, Van Buren exceeded the average in education, intellect, and expertise.

- ○ profundity
- ○ stoicism
- ○ mediocrity
- ○ aptitude
- ○ malleability

Some argue that profiting from terrible suffering by publishing photographic books about natural disasters is _____(i)_____, but perhaps the practice has the _____(ii)_____ effect of helping us to appreciate the humanity of people living far way.

Blank (i)	Blank (ii)
presumptuous	salutary
idolatrous	specious
pernicious	sedulous

While she may have answered him truthfully—in the strictest sense of the word—it became clear to Sergei after the incident that Sheryl had actually been trying to ------.

- ○ vituperate
- ○ obfuscate
- ○ illuminate
- ○ covet
- ○ desiccate

Certainly a roundabout narrative, the book—much like the others in the author's pseudo-autobiographical series—proved to be unpopular among those who preferred ------ to loquaciousness.

- ○ succinctness
- ○ enlargement
- ○ garrulousness
- ○ gregariousness
- ○ perspicacity

Holding that life is essentially ------ truth, value, or objective meaning, nihilism ------ the notion of absolute moral principles.

- ○ resplendent with. .discards
- ○ devoid of. .disavows
- ○ replete with. .defends
- ○ lacking in. .applauds
- ○ enigmatic of. .exonerates

Although they stood with the congressman in a tenuous display of solidarity, the incensed commissioners could not conceal their ——.

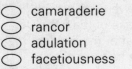 camaraderie
○ rancor
○ adulation
○ facetiousness
○ hubris

Pearson's equanimity as he listened to the evidence of his fraudulent schemes caused his erstwhile supporters to question his _____(i)_____; indeed, Pearson seemed to have a penchant for _____(ii))_____ that would impress even the most _____(iii)_____ of hucksters.

Blank (i)	Blank (ii)	Blank (iii)
indolence	petulance	recumbent
alacrity	chicanery	ardent
probity	recidivism	fetid

Though Fenster tended to ——, making proclamations that veered in many directions, he always managed to convey the —— part of the topic he chose to discuss.

○ calumniate. .constitutive
○ maunder. .pithy
○ pontificate. .tritest
○ recapitulate. .elaborated
○ digress. .grandiloquent

SENTENCE COMPLETIONS: DRILL 5

Both the local environmental group and the owner of the land agreed that last week's fundraiser was ------; thus, another event would not have to be scheduled in order to ------ the necessary funds to purchase the marshland.

- ⭘ ample. .deplete
- ⭘ sufficient. .garner
- ⭘ allowable. .hedge
- ⭘ necessary. .broker
- ⭘ successful. .disburse

The defense attorney's ------ closing statement was not enough to sway the jurors in his client's favor; stirring words could not conceal the defendant's evident guilt.

- ⭘ deceptive
- ⭘ eloquent
- ⭘ lengthy
- ⭘ crafty
- ⭘ impromptu

A recent Harris Poll indicated that many professions have seen a decline in their ------ over the past several years; teaching, in contrast, has ------ more respect over the same time period.

- ⭘ ranks. .lost
- ⭘ prestige. .garnered
- ⭘ visibility. .withheld
- ⭘ cachet. .improved
- ⭘ disrepute. .dwindled

In 1770s colonial New England, Puritans ------ the celebration of Christmas, which they considered to be an odious reminder of the Pope's tyranny.

- ⭘ placated
- ⭘ extolled
- ⭘ circumscribed
- ⭘ tempered
- ⭘ repudiated

Michael was ------ because although the couch was by far the nicest in his price range, he knew that the country in which it was made often did not enforce safe labor practices and he did not want to be complicit in ------ unsafe working conditions.

- ⭘ excited. .repudiating
- ⭘ apoplectic. .sustaining
- ⭘ despondent. .supporting
- ⭘ apathetic. .championing
- ⭘ uncertain. .enforcing

Many dog owners treat their pets too ------, forgetting that canines have evolved in competitive environments in which emotional coddling was a sign of weakness.

- ⭘ aggressively
- ⭘ quixotically
- ⭘ fortuitously
- ⭘ indulgently
- ⭘ belligerently

Because Ted's boss Amy could be, at times, rather ------; Ted found himself unable to interpret whether Amy's immutable expressions and tone indicated encomium or ------ of Ted's work performance.

- ⭘ stolid. .opprobrium
- ⭘ erratic. .prescience
- ⭘ mercurial. .denigration
- ⭘ stoic. .guile
- ⭘ quixotic. .obloquy

Repulsed by ------ employees, the executive informed his staff that he preferred constructive criticism to calculated flattery.

- ⭘ natty
- ⭘ profligate
- ⭘ rapacious
- ⭘ sententious
- ⭘ obsequious

Students may consider Modernist works such as James Joyce's *Finnegan's Wake* to be more ------ than Victorian prose: Victorian narratives are linear and predictable, while Joyce's tortuous plots are fragmented and fickle, and they confound the reader.

- ⭘ banal
- ⭘ recondite
- ⭘ elegiac
- ⭘ mundane
- ⭘ panegyric

It struck Professor Steele as _____(i)_____ that the eighteenth-century Bavarians devoted such effort to building houses of worship because at the same time, the rest of Europe's religious fervor was _____(ii)_____, while movements such as nihilism gained steam.

Blank (i)	Blank (ii)
felicitous	weltering
anomalous	forswearing
querulous	dissipating

Ancient generals, lacking modern technologies such as radio and satellite communication, often found that one of the most significant challenges in warfare was accurate ------ of the myriad of changes on the battlefield or in the campaign.

- ⭘ fortification
- ⭘ adulteration
- ⭘ appraisal
- ⭘ accretion
- ⭘ adumbration

In psychological literature, the "sleeper effect" refers to the phenomenon in which a persuasive message by a trustworthy source loses ------ over time, while the efficacy of a message from a less credible source simultaneously increases.

- ⭘ prescience
- ⭘ erudition
- ⭘ effrontery
- ⭘ control
- ⭘ tenability

Pundits do not believe that the sporadic calls for her ouster—outcries spurred by both her unusual lifestyle and social policies—have compelled the monarch to seriously consider ——.

- ⭘ abnegation
- ⭘ vacillation
- ⭘ castigation
- ⭘ asceticism
- ⭘ misanthropy

For some time, scientists refused to believe that Earth's continents are made of moving tectonic plates; physicists, who could not devise a theory to explain the now-accepted process, rejected the theory outright, as did geologists, who were far too _____(i)_____ in their thinking, thereby _____(ii)_____ the advancement of science for a time.

Blank (i)	Blank (ii)
officious	checking
peremptory	limning
supine	asseverating

Though presented as a —— during the first few chapters of the book, the main character is later shown to be entirely ——, a revelation made particularly surprising by the deft way in which the author weaves his story.

- ⭘ degenerate. .incorrigible
- ⭘ prodigy. .ambitious
- ⭘ vagabond. .peripatetic
- ⭘ scamp. .august
- ⭘ provident. .discursive

SENTENCE COMPLETIONS: DRILL 6

Dolly Madison, the wife of President James Madison, was known especially for her ------, remaining calm even as the British invaded Washington D.C. during the War of 1812.

- ⭘ impracticality
- ⭘ cynicism
- ⭘ equanimity
- ⭘ zeal
- ⭘ malevolence

Seth was extremely ------, and did not enjoy activities that required effort to meet new people.

- ⭘ extroverted
- ⭘ introverted
- ⭘ gregarious
- ⭘ lackluster
- ⭘ jaded

After the Corinthian war, during which the Athenian Empire and the Persian army ------ forces to attack Sparta together, the Athenians' acquisition of additional territories on their own alarmed the Persians and prompted the latter to ------ the alliance and join forces with Sparta instead.

- ⭘ clashed. .forsake
- ⭘ combined. .belittle
- ⭘ amalgamated. .renounce
- ⭘ splintered. .disabuse
- ⭘ diverted. .demur

Some religious leaders have declared inaction on environmental issues to be ------, because it may now be considered a sin to pollute the earth.

- ⭘ noxious
- ⭘ splenetic
- ⭘ iniquitous
- ⭘ diaphanous
- ⭘ dilatory

Because he ate high-calorie snacks while riding the exercise bike, Julie ridiculed DeRay's workout philosophy as ------.

- ⭘ fatuous
- ⭘ pithy
- ⭘ indolent
- ⭘ hackneyed
- ⭘ precarious

Marty could not help but to view the glass as half-empty; for example, when the economy turned around and number of jobs began to _____(i)_____, Marty insisted to all who would listen that the good news would be quite transient, another recession was _____(ii)_____, and those who doubted him would appreciate his unwillingness to celebrate.

Blank (i)	Blank (ii)
proliferate	superfluous
aggrandize	imminent
pique	odious

The recent convert, still a ------ with respect to the rites of her church, did not yet feel completely comfortable in her new faith.

- ⬭ pilgrim
- ⬭ iconoclast
- ⬭ ascetic
- ⬭ tyro
- ⬭ poseur

When questioned about her ------ preparation for the test, Ginger explained that she did not believe that the exam required a ------ course of study.

- ⬭ tenuous. .salubrious
- ⬭ cursory. .sedulous
- ⬭ perfunctory. .erudite
- ⬭ tenacious. .thorough
- ⬭ arduous. .assiduous

Marked by ------, the dictator's speech may have been inspiring to those already ------ by the regime's false propaganda, but it seemed intentionally oblique to impartial international political observers.

- ⬭ prevarication. .inculcated
- ⬭ canards. .irked
- ⬭ rhetoric. .emboldened
- ⬭ fallacies. .scandalized
- ⬭ redolence. .indoctrinated

Video game enthusiasts know that, while the astounding advances in technological innovation might increase the level of fun of the gaming experience, such a result is by no means ------.

- ⬭ desultory
- ⬭ endemic
- ⬭ salient
- ⬭ ineluctable
- ⬭ seminal

Middlemarch author George Eliot reportedly bemoaned the dearth of brainy, well-educated women, of which her main character, Dorothea, was ------; thus, Eliot scholars have debated the author's meaning in marrying Dorothea to the elderly preacher Casaubon and having him exploit his bride for mundane and ------ needs.

- ⬭ an epitome. .perverted
- ⬭ an archetype. .detestable
- ⬭ a paradigm. .menial
- ⬭ a misogynist. .servile
- ⬭ a chimera. .clerical

With its maverick approach to the subject, Shere Hite's book has been widely debated and even criticized, thanks in no small part to the media's role in bringing the author's ------ opinions to the public.

- ⬭ iconoclastic
- ⬭ blithe
- ⬭ inveterate
- ⬭ meretricious
- ⬭ raffish

By far not the most ------ of men, Wilbert nonetheless enjoyed a renown that was unimpeded by his inherent petulance and ------.

- ⬭ estimable. .gregariousness
- ⬭ pedantic. .celebrity
- ⬭ irritable. .pugnacity
- ⬭ jocose. .irascibility
- ⬭ garrulous. .amenability

Sarah Grand's short story "The Tenor and the Boy" was ------ account of her popular novel *The Heavenly Twins*, for it was published years before the novel was completed; unlike the novel's characters, who were drawn with rich detail, the short story contained mere ------ caricatures.

- ⬭ an unformed. .derivative
- ⬭ an infelicitous. .superficial
- ⬭ a fallow. .dynamic
- ⬭ a nascent. .unbedizened
- ⬭ a parochial. .fractious

One might sometimes wonder whether some of the stories passed down through generations are veritable or _____(i)_____, whether the heroes had such endless mettle or were, in their hearts, occasionally _____(ii)_____, whether the times described were really so _____(iii)_____ or perhaps tinged with a bit of guile.

Blank (i)	Blank (ii)	Blank (iii)
heretical	pusillanimous	gossamer
jejune	arrant	ingenuous
apocryphal	insouciant	piquant

SENTENCE COMPLETIONS: DRILL 7

Although his latest project was relatively
------ —little more than a few basic plot points
scribbled on a napkin—the veteran screenwriter easily sold the story to a major
Hollywood studio.

- ○ undeveloped
- ○ polished
- ○ convoluted
- ○ prosaic
- ○ tortuous

Despite being located in hot and sunny
California, San Francisco is famous for its
------ weather, engendered by the confluence
of two different meteorological systems in
the Bay Area.

- ○ stimulating
- ○ dreary
- ○ balmy
- ○ appealing
- ○ duplicitous

Possessing few natural resources upon its
newly-granted independence in 1863,
Singapore remained economically ------
until an influx of industrialization and foreign
investment took hold there.

- ○ powerful
- ○ prosperous
- ○ solvent
- ○ fortuitous
- ○ dubious

Wealth and technology wrought by industrialization gave nations in the northern
hemisphere ------, including sophisticated
weaponry that could easily overpower the
more ------ arms possessed by peoples of the
southern hemisphere.

- ○ palpable advantages. .rudimentary
- ○ unexpected consequences. .malevolent
- ○ undeserved exoneration. .pernicious
- ○ fawning adoration. .intricate
- ○ meritorious regard. .fundamental

Even though legislators claimed the Contagious Diseases Acts strengthened the
nation, social purists argued the Acts ------ the
nation's moral growth by encouraging licen-
tious behavior.

- ○ advanced
- ○ ameliorated
- ○ hampered
- ○ supplanted
- ○ enhanced

The new lecture hall's ------ design, both
inside and out, emphasized that it was solely
a place of serious inquiry.

- ○ posh
- ○ intricate
- ○ unadorned
- ○ refulgent
- ○ grandiose

Knowing that the final presentation requirements would perplex many students, the professor wanted to ------ the students' anxieties, so he spent a significant amount of class time discussing the final project.

- ○ fawn
- ○ coddle
- ○ obfuscate
- ○ obviate
- ○ pervade

The grave accusations made by the plaintiff were almost entirely _____(i)_____ the testimony of two witnesses. Therefore, when the court _____(ii)_____ the credentials of those witnesses, the plaintiff's case disintegrated, and the relevant claims were shown to be _____(iii)_____.

Blank (i)	Blank (ii)	Blank (iii)
subservient to	vindicated	facetious
isolated from	repudiated	unerring
dependent on	debated	specious

Modern tennis fans have come to realize that, although, quantum technological leaps in racquet technology have lead to ------ increases in the speed and power with which players can hit the ball, this has not necessarily lead to a more entertaining game.

- ○ innocuous
- ○ halcyon
- ○ malleable
- ○ commensurate
- ○ tractable

Many Major League Baseball relief pitchers choose an electrifying theme song to play as they take the mound; the song ------ their fans and instills fear in their opponents.

- ○ eviscerates
- ○ enervates
- ○ assuages
- ○ innervates
- ○ pervades

Emmet Ray, a fictional jazz guitarist in Woody Allen's film *Sweet and Lowdown*, is a paradoxical character; while he displays sophisticated musical artistry, his personality is typically ------.

- ○ petulant
- ○ elegant
- ○ audacious
- ○ maladroit
- ○ multi-faceted

The editorial, intending to _____(i)_____ the current policy, inadvertently _____(ii)_____ several claims formerly made against the regime that was suggested as a preferable alternative to the current one, effectively _____(iii)_____ any plans for a change in leadership.

Blank (i)	Blank (ii)	Blank (iii)
impugn	laud	abrogating
bolster	substantiated	metamorphosing
vitiate	aggrandized	castrating

While Professor Alberts' past transgressions had been impassively weathered by university administrators, his latest gaffe was ------ enough that the school's president felt compelled to take action.

- ⃝ inimical
- ⃝ complaisant
- ⃝ innocuous
- ⃝ quotidian
- ⃝ reverent

Who could have predicted that the class president's downfall would follow so closely upon the heels of her landslide election victory, and that the only ------ of her abdication would be her defeated opponent's concession speech?

- ⃝ equivocation
- ⃝ malingerer
- ⃝ reagent
- ⃝ desiccant
- ⃝ portent

Despite the fact that Dutch law did not ------ slavery, by the middle of the 18th Century, the ports of Vlissingen and Middleburg in the State of Zeeland were unparalleled in the speed of their development, and even ------ London as centers of slave commerce.

- ⃝ countenance. .approached
- ⃝ relegate. .dominated
- ⃝ condone. .alleviated
- ⃝ impugn. .challenged
- ⃝ prepossess. .surpassed

ANSWERS

Drill 1

1. E
2. B
3. A
4. B
5. distinction between, interchangeably
6. B
7. C
8. C
9. E
10. A
11. E
12. A
13. pecuniary, panacea
14. B
15. B

Drill 2

1. A
2. D
3. B
4. D
5. A
6. B
7. C
8. A
9. D
10. esteem, accolades
11. C
12. D
13. pilloried, deride
14. E
15. B

Drill 3

1. D
2. A
3. C
4. C
5. E
6. E
7. B
8. A
9. deride, heretical, separate
10. D
11. B
12. D
13. squandered, impugned
14. D
15. A

Drill 4

1. B
2. A
3. A
4. B
5. D
6. B
7. D
8. C
9. pernicious, salutary
10. B
11. A
12. B
13. B
14. probity, chicanery, ignominious
15. B

Drill 5

1. B
2. B
3. B
4. E
5. B
6. D
7. A
8. E
9. B
10. anomalous, dissipating
11. C
12. E
13. A
14. supine, checking
15. D

Drill 6

1. C
2. B
3. C
4. C
5. A
6. proliferate, imminent
7. D
8. B
9. A
10. D
11. C
12. A
13. D
14. D
15. apocryphal, pusillanimous, ingenuous

Drill 7

1. A
2. B
3. D
4. A
5. C
6. C
7. E
8. dependent on, repudiated, specious
9. D
10. D
11. D
12. impugn, substantiated, castrating
13. A
14. E
15. A

EXPLANATIONS

Drill 1

1. **E**   If you notice the same direction trigger *so too*, you can recycle the clue *personalities* for the blank. None of *initiations*, *implementations*, or *rationalizations* means *personalities*, so eliminate choices (A), (B), and (D). Although *characteristics* can sometimes be used to describe aspects of someone's personality, the word can also be used to describe one's physical aspects. *Temperaments*, on the other hand, means *personalities*, so eliminate choice (C) and select choice (E).

2. **B**   Begin with first blank because it is easier. With the opposite direction trigger *although* and the clue *resumption of unrestricted submarine warfare*, the first blank must mean something like opposed. None of *championed*, *debated*, or *imagined* means opposed, so eliminate choices (A), (C), and (E). For the second blank, ask yourself what role the *submarine warfare* played in Wilson's *change in position*. The second blank must mean something similar to reason. Because *mitigation* has nothing to do with reason, and *catalyst* is quite similar, eliminate choice (D) and select choice (B).

3. **A**   Begin with the first blank because it is easier. With the clue that the diplomat *did not underestimate the importance of language*, the first blank must mean something like carefully. None of *indifferently*, *mindlessly*, or *carelessly* mean carefully, so eliminate choices (B), (C), and (D). For the second blank, ask yourself what the diplomat planned for *each word*. The second blank must mean something similar to expressed. *Invoked* does not relate exclusively to the expression of words, so eliminate choice (E). *Meticulously* means carefully and *articulated* means expressed, so select choice (A).

4. **B**   With the opposite direction trigger *but in fact*, you can recycle the opposite of the descriptive clue *much less well-known*, by filling the blank with well-known. None of *contingent*, *cogent*, or *insistent* means well-known, so eliminate choices (C), (D), and (E). *Infamous* means well-known, but in a negative way, so eliminate choice (A). *Renowned* means well-known, so select choice (B).

5.   **distinction between, interchangeably**   For the first blank, the clues *difference* and *has become unimportant* require something like difference between. *Similarity of* and *usefulness* of do not mean difference between; *distinction between* does. For the second blank, the opposite-direction trigger *but* and the clue *difference* require something like similar. *Statistically* and *differentially* do not mean similar, but *interchangeably* does. Select *distinction between* and *interchangeably*.

6. **B**   The clue is that Klemfuss *created Secretaries' Day*, so he must have appreciated the *value and significance of administrative assistants*. None of *proscribed*, *refuted*, *undermined*, or *admonished* means appreciated, so eliminate choices (A), (C), (D), and (E). Although *touted* does not—strictly speaking—mean appreciated, a person touts only something that is appreciated, so select choice (B).

7. **A** Begin with the first blank because it is easier. A semi-colon is a same-direction trigger, and you have the clue *differences among the extant editions of the same work*, so recycle the word *differences*. None of *parodies*, *conformities*, or *congruities* means *differences*, so eliminate choices (B), (D), and (E). For the second blank, ask yourself what type of texts would be *difficult to publish* because of these *differences*. If all of the original texts were *different*, it would be *difficult* to publish one original text. *Original* works, *cosmetic* does not. The correct answer is choice (C).

8. **C** The clue is the CD is *similar* to the painting, so you can fill the blank with something like reminds people of. None of *obfuscates*, *disenchants*, or *sanctions* means reminds people of, so eliminate choices (B), (D), and (E). Although the designer of the CD may *admire* the painting, the CD itself does not. Moreover, *admires* does not mean reminds people of. *Evokes* means reminds people of, so eliminate choice (A) and select choice (C).

9. **E** Despite the use of the word *although*, the structure of this sentence, including the colon, makes clear that you need a word that goes in the same direction as the clue. Whether you look to *known* or the phrase after the colon (or both), the blank must mean something like recognized. None of *relegated*, *abrogated*, *annulled*, or *criticized* means recognized, so eliminate choices (A), (B), (C), and (D). Someone who is positively *recognized* for something would be *apotheosized*, so select choice (E).

10. **A** With the opposite-direction trigger *though*, and the clue that Dan wanted *honest criticism*, the blank can mean something like yes-men. None of *pedants*, *benefactors*, *adversaries*, or *mavericks* means yes-men, so eliminate choices (B), (C), (D), and (E). *Sycophants* means yes-men, so select choice (A).

11. **E** If you try to begin with the easier blank, you will realize that you need one blank as the clue for the other (and vice versa), so identify the relationship between the blanks. The opposite-direction triggers *although* and *not* cancel each other out; the two blanks must run in the same direction. *Exonerated* and *maintained* are not related, so eliminate choice (A). *Unwieldy* and *adorned* are not related, so eliminate choice (B). *Slandered* and *honored* run in the opposite direction, as do *abhorred* and *desired*, so eliminate choices (C) and (D). *Prized* and *coveted* run in the same direction, so select choice (E).

12. **A** Begin with the second blank because it is easier. The opposite-direction trigger *although* affects the first blank, not the second. The clues are the specified examples of *ideas*, which are complex. None of *obtuse*, *poignant*, or *straightforward* mean complex, so eliminate choices (C), (D), and (E). For the second blank, the opposite-direction trigger *although* calls for the opposite of complex, or simple. *Difficult* is the opposite of simple, so eliminate choice (B). *Elementary* means simple, and *abstruse* means complex, so select choice (A).

13. **pecuniary, panacea** For the first blank, the information regarding the type of *resources* that were *expended* are the clues *financial albatross* and *bankrupted*. Thus, the first blank must mean something like *financial. Assiduous* and *wholesome* do not mean *financial; pecuniary* does. For the second blank, you learn that the drug is supposed to be *used to treat numerous physical and mental ailments.* Thus, the second blank must mean something like cure-all. *Sinecure* and *mendicant* do not mean cure-all, but *panacea* does. Thus, select *pecuniary* and *panacea.*

14. **B** Recycle the clue that Sheila made what seemed like *bitter complaints.* None of to *waffle, dissemble,* or *mince* mean to make *bitter complaints,* so eliminate choices (A), (C), and (E). You might have associated *grieve* with the word grievance, but it actually means to mourn, so eliminate choice (D). To *rail* is to make *bitter complaints,* so select choice (B).

15. **B** Begin with the first blank because it is easier. The clue is that the *victims* believed that *the accused had been punished enough,* so the first blank must be something like leniency. None of *approbation, enervation* or *delay* mean leniency, so eliminate choices (A), (C), and (E). The clue for the second blank is that the judge *imposed a more severe penalty.* Thus, the second blank must mean something like agree to. *Hinder* does not mean agree to, so eliminate choice (D). *Clemency* means lenience and *countenance* means agree to, so select choice (B).

Drill 2

1. **A** Recycle the clue *bickering.* None of *laudations, affectations, procrastinations,* or *humor* mean *bickering,* so eliminate choices (B), (C), (D), and (E). To *squabble* means to *bicker,* so select choice (A).

2. **D** The clues that the *Mayor* was involved in a *long trial* and as a result suffered *failing health* require that the blank mean something like sick. None of *distraught, exonerated, inspired,* or *vindicated* mean sick, so eliminate choices (A), (B), (C), and (E). *Debilitated* means sick, so select choice (D).

3. **B** Begin with the first blank because it is easier. The same-direction trigger *thus* and the clue that *Festivus* is associated with a *situation comedy* require that the blank mean something like fictional. Neither *hackneyed* nor *archaic* means fictional, so eliminate choices (D) and (E). *Deceptive* does not quite mean fictional either, but in a two-blank question, it is okay to be flexible when dealing with the first blank. For the second blank, the trigger *however* changes direction from the first half of the sentence. Moreover, the clue that *Festivus* is *based on a celebration dating back thousands of years* requires that the blank mean something like celebrated. Neither *ridiculed* nor *forgotten* means celebrated, so eliminate choices (A) and (C). *Fictitious* means fictional and *observed* means celebrated, so select choice (B).

4. **D** The clue that the goal is *to prevent breaking* the *shell* requires that the blank mean something like strong. None of *tenuous, pristine, permeable,* or *obtuse* mean strong, so eliminate choices (A), (B), (C), and (E). *Resilient* means strong, so select choice (D).

5.   A   Begin with the second blank because it is easier. The clues *former aficionado* and *dangerous accident* require that the second blank mean something like stopped. Neither *emboldened* nor *encouraged* means stopped, so eliminate choices (C) and (D). *Cautioned* does not quite mean stopped either, but in a two-blank question, it is okay to be flexible when dealing with the first blank. For the second blank, the clues *former aficionado* and *interest* require that the blank mean something like gave up. Neither *redoubled* nor *developed* means gave up, so eliminate choices (B) and (E). *Abjured* means gave up and *dissuaded* means stopped, so select choice (A).

6.   B   Begin with the first blank because it is easier. The clues *willingness to publicly* and *easy target for censure and condemnation* require that the first blank mean something like reject. None of *bolster, support,* or *divulge* mean reject, so eliminate choices (A), (C), and (D). For the second blank, the clues *those whose values were based on conventional wisdom* and *found the author's radical ideas* require that the second blank mean something like *offensive. Titillating* does not mean horrible, so eliminate choice (E). *Flout* means reject and *repugnant* means horrible, so select choice (B).

7.   C   Recycle the clue *dominion.* None of *heterodoxy, methodology, impotence,* or *timorousness* means *dominion,* so eliminate choices (A), (B), (D), and (E). *Hegemony* means *dominion,* so select choice (C).

8.   A   Begin with the second blank because it is easier. The clues *legitimate* and *commensurate with respected word of literature or film* requires that the second blank mean something like *artistic.* None of *lucrative, pugnacious,* or *wry* means artistic, so eliminate choices (B), (C), and (D). For the second blank, the trigger *although* requires that the clue used in the second blank be reversed, to something like artless. *Specialized* does not mean artless, so eliminate choice (E). *Tawdry* means tasteless and *aesthetic* means artistic, so select choice (A).

9.   D   Begin with the first blank because it is easier. The clue *abuse their powers* requires that the first blank mean criticized. Neither *trumpets* nor *commends* means criticized, so eliminate choices (B) and (E). *Bemoans* does not quite mean criticized either, but in a two-blank question, it is okay to be flexible when dealing with the first blank. For the second blank, the same-direction trigger *thus* and the clues *only beauty of language* and *bereft of facts and evidence* require that the blank mean something like deception. Neither insightfulness nor *naiveté* means deception, so eliminate choices (A) and (C). *Excoriates* means criticize and *chicanery* means deception, so select choice (D).

10.   **esteem, accolades**   For the first blank, the opposite-direction triggers *although* and *not* cancel each other out, so you can recycle the clue *honored.* Neither *decorum* nor *ennui* means *honor,* but *esteem* does. For the second blank, the semicolon trigger indicates than an explanation will be given about how Father's Day became *an honored tradition.* Ask yourself what was *required* from *prominent figures* before Americans *embraced the holiday.* The second blank must mean something like praise. Neither *opprobrium* nor *hyperbole* means praise, but *accolades* means to praise. Thus, select *esteem* and *accolades.*

11. C Begin with the first blank because it is easier. The opposite-direction trigger *although* and the clue that a *return* to prior *practices* would *cause* a *rapid extinction* require that the first blank mean something like recover. Neither *dwindle* nor *atrophy* means recover, so eliminate choices (D) and (E). For the second blank, ask yourself what type of statement *marine biologists* would give in the context of the same clue used for the first blank. The second blank must mean something like warn. Neither *extol* nor *laud* means warn, so eliminate choices (A) and (C). *Rebound* means recover and *admonish* means warn, so select choice (C).

12. D If you try to begin with the easier blank, you will realize that you need one blank as the clue for the other (and vice versa), so identify the relationship between the blanks. The triggers *unlike* and *thus*, when read in the context of the entire sentence, tell you that the words in the blanks must run in the opposite direction. *Eager* and *aggression* are not related, so eliminate choice (A). Likewise, *not keen* and *bombast* are not related, so eliminate choice (E). *Late* and *warmth* run in the same direction, as do *loathe* and *trepidation*, so eliminate choices (B) and (C). *Prepared* and *disquiet* run in the opposite direction, so select choice (D).

13. **pilloried, deride** Start with the first blank because it is easier. The clue *disruptive child* tells you the mother probably *punished* the child. *Touted* would provide you with a sentence that was opposite in meaning and *calumniated* has a similar negative connotation, but it would not be appropriate. The second blank's clue *mock* can be recycled for the blank. *Laud* is opposite of *mock*, and *renege* simply doesn't make sense. Select *pilloried* and *deride*.

14. E The same direction trigger provided by the colon and *indeed*, and the clue that some people *have never even seen a live chicken or cow* requires that the blank mean something like absence. None of *pith*, *dross*, *surfeit*, or *dirge* mean absence, so eliminate choices (A), (B), (C), and (D). *Dearth* does mean absence, so select choice (E).

15. B The same direction trigger *as* and the clues *hoax* and *feigned* require that the blank mean something like tricked. None of *reconnoitered*, *lambasted*, *vitiated*, or *derided* mean tricked, so eliminate choices (A), (C), (D), and (E). *Hoodwinked* does mean tricked, so select choice (B).

Drill 3

1. **D** The same-direction semi-colon and the clues that an aloe plan is an *excellent choice* for someone who lacks time for frequent *watering or careful maintenance* requires that the blank mean something like thrive. None of *facilitate*, *ingest*, *consume*, or *advance* means thrive, so eliminate choices (A), (B), (C), and (E). *Flourish* means thrive, so select choice (D).

2. **A** The trigger *although* indicates that opposite meanings of the clues will be needed. The structure of this sentence calls for the first clue to be assigned to the first blank and the second clue to be assigned to the second blank. Thus, the opposites of *unique* and *engaging* will be assigned the first and second blanks, respectively. Do your POE one blank at a time. The first blank must mean something like ordinary. None of *unusual*, *excessive*, or *matchless* mean ordinary, so eliminate choices (B), (D), and (E). The second blank must mean something like boring. *Convoluted* does not mean boring, so eliminate choice (C). *Mundane* means ordinary and *lackluster* means boring, so select choice (A).

3. **C** Recycle the clue *peaceful pasture* for the blank. None of *halcyon*, *perennial*, *eclectic*, or *quiescent* mean relating to a *peaceful pasture*, so eliminate choices (A), (B), (D), and (E). *Bucolic* does mean relating to a *peaceful pasture*, so select choice (C).

4. **C** Begin with the first blank because it is easier. The opposite-direction trigger *although* and the clue *professional* requires that the first blank mean something like amateur. None of *illustrious*, *famous*, or *eager* mean amateur, so eliminate choices (A), (B), and (D). For the second blank, the opposite direction trigger *although* and the clue *fake* require the blank to mean something like authentic. *Counterfeit* does not mean authentic, so eliminate choice (D). *Neophyte* means amateur and *archetypal* means representative; as something representative is authentic, select choice (C).

5. **E** The same-direction trigger *and* as well as the clue *nothing but contempt* requires that the blank mean something like disrespectfully. None of *didactically*, *affably*, *jocularly*, or *morosely* means disrespectfully, so eliminate choices (A), (B), (C), and (D). Disdainfully does mean disrespectfully, so select choice (E).

6. **E** Begin with the second blank because it is easier. The opposite direction trigger *rather than* and the clue *significant religious* require that the second blank mean something opposite religious. *Poignant*, *transcendent*, or *dramatic* mean the opposite of religious, so eliminate choices (B), (D), and (C). For the first blank, the same direction trigger *because* and the clue *disparaging* call for a word meaning something like suggests. *Belies* does not mean suggests, so eliminate choice (A). *Insinuates* means suggests as does *imply*, so select choice (E).

7. **B** The clue *unsure whether to ask* and the conflicting reasons in the first part of the sentence require that the blank means something like went back and forth. None of *dissembled*, *equivocated*, *disparaged*, or *concurred* mean went back and forth, so eliminate choices (A), (C), (D), and (E). *Vacillated* means went back and forth, so select choice (B).

8. **A**   Begin with the second blank because it is easier. The opposite direction trigger *but* and the clue *outline* require that the blank mean something like complete. None of *intractable*, *indefatigable*, or *grandiloquent* means complete, so eliminate choices (B), (C), and (D). While *fulsome* often has a negative connotation, it is worth holding at this stage. For the first blank, the same-direction semi-colon trigger and the clue *outline* require a word meaning something like in an early stage. *Ingenious* does not mean in an early stage, so eliminate choice (E). *Inchoate* means in an early stage and *comprehensive* means complete, so select choice (A).

9. **deride, heretical, separate**   For the first blank, the opposite-direction trigger *while* and the contrast between the clues *modernist* and *traditional* require that the blank mean something like criticize. *Venerate* and *celebrate* do not mean criticize, but *deride* does. For the second blank, the clue *traditional* as well as the completed first blank require that the second blank mean something like radical. *Dogmatic* and *axiomatic* do not mean radical, but *heretical* does. For the third blank, the opposite direction trigger *while* and the clue *inherently related* require that the blank mean something like distinct. *Logical* and *intertwined* do not mean distinct, but *separate* does. Thus, select *deride*, *heretical*, and *separate*.

10. **D**   Recycle the clues *common* and *everyday events*. None of *erudite*, *reticent*, *urbane*, or *quixotic* means common or everyday events, so eliminate choices (A), (B), (C), and (E). *Quotidian* does mean relating to everyday events, so select choice (D).

11. **B**   Begin with the first blank because it is easier. The opposite direction trigger *no* and the clue *persisted for more than a century and a half* require that the blank mean something like new. None of *inveterate*, *imminent*, or *archaic* mean new, so eliminate choices (A), (B), and (E). For the second blank, the opposite-direction trigger *albeit* might seem to call for something like did not persist, but the sentence cannot support such a meaning. So ask yourself what is different from long-lasting but doesn't mean did not persist. The second blank must mean something like with breaks during the time. *Consistently* is the opposite of breaks during the time, so eliminate choice (C). *Neoteric* means new, and *intermittently* means with breaks during the time, so select choice (B).

12. **D**   Begin with the second blank because it is easier. Recycle the clue *diligence*. Neither creativity nor perspicacity mean diligence, so eliminate choices (C) and (E) without regard to the second words. For the second blank, the clue *diligence* is negated by the opposite-direction trigger *while*, and another clue, *unpredictable*, provides additional information; the blank must mean something like admit. Neither *diminish* nor *condemn* means admit, so eliminate choices (A) and (B). *Assiduity* means diligence and *concede* means admit, so select choice (D).

13. **squandered, impugned**   For the first blank, the clues that Garlin has a *diminutive attention span* and *uncompleted projects* require a word that means something like wasted. *Evinced* and *burnished* do not mean wasted, but *squandered* does. For the second blank, the opposite-direction trigger *while* and the clue *venerating* require a strong word such as scored. *Parried* and *defalcated* do not mean scored, but *impugned* does. Thus, select *squandered* and *impugned*.

14. **D**   The clues *origins* and the entire phrase following the comma requires that the blank mean something like uncertain. None of *esoteric*, *ephemeral*, *apposite*, or *ubiquitous* means uncertain, so eliminate choices (A), (B), (C), and (E). *Enigmatic* means mysterious which is close enough to unknown, so select choice (D).

15. **A**   The clue *made concentrating difficult* requires that the blank mean something like noisy. None of *quiescent*, *rapacious*, *enervated*, or *antagonistic* means noisy, so eliminate choices (B), (C), (D), and (E). *Obstreperous* means noisy, so select choice (A).

Drill 4

1. **B**   The same-direction semi-colon trigger and the clue *bought tickets for all the show* require that the blank mean something like loved. None of *abhorred*, *owned*, *loathed*, or *managed* means loved, so eliminate choices (A), (C), (D), and (E). *Cherished* means loved, so select choice (B).

2. **A**   Begin with the second blank because it is easier. Recycle the clue *everywhere*. None of *scarce*, *pedestrian*, or *meager* means everywhere, so eliminate choices (B), (C), and (E). For the first blank, the clue *consistently reliable reception* and the clue provided by the second blank require a word meaning something like increase. *Dwindling* does not mean increase, so eliminate choice (D). *Proliferation* means increase and u*biquitous* means everywhere, so select choice (A).

3. **A**   Even if you do not know the words *philately* and *numismatist*, the clue is *new hobby*, with yet additional information provided by the opposite-direction time trigger *had already become* and associated clue *expert*. Therefore, the blank must mean something like amateur. None of *philanderer*, *mentor*, *specialist*, or *eccentric* means amateur, so eliminate choices (B), (C), (D), and (E). *Dilettante* means amateur, so select choice (A).

4. **B**   Begin with the second blank because it is easier. The opposite direction trigger *while* and the clue *swiftly, fueled by their fervent inspiration* require that the second blank mean something like slowly and thoughtfully. Neither *audaciously* nor *expeditiously* mean slowly and thoughtfully, so eliminate choices (A) and (E). *Timorously* is not an ideal choice either, but it is okay to be flexible when dealing with the first of the two blanks you select, so hold onto the word. For the first missing word, the same-direction trigger semi-colon and the following part of the sentence require that the blank mean something like unique. Neither *archetypal* nor *quotidian* mean unique, so eliminate choices (C) and (D). *Idiosyncratic* means unique and *meticulously* means slow and thoughtfully, so select choice (B).

5. **D**   The same-direction semi-colon trigger and the clues *arduous combat*, *two battles in two days* and *subsequent defeat* require that the blank mean something like exhaustion. None of *bellicosity*, *pugnacity*, *pacification*, or *aggravation* means exhaustion, so eliminate choices (A), (B), (C), and (E). *Enervation* means weakening, so select choice (D).

6. **B** Begin with the first blank because it is easier. The clue *accolades* requires that the blank mean something like expertise. Neither *sophistry* nor *limitations* means expertise, so eliminate choices (C) and (E). The opposite-direction triggers *would have* and *were*—which negate the prior blank—and the clue *alleged involvement*—which relate to the second blank—require that the second blank mean something like shady. Neither *stellar* nor *novice* means shady, so eliminate choices (B) and (D). *Acumen* means expertise and *bankrupt* means the bank failed, so select choice (B).

7. **D** Begin with the second blank because it is easier. The clue *biting comic plays* requires that the blank mean something like satires. Neither *sermons* nor *soliloquies* means satires, so eliminate choices (B) and (E). *Burlesque* does not quite work either, but it is okay to be flexible when dealing with the first blank, so hold on to it for now. For the first blank, the opposite-direction trigger *despite* and the clue *short* satires require the blank to mean something like heavy and serious. Neither *maudlin* nor *whimsical* means heavy and serious, so eliminate choices (A) and (C). *Morose* means heavy and serious, so select choice (D).

8. **C** The word *ironically* acts as an opposite-direction trigger. The clue following the semi-colon is *exceeded the average in education, intellect and expertise.* Therefore, the blank must mean something like below average in those attributes. None of *profundity, aptitude, fervency,* or *malleability* mean below average, so eliminate choices (A), (B), (D), and (E). *Mediocrity* does mean below average, so select choice (C).

9. **pernicious, salutary** For the first blank, the opposite-direction trigger *but* and the clue *helping us to appreciate the humanity of people* require that the blank mean something like hurtful. *Presumptuous* and *idolatrous* do not mean hurtful, but *pernicious* does. For the second blank, the clue *helping us to appreciate the humanity of people* requires a word meaning something like helpful. *Specious* and *sedulous* do not mean helpful, but *salutary* does. Thus, select *pernicious* and *salutary*.

10. **B** The opposite-direction trigger *while* and the opposite-direction time trigger *after the incident*, along with the clue *answered him truthfully* require that the second blank mean something like mislead. None of *vituperate, illuminate, covet,* or *desiccate* mean mislead, so eliminate choices (A), (C), (D), and (E). *Obfuscate* does mean mislead, so select choice (B).

11. **A** The words *unpopular* and *preferred* act as opposite-direction triggers. The clues *roundabout* and *loquaciousness* require that the blank mean something like briefness. None of *enlargement, garrulousness, gregariousness,* or *perspicacity* means brevity, so eliminate choices (B), (C), (D), and (E). *Succinctness* does mean brevity, so select choice (A).

12. **B** It is not necessary to know the definition of *nihilism* because you may consider the relationship between the blanks. The clue *holding that* and the general structure of the sentence indicate that the two blanks must run in the same direction. The words in choices (A), (C), and (E) are unrelated so eliminate them. *Lacking in* and *applauds* run in the opposite direction, so eliminate choice (D). *Devoid of* and *disavows* run in the same direction, so select choice (B).

13. **B** The opposite-direction trigger *although* and the clue *tenuous display of solidarity* indicate that the remainder of the sentence will explain that the solidarity is not heartfelt. Thus, the clue *incensed* requires that the blank mean something like anger. None of *camaraderie*, *adulation*, *facetiousness*, or *hubris* means anger, so eliminate choices (A), (C), (D), and (E). *Rancor* does mean anger, so select choice (B).

14. **probity, chicanery, ardent** For the first blank, the opposite-direction trigger *erstwhile* and the clue *fraudulent schemes* require a word similar to honesty. *Indolence* and *alacrity* do not mean honesty, but *probity* does. For the second blank, the same-direction trigger *indeed* and the clues *fraudulent schemes* and huckster require a word like trickery. *Petulance* and *recidivism* do not mean trickery, but *chicanery* does. The third blank modifies the word huskster. It needs a word that even the most serious or hard core huckster would be impressed. *Recumbent* or *fetid* can't be used to describe a huckster, but *ardent*—which means intensly devoted—can. Thus, select *probity*, *chicanery*, and *ardent*.

15. **B** Begin with the first blank because it is easier. The clue *making proclamations that veered in many directions* requires the first blank to mean something like ramble. None of *calumniate*, *pontificate*, or *recapitulate* means ramble, so eliminate choices (A), (C), and (D). For the second blank, the opposite direction trigger *though,* along with the clue from the prior part of the sentence require that the blank means something like central. *Grandiloquent* does not mean central, so eliminate choice (E). *Maunder* means ramble and *pithy* means central, so select choice (B).

Drill 5

1. **B** Begin with the first blank because it is easier. The same-direction trigger *thus* and the clue *another event would not have to be scheduled* require that the blank means something like successful or enough. Neither *allowable* nor *necessary* means successful or enough, so eliminate choices (C) and (D). For the second blank, the first part of the sentence and the clue *necessary funds* require a word meaning something like raise. Neither *deplete* nor *disburse* means raise, so eliminate choices (A) and (E). *Sufficient* means enough and *garner* means collect, so select choice (B).

2. **B** The clues *stirring words* and *not enough* require that the blank mean something like eloquent. None of *deceptive, lengthy, crafty*, or *impromptu* means eloquent, so eliminate choices (A), (C), (D), and (E), and select choice (B).

3. **B** Begin with the second blank because it is easier. The opposite-direction trigger *in contrast* and the clue *decline* require that the blank mean something like increased. None of *lost, withheld*, or *dwindled* mean increased, so eliminate choices (A), (C), and (E). For the first blank, the trigger *in contrast* no longer applies; recycle the clue *respect*. *Cachet* does not mean respect, so eliminate choice (D). *Prestige* means respect and *garnered* means increase, so select choice (B).

4. **E**   The clue *odious reminder* requires that the blank mean rejected. None of *placated*, *extolled*, *circumscribed*, or *tempered* mean rejected, so eliminate choices (A), (B), (C), and (D). *Repudiated* does mean rejected, so select choice (E).

5. **B**   Begin with the second blank because it is easier. The clues *he did not want to be complicit in* and *unsafe working conditions* require that the blank mean supporting. Neither *repudiating* nor *enforcing* means supporting, so eliminate choices (A) and (E). For the first blank, the entire sentence starting with *although* sets up a contrast of goals. Therefore, the blank should mean something like uncertain. Neither *apoplectic* nor *apathetic* means uncertain, so eliminate choices (C) and (D). *Ambivalent* means uncertain, and *sustaining* means supporting, so select choice (B).

6. **D**   The same-direction trigger *too* and the clue *emotional coddling* (and the opposite-direction trigger *forgetting* and its clue *competitive environments*) require that the blank mean something like leniently. None of *aggressively*, *quixotically*, *fortuitously*, or *belligerently* mean leniently, so eliminate choices (A), (B), (C), and (E). *Indulgently* does mean leniently, so select choice (D).

7. **A**   Begin with the second blank because it is easier. The clue *whether Amy's expression indicated encomium or* requires that the second blank mean something like harsh criticism. Neither *prescience* nor *guile* means harsh criticism so eliminate choices (B) and (D). For the second blank, the clue *Ted was unable to interpret Amy's expressions* requires a word similar to unemotional. Neither *mercurial* nor *quixotic* mean unemotional, so eliminate choices (C) and (E). *Stolid* means unemotional and *opprobrium* means harsh criticism, so select choice (A).

8. **E**   The clues *repulsed by* and *calculated flattery* require that the blank means something like flattering. None of *natty*, *profligate*, *rapacious*, nor *sententious* means flattering, so eliminate choices (A), (B), (C), and (D). *Obsequious* means flattering, so select choice (E).

9. **B**   The same-direction trigger colon and the clues *tortuous* and *confound* require that the blank mean something like complex. None of *banal*, *elegiac*, *mundane*, or *panegyric* means complex, so eliminate choices (A), (C), (D), and (E). *Recondite* does mean complex, so select choice (B).

10. **anomalous, dissipating**   For the first blank, the clue is the contrast the established between the *Bavaria* and *the rest of Europe*. Thus, the blank must mean something like weird. *Felicitous* and *querulous* do not mean weird, but *anomalous* does. For the second blank, the opposite-direction trigger *while*, and the clue *gained steam* require a word meaning something like diminishing. *Weltering* and *forswearing* do not mean diminishing, but *dissipating* does. Thus, select *anomalous* and *dissipating*.

11. **C**   The clues *lacking radio and satellite*, *significant challenges*, and *changes on the battlefield* require that the blank mean something like information about. None of *fortification*, *adulteration*, *accretion*, or *adumbration* of means information, so eliminate choices (A), (B), (D), and (E). *Appraisal* means review or evaluation, so choice (C) is the best answer.

12. E The opposite-direction trigger *while* and the clue *increases* (referring to *efficacy* of a *less credible source*) require that the blank mean something like believability. None of *prescience*, *erudition*, *effrontery*, or *control* mean believability, so eliminate choices (A), (B), (C) and (D). *Tenability* means plausibility, so select choice (E).

13. A The clue *ouster* requires that the blank mean something like resignation. None of *vacillation*, *castigation*, *asceticism*, or *misanthropy* means resignation, so eliminate choices (B), (C), (D), and (E). *Abnegation* means resignation of the throne, so select choice (A).

14. **supine, checking**   For the first blank, the clue that geologists *rejected* a theory later to be *accepted* requires a word meaning something like limited in thought. *Officious* and *peremptory* do not mean limited in thought, but *supine* does. For the second blank, the same-direction trigger *thereby* and the clues that physicists and geologists *rejected* something later *accepted* as true requires a word meaning something like slowing down. *Limning* and *asseverating* do not mean slowing down, but *checking* does. Thus, select *supine* and *checking*.

15. D If you try to begin with the easier blank, you will realize that you need one blank as the clue for the other (and vice versa), so identify the relationship between the blanks. The opposite-direction triggers *though* and *later* tell you that the two blanks must run in the opposite direction. *Degenerate* and *incorrigible* run in the same direction, as do *vagabond* and *peripatetic*, so eliminate choices (A) and (C). *Prodigy* and *ambitious* are not related, so eliminate choice (B). *Provident* and *discursive* are not related, so eliminate choice (E). *Scamp* and *august* run in the opposite direction, so select choice (D).

Drill 6

1. C Recycle the clue *remaining calm*. None of *impracticality*, *cynicism*, *zeal*, or *malevolence* means remaining calm, so eliminate choices (A), (B), (D), and (E). *Equanimity* means remaining calm, so select choice (C).

2. B The clue that Seth *did not enjoy activities that required effort to meet new people* requires that the blank mean something like shy. None of *extroverted*, *gregarious*, *lackluster*, or *jaded* mean shy, so eliminate choices (A), (C), (D), and (E). *Introverted* means shy, so select choice (B).

3. C Begin with the first blank because it is easier. The clue *together* requires that the blank mean something like joined. None of *clashed*, *splintered*, or *diverted* mean joined, so eliminate choices (A), (D), and (E). For the second blank, the clues *alarmed* and *joined forces with Sparta* require a word meaning something like give up. *Belittle* does not mean give up, so eliminate choice (B). *Amalgamated* means joined and *renounce* means give up, so select choice (C).

4. **C**   The same-direction trigger *because* and the clue *sin* require that the blank mean something like sinful. None of *noxious*, *splenetic*, *diaphanous*, or *dilatory* means sinful, so eliminate choices (A), (B), (D), and (E). *Iniquitous* means sinful, so select choice (C).

5. **A**   The clue *ridiculed*, as well as the idea of eating snacks while working out, requires that the blank mean something like foolish. None of *pithy*, *indolent*, *precarious*, or *hackneyed* means foolish, so eliminate choices (B), (C), (D), and (E). *Fatuous* means foolish, so select choice (A).

6. **proliferate, imminent**   For the first blank, the clue is that the *economy turned around*. Thus, the blank must mean something like increase. *Aggrandize* and *pique* do not mean increase, but *proliferate* does. For the second blank the contrast between *good news* and *recession* and the clue *transient* require a word meaning something like coming soon. *Superfluous* and *odious* do not mean coming soon, but *imminent* does. Thus, select *proliferate* and *imminent*.

7. **D**   The clues *recent* and *new* require that the blank mean something like beginner. None of *pilgrim*, *iconoclast*, *ascetic*, or *poseur* mean beginner, so eliminate choices (A), (B), (C), and (E). *Tyro* does mean beginner, so select choice (D).

8. **B**   If you try to begin with the easier blank, you will realize that you need one blank as the clue for the other (and vice versa), so just identify the relationship between the blanks. The trigger *did not believe* tells you that the two blanks must run in the opposite direction. *Tenuous* and *salubrious* are not related, so eliminate choice (A). *Perfunctory* and *erudite* are also not related, so eliminate choice (C). *Tenacious* and *thorough* run in the same direction, as do *arduous* and *assiduous*, so eliminate choices (D) and (E). *Cursory* and *sedulous* run in the opposite direction, so select choice (B).

9. **A**   Begin with the second blank because it is easier. The opposite-direction trigger *but* and the clue *impartial*, along with the additional information provided by *propaganda*, require that the blank mean something like taken in. None of *irked*, *emboldened*, or *scandalized* means taken in, so eliminate choices (B), (C), and (D). For the second blank, the clues *propaganda* and *intentionally oblique* require a word meaning something like untruths. *Redolence* does not mean untruths, so eliminate choice (E). *Prevarication* means untruths and *inculcated* means taken in, so select choice (A).

10. **D**   The opposite-direction trigger *while* and the clue *might* require that the blank mean something like inevitable. None of *desultory*, *endemic*, *salient*, or *seminal* means inevitable, so eliminate choices (A), (B), (C), and (E). *Ineluctable* means inevitable, so select choice (D).

11. **C**   Begin with the second blank because it is easier. Recycle the clue *mundane* for the blank. Neither *perverted* nor *detestable* mean mundane, so eliminate choices (A) and (B). For the first blank—based on the *debate* over Dorothea's treatment and Eliot having *bemoaned the dearth of brainy, well-educated women*—you can conclude that Dorothea was such a person. Thus, the first blank must mean something like example. Neither *misogynist* nor *chimera* mean example, so eliminate choices (D) and (E). *Paradigm* means example and *menial* means mundane, so select choice (C).

12.   **A**   The clues *maverick*, *debated*, and *criticized* require that the blank mean something like unorthodox. None of *blithe*, *inveterate*, *meretricious*, or *raffish* mean unorthodox, so eliminate choices (B), (C), (D), and (E). *Iconoclastic* means unorthodox, so select choice (A).

13.   **D**   Begin with the second blank because it is easier. Recycle the clue *petulance*. None of *gregariousness*, *celebrity*, or *amenability* means *petulance*, so eliminate choices (A), (B), and (E). For the first blank, the opposite-direction trigger *by far not* and the clue provided by the second blank require a word meaning something like friendly. *Irritable* does not mean friendly, so eliminate choice (C). *Jocose* means humorous and *irascibility* means *petulance*, so select choice (D).

14.   **D**   Begin with the second blank because it is easier. The opposite-direction trigger *unlike* and the clue *drawn with rich detail* require that the second blank means something like lacking in detail. None of *derivative*, *dynamic*, or *fractious* mean lacking in detail, so eliminate choices (A), (C), and (E). For the first blank, the clue that the short story came *years before the novel was complete* and the information contained in the second part of the sentence require a word that also means something like incomplete. *Infelicitous* does not mean incomplete, so eliminate choice (B). *Nascent* means emerging and *unbedizened* means unadorned, so select choice (D).

15.   **apocryphal, pusillanimous, ingenuous**   Each blank is associated with the opposite-direction trigger *or*. For the first blank, the clue *veritable* requires a word meaning something similar to untrue. *Heretical* and *jejune* do not mean untrue, but *apocryphal* does. For the second blank, the clue *mettle* requires a word meaning something like cowardly. *Arrant* and *insouciant* do not mean cowardly, but *pusillanimous* does. For the third blank, the clue *guile* requires a word meaning something like innocent; *gossamer* and *piquant* do not mean innocent, but *ingenuous* does. Thus, select *apocryphal*, *pusillanimous*, and *ingenuous*.

Drill 7

1. **A** The missing word refers to a *project*—in this case a screenwriter's story—which consists of *little more than a few basic plot points*. Therefore, the missing word might mean something like incomplete, so you can immediately eliminate choice (B). There is not enough information to suggest that the story is *convoluted*, *prosaic*, or *tortuous*, so eliminate choices (C), (D), and (E). *Undeveloped* means "incomplete," so choice (A) is the best answer.

2. **B** The blank is describing the weather in San Francisco. The clue *hot and sunny* with the trigger *despite* indicate that the blank means the opposite. *Cold* or *rainy* would be a good replacement. *Balmy* and *appealing* are similar to *hot and sunny*, so eliminate choices (C) and (D). *Duplicitous* and *stimulating* are not related to being cold and rainy, so *dreary* is the best answer.

3. **D** From the clues in this sentence, you know that Singapore's independence was *newly-granted* and that *industrialization and foreign investment* had not yet taken root. You need a word that means something like unstable or weak for the blank. Choices (A), (B), and (C) all go in the opposite direction of what you're looking for, so eliminate them. *Fortuitous* doesn't fit in the context of your clues, making *dubious* the best answer.

4. **A** Start with the second blank. The clue *sophisticated weaponry that could easily overpower* suggests a word similar to less sophisticated. *Malevolent*, *pernicious*, and *intricate* do not match, so eliminate choices (B), (C), and (D). The nations in the north overpowered the peoples of the south, so you need a choice meaning an edge for the first blank. Choice (A) is the best fit.

5. **C** While the *legislators claimed the Contagious Diseases Acts strengthened the nation*, the change-direction trigger *even though* shows that the social purists disagreed. You want a word similar to harm or weaken for the blank. *Hampered* is similar to harm and provides you with an equivalent sentence; *advanced* and *enhanced* go in the opposite direction, so eliminate choices (A) and (E). *Ameliorated* and *supplanted* don't make sense in the context of the sentence, so eliminate choices (B) and (D) and select choice (C).

6. **C** The hall's design was likely plain or functional, given the clue *solely a place of serious inquiry*. Choices (A), (B), and (E) are easy eliminations, as they are clearly opposite in meaning. You can eliminate choice (D) if you know that *refulgent* is the opposite of *plain*. *Unadorned* is the best match.

7. **D** The blank refers to the professor's actions in regards to the final paper. You know that the students were *perplexed* and had *anxieties*, for which reason the professor spent time *discussing the final project*. You might use a word similar to prevent for the blank. Choices (A), (B), (C), and (E) do not work, so eliminate them. *Obviate* would show that he tried to calm their anxieties, so choice (D) is the best answer.

8. **dependent on, repudiated, specious**   Start with the last blank because it is the easiest. The clue tells you that *the plaintiff's case disintegrated*. Therefore, the claims must have been shown to be false. *Facetious*, though somewhat negative, does not mean *false* but does not go far enough. *Unerring* goes in the opposite direction. *Specious* is the best match. The first blank is the easiest one to attempt next. The case fell apart when something happened to the witnesses' credentials, so a good phrase for the first blank—which described the role of the witnesses in the plaintiff's case—is "based on." *Dependent on* is the only match. If the plaintiff's claims were based on the witnesses, and the case fell apart, logically the witnesses must have been discredited somehow. A good word for the second blank—which describes what the court decided about the witnesses' credentials—is denied. *Vindicated* goes in the opposite direction. *Repudiated* is the best match.

9. **D**   The sentence states that *increases in technology have led to increases in speed and power*. The blank, therefore, requires something along the lines of similar or proportional. Only *commensurate* fits. The answer is choice (D).

10. **D**   Look for the clue in the strong adjective *electrifying*. The song must pump up the pitchers' fans. *Eviscerates* and *enervates* are the opposite of what you want, so eliminate choices (A) and (B). *Pervades* is unrelated to the clue, and *assuages* sounds like a possibility, but has nothing to do with excitement; eliminate choices (C) and (E). You're left with choice (D), *innervates*, which means to pump up.

11. **D**   The blank refers to Emmet Ray's *paradoxical* character. The trigger *while* follows the clue, indicating that his *sophisticated musical artistry* is contrary to some other aspect of his personality. Look for a word that means unsophisticated, and use POE to eliminate choices (B) and (E). *Petulant* and *audacious* have appropriately negative meanings, but are unrelated to sophistication in the context of *artistry*. *Maladroit* means clumsy, so choice (D) is the best match.

12. **impugn, substantiated, castrating**   Start with the first blank because it is easier. It describes the intention of the editorial, which you know suggested a *preferable alternative* to the current leadership. A good word to describe the article's intention toward the current policy is a word similar to undermine. *Bolster* goes in the wrong direction. *Vitiate* might look appealing, but is a bit too strong for an editorial. *Impugn* is the best choice. Now look at the second blank. The second blank describes *claims made against* the alternative group, and the actions were *inadvertent*, so a good word for the blank is something similar to supported or proved. *Laud* and *aggrandized* go in the wrong direction. *Substantiated* is the best match. Now look at the third blank. The editorial ended by damaging the opposition party, which was the *preferable alternative*, so a good word for this blank is halted. *Metamorphosing* and *abrogating* go in the wrong direction. *Castrating* is the best choice.

13.   **A**   The sentence talks about Professor Alberts' bad behavior and how it was overlooked by school administrators. Given the reverse-direction trigger *while* and the clue *had been impassively weathered*—along with the clue after the blank: *the school's president felt compelled to take action*—you know that Alberts' latest escapade was too serious to be overlooked. Use a word similar to serious or threatening for the blank. *Inimical* fits, but *complaisant, innocuous,* and *quotidian* would take the sentence in the wrong direction so eliminate choices (B), (C), and (D). *Reverent* is unrelated so eliminate choice (E). Thus, choice (A) is the best match.

14.   **E**   It's tricky to tease out what the missing word should be here, but from the clue *who could have predicted*, you might infer that the missing word relates to prediction. Choosing the right answer depends largely on vocabulary here, as *malingerer, reagent, desiccant,* and *equivocation* are all unrelated to prediction. *Portent* is the best answer.

15.   **A**   This sentence is rather complicated with two triggers—*despite* and *did not*—for the first blank. These indicate that even though they rapidly developed ports for slave commerce, the practice was not officially condoned. Use POE and eliminate choices (B), (D), and (E). The trigger *even* connected with the second blank tells you that Dutch slave commerce must have been similar to London commerce, so eliminate choice (C) and select choice (A).

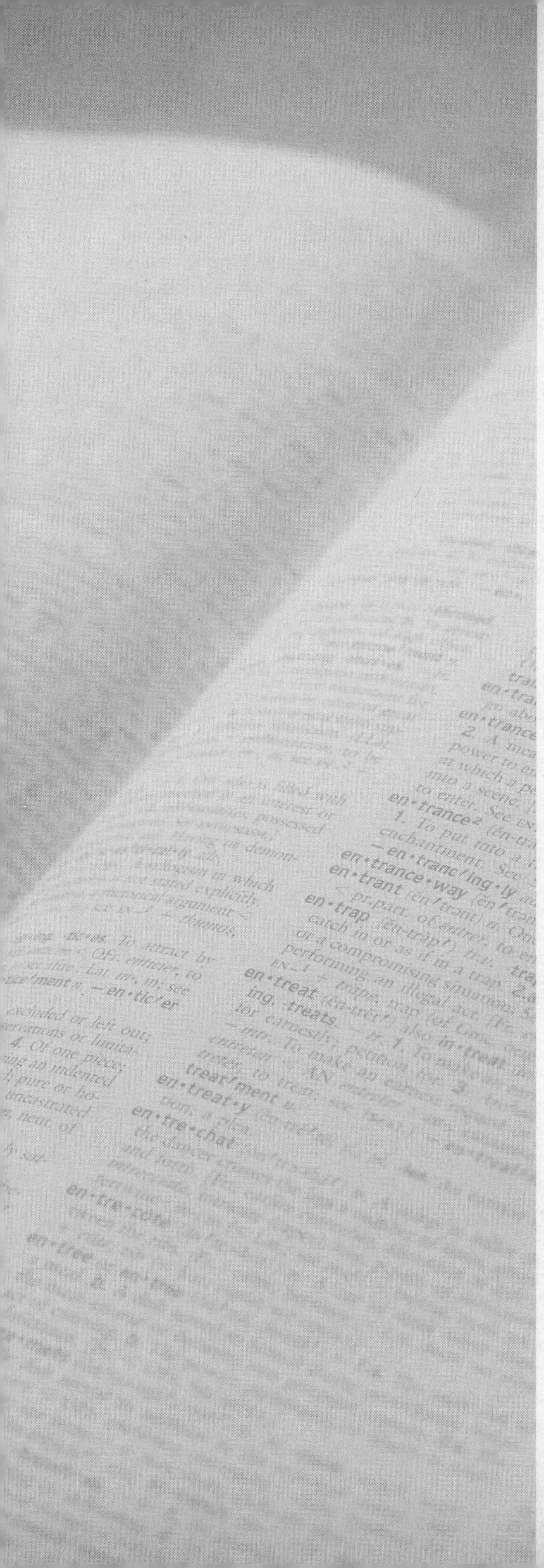

Reading Comprehension

READING COMPREHENSION

On any CAT exam there are always trade offs between speed and accuracy. Nowhere is this truer than on Reading Comprehension (RC). RC is an open-book test, so with unlimited time you should never get an RC question wrong. The first step to improving performance on RC questions, therefore, is to find that time. By improving your speed and efficiency with Analogy, Sentence Completion, and Antonym questions, you leave yourself more time to spend on RC. When you become a master of the other three question types, you free yourself up to relax and take your time on RC, where time equals points.

HOW MUCH TO READ

RC is the most time intensive portion of the verbal test. Deciding how much time to allocate to the passage is another way to pick up valuable time without sacrificing accuracy. The amount of time you devote will depend upon four primary factors. They are Location, Length, Skill Set, and Number of Questions.

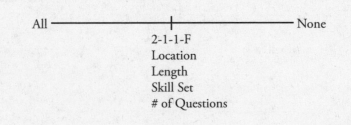

> **RULES TO LIVE BY:** You can always read more *IF* you have to, but you never want to read more THAN you have to.

Location

Location means the location of the question on the test. Getting the first 10 questions on the CAT correct is too important to risk missing crucial details in the passage. You are guaranteed to get at least one, more likely two, RC questions in your first ten. When you are working RC questions, read as much as you need and take as much time as you require to ensure that you get these early questions correct.

At the tail end of the test, on the other hand, you may have two minutes and five questions left. In this case, generating answers for all five questions is far more important than getting any one question correct. The uncoached test taker is likely to burn all two minutes looking for the correct answer to a single RC question, rather than using that same two minutes to correctly answer four Analogy, Antonym, or Sentence Completion questions. Be more strategic than that. It is far smarter to bubble in an RC late in the test and to use the few remaining minutes to get accurate answers on the four other question types.

Length

Passages on the GRE are one of two lengths: those that fit on a screen and those that force you to scroll. Scrolling is a nuisance. If the passage is so short that it fits on one screen, you might as well just read it. You'll probably end up reading the whole thing anyway.

Skill Set

Some people can skim, some cannot. Which are you? Can you skim quickly and still pick up the main idea of a passage? Or, when you skim do you either miss the main idea or get sucked into the details? If you are inclined to get sucked in, you shouldn't try to skim. Use 2-1-1-F instead. This means that you read the first two sentences of the first paragraph, the first sentence of each additional paragraph, and the final sentence of the passage. This should be sufficient to get the gist of the passage.

Number of Questions

The test will tell you how many questions are associated with a particular passage. If the next two or three questions are based upon the same passage, it's worth your time to read more of it.

HOW MUCH YOU SHOULD READ

All ————————————|———————————— None

2-1-1-F

Questions in the first 10 minute	Location	Questions in the last five minutes
Passages that fit on one screen	Length	Passages for which you have to scroll
I can skim effectively	Skill Set	I get sucked into details and end up burning time
> two questions per passage	# of Questions	</= two questions per passage

Reading Strategy Cont.

You can always read more *if* you need to, but you don't ever want to read more than you have to in order to answer a particular question. If you see a short passage with two questions in the first ten, you should read the whole thing. If you see a long passage with one question in the last few minutes, and you have more questions to get to, just bubble in and move on. For anything else, you will need a moderated approach. A great place to start is 2-1-1-F. Remember, if you need to read more, you always can.

BASIC QUESTION APPROACH

If you get a RC question wrong, it is for one of the three reasons: either you misread something in the passage, misread the question, or misread one of the answer choices. The basic four-step approach is designed to give some rigor to your interaction with each of these main components.

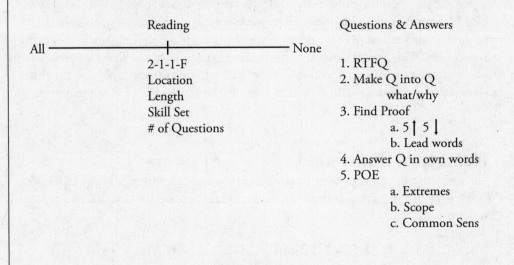

	Reading		Questions & Answers
All		None	1. RTFQ
	2-1-1-F		2. Make Q into Q
	Location		what/why
	Length		3. Find Proof
	Skill Set		a. 5↑ 5↓
	# of Questions		b. Lead words
			4. Answer Q in own words
			5. POE
			a. Extremes
			b. Scope
			c. Common Sens

Step 1: Read the Question (RTQ)

The first thing to do, naturally, is to read the question. Specifically, you should put your finger or pencil literally on the screen and read the question word for word. Misreading the question is one of the most common causes of errors. Reading with a pencil or finger, word for word, is a good habit, especially for strong readers who tend to skip over words without even noticing.

Step 2: Turn the Question into a Question

After a few hours of testing, it is all too easy for the eyes to glaze over and to read without really comprehending. To ensure that the words aren't simply going in one eyeball and out the other, you will want to engage in the question in a qualitative way. Most questions, you will notice, aren't really questions at all. They are incomplete sentences. The easiest way to own the question is to actually turn it back into a question. The easiest way to do that is to simply start with "what" or "why" and then to let the rest follow (any question-word will do, but the vast majority of questions either ask "What was stated in the passage?" or "Why was it said?").

Step 3: Read 5 Up, 5 Down

Never attempt to answer a question from memory. The minute you stop reading you start forgetting. ETS counts on this and plays with the answer choices to change your recollection of the information. You must look at the information in context, but you don't have to read the whole paragraph. Choose a word from the question that will be easy to find in the passage, skim for it, and then read five lines above it to five lines below it. That should be sufficient to answer the question.

Step 4: Answer the Question in Your Own Words

Before you get to the answer choices, stop and answer the question in your own words. When you do this, you will know exactly what you are looking for in the answer choices. With your own answer choice in mind, you will be protected from the tricks and traps that ETS has laid for you. Answering in your own words and turning the question into a question are perhaps the most frequently ignored steps in RC, but the truth is that these are two of the most important things you can do. If you have followed steps one through four, typically, one answer choice will look correct, and the other four will look ridiculous. This is precisely what you want.

POE: THE ANSWER CHOICES

There are three general characteristics that separate correct answers from incorrect ones. As you work through the drills, note these characteristics whenever you see them. Over time you will develop an instinct for right versus wrong answers.

Extremes

ETS plays it safe. Correct answers are wishy-washy or very difficult to prove false. It is too easy to find exceptions to extreme answer choices. For this reason, such extreme choices are almost never correct. Remember, to ETS it doesn't matter what the passages say. They don't write the passages, but they do write the questions and the answers. They can choose to create correct or incorrect answers in any way they like. They choose to do it in a way that won't put them on the phone with dozens of experts in various fields who beg to differ with them.

Examples

    (A) Disprove the view that amphibians are less intelligent than other vertabrates.

Can this even be done? Prove or Disprove is a very extreme word.

    (B) James was the first American author to focus on society as a whole as well as on individual characters.

This is too definitive a statement for a subjective view.

    (C) The public is not interested in increasing its awareness of the advantages and disadvantages of raw, as opposed to cooked, food.

Really? Says who? The whole of the public?

Scope

If you cannot physically put your finger on a specific word, line, phrase, or sentence that proves that your answer choice is correct, you cannot choose it. ETS loves to add information to answer choices little bits and bobs that was never stated in the passage. If a passage is about a recent immigrant's first experience of America, ETS will widen the scope of an answer choice to include *all* immigrants. If the passage is about the existence of heavy metals on some planets, an incorrect answer choice will talk about all planets.

Examples

MAIN IDEA OF PASSAGE	OUT OF SCOPE ANSWER CHOICE
How a species of evergreen flourished in South Florida	1. Resolving a dispute about the adaptability of plant seeds to bird transport
	2. Refute the claim that Floridian flora evolved independently from flora in other parts of the world
	3. Why more varieties of plant seeds adapted to external rather than to internal bird transport

What's wrong with the answer choices?

1. *Resolving a dispute* is a very strong opening verb phrase for this answer choice, but this answer choice is all about the nature of seeds, not about how seeds got to Hawaii. If the passage is about Hawaii, then the correct answer better say Hawaii.
2. The question is talking about Hawaii and seed transport, not about other parts of the world and evolution.
3. Again, this one is all about seeds and adaptation, not about Hawaii and transportation.

Common Sense

Many of the answer choices simply don't make any sense. Just because you see it on the GRE doesn't mean you have to take it seriously. Science passages may have answer choices that are highly illogical or physically impossible. Humanities passages may have answer choices that support different or even opposite views than those of the author, and are certainly answers that ETS could never stand behind. And some answer choices are just downright ridiculous.

> (A)   The public has been deliberately misinformed about the advantages and disadvantages of uncooked vegetables.

The GRE is not your typical forum for exposing government cover-ups.

> (B)   An interpretation of a novel should primarily consider those elements of novelistic construction of which the author of the novel was aware.

Unless someone can call up dead novelists from the grave, exactly how is the good critic to know which elements of novelistic construction the authors were aware of?

> (C)   Hawthorne, more than any other novelist, was aware of the difficulties of novelistic construction.

Extreme language aside, are there measurable degrees of awareness? Do we know how aware every novelist in history is or was? Is James really the Michael Jordan of Awareness of Novelistic Construction?

> **RULES TO LIVE BY:** If you cannot physically put your finger on a specific word, line, phrase, or sentence that proves that your answer choice is correct, you cannot pick it.

POE: THE PROCESS

In general, you want to be doing, not thinking. Thinking gets you into trouble. The best way to tell if you are thinking rather than doing is to pay attention to your hand. If your hand is not moving, you are either spacing out, lost, or attempting to do work in your head—all are bad. The use of scratch paper, therefore, is as critical to the verbal portion as it is to the math. Proper use of the scratch paper will help you stay on track; organize your thinking; and maintain an efficient, meticulous, and systematic approach.

Process Of Elimination is, in essence, a two-pass approach. In the first pass, walk through the answer choices asking a simple question: maybe or gone? "Gone" refers to the answer that can be eliminated with confidence; "Maybe" refers to everything else. This pass should take no more than 15 seconds. You are not looking for the correct answer. On this pass, you don't want to invest a lot of time in any one answer choice. If you have already found proof in the passage and answered the question in your own words, you will often find either that one answer choice is very clearly correct, or that the other four answer choices can very clearly be eliminated. Correct and incorrect answers should leap out at you. Only if you are left with two or three possibilities do you need to investigate further.

Make sure that you park your thinking on the page as you go, otherwise you are doing two separate jobs: assessing the answer choices and keeping track of what you've already decided about prior answer choices. This is confusing and inefficient. It is much better to simply park your thoughts on the page.

To do this, use these three basic symbols.

~~(A) WRONG~~
✓ (B) LOOKS GOOD
m (C) MAYBE OR DON'T KNOW
(D)
(E)

"Wrong" means that it is clearly wrong and needs to be gone. You never need to spend any time on this answer choice again. "Maybe" simply means that it is possible or you're not sure. "Yes" means that it looks good. You make these assessments through a combination of information you have acquired in the passage and the three elimination techniques listed above. If you are in the last ten questions, you might even stop here if you have two maybes or a clear winner. If you are in the first ten, you must go back to the passage to find proof.

Here is what the two passes might look like on a short passage in the first ten questions.

First Pass

Main Idea:
Pros and Cons of a unified assessment of the two halves of *Wuthering Heights*

Q: **The author of the passage would be most likely to agree that an interpretation of a novel should**

(A) not try to unite heterogeneous elements in the novel

Half of the passage is about why this is a good thing!

m (B) not be inflexible in its treatment of the elements in the novel

Wording is ridiculous, but "be flexible," ok, that makes sense.

m (C) not argue that the complex use of narrators or of timeshifts indicates a sophisticated stucture

Umm. Not sure, it's got to stay in for now.

(D) concentrate on the elements recalcitrant of the novel that are outside the novel's main structure

No, the author definitely didn't proscribe what someone should or shouldn't concentrate on.

(E) primarily consider those elements of novelistic construction of which the author of the novel was aware

Common sense.

This first pass took about 15–20 seconds. You eliminated some obvious choices and are now down to two. On the second pass, go back to the passage to check your proof. Paraphrase the remaining answer choices to make sure you are reading them correctly. Remember that there is only one correct answer. If you are absolutely sure that both are correct, you are misreading something.

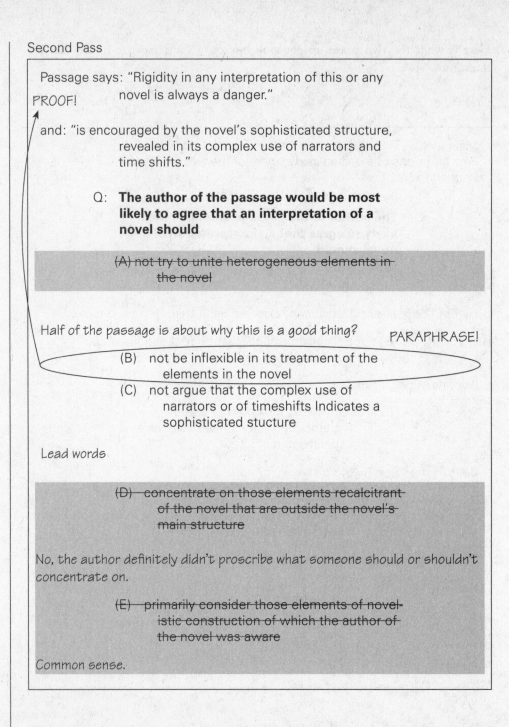

Second Pass

Passage says: "Rigidity in any interpretation of this or any novel is always a danger."

PROOF!

and: "is encouraged by the novel's sophisticated structure, revealed in its complex use of narrators and time shifts."

Q: **The author of the passage would be most likely to agree that an interpretation of a novel should**

(A) not try to unite heterogeneous elements in the novel

Half of the passage is about why this is a good thing?   PARAPHRASE!

(B) not be inflexible in its treatment of the elements in the novel

(C) not argue that the complex use of narrators or of timeshifts Indicates a sophisticated stucture

Lead words

(D) concentrate on those elements recalcitrant of the novel that are outside the novel's main structure

No, the author definitely didn't proscribe what someone should or shouldn't concentrate on.

(E) primarily consider those elements of novelistic construction of which the author of the novel was aware

Common sense.

As usual, the correct answer is a clear, if awkward, paraphrase of something stated in the passage (the awkwardness is an obvious attempt to steer you away from this answer choice). The second choice is stated, but the wording is encouraging, not discouraging. This is the choice that ETS will try to steer you toward.

In the second pass, pay no attention to choices (A), (D), or (E) because they have already been eliminated. Occasionally, you will end up eliminating all five; only in this case will you go back and reassess an answer choice you have already eliminated.

Strategy Summary

To sum up, read only as much as you have to and follow these five steps for all questions.

1. RTQ
2. Turn the question back into a question
3. Find proof
4. Answer the question in your own words
5. Process of Elimination

For more practice and a more in-depth look at The Princeton Review Reading Comprehension techniques, check out our student-friendly guidebook, *Cracking the GRE*.

READING COMPREHENSION: DRILL 1

Questions 1–2 refer to the following passage.

    Little is known about the elusive section of the earth's atmosphere known as the mesosphere. Located between the stratosphere (the maximum altitude that airplanes can achieve) and the thermosphere (the minimum altitude of space crafts), the mesosphere is poorly understood and little explored. The most significant feature of the mesosphere is the various tides and waves that propagate up through the troposphere and stratosphere. The dissipation of these waves is largely responsible for propelling the mesosphere around the globe. These wave patterns are further affected when gas particles in the mesosphere collide with meteors, producing spectacular explosions. These explosions usually generate enough heat to consume the meteor before it can fall to earth. The conflagration leaves behind a trace of iron and other metals and creates momentum that fuels the atmospheric tides radiating outward from the mesosphere.

In the last sentence, the word "fuels" refers to
- ◯ a process that changes the momentum of the atmosphere.
- ◯ a shift in the pressure of the mesosphere.
- ◯ a series of violent explosions in the mesosphere.
- ◯ a system that pushes the mesosphere around the earth.
- ◯ the presence of metals in the atmosphere.

Which of the following can be inferred from the passage?
- ◯ Without the mesosphere's mix of chemicals, falling meteors would be a serious threat to life on Earth.
- ◯ The turbosphere serves as a cap, containing the elements life needs to survive on Earth.
- ◯ Scientists lack appropriate methods for exploring our atmosphere.
- ◯ Little is known about atmospheric conditions above the thermosphere.
- ◯ Scientists may lack appropriate vehicles for manned exploration of the mesosphere.

Questions 3–4 refer to the following passage.

Television programming is big business, with sales of interstitial advertising reaching billions of dollars annually. Advertising rates are determined by the viewership of the program in question, which has traditionally been determined by the ACNielsen Company. Nielsen wields an immoderate amount of industry clout considering its questionable methods of statistics gathering.

The Nielsen Company relies on selected households to catalog their television watching habits in "diaries." The ratings are then reported as a percentage that indicates the number of viewers watching a television program at a given time. The company has come under criticism for choosing residences that underreport daytime and late-night television viewing and for over-representing minorities in sample populations. Critics also point to the nonviable practice of measuring how many individuals are watching a given television set and of gauging how attentive the audience is to a program or its advertising.

It can be inferred from the passage that the author considers the Nielsen Company's techniques

- ○ intentionally biased
- ○ dubious
- ○ worthless
- ○ unscrupulous
- ○ boastful

According to the passage, which of the following is true of the household members who report their viewing habits?

- ○ They are not always accurate when it comes to recording their viewing habits.
- ○ They are counted only as one person, no matter how many people make up the household.
- ○ They are required to record the channel to which the television is tuned during certain times of day.
- ○ They work in conjunction with the Nielsen Company to skew the viewership information and alter the ratings.
- ○ They give feedback about how advertising influences their spending habits.

Questions 5–8 refer to the following passage.

Although multi-organ transplants have become more common, scientists and surgeons continue to face the ineluctable obstacle of time. Current donor organ preservation times hover around five to six hours. Because of the complicated tissue-matching process, oftentimes organs are unable to reach their beneficiaries, wasting valuable, viable organs. However, scientists are hopeful that a certain substance, called the Hibernation Induction Trigger (HIT), will extend the life of a potential transplant organ.

HIT is an opiate-like substance found in the blood of hibernating animals. Previous experiments have shown that opioids act as an autoperfusion block, preventing blood from flowing through the lymphatic system to organs, a phenomenon known as ischemia. In a preliminary experiment, an infusion of plasma with the Delta opioid delayed hemorrhaging in certain laboratory animals. When this arresting of activity was applied to the transplantation of organs, physicians reported preservation times up to 15 hours, a more than two-fold increase over standard conservation.

Scientists have extrapolated from these findings, further identifying the opioid DADLE as integral to triggering the hibernation process. Infusing HIT-molecule-containing plasma from hibernating woodchucks into canine lungs increased preservation times more than three-fold from previous findings. This experiment suggests that, should a potential donor organ be infused with these trigger molecules before the organ is harvested, the organ would remain transplantable for up to 45 hours, greatly increasing the chance for doctors to find a suitable recipient.

Though these results are exciting, they do nothing to increase survival rates from an organ transplant operation, which currently hover at 60 percent over four years, because patients are still susceptible to infection and rejection. Scientists are a long way from declaring HIT-molecules a safe and consistent method of organ preservation. Still, other areas of science have taken an interest in this research. NASA, for example, is considering the implications of human hibernation for deep space travel.

Which of the following can be inferred from the passage?

○ Ischemia is essential to the organ transplantation process.
○ The same process by which HIT induces hibernation might work in donor organs.
○ The biggest obstacle facing physicians in the science of organ transplantation is the difficulty of matching suitable donors and recipients.
○ Additional time could be saved by computerizing the tissue-matching process.
○ HIT could also be administered to patients awaiting an organ transplant, thereby lengthening the amount of time they are eligible for surgery.

Given the information in the passage about blocking autoperfusion, which of the following could also be true?

○ DADLE and HIT must be present in an organ at the same time in order for autoperfusion to be prevented for any length of time.
○ If scientists could circumvent the passage of blood through the lymphatic system, organs would cease to deteriorate.
○ Scientists are close to developing a method to induce production of HIT in a non-hibernating animal.
○ Administering HIT after transplantation is likely to lower the current rates of infection and organ rejection.
○ Isolating and infusing opioids may be the key to retarding the progression of decay in transplant organs.

The author refers to the experiment with the woodchuck in order to

- ⬭ illustrate successful preliminary experiments.
- ⬭ suggest genetic similarity between species.
- ⬭ warn that the findings are preliminary at best.
- ⬭ explain why other scientists may be interested in the findings.
- ⬭ suggest the feasibility of inter-species transplant.

According to the passage, which of the following is true of Hibernation Induction Trigger?

- ⬭ It is a newly discovered substance.
- ⬭ It prevents ischemia.
- ⬭ It is found primarily in opioids.
- ⬭ It may be possible to isolate its molecules.
- ⬭ It is solely responsible for creating hibernation-like effects in animals.

Questions 9–11 refer to the following passage.

It might seem illogical that the development of modern currency rests on a scientific discovery, but the invention of the "touchstone" allowed ancient societies to create a standard by which valuable metals could be judged. In its most basic form, a touchstone is any dark, finely grained stone upon which soft metals leave traces. When rubbed, a process known as "probing," precious metal alloy cleaves to the stone, leaving a stripe. The color of the stripe (which reveals the percentage of its content that is base metal) can then be compared to a stripe of a known grade of standard alloy. Despite its primitiveness, this probing process allowed merchants to examine alloys quickly and with reasonable certainty. Though civilizations were using gold and silver currencies as early as 500 B.C., coins were easily forged or diluted with less valuable metals, such as tin or lead. The invention and popularization of the touchstone ensured that pure gold and silver could become a standard expression of value.

The primary purpose of the passage is to
- ○ demonstrate that science can influence non-scientific progress
- ○ underline the touchstone's importance in the history of currency
- ○ explain how the touchstone is able to measure the purity of an alloy
- ○ explore the etymology of the word "touchstone"
- ○ refute an historical misconception

The author's description of how coins were adulterated is included in the passage in order to
- ○ illustrate the historical precedent replaced by the invention
- ○ outline for the reader the chronology of the events in the passage
- ○ explain the larger importance of the details just provided
- ○ give the passage a cultural context
- ○ dismiss a misleading counterargument

According to the passage, the probing process allowed for which of the following advances?
- ○ It revealed the type of impurities in a given alloy.
- ○ It offered a means by which governments could standardize currency values.
- ○ It allowed the common merchant a means to accept payment in the form of currency.
- ○ It provided merchants an efficient means of ascertaining the purity of a metal.
- ○ It furnished an infallible method of testing the density of alloy.

Women played a substantial role in the furthering of the Polish art song in the late eighteenth and early nineteenth centuries. One notable woman from this time period was Maria Szymanowska, who was both a concert pianist and a composer.

Szymanowska was a member of the Warsaw Music Society who contributed pieces to a cycle entitled Historical Songs. Her songs are by far the most creative and individualistic of the cycle. In addition, Szymanowska composed more than one hundred other pieces, mostly for the piano, including six romances.

Her songs most resemble French romances, and she also employs Polonaise rhythms in two of her songs. In all her works, the melodic line is technically superior. She employs idiomatic keyboard writing, wide chord-spacing, broad cantilenas, and interesting modulations. She also uses the most compelling registers of the instrument and pianistic keys. Her romances are on par with those of Beethoven, Schubert, and Mozart. In fact, Szymanowska was praised by her contemporaries, such as Schumann, who lauded her etudes. Her piano playing was frequently equated to that of Hummel, though Szymanowska's was said to be more ethereal. Thus, she is a progenitor of Chopin in both piano technique and composition.

Female contributors to the development of Polish music have been chiefly ignored. From the meager records which have been preserved, it is incontrovertible that Polish women were, in fact, playing, instructing, and writing music as early as the fifteenth century. However, patriarchal societal structures have precluded adequate documentation about, and preservation of, their work. Unless changes take place, human society will be made poorer for its inability to recognize the expertise and inventiveness of these women.

What idea does the author put forward that would most strengthen the argument that Szymanowska's work laid the foundation for future composers?

- ◯ The author decries the constraints put on Szymanowska's fame by the patriarchy in which she lived.
- ◯ The author extols the fine qualities of her contributions to Historical Songs.
- ◯ The author favorably compares Szymanowska's work to that of her contemporary, Hummel.
- ◯ The author notes the critical acclaim that Szymanowska received from Schumann.
- ◯ The author describes Szymanowska as a foremother to another composer, Chopin.

Which of the following can be correctly inferred from the author's description of Szymanowska's style?

- ◯ Szymanowska exploited the capabilities of the piano.
- ◯ Szymanowska wrote for all types of vocal registers.
- ◯ Szymanowska used various techniques that made her the premier pianist of her era.
- ◯ Szymanowska developed a new method of playing piano that further enhanced the sound capabilities of the keys.
- ◯ Szymanowska deferred to the accepted standards of piano performance established in her time.

According to the passage, the musical contributions of Polish women have been neglected due to

○ an absence of any documentation of the efforts of female composers

○ improper preservation of musical scores produced by women

○ the male-dominated social order that has existed since at least the fifteenth century

○ society willfully ignoring the talent and hard work of female composers

○ the fact that people did not realize the genius and creativity of female composers

Which of the following statements can be properly inferred from the passage?

○ Szymanowska's piano playing rivaled that of Hummel and Schubert.

○ Szymanowska composed numerous works that were appreciated in her time.

○ Szymanowska opposed the evolution of Polish art songs and romances.

○ Szymanowska was an inspiration for Chopin and shaped the formation of his personal musical style.

○ Szymanowska demonstrated her support of egalitarian feminism by advancing the music of Polish art songs in spite of patriarchal pressure.

READING COMPREHENSION: DRILL 2

Questions 1–2 refer to the following passage.

Historically, sociologists have presumed that people will attribute certain characteristics to a member of a particular group when it is generally believed that most members of that group possess the characteristics in question. For sociologists Hepburn and Locksley, such social stereotyping has led to the broader question of whether people are cognizant of their own stereotyping behavior. Seemingly, if one knows that one holds a stereotypical notion such as "all members of a certain ethnic group are natural musicians," then one might also be aware that the notion that "a particular musician of that ethnic group is a great musician" is a corollary of that stereotype. However, people are most aware of their stereotyping when they have no information. When given information that conforms to their beliefs and the individual case observed, people become less aware of their tendency to stereotype and therefore more likely to engage in stereotyping.

Which of the following best describes the function of the first sentence?

○ to present a criticism of Hepburn and Locksley's conceptualization of why individuals stereotype

○ to provide evidence to support Hepburn and Locksley's claims about the problems inherent with stereotyping

○ to provide the backdrop for Hepburn and Locksley's study

○ to provide an overview of a social phenomenon and its contributions to Hepburn and Locksley's area of inquiry

○ to provide a history of social stereotyping alongside Hepburn and Locksley's reservations about the practice

The author of the passage is primarily concerned with

○ investigations into stereotyping and an awareness of stereotyping by individuals

○ an examination of the relative truths behind well known stereotypes

○ an attempt to prove that stereotypes are a result of ignorance

○ a refutation of a broader question surrounding stereotypes

○ a detailed list of when individuals are likely to be aware that they are applying stereotypes

Questions 3–6 refer to the following passage.

The literature of the American West ranges from lowbrow entertainment to great works of fiction. The extremes are obvious enough, but the middle tends to blur. The dime-store Western never aspired to be anything but entertainment. James Fenimore Cooper and Willa Cather, however, used themes of westward expansion in works clearly intended as highbrow literature. The novels of modern writer Larry McMurtry broke new ground: He took the Western and created a great piece of fiction, without changing its fundamental genre appeal or its accessibility to the general reader.

As an example of his retooling of the Western genre, consider McMurtry's themes. While the Western myth is fundamentally about resettlement to new lands, McMurtry's novels combine elements of the Western myth with less traditional motifs: profound reluctance to face change, conflict between urbanization and the Western ideal, the importance of place, and the role of the land itself. While the traditional Western is rooted in the past, McMurtry's themes combine nostalgia for that past with a sense of emptiness in the present and hopelessness for the future.

Or consider McMurtry's treatment of character. The traditional Western formula depicts mainly masculine characters and portrays them as both heroic and human. In his novels, McMurtry creates strong female characters, transmuting the conventional plot of the trials and dangers of the frontier by folding in deeper ideological insights. Critics rightly credit his novels with reshaping the Western genre, praising his work and its meticulous attention to the Western mise en scene as a subversive but sincere tribute to the American West.

It can be inferred from the passage that the author regards reliance on masculine characters in traditional Westerns as

○ an idealized but fundamentally accurate picture of frontier life
○ a limitation in the traditional construct of the Western
○ a convention largely seen to be irrelevant by readers
○ a trait that was embraced by McMurtry
○ a symbolic representation of the Western myth

The author refers to James Fenimore Cooper and Willa Cather in order to suggest

○ that their works are examples of entertaining literature
○ that their literary achievements were no less impressive than those of McMurtry
○ that the themes of the Western genre could be employed in literature meant to appeal to a more sophisticated reader
○ that they were contemporaries of McMurtry
○ that the theme of westward expansion was a multicultural concept

According to the passage the ideological undertones in McMurtry's novels stem from the

- ◯ introduction of strong·female characters
- ◯ reader's familiarity with other Westerns
- ◯ portrayal of the dangerous nature of the Western frontier
- ◯ heroic nature of the masculine characters
- ◯ verisimilitude of the characters

It can be inferred that the author regards McMurtry's treatment of character with

- ◯ regret that he did not adhere to Western novelistic conventions
- ◯ concern that the characterizations altered the nature of the Western formula
- ◯ approval for the manner in which their inclusion transformed the Western genre
- ◯ puzzlement, because the characters seem insignificant to the plot
- ◯ enthusiasm, because the characters reform the conventionality of Western plots

Questions 7–10 refer to the following passage.

"Hydrothermal vent" is the term that scientists use to describe a crack in a planet's surface from which geothermally heated water emerges. Because these vents are common in places that are volcanically active, they are plentiful on Earth. While the most famous hydrothermal vent is probably the geyser at Yellowstone National Park in the United States, there are several different types of vents, existing both on land and underwater. Black Smokers, for instance, are a common type of submarine vent. The National Oceanic and Atmospheric Administration first discovered these in the vicinity of the Galapagos Islands in 1977. Underwater vents such as these form when water that has been heated by magma beneath the earth's crust exits through cracks in the ocean floor. Scientists are interested in these vents primarily for their ability to host biologically dense communities in areas that are otherwise hostile to life. Studies show that Chemosynthetic archaea, a life form similar to bacteria, allows these areas to support such diverse organisms as clams and shrimp. Black Smokers are also visually striking. Minerals in the water that emerge from the earth's crust crystallize around each vent to create their distinctive black chimney-like formations.

While on a vessel exploring the Atlantis Massif in the mid-Atlantic Ridge, scientists recently discovered a completely new kind of hydrothermal system, which they dubbed "Lost City." Here, a "forest" of white limestone pillars rises 180 feet above the sea floor. There are several important differences that distinguish the hydrothermal vents in Lost City from the more familiar Black Smokers. The heat and fluid flow at Lost City is driven by the intermingling of seawater and mantle rocks on the sea floor, rather than by hot magma. As these fluids mix with magnesium-rich sea water, they deposit calcium carbonate and magnesium hydroxide, thereby creating the stunning white structures of Lost City. The fluids here are also much cooler (less than 100 degrees Celsius) and are composed of substances and gases that are different from those of Black Smokers. For instance, the fluids here have high pH content and contain significant amounts of hydrogen and methane gas.

The discovery of Lost City is still a fairly recent one, and scientists currently have more questions than answers. However, they hope that the insights they gain from this study will provide information that will lead to a better understanding of some of the earliest hydrothermal systems on earth and the life they supported.

The primary purpose of the passage is to
- ⚪ refute a well-established theory
- ⚪ describing a newly discovered natural phenomenon and compare it to another
- ⚪ explaining how the study of a certain natural phenomenon has changed over time
- ⚪ evaluating opposing theories
- ⚪ reconsidering a natural phenomenon in light of new discoveries

The author most likely introduced Black Smokers in the first paragraph in order to
- ⚪ summarize the main points made over the course of the passage about a natural phenomenon
- ⚪ provide a specific example that proves the hypothesis made in the preceding sentence
- ⚪ present an example that invalidates a commonly held belief regarding a natural phenomenon
- ⚪ detail the discovery of a previously unknown natural phenomenon
- ⚪ substantiate the general idea presented in the preceding sentence

The passage suggests that the hydrothermal vents that constitute Lost City are different from Black Smokers in which of the following ways?

○ Magma propels the heat and water of Black Smokers, whereas the vents at Lost City are driven by the merging of seawater and mantle rocks.

○ Black Smoker vents release water that is much cooler than the water released at Lost City.

○ Chemosynthetic archaea fosters many different life forms around Black Smokers but is not present at Lost City.

○ The Lost City vents are of greater geological interest because they have been studied longer and more extensively than the Black Smoker vents.

○ The communities of organisms supported by the Lost Vents are more diverse than the communities of the Black Smokers.

Each of the following is true of Black Smokers EXCEPT

○ Black chimney-like structures form around each vent.

○ Black Smokers host biologically dense communities.

○ As water emerges from the vents it deposits calcium carbonate and magnesium hydroxide.

○ Magma drives the fluid flow of Black Smokers.

○ Black Smokers were discovered near the Galapagos Islands in the latter part of the twentieth century.

Questions 11–12 refer to the following passage.

The paintings of Eugene Delacroix are as political, complex, tumultuous, and vivid as the life of Lord Byron, who inspired some of Delacroix's best works, such as Greece Expiring on the Ruins of Missolonghi and Scènes des massacres de Scio. Simultaneously, the paintings boast an incredible mélange of the artistic traditions of prior masters and movements—such as a preoccupation with terribilitas from Michelangelo; a flair for color from Titian; and power, strength, and exuberance from Rubens—all underlain by the harmony and balance of classical artists and tinted with the Baroque. Delacroix combined eclectic elements and infused them with his own genius, creating a unique expression of Romanticism, and in so doing, inspired yet another style, Symbolism.

What can be inferred about Delacroix's work by the phrase "tinted with the Baroque"?

○ Delacroix frequently used unusual colors patented by Titian.
○ Delacroix preferred highly elaborate frames with gold tint for his pictures.
○ Delacroix often painted bizarre figures and scenes.
○ Delacroix used sketches made by one of his student as models for his paintings.
○ Delacroix included in his paintings some elements of the Baroque movement in his paintings.

According to the passage, which of the following is most likely a non-painter who inspired Delacroix?

○ Titian
○ Lord Byron
○ Michelangelo
○ Rubens
○ Missolonghi

Sociobiologists, the most well known of whom is Edward O. Wilson, contend that there is a biological basis for the social behavior of animals, and they test their hypotheses through observation of animals in situations. Species studied have varied as widely as to encompass both termites and rhesus macaques. Sociobiologists further argue that students of human behavior cannot adequately account for the panoply of human nature through only such traditional variables as culture, ethnicity, and environment but must also include evolutionary processes. However, many scientists, notably Stephen Jay Gould and Richard Lewontin, have criticized this approach to the study of humans on a number of grounds: for example, that it is based on Eurocentric notions and that it is plagued by methodological problems. These detractors label it a pseudo-science because sociobiological theories are not falsifiable and thus, in this respect, are similar to alchemy or astrology.

Based on the critique by Gould and Lewontin, it can be inferred that they might agree with which of the following statements about a sociobiological approach to the study of humans?

○ Studying termite colonies and rhesus macaques is important since this comparison might lead to a general theory of sociobiology.

○ It is one of the most important developments in science and has provided valuable insights into the social behavior of animals and humans.

○ When applied to the study of humans, sociobiology is problematic because it is rooted in a Western worldview and because it does not comport with proper scientific methodology.

○ Sociobiology should never be applied to the study of animals or humans because it is Eurocentric and is plagued with methodological problems.

○ Scientists cannot adequately explain human behavior through the consideration of cultural, ethnic, and environmental factors alone; therefore, they must resort to sociobiological explanations.

The author mentions culture, ethnicity, and environment in order to

○ offer justification for a comparative study between termite colonies and rhesus macques

○ assert that sociobiology is problematic because it is Eurocentric and beset by methodological complications

○ illustrate that sociobiology is an inappropriate method for studying humans

○ enumerate some variables that sociobiologists believe are insufficient in the study of humans and thus necessitate the addition of biological considerations

○ provide a comprehensive list of the factors that influence human behavior

The primary purpose of the passage is to

○ offer praise for an influential scientific approach to the study of animal and human behavior

○ argue for a sociobiological approach to the study of human behavior

○ dispute a sociobiological approach to the study of human behavior

○ justify a sociobiological approach to the study of termite colonies and rhesus macaques

○ set forth an influential approach to the study of animal and human behavior and discuss some objections to this approach

READING COMPREHENSION: DRILL 3

Questions 1–2 refer to the following passage.

In *The Federalist Number Ten*, James Madison forewarned against the dangers of factions—groups of people with a common interest adverse to the overall good of the nation, what today are referred to as "special interest groups." Madison described two hypothetical ways to check a faction: Either eliminate the causes or mitigate the effects of the faction. To eliminate the causes, the government would either have to make all people perfectly equal, an impossible goal, or take away people's liberty and thus defeat the purpose of having a republican form of government. Madison argued, alternatively, for ameliorating the effects of factions by enlarging the population of the country and thus diluting their influence. If there are a sufficient number of diverse peoples, it will be difficult for a majority to share a common interest at the same time.

According to the passage, why does Madison believe it necessary to check a faction?

- ◯ Madison considered factions to be detrimental to the common welfare.
- ◯ Madison thought factions were a way to encourage population growth.
- ◯ Madison relied on factions to support the republican style of government.
- ◯ Madison accepted factions as a consequence of allowing people to participate in government.
- ◯ Madison evaluated the impact of factions on liberty.

Which of the following can be most correctly inferred from the passage?

- ◯ Madison solved the problem of factions in the United States.
- ◯ Madison thought that the best solution was to make all citizens equal.
- ◯ Madison argued against a republican government in *The Federalist Number Ten*.
- ◯ Madison analyzed the effects of increased population.
- ◯ Madison considered more than one way to constrain factions.

Questions 3–4 refer to the following passage.

William Le Baron Jenney is considered the founder of the Chicago School of architecture, as well as the father of the American skyscraper. He served as an engineering officer during the Civil War but by 1868 was a practicing architect. His greatest accomplishments were his mammoth commercial buildings, including the Home Insurance Building in Chicago, which was one of the first buildings to use a metal skeleton. This structure, in fact, would become the archetypical American skyscraper design. Other notable accomplishments included his 16-story Manhattan Building, which was the first edifice ever to achieve that height, and the Horticultural Building, which was the largest botanical conservatory ever erected.

William Holabird also assisted in the evolution of the Chicago School, beginning as a draftsman for Jenney and then founding his own practice in 1880. Holabird invented the "Chicago window," which made buildings appear to be constructed of glass.

According to the passage, all of the following describe William Jenney EXCEPT

○ He worked extensively on commercial properties during his career.

○ He is credited with the development of a much-copied design for skyscrapers.

○ He influenced the careers of other architects.

○ He designed buildings that pushed boundaries in construction as well as architecture.

○ He served as an architect for the Union Army during the Civil War.

The author mentions the "Chicago window" in order to

○ highlight a feature of glass buildings

○ strengthen the argument that Holabird developed the Chicago School

○ argue that Holabird was a better inventor than Jenney

○ provide an example of Holabird's contributions to the 'Chicago School'

○ demonstrate the artistry of architecture

READING COMPREHENSION: DRILL 3

Questions 1–2 refer to the following passage.

In *The Federalist Number Ten*, James Madison forewarned against the dangers of factions—groups of people with a common interest adverse to the overall good of the nation, what today are referred to as "special interest groups." Madison described two hypothetical ways to check a faction: Either eliminate the causes or mitigate the effects of the faction. To eliminate the causes, the government would either have to make all people perfectly equal, an impossible goal, or take away people's liberty and thus defeat the purpose of having a republican form of government. Madison argued, alternatively, for ameliorating the effects of factions by enlarging the population of the country and thus diluting their influence. If there are a sufficient number of diverse peoples, it will be difficult for a majority to share a common interest at the same time.

According to the passage, why does Madison believe it necessary to check a faction?

○ Madison considered factions to be detrimental to the common welfare.
○ Madison thought factions were a way to encourage population growth.
○ Madison relied on factions to support the republican style of government.
○ Madison accepted factions as a consequence of allowing people to participate in government.
○ Madison evaluated the impact of factions on liberty.

Which of the following can be most correctly inferred from the passage?

○ Madison solved the problem of factions in the United States.
○ Madison thought that the best solution was to make all citizens equal.
○ Madison argued against a republican government in *The Federalist Number Ten*.
○ Madison analyzed the effects of increased population.
○ Madison considered more than one way to constrain factions.

Questions 3–4 refer to the following passage.

William Le Baron Jenney is considered the founder of the Chicago School of architecture, as well as the father of the American skyscraper. He served as an engineering officer during the Civil War but by 1868 was a practicing architect. His greatest accomplishments were his mammoth commercial buildings, including the Home Insurance Building in Chicago, which was one of the first buildings to use a metal skeleton. This structure, in fact, would become the archetypical American skyscraper design. Other notable accomplishments included his 16-story Manhattan Building, which was the first edifice ever to achieve that height, and the Horticultural Building, which was the largest botanical conservatory ever erected.

William Holabird also assisted in the evolution of the Chicago School, beginning as a draftsman for Jenney and then founding his own practice in 1880. Holabird invented the "Chicago window," which made buildings appear to be constructed of glass.

According to the passage, all of the following describe William Jenney EXCEPT

- ⃝ He worked extensively on commercial properties during his career.
- ⃝ He is credited with the development of a much-copied design for skyscrapers.
- ⃝ He influenced the careers of other architects.
- ⃝ He designed buildings that pushed boundaries in construction as well as architecture.
- ⃝ He served as an architect for the Union Army during the Civil War.

The author mentions the "Chicago window" in order to

- ⃝ highlight a feature of glass buildings
- ⃝ strengthen the argument that Holabird developed the Chicago School
- ⃝ argue that Holabird was a better inventor than Jenney
- ⃝ provide an example of Holabird's contributions to the 'Chicago School'
- ⃝ demonstrate the artistry of architecture

Questions 5–8 refer to the following passage.

"Solar wind" is the term scientists use to describe the stream of particles that the sun's corona constantly emits. These solar winds, which consist mainly of hydrogen and helium, are intensely hot, fully ionized plasma. Because of the corona's intense heat, these particles continuously escape the sun's gravitational attraction, flowing away from the sun at extreme velocities. Solar winds, though, are not without variation, because they contain faster and slower moving pockets. For instance, solar winds that originate from streamers are slower moving winds at approximately 300 km/second, as opposed to the winds that originate from corona holes and reach speeds of 800 km/second. As they flow away from the sun, tangential discontinuities and interplanetary shocks form, producing pressure variations. Moreover, researchers also know that solar winds are directly related to geomagnetic storms, auroras, and comets. It is these winds that cause comet tails to bend away from the sun, as Kepler accurately predicted in the early 1600s.

Studies have been done on the effect of solar winds on the planets in the solar system. While all the planets are surrounded by this hot, super-charged plasma, the Earth's magnetic field protects it from the solar wind by deflecting the particles. However, solar winds are responsible for the Earth's magnetosphere, and changes in their speed and direction strongly influence Earth's space environment. As the planet closest to the sun, Mercury endures the main impact of solar winds. If Mercury had an atmosphere, these winds would have stripped it away, leaving the planet bathed in radiation. Though Mars is much further from the sun than Mercury, solar winds have also greatly reduced its atmosphere. While Venus has a substantial atmosphere—100 times denser than ours—solar winds reduce its clouds. It is not just those planets nearest the sun which bear the effects of solar winds: The winds travel far beyond the limits of Pluto. Interestingly, while much is now known about solar winds, scientists still do not fully understand how the gases and particles in the sun's corona reach such high velocities.

According to the passage, which of the following is true of the effect of solar winds on the Earth?

- ⬭ Solar winds long ago stripped away Earth's upper atmosphere, leaving it bathed in radiation.
- ⬭ Solar winds play a significant role in the formation and intensity of aurora borealis and geomagnetic storms in the earth's space environment.
- ⬭ Though the Earth's magnetic field largely protects it from the full effects of solar winds, the winds are responsible for its magnetosphere and its space environment.
- ⬭ Because of the corona's intense heat, solar wind particles continuousl escape the sun's gravitational attraction, flowing away from the corona at extremely high velocities and surrounding the Earth with hot, super-charged plasma.
- ⬭ According to one recent theory, solar winds may move at incredibly high speeds and travel great distances, but they have little effect on the Earth because it is too distant from the sun.

It can be inferred from the passage that the Earth's magnetic field acts to

- ⬭ absorb the particles blown by solar winds
- ⬭ incinerate the particles present in solar winds
- ⬭ assimilate the particles in solar winds into the Earth's atmosphere
- ⬭ divert the particles in solar winds from the Earth
- ⬭ re-orient the particles in solar winds toward a central collection point

The author most likely discusses Kepler's observations of solar winds in order to

- present an example of the surprisingly accurate work performed by an early astronomer
- denounce Kepler's work as unreliable because the technology required to study solar winds directly has only been developed within the last century
- describe more generally the first major contribution to the study of solar winds and the sun
- disprove Kepler's theories on the motion of comets and auroras
- establish a standard against which to compare the observations concerning the atmospheres of Mars and Mercury

The primary purpose of this passage is to

- discuss the difficulties in providing accurate information on a phenomenon that cannot be observed firsthand
- provide information on solar winds and discuss their effects on planets in the solar system
- describe the effects of solar winds on planets in the solar system and how this knowledge impacts other scientific studies
- contrast and critique two competing theories concerning the origins and causes of solar winds
- point out the gaps in a scientific study and discuss the reasons for these gaps

Questions 9–10 refer to the following passage.

The American people have an incorrect understanding of what it means to be at war. At least, so argues T.H. Pickett in his conservative interpretation of American military history.

Pickett does present a wealth of examples, along with a refreshingly candid argument that America often goes to war for an abstract ideal such as democratization of societies, world peace, liberty, or freedom. For instance, the Spanish-American War of 1898 was ostensibly a consequence of national enthusiasm for the cause of Cuban liberty. And, more obviously, America's entry into World War I stemmed from a desire to "make the world safe for democracy." Although these observations are supportable, Pickett overstates the case when he argues that these abstract causes typically lead to a war hysteria in which American leadership can no longer enforce any measured policies.

It can be inferred from the description of Pickett's work that the author believes all of the following EXCEPT

- ◯ Pickett provides a plethora of examples to support his case.
- ◯ Picket should be lauded for his understanding of the rationale behind America's decisions to enter certain battles.
- ◯ The desire for tangible rewards is not always the primary reason that America enters into warfare.
- ◯ Democratization of a foreign country is a rationale for at least one of the wars America has waged.
- ◯ Pickett ineffectively supports his argument with abstract examples.

Which of the following best states the author's main point?

- ◯ Pickett's study overturned the conventional understanding of why America engages in warfare.
- ◯ Pickett's study is valuable primarily because it provides a thorough understanding of the causes of American warfare.
- ◯ The rationale for American warfare is well documented.
- ◯ Pickett provides a cogent rationale for why America engages in warfare; however, he draws conclusions that the author does not fully support.
- ◯ Pickett's analysis of American military history provides the definitive historical record of the period from the Spanish-American War to World War I.

Though artist Chuck Close has devoted his life to portraiture, his paintings rarely comport with that genre's traditional purpose. His early photorealist images, which are created by overlaying a grid on a photograph and painstakingly copying the image cell by cell, are, to the naked eye, nearly undifferentiable from photographs. Close's emphasis is on the disembodied head itself, expressionless and devoid of any overt personality. He has never acceded to commissions, relying on both his own image and his friends as models. In 1988, a collapsed spinal artery caused almost total paralysis, but Close has continued to work. His freer paintings evince a natural extension of an augmented interest in the minute grid over the total work that predated his illness. This non-privileging of any particular part of the canvas finds its inspiration, oddly enough, in abstract expressionism, despite the apparent inconsonance of the two techniques.

What is the author's intent when discussing Close's focus on the head of his subjects?

○ The author compares the artistic impact of photographs of heads to abstract paintings of the same heads.

○ The author ruminates on what early experiences led to Close's focus on the head as a unifying theme in his work.

○ The author expounds upon how, by not accepting commissions, Close's work has remained free of commercial influences.

○ The author deconstructs the impact that Close's illness had on the content of his paintings.

○ The author believes that Close's approach of depicting the head but none of the personality of the subject is unique.

According to the passage, which of the following statements is true?

○ Close's portraits are so realistic that they are sometimes mistaken for photographs.

○ By the late 1980s, Close was beginning to forgo the rigid photorealism that characterized his early work.

○ Close's change of style was influenced primarily by his crippling illness.

○ Close claims to be inspired by abstract impressionism; though critics say there is no relationship between the two genres.

○ Close's photorealistic process takes longer to complete than other forms of painting.

The anti-foundationalist belief that there is no secure basis for knowledge was worked out philosophically in the somewhat wearisome tracts of Jacques Derrida. Difference, Derrida tells us, is the idea that any attempts to discuss universal features of human nature are merely products of local standards, often serving the vested interests of the status quo, and should rightly be dismantled and critiqued. Derrida was considered the originator of a profound challenge to the history of human thought. However, a century before Derrida, Darwin's theory of natural selection had made anti-foundationalism almost an inevitable consequence. From an evolutionary point of view, our understanding of the world depends on earlier and less-developed forms of understanding; meaning is continuously referred or deferred to other terms or experiences.

Derrida's definition of difference suggests that he would most likely subscribe to which of the following beliefs?

- ◯ The interests of the status quo originate from local standards.
- ◯ Ideas expressed by those who are part of the status quo do not necessarily represent a universally accepted truth.
- ◯ Any attempts to discuss human nature serve the interests of the status quo.
- ◯ The interests of the status quo should be critiqued and dismantled by those who are part of the status quo.
- ◯ Ideas that are a product of local standards cannot contain elements of a universal truth.

The author mentions "an evolutionary point of view" in the last sentence in order to do which of the following?

○ Expand his argument to include the field of evolutionary science.

○ Indicate his disagreement with Derrida's theory of anti-foundationalism.

○ Support his point that anti-foundationalism had been a theoretical construct before Derrida expounded its tenets.

○ Explain the elements of evolutionary theory that embraced anti-foundationalism.

○ Show the increasing sophistication of evolutionary biologists.

The passage implies that which of the following beliefs is embraced by anti-foundationalists?

○ In many cases humans cannot be completely secure in thinking that they fully understand a given situation.

○ The meaning of an experience can best be understood outside the cultural context in which it occurs.

○ Those who are part of the status quo are best able to dismantle and critique society.

○ Derrida's work would not have been possible without the prior ruminations of Darwin a century earlier.

○ Darwin's faith in the status quo is sufficient grounds to develop universal truths about cultural experiences.

READING COMPREHENSION: DRILL 4

Questions 1–2 refer to the following passage.

Some readers categorize Maxine Hong Kingston as a great Asian-American writer, a classification that is ultimately too narrow for her body of work. However, the subject matter of Kingston's novels and autobiographies espouses the Asian immigrant experience, as the following characters suggest: immigrant laborers in California and Hawaii, railroad laborers, and Chinese doctors. In natural harmony with her choice of subject matter are the personal sensibilities of a first-generation American writer who endeavors to explain her mother's alien sensibility and her relationship with her silent, angry father.

Kingston's Asian influences are present in another type of work, Chinese myths in the guise of "talk stories." A character in her novel Tripmaster Monkey is based on Sun Wu Kong, a mythical Chinese figure. In response to this work, Herbert Gold notes that the author "invigorates her novel with an avid personal perspective, doing what the novel is supposed to do—she brings us the news of the world and makes magic of it."

It can be inferred that Kingston uses the term "talk stories"

- ◯ to honor the legacy of Sun Wu Kong
- ◯ to provide an outlet for critiques of her work
- ◯ as a way to present Chinese myths in her novels
- ◯ to distance herself from her own cultural heritage
- ◯ as a method of engaging children who are not yet reading on their own

The author focuses on the content of Kingston's work primarily to

- ◯ illustrate why one might be tempted to call Kingston an Asian-American author
- ◯ assert why Kingston's work is difficult to categorize
- ◯ explain why Kingston's work is thought by many to have universal appeal
- ◯ illustrate how Kingston's work is affected by her parental influences
- ◯ show what makes Kingston unique among Asian-American writers

Questions 3–6 refer to the following passage.

Préciosité, "preciousness," or the manifestation of the Baroque in literature, is often dismissed as a "feminine concoction," mocked by Molière and thought to be ridiculous by modern standards. Preferring appearance to substance and excess to moderation, baroque expression is given to wild exaggeration and purple description. However, when one considers its historical context, the movement can be seen as a subtle rebellion by an otherwise powerless sex against its restrictive society.

Crippled and stunned from a series of religious wars, seventeenth-century France under Louis XIII was characterized by political intrigue and violence. Escaping the crude court, a group of cultured and educated ladies met to discuss—in a fantastically embellished and witty manner—literature, art, and philosophy. They rejected the predominant emphasis on vulgarity and sought the elevation of l'éducation, or "manners" they considered essential to society. More salons followed, and these précieuses (literally, "precious ones") produced works of literature that are still widely read, such as novels, essays, and poems that elevated the ideal of courtly, or Platonic, love with an emphasis on sensuality and scrupulous rules of behavior.

Though men scoffed at their wives' pretensions, baroque literature as a reaction to political instability reawakened French proclivities for cultural expression. When Louis XIV ascended to the throne in 1661, French society was primed for the reestablishment of the arts. Baroque ideals served important roles regarding the criticism of the political situation and the influence of cultural trends. Louis XIV's peace provoked the cultural pendulum to swing to the other direction, ushering in a neo-classical movement that elevated simplicity and minimalism. It is surely no coincidence that it was the performance of "Les Précieuses Ridicules" ("The Conceited Ladies"), Moliere's play mocking préciosité, that first gained him wide acclaim and established him as the preeminent father of French theater.

It can be inferred from the passage that the author most likely believes that

○ censorship sometimes serves as inspiration.

○ literature was the only means of protest available to women in the seventeenth century.

○ literature is a valuable weapon of protest.

○ Baroque literature played a role in reviving France's interest in politics.

○ it is necessary to look at a movement's historical context to glean its importance.

The primary purpose of the passage is to

○ demonstrate the importance of the role of a specific artistic movement to a culture

○ show that women had a greater influence on history than was previously thought

○ define and explain the origins of an obscure art forms

○ correct a commonly held historical misconception about the origins of a literary movement

○ emphasize the influence of a nation's ruler on its arts and culture

The author suggests which of the following about how préciosité was viewed during the seventeenth century?

- ○ It became the preferred method of communication for all members of French society.
- ○ It can be dismissed as a mere pastime for women of leisure.
- ○ It was ridiculed, but some thought its influence would endure.
- ○ It was tolerated until Molière's popular play mocked it.
- ○ Its importance as a cultural force was not understood.

The author places quotation marks around "feminine concoction" most likely in order to

- ○ cite a source of information
- ○ imbue the phrase with irony
- ○ isolate the phrase as a term to be defined
- ○ show that it is a foreign term
- ○ emphasize its gendered phrasing

Questions 7–8 refer to the following passage.

The mid-nineteenth century witnessed two major wars on U.S. soil: the Mexican-American War and the Civil War. That Abraham Lincoln would commit the country to civil war appears to require little explanation, since he endorsed the abolition of slavery and the preservation of the young nation. However, Lincoln's disdain for the Mexican-American War, which was ostensibly fought to keep Texas in the Union, requires some examination. After all, Lincoln's swift military response to the Southern secessionists at the beginning of the Civil War illustrates that Lincoln would not shrink from battle if the war could ensure a united country. Perhaps Lincoln's resistance to the Mexican-American War can best be seen in light of his sincere belief that President Polk had overstepped his constitutional boundaries in declaring war against Mexico, a sovereign nation. In this light, it is perhaps ironic that Lincoln's own presidential legacy includes a greater centralization of federal government power.

According to the passage, which of the following is true of the Mexican-American War?

○ Lincoln was not president during that war.

○ It was supported by those who lived in Texas.

○ It was fought ostensibly to abolish slavery.

○ It resulted in a centralization of government power.

○ It was unconstitutional.

Which of the following best describes the function of the sentence about Lincoln's swift military response in the passage?

○ It provides evidence that Lincoln generally did not oppose wars.

○ It explains that Lincoln, despite his pacifist tendencies, was not convinced that the Mexican-American War effort was wrong.

○ It confirms that Lincoln's belief in the wisdom of entering a war was formulated on the basis of what is good for a united country.

○ It suggests that Lincoln's opinions on the Mexican-American War were not based solely on a belief in unification.

○ It illustrates that opponents of United States foreign policy within the federal government convinced Lincoln to enter the Civil War.

The increasing pressure on American businesses to pursue cost-cutting measures will eventually lead to an increase in the outsourcing of business processes to venues with lower overhead, such as India. However, this shift may not provide the dramatic gains for American business that might have been expected by an enterprise with an ethos for change that is oriented to preserving bottom-line profits. The difficulty is that a significant portion of American society remains uncomfortable with shifting business tasks overseas. Therefore, American businesses will predominantly opt for outsourcing opportunities for repetitive tasks that can easily be brought back to the United States if necessary. Nevertheless, opportunities for Indian firms to get a larger piece of the pie seem certain to arise. The growing emphasis on bringing down the cost of back-office operations is bound to offer increasing scope for Indian firms to become involved in novel types of ever more complex business processes.

The attitude held by a significant portion of American society and the opportunities for Indian firms to get a larger piece of the pie are logically related to each other inasmuch as the author presents the former as

- ⬭ a public response to the achievements of Indian firms
- ⬭ a reason for the loss of a majority of the opportunities for Indian firms
- ⬭ a precondition for any hopes of achieving the latter
- ⬭ a catalyst for a further extension of the latter
- ⬭ a factor hindering the latter

The primary purpose of the passage is to
- ⬭ present an overview of the different types of business opportunities available to Indian firms
- ⬭ present a reasoned prognosis of the business opportunities that may become available to Indian firms
- ⬭ present the trend toward outsourcing business operations as a model case of business operations in action
- ⬭ analyze how opportunities available to Indian firms were necessitated by an increasing number of American firms
- ⬭ analyze the use of cost-cutting measures as a substitute for outsourcing in the new American business climate

According to the passage, despite the increasing pressure on American businesses to pursue cost-cutting measures, certain other factors preclude Indian firms'
- ⬭ benefiting from the new preoccupation with cost-cutting among American businesses
- ⬭ reassuring the American public that performing a business's activities can be done even better in India than in America
- ⬭ performing all of the business processes currently being performed onshore by American businesses
- ⬭ outsourcing more complex tasks to American firms in order to create an interconnected hierarchy of business needs
- ⬭ lobbying for favored nation trading status in order to make doing business in India more financially appealing to American companies

Questions 12–15 refer to the following passage.

Scientists are growing increasingly concerned that coral, which grows abundantly in the circumtropical shallow waters near bodies of land, is evincing a paling, or bleaching effect. Though experts are still at odds over what has precipitated this event, most agree that it is a stress response to changes in habitat and water quality, including temperature variations and salination percentage, and predict a loss of 95 percent of existing coral populations.

An exemplary symbiotic entity, scleractinian coral lives harmoniously with vertebrates, invertebrates, and plants. Corals receive nutrients in two ways: by capturing planktonic organisms with nematocyst-capped tentacles and by resource-sharing and recycling with single-celled algae called zooxanthellae. These algae live within the polyps of the coral, using photosynthesis to increase (and thereby strengthen) coral calcification, and providing energy for coral growth. The zooxanthellae benefit from the relationship through protection from predators and a steady supply of necessary carbon dioxide. Interestingly, it is the zooxanthellae that provide coral with its brilliant coloration.

When coral loses its color, it is a sign that the single-celled algae are not able to thrive. Though not necessarily a sign of mortality, a pale, wan color indicates imminent danger and is considered a stress response. The zooxanthellate invertebrates lose their concentration of pigmentation or die altogether when stressed, turning translucent and allowing the slightly darker coral skeleton to show through the decaying tissue. Whether this response stems from anthropogenic pollutions such as overharvesting coral for the exotic travel market, overfishing coral waters, and increased water temperatures due to global warming, or from natural disturbances (storms, temperature extremes, and diseases), scientists fear for the future of the radiant corals. If zooxanthellate populations continue to decrease without recovery, their host corals will eventually follow suit, triggering a cascade of unanticipated biological events.

It can be inferred from the passage that zooxanthellae are

- able to camouflage to blend into their surroundings
- able to use carbon dioxide to affect their coloration
- unable to live without coral hosts
- considered parasitical to coral
- algae that lack intrinsic defense mechanisms

The author attributes the pollution cited as being detrimental to coral to

- overpopulation by large sea mammals, such as dolphins
- activities of humans
- purely accidental causes which cannot be influenced
- overpopulation by photosynthetic archaebacteria
- natural phenomena, such as changes in weather

What does the author cite as the best explanation of the biological mechanisms behind coral bleaching?

○ The disappearance of pigmentation from zooxanthellae invertebrates

○ The displacement of zooxanthellae invertebrates to new habitats

○ The alteration in feeding schedule and diet of zooxanthellae invertebrates

○ The appearance of competitive species of zooxanthellae invertebrates

○ Zooxanthellae invertebrates' sensitivity to changes in salination

It can be inferred from the passage that which of the following situations is a possible contributing factor to coral bleaching?

○ The proliferation of large-scale freight ships in circumtropical regions

○ Modern civilization's dependence on fossil fuels

○ The increase in tourism in areas where coral is a popular souvenir

○ Governmental apathy due to more pressing problems

○ Coral's unusual sensitivity to the vagaries of natural climate changes

READING COMPREHENSION: DRILL 5

Questions 1–2 refer to the following passage.

Country music scholars generally overlook the role that African-Americans played in the formation of this genre. Typically, scholars trace the birth of country music to the recording sessions that record producer and talent scout Ralph Peer held in Bristol, Tennessee, in 1927. However, the origins of country music go back much further and owe a great deal to African-American musicians, some known and some anonymous and unheralded. The banjo, field hollers, and gospel music are examples of country genre staples that are rooted in the African-American experience. Moreover, some of the "stars" of country music learned their trade from African-American musicians. Rufus "Tee Tot" Payne, for instance, educated Hank Williams. In addition to jazz, gospel, and the blues, country music now clearly needs to be included in the list of musical genres that have an African-American lineage.

It can be inferred from the passage that the author would be most likely to agree with which of the following statements concerning the contributions of African-Americans to country music?

○ While they were instrumental in developing jazz, gospel, and the blues, African-Americans had only a minor impact on the development of country music.

○ African-Americans are also responsible for developing hip hop, a musical genre and cultural movement common in urban communities within the last quarter century.

○ Though all of the well-known country music singers are of European ancestry, African-Americans are solely responsible for the sound of country music.

○ Rufus "Tee Tot" Payne is responsible for teaching Hank Williams the banjo, field holler, and gospel.

○ African-Americans were instrumental in developing country music and for teaching it to some of the well-known musicians in the field.

According to the passage, the "African-American experience" (line 6) is crucial to country music because

○ other previously established African-American genres provided the instrumental and vocal basis for country music

○ other previously established African-American genres were not as well developed as country music

○ other previously established African-American genres preceded country music

○ other previously established African-American genres weakened the popularity of country music

○ other previously established African-American genres were more accepted and conventional than country music

Questions 3–4 refer to the following passage.

Face perception is the mind's ability to recognize and register another visage. It plays a significant role in social interactions. Through it we distinguish the familiar from the strange and formulate nuanced readings of people's moods and characters. However, controversy surrounds the process of face perception. Psychologists argue that it involves a series of stages: Individuals recognize physical features, make broad inferences regarding gender and age, and finally recall meaningful information regarding the face they perceive, such as a name. Cognitive neuroscientists, on the other hand, posit the idea that face perception works through analogy: The mind has an inherent ability to connect similar objects. While the exact process of face perception is still unclear, evidence suggests that it involves a specific set of skills and that the fusiform gyrus, a part of the brain, is necessary for it to occur.

The author mentions cognitive neuroscientists in order to

- ◯ provide a specific example of a general idea the author mentions in the preceding sentence
- ◯ present one side in the debate surrounding the issue of how minds identify and understand faces
- ◯ trace the development of scientific inquiry into the phenomenon of face perception
- ◯ compare the process of face perception with the process of visual recognition more generally
- ◯ reconcile two contradictory view points

Question 4 of 15

What can be inferred from the use of the word "analogy" to describe face perception?

- ◯ Cognitive neuroscientists believe face perception works via a process of comparison.
- ◯ Psychologists believe face perception works via a process of dissemblance.
- ◯ Cognitive neuroscientists believe face perception works via a process of analysis.
- ◯ Psychologists believe face perception works via a process of resolving discrepancies.
- ◯ Cognitive neuroscientists believe it works via contraposition.

Questions 5–8 refer to the following passage.

It has frequently been argued that freeing schools from the rigid rules, regulations, and statutes that have traditionally fettered them would have a revolutionary effect on academic achievement. For example, it has been suggested that schools embodying this idea could develop new teaching methods that could then be replicated in other schools for the benefit of all children. Charter schools—public schools that operate under a contract, or "charter"—were given just such an opportunity beginning in 1991, when Minnesota passed the first charter school law. At that time, many critics warned of deleterious rather than beneficial effects that such free-wheeling schools could have on the academic achievement of students. Observers thus differed concerning the social desirability of charter schools, even though they agreed that there would be a pronounced effect.

Surprisingly, educators who study educational reform now seriously question the degree to which charter schools have made an impact. They conclude that freedom from many of the policies and regulations affecting traditional public schools and the concomitant control over decisions that guide the day-to-day affairs of the school have not resulted in equally dramatic changes in students' academic performance. In some states, charter schools are less likely to meet state performance standards than traditional public schools. It is, however, impossible to know whether this difference is due to the performance of the schools, the prior achievement of the students, or some other factor.

Educational accountability has changed considerably in the past decade, moving increasingly to performance as measured by state mandated tests of individual student achievement. Fundamentally, however, the challenging conditions under which schools operate, be they traditional or charter, have changed little: the struggle for resources, low pay for teachers, accountability to multiple stakeholders, and the difficulty of meeting the educational requirements of children with special needs all persist.

Which of the following statements best summarizes the main point of the passage?

○ Assessments of charter schools' performance have not borne out the frequently held assumption that schools that have been freed of the rules and regulations that generally govern schools will have a revolutionary effect on education.

○ Recent studies have shown that charter schools have had a revolutionary effect on student achievement.

○ Freeing schools from some of the restrictions that govern them has caused a change in education since 1991.

○ Charter schools have created a whole new way of educating children that did not previously exist.

○ Freeing schools of rules and regulations, while extremely revolutionary in its effects, has not, on the whole, had the deleterious effect that some critics had feared.

Which of the following best describes the function of the concluding paragraph of the passage?

○ It sums up the general points concerning charter schools made in the passage as a whole.

○ It draws a conclusion concerning the challenges that schools face that goes beyond the information provided in the rest of the passage.

○ It restates the point concerning the challenges that schools face made in the previous paragraph.

○ It qualifies the author's agreement with those academics who question the degree to which charter schools have made an impact.

○ It suggests a compromise between those academics who believe that charter schools have had a revolutionary impact, and those who do not.

In the last paragraph the author mentions all of the following as challenges faced by all schools EXCEPT

- ◯ the difficulty of securing the wherewithal
- ◯ the challenge of providing appropriate conditions for special-needs students
- ◯ the necessity to answer to different interest groups
- ◯ the manner in which student performance is measured
- ◯ poor compensation for teachers

It can be inferred from the passage that the author would consider which of the following an indication of a fundamental alteration in education, if it were to occur?

- ◯ Statistics showing that the majority of children who attended charter schools in the 1990s are now attending college
- ◯ Studies showing that children attending public schools consistently outperform students who attend charter schools
- ◯ Increasing the pay for teachers working in charter schools with a concurrent rise in scores on standardized assessments and in grade point averages
- ◯ The creation of a national standard of academic performance to which all students in every type of school must adhere, regardless of the state in which they live
- ◯ A consistent score improvement in state-mandated standardized tests by children who attend charter schools, but not by those children who attend traditional schools

Questions 9–12 refer to the following passage.

Many scholars consider Marcel Proust's *Remembrance of Things Past* (1913–1927) a significant literary achievement. For instance, Harold Bloom states that it is "widely recognized as the major novel of the twentieth century." In addition to noting its length—it spans seven volumes and 3,200 pages—many commentaries have focused on Proust's treatment of two kinds of memory, involuntary and voluntary. Involuntary memory occurs through the stimulation of the senses, while voluntary memory is a deliberate effort to remember the past. For Proust, involuntary memories are superior because they contain the spirit of the past in a way that voluntary memories do not; the former are more vivid, and they have the power to erase the temporal distance between the present moment and past experiences. More recently, scholars such as André Benhaïm have explored the relationship between Proust's treatment of memory and his representation of France and French culture. According to Benhaïm, memory functions within this text to reconfigure both.

Proust describes France in ways that one would not expect. In his work, French cities are archaic and exotic. As a result, the narrator becomes a stranger to, or is estranged from, his homeland, and lives the life of an exile. For instance, when recalling his travels through the fictional French town of Balbec, he states, "These strangely ordinary and disdainfully familiar cathedrals cruelly stunned my unconsidered eyes and stabbed my homesick heart." Words such as "stun" and "stab" suggest the hostility the narrator feels from this French territory. Proust's suggestion of Middle Eastern influences further distorts the idea of a singular French experience. First, the town's name refers to the ancient city of Baalbek, located in what is now Lebanon. Second, Balbec is populated by Jewish residents. Proust is widely recognized as an icon of French literature and culture, but ultimately his mysterious representations of this place and its culture call into question the existence of a single Francophone literature or a single French identity.

It can be inferred that Benhaïm might agree with which one of the following statements about the role of memory in *Remembrance of Things Past*?

○ The study of memory in Proust's novel is the most important approach to this text and has led to valuable insights regarding the human condition.

○ The study of memory in Proust's novel is overdone and has led to few insights regarding the workings of the human mind.

○ Proust's representations of France, through the recollections of the narrator of this novel, function to reshape conceptions of the country and of Francophone literature.

○ While the study of memory in Proust's novel once yielded interesting insights into the workings of the human mind, new approaches to this text have proven to be more useful.

○ The study of Proust's exploration of memory is a useful starting place with which to consider other issues, such as French culture and traditions.

The author uses the quotation from *Remembrance of Things Past* in order to

○ illustrate how Proust's concept of involuntary memory

○ exemplify an assertion regarding the narrator's relationship to his homeland, which the author mentions in the preceding sentence

○ mark a turning point in the passage in which the author switches from describing life in France to exploring Proust's representation of it

○ bolster Proust's disdain for reliance on personal memories when returning to the locales of childhood

○ dissuade the reader from accepting Proust's characterizations of voluntary memory

The passage refers to which of the following as a feature of the French town of Balbec, as Proust represents it?

○ mausoleums
○ itinerants
○ bazaars
○ nomads
○ basilicas

The passage supports which of the following statements regarding Proust's *Remembrance of Things Past*?

○ There is very little agreement among critics about its contributions to twentieth century literature.
○ The relationship between Proust's images of French cities and the realities of French life and history is tenuous.
○ Literary scholars have focused too heavily on memory in this text and have largely ignored other aspects of it.
○ Proust's concept of voluntary memory was groundbreaking at the time and had a significant impact on modern psychology.
○ For many critics, it is text in which Proust explores his formative years before he discovered his vocation as a writer.

According to scholars, the indigenous peoples of ancient Mesoamerica, specifically the Nahuas, developed a rich and complex philosophy comprising four interrelated and overlapping branches of knowledge: metaphysics, epistemology, theory of value, and aesthetics. At the core of their philosophy was teotl, which, rather than an immutable supernatural being like the Judaeo-Christian deity, was an ever-moving and ever-changing, self-producing sacred power that animated the universe and its contents. It was responsible for all things in nature—animals, rocks, rain, and so on—and permeated the details of everything. There was no distinction between teotl and the natural world; teotl was in every entity, and every entity was also teotl. Unlike Western philosophy, which fosters dichotomies such as the personal versus the impersonal, that of the Nahuas posited a sacred power that was united with everything; it was both intrinsic and transcendent.

The definition of teotl and its comparison to the Judaeo-Christian deity plays which of the following roles within the passage?

○ It compares a lesser-known idea to a more common one to further understanding.

○ It contrasts the sacred power of teotl with a more familiar object of veneration in order to illustrate that cultures often possess diverging narratives on the origins of the world and the organisms therein.

○ It provides an explanation of the origins of the cosmos according to some of the proponents of Western philosophy.

○ It bolsters the case for accepting an aboriginal explanation for the creation of the universe over a Western one.

○ It encourages further inquiry into a lesser known understanding of the world.

The primary purpose of the passage is to
- ◯ describe the spirituality common to many Nahua thinkers
- ◯ posit a theory on the universality of narratives explaining the origins of the universe
- ◯ describe the central beliefs of a society that lived in the ancient world
- ◯ delineate the function of teotl in Nahua society
- ◯ trouble the Christian notion that there is a single omnipotent deity behind the creation of the world and its inhabitants

According to the passage, the ancient philosophy of the Nahua people is different from European-based philosophy in that
- ◯ at the center of Nahua philosophy was a detached and unmoving deity, whereas Christianity is based on the notion of a dynamic, ever-flowing supernatural force
- ◯ Nahua philosophy consisted of several interlocking concepts, whereas Western philosophy is composed only of dichotomies
- ◯ Nahua philosophy was based on the notion that a vivifying and mutable force saturated all matter, whereas in Western religion there is little or no division between supernatural powers and the natural world
- ◯ rather than promoting mutually exclusive but dependent binaries, Nahua philosophy fostered an integrated and holistic worldview
- ◯ within Nahuas society there was not a strong sense of individualism, whereas in Western societies, worldviews based on dichotomies engender excessive concern for self

READING COMPREHENSION: DRILL 6

Questions 1–2 refer to the following passage.

The wombat is a muscular quadruped, about 3 feet in length with a short tail. The animal, which is not a mythical creature but an Australian marsupial, has a name derived from the language of the native peoples of the Sydney area, the Eora aboriginals. Wombats are herbivores and leave cubic scats that are easily recognized. Because wombats are seldom seen, attributed to the fact that they are nocturnal, the scats provide crucial evidence regarding territory. This large, burrowing mammal is not related to the badger, whose habits are similar. In fact, the koala is the wombat's closest relative. The principal burrowing instrument of the latter is its incisors which, like those of other rodents with orange enamel, are never worn down. Burrows can be extensive and shared by more than one wombat, despite the generally solitary nature of the creature. Territories within the burrow are marked by scent, vocalizations, and aggressive displays.

According to the passage, which of the following is NOT true regarding wombats?

○ Wombats are not usually abroad in the daylight.

○ The question of how much territory a wombat covers is of concern to some scientists.

○ Scats are the only way to determine territorial limits of wombats.

○ Orange enamel is not distinctive to the teeth of wombats.

○ Wombats can be territorial about the space in their burrows.

The author states that the wombat is an Australian marsupial in order to

○ describe the role of stories about the wombat as part of the Eora's oral tradition

○ dispel the belief of some people that the wombat is not a real animal

○ create parallels between the Eora culture and the mythology of the ancient Greeks

○ contrast the behavior of wombats with that of other rodents

○ undermine the validity of research surrounding naming standards

Questions 3–4 refer to the following passage.

Theorists are divided about the cause of the Permian mass extinctions. Some hypothesize that the impact of a massive asteroid caused a sudden disappearance of species. However, a look at the carbon-isotope record suggests that existing plant communities were struck down and re-formed several times. To produce such a pattern would require a succession of asteroid strikes thousands of years apart. Other theorists have proposed that volcanic explosions raised the CO_2 levels, leading to intense global warming. One problem with this theory is that it cannot explain the massive marine extinctions at the end of the Permian period. A new theory posits that rising concentrations of toxic hydrogen sulfide in the world's oceans plus gradual oxygen depletions in the surface waters caused the extinctions. Fortunately, this theory is testable. If true, oceanic sediments from the Permian period would yield chemical evidence of a rise in hydrogen sulfide-consuming bacteria.

The primary purpose of the passage is to

○ present several hypotheses concerning the cause of the Permian mass extinctions

○ discuss the strengths and weaknesses of the asteroid hypothesis of the Permian mass extinctions

○ propose that theories regarding the cause of the Permian mass extinctions be tested

○ argue that Permian mass extinctions could not have been caused by a volcanic explosion

○ describe one reason that a rise in hydrogen sulfide would cause massive marine extinctions

Which of the following, if true, would most likely weaken the author's conclusion about the hydrogen sulfide theory?

○ The oceanic sediment is geologically inactive.

○ The oceanic sediment has changed its chemical composition several times since the Permian period.

○ The oceanic sediments of the Permian period contain high levels of carbon.

○ The oceanic sediments contain more toxic chemicals than simple hydrogen sulfide.

○ The oceanic sediments mask populations of other types of bacteria.

Questions 5–6 refer to the following passage.

In her self-portraits, Frida Kahlo blends realism and fantasy to capture the psychological and physical pain she constantly endured as a result of the trolley car accident she experienced as a young woman. This self-representation sets her apart from her contemporaries, who were more interested in public forms of art, such as murals. This was the time of the Mexican revolution, after all, a period that fostered an interest in nationalistic themes.

The more well-known artists of this period included David Alfaro Siqueiros, Diego Rivera, Jose Clemente Orozco, and Juan O'Gorman. These figures dominated the Mexican art world in the 1920s and 1930s. Unlike her contemporaries, Kahlo's work did not achieve recognition until long after her death. In the late twentieth century, she became a feminist icon, a phenomenon attributable to the candor with which she portrayed issues relating to women.

The purpose of the author's discussion of the Mexican revolution is to
⬭ provide a historical context for the reader to clarify what distinguished Kahlo's art from her contemporaries' art
⬭ discuss aspects of Mexican history, such as the revolution and nationalism, which were irrelevant to Kahlo's art
⬭ contrast the way male and female artists responded to a tumultuous time in Mexican history
⬭ explain why it was not until after Kahlo's death that her work received greater acknowledgment
⬭ highlight the differences between feminists and revolutionaries at the time that Kahlo was painting

It can be inferred from the passage that the author would characterize Kahlo's style of painting as
⬭ public and nationalistic
⬭ intensely realistic
⬭ fanciful and obscure
⬭ abstruse and feminine
⬭ natural and imagined

Questions 7–8 refer to the following passage.

The controversial concept of terraforming, or changing a planet's atmosphere to make it more habitable for humans, is still no more than a theoretical debate. However, the most recent data from two American Mars Rovers suggest that the terraforming of Mars may be more feasible than previously thought. The rovers found evidence of stratification patterns and cross bedding (indicating a history of sediment deposited by water) in rocks on the edges of craters, as well as chlorine and bromine, suggestive of a large body of salt water. If Mars once held water, it is possible that its atmosphere was at one time somewhat similar to Earth's. Even if this theory were true, however, scientists would have to prevent a recurrence of the desiccation of the Martian atmosphere once it is made habitable, as well as endeavor to preserve any extant life. Of course, until a reliable method of transporting humans to Mars is developed, any possibility of terraforming is mere conjecture.

It can be inferred from the passage that the author would be most likely to agree with which of the following statements?

○ Before we contemplate travel to Mars, we must make space travel reliable and safe.

○ It is highly likely, according to recent data, that there is, or was at one time, life on Mars.

○ If life on Mars existed at one time, then there may be other life in the universe.

○ If we terraform Mars, it will be important to think about the long-term effects of changing a planet's climate.

○ Preservation of Mars' natural resources should be of paramount concern.

Which of the following statements, if true, would most likely make terraforming Mars more feasible?

○ Scientists have devised a technique to provide a layer of carbon dioxide in the Martian atmosphere, which would trap solar radiation and thus modify temperature.

○ Mars has stronger solar winds than does Earth, thus, making it difficult to retain atmospheric gases.

○ Mars' core has cooled faster than Earth's, and its temperature is much lower than Earth's.

○ Terraforming Mars is likely to have a galvanizing effect on Earth's governments.

○ Terraforming Mars is unlikely to disturb life on other planets, should it exist.

Questions 9–12 refer to the following passage.

The harshness and extreme unpopularity
of the "war communism" system imposed in
Russia from 1918 to 1921 led the Soviet leadership to adopt the New Economic Policy (NEP)
in March of 1921. Under the NEP, the prodna-
log system of tax in kind was begun, and a
semi-market economy was allowed to develop
alongside government control of what Lenin
had called the "commanding heights industries."
When the NEP was abandoned in 1927, the
state declared it a failure as a result of several
adverse events: the scissors crisis, the goods
famine, and speculation by "NEPmen."

The scissors crisis of 1923 was caused by
high industrial prices relative to agricultural
prices. When these two sets of prices are
graphed, the wide disparity resembles an open
pair of scissors. The government had been
spurring industry but felt that this price disparity had to be immediately addressed. To do so,
it adopted policies favoring agriculture. There is
some speculation by economists, however, that
the scissors would have closed on their own.

The goods famine occurred at roughly the
same time. Because of burgeoning industry,
demand for industrial and consumer products
skyrocketed. The state could not produce goods
equal to demand, forcing prices up. In the
midst of shortages, the state found itself in a
losing contest with "NEPmen," small entrepre-
neurs who sold goods at prices often higher
than those of the state. NEPmen were seen as
capitalists who sought to return the Soviet state
to its position as lapdog to the Western capitalist states. Since the state could not produce or
profit as well as the NEPmen, it adopted measures to put the NEPmen out of business. By
1926, speculating on pricing was a crime. As a
result, profits and incentives had fallen, and the
speculation crisis was somewhat alleviated.

The author describes the former Soviet state
as a lapdog in order to

○ emphasize the extent to which Russia
relied on the Western capitalist states

○ highlight the subservient position that
Russia had held in relation to Western
states

○ demonstrate the contempt with which
Russia viewed capitalist states

○ contrast Russia's communist economy
with the capitalist economies of the
West

○ criticize the way the United States had
treated Russia as an inferior partner

The speculation by economists refers to
which of the following beliefs?

○ The government's belief that the crisis
would one day have ended, even if the
government had not moved to support
agriculture

○ Economists' belief that the government
was mistaken in supporting agriculture
over industry

○ Economists' belief that the scissors
crisis could have been averted without
government intervention

○ Economists' belief that the price disparity
would have eventually resolved itself
without action by the government

○ The government's belief that agricultural and industrial prices would have
balanced each other, but not in time to
stop a crisis from occurring

Which of the following would make the most appropriate title for this passage?

- ⃝ The Fall of the New Economic Policy
- ⃝ An End to War Communism
- ⃝ Why the New Economic Policy Failed
- ⃝ Three Crises that Ended an Era
- ⃝ Soviet Economic Systems: an Overview

It can be inferred that all of the following accurately represent the author's opinions EXCEPT

- ⃝ The government acted hastily in the scissors crisis, which would probably have resolved itself without government interference.
- ⃝ In dealing with the three main crises of the NEP era, the government did not always choose appropriate responses.
- ⃝ The government was partially responsible for the goods famine, due to its inability to control supply and demand.
- ⃝ The government could not compete with the NEPmen in either the production or sale of goods.
- ⃝ NEPmen were like capitalists, who sought to earn their fortune at the expense of others and helped bring about the downfall of the NEP.

Questions 13–16 refer to the following passage.

The determination of the age of KNM-ER 1470, a humanoid skull, would add greatly to our knowledge of mammalian evolution. Anthropologists originally dated the habilis skull at 3 million years old. This age seemed unlikely because it was older than the age of any known australophithecines, which are presumed to be the habilis's ancestor. Further attempts to date the skull have led to speculative results.

An elemental property of all living things is that they contain a certain portion of their carbon as the radioactive isotope carbon-14. Carbon-14 is created when solar radiation blasts nuclei in the upper atmosphere, in turn producing neutrons that bombard nitrogen-14 at lower altitudes, turning it into carbon-14. All living things maintain an equilibrium of carbon-14 as they exchange carbon with their surrounding atmosphere. Presuming the rate of production to be constant, the activity of a sample can be compared to the equilibrium activity of living matter, and thus the age can be calculated. However, carbon-14 decays at a half-life of 5730 years, limiting age determinations to the order of 50,000 years. This time frame can be extended to perhaps 100,000 years using accelerator techniques. Even so, at these ages carbon dating is increasingly unreliable as a result of changes in the carbon-isotope mix. Over the last century, the burning of fossil fuels, which have no carbon-14 content, have had a diluting effect on the atmospheric carbon-14. As a countervailing effect, atmospheric testing of nuclear weapons in the 1950s may well have doubled the atmosphere's carbon-14 content.

Other radiometric dating methods, using relative concentrations of parent-daughter products in radio decay changes of other elements, such as argon, may prove to be of greater benefit for dating such ancient samples as habilis. However, the assumption that the decay rates of these isotopes have always been constant would first have to be substantiated.

The author suggests that the burning of fossil fuels has had which of the following effects on the efficacy of carbon dating techniques?

○ It lessens the rate at which carbon-14 decays.

○ It may make items subjected to carbon dating appear to have died later than is the case.

○ It may increase the carbon-isotope mix of the object being dated.

○ It may tilt the fragile equilibrium activity of living matter.

○ It may inhibit radiometric dating methods that utilize parent-daughter relationships.

The author first mentions the half-life of carbon in order to

○ provide a reason why carbon dating techniques fail to give an age for the habilis skull

○ explain the success of carbon dating techniques

○ illustrate the difference between carbon dating and other techniques

○ show the need for extending carbon dating results with accelerator techniques

○ illustrate the carbon equilibrium that all living things maintain

What can be inferred about the proposed solution mentioned in the final paragraph?

- ◯ Continued experimentation with nuclear weapons could restore the expected carbon-14 content to the atmosphere to ensure accuracy of carbon dating.
- ◯ Alternatives to fossil fuels should be pursued to prevent further interference with carbon dating procedures.
- ◯ Decay rates of isotopes involved in radiometric methods need to be invariable.
- ◯ Carbon-14 levels could be artificially restored to previous historical levels to allow an appropriate basis of comparison.
- ◯ Appropriate technology to implement radiometric methods needs to be engineered.

The primary purpose of the passage is to

- ◯ discuss the techniques of carbon dating
- ◯ describe the deficiencies of currently used methodologies to date living matter
- ◯ resolve a dispute concerning the use of carbon dating techniques
- ◯ to indicate that a reliable way to date a certain find has yet to be determined
- ◯ offer an interpretation of KNM-ER 1470's paleontological record

ANSWERS

Drill 1

1. D
2. E
3. B
4. A
5. B
6. E
7. A
8. D
9. B
10. C
11. D
12. E
13. A
14. C
15. B

Drill 2

1. C
2. B
3. B
4. C
5. A
6. C
7. B
8. E
9. A
10. C
11. E
12. B
13. C
14. D
15. E

Drill 3

1. A
2. E
3. E
4. D
5. C
6. D
7. A
8. B
9. E
10. D
11. E
12. B
13. B
14. C
15. A

Drill 4

1. C
2. A
3. C
4. A
5. E
6. B
7. A
8. D
9. E
10. B
11. C
12. E
13. B
14. A
15. C

Drill 5

1. E
2. A
3. B
4. A
5. A
6. B
7. D
8. E
9. C
10. B
11. E
12. B
13. A
14. C
15. D

Drill 6

1. C
2. B
3. A
4. B
5. A
6. E
7. D
8. A
9. B
10. D
11. C
12. E
13. B
14. A
15. C
16. D

EXPLANATIONS

Drill 1

1. **D** The key here is to read further along in the sentence; the scale heights are described as *rates of atmospheric pressure that vary,* so the answer choice needs to describe a change in this pressure. Choice (D) is the best match. Choices (B) and (C) are specific to the mesosphere, while choices (A) and (E) do not address pressure.

2. **E** The fact that the mesosphere is located between the stratosphere (the maximum altitude that airplanes can achieve) and the thermosphere (the minimum altitude for space flight), the passage raises the possibility that the reason this region is poorly understood is because we do not have a vehicle that can adequately explore it, as in choice (E). Choice (A) goes too far; the passage doesn't talk about the threat of meteors. Choice (B) draws a faulty conclusion, because the turbosphere is not described as a *cap.* Other parts of the atmosphere can be explored, so choice (C) is too broad. The passage does not give evidence that we know little about outer atmospheric conditions, as suggested by choice (D).

3. **B** The author says the Nielsen Company has *questionable methods* and has *come under criticism,* and puts the word *diaries* in quotes as though to make fun of its methodology as quaint or clunky, so choice (B) is the best answer. There is no indication that Nielsen's bias is intentional, so eliminate choice (A). Choices (C) and (D) are extreme because the passage does not suggest that Nielsen's research is so bad as to be worthless or unscrupulous. The passage does not offer any information about Nielsen's opinion of itself, boastful or otherwise choice (E).

4. **A** The passage says that residences *underreport daytime and late-night television viewing,* so choice (A) is true. The passage does not say that each household counts as one person, so eliminate choice (B). Viewers must record the channel whenever the television is on, not only at particular times, so eliminate choice (C). Choices (D) and (E) both describe a corrupt relationship between the viewers and the Nielsen company, which is not described in the passage.

5. **B** The woodchuck example is provided to show that the same molecules that induce hibernation might have applications in organs being readied for transplants. Therefore, choice (B) is the best answer. There is no evidence that ischemia plays any role in the transplantation process, so choice (A) is incorrect. Choice (C) is too extreme; nothing is identified as the biggest obstacle. The passage does not comment on the feasibility of changing the tissue-matching process, so choice (D) is not a well-supported answer choice. The passage does not mention the effects of HIT on patients awaiting transplants, so choice (E) is wrong.

6.   **E**   The highlighted passage describes an experiment wherein infusing opioids delayed decay, so choice (E) is true. Choice (B) is incorrect because the passage does not state that the lymphatic system is what causes organs to deteriorate. There is no information in the passage on when HIT will be produced in a lab, so choice (C) can be eliminated. Choice (D) extrapolates too far on the effects of HIT, and there is not enough information in the passage to support the relationship in choice (A).

7.   **A**   Choice (A) is the best answer because the author cites the experiment with woodchucks to give an example of a promising line of research. There is no suggestion of genetic similarity, so choice (B) is incorrect. Though the author does warn that the findings are preliminary, he/she does so in another context in the passage, which makes choice (C) wrong. Similarly, other areas of science are not mentioned in conjunction with this experiment, but rather later on in the passage, so choice (D) is incorrect. Though an interspecies infusion of HIT is mentioned, that is not the primary purpose of the woodchuck experiment, and choice (E) is incorrect as well.

8.   **D**   Scientists are able to isolate HIT and inject it into other animals, so it must be possible to isolate its molecules; choice (D) is the best answer. There is no evidence that HIT is newly discovered, which discounts choice (A). Opioids, not HIT, cause ischemia, so choice (B) is wrong. HIT is described as an *opiate-like substance*, which is not close enough to choice (C) to make it correct. Finally, choice (E) is wrong because the passage does not specify whether HIT is the only substance that causes hibernation.

9.   **B**   The text is primarily concerned with showing the ancient origin of modern currency and underlines the touchstone's importance within this history; therefore, choice (B) is correct. Choice (A) is too broad—the passage is concerned only with currency, not science in general. Conversely, choice (C) is too narrow; the passage talks about the touchstone's historical importance, not just the science behind it. The passage does not discuss where the word came from, so choice (D) is incorrect. Choice (E) is also wrong because there is no historical misconception that needs to be cleared up.

10.   **C**   Choice (C) accurately describes the reason for including the details concerning the inclusion of lesser metals in early coins: It takes the details of how the touchstone works and shows why the touchstone was important for trade. The passage does not state how individuals previously tested metals, so choice (A) cannot be true. Choice (B) is also incorrect because the date given in the passage is of the earliest use of coins; it does not talk about the date of the touchstone. The purpose of the sentence is not to give a cultural context because the passage does not identify the cultures involved, so eliminate choice (D). There is no counterargument given, making choice (E) incorrect.

11. **D** Choice (D) is correct because it paraphrases the information given in the passage: *This priming process allowed for merchants to examine alloys quickly and with reasonable certainty*. Choice (A) is not explicitly stated in the passage; probing revealed the degree of purity, not which impurities it contained. The standardizing of currency values was not stated to be a direct result of the probing process, besides which there is no mention of any government, so eliminate choice (B). Choice (C) is also incorrect because the passage doesn't explicitly state that merchants were paid in currency, just that they were able to have confidence in the purity of their metals. Choice (E) is too extreme; the passage does not suggest that the method was foolproof.

12. **E** The author explains that Szymanowska is may have been a *progenitor of Chopin*, indicating that she came before him; therefore choice (E) the best answer. While choices (A) and (B) are true, they don't address the question. Choices (C) and (D) both mention composers who worked at the same time as Szymanowska.

13. **A** Choice (A) is the best, answer because it is a simplification of *uses the most compelling registers of the instrument and pianistic keys.* If you picked choice (B), you may have confused registers of instruments with vocal registers. Choice (C), while probably true, cannot be inferred because the highlighted sentence is about her compositions, not her piano playing. Choice (D) misinterprets the intent of the statements, while choice (E) goes against the main thrust of both these statements and the passage.

14. **C** Choice (A) describes a problem, but it is too extreme because some documentation must exist for people to know about Szymanowska's work. Choice (B) also describes a problem but is too specific—musical scores were never mentioned. Choice (C) provides a good paraphrase of the second and third sentences of the last paragraph and is, therefore, the best choice. Choice (D) is too extreme. If you chose choice (E), you probably were looking at the last line of the passage, which talks about the future, not about the past and present.

15. **B** Choice (B) is the only correct inference based on the passage, as it is supported by the number of works attributed to Szymanowska and by the statement that she was praised by her contemporaries. Choice (A) cannot be inferred because the passage does not state that Schubert played piano (though he did). It merely compares Szymanowska's composed romances to those of Schubert. Choice (C) goes against the main idea of the passage. The passage describes her as a progenitor of Chopin, but does not discuss his awareness of her work, thus choice (D) can be eliminated. Choice (E) goes too far in ascribing a particular belief system to Szymanowska.

Drill 2

1. C The first sentence states that sociologists have historically held the view that individuals stereotype. The rest of the paragraph delves into Hepburn and Locksley's study, which investigates the extent to which people are aware of their own stereotyping behavior. Therefore, the first sentence provides the historical background for Hepburn and Locksley's study. The closest answer is therefore choice (C).

2. B The passage starts with a historical overview of stereotypes and then focuses on two investigators who look at the related issue of whether or not individuals are aware that they are applying stereotypes. Choice (A) sums this up the best. Choice (B) is out of scope. Choices (C) and (D) are too strong; it is neither an attempt to prove nor to refute anything. Choice (E) is too specific, and the passage doesn't contain any detailed lists.

3. B In the passage, the author notes that traditional Westerns focus on masculine characterizations while McMurtry included depictions of strong female characters. The author argues that this inclusion changed the traditional plot of the Western and allowed for an exploration of deeper ideological issues. We can infer from this that the focus on male characters in traditional Westerns hindered an exploration of these deeper ideological issues. Therefore the best answer is choice (B).

4. C In the first paragraph the author notes how Western literature ranges from lowbrow entertainment to great literature and offers the dime-store novel as an example of writing that is merely entertaining. At the other end of the spectrum, the author states that *James Fenimore Cooper and Willa Cather, however, used themes of westward expansion in works clearly intended as highbrow literature.* In other words, they wrote literature that expects the reader to be more sophisticated, so the best answer is choice (C). Choice (A) is incorrect, choices (B) and (D) are not discussed in the passage, and choice (E) is off the topic.

5. A In the third paragraph the author writes, *In his novels McMurtry creates strong female characters, transmuting conventional plot of the trials and dangers of the frontier by folding in deeper ideological insights.* In other words, the strong female characters McMurtry creates add deeper ideological issues to his writing. Therefore, the best answer is choice (A).

6. C In the last paragraph the author talks about McMurtry's use of character, stating that *In his novels McMurtry creates strong female characters, transmuting the conventional plot of the trials and dangers of the frontier by folding in deeper ideological insights.* When referring to the critics, the author notes that they rightly credit his novels with reforming the Western genre. The use of the word *rightly* suggests that the author agrees with the critics, thereby making choice (C) the best answer.

7. B Choice (A) isn't supported in the text. Eliminate choice (C) because, while the passage suggests that the body of knowledge relating to hydrothermal vents is expanding due to a recent discovery, the author doesn't really look at how scientists study hydrothermal vents or mention how these studies might have changed. Choice (D) isn't supported in the passage. In choice (E), while the author discusses the discovery of a new natural phenomenon, the author doesn't reconsider or reevaluate previous studies on similar natural phenomenon. Choice (B) is the correct answer and is an accurate summary of the author's purpose over the course of the passage.

8. E In the sentence immediately before the highlighted text, the author discusses hydrothermal vents in general terms, stating that they *[exist] on land and underwater.* In the following sentence the author discusses a specific example of underwater hydrothermal vents: Black Smokers. Thus, choice (E) is the best match.

9. A Support for choice (A) can be found in the second paragraph. Take a look at the sentences beginning with *[t]he heat and fluid flow,* and *[t]he fluids here,* respectively. The opposite of choice (B) is true, so eliminate it. Eliminate choice (C), because it mixes up information from the passage. It combines the information about Chemosynthetic archaea, which the author mentions in paragraph one, with information from the final paragraph. There is no comparison of geological importance, but the Lost City was a recent discovery so it could not have been studied for as long; therefore eliminate choice (D). Similarly, there is not enough information to compare biological diversity, so choice (E) can be eliminated.

10. C The first paragraph deals with Black Smokers. You can find support for choices (A), (B), (D), and (E) here. Choice (C) is information that the author provides about the hydrothermal vents at Lost City. Calcium carbonate and magnesium hydroxide help create the white chimney-like structures there, as opposed to the black ones found surrounding Black Smokers.

11. E The sentence in which this phrase occurs is referring to the mixture of artists and movements that inspired Delacroix, so *Baroque* must be either an artist or a movement. It is most likely a movement given the structure of the sentence, which lists specific traditions with specific artists and then notes movements. Choice (E) captures this notion most closely. The other choices are not supported by the passage.

12. B The passage opens by discussing the influence of Lord Byron's life on Delacroix and puts that influence in a political context, not artistic. Thus, choice (B) is the most likely non-painter. Titian, Michelangelo, and Rubens are all identified as painters, so choices (A), (C), and (D) are not correct. Choice (E) appears to refer to the name of a place that Delacroix painted.

13. **C** The second half of the final sentence expresses Gould's and Lewontin's position on sociobiology, at least as it applies to humans. Look for an answer that is similar to this statement. Choice (A) is not supported by the text. The author states only that sociobiologists test their theories on termites and rhesus macaques and doesn't say why this fact is important or what it might lead to, much less what Gould or Lewonton might say. Choice (B) contradicts the passage. Choice (D) is an extreme answer. The author only states that Gould and Lewontin find sociobiology problematic when scientists apply it to humans; animals are not mentioned. Choice (E) mixes up information in the passage—this is what sociobiologists say. Choice (C) is the only remaining answer and is an accurate paraphrase of Lewontin and Gould's position.

14. **D** The author discusses *culture, ethnicity, and environment* in relation to the justification offered by sociobiologists when applying sociobiology to humans: In their view, these factors don't adequately explain human behavior. Choice (D) is a good paraphrase of this justification. Choice (A) isn't supported in the passage. Choice (B) is Gould's and Lewontin's position on sociobiology. Choice (C) contradicts the sociobiologists' view. Choice (E) is incorrect because, although the list comprises some factors that influence human behavior, the author intends it to serve a greater purpose in the passage. In addition, it would be extreme to assert that the list is *comprehensive*.

15. **E** The author doesn't praise either side in the debate, so eliminate choice (A). Both choices (B) and (C) suggest that the author has a point of view, while the passage offers no indication as to which side the author may favor. Eliminate choice (D) because no such justification is made, and the thrust of the passage is on human, not animal, behavior. Choice (E) is an accurate summary of the entire passage because it takes into account both sociobiological theories and their critics in an impartial fashion.

Drill 3

1. **A** The reason for controlling factions is described in the previous sentence with Madison's claim that they are *adverse to the overall good of the nation*. Choice (A) is the best answer. Choices (B), (C), and (D) are not accurate based on the information in the passage. Choice (E) is not specific enough to answer the question.

2. **E** The passage discusses Madison's theories on constraining factions by controlling either their causes or effects. Choice (A) goes too far; the passage does not solve the problem. Choices (B) and (C) are contrary to the passage. Choice (D) is overly broad; the passage considers only one effect of increased population. Choice (E) is the best answer because it encompasses the scope of Madison's ideas in *The Federalist Number Ten*.

3. **E** Jenney's work on the Home Insurance and Manhattan Buildings, among others, supports choice (A), and the passage's description of his work as *archetypical* supports choice (B). His relationship with Holabird supports choice (C); choice (D) is supported by the discussion of the Manhattan and Horticultural Buildings. The passage does not provide information about which side Jenney worked for during the Civil War nor the specific responsibilities of an engineering officer. Thus the best answer is choice (E).

4. **D** Choice (D) is the best answer. The *Chicago window* is a development of Holabird's; it is the only specific feature mentioned, so it must be significant. Choice (A) is partially correct, in that a feature is highlighted, but the buildings are not made of glass; they merely *appear* to be glass. Choice (B) says Holabird developed the Chicago School, but the passage says he helped Jenney do so. Choice (C) goes against the tone of the passage, which does not make that argument at all. Choice (E) is too broad to be the purpose of this small detail.

5. **C** Choice (A) is not supported in the passage. Choices (B) and (D) are paraphrases of statements that the author makes in the passage, but neither one of them addresses the question at hand: What is the effect of the solar winds on the earth? Choice (E) contradicts the passage, which states that solar winds travel as far as Pluto. Choice (C) is the correct answer and is a paraphrase of the third sentence in paragraph two: *[S]olar winds are responsible for the earth's magnetosphere, and changes in their speed and direction strongly influence Earth's space environment.*

6. **D** The author uses the word *deflecting* to describe the action of Earth's magnetic field in the face of the solar winds. In other words, the earth's magnetic field protects the earth by turning aside the harmful, radiation-filled solar winds. Look for an answer choice that has a similar meaning. Eliminate choices (B) and (E) because they are not supported by the text. Eliminate choices (A) and (C), which contradict the passage. Choice (D) is the correct answer because the word *avert* is a synonym for the word *deflect,* and this action would provide the protection that is observed.

7. **A** Eliminate choice (B) because it is not supported by the text; the author makes no mention of the technology required for scientists to observe solar winds. Eliminate choice (C) for similar reasons; while Kepler made an accurate guess regarding comet tails and the reasons for which they bend away from the sun, one cannot infer that these observations constitute the first major contribution to the study of solar winds or the sun more generally. Choice (D) goes beyond the scope of the text in discussing Kepler's work, and choice (E) compares two different types of information. The correct answer is choice (A).

8. **B** Eliminate choice (A), (D), and (E) because they are not supported by the text. Choice (C) is incorrect because, while the first part seems good, it goes wrong in the second half of the sentence; the author never considers the relationship between research on solar winds and other studies. The correct answer is choice (B) because this choice provides the most accurate summary of what the passage accomplishes.

9. **E** For EXCEPT questions, use POE to eliminate choices that are true. The author states that Pickett presents *a wealth of examples*, so eliminate choice (A). The author notes that Pickett provides *a refreshingly candid argument* for why America goes to war, eliminating choice (B). You are told that *America often goes to war for an abstract ideal*, so eliminate choice (C). Among the reasons that Pickett cites for war (and the author clearly agrees) is *democratization of societies*, so eliminate choice (D). Choice (E) is the credited response; the examples given are not abstract but concrete, and the passage hardly portrays them as ineffective.

10. **D** The topic of the passage is Pickett's interpretation of American military history. In the second paragraph, the author states that while Pickett's work provides a *refreshingly candid understanding* of why America goes to war, he *overstates the case when he argues that these abstract causes typically lead to a war hysteria in which American leadership can no longer enforce any measured policies*. In other words, while the author believes that some of the ideas Pickett presents are correct, the author also notes that Pickett's conclusions cannot be fully supported. The best answer is therefore choice (D). All the other answers are outside the scope of the passage. Additionally, choices (B) and (E) are extreme.

11. **E** The author lists the ways in which Close's ideas of portraiture differ from tradition. Close's emphasis on a head without expression or personality is the opposite, then, of traditional portraiture. Thus the best answer is choice (E) because this addresses unique approach. Choices (A) and (B) are not suggested in this passage. There is not enough information to support choice (C), and choice (D) is only partially addressed later in the passage.

12. **B** According to the passage, Close's freer lines came before his illness, so choice (B) is the correct answer. Therefore, his change of style was not primarily caused by his illness, which makes choice (C) incorrect. The paintings are *nearly undifferentiable* to the naked eye from photographs—the passage does not suggest that people sometimes get confused—which discounts choice (A). Though abstract expressionism and photorealism appear to be unrelated, they both do not favor any one particular part of the canvas; therefore, critics do not consider them incompatible so choice (D) is incorrect. Eliminate choice (E) because, even though the process is described as *painstaking*, the time required is not comparable to other forms of painting.

13. **B** The second sentence of the passage provides Derrida's description of the concept of difference and includes *attempts to discuss universal features of human nature are merely products of local standards*. Thus the answer needs to make clear that acceptance does not equate truth. This is best summarized in choice (B). The other answers all discuss some aspect of the status quo, but none sufficiently debunk it as the accepted standard.

14. **C** You learn in the passage that Derrida was thought to be the originator of anti-foundationalism. In the second-to-last sentence the author states, *However, a century before Derrida, Darwin's theory of natural selection had made anti-foundationalism almost an inevitable consequence.* The study of evolution is therefore mentioned as support for the notion that Derrida did not originate the idea of anti-foundationalism, thus making choice (C) the best answer.

15. **A** The author states that anti-foundationalists believe that *there is no secure basis for knowledge.* Therefore, answer choice (A) is correct. The author states that Derrida held the belief that *any attempts to discuss universal features of human nature are merely products of local standards.* In other words, meaning is understood within a cultural context, thus eliminate choice (B). Choice (C) misquotes the information in the passage. Though the passage talks about Darwin's work, almost making Derrida's inevitable, choice (D) is too extreme. Eliminate choice (E) because it does not address the question.

Drill 4

1. **C** The use of the word *guise* means that the *talk stories* are a way to convey other information, namely the myths of Kingston's cultural background. Thus, choice (C) is the best answer because it restates this point. Choices (A), (B), and (E) are unrelated; choice (D) is basically the opposite of what the passage is discussing.

2. **A** In the first paragraph the author notes that some readers categorize Kingston as a great Asian-American writer. The author follows this statement by referencing examples in her writing that support the contention, so the best answer is choice (A). The other choices are not supported by the passage. In addition, choice (E) is extreme in its use of the word *unique.*

3. **C** Because the movement is described as *a subtle form of protest,* it is reasonable to infer that the author believes that literature can act in such a capacity, as stated in choice (C). Choice (A) is incorrect because there is no indication that censorship serves as inspiration. Other forms of protest are not explored, so there is no indication that literature is the only means of protest, therefore discounting choice (B). Choice (D) misstates information from the passage; baroque literature reawakened feelings of *cultural expression,* not an interest in politics. The methods of judging a movement's importance are not discussed in the passage, so choice (E) is incorrect.

4. **A** The passage is primarily concerned with how *préciosité* paved the way for a resurgence of interest in the arts in seventeenth-century France, which makes choice (A) the best answer. Though the passage does highlight the role of women in the Baroque movement, it does not attempt to make any larger statements about women in history, therefore, choice (B) is incorrect. The passage does define and explain the origins of a literary movement, but that is not the primary purpose, so eliminate choice (C). The primary purpose of the passage is not a discussion of how nations' rulers affect the arts, which makes choice (D) incorrect. Finally, choice (E) is not suggested in the passage.

5. **E**   It is clear from the passage that no one at the time understood the importance of *préciosité* (men scoffed; mocking plays were written). Therefore, choice (E) is the best answer. Eliminate choice (A) because *préciosité* required considerable education and therefore was only *spoken* by the upper class. Although the author mentions critics and husbands who dismissed *préciosité* as frivolous, choice (B) is too sweeping a generalization. Choice (C) does not work because, although *préciosité* was ridiculed, there is no mention of people's predictions for its durability. Finally, choice (D) is wrong because Molière was not the first to mock it; it was ridiculed long before he wrote his play.

6. **B**   The author spends the rest of the passage proving that *préciosité* was an important force, so he/she clearly does not believe that it is unimportant. Choice (B) is the best answer because the quotation marks let the reader know that the author means the opposite: an ironic use of quotes. Choice (A) is incorrect because it is not a direct quotation. "Feminine concoction" is also not a term that needs a definition, so choice (C) is wrong. Eliminate choice (D) because the term is not foreign. Finally, choice (E) is incorrect because the entire phrase is in quotations and not just the word "feminine;" therefore, the quotes do not emphasize gender.

7. **A**   According to the passage, Lincoln had a *sincere belief that President Polk had overstepped his constitutional boundaries by declaring war.* You can infer that Polk was president at the time of the Mexican-American War, not Lincoln. Therefore the correct answer is choice (A). There is no support in the passage for choices (B), (C), and (D). Choice (E) is given by the author as Lincoln's belief and therefore may or may not have been true.

8. **D**   It is important to read the lines within the context of the passage. Earlier in the passage the author informs us that Lincoln felt *disdain* for the Mexican-American War. The author notes that given Lincoln's willingness to fight the Civil War, this seeming inconsistency bears some explanation. From this text, you can infer that one of the goals of both the Mexican-American War and the Civil War was to ensure a united country. Therefore, given that Lincoln supported the Civil War, you can assume that he had reasons for opposing the Mexican-American War on grounds other than unification. Therefore, the correct answer is choice (D).

9. **E**   This is an extremely complicated question. Take the time to understand what the question is asking. A good paraphrase of the question might be: How are the two statements related to each other? According to the passage, *a significant portion of American society remains uncomfortable shifting business tasks overseas.* Logically, this discomfort hinders American businesses from offshoring more of their business processes. As a result, Indian firms aren't yet getting a larger piece of the pie, making choice (E) a good paraphrase of this connection. There is no suggestion that this attitude is in response to anything about India in particular, so choice (A) can be eliminated. Choices (B) and (C) are too extreme, and choice (D) goes against the author's point. Choice (B) is a close second answer, but the word *majority* makes this answer somewhat too strong.

10. B   The author's purpose is sometimes presented at the end of the passage, as is the case with this passage, which ends with *[t]he growing emphasis on bringing down the cost of back office operations is bound to offer increasing scope for Indian firms to become involved in novel types of ever more complex business processes.* Choice (B) presents the best paraphrase of this statement. Choices (A) and (C) are too broad; choices (D) and (E) are not supported by the passage.

11. C   Be sure that you understand the question before you attempt to answer it. A good paraphrase of this question might be: "What are Indian firms not able to do?" According to the passage, *American society remains uncomfortable shifting business tasks overseas.* Choice (C) provides a good paraphrase for this general discomfort that Americans have. Choice (A) addresses the trend toward outsourcing generally but does not answer the question. The passage does not give enough information to evaluate choice (B). Choices (D) and (E) go beyond the scope of the passage; outsourcing is already financially favorable, so choice (E) has another strike against it.

12. E   Because coral offers the zooxanthellae protection, it is reasonable to infer that they do not have their own defense mechanisms, making choice (E) correct. Eliminate choice (A) because the passage states only that zooxanthellae cause coral coloration but does not mention camouflage. The zooxanthellae need carbon dioxide, but its purpose is not stated in the passage, so choice (B) is incorrect. Choice (C) is also wrong because there is no indication that they cannot live outside coral. Finally, the relationship is mutualistic, not parasitical, so choice (D) is incorrect.

13. B   The pollutions referred to are described as *anthropogenic*; the root means that they are linked to humans. Thus choice (B) is the best answer. The pollutions are not linked to any other type of organism, so eliminate choices (A) and (D). Choice (C) is incorrect because overfishing, etc., is not an accident. Choice (E) is wrong because the pollutions are not natural.

14. A   The third paragraph discusses why the coral appear bleached and directly links this to a loss of color in the zooxanthellae invertebrates. This process is best summarized in choice (A). The passage does not discuss a displacement of the invertebrates, as in choice (B), a change in their habits, as in choice (C), or the arrival of a new species, as in choice (D). Choice (E) describes an issue for coral in general, but the question is about pigmentation specifically.

15. C   One of the causes of coral bleaching is overharvesting of coral, so increased tourism (in areas where tourists purchase coral souvenirs) may be contributing to coral bleaching. Therefore, choice (C) is the best answer. There is no mention of shipping as a cause of bleaching, so eliminate choice (A). There is no direct connection in the passage between the consumption of fossil fuels and coral bleaching, which makes choice (B) incorrect. Choice (D) is also wrong because the government is not mentioned, nor does the passage rank environmental concerns. Finally, the passage does not state that coral is unusually sensitive, merely that it is sensitive to change, so choice (E) is incorrect as well.

Drill 5

1. E At the conclusion of this passage the author asserts that African-Americans played an important role in the development of country music. Choice (A) states they had a minimal impact on this genre, so this choice contradicts the passage. Choice (B) might be an accurate statement, but there is no mention of hip hop in the passage; therefore, there is no support for this answer. Choice (C) is an extreme answer. While African-Americans played a key role in developing country music, the author does not claim that they are the only ones responsible for it. Choice (D) is a partial answer; while Rufus "Tee Tot" Payne instructed Hank Williams, the passage does not give any specifics regarding what he taught Williams. Choice (E) is a good paraphrase of the author's position. See the sentence beginning with *[t]he banjo* and the following sentence.

2. A The line reference draws attention to the sentence naming some African-American musical traditions that shaped country music; thus, the answer needs to describe that relationship. Only choice (A) depicts this previous music as the source from which country music arose. There is nothing in the passage to support choices (B), (D), or (E), choice (C) is true but does not answer the question.

3. B The preceding sentence (the one that details the possible steps in face perception) is a more specific description of the psychologists' theory so eliminate choice (A). The author never provides the history described in choice (C) so it is also incorrect; he/she merely provides two arguments on the phenomenon. The author never discusses visual perception more generally; thus choice (D) goes beyond the scope of the passage. The author never reconciles the psychologists' and cognitive neuroscientists' views, and so choice (E) is not supported. Choice (B) is the best match.

4. A *Analogy* describes the way cognitive neuroscientists believe the brain functions when confronted with faces. In the following sentence the author discusses the way in which brains have a natural ability to recognize things of the same character or quality. Eliminate choices (B) and (D) because they discuss psychologists Choice (C) is too unspecific, and choice (E) leaves out the comparison factor. The best match is choice (A) because it addresses the matching that neuroscientists think is happening.

5. A When looking for the main idea, you need to consider the entire passage. In the first paragraph the author states that some people had assumed that schools that were freed from rules and regulations (such as charter schools) would revolutionize education. In the second paragraph the author states that those who study educational reform have found that charter schools did not in fact have a revolutionary impact on education—either for better or worse—although students who attend charter schools sometimes do not seem to do as well academically. In the last paragraph the author talks about the challenges that schools face in general, be they charter schools or traditional schools. Choice (A) gets closest to summarizing the entire passage. Choices (B) and (E) contradict the passage, choice (D) is too extreme, and choice (C) is not the whole point.

6. **B**   Always answer the question in your own words first to avoid being distracted by trap answer choices. In this passage the author provides background on the charter school movement in the first paragraph. In the second paragraph the author states that those who study educational reform have found that the students who attend charter schools have not performed better than other students. In the last paragraph the author discusses education in more general terms, stating that schools continue to face some of the same challenges they have always faced. The last paragraph therefore links to the other paragraphs only insofar as it is on generally the same theme, but it provides entirely new information. Therefore, choice (B) is the best answer.

7. **D**   At the end of the final paragraph the author lists the challenges that schools face. Choices (A), (B), (C), and (E) are paraphrases of these points. While the paragraph does discuss how student performance is measured, this information is not presented as a particular challenge that schools face; thus choice (D) is the best answer.

8. **E**   According to the second paragraph of the passage, those who study educational reform question whether charter schools have made a revolutionary impact, and as evidence, they note that students who attend charter schools have often not met state performance standards. Although attending college—which is suggested by choice (A)—may suggest academic achievement, college attendance is outside the scope of this passage. Choice (B) talks about the performance of students who attend traditional schools, and therefore it goes in the wrong direction. Low pay is raised as an issue, but the passage does not link it to student performance, so eliminate choice (C). The idea of a national standard goes beyond the scope of the passage; thus choice (D) is not only too extreme but also does not address the question. Only choice (E) mentions performance measurements on a state level.

9. **E**   Eliminate choice (A) because it is an extreme answer. Choice (B) can be eliminated because it is also an extreme answer, but in the opposite direction. Eliminate choice (C) because this is Benhaïm's argument about the novel, not the approach that other critics have taken. Choice (D) is incorrect because, while Benhaïm's approach may mark a turning point in Proustian scholarship, the author doesn't state that studies on memory in these texts are no longer useful. Therefore, choice (E) is the best match.

10. **B**   The second paragraph focuses on Benhaïm's study of Proust's text. Because of Proust's mysterious and, at times, hostile representations of French cities, the narrator is turned into an exile in his homeland. The quotation illustrates this point using the narrator's perception of Balbec, which for him is strange and cruel. Choice (B) is the best match. Eliminate choice (A) because it uses information from the passage but doesn't answer the question. Eliminate choice (C) because the author never discusses the realities of living in France. Choice (D) goes beyond the scope of the question, and choice (E) is unrelated to the quoted text.

11. **E** Most of the second paragraph focuses on Proust's portrayal of the French town of Balbec, which has cathedrals. Therefore, the answer is choice (E) because "basilicas" is another word for "cathedrals." Eliminate choice (A) because the quote does not mention graves. Eliminate choices (B) and (D) because these are slightly obscure synonyms for travelers and, while the narrator feels like an exile in his own land, the author doesn't mention travelers as features of Balbec. Finally, choice (C) is incorrect because this word means marketplace, which is also not mentioned.

12. **B** Eliminate choice (A) because this isn't supported in the passage. If anything there is a significant amount of agreement regarding the value of this text. Eliminate choice (C); while critics have focused much of their attention on memory in these texts, the author doesn't suggest that it has been ignored in other ways. Eliminate choice (D) because it was Proust's theories on involuntary memory, not voluntary memory, which caught people's attention. Eliminate choice (E) because the autobiographical nature of the text isn't mentioned in the passage. Choice (B) is the best match because the text states that Proust's representations of France are *exotic* and *mysterious* and not what *one expects*.

13. **A** Eliminate choice (B); while the author compares the Judaeo-Christian concept of god with the Nahuas' belief in the sacred power of *teotl*, the author never discusses any Christian stories that explain the beginnings of the world. *Teotl* is not a concept in Western philosophy, so eliminate choice (C). Though the author's definition of *teotl* makes a comparison, one isn't supported over the other, eliminating choice (D). While this definition may spark curiosity, the role of this statement is not to advocate action, so choice (E) is eliminated. Thus, the best answer is choice (A).

14. **C** While the author describes the spirituality of this ancient culture, he/she never attributes this spirituality specifically to *thinkers*, so eliminate choice (A). Eliminate choice (B), as the author makes no such claim. While the author describes a key concept within Nahau philosophy, the author never discusses how this idea might have functioned in the lives of men and women in the ancient world; thus choice (D) is eliminated. There is no evidence to suggest that the author intends to trouble anyone's belief system, so eliminate choice (E). Choice (C) is the best match.

15. **D** Eliminate choice (A) because this answer clearly mixes up a couple of the central ideas in the passage. According to scholars, Nahua philosophy was complex and interrelated, but the author doesn't say that Western philosophy consists *only* of dichotomies, so eliminate choice (B) as this is an extreme answer. The first part of choice (C) is great, but the second part is very wrong; half bad is all bad, so eliminate it. Eliminate choice (E) because it is too extreme. Within the Nahuas' worldview, the supernatural force was united with the natural world, so choice (D) is the best match.

Drill 6

1. **C**   The passage states that wombats are nocturnal, so choice (A) is true. The fact that scats *provide crucial evidence* indicates that the issue of territory is worthy of study, thus supporting choice (B). The passage refers to other rodents as having orange enamel, and the aggressive displays would be a sign of being territorial, so both choices (D) and (E) are true. While the passage does not discuss alternatives, it cannot be assumed—based on this passage that studying the scats are the only way to determine limits on territory, thus, choice (C) is the credited response.

2. **B**   By saying that the wombat is not mythical, the passage suggests that someone must have thought that the wombat does not really exist; thus the correct answer is choice (B). This passage does not tie the wombat to the Eora culture, nor does it extend that culture to any other civilization, thus eliminating choices (A) and (C). The passage also does not provide any contrast with other rodents, so choice (D) is incorrect. Eliminate choice (E) because, while the passage addresses the derivative of the wombat's name, it does not refer to naming standards.

3. **A**   The right answer to a main idea question will cover the entire passage. This passage describes three theories for the cause of the Permian mass extinctions: asteroid impact, volcanic eruption, and rising concentrations of hydrogen sulfide in the earth's oceans. The first two of these theories are shown to be problematic. All you are told about the third theory is that it can be tested. The answer that best covers all three theories is choice (A).

4. **B**   According to the passage, to test the hydrogen sulfide theory the oceanic sediments from the Permian period would yield evidence of a rise in hydrogen sulfide consuming bacteria. However, if the chemical composition of the oceanic sediment has changed since the Permian period, then testing that sediment would provide unreliable results, so choice (B) is the best answer.

5. **A**   Eliminate choice (B) because is an extreme answer and not supported by the text. While Kahlo focused on self-representation, it is too much of a leap to infer that the Mexican revolution and/or nationalism were irrelevant to Kahlo's art. Eliminate choice (C) because it is too broad. This passage focuses on Kahlo and some of her male contemporaries, not female and male artists in general. The information about the war does not explain Kahlo's relative obscurity nor does it address issues of feminist beliefs, so eliminate choices (D) and (E). The correct answer is choice (A).

6. **E**   Though the author makes a range of comments, he/she discusses Kahlo's painting style in the first sentence. Look for an answer that matches the author's description of Kahlo's painting as a blend of *realism and fantasy*. Choice (E) is a rewording of this discussion. Choice (A) contains the words the author uses to describe the male painters. Choices (B) and (C) are partial answers. Finally, choice (D) is not supported in the passage.

7. **D** The passage is primarily concerned with the possibility and consequences of terraforming, so choice (A), though an issue, is secondary in this discussion. Besides, we clearly are at least *thinking* about going to Mars. Just because there is water doesn't necessarily mean that life once existed on Mars, making choice (B) untrue. Choice (C) is incorrect because the passage speaks only about Mars, not about the rest of the universe. The author is worried about preserving life; he/she does not mention natural resources, so eliminate choice (E). The author is worried about the atmosphere dehydrating again; therefore he/she considers the long-term important, and choice (D) is the best answer.

8. **A** One of the major obstacles to terraforming Mars as mentioned in the passage is the lack of a life-sustaining atmosphere; if the carbon dioxide layer were able to retain atmospheric heat, terraforming would be more feasible. Thus, choice (A) is the best answer. Choice (B) makes terraforming less feasible; without an atmosphere it would be inhospitable to man. Choice (C) makes terraforming neither more nor less likely—the point of terraforming is to change the environment. The passage is not concerned with governments on Earth, making choice (D) incorrect. Choice (E) is incorrect because the passage is not concerned with other planets.

9. **B** This question has several attractive answer choices. The best way to deal with this challenge is to state the purpose in your own words and then eliminate any choices that don't match. You might have said that the author called Russia a *lapdog* to show that Russia was like a dog, begging at the feet of the West. That paraphrase would eliminate choice (D). Choice (A) is not quite a match either. Choice (C) uses the word *contempt,* which is a bit too strong, so you would eliminate it, too. Once you have done that, compare the remaining choices to each other. What is the difference between choices (B) and (E)? In choice (E), the focus is on how the West treated Russia. In the passage, the focus is more on Russia's position. Choice (B) is the best answer.

10. **D** Choices (A) and (E) can be eliminated, because the sentence does not refer to the government's view. Choice (B) may look attractive, but the word *mistaken* is too strong. Choices (C) and (D) are quite similar, so compare them to each other. The only real problem is that choice (C) says the crisis could have been averted. The passage does not say the crisis was preventable. Choice (D) is the best answer.

11. **C** Choice (B) is too narrow because it refers only to the beginning of the passage. Choice (E) is too broad; only a few systems are mentioned and only one is the focus. Choices (A), (C), and (D) are similar, so compare them to each other. If you can't decide which one to choose, make a guess and move on. Choice (C) is best because it captures the real focus of the passage: *why* the NEP failed. Choice (D) is close, but the three crises ended a policy, not a whole era.

12. **E** The author would likely agree with each of the statements, except for choice (E). The passage presents the popular view of NEPmen, which is not necessarily the author's view. Choice (D) seems extreme but is supported by the passage.

13. B   According to the passage, *the burning of fossil fuels, which have no carbon-14 content, has diluted the atmospheric carbon-14 content.* You are told in the passage that carbon dating works by measuring the percentage of carbon remaining in an ancient object, compared to that found in living matter. However, because the burning of fossil fuels has decreased the ratio of carbon-14 in the atmosphere, living matter that died more than a century ago (prior to the burning of fossil fuels) would have more carbon-14 content when it died, and would appear, therefore, to have died more recently. Thus, choice (B) is supported. There is no information in the passage to justify any of the other answers.

14. A   In the first paragraph, the author discusses the trouble that anthropologists have had in dating the *habilis* skull, which at first they thought to be 3 million years old. In the second paragraph, the author describes how carbon dating techniques work; objects are dated by the ratio of carbon-14 they possess. However, the author goes on to show that the half-life of carbon can date objects only up to 50,000 years old, or 100,000 years at most if accelerator techniques are used. This limitation suggests that carbon dating is unsuitable for providing the exact age of the *habilis* skull, making choice (A) the best answer. Choice (B) is actually the opposite of what the author suggests for the time frame being discussed. Choice (C) does not answer the question; while the difference is indeed highlighted, this answer ignores the *purpose* of the contrast. In choice (D), accelerator techniques would still not be adequate to date *habilis*. Choice (E) is off the mark; the half-life in itself does not *illustrate the equilibrium*.

15. C   The proposed solution comes at the end of the passage, where the author discusses radiometric dating methods, so the answer needs to address the requirements of this solution. There is an assumption in this method that the isotopes being measured decay at a consistent rate, and this issue is best addressed in choice (C). While choice (D) addresses radiometric methods, the author does not discuss the equipment involved in the process. The remaining answers do not cover this proposed solution.

16. D   The first paragraph of the passage talks about the difficulties that anthropologists have had in dating KNM-ER 1470. The second paragraph discusses the limitations of carbon-14 dating, most notably that it can be reliably used only for objects that are up to 100,000 years old. The final paragraph proposes other radiometric methods and suggests that these might be of *greater benefit*. Therefore, the primary purpose of the passage can best be expressed as proposing a methodology to measure the age of KNM-ER 1470, closest to choice (D). Choices (A) and (B), while true of the passage, are too narrow. Neither choice (C) nor choice (E) is addressed in the passage.

Antonyms

ANTONYMS

There are five techniques for antonyms, and the first four are vocabulary-based. Do not even think about taking the real GRE until you have mastered a reliable list of GRE specific vocabulary. That means make flashcards now and start carrying them around with you. Don't try to do it all at once. Learn three or four new words a day and use them in conversation, that way you will never forget them. It is a very different test when you know all of the words.

It is very likely that the first question you will see will be an antonym question. Your first five questions will likely be a mix of antonyms and analogies. This is the computer's way of taking your vocabulary temperature.

The nice thing about antonyms is that they are relatively quick. No single antonym question should take more that thirty to forty seconds. Mastering your approach to antonyms is a good way to give yourself more time on the reading comprehension. As with the rest of the test, scratch paper is a crucial tool to assist you with the clarity and the efficiency of your approach. Another similarity between antonyms and the rest of the test is that the answer choices are very carefully selected and tested to mess with your head. The best protection against ETS: traps is to know what you're looking for before you get there. This puts you in charge. You are assessing each answer choice based upon how well it fits your needs, as opposed to seeing them as a series of compelling suggestions.

> The answer choices represent ETS's suggestions. We don't like their suggestions, we don't want them, and we don't trust them. Know what you're looking for before you get there.

BASIC APPROACH

- **If you know the word, simplify it.** Come up with an easy synonym.
- **Find the opposite of your synonym.** This is the filter you will use to test the answer choices.
- **Compare your word to each answer choice.** Use a two-pass approach and park your thinking on the page. Remember, on the first pass you are not looking for the correct answer. You are simply deciding "Maybe," or "Gone." Don't be afraid of the "Maybe," and don't get stuck on any one answer choice in the first pass; try to make your decision in 15 seconds or less. Make sure your hand is moving.

SECONDARY TECHNIQUES

If you are down to two or three answer choices, it must be because you don't know some of the words well enough to eliminate them. Here are a few ways to whittle down the last few.

Good Word or Bad Word (Positive/Negative)

If your stem word is a good word, then your answer choice must be a bad word. If you don't know a word well enough to define it, you may at least know if it is good or bad. Often you can tell if a word is good or bad just by its context. You might not know what the word "fester" means, but you've heard it as the name for the creepy uncle in *The Addams Family,* therefore, it must be bad. You may not know what the word zenith means, but they named a brands of TVs after it, so it must be good.

Context

Use context if you've heard a word in a common phrase. Some words, such as *alleviate* or *proliferation,* you can't define, but you may have heard them in context (alleviate pain is frequently heard on TV commercials, and nuclear proliferation is frequently heard on the nightly news). Make a simple synonym and then a simple antonym of the stem word or answer choice and plug it into your phrase to see if it makes sense.

PROLIFERATION:

- ○ egress
- ○ detraction
- ○ boisterousness
- ○ containment
- ○ bilge

choice (A)   *Egress* means an exit. The opposite is entrance. Does nuclear entrance make sense? No. Cross it off.

choice (B)   *Detraction* means to put someone or something down. The opposite is to compliment. Does nuclear compliment make sense? No. Cross it off.

choice (C)   *Boisterousness* means rowdiness. The opposite would be quietness or calmness. Does nuclear calmness make sense? No. Cross it off.

choice (D)   The opposite would be spread. Does nuclear spread make sense? Sort of. Keep it in.

choice (E)   *Bilge* is the bottom of a boat where all of the nasty water collects. It doesn't have a clear opposite. You can eliminate it.

Lack of Opposites

Some words like salt, chair, arithmetic, just don't have clear opposites. Cross these off.

Secondary Definition/Part of Speech

Part of speech will remain consistent. If one word is a noun, they will all be nouns. If you see a word, such as the word *milk*, which looks out of place, check the part of speech. Milk as a verb might show up as an antonym. Milk as a noun will not. Part of speech is often a clue that secondary definitions are being tested.

Roots and Prefixes

Use these aggressively when you are stuck. Hey, you have to guess anyway. A word like Maladroit has "*mal*" as a prefix; it must be bad, right? Incredulity has "*-cred*" as a root. Incredible, credible (witness), and credit all have the same root. Credible means believable. Incredulity probably means something like not believable. As long as you must pick an answer, be aggressive with your guessing.

Extremes

Extreme words are more likely to have clear opposites. *Hot*, *scalding*, or *torrid* all have clear opposites, but what's the opposite of *tepid*?

STRATEGY SUMMARY

Any technique that applies to the answer choices also applies to the stem words. If you're not sure about the stem word, try making simple antonyms of the answer choices and comparing them to the stem word to see if anything makes sense. If that doesn't work, see if you can figure out if it is at least positive or negative. If you really have no idea, the good news is that you're doing well enough to have some really hard words thrown your way. Don't spend too much time trying to figure out what you don't know. Eliminate any answer choice that doesn't have a clear opposite and pick words that look more extreme. Remember that no antonym, easy, medium, or hard, should take more that 30–40 seconds. Never try to go fast, just practice until the approach becomes second nature.

For more practice using these techniques, check out our student-friendly guidebook, *Cracking the GRE*.

ANTONYMS: DRILL 1

DILATE:
- ○ raise higher
- ○ shrink down
- ○ set right
- ○ line up
- ○ make bigger

TURBULENCE:
- ○ landing
- ○ balance
- ○ territory
- ○ stability
- ○ commotion

ANARCHY:
- ○ order
- ○ altruism
- ○ imprudence
- ○ lawlessness
- ○ immersion

ADULTERATION:
- ○ matrimony
- ○ eloquence
- ○ sanctification
- ○ inflection
- ○ befoulment

DISARM:
- ○ ameliorate
- ○ pacify
- ○ attest
- ○ incense
- ○ apprehend

CONVERSANCE:
- ○ obliviousness
- ○ reticence
- ○ versed
- ○ illiteracy
- ○ acquaintance

TACIT:
- ○ deposed
- ○ mercurial
- ○ implicit
- ○ untenable
- ○ articulate

RIFT:
- ○ tributary
- ○ unification
- ○ fissure
- ○ bridge
- ○ depletion

OUTSET:
- ○ hesitation
- ○ culpability
- ○ plethora
- ○ culmination
- ○ inception

SPLENDOR:
- ○ dreariness
- ○ magnificence
- ○ hubris
- ○ garishness
- ○ austerity

MERCURIAL:
- ⬭ trenchant
- ⬭ malingering
- ⬭ capricious
- ⬭ immutable
- ⬭ episodic

SENTIENT:
- ⬭ insipid
- ⬭ cognizant
- ⬭ nascent
- ⬭ reverent
- ⬭ insensate

QUIESCENCE:
- ⬭ listlessness
- ⬭ kinesis
- ⬭ cacophony
- ⬭ iniquity
- ⬭ latency

EFFRONTERY:
- ⬭ diffidence
- ⬭ iniquity
- ⬭ reticence
- ⬭ mettle
- ⬭ audacity

INVETERATE:
- ⬭ untoward
- ⬭ tawdry
- ⬭ unaccustomed
- ⬭ noisome
- ⬭ ineradicable

ERUDITE:
- ⬭ fallow
- ⬭ benighted
- ⬭ lettered
- ⬭ fatuous
- ⬭ ingenuous

LIBERTINE:
- ⬭ prig
- ⬭ mendicant
- ⬭ ascetic
- ⬭ rake
- ⬭ prodigal

TYRO:
- ⬭ pedagogue
- ⬭ despot
- ⬭ adulator
- ⬭ neophyte
- ⬭ veteran

VENAL:
- ⬭ pulmonary
- ⬭ turbid
- ⬭ stolid
- ⬭ ethical
- ⬭ intense

NATTY:
- ⬭ indefatigable
- ⬭ sordid
- ⬭ dapper
- ⬭ ineluctable
- ⬭ unkempt

ANTONYMS: DRILL 2

EXCESSIVE:
- ◯ inadequate
- ◯ vivacious
- ◯ arrogant
- ◯ overflowing
- ◯ indifferent

CONSTRAIN:
- ◯ conjure
- ◯ restrict
- ◯ release
- ◯ identify
- ◯ enflame

CONSOLE:
- ◯ ascertain
- ◯ solace
- ◯ pilfer
- ◯ dishearten
- ◯ belabor

ANALOGOUS:
- ◯ disparate
- ◯ comparable
- ◯ variegated
- ◯ mundane
- ◯ prosperous

CESSATION:
- ◯ deprecation
- ◯ continuation
- ◯ endorsement
- ◯ induction
- ◯ termination

EULOGY:
- ◯ wake
- ◯ tirade
- ◯ lament
- ◯ canticle
- ◯ oration

DISPOSED:
- ◯ apt
- ◯ mitigated
- ◯ salvaged
- ◯ prone
- ◯ averse

PLASTICITY:
- ◯ vexation
- ◯ authenticity
- ◯ innelasticity
- ◯ malleability
- ◯ hubris

CRYPTIC:
- ◯ deathly
- ◯ inscrutable
- ◯ feasible
- ◯ fathomable
- ◯ vital

ANOMALOUS:
- ◯ quotidian
- ◯ sporadic
- ◯ equable
- ◯ aberrant
- ◯ superfluous

OBDURATE:

- ○ caustic
- ○ tractable
- ○ obsequious
- ○ recalcitrant
- ○ onerous

MENDACITY:

- ○ parody
- ○ perspicacity
- ○ veraciousness
- ○ sagacity
- ○ subterfuge

TENDENTIOUS:

- ○ impassive
- ○ desultory
- ○ disinterested
- ○ uninterested
- ○ prepossessed

ACCRETION:

- ○ equanimity
- ○ attenuation
- ○ proliferation
- ○ perfidy
- ○ attrition

FATUITY:

- ○ asininity
- ○ recalcitrance
- ○ sapience
- ○ dearness
- ○ gauntness

PROLIXITY:

- ○ concavity
- ○ turpitude
- ○ bombast
- ○ pugnacity
- ○ taciturnity

VERDANT:

- ○ defoliated
- ○ fetid
- ○ lush
- ○ feckless
- ○ arid

TRACTABILITY:

- ○ insouciance
- ○ frowardness
- ○ inimicality
- ○ docility
- ○ desuetude

BLITHE:

- ○ sanguine
- ○ rapacious
- ○ irascible
- ○ saturnine
- ○ indolent

VERITABLE:

- ○ spurious
- ○ indubitable
- ○ fallacious
- ○ authentic
- ○ circumstantiated

ANTONYMS: DRILL 3

CONTAMINATE:
- ◯ discourage
- ◯ purify
- ◯ institute
- ◯ perpetuate
- ◯ pollute

CONSTRICT:
- ◯ repeal
- ◯ liberate
- ◯ augment
- ◯ cramp
- ◯ protract

BOISTEROUS:
- ◯ succulent
- ◯ rambunctious
- ◯ sedate
- ◯ cerebral
- ◯ wistful

JOCULAR:
- ◯ perilous
- ◯ solemn
- ◯ cantankerous
- ◯ indignant
- ◯ jovial

AUTONOMY:
- ◯ tenacity
- ◯ decorum
- ◯ sovereignty
- ◯ hubris
- ◯ dependence

CONVOLUTED:
- ◯ perspicuous
- ◯ byzantine
- ◯ ardent
- ◯ egregious
- ◯ amenable

PROFUNDITY:
- ◯ sagaciousness
- ◯ insipidness
- ◯ superficiality
- ◯ illegitimation
- ◯ asperity

INDIGENOUS:
- ◯ affluent
- ◯ extrinsic
- ◯ proximate
- ◯ aboriginal
- ◯ inimical

OCCULT:
- ◯ precipitate
- ◯ surreptitious
- ◯ supernatural
- ◯ manifest
- ◯ stoic

MALAPERT:
- ◯ impudent
- ◯ diffident
- ◯ stolid
- ◯ obsequious
- ◯ arrant

INCHOATE:

- ○ embryonic
- ○ mature
- ○ seasoned
- ○ inordinate
- ○ incipient

SOMATIC:

- ○ cerebral
- ○ medicinal
- ○ corporeal
- ○ illustrative
- ○ loquacious

GARRULITY:

- ○ aloof
- ○ lassitude
- ○ reticence
- ○ peregrination
- ○ loquacity

REFULGENT:

- ○ torpid
- ○ lackluster
- ○ evanescent
- ○ effulgent
- ○ saturnine

BANAL:

- ○ bombastic
- ○ jejune
- ○ noteworthy
- ○ bromidic
- ○ novel

SALUBRIOUS:

- ○ mendacious
- ○ noisome
- ○ nebulous
- ○ minacious
- ○ salutary

MACULATED:

- ○ unsullied
- ○ adulterated
- ○ minimized
- ○ ameliorated
- ○ agonized

IMPECUNIOUS:

- ○ flush
- ○ incipient
- ○ penurious
- ○ ingenuous
- ○ deficient

ATTENUATE:

- ○ impute
- ○ rarefy
- ○ impugn
- ○ vivify
- ○ wax

PUISSANCE:

- ○ thew
- ○ paucity
- ○ pusillanimity
- ○ cravenness
- ○ impotence

ANTONYMS: DRILL 4

COLLECT:
- demote
- assemble
- entangle
- disperse
- incorporate

ABHOR:
- adore
- vex
- substantiate
- foster
- despise

MUNDANE:
- pedestrian
- whimsical
- biased
- atypical
- energetic

ZENITH:
- pinnacle
- median
- nadir
- vertex
- intersection

AMALGAMATE:
- squander
- commingle
- preclude
- laud
- segregate

OBSTINATE:
- participatory
- dogged
- svelte
- rational
- complaisant

FLOURISH:
- languish
- reconnoiter
- brandish
- deplete
- blossom

TIMOROUS:
- brash
- valiant
- craven
- fervent
- volatile

TIRADE:
- buttress
- diatribe
- fusillade
- panegyric
- dynamo

NASCENT:
- latent
- extant
- dormant
- inchoate
- moribund

ABATE:

- ◯ proselytize
- ◯ wane
- ◯ protract
- ◯ tout
- ◯ proliferate

UBIQUITOUS:

- ◯ vociferous
- ◯ omnipresent
- ◯ nonexistent
- ◯ obstreperous
- ◯ differentiable

ABERRANT:

- ◯ nugatory
- ◯ accurate
- ◯ deviant
- ◯ tranquil
- ◯ wonted

TRACTABLE:

- ◯ vituperative
- ◯ implacable
- ◯ mellifluous
- ◯ venal
- ◯ courteous

OPPROBRIOUS:

- ◯ disreputable
- ◯ encomiastic
- ◯ salacious
- ◯ calumnious
- ◯ endemic

BALEFUL:

- ◯ redolent
- ◯ malefic
- ◯ salubrious
- ◯ recumbent
- ◯ propitious

FLAG:

- ◯ contravene
- ◯ quibble
- ◯ lag
- ◯ dissemble
- ◯ semaphore

VERITABLE:

- ◯ ambiguous
- ◯ caustic
- ◯ splenetic
- ◯ indubitable
- ◯ spurious

PERIPATETIC:

- ◯ awe-inspiring
- ◯ sedentary
- ◯ impecunious
- ◯ itinerant
- ◯ captious

CAKE:

- ◯ attenuate
- ◯ inveigh
- ◯ desiccate
- ◯ limn
- ◯ ostracize

ANTONYMS: DRILL 5

VAGUE:

- ⬭ condensed
- ⬭ reclusive
- ⬭ concrete
- ⬭ superb
- ⬭ murky

TAINTED:

- ⬭ robust
- ⬭ uncorrupted
- ⬭ magnanimous
- ⬭ contaminated
- ⬭ negligible

PUNGENCY:

- ⬭ acridity
- ⬭ vigilance
- ⬭ intelligence
- ⬭ opulence
- ⬭ insipidness

DISPERSION:

- ⬭ dissipation
- ⬭ deification
- ⬭ absolution
- ⬭ indemnification
- ⬭ amalgamation

FLEDGLING:

- ⬭ novice
- ⬭ cynic
- ⬭ veteran
- ⬭ misanthrope
- ⬭ ingénue

SPARSE:

- ⬭ languorous
- ⬭ fetid
- ⬭ meager
- ⬭ serried
- ⬭ true

MITIGATE:

- ⬭ exacerbate
- ⬭ concentrate
- ⬭ annul
- ⬭ obviate
- ⬭ allay

PALPABILITY:

- ⬭ proclivity
- ⬭ magnanimity
- ⬭ discernibleness
- ⬭ intangibility
- ⬭ abstruseness

OCCLUDED:

- ⬭ luminous
- ⬭ unimpeded
- ⬭ obstructed
- ⬭ inundated
- ⬭ breached

PENCHANT:

- ⬭ mode
- ⬭ flair
- ⬭ repugnance
- ⬭ ambivalence
- ⬭ proclivity

POLEMICAL:

- ○ unequivocal
- ○ imminent
- ○ veracious
- ○ untenable
- ○ disputable

GERMANE:

- ○ extraneous
- ○ tractable
- ○ cogent
- ○ corrigible
- ○ apposite

STEEP:

- ○ subsume
- ○ adulterate
- ○ desiccate
- ○ suffuse
- ○ level

LOQUACIOUS:

- ○ meretricious
- ○ garrulous
- ○ taciturn
- ○ risible
- ○ inarticulate

PERUSE:

- ○ rifle
- ○ scuttle
- ○ inspect
- ○ skate
- ○ scrutinize

RIPE:

- ○ antediluvian
- ○ inchoate
- ○ indefatigable
- ○ emergent
- ○ infelicitous

VENERATION:

- ○ anathema
- ○ impudence
- ○ reverence
- ○ apotheosis
- ○ antipathy

CHARY:

- ○ dauntless
- ○ insouciant
- ○ precipitate
- ○ circumspect
- ○ intrepid

OBLOQUY:

- ○ peroration
- ○ ignominy
- ○ perigee
- ○ esteem
- ○ approbation

TENUOUS:

- ○ imposing
- ○ pulchritudinous
- ○ puissant
- ○ insubstantial
- ○ preternatural

ANTONYMS: DRILL 6

INSERT:
- ◯ detract
- ◯ inject
- ◯ expose
- ◯ withdraw
- ◯ enlist

STABILITY:
- ◯ inflection
- ◯ pessimism
- ◯ intensity
- ◯ fluctuation
- ◯ permanence

AERATE:
- ◯ smother
- ◯ infer
- ◯ lubricate
- ◯ ventilate
- ◯ embed

ALLY:
- ◯ maverick
- ◯ foe
- ◯ connoisseur
- ◯ noncombatant
- ◯ comrade

FALLACIOUS:
- ◯ erroneous
- ◯ inept
- ◯ somber
- ◯ austere
- ◯ valid

HYPERBOLE:
- ◯ equivocation
- ◯ overstatement
- ◯ veraciousness
- ◯ minimization
- ◯ equanimity

DIFFIDENT:
- ◯ refulgent
- ◯ truculent
- ◯ demure
- ◯ tractable
- ◯ gregarious

COMELINESS:
- ◯ propriety
- ◯ exodus
- ◯ inaccessibility
- ◯ obscurity
- ◯ homeliness

DERIDE:
- ◯ bolster
- ◯ censure
- ◯ goad
- ◯ gibe
- ◯ laud

PERENNIAL:
- ◯ ephemeral
- ◯ seasonal
- ◯ diffuse
- ◯ distrait
- ◯ centennial

ASSUAGE:

- ◯ placate
- ◯ enervate
- ◯ nettle
- ◯ beatify
- ◯ belittle

DISAFFECT:

- ◯ conciliate
- ◯ allure
- ◯ maunder
- ◯ estrange
- ◯ malinger

HEGEMONY:

- ◯ polemic
- ◯ prepotency
- ◯ obsequiousness
- ◯ paramountcy
- ◯ subordinance

HAPLESS:

- ◯ opportunistic
- ◯ profligate
- ◯ ill-fated
- ◯ providential
- ◯ refractory

CASTIGATION:

- ◯ excoriation
- ◯ reconnaissance
- ◯ obeisance
- ◯ expurgation
- ◯ encomium

ANTIPATHY:

- ◯ enmity
- ◯ adoration
- ◯ desuetude
- ◯ apathy
- ◯ delectation

EBULLIENCE:

- ◯ virago
- ◯ tepidness
- ◯ effervescence
- ◯ cowling
- ◯ vitriol

SEDULOUS:

- ◯ languorous
- ◯ assiduous
- ◯ pellucid
- ◯ indolent
- ◯ peripatetic

DIATRIBE:

- ◯ filibuster
- ◯ elegy
- ◯ allocution
- ◯ fulmination
- ◯ panegyric

SINECURE:

- ◯ confabulation
- ◯ solicitude
- ◯ moil
- ◯ turpitude
- ◯ quagmire

ANTONYMS: DRILL 7

GLOBAL:
- ⬭ comprehensive
- ⬭ personable
- ⬭ cheerful
- ⬭ provincial
- ⬭ superstitious

REPULSION:
- ⬭ disgust
- ⬭ lavishness
- ⬭ brevity
- ⬭ attraction
- ⬭ conviction

LOLL:
- ⬭ recline lazily
- ⬭ climb slowly
- ⬭ sit stiffly
- ⬭ grab eagerly
- ⬭ view longingly

FRINGE:
- ⬭ rhetoric
- ⬭ ornament
- ⬭ hub
- ⬭ plethora
- ⬭ periphery

SERRATED:
- ⬭ smooth
- ⬭ convoluted
- ⬭ mundane
- ⬭ jagged
- ⬭ eloquent

ELASTICITY:
- ⬭ fidelity
- ⬭ pliancy
- ⬭ intransigence
- ⬭ dogmatism
- ⬭ aptitude

SAP:
- ⬭ bolster
- ⬭ defoliate
- ⬭ enervate
- ⬭ invigorate
- ⬭ sate

ARRHYTHMIC:
- ⬭ caustic
- ⬭ erratic
- ⬭ symphonic
- ⬭ cadenced
- ⬭ fortuitous

BURGEON:
- ⬭ flourish
- ⬭ ameliorate
- ⬭ eviscerate
- ⬭ ebb
- ⬭ elicit

INDIGENCE:
- ⬭ penury
- ⬭ ambiguity
- ⬭ nonchalance
- ⬭ duplicity
- ⬭ affluence

DESSICATE:
- ○ saturate
- ○ exculpate
- ○ deluge
- ○ satiate
- ○ parch

FORESTALL:
- ○ obviate
- ○ embark
- ○ precipitate
- ○ obfuscate
- ○ thwart

RECONDITE:
- ○ monotonous
- ○ lucid
- ○ abstruse
- ○ erudite
- ○ benighted

ABJURE:
- ○ recant
- ○ wheedle
- ○ abnegate
- ○ evince
- ○ asseverate

RUE:
- ○ exult
- ○ lament
- ○ eschew
- ○ maunder
- ○ exude

SURFEIT:
- ○ superfluity
- ○ modicum
- ○ succor
- ○ dearth
- ○ din

PERFIDY:
- ○ staunchness
- ○ treachery
- ○ ignominy
- ○ decrepitude
- ○ haleness

HOODWINK:
- ○ disabuse
- ○ cozen
- ○ apprise
- ○ digress
- ○ calumniate

NICE:
- ○ adjunct
- ○ free
- ○ lost
- ○ terse
- ○ dull

APOTHEOSIS:
- ○ effluvia
- ○ exaltation
- ○ ostracism
- ○ abasement
- ○ odium

ANSWERS

Drill 1

1. B
2. D
3. A
4. C
5. D
6. A
7. A
8. B
9. D
10. E
11. D
12. E
13. B
14. A
15. C
16. B
17. C
18. E
19. D
20. E

Drill 2

1. A
2. C
3. D
4. A
5. B
6. B
7. E
8. C
9. D
10. A
11. B
12. C
13. C
14. E
15. C
16. E
17. A
18. B
19. D
20. A

Drill 3

1. B
2. B
3. C
4. B
5. E
6. A
7. C
8. B
9. D
10. B
11. B
12. A
13. C
14. B
15. E
16. B
17. A
18. A
19. E
20. E

Drill 4

1. D
2. A
3. D
4. C
5. E
6. E
7. A
8. B
9. D
10. E
11. E
12. C
13. E
14. B
15. B
16. E
17. D
18. E
19. B
20. A

Drill 5

1. C
2. B
3. E
4. E
5. C
6. D
7. A
8. D
9. B
10. C
11. A
12. A
13. C
14. C
15. D
16. B
17. B
18. D
19. E
20. C

Drill 6

1. D
2. D
3. A
4. B
5. E
6. D
7. E
8. E
9. E
10. A
11. C
12. A
13. E
14. D
15. E
16. B
17. B
18. D
19. E
20. C

Drill 7

1. D
2. D
3. C
4. C
5. A
6. C
7. D
8. D
9. D
10. E
11. A
12. C
13. B
14. E
15. A
16. D
17. A
18. A
19. B
20. D

EXPLANATIONS

Drill 1

1. **B** *Dilate* means to enlarge or widen, so the opposite is to make smaller. *Make bigger* is a synonym. *Shrink down* means to make smaller, so the best answer is choice (B).

2. **D** *Turbulence* is irregular motion, so the opposite is lack of motion. *Commotion* is a synonym. *Balance* means consistent motion, not lack of motion. *Stability* means lack of motion, so the best answer is choice (D).

3. **A** *Anarchy* means chaos, so the opposite is order. *Lawlessness* is a synonym. *Order* is what you're looking for, so the best answer choice (A).

4. **C** *Adulteration* is the act of making impure, so the opposite is purification. *Befoulment* is a synonym. *Matrimony* is a trap answer; it has a relationship to *adultery*—a related, but different, word. *Sanctification* means purification, so the best answer is choice (C).

5. **D** *Disarm* means to reduce hostility or suspicion, so the opposite is to increase hostility. *Pacify* is a synonym. *Incense* means to increase hostility, so the best answer is choice (D).

6. **A** *Conversance* means familiarity with a subject, so the opposite is unfamiliarity. *Acquaintance* is a synonym, and *illiteracy* means the inability to read, so it's not quite right. *Reticence* means the reluctance to speak; it's a trap answer if you are thinking *conversance* has something to do with conversation. *Obliviousness* means lacking awareness, so the best answer is choice (A).

7. **A** *Tacit* means implied, or unspoken so the opposite is stated or spoken. *Implicit* is a synonym. *Articulate* is a trap answer; both *articulate* and *tacit* concern speech, but the words are not antonyms. If you've heard the expression "tacit agreement," you may be able to use word association. *Deposed* means stated under oath, so the best answer is choice (A).

8. **B** A *rift* is a gap or separation, so the opposite is joining together. *Fissure* is a synonym. Choice (D) is attractive because you might use a *bridge* in order to cross a *rift*, but the opposite of a gap is not the thing that crosses the gap; it is the absence of that gap. *Unification* means joining together, so the best answer is choice (B).

9. **D** *Outset* means beginning, so the opposite is end. *Inception* is a synonym. *Culmination* means end, so the best answer is choice (D).

10. **E** *Splendor* means glory or grandeur, so the opposite is plainness or simplicity. *Magnificence* is a synonym. *Dreariness* means gloominess or sadness, so it's not quite right. *Garishness* is a negative version of *splendor*, but not an antonym. *Austerity* means severity or plainness, so the best answer is choice (E).

11.　D　*Mercurial* means unpredictable or rapidly changing, so the opposite is unchanging or predictable. *Capricious* is a near synonym of *mercurial*. If you're not sure what *mercurial* means you may be able to guess using word association. Think of mercury in a thermometer; it's always changing. *Immutable* means unchanging, so the best answer is choice (D).

12.　E　*Sentient* means having sense perception or consciousness, so the opposite is unconscious. *Cognizant* is a synonym. *Nascent* means coming into existence, so it's not quite right. Eliminate *insipid* also, because it means bland or uninteresting. You may be able to use roots to guess that *insensate* means without sensation. Thus, the best answer is choice (E).

13.　B　*Quiescence* means stillness, so the opposite is activity. *Latency* is a synonym. *Cacophony* means harsh, jarring sound, so it's a trap answer, in case you're thinking *quiescence* means quietness. *Quiescence* is on the neutral side, so try eliminating answers that are strongly positive or negative. *Listlessness*, *cacophony*, and *iniquity* are negative, so eliminate choices (A), (C), and (D). *Kinesis* means activity, so the best answer is choice (B).

14.　A　*Effrontery* means extreme boldness, so the opposite is timidity or shyness. *Audacity* is a synonym. *Reticence* means reluctance to speak, not necessarily shyness, so it's not quite right. If you know *effrontery* has a negative connotation, you can eliminate negative answers. *Iniquity* and *audacity* are negative, so eliminate choices (B) and (E). *Diffidence* means timidity, so the best answer is choice (A).

15.　C　*Inveterate* means habitual or routine, so the opposite is not habitual. If you know *inveterate* is neutral you can cross off answers that are strongly positive or negative. *Untoward*, *tawdry*, and *noisome* are negative so eliminate choices (A), (B), and (D). *Ineradicable* is on the positive side. It's also unlikely that two words that start with "*in-*" would be antonyms, so eliminate choice (E). *Unaccustomed* means not habitual, so the best answer is choice (C).

16.　B　*Erudite* means learned, so the opposite is ignorant. *Lettered* is a synonym. *Fatuous* means foolish, and *ingenuous* means naïve, so they're not quite right. If you know that *erudite* is positive, you know you need a negative word. *Lettered* and *ingenuous* are positive, so you can eliminate choices (C) and (E). Now guess the hardest/weirdest word. *Benighted* means ignorant, so the best answer is choice (B).

17.　C　A *libertine* is a person who is morally unrestrained, so the opposite is someone who is morally restrained. *Rake* is a synonym. *A prig* is someone who is excessively concerned with propriety, so choice (A) is not quite right. If you know that *libertine* is negative, then you know you need a positive answer. *Prig*, *mendicant*, *rake*, and *prodigal* are negative. Eliminate choices (A), (B), (D), and (E). An *ascetic* is someone who is morally restrained, so the best answer is choice (C).

18.　E　A *tyro* is a novice or beginner, so the opposite is someone with experience. *Neophyte* is a synonym. A *pedagogue* is teacher, who often has experience, but not always, so choice (A) is not quite right. *Despot* is trap, because *tyro* looks like tyrant. A *veteran* is someone with experience, so the best answer is choice (E).

19. D *Venal* means morally corrupt or able to be bribed, so the opposite is uncorrupt. *Pulmonary* is a trap, in case you're associating *venal* with veins. If you know that *venal* is negative, you know you need a positive answer. Choice (B) is negative, so it can be eliminated. *Ethical* means uncorrupt, and it's the most positive word, so the best answer is choice (D).

20. E *Natty* means stylish, so the opposite is unstylish or sloppy. *Dapper* is a synonym. *Sordid* means filthy, so it's not quite right. If you know *natty* is positive, you know you need a negative answer. *Indefatigable* and *dapper* are positive and *ineluctable* is neutral; eliminate choices (A), (C), and (D). *Unkempt* means messy, so the best answer is choice (E).

Drill 2

1. A *Excessive* means too much, so the opposite is not enough. *Overflowing* is a synonym. *Inadequate* means not enough, so the best answer is choice (A).

2. C *Constrain* means to restrict or control, so the opposite is to set free. *Restrict* is a synonym. *Release* means to set free, so the best answer is choice (C).

3. D *Console* means to comfort, so the opposite is to upset. *Solace* is a synonym. *Dishearten* means to upset, so the best answer is choice (D).

4. A *Analogous* means similar to, so the opposite is different from. *Comparable* is a synonym. *Disparate* means different, so the best answer is choice (A).

5. B *Cessation* means stopping, so the opposite is continuing. *Termination* is a synonym. *Continuation* is what you're looking for, so the best answer is choice (B).

6. B A *eulogy* is a speech of praise, so the opposite is a critical speech. *Wake* and *lament* are trap answers; *eulogy* might remind you of a funeral. If you know that *eulogy* is positive, you know you need a negative word. *Canticle* and *oration* are neutral, so you can eliminate choices (D) and (E). A *tirade* is a harshly critical speech, so the best answer is choice (B).

7. E *Disposed* means having a tendency toward something, so the opposite is having repulsion toward something. *Apt* and *prone* are synonyms and *salvaged* is a trap answer. If you know that *disposed* is on the positive side, you know you need a negative word. Choices (A), (B), (C), and (D) are positive, so eliminate them. *Averse* means feeling dislike or reluctance, so the best answer is choice (E).

8. C *Plasticity* is the ability to be shaped or molded, so the opposite is rigidity. *Malleability* is a synonym. *Authenticity* is a trap answer, because its opposite is fakeness, which may make you think of the colloquial use of the word plastic. *Inelasticity* means rigidity, so the best answer is choice (C).

9. D *Cryptic* means puzzling or difficult to understand, so the opposite is easy to understand. *Inscrutable* is a synonym. *Deathly* is a trap answer, because it may remind you of the word crypt. *Fathomable* means possible to understand, so the best answer is choice (D).

10. **A** *Anomalous* means deviating from what is normal, so the opposite is commonplace or normal. *Aberrant* is a synonym. *Anomalous* has a prefix "*a-*," so any answer with the same prefix can't be its opposite; eliminate choice (D). *Quotidian* means commonplace, so the best answer is choice (A).

11. **B** *Obdurate* means unyielding, so the opposite is pliable. R*ecalcitrant* is a synonym. If you know that *obdurate* is negative, you know you need a positive answer. *Caustic*, *obsequious*, *recalcitrant*, and *onerous* are negative, so eliminate choices (A), (C), (D), and (E). *Tractable* means pliable, so the best answer is choice (B).

12. **C** *Mendacity* means untruthfulness, so the opposite is truthfulness. *Subterfuge* is a near synonym of *mendacity*. *Perspicacity* relates to the ability to discern the truth, and it does not in itself mean truthfulness, so it's not quite right. If you know that *mendacity* is negative, you know you need a positive answer. *Parody* is neutral and *subterfuge* is negative, so you can eliminate choices (A) and (E). You might be able to use word roots to determine that *veraciousness* means truthfulness, so the best answer is choice (C).

13. **C** *Tendentious* means biased, so the opposite is unbiased. *Prepossessed* is a synonym. *Impassive* means without emotion, so it's not quite right. *Uninterested* and *disinterested* may seem like synonyms, but *uninterested* means not interested in the sense of being bored, while *disinterested* means unbiased, so the best answer is choice (C).

14. **E** *Accretion* means an increase, so the opposite is a decrease. *Proliferation* is a synonym. *Attenuation* is the act of thinner, so it's not quite right. If you know *accretion* is positive, then you know you need a negative answer. *Equanimity* and *proliferation* are positive, so eliminate choices (A) and (C). *Attrition* means decrease, so the best answer is choice (E).

15. **C** *Fatuity* means foolishness, so the opposite is wisdom. *Asininity* is a synonym. If you know that *fatuity* is negative, you know you need a positive answer. *Asininity*, *recalcitrance*, *dearness* (which means expensiveness in this context), and *gauntness* are all negative; eliminate choices (A), (B), (D), and (E). *Sapience* means wisdom or great judgment, so the best answer is choice (C).

16. **E** *Prolixity* means excessive wordiness, so the opposite is using few words. *Bombast* is a synonym. Choice (A) may be tempting, because the prefix "*con-*" is the opposite of "*pro-*," but *concavity* does not mean the use of very few words, so choice (A) is a trap answer. *Pugnacity* means a lack of sociability, so choice (D) is not quite right. *Taciturnity* means using few words, so the best answer is choice (E).

17. **A** *Verdant* means green with vegetation, so the opposite is lacking vegetation. *Lush* is a synonym. *Arid* means dry, so it's not quite right. If you're not sure what *verdant* means, try using roots. The base "*verd*" in *verdant* means green, so the correct answer must mean something that is not green. *Defoliated* means lacking in vegetation, so the best answer is choice (A).

18. **B** *Tractability* is the quality of being easily managed, so the opposite is the quality of being difficult to manage. *Docility* is a synonym. *Inimicality* means hostility, so it's not quite right. If you know the root "*tract*" means pull, you may be able to guess the meaning of the stem word. *Frowardness* is the quality of being difficult to manage, so the best answer is choice (B).

19. **D** *Blithe* means happy or carefree, so the opposite is sad. *Sanguine* is a synonym. If you know that *blithe* is positive, you know you need a negative answer. *Sanguine* is positive, so eliminate choice (A). Guess the hardest/weirdest word. *Saturnine* means sad, so the best answer is choice (D).

20. **A** *Veritable* means genuine, so the opposite is not genuine. *Authentic* is a synonym. *Fallacious* means inaccurate, so it's not quite right. If you're not sure what *veritable* means, try using roots. The root "*ver*" means truth, so *veritable* must mean something like true; the correct answer must mean something like false. *Spurious* means not genuine, so the best answer is choice (A).

Drill 3

1. **B** *Contaminate* means to reduce the purity of, so the opposite is increase the purity of. *Pollute* is a synonym. *Purify* means to increase purity, so the best answer is choice (B).

2. **B** A secondary definition of *constrict* is to restrict freedom, so the opposite is to increase freedom. *Cramp* is a synonym. *Protract* means to draw out, so it's not quite right. *Liberate* means to increase freedom, so the best answer is choice (B).

3. **C** *Boisterous* means rowdy, so the opposite is calm. *Rambunctious* is a synonym. *Sedate* means calm, so the best answer is choice (C).

4. **B** *Jocular* means humorous, so the opposite is serious. *Jovial* is a synonym. *Solemn* means serious, so the best answer is choice (B).

5. **E** *Autonomy* means independence, so the opposite is dependence. *Sovereignty* is a synonym. *Dependence* is what you're looking for, so the best answer is choice (E).

6. **A** *Convoluted* means complicated or complex, so the opposite is direct or straightforward. *Byzantine* is a synonym. You might know that the roots "*per*" and "*spic*" mean through and sight, which would suggest that *perspicuous* is a good fit for what you're looking for. *Perspicuous* is the only word that means straightforward, so the best answer is choice (A).

7. **C** *Profundity* means *depth*, so the opposite is shallowness. *Sagaciousness* is a synonym. *Insipidness* means bland, so it's not quite right. If you know that *profundity* is positive, you know you need a negative word. *Sagaciousness* is positive, so you can eliminate choice (A). *Superficiality* means shallowness, so the best answer is choice (C).

8. **B** *Indigenous* means native to a certain area, so the opposite is *foreign*. *Aboriginal* is a synonym. *Affluent* is a trap because you may have confused *indigenous* with indigent, which means poor. If you're not sure of the meaning of the stem word, look at the prefix "*in-*." Do any of the answers have an opposite prefix? Yes, *extrinsic* does, and it means something foreign. The other answer choices do not match, so the best answer is choice (B).

9. **D** A secondary meaning for *occult* is hidden, so the opposite means apparent. *Surreptitious* is a synonym. *Supernatural* is a synonym for another meaning of *occult*, making it, is a trap answer. *Manifest* means apparent, so the best answer is choice (D).

10. **B** *Malapert* means rudely outspoken, so the opposite is shy. *Impudent* is a synonym and *obsequious* means subservient, so they're not quite right. If you aren't familiar with *malapert*, you may still recognize its root, "*mal*," meaning bad, and the word "*pert*," meaning bold—take a guess at its meaning. *Diffident* means shy, so the best answer is choice (B).

11. **B** *Inchoate* means unformed, so the opposite is fully formed. *Embryonic* and *incipient* are synonyms. *Seasoned* means experienced, so it's not quite right. *Inordinate* and *incipient* have the same prefix as the stem, so are unlikely to be its opposite; eliminate choices (D) and (E). *Mature* means fully formed, so the best answer is choice (B).

12. **A** *Somatic* means related to the body, so the opposite is related to the mind or spirit. *Corporeal* is a synonym. If you're not sure what the stem word means, you may be able to use roots to guess its meaning, because "*soma*" means body. *Cerebral* means related to the mind or intellect, so the best answer is choice (A).

13. **C** *Garrulity* means talkativeness, so the opposite is talking little. *Loquacity* is a synonym. *Aloof* means standoffish, so it's not quite right; eliminate choices (A) and (E). If you're not sure what *garrulity* means, but know it has something to do with talking, you know the correct answer will have to do with not talking. *Aloof*, *lassitude*, and *peregrination* have nothing to do with talking, so eliminate choices (A), (B) and (D). *Reticence* means talking little, so choice (C) is the best answer.

14. **B** *Refulgent* means brilliant or shiny, so the opposite is dull or not shiny. *Effulgent* is a synonym and looks a lot like *refulgent*, so it's a trap answer. *Torpid* means sluggish, not physically dim, so it's not quite right. If you know that *refulgent* is positive, you know you need a negative answer. *Effulgent* is positive, so eliminate choice (D). *Lackluster* means dull, so the best answer is choice (B).

15. **E** *Banal* means trite and overused, so the opposite is fresh and new. *Bromidic* is a synonym. *Noteworthy* means worthy of recognition, so it's not quite right. If you know *banal* is negative, then you know you need a positive answer. *Bombastic*, *jejune*, and *bromidic* are negative, so eliminate choices (A), (B), and (D). *Novel* means new and different, so the best answer is choice (E).

16. **B** *Salubrious* means good for one's health, so the opposite is bad for one's health. *Salutary* is a synonym. *Minacious* means menacing, so it's not quite right. If you know that *salubrious* is positive, you know you need a negative answer. *Nebulous* is neutral and *salutary* is positive, so eliminate choices (C) and (E). *Noisome* means harmful, so the best answer is choice (B).

17. **A** *Maculated* means polluted or blemished, so the opposite is pure. *Adulterated* is a synonym. *Ameliorated* means made better, not pure, so eliminate choice (D). If you don't know *maculated* you may be able to recognize the root *maculate* from the word immaculate, which means pure. The prefix *im* means not, so *maculated* must mean impure. *Unsullied* means pure, so the best answer is choice (A).

18. **A** *Impecunious* means penniless or having very little money, so the opposite is wealthy. If you don't know *impecunious*, the *im-* prefix may help you guess that the word has a negative connotation or that it implies some kind of lack. Choices (B), (C), and (E) all also involve some kind of lack, so they're probably not antonyms of the stem. A secondary definition of *flush* is having lots of money, so the best answer is choice (A).

19. **E** *Attenuate* means to weaken, so the opposite is to strengthen. *Rarefy* is a synonym. *Vivify* means to give life to, so it's not quite right. If you know that *attenuate* is negative, you know you need a positive answer. *Impute* is neutral and *rarefy* and *impugn* are negative; eliminate choices (A), (B), and (C). A secondary meaning of *wax* is to gradually strengthen, so the best answer is choice (E).

20. **E** *Puissance* means power, so the opposite is powerlessness. *Thew* is a synonym. *Pusillanimity* means timidity and *cravenness* means cowardice, so they are not quite right. If you know that *puissance* is positive, you know you need a negative answer. *Thew* is positive, so you can eliminate choice (A). *Impotence* means powerlessness, so the best answer is choice (E).

Drill 4

1. **D** *Collect* means to gather, so the opposite is to scatter. *Assemble* is a synonym. *Disperse* means to scatter, so the best answer is choice (D).

2. **A** *Abhor* means hate, so the opposite is love. *Despise* is a synonym. *Adore* means love, so the best answer is choice (A).

3. **D** *Mundane* means common or ordinary, so the opposite is *atypical*. *Pedestrian* is a synonym. *Whimsical* means unpredictable or capricious, so it's not quite right. *Atypical* is what you're looking for, so the best answer is choice (D).

4. **C** *Zenith* means the highest point, so the opposite is the lowest point. *Pinnacle* is a synonym. *Nadir* means the lowest point, so the best answer is choice (C).

5. **E** *Amalgamate* means to combine or mix, so the opposite is to separate. *Commingle* is a synonym. *Segregate* means to separate, so the best answer is choice (E).

6. **E** *Obstinate* means stubborn, so the opposite is accommodating or flexible. *Dogged* is a synonym. *Participatory* means willing to participate, which isn't exactly the same as flexible, so it's not quite right. *Rational* is a trap answer, in case you're thinking stubborn people aren't rational. *Complaisant* means accommodating, so the best answer is choice (E).

7. **A** *Flourish* means to *thrive*, so the opposite is to fade or decline. *Blossom* is a synonym and *brandish*—which means to wave menacingly—is a secondary meaning of *flourish*. *Deplete* means to use up, so it's not quite right. If you know that *flourish* is positive, you know you need a negative word. *Reconnoiter* is neutral and *blossom* is positive, so you can eliminate choices (B) and (E). *Languish* means to fade or waste away, so the best answer is choice (A).

8. **B** *Timorous* means timid, so the opposite is brave. *Diffident* is a synonym. *Brash* means rash, *volatile* means explosive and *fervent* means passionate, so they're not quite right. If you're not sure of the answers, try using word association—you may remember *valiant* from the *Prince Valiant* comic. Word roots could also be helpful here. *Valiant* means brave, so the best answer is choice (B).

9. **D** A *tirade* is an abusive speech, so the opposite is a supportive speech. *Diatribe* is a synonym. *Fusillade* is a continuous discharge of firearms—not exactly praise. A *buttress* is a physical object used for support, not a speech of support. A *panegyric* is a speech of praise, so the best answer is choice (D).

10. **E** *Nascent* means coming into being, so the opposite is about to die. *Inchoate* is a synonym. *Latent* and *dormant* both mean inactive, so they're not quite right. You may be able to guess the meaning of *moribund* by looking at the root "mor/mort," which means death. *Moribund* means dying or becoming obsolete, so the best answer is choice (E).

11. **E** *Abate* means to decrease, so the opposite is to increase. *Wane* is a synonym. *Protract* means to draw out, so it's not quite right. If you know *abate* is negative, you know you need a positive answer. *Wane* is negative; *proselytize* and *protract* are neutral, so you can eliminate choices (A), (B), and (C). *Proliferate* means to increase, so the best answer is choice (E).

12. **C** *Ubiquitous* means existing everywhere, so the opposite means existing nowhere. *Omnipresent* is a synonym. *Vociferous* and *obstreperous* both mean loud or noisy. If two answers have identical meanings, neither of them is likely to be correct, so you can eliminate choices (A) and (D). *Nonexistent* means existing nowhere, so the best answer is choice (C).

13. **E** *Aberrant* means deviating from the norm, so the opposite is normal. *Deviant* is a synonym. *Accurate* is a trap answer, in case you guess that *aberrant* means incorrect. If you know *aberrant* is negative, you know you need a positive answer, so eliminate choices (A) and (C). *Wonted* means usual, so the best answer is choice (E).

14. **B** *Tractable* means easily managed, so the opposite is not easily managed. If you know that *tractable* is positive, then you know you need a negative word, so eliminate choices (C) and (E). *Implacable* means not easily managed, so the best answer is choice (B).

15. **B** *Opprobrious* means scornful or abusive, so the opposite is complimentary or laudatory. *Calumnious* is a synonym. *Disreputable* is a synonym for a secondary meaning of *opprobrious,* so that's a trap answer. If you know that *opprobrious* is negative, you know you need a positive answer. *Disreputable*, *salacious*, and *calumnious* are negative and *endemic* is neutral, so eliminate them. You may recognize the root of *encomiastic* in "*encomium*," which means "praise." *Encomiastic* means expressing praise, so the best answer is choice (B).

16. **E** *Baleful* means menacing or foreboding evil, so the opposite means predicting something good. *Malefic* is a synonym. *Salubrious* means promoting health, so it's not quite right. If you know that *baleful* is negative, you know you need a positive answer. *Malefic* is negative and *recumbent* is neutral, so you can eliminate choices (B) and (D). *Propitious* means favorable, so the best answer is choice (E).

17. **D** A secondary definition of *flag* is to mark something or draw attention to it, so the opposite is to take attention away or conceal. *Dissemble* means to disguise or draw attention away from, so the best answer is choice (D).

18. **E** *Veritable* means authentic, so the opposite is inauthentic. *Indubitable* is a synonym. *Caustic* means harsh or biting, so it's not right. If you know that *veritable* is positive, then you know you need a negative answer. *Indubitable* is positive, and *ambiguous* is neutral, so eliminate choices (A) and (D). *Spurious* means inauthentic, so the best answer is choice (E).

19. **B** *Peripatetic* means walking about or nomadic, so the opposite is staying still. *Itinerant* is a synonym. *Awe-inspiring* is a trap answer, in case *peripatetic* makes you think of pathetic. If you're not sure of the stem word, the prefix *peri-* may be some help here; it means "around" which may help you realize that the stem word has something to do with motion, so the antonym may have something to do with stillness. *Sedentary* means staying still, so the best answer is choice (B).

20. **A** *Cake* means to thicken, so the opposite is to make less thick. *Limn* means to draw with lines; this word doesn't have a clear opposite, so eliminate choice (D). *Attenuate* means to make thin or weak, so the best answer is choice (A).

Drill 5

1. **C** *Vague* means not definite, so the opposite is definite. *Murky* is a synonym. *Absolute* means with certainty, so it's not quite right. *Concrete* means definite, so the best answer is choice (C).

2. **B** *Tainted* means contaminated, so the opposite is pure. *Contaminated* is a synonym. *Uncorrupted* means pure, so the best answer is choice (B).

3. **E** *Pungency* means having a harsh quality, so the opposite is blandness. *Acridity* is a synonym. *Insipidness* means blandness, so the best answer is choice (E).

4. **E** *Dispersion* is the scattering of something, so the opposite is consolidation. *Dissipation* is a synonym. *Amalgamation* means consolidation, so the best answer is choice (E).

5. **C** A *fledgling* is an inexperienced person, so the opposite is an experienced person. *Novice* is a synonym. A *veteran* is an experienced person, so the best answer is choice (C).

6. **D** *Sparse* means spread out, so the opposite is dense. If you're having trouble, try working backwards to see whether your antonyms for the answer choices could mean *sparse*. *Serried* means dense, so the best answer is choice (D).

7. **A** *Mitigate* means to make less severe, so the opposite is to make more severe. *Allay* is a synonym. If you're not sure of the stem word, try word association. "Mitigating circumstances" might make punishment less severe, so *mitigate* means to lessen the severity of. *Exacerbate* means to make worse, so the best answer is choice (A).

8. **D** *Palpability* is the ability to be perceived or felt, so the opposite is the inability to be perceived or felt. *Discernibleness* is a synonym. *Abstruseness* is the inability to be understood, so choice (E) is not quite right. If you know that *palpability* is on the neutral side, you can eliminate answers that are clearly positive or negative. *Magnanimity* is positive and *abstruseness* is negative. *Intangibility* is the inability to be felt, so the best answer is choice (D).

9. **B** *Occluded* means blocked, so the opposite is free from obstruction. *Obstructed* is a synonym. If you're not sure of the stem word, you may be able to use word association if you've heard the word *occlusion* at the dentist; it means aligning the upper and lower teeth. *Unimpeded* means unobstructed, so the best answer is choice (B).

10. **C** *Penchant* means strong inclination or liking, so the opposite is aversion. *Proclivity* is a synonym. If you know that *penchant* is positive, you know you need a negative word. *Flair* and *proclivity* are positive and *mode* is neutral, so you can eliminate choices (A), (B), and (E). *Repugnance* means aversion, so the best answer is choice (C).

11. **A** *Polemical* means controversial, so the opposite is not controversial. *Disputable* is a synonym. If you know that *polemical* is negative, you know the correct answer must be positive. *Imminent* is neutral and *untenable* and *disputable* are negative; eliminate choices (B), (D), and (E). *Unequivocal* means not disputable, so the best answer is choice (A).

12. **A** *Germane* means relevant, so the opposite is irrelevant. *Apposite* is a synonym. If you know that *germane* is positive, you know you need a negative word. *Tractable, cogent, corrigible*, and *apposite* are all positive, so you can eliminate choices (B), (C), (D), and (E). *Extraneous* means irrelevant, so the best answer is choice (A).

13.   C   The verb meaning of *steep* is to immerse or saturate, so the opposite is to dry out. *Steep* has a common meaning as a sharp incline, but all of the answer choices are verbs. *Suffuse* is a synonym. *Level* is a trap in case you're thinking of the primary meaning of *steep*. *Desiccate* means to dry out, so the best answer is choice (C).

14.   C   *Loquacious* means talkative, so the opposite is not talkative. *Garrulous* is a synonym. *Inarticulate* means not well spoken, so it's not quite right. If you're not sure of the stem word, you may be able to guess its meaning using roots. The root "*loq*" means word or speech, so *loquacious* must have something to do with speech. *Taciturn* means not talkative, so the best answer is choice (C).

15.   D   *Peruse* means to examine carefully, so the opposite is to skim. *Scrutinize* and *inspect* are synonyms and special trap answers, because *peruse* is commonly misunderstood to mean skim. Also, if two different answers mean the same thing, it is unlikely that either is correct, so eliminate choices (C) and (E). *Rifle* is also a trap answer, because you may think of rifling through someone's things. *Skate* means to skim or briefly glance through, so the best answer is choice (D).

16.   B   *Ripe* means not fully formed, so the opposite is fully formed. *Emergent* is a synonym. A secondary definition of *inchoate* is fully formed, so the best answer is choice (B).

17.   B   *Veneration* means great honor, so the opposite is disrespect. *Reverence* is a synonym. *Antipathy* is a strong feeling of dislike, so it's not quite right. If you know that *veneration* is positive, you know you need a negative answer. *Reverence* and *apotheosis* are positive, so eliminate choices (C) and (D). *Impudence* means disrespect, so the best answer is choice (B).

18.   C   *Chary* means wary or cautious, so the opposite is reckless or rash. *Circumspect* is a synonym. *Insouciant* is very close, but it means carefree or nonchalant, so it's not quite right. Similarly, *dauntless* and *intrepid*, both of which mean fearless, are not quite right; because they both mean the same thing, it is unlikely that either of them is the answer. *Precipitate* means recklessly daring, so the best answer is choice (C).

19.   D   *Obloquy* means disgrace or infamy, so the opposite is high regard. *Ignominy* is a synonym. *Approbation* means approval, so it's not quite right. If you know that *obloquy* is negative, you know you need a positive answer. *Peroration* and *perigee* are neutral and *ignominy* is negative; eliminate choices (A), (B), and (C). *Esteem* means high regard, so the best answer is choice (D).

20.   C   *Tenuous* means weak or flimsy, so the opposite is not flimsy or strong. *Insubstantial* is a synonym. *Imposing* means impressive, so it's not quite right. If you're not sure what *tenuous* means, try using word association. You may have heard about someone having a *tenuous* grasp on things, meaning a weak grasp, so look for an antonym that means strong. *Puissant* means powerful, so the best answer is choice (C).

Drill 6

1. **D** *Insert* means to put in, so the opposite is to remove. *Inject* is a synonym. *Withdraw* means to remove, so the best answer is choice (D).

2. **D** *Stability* means staying the same, so the opposite is changing. *Permanence* is a synonym. *Fluctuation* means changing, so the best answer is choice (D).

3. **A** *Aerate* means to air out, so the opposite is to keep air in. *Ventilate* is a synonym. *Smother* means to keep air in, so the best answer is choice (A).

4. **B** An *ally* is a supporter, so the opposite is an enemy. *Comrade* is synonym. A *foe* is an enemy, so the best answer is choice (B).

5. **E** *Fallacious* means illogical or invalid, so the opposite is logically sound or well-founded. *Erroneous* is a synonym. *Valid* means logically sound, so the best answer is choice (E).

6. **D** *Hyperbole* means exaggeration, so the opposite is understatement. *Overstatement* is a synonym. If you're not sure of the answer choices, try using roots; "*equi*" means equal and "*voc*" means voice, so you can eliminate choice (A). The root "*anim*" means spirit, so *equanimity* means something close to equal spirit (in actuality, even-tempered), so you can eliminate choice (E). The root "*ver*" means truth and *veraciousness* means accuracy, so choice (C) is not quite right. *Minimization* is close to understatement, so the best answer is choice (D).

7. **E** *Diffident* means shy, so the opposite is outgoing. *Demure* is a synonym. *Refulgent* means shining brightly. *Effusive* means expressive, so it's not quite right. *Truculent* means fierce, so choice (B) isn't right either. *Gregarious* means sociable, so choice (E) is the best answer.

8. **E** *Comeliness* means attractiveness, so the opposite is ugliness. *Exodus* and *inaccessibility* are traps, because you might be guessing based on the root "*come*" in the stem word. If you know that *comeliness* is positive, you know you need a negative word. *Propriety* is positive and *exodus* is neutral, so you can eliminate choices (A) and (B). *Homeliness* means ugliness, so the best answer is choice (E).

9. **E** *Deride* means to mock, so the opposite is to praise. *Gibe* is a synonym. *Bolster* means to provide support, so choice (A) is not quite right. If you know *deride* is negative, you know you need a positive word. *Censure*, *goad*, and *gibe* are all negative, so you can eliminate choices (B), (C), and (D). *Laud* means to praise, so the best answer is choice (E).

10. **A** *Perennial* means perpetual or everlasting, so the opposite is temporary or fleeting. *Seasonal* is a trap, because it may make you think of *perennial* plants. If you're not sure what the stem word means, try working backwards. The root "*cent*" in *centennial* should make you think 100; that does not have a clear opposite, so eliminate choice (E). The opposites of *seasonal*, *diffuse*, and *distrait* don't match the stem, so you can eliminate choices (B), (C), and (D). *Ephemeral* means temporary or fleeting, so the best answer is choice (A).

11.   C   *Assuage* means to soothe, so the opposite is to agitate. *Placate* is a synonym. *Belittle* means to portrey or regard as less impressive, so it's not quite right. If you know *assuage* is positive, you know you need a negative word. *Placate* and *beatify* are positive, so eliminate choices (A) and (D). *Nettle* means to provoke, so the best answer is choice (C).

12.   A   *Disaffect* means to alienate affection or loyalty, so the opposite is to make closer or friendlier. *Estrange* is a synonym. If you know *disaffect* is negative, then you know you need a positive answer. *Maunder*, *estrange*, and *malinger* are all negative, so you can eliminate choices (C), (D), and (E). A secondary meaning of *allure* is to attract, but that's not quite right, so eliminate (B). *Conciliate* means to win over or reconcile, so the best answer is choice (A).

13.   E   *Hegemony* is the consistent dominance of one state over another, so the opposite is deference to another state. *Prepotency* and *paramountcy* are both synonyms of *hegemony*, so eliminate choices (B) and (D). *Obsequiousness* is excessively deferential behavior, so it's not quite right. *Subordinance* means deference to another state or person, so the best answer is choice (E).

14.   D   *Hapless* means unlucky, so the opposite is lucky. *Ill-fated* is a synonym. *Opportunistic* means to take advantage of an opportune moment, so it's not quite right. If you know that *hapless* is negative, you know you need a positive answer. *Profligate*, *ill-fated*, and *refractory* are negative, so you can eliminate choices (B), (C), and (E). Guess the hardest/weirdest word. *Providential* means lucky, so the best answer is choice (D).

15.   E   *Castigation* means harsh criticism, so the opposite is praise. *Excoriation* is a synonym. *Obeisance* means deference or homage, so it's not quite right. If you know that *castigation* is negative, you know you need a positive word. *Reconnaissance* is neutral, and *excoriation* and *expurgation* are negative, so you can eliminate choices (A), (B), and (D). *Encomium* means high praise, so the best answer is choice (E).

16.   E   *Antipathy* is a feeling of intense dislike or aversion, so the opposite is a feeling of great affection. *Enmity* is a synonym. *Delectation* means great enjoyment, so it's not quite right. *Apathy* is a trap answer, in case the "*path*" in *antipathy* reminds you of the "*path*" in *apathy*. If you are unsure of the stem word's definition, use its roots; "*anti*" means against and "*path*" means feelings. (Think of words such as empathy and sympathy.) Therefore, *antipathy* must mean something like against feelings, and its opposite must mean something like for feelings. *Adoration* means great affection, so the best answer is choice (B).

17.   B   *Ebullience* means intense enthusiasm, so the opposite is lacking enthusiasm. *Effervescence* is a synonym. Choice (D) is a trap answer, in case the "*cow*" in *cowling* reminds you of the "*bull*" in *ebullience*. If you know that *ebullience* is positive, you know you need a negative answer. *Effervescence* is positive and *cowling* is neutral, so you can eliminate choices (C) and (D). *Tepidness* means lacking enthusiasm, so the best answer is choice (B).

18. D *Sedulous* means hard working, so the opposite is lazy. *Assiduous* is a synonym. *Languorous* means listless, so it's not quite right. If you know that *sedulous* is positive, you know you need a negative answer. *Assiduous* is positive, *pellucid* is positive (or neutral, depending on the context), and *peripatetic* is neutral, so you can eliminate choices (B), (C), and (E). *Indolent* means lazy, so the best answer is choice (D).

19. E A *diatribe* is a speech of harsh denunciation, so the opposite is a speech of praise. *Fulmination* is a synonym. A *filibuster* is a long speech, but not necessarily a speech of praise, so choice (A) is not quite right. *Elegy* and *allocution* are also related to speech, but neither means a speech of praise, so eliminate choices (B) and (C). A *panegyric* is a speech of praise, so the best answer is choice (E).

20. C A *sinecure* is a job that pays well but requires little work, so the opposite is a position that requires hard work for little pay. If you don't know *sinecure*, try breaking it down by its roots; "*sin*" or "*sine*" means without and "*cure*" means care, or concern, like in the words cure and curator. Thus, *sinecure* means something like without care and the opposite means with great care. Otherwise, guess the hardest/weirdest word. *Moil* means tedious, unpleasant, or menial work, so the best answer is choice (C).

Drill 7

1. D *Global* means universal, so the opposite is local. *Comprehensive* is a synonym. *Provincial* means local, so the best answer is choice (D).

2. D *Repulsion* means feeling an aversion towards something, so the opposite is feeling an attraction toward something. *Disgust* is a synonym. *Attraction* is what we want, so the best answer is choice (D).

3. C *Loll* means to lounge or to hang loosely, so the opposite is to remain erect. *Recline lazily* is a synonym. *Sit stiffly* means to remain erect, so the best answer is choice (C).

4. C *Fringe* means edge or border, so the opposite is center. *Periphery* is a synonym. *Hub* means center, so the best answer is choice (C).

5. A *Serrated* means saw toothed, so the opposite is smooth. *Jagged* is a synonym. *Smooth* is what you're looking for, so the best answer is choice (A).

6. C *Elasticity* means flexibility, so the opposite is rigidity. *Pliancy* is a synonym. *Dogmatism* means stubborn adherence to insufficiently proved beliefs, so it's not quite right. If you're not sure of the answer choices, try using roots. *Fid* in *fidelity* means faith, so choice (A) is not quite right. *Intransigence* has the prefix *in-* meaning not and the base *trans* meaning moving across. Intransigence means inflexibility, so the best answer is choice (C).

7.   D   *Sap* means to weaken the vitality of, so the opposite is to energize. *Enervate* is a synonym. *Bolster* means to support, so it's not quite right. *Defoliate* is a trap answer, because you may be thinking of tree *sap*, which is a noun, not a verb. If you know that *sap* is negative, you know you need a positive word. *Defoliate* and *enervate* are negative, so you can eliminate choices (B) and (C). *Invigorate* means to energize, so the best answer is choice (D).

8.   D   *Arrhythmic* means without rhythm, so the opposite means having rhythm. *Erratic* is a synonym and *symphonic* is a trap answer. You may be able to guess the meaning of *arrhythmic* if you know that the prefix "*a-*" means without. *Cadenced* means having rhythm, so the best answer is choice (D).

9.   D   *Burgeon* means to grow rapidly or blossom, so the opposite is to decline or decrease in number. *Flourish* is a synonym. If you notice that choices (A) and (D) are opposites, you know there is a fairly good chance that one of them is the correct answer. *Ebb* means to decline or decrease, so the best answer is choice (D).

10.   E   *Indigence* means poverty, so the opposite is wealth. *Penury* is a synonym. If you know *indigence* is negative, you know your answer needs to be positive. *Penury* and *duplicity* are negative and *ambiguity* is neutral, so you can eliminate choices (A), (B), and (D). Of the remaining two, *nonchalance* is not as strongly positive as *affluence*, so eliminate choice (C). *Affluence* means wealth, so the best answer is choice (E).

11.   A   *Desiccate* means to dry out, so the opposite is to fill with fluid. *Parch* is a synonym. *Deluge* means to flood, so it's not quite right; eliminate choices (C) and (E). *Satiate* means to satisfy, so it doesn't work either. *Saturate* means to fill with fluid, so the best answer is choice (A).

12.   C   *Forestall* means to prevent from happening, so the opposite is to cause to happen. *Thwart* is a synonym. *Embark* means to start something, so it's not quite right; eliminate choices (B) and (E). If you're not sure about the stem word, you may be able to guess its meaning by looking at the root "*stall*" in *forestall*. *Precipitate* means to cause to happen, so the best answer is choice (C).

13.   B   *Recondite* means concealed or difficult to understand, so the opposite is obvious or easy to understand. *Abstruse* is a synonym. If you know that *recondite* is negative, you know you need a positive answer. *Monotonous*, *abstruse*, and *benighted* are negative, so eliminate choices (A), (C), and (E). *Lucid* means easily understood, so the best answer is choice (B).

14.   E   *Abjure* means to renounce or retract, so the opposite is to affirm. *Recant* is a synonym. If you don't know the stem word, you could still eliminate a*bnegate*; it has the same prefix as the stem, so it probably has a meaning that is similar to (instead of opposite of) *abjure*. Guess the hardest/weirdest word. *Asseverate* means to affirm, so the best answer is choice (E).

15. **A** *Rue* means regret, so the opposite means celebrate. *Lament* is a synonym. If you've heard the expression "rue the day," you may know that *rue* is negative. The correct answer must be positive, so eliminate choices (B) and (C), which are negative, and choices (D) and (E), which are neutral. *Exult* means rejoice over, so the best answer is choice (A).

16. **D** *Surfeit* means excess, so the opposite is scarcity. *Superfluity* is a synonym. *Modicum* means a small amount, not necessarily scarcity, so it's not quite right; eliminate choices (A) and (B). If you're not sure what *surfeit* means, you may recognize the prefix *sur-* from words like surplus and surtax; thus, *surfeit* must mean something like extra, and its opposite must mean something like not enough. *Dearth* means scarcity, so the best answer is choice (D).

17. **A** *Perfidy* means betrayal or breach of faith, so the opposite is continuation of faith. *Treachery* is a synonym. If you're not sure what *perfidy* means, try using roots; *per* means against and *fid* means faith, as seen in the word fidelity. If the stem word means to go against faith, then the correct answer must mean to support faith. *Staunchness* means steadfast or true, so the best answer is choice (A).

18. **A** *Hoodwink* means to deceive, so the opposite is to undeceive. *Cozen* is a synonym. *Apprise* means to inform, so it's not quite right. If you know *hoodwink* is negative, you know you need a positive answer. *Cozen*, *digress*, and *calumniate* are negative; eliminate choices (B), (D), and (E). *Disabuse* means to undeceive, so the best answer is choice (A).

19. **B** A secondary meaning of *nice* is showing great precision, so the opposite is inexact. If you do not recognize this meaning for *nice*, you can try to work backwards. *Adjunct* means next to, so its opposite is far away from; eliminate choice (A). The opposite of *lost* is found, so eliminate choice (C). *Terse* means not using many words, so the opposite is talkative; eliminate choice (D). *Dull* means boring or lacking brilliance, so its opposite is interesting or brilliant; eliminate choice (E). A secondary meaning for the word *free* is inexact, so the correct answer is choice (B).

20. **D** *Apotheosis* means glorification, so the opposite is degradation. *Exaltation* is a synonym. *Ostracism* means banishment or exclusion, so it's not quite right. If you don't know *apotheosis*, try using roots. *Theo* means god, so *apotheosis* must mean something lofty, and its opposite must mean something low. *Abasement* means degradation, so the best answer is choice (D).

Math

Plugging In & PITA

PLUGGING IN

Math on the GRE can be quite simple. A question may give you the price of an item and the amount of money to be used and then ask you to figure out how much change should be given. What makes it difficult, however, is that the price will be given as x cents and the amount to be spent as y dollars. In other words, the numbers will be expressed as abstract symbols, a.k.a. algebra; x dollars is an algebraic concept. It is far more difficult to think about and to manipulate x dollars (What do you do with the decimal?), than the actual quantity of $10. Anytime a symbol appears on the test, it can be replaced by a number. When you do this, what was abstract and fuzzy instantly becomes concrete and easy to work with.

Example:

> Eleven years ago, Lauren was half as old as Mike will be in 4 years. If Mike is m years old now, how old is Lauren now in terms of m ?
>
> ⬭ $4m - 11$
>
> ⬭ $\frac{1}{2}(m + 4) + 11$
>
> ⬭ $\frac{1}{2}(m - 11)$
>
> ⬭ $4m + \frac{11}{2}$
>
> ⬭ $2m - 7$

No one has ever heard of someone being m years old. To turn this from an abstract problem of algebra, back into a simple problem of arithmetic, replace the variable with an actual number. In this case, try 10. The question asks you to find out how old Lauren is now. If you set Mike's age to 10, it's not too difficult to figure out how old he will be in four years, and then to figure out that Lauren was half as old as that, eleven years ago. If Mike is 10, Lauren is now 18. This is what you were asked to find; therefore, 18 is your Target Number. In the answer choices, when you replace all m's with 10, the correct answer should equal 18.

The answers now look like this.

⬭ $4(10) - 11 = 29$

⬭ $\frac{1}{2}(10 + 4) + 11 = 18$

⬭ $\frac{1}{2}(10 - 11) = -\frac{1}{2}$

⬭ $4(10) + \frac{11}{2} = 45.5$

⬭ $2(10) - 7 = 13$

Only one of them is equal to 18. That is the correct answer. This technique is called Plugging In.

When you see variables in the answer choices, Plug In.

Once you have recognized this opportunity, you can set up your scratch paper.

It should look like this.

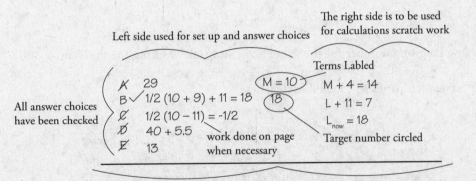

Here are some elements of this set-up to note.

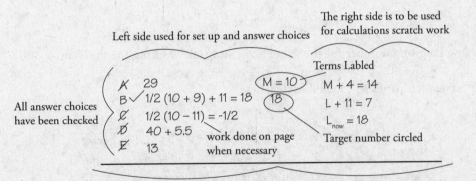

Left side used for set up and answer choices

The right side is to be used for calculations scratch work

Terms Labled

All answer choices have been checked

work done on page when necessary

Target number circled

Line drawn underneath problem so that next problem can be started on clean space

When you are Plugging In for a multiple choice question, you must have your terms labeled and a target number circled. This all happens on your scratch paper. The minute you see variables, write down the answer choices and Plug In.

Try to Plug In nice happy numbers that will make your life easier. Avoid Plugging In 1 or 0, not because they are wrong, but only because they may lead to multiple correct answers. If this happens, it's not a big deal. Just change your Plug In number, and check the remaining answer choices.

Plugging In is equally effective on Quantitative Comparisons. In this case, your response should be just as automatic. When that problem pops up, the minute you see that it is Quant Comp and it includes variables, make your set up. You do this even before you have read and understood the problem. It is an automatic response. See variables, make set up.

Example

> Wendy purchased n napkins and Juan purchased 2 fewer than half as many napkins as Wendy.
>
> <u>Column A</u>   <u>Column B</u>
>
> The number of napkins $\dfrac{n-4}{2}$
> Juan purchased
>
> ◯   The quantity in Column A is greater.
> ◯   The quantity in Column B is greater.
> ◯   The two quantities are equal.
> ◯   The relationship cannot be determined
>   from the information given.

Before you have even read the problem your hand should be moving. Your set up should look like this.

$$\underline{A} \quad\quad A\ B\ C\ D \quad\quad \underline{B}$$

$$n =$$

$$n =$$

$$n =$$

Now Plug In a number for the variable, *n*, and start working the problem.

Your scratch paper will look like this.

$$\underline{A} \quad A\ \cancel{B}\ \textcircled{C}\ \cancel{D} \quad \underline{B} \quad\quad \text{half Wendy} = 5 \quad 2\overline{)\,196}$$
$$3 \quad n = 10 \quad 3 \quad\quad 200 - 4 = 196 \quad\quad 16$$
$$-2 \quad n = 0 \quad -2 \quad\quad \text{half Wendy} = \cancel{100}\ 4$$
$$98 \quad n = 200 \quad 98$$

Here are some things to note.

$$\frac{A}{}$$

A $\cancel{B}$ $\textcircled{C}$ D

half wendy = S

$\frac{A}{}$ n = 10 $\frac{B}{}$ 200 − 4 = 196   2$\overline{)196}$

3   n = 10   3

−2   n = 0   −2   half wendy = 1̶0̶0̶ ̶4   16

98   n = 200   98

On a regular Plugging In problem, use numbers that are easy to work with and calculate. On Quant Comp you must always Plug In more than once. Your first Plug In will be something simple, like 2 or 10. Plug in something nice and easy and then eliminate. If B is bigger, eliminate choices (A) and (C). If they are both the same, eliminate choices (A) and (B). Remember that choice (A) means that Column A is always larger, *no matter what numbers you Plug In for the variables.* That means that you have to Plug In all kinds of weird stuff to make sure that Column A always stays larger. For your second and third Plug In, look for numbers that will generate a different answer. If after your first Plug In you are left with choices (B) and (D), try to prove choice (B) wrong. If you can Plug In something that makes Column B smaller than Column A, then you can eliminate and the answer is choice (D). If you can't, then the answer is choice (B). In other words, when Plugging In on Quant Comp, you are trying to find out whether choice (D)—which really means that neither A, B, nor C is always correct—is the correct answer. If you can't prove choice (D), then the remaining answer choice is the correct answer. You prove choice (D) by Plugging In different types of numbers and eliminating answer choices as you go. These include **Z**ero, **O**ne, **N**egative numbers, **E**xtremely large numbers, and **F**ractions. ZONEF is a mental checklist to help you remember what to Plug In. If you continue to get choices (A), (B), or (C)—after plugging in everything listed in ZONEF—then that's your answer.

For a more thorough explanation of Plugging In, check our student friendly guidebook *Cracking the GRE* book.

PITA (PLUGGING IN THE ANSWERS)

ETS has given you the answers, which makes the test easier. On a multiple-choice test, one of those answer choices has to be correct; therefore, you can use the answer choices to solve the problem.

Example.

> Vicken, Roger, and Adam went to buy a $90 radio. If Roger agrees to pay twice as much as Adam, and Vicken agrees to pay three times as much as Adam, how much must Roger pay?
>
> ○ 10
> ○ 20
> ○ 30
> ○ 45
> ○ 65

One of those answer choices must be the correct one. Pick the one in the middle, assume that it is correct, and use that number to work the rest of the problem in bite-sized pieces. The question asks you how much Roger must pay, so label the answer choices "Roger." This is your first column. For every additional step in the problem, make and label an additional column on your scratch paper.

It should look like this:

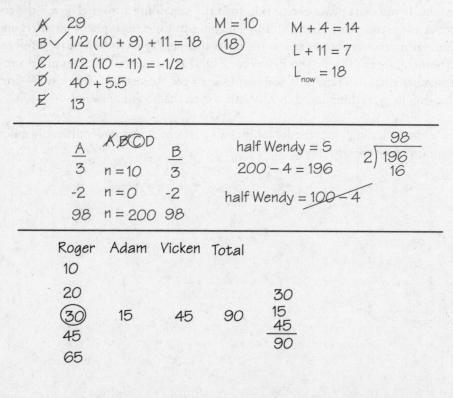

You've set up a small spreadsheet using the steps of the problem as your column headings. Once you have made your set-up, the thinking is done for you. All you have to do is fill it in until you come up with an answer choice that works. In this case, according to the question, if Roger pays $30, Adam will pay half that, or $15. Vicken pays three times the amount that Adam does, or $45. The three together pay $90. The radio costs $90, so it works, and you're done. Only one answer choice will work; therefore, when you find it, you are done, and you don't have to check the others.

The only tricky thing about this technique is recognizing the opportunity. If the question asks, "How much," "How many," or "What is the value of," Plug In The Answers. If you have specific numbers in the answer choices, and you find yourself oddly compelled to make a formula, Plug In The Answers. Once you recognize the opportunity, get your hand moving and write down the answer choices on the left side of your scratch paper. This is your first column; label it. At this point, you are already halfway into the problem. No time spent thinking; no time spent wondering how to go about solving it. Before you even fully understand the problem, you are already halfway to the answer.

STRATEGY SUMMARY

Once you spot the opportunity, whether you are Plugging In the Answers or Plugging In for variables in the question, the technique begins with recognizing the opportunity and ends with your scratch paper. Variables in the answer choices are a trigger that should provoke the instant response of writing out your answer choices and labeling your terms. You should do this before you have even fully read the question because it will help organize your approach, give you a place to park the information, and set you up to succeed on the problem, no matter how difficult the problem is. The same is true for Plugging In the Answers. The hardest part is recognizing the opportunity. Once you see the phrase "How Much," "How Many," or "What is the Value of," write out A, B, C, D, and E on your scratch paper, label the first column, and assume choice (C) to be the correct answer. Once you do this, you are already halfway through the problem. You must get your hand moving and make your set ups on the scratch paper. When you get good at it, this will become an automatic habit and even the hardest problems will unfold quickly and accurately. Remember that practice and repetition make the habit, and scratch paper ensures that it happens, and happens correctly.

PLUGGING IN DRILL

The profit from selling y units of a product is given by the formula $4y - 2$. $y \neq 0$

Column A	Column B
4 times the profit from selling y units	$16y - 4$

○ Quantity in Column A is greater.
○ Quantity in Column B is greater.
○ The two quantities are equal.
○ The relationship cannot be determined from the information given.

J is the set of all fractions in the form of $\dfrac{a}{a^2}$, where $a \neq 0$.

Column A	Column B
a (any member of set J)	1

○ The quantity in Column A is greater.
○ The quantity in Column B is greater.
○ The two quantities are equal.
○ The relationship cannot be determined from the information given.

$$x^3 = 27$$
$$y^2 = 16$$

Column A	Column B
x	y

○ The quantity in Column A is greater.
○ The quantity in Column B is greater.
○ The two quantities are equal.
○ The relationship cannot be determined from the information given.

$$x > y > 0$$

Column A	Column B
$4x$	$5y$

○ The quantity in Column A is greater.
○ The quantity in Column B is greater.
○ The two quantities are equal.
○ The relationship cannot be determined from the information given.

If $7(q - r) = 10$, what is q in terms of r ?

○ $r + \dfrac{10}{7}$

○ $r - \dfrac{10}{7}$

○ $7r + 10$

○ $10 - 7r$

○ $7r + \dfrac{10}{7}$

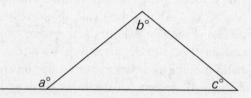

In the figure above, what is a in terms of b and c ?

○ $180 - (b + c)$
○ $180 + (b + c)$
○ $(b + c)$
○ $(b + c) - 180$
○ $(b + c) + 180$

Column A	Column B
$3a^5$	$(3a)^5$

- ◯ The quantity in Column A is greater.
- ◯ The quantity in Column B is greater.
- ◯ The two quantities are equal.
- ◯ The relationship cannot be determined from the information given.

$$2a = 12 - 2b$$
$$2a = -8 + 2b$$

Column A	Column B
a	b

- ◯ The quantity in Column A is greater.
- ◯ The quantity in Column B is greater.
- ◯ The two quantities are equal.
- ◯ The relationship cannot be determined from the information given.

$$0 < a < 3$$
$$-3 < b < 0$$

a and b are integers.

Column A	Column B
$a + b$	$a - b$

- ◯ The quantity in Column A is greater.
- ◯ The quantity in Column B is greater.
- ◯ The two quantities are equal.
- ◯ The relationship cannot be determined from the information given.

$$0 < a < b < 1$$

Column A	Column B
0	$2(a - b)$

- ◯ The quantity in Column A is greater.
- ◯ The quantity in Column B is greater.
- ◯ The two quantities are equal.
- ◯ The relationship cannot be determined from the information given.

Rachel, David, and Kristen decide to pool their money to buy a video game system. David contributes 4 dollars more than twice what Kristen does, and Kristen contributes 3 dollars less than Rachel does. If Rachel contributes r dollars, then, in terms of r, how much does David contribute?

- ◯ $\dfrac{r - 7}{2}$
- ◯ $\dfrac{r - 2}{2}$
- ◯ $\dfrac{2r + 7}{2}$
- ◯ $2r - 2$
- ◯ $2r + 7$

If $x \neq 0$ and $y = \dfrac{x + 1}{x} - 1$, what is $\dfrac{1}{y}$?

- ◯ x
- ◯ $\dfrac{1}{x}$
- ◯ $-x + 1$
- ◯ $\dfrac{x + 1}{x - 1}$
- ◯ $-(x + 1)$

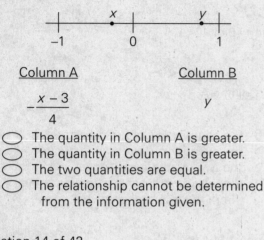

Column A	Column B
$-\dfrac{x-3}{4}$	y

○ The quantity in Column A is greater.
○ The quantity in Column B is greater.
○ The two quantities are equal.
○ The relationship cannot be determined from the information given.

Column A	Column B
$x + y - 1$	$x - y + 1$

○ The quantity in Column A is greater.
○ The quantity in Column B is greater.
○ The two quantities are equal.
○ The relationship cannot be determined from the information given.

$$x > 1$$

Column A	Column B
$5^x + 1$	6^x

○ The quantity in Column A is greater.
○ The quantity in Column B is greater.
○ The two quantities are equal.
○ The relationship cannot be determined from the information given.

At a crafts supply store, the price of a type of decorative string is c cents per foot. At this rate, what would be the price, in dollars, of y yards of this string?

○ $\dfrac{cy}{300}$

○ $\dfrac{100}{3cy}$

○ $\dfrac{3y}{100c}$

○ $\dfrac{3cy}{100}$

○ $\dfrac{300}{cy}$

$$x^2 = |y|$$

Column A	Column B
$|x|$	y

○ The quantity in Column A is greater.
○ The quantity in Column B is greater.
○ The two quantities are equal.
○ The relationship cannot be determined from the information given.

Column A	Column B
$\dfrac{a+b+c}{5}$	$\dfrac{1}{5ab} + \dfrac{c}{5}$

○ The quantity in Column A is greater.
○ The quantity in Column B is greater.
○ The two quantities are equal.
○ The relationship cannot be determined from the information given.

Going into the last exam, a student has an average test score of x. The student scored $x + 12$ on his last test.

Column A	Column B
The student's overall average with a total of 5 exams	The student's overall average with a total of 7 exams

○ The quantity in Column A is greater.
○ The quantity in Column B is greater.
○ The two quantities are equal.
○ The relationship cannot be determined from the information given.

If a and b are positive and $\dfrac{ab}{x} = \sqrt{a}$, then $\dfrac{x}{\sqrt{b}} =$

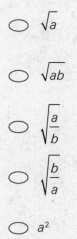

○ $\sqrt{a}$

○ $\sqrt{ab}$

○ $\sqrt{\dfrac{a}{b}}$

○ $\sqrt{\dfrac{b}{a}}$

○ a^2

If m is an odd integer, which of the following expresses the number of even integers between m and $2m$ inclusive?

○ $\dfrac{m}{2} + 1$

○ $\dfrac{m}{2} - 1$

○ $\dfrac{m+1}{2}$

○ $\dfrac{m-1}{2}$

○ $2m + 1$

$$\frac{4+5}{5} > \frac{4}{5y}$$

Column A	Column B
$\dfrac{8}{9y}$	2

○ The quantity in Column A is greater.
○ The quantity in Column B is greater.
○ The two quantities are equal.
○ The relationship cannot be determined from the information given.

$$x < 0 < y$$
x and y are integers.

Column A	Column B
$-\dfrac{w}{x}$	$\dfrac{y}{w}$

○ The quantity in Column A is greater.
○ The quantity in Column B is greater.
○ The two quantities are equal.
○ The relationship cannot be determined from the information given.

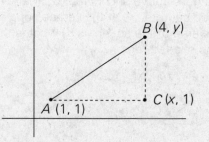

Line AB has a slope of 1.

Column A	Column B
x	y

○ The quantity in Column A is greater.
○ The quantity in Column B is greater.
○ The two quantities are equal.
○ The relationship cannot be determined from the information given.

Two children named Peter and Wanda are playing a number game. If Peter's number z is 200 percent of Wanda's number, what is 20 percent of Wanda's number, in terms of z ?

○ $10z$

○ $2z$

○ $\dfrac{z}{5}$

○ $\dfrac{z}{10}$

○ $\dfrac{z}{20}$

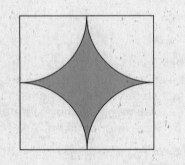

The figure above shows four quarter circles whose centers are at the vertices of a square. If the area of the square is K, what is the area of the shaded region?

○ $\dfrac{4-\pi}{4}K$

○ $\dfrac{\pi-2}{\pi}K$

○ $\dfrac{4-\pi}{2}K$

○ $\dfrac{\pi-2}{2}K$

○ $\dfrac{2}{\pi}K$

What is the area of a circle whose circumference is x ?

○ $\dfrac{x^2}{4\pi}$

○ $\dfrac{x^2}{2\pi}$

○ $\dfrac{x}{4\pi}$

○ $\dfrac{x}{2\pi}$

○ $2\sqrt{\pi x}$

A rectangle has length $2x$ and width x. If each diagonal of the rectangle has length d, what is the area of the rectangle, in terms of d ?

○ $\dfrac{2}{5}d$

○ $\dfrac{5}{2}d$

○ $\dfrac{4}{25}d^2$

○ $\dfrac{2}{5}d^2$

○ $\dfrac{5}{2}d^2$

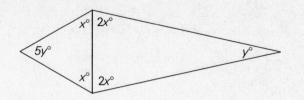

In the figure above, which one of the following is true?

○ $x = 2y$
○ $y = 2x$
○ $x + y = 80$
○ $x - y = 30$
○ $x = y$

$$130 < x < 150$$

Column A	Column B
the greatest odd factor of x	the greatest even factor of x

○ The quantity in Column A is greater.
○ The quantity in Column B is greater.
○ The two quantities are equal.
○ The relationship cannot be determined from the information given.

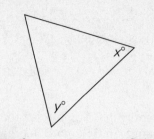

Column A	Column B
$358 - 2(x + y)$	$180 - (x + y)$

○ The quantity in Column A is greater.
○ The quantity in Column B is greater.
○ The two quantities are equal.
○ The relationship cannot be determined from the information given.

$$pq \neq 0$$

Column A	Column B
$(p + q)^3$	$p^3 + q^3$

○ The quantity in A is greater.
○ The quantity in B is greater.
○ The two quantities are equal.
○ The relationship cannot be determined from the information given.

$\dfrac{y^2}{x^{12}}$ is an integer, $y > x > 1$.

Column A	Column B
x^2	$\sqrt{y}$

◯ The quantity in Column A is greater.
◯ The quantity in Column B is greater.
◯ The two quantities are equal.
◯ The relationship cannot be determined
   from the information given.

Let x, y, and z be non-zero numbers such that the average (arithmetic mean) of x and twice y is equal to the average (arithmetic mean) of y and twice z. What is the average (arithmetic mean) of x and y ?

◯ $\dfrac{z}{2}$

◯ z

◯ $2z$

◯ $z - x$

◯ $z - y$

If $b = \dfrac{c + d^2}{c}$ and $a = \dfrac{c}{d^2}$, what is b in terms of a ?

◯ $1 + \dfrac{1}{a}$

◯ $1 + a$

◯ $\dfrac{1}{1 + a}$

◯ $a^2 + 1$

◯ $\dfrac{a}{a + 1}$

$\dfrac{1}{r}$ of a circular pizza has been eaten. If the rest of the pizza is divided into m equal slices, then each of these slices is what fraction of the whole pizza?

◯ $\dfrac{r}{rm}$

◯ $\dfrac{r - 1}{rm}$

◯ $\dfrac{1}{m}$

◯ $\dfrac{m - 1}{rm}$

◯ $\dfrac{m - r}{rm}$

A certain heavenly body moves k kilometers in d days and h hours. What is the speed of the heavenly body in kilometers per day?

○ $\dfrac{24k + d}{h}$

○ $\dfrac{24(k + d)}{h}$

○ $\dfrac{24k}{24d + h}$

○ $\dfrac{24k}{24d + 12h}$

○ $\dfrac{24k}{24(d + h)}$

The total number of girls in a club is g. There are twice as many boys in the club as there are girls in the club. The total number of members in the club is 200.

Column A	Column B
$200 - 3g$	The number of adults in the club

○ The quantity in A is greater.
○ The quantity in B is greater.
○ The two quantities are equal.
○ The relationship cannot be determined from the information given.

Column A	Column B
$(x + y)^2 - 2xy$	$x^2 + y^2$

○ The quantity in A is greater.
○ The quantity in B is greater.
○ The two quantities are equal.
○ The relationship cannot be determined from the information given.

If $\dfrac{1}{x} < x < 0$, then which one of the following must be true?

○ $1 < x^2$

○ $x^2 < x$

○ $-1 < x^3 < 0$

○ $\dfrac{1}{x} > -1$

○ $x^3 > x$

If $A = q - r$, $B = r - s$, and $C = q - s$, what is the value of $A - (B - C)$?

○ $-r$
○ 0
○ 1
○ $q + r$
○ $2(q - r)$

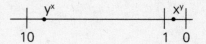

x and y are both integers

Column A	Column B
xy	6

○ The quantity in Column A is greater.
○ The quantity in Column B is greater.
○ The two quantities are equal.
○ The relationship cannot be determined from the information given.

ANSWERS

1. B
2. C
3. D
4. D
5. A
6. C
7. D
8. B
9. B
10. A
11. D
12. A
13. D
14. D
15. B
16. D
17. D
18. D
19. A
20. B
21. C
22. B
23. D
24. C
25. D
26. A
27. A
28. D
29. A
30. A
31. D
32. C
33. B
34. B
35. A
36. B
37. C
38. C
39. C
40. C
41. E
42. E

14. **C**   The minute you see variables in a Quant Comp, make your set up. Start with something simple such as $x = 10$ and $y = 1$. Column A equals 10 and Column B equals 10. Cross off Choices (A) and (B). You're adding and subtracting so try flipping the numbers to see if you can get a negative number, so $x = 1$ and $y = 10$. Now Column A still equals 10, but Column B equals -8. Your answer is (C).

15. **B**   The minute you see variables, make your set up. Start with something nice and happy such as $x = 2$. On the left you get 26 and on the right you get 36. Cross off Choices (A) and (C). The bigger x gets, the more it will exaggerate the difference. 6 to the 50th power, for example, will be way bigger than 5 to the 50th power plus 1. Can you get smaller? X still has to be greater than 1 so try $x = \dfrac{3}{2}$. It's a bit of a pain, but it's worth it just to make sure At $x = \dfrac{3}{2}$, Column A = 12 and Column B = 14.69. Column B is still bigger. It's safe to pick choice (B),

16. **D**   If the string costs c cents per foot, then it costs $3c$ cents per yard (because 1 yard = 3 feet). So the price of y yards of the string will be $3cy$ cents. Dividing this by 100 (to convert from cents per dollars), the cost of the string will be $\dfrac{3cy}{100}$ dollars, choice (D). Alternatively, you can plug in values for the variables; for example, let $c = 100$ and $y = 2$. Then the price of the string is 100 cents (or 1 dollar) per foot. It follows that the string is 3 dollars per yard, so the price of 2 yards would be 6 dollars. If you now Plug In $c = 100$ and $y = 2$ into the answer choices, the only one that equals 6 is choice (D).

17. **D**   The minute you see variables, make your set up. Try something easy first, like 2. When $x = 2$, then $y = 4$; eliminate choices (A) and (C). Generally when you square something it gets larger, but that is not always the case. You have been given no rules for what you can plug in, therefore use ZONEF and try 1 or 0 or a fraction. Any of those options will allow you to eliminate choice (B). Therefore, the answer must be choice (D).

18. **D**   The minute you see variables, make your set up. Start with some basic numbers such as 2, 3, and 5. Column A is 2 and Column B is $1\dfrac{1}{30}$. Eliminate choices (B) and (C). How could you make Column B bigger? Negative numbers might help by making Column A smaller and Column B bigger. Try -2, -3, and something much larger like 20. Now Column A is 3 and Column B is $4\dfrac{1}{30}$, so eliminate choice (A), leaving you with choice (D) for the answer.

19. **A** The minute you see variables, make your set up. Try something simple for x, like 10. The minute you see the word average, draw your average pie. The student averaged 10 on each of the first four tests, so his total points are 40. On the fifth test he scored 22 so his total is 62 and the number of tests is 5. This makes his average 12.4. In Column B, he had a total of 60 after the first 6 tests. For his overall average, therefore, he had a total of 82 over 7 tests for an average 11 point something (don't divide it all out, it's already smaller than Column A). Eliminate choices (B) and (C). Now try a bigger number, like 100 and repeat the process. Column A is still bigger. At this point, you may realize that a 12 point increase will pull the average up higher when it is part of a smaller pool. If there were 1,000 tests, an extra 12 points wouldn't affect the pool much at all. The answer is choice (A).

20. **B** You have variables in the question and in the answer, so clearly you're plugging in. Since you have an a on both sides of the equal sign, start there with something nice and happy, such as $a = 4$. You know you're going to have to square b, so plug in a perfect quare such as $b = 9$. This makes $x = 18$. Your target number, therefore, is 6. Only choice (B) works.

21. **B** As usual, when you see variables on a Quant Comp, make your set up. First you must solve for y. When you multiply both sides by 4 you get $\frac{45}{20} < \frac{1}{y}$, so $\frac{20}{45}$ or $\frac{4}{9} > y$. If you were to assume that $y = \frac{4}{9}$ and you plugged that into Column A you would get 2 and both would be equal. However, y is greater than $\frac{4}{9}$, so 8 divided by a larger number will yield something less than 2. The answer is Choice (B).

22. **B** The minute you see variables, make your set up. The first thing to do is to clean up the expression and isolate the variable. When you do this, you end up with $\frac{4}{9} > y$. Now you can start plugging in. Try something nice and easy for y. Column B is 2, so start by Plugging In 2, making Column A $1\frac{7}{8}$, while Column B is 2. Eliminate choices (A) and (C). Can you beat 2 in Column A? Plug In something larger than 2 for y, but remember that you can't go above $\frac{9}{4}$. Try $\frac{17}{8}$. This gets you closer, but doesn't close the gap. How about $\frac{35}{16}$? Closer still, but you're still running a losing race. As long as you can only use $\frac{8}{9}$ of y, you'll never make it back to 2, so select choice (B).

23. **D** The minute you see variables, make your set up. Plug In some nice easy numbers to start. Try $w = 1$, $x = -2$, and $y = 1$. Column A works out to $\frac{1}{2}$ and Column B works out to 1. Eliminate choices (A) and (C). You've been given a rule for what you can Plug In for x and y, but no rules for w. The question addresses positive versus negative numbers, so plug in a negative number for w. Try $w = -1$, $x = -2$, and $y = 4$. When you do this Column A is $-\frac{1}{2}$ and Column B is -4. $-\frac{1}{2}$ is bigger, so eliminate choice (B). The answer is choice (D).

24. **C** The minute you see variables, make your set-up. Because this is a geometry question, draw your shape and fill in what you know. In this case x must equal 4. If AB has a slope of 1, then angles BAC and ABC must both equal 45 degrees. This is a right isosceles triangle, so $y = 3$. The answer is choice (C).

25. **D** Plug In 100 for z: now, Wanda's number is 50 and 20 percent of her number is 10. Now Plug In 100 for z in the answer choices; only choice (D) hits your target answer of 10.

26. **A** If the area of the square is K, then each side of the square has length $\sqrt{K}$. Therefore, half the length of each side of the square, which is the radius of each quarter circle, is $\frac{1}{2}\sqrt{K}$. Because the 4 quarter circles equal 1 full circle in area, the total area of the 4 quarter circles is $\pi r^2 = \pi\left(\frac{1}{2}\sqrt{K}\right)^2 = \frac{\pi}{4}K$. The area of the shaded region is equal to the area of the square minus the total area of the 4 quarter circles: $K - \frac{\pi}{4}K = \frac{4-\pi}{4}K$, choice (A).

27. **A** If r is the radius of the circle, then $2\pi r = x$. Solving for r, you get $r = \frac{x}{2\pi}$. The area of the circle is then $\pi r^2 = \pi\left(\frac{x}{2\pi}\right)^2 = \pi\frac{x^2}{4\pi^2} = \frac{x^2}{4\pi}$, choice (A).

28. **D** By the Pythagorean theorem, you have $x^2 + (2x)^2 = d^2$, so $5x^2 = d^2$. The area of the rectangle is $(2x)(x) = 2x^2$, which is $\frac{2}{5}$ of $5x^2$—that is, $\frac{2}{5}$ of d^2. Thus, in terms of d, the area of the rectangle is $\frac{2}{5}d^2$, choice (D).

29. **A** In the left triangle, you have $x + x + 5y = 180$, and in the right triangle, you have $2x + 2x + y = 180$. Because both these sums equal 180, they must be equal to each other: $x + x + 5y = 2x + 2x + y$. This equation simplifies to become $x = 2y$, choice (A).

30. **A** The minute you see variables, make your set up. The question here is what to Plug In. You could start with any integer between 130 and 150. You are looking for the greatest factors, so you might as well start with the greatest integer which is 149. The largest factor of 149 is 149, which is odd. If you use 148, the largest factor is 148, but that is smaller than 149. If you use 147, the largest factor is 147, still smaller. 149 is the largest factor of the largest number in your set, so you are done. The answer is choice (A).

31. **D** The minute you see variables, make your set up. When you draw your shape, label the third angle of the triangle z. In general, when you have 2 angles of a triangle, go ahead and find the third angle, because it is likely to come in handy. For this problem, it might be easier to Plug In for angle z. When you have geometry on Quant Comp, you usually need to draw your shape in different ways and really exaggerate the differences. In this case, make z something really small, like 2. Column A will be 2 and Column B will also be 2. Eliminate choices (A) and (B). Now exaggerate the difference between possible triangles and make z a really large value, like 178. Column A will be 354 and Column B will be 178. Eliminate choice (C) and select choice (D).

32. **C** The minute you see variables, make your set up. You don't have many options for things you can plug in that will yield a graph that looks like this. In fact, the first thing you will realize is that you must use negative numbers for this to work. Try $x = 2$ and $y = 3$. When you do this you will end up with a chart of 9 and $\frac{1}{8}$, but this chart is to the left of zero, so try $x = -2$ and $y = -3$. When you do this you end up with a graph of -9 and $-\frac{1}{8}$. This works. $-2 \times -3 = 6$, So the Columns are equal.

33. **B** The minute you see variables, make your set up. Because x^{12} is such a large number use a small value for x, such as 2. You now have a fraction with twelve 2's on the bottom. For this fraction to be an integer, y must be a number that contains at least six 2's. To keep it simple, try $y = 2^6$. Column A is 4 and Column B is 2^3 or 8. Eliminate choices (A) and (C). You can add more 2's or any other number to the top of this fraction as long as y contains six 2's. Therefore, y can only get bigger; it cannot get smaller. The answer is choice (B).

34. **B** According to the information given in the question, you have $\frac{x+2y}{2} = \frac{y+2z}{2}$. Multiplying both sides by 2 gives $x + 2y = y + 2z$, so after subtracting y from both sides, you get $x + y = 2z$. It now follows that $\frac{x+y}{2} = z$—that is, the average (arithmetic mean) of x and y is z, choice (B).

35. **A** Plug In for c and d, in both equations, and solve for a and b. If $c = 8$ and $d = 4$, then $a = \frac{1}{2}$ and $b = 3$. Now Plug In 8 for c and 4 for d in the answer choices; only choice (A) hits your target answer of 3.

36. **B** To solve this one, Plug In for r and m: try $r = 2$ and $m = 4$. If $\frac{1}{2}$ of the pizza has been eaten, and the remaining $\frac{1}{2}$ is divided into 4 equal slices, then each of those remaining pieces is $\frac{1}{8}$ of the whole pizza. Now Plug In 2 for r and 4 for m in the answer choices; only choice (B) hits your target answer of $\frac{1}{8}$.

37. **C** Because the answer choices are full of variables, this is a good opportunity to Plug In: try $k = 100$, $d = 2$, and $h = 12$. If the heavenly body moves 100 kilometers in 2 days and 12 hours, or $2\frac{1}{2}$ days, then a proportion can be set up to determine its speed per day: $\frac{100 \ kilometers}{2\frac{1}{2} \ days} = \frac{x \ kilometers}{1 \ day}$, so $2\frac{1}{2}x = 100$, thus, $x = 40$. Only the correct answer, choice (C), will yield the target answer of 40.

38. **C** Try Plugging In. If there are $g = 20$ girls, then there are $20 \times 2 = 40$ boys. That makes $20 + 40 = 60$ kids. The number of adults is $200 - 60 = 140$. So, Column B is 140. Plug In $g = 20$ into Column A to find $200 - 3(20) = 140$. The Columns are equal. Try another number to make sure. You'll find that the Columns are always equal.

39. **C** If you recognize the common quadratics, you know that $(x + y)^2 = x^2 + 2xy + y^2$; hence, $x^2 + 2xy + y^2 - 2xy = x^2 + y^2$. Thus, the two quantities are equal. Alternately, you could Plug In values for x and y: if $x = 2$ and $y = 3$, then Column A equals $25 - 12 = 13$, and Column B equals $4 + 9 = 13$. Any set of values gives the same outcome, so select choice (C).

40. **C** Choose a value for x that satisfies the conditions of the question: $x = -\dfrac{1}{2}$, for example. Substituting this value into the answer choices, you see that all of the choices are false, except for choice (C).

41. **E** It's very easy to make a careless error on this one. Make sure to Plug In and write your work down in an organized manner. Try $q = 10$, $r = 5$, and $s = 2$. So, $A = 10 - 5 = 5$, $B = 5 - 2 = 3$, and $C = 10 - 2 = 8$. So, $A - (B - C) = 5 - (3 - 8) = 5 - (-5) = 10$. Only choice (E) yields 10 when you Plug In 10 for q and 5 for r.

42. **E.** The minute you see variables in a Quant Comp, make your set up. Start with some nice happy numbers such as $p = 1$ and $q = 2$. This will knock out choices (B) and (C). Now, try the weird stuff. How about fractions? Try $p = \dfrac{1}{2}$ and $q = \dfrac{1}{4}$. Column A is still bigger. How about negative numbers? Try $p = -2$ and $q = -1$. Now Column B is bigger. You can eliminate Choice (A) and pick Choice (D).

PITA AND HIDDEN PLUG-IN DRILL

A new release DVD rental costs d dollars for 1 day and $5.00 for each additional day. The first two days of standard release rental costs $3.00 less than the first day of a new release rental, and $2.25 for each day thereafter. Carl rented two new releases and one standard release for five days and it cost him $61.75. What is the value of d ?

- ○ < $5.25
- ○ $4.50
- ○ $5.25
- ○ $6.00
- ○ $6.75

If 3 less than twice a certain number is equal to 2 more than 3 times the number, then 5 less than 5 times the number is

- ○ −30
- ○ −20
- ○ −5
- ○ 0
- ○ 20

A sports league encourages collaboration by awarding 3 points for each goal scored without assistance and 5 points for each goal scored with assistance. A total of 48 points were scored by a team in a single game. Which of the following CANNOT be the number of goals scored without assistance by this team in this game?

- ○ 1
- ○ 6
- ○ 11
- ○ 12
- ○ 16

Melinda and Shirley worked together to make hamburger patties. Shirley worked for 1 hour and 45 minutes, Melinda worked for 45 minutes, and they split their earnings according to the amount of time each spent working. Melinda's hourly rate, however, is twice that of Shirley's. If the two together earned $45.75, what was Shirley's hourly rate?

- ○ $15
- ○ $20
- ○ $25
- ○ $30
- ○ $35

The 200 seventh graders at John Witherspoon Middle School raised 80% of the funds needed for a field trip. The school donated the remaining 20%. When they went to purchase the tickets, however, they were given a 10% bulk rate discount after a $20 processing fee. Faced with an unexpected surplus the students chose to buy each member of the class one cookie and were still left with $18, which they gave to the bus driver. If each of the cookies cost $0.30, how much did the trip cost the school?

- ○ $40
- ○ $80
- ○ $120
- ○ $160
- ○ $200

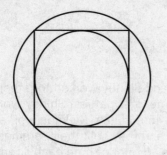

The figure above shows a circle inscribed in a square which is in turn inscribed within a larger circle. What is the ratio of the area of the larger circle to that of the smaller circle?

○ $\sqrt{2}$

○ $\dfrac{\pi}{2}$

○ $\dfrac{\pi^2}{4\sqrt{2}}$

○ 2

○ $\dfrac{\pi}{\sqrt{2}}$

At a restaurant, all tips are added together

to be split among the employees at the end

of a shift. The 4 waiters combined get $\dfrac{2}{3}$ of

the money, the manager receives $\dfrac{1}{4}$, and the

busboy receives the remainder. If 1 waiter

and the busboy together receive $30, how

much money was earned in tips for the

entire shift?

○ $90
○ $96
○ $108
○ $120
○ $180

If $\sqrt{x+3} = \sqrt{x} + \sqrt{3}$, then x is

○ −3

○ 0

○ $\sqrt{3}$

○ 3

○ any non-negative real number

If n is positive, $\dfrac{n}{m} = 4$, and $mn = 9$, then $m =$

○ $\dfrac{1}{6}$

○ $\dfrac{2}{3}$

○ $\dfrac{3}{2}$

○ 6

○ $\dfrac{27}{2}$

During a sale, the original price of a garment is lowered by 20%. Because the garment did not sell, its sale price was reduced by 10%. The final price of the garment could have been obtained with a single discount by x% from the original price, where $x =$

○ 25
○ 26
○ 27.5
○ 28
○ 30

At Betty's Bagels, bagels normally cost x each, but with each purchase of a dozen the customer receives a discount of 1.40 dollars. Billy buys 56 bagels and calculates that he spends an average of 90 cents per bagel. What is the value of x ?

○ $1.00
○ $1.40
○ $1.60
○ $2.20
○ $2.75

A bookstore stocks $\frac{1}{5}$ of its books as fiction works, and $\frac{1}{3}$ less than the fiction books as self-help books. What fraction of the total books are the fiction and self-help books?

○ $\frac{3}{5}$

○ $\frac{11}{30}$

○ $\frac{4}{15}$

○ $\frac{2}{15}$

○ $\frac{1}{3}$

Reservoir A contains 450 million gallons of water more than does Reservoir B. If 100 million gallons of water were to be drained from Reservoir A into Reservoir B, then Reservoir A would contain twice as much water as would Reservoir B. How many million gallons of water does Reservoir A currently contain?

○ 500
○ 600
○ 700
○ 800
○ 900

The New Age Entertainment Company produces x mood rings at a cost, in cents, of $80x + 9,000$. These x mood rings can be sold for a price, in cents, of $260x$. What is the least value of x for which the New Age Entertainment Company does not lose money?

○ 107
○ 82
○ 63
○ 51
○ 50

Let S be a point on a circle whose center is R. If PQ is a chord that passes perpendicularly through the midpoint of RS, then the length of arc PSQ is what fraction of the circle's circumference?

○ $\frac{1}{\pi}$

○ $\frac{1}{3}$

○ $\frac{\sqrt{3}}{\pi + 2}$

○ $\frac{1}{2\sqrt{2}}$

○ $\frac{2\sqrt{3}}{3\pi}$

Assume that at a particular zoo, $\frac{2}{5}$ of all the animals are mammals, and $\frac{2}{3}$ of the mammals are allowed to interact directly with the public. If 24 mammals are allowed to interact directly with the public, how many animals in this zoo are NOT mammals?

- ○ 36
- ○ 48
- ○ 54
- ○ 60
- ○ 72

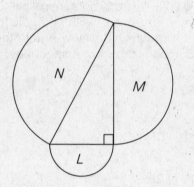

In the figure above, the letters L, M, and N denote the areas of the semicircular regions whose diameters are the sides of the triangle, as shown. What is the value of $\frac{L+M}{N}$?

- ○ $\frac{1}{2}$
- ○ $\frac{\sqrt{2}}{2}$
- ○ 1
- ○ $\frac{\pi}{2\sqrt{2}}$
- ○ $2\sqrt{2}$

A square region has an area of b square inches and a perimeter of n inches. If $n = \frac{b}{3}$, what is the length, in inches, of the side of the square?

- ○ 12
- ○ $12\sqrt{2}$
- ○ 48
- ○ $48\sqrt{2}$
- ○ 144

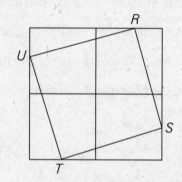

The figure above shows four adjacent small squares, forming one large square. The vertices of square $RSTU$ are midpoints of the sides of the small squares. What is the ratio of the area of $RSTU$ to the area of the large outer square?

- ○ $\frac{1}{2}$
- ○ $\frac{5}{9}$
- ○ $\frac{7}{12}$
- ○ $\frac{3}{5}$
- ○ $\frac{5}{8}$

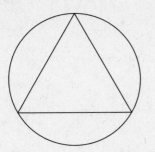

In the figure above, an equilateral triangle is inscribed in a circle. How many times greater is the area of the circle than the area of the triangle?

○ $\dfrac{\pi}{\sqrt{3}}$

○ $\dfrac{3\pi}{4}$

○ $\dfrac{4\pi}{3\sqrt{3}}$

○ 3

○ $\dfrac{2\pi}{\sqrt{3}}$

If $4x^2 + 24x + 27 = 0$, then $|x + 3|$ could =

○ $\dfrac{1}{2}$

○ $\dfrac{3}{2}$

○ $\dfrac{5}{2}$

○ 3

○ $\dfrac{7}{2}$

If $\dfrac{(x + 2)(x - 5)}{(x - 3)(x + 4)} = 1$, then $x =$

○ -2

○ $-\dfrac{1}{2}$

○ 1

○ $\dfrac{1}{2}$

○ 2

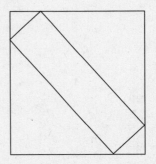

The figure above shows a rectangle inscribed within a square. How many times greater is the perimeter of the square than the perimeter of the inscribed rectangle?

○ $\sqrt{2}$

○ $\dfrac{2 + \sqrt{2}}{2}$

○ 2

○ $2\sqrt{2}$

○ It cannot be determined from the information given.

ANSWERS

1. A
2. A
3. D
4. B
5. A
6. D
7. D
8. B
9. C
10. D
11. A
12. E
13. B
14. E
15. B
16. C
17. C
18. A
19. E
20. C
21. B
22. D
23. A

EXPLANATIONS

1. **D** The minute you see the phrase "what value of d," list the answer choices on your scratch paper and label the first column. In this case, the answer choices, (Column 1) represent the price of a new release, *d*. If you assume choice (C) to be the correct answer, a new release costs $5.25. That means that a standard release (Column 2) costs $2.25. Carl rented two new releases for five days (Column 3), at a cost of $50.50 (2[$5.25 + (4)$5.00]). His standard release cost him $9 (Column 4), for a total of $59.50. It's too low, so the initial price of the DVD must be too low. Cross off choices (C), (B) and (A). You now have instructions for exactly what to do with each of the remaining answer choices. Start with $6 and follow the exact same process. The answer is choice (D).

2. **A** The problem wants you to figure out "five less than five times the number." When the question asks for "the number," Plug In the answers and work backwards. Start with choice (C) and carefully work through the problem, one step at a time. Remember to write out the steps on your scratch paper to make things easier to follow. Choice (C) is –5. This number is "5 less" than "5 times the number," so first add 5 to –5. That yields 0. 0, then, is "5 times the number" you're looking for. The only number you can multiply by 5 to get 0 is 0 itself, so that's the number you want. But does 0 work in the problem? No, because "three less than two times" 0 is just 2(0) – 3, or –3. This doesn't equal "two more than three times the number," which is 3(0) + 2, or 2. For a problem like this, it's tough to figure out if you need a bigger or smaller number, so just pick one and go. Try choice (A), which is –30. –30 is 5 less than the number you want, so you need to add 5. That gives you –25. And –25 is five times the number you're looking for, so what number times 5 yields –25? It's –5 (because 5 × -5 = –25, so –25 is five times –5). Now check –5 in the first part of the question. 2(–5) – 3 = –13. And 3(–5) + 2 is also –13, so they're equal and the best answer is choice (A).

3. **D** Plug In each of the answer choices to see which value cannot work. If 1 goal for 3 points is scored, then the team scored 45 points on unassisted goals (because the team had 48 points and 1 goal was worth 3 points, that leaves 48 – 3 = 45) To score 45 points, the team would need 9 assisted goals (9 goals at 5 points each gives us 9 × 5 = 45), so choice (A) cannot be correct. If 6 goals for 3 points are scored, then there are 18 points scored on unassisted goals and 30 points remain to be accounted for. 30 points can be achieved by 6 goals scored with assistance, so choice (B) cannot be correct. If 11 goals for 3 points are scored, there are 33 points scored and 15 left over, so that equals 3 goals scored without assistance, making choice (C) incorrect. If 12 goals for 3 points are scored, then 36 points have been scored and there are 12 points remaining. This is not divisible by 5, so choice (D) does not work and is the correct answer.

4. **A** List your answer choices in a column on your scratch paper and label it "Shirley's hourly." Assume Shirley's hourly is $25; Melinda's hourly (Column 2), therefore, must be twice that, or $50. Shirley worked at that rate for 1.75 hours and earned $43.76 (Column 3). Melinda worked for $\frac{3}{4}$ of an hour and earned $37.50 (Column 4). The two together, therefore, earned $81.25 (Column 5), which is almost double what it should be. Cross off choices (C), (D), and (E) and try jumping to Choice (A). Choice (A) is the correct answer.

5. **D** As soon as you see the phrase "how much" write your answer choices in a column and label it "Cost to the School" (Column 1). If the $120 the school pitched in represents $\frac{1}{5}$ of the cost of the trip, then the trip must have cost $600 (Column 2). Subtract $20 for the processing fee, then 10% for the discount, then add the processing fee back on. This gives you the actual cost of $542 (Column 3) and the students a surplus of $58 (Column 4). Subtract the $18 they had left over and divide the rest by 200, this will give you the price per cookie (Column 5), $0.80. This is way too much per cookie. To pay less per cookie you need to have more left over, so the school must have chipped in more money. Cross off Choices (C), (B) and (A). Don't be afraid of lots of columns. Combining steps means that you are doing work in your head, and this is where mistakes happen. Keep each step simple and methodical. Limit yourself to one operation per step. This will help prevent errors. Plug In $160 into your new spreadsheet. It works. You're done.

6. **D**

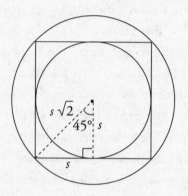

There are two important things to notice about this problem. The first is that it contains no values whatsoever. The second is that it asks for a ratio, which is just a special type of fraction. A fraction question with missing numbers equals a hidden plug in. Plug In a number for the radius of the smaller circle—say 2. If the radius of the smaller circle is equal to 2, then the area of the smaller circle is 4π. To find the area of the larger circle, make a right triangle. The legs of the triangle are 2 each and the diagonal is $2\sqrt{2}$. This is equal to the radius of the larger circle, which therefore has an area of $(2\sqrt{2})^2\pi$, or 8π. The ratio of these two numbers is equal to 2.

7. **D** The question wants the total amount of tips, so try Plugging In the Answers. In choice (D), if the total earned in tips was $120, then the 4 waiters combined receive $\frac{2}{3}$ of $120, or $80. The manager receives $\frac{1}{4}$ of $120, or $30, and the busboy receives the remaining $10. Because 4 waiters received $80, and 1 waiter received $20, 1 waiter and the busboy together receive $30.

8. **B**   Don't attempt messy algebra on the GRE if you can avoid it! The question wants to know the value of x, and it must be one of the answers provided. So just Plug In the answers. Normally, you'd start with choice (C), but that's a messy radical, so start with choice (B) instead. Plug In 0 for x and you get $\sqrt{0+3} = \sqrt{0} + \sqrt{3}$. These two are equal, so choice (B) is the answer.

9. **C**   This is another question on which you can avoid algebra by simply plugging in the answers. The question asks for the value of m, so see which of the choices works in the problem. Start with choice (C), which is $\frac{3}{2}$. The problem states that $mn = 9$, so that means $\frac{3}{2}n = 9$. Solve for n, you get 6. Now you just have to make sure that $\frac{n}{m} = 4$. It does, because $\frac{6}{\frac{3}{2}} = 6 \times \frac{2}{3}$, which is 4. Thus, choice (C) is the answer.

10. **D**   A percent question with no specific values indicates a hidden Plug In question. The question mentions "the original price," but gives no actual number, so assume that the original price of the garment was $100. After the first reduction, the sale price was $100 – (20% of $100) = $80. After the second reduction, the final price was $80 – (10% of $80) = $72. The total reduction from the original price was therefore $28, which is 28% of the original price. Choice (D) is the answer.

11. **A**   When you see, "What is the value of x," you know what to do. The answers (Column 1) represent the price of a bagel. If one bagel costs $1.60, then 56 bagels would cost $89.60 (Column 2). Fortunately there is a discount of $1.40 per dozen, so the total discount is $5.60 (Column 3). The actual price paid, therefore is $84 (Column 4) or an aveage of $1.50 per bagel (Column 5). This is too much, so cross off Choices (C), (D) and (E). It's too much by a lot, so try choice (A). It works.

12. **E**   This is another hidden Plug In problem. It asks for a fraction of an unknown total, so just make up your own number. Plug In 15 for the total. So $\frac{1}{5}$ of 15 = 3 fiction books. Then $\frac{1}{3}$ of 3 is 1, so there's 1 fewer self-help than fiction, or 3 – 1 = 2 self-help books. Together, there are 3 + 2 = 5 fiction and self-help books out of 15 total books so $\frac{5}{15} = \frac{1}{3}$.

13. **B**   This algebra problem has numbers in the answers, so solve it by Plugging In the Answers. Start with choice (C): if Reservoir A contains 700 million gallons of water, then Reservoir B has 450 million gallons less, or 250 million gallons. When 100 million gallons are drained from Reservoir A to Reservoir B, then the reservoirs will hold 600 million and 350 million gallons of water, respectively. That's not the relationship you're looking for—Reservoir A should have twice the water as Reservoir B—so eliminate choice (C). Try choice (B): if Reservoir A contains 600 million gallons of water, then Reservoir B has 450 million gallons less, or 150 million gallons. When 100 million gallons are drained from Reservoir A to Reservoir B, then the reservoirs will hold, respectively, 500 million and 250 million gallons of water. That's the relationship you're looking for—Reservoir A has twice as much water as Reservoir B—so select choice (B).

14.   E   The problem asks for the least value of *x*. Instead of doing the messy algebra, simply Plug In the answers. The question asks for the least value, so start with the smallest value given and work your way up. Start with choice (E). If *x* equals 50, then the cost is 80(50) + 9,000, which is 13,000. The money made from the sale of the rings is 260(50), or 13,000. The problem says the company must not lose money (which is not the same as making money), so choice (E) is correct.

15.   B

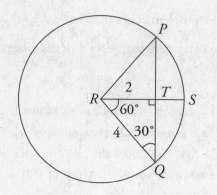

Make sure to draw the picture first. The question asks for a fraction, so Plug In any numbers you want, as long as they make sense with the problem. Make the radius of the circle 4. That means that *RQ* and *RP* are both equal to 4. *RS* is also 4, because it is a radius as well. The problem states that a line goes through the midpoint of *RS*, so *RT* must be 2. Now you have a right triangle with leg 2 and hypotenuse 4. If you use the Pythagorean Theorem to find the third side, it will be $2\sqrt{3}$. Thus, you have 30-60-90 triangles for *RTQ* and *RTP*. This means angle *R* is 120 degrees and the arc is $\frac{1}{3}$ of the circumference. Thus, choice (B) is correct.

16.   C   This problem is a bit tricky because at first it looks like a hidden Plug In. The question does not tell you the number of animals in the zoo and gives you a bunch of fractions. But, in fact, this is a Plugging In the Answers problem, because the question asks for the total number of non-mammals in the zoo and the answer choices are real numbers, not fractions or percents. Start by Plugging In choice (C), 54, for the number of non-mammals. Now, use the information in the problem to find the number of mammals. According to the problem, 24 mammals are allowed to interact with the public, and this is $\frac{2}{3}$ of all the mammals. Thus, there must be 36 total mammals in the zoo (because 24 is $\frac{2}{3}$ of 36). If there are 36 mammals and 54 non-mammals, then there are 90 animals in the zoo. Now, check this number against the information in the problem. The problem says that $\frac{2}{5}$ of all the animals are mammals and 36 is $\frac{2}{5}$ of 90. Choice (C) is the correct answer.

17.   C

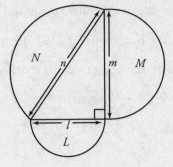

Don't be intimidated by the lack of numbers in the problem—that just means you can plug in. The question asks for a fraction, so any numbers that you plug in will work, provided they make sense in the problem. The triangle is a right triangle, so use some familiar numbers for the legs: 6, 8, and 10. If l is 6, then the radius of the semicircle is 3 and the area is 4.5π (remember, it's half of a circle, so you need to take half of the area). Similarly, m is 8, so the radius of the circle is 4 and the area of the semicircle is 8π. Lastly, n is 10, which means the radius is 5 and the area is 12.5π. If you add $L + M$, you get 12.5π. If you put this over N, you get a fraction equal to one, which is choice (C).

18.   A   This problem is a great opportunity to Plug In the answers: For any given side, simply find b (the area, or the square of the side) and n (the perimeter, or 4 times the length of the side), and then determine whether they meet the given condition of $n = \dfrac{b}{3}$. Only choice (A) will give the desired results. If the side of the square is 12, then $b = 144$, $n = 48$, and $48 = \dfrac{144}{3}$.

19.   D

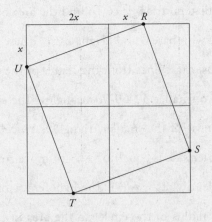

Remember, a ratio is just another type of fraction. No numbers are provided, so plug in anything you want and see what happens. Make the side of each smaller square 4. To find the area of the square in the middle, you need the length of one of its sides. Get this by using the Pythagorean Theorem. You have a right triangle formed by the length of one smaller square plus half of the length of the adjacent square (because points R, S, T, and U are all midpoints according to the problem). So if the length of a side of a smaller square is 4, you have a triangle with legs 6 and 2. By the Pythagorean theorem, the hypotenuse is $\sqrt{40}$. This is the length of one of the sides of the square in the middle. The area of this inner square is therefore 40, which is $\sqrt{40}$ squared. The area of the big square is going to be 64, or 8 squared. The ratio of areas is $\frac{40}{64}$, which is equal to $\frac{5}{8}$, which is choice (E).

20.   C

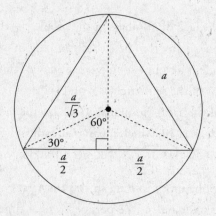

Don't attempt this problem without Plugging In some numbers. The problem wants to know "how many times" greater is the area of the circle than the area of the triangle. This is same as asking what the ratio of the two areas is. A ratio is a fraction, so Plug In numbers and work from there. Make each side of the equilateral triangle 6. To find the area of the triangle, draw in the height to create a 30-60-90 triangle with base 6 and height $3\sqrt{3}$. These values yield an area of $9\sqrt{3}$ for the triangle. To find the radius, draw lines from the center of the circle to each vertex of the triangle. Thus, you have created two smaller 30-60-90 triangles. The side opposite the 60 degree angle is equal to 3, so the hypotenuse of the smaller triangle is twice the length of the side opposite the 30 degree angle. This shorter side is equal to $\frac{3}{\sqrt{3}}$ (to move from the medium side of a 30-60-90 triangle to the shortest side, divide by $\sqrt{3}$). The hypotenuse of the triangle is twice this value, or $\frac{6}{\sqrt{3}}$. This is equal to the radius of the circle, so the area of the circle is $\pi \frac{6}{\sqrt{3}}$ squared or 12π. Finally, the ratio of the areas is $\frac{12\pi}{9\sqrt{3}}$. This reduces down to choice (C).

21. **B** Factoring the quadratic polynomial, the equation becomes $(2x + 9)(2x + 3) = 0$, so $x = -\dfrac{9}{2}$ or $-\dfrac{3}{2}$. In either case, the value of $\left| x + 3 \right|$ is $\dfrac{3}{2}$, choice (B). If you like factoring, this is the way to go. If you don't like factoring, you can always Plug In. The answers represent the value of $\left| x + 3 \right|$, so work backwards. For example, if you Plug In choice (B), you can solve for x and get $-\dfrac{3}{2}$. If you plug this back into the original equation, it works.

22. **D** Plug in the values in the answer choices and see which one works. Start with choice (C), which is 1. That makes the top of the fraction $(3)(-4)$ and the bottom $(-2)(5)$. This doesn't equal 1. Try choice (D). The top of the fraction becomes $(2.5)(-4.5)$ and the bottom becomes $(-2.5)(4.5)$. This does equal 1, so choice (D) is correct.

23. **A**

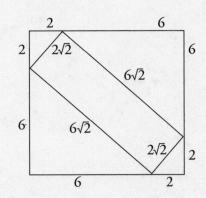

This problem is another hidden Plug In. There are no numbers provided and the question asks for the ratio of the perimeters, so Plug In your own numbers according to the ratio you've been given. Make the length of the side of the square 8. Assume the sides of the small triangles in the corners are 2. That leaves 6 for the length of the rest of the side. The sides of the rectangle are the hypotenuses of the right triangles. The smaller right triangle is 2 by 2, so the hypotenuse is $2\sqrt{2}$. The larger triangles are 6 by 6, so the hypotenuses are $6\sqrt{2}$. Now, you just need to add up the sides to get the perimeters. The square is simply $8 + 8 + 8 + 8$, which equals 32. The rectangle is $2\sqrt{2} + 2\sqrt{2} + 6\sqrt{2} + 6\sqrt{2}$. This simplifies to $16\sqrt{2}$. 32 is $\sqrt{2}$ times greater than $16\sqrt{2}$, making choice (A) correct.

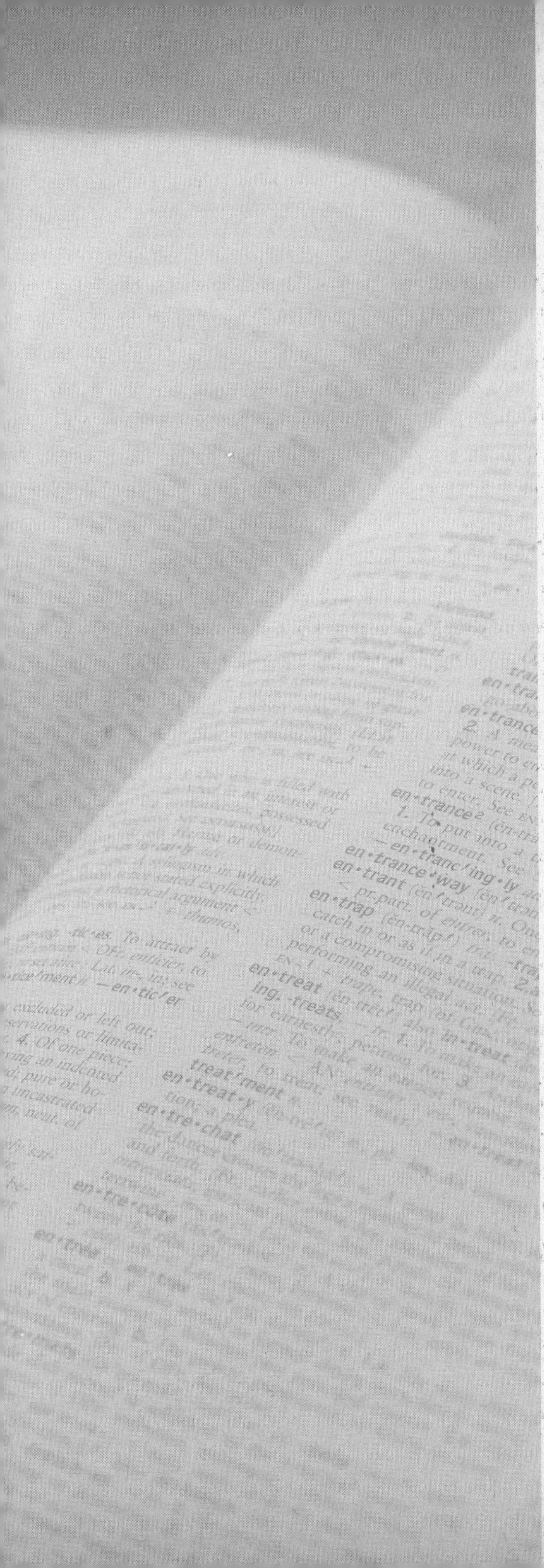

Number Properties

NUMBER PROPERTIES

The math section on the GRE is as much a test of reading comprehension as it is a test of math. Many of the problems you will see involve pieces of information given to you in prose format. Good readers read quickly and holistically, reading for overall meaning but not necessarily reading every word. This is how most of you were trained. Unfortunately, this method does not work so well on the GRE when you are under time pressure, you're reading off a screen (not a printed page), and every word counts. When you are reading math problems, mouth the words to yourself and use your finger or your pencil to track the text on the screen. It may feel silly, but it will protect you from the reading errors that are inevitable on a four-hour test.

MATH VOCABULARY

You must also know your math vocabulary. Your ability to get the correct answer on many questions will rest entirely on your knowledge of key math terms. If you have a question that states, "Set A consists of consecutive, single digit, non-negative, even integers," you will have one answer choice that contains 0 and one that does not. Which one is correct? Is zero positive or negative? Is it odd or even? Is it an integer? In order to maximize your score, you must know your math vocabulary.

Here is a list of common math terms tested on the GRE.

Term	Definition	Examples
Integer	a "whole" number that does not contain decimals, fractions, or radicals; can be positive, negative, or zero	−500, 0, 1, 28
Positive	greater than zero	$0.5, 25, \frac{5}{3}$
Negative	less than zero	$-72.3, \frac{-7}{4}, -2$
Even	an integer divisible by two	−40, 0, 2
Odd	an integer not divisible by two	−41, 1, 3
Divisible	when a number divides into another number with nothing leftover	10 is divisible by 2, but not by 3.
Remainder	the "leftovers" when one number doesn't divide evenly into another number	When 10 is divided by 3, the remainder is 1.
Divisor	a number that divides into another number	In the statement "24 divided by 6," 6 is the divisor.
Sum	the result of adding	The sum of 3 and 4 is 7.
Difference	the result of subtracting	The difference between 7 and 2 is 5.
Product	the result of multiplying	The product of 5 and 7 is 35.
Quotient	the result of dividing	The quotient of 8 and 2 is 4.
Prime	a number that is only divisible by itself and 1; 1 is not considered prime (because 1 is itself); negative numbers and zero are not prime	2, 3, 5, 7
Consecutive	in a row, usually ascending	1, 2, 3, 4; −3, −2, −1, 0
Digits	0–9; the numbers on the phone pad	1, 2, 3, 4, 5, 6, 7, 8, 9, 0
Distinct	different	2 and 3 are distinct; 6.25 and 6.26 are distinct; 4 and 4 are not distinct.

CALCULATING

For any GRE problem without a variable, you can always calculate the answer. In fact, ETS will always give you that option. You will be able to calculate your way to the answer, but it will take you 1–2 minutes and increase your opportunity for error tenfold. Instead, look for shortcuts. Remember the GRE is a test of thinking, not of calculating. Here are some shortcuts that will help expedite your thinking.

negative × negative = positive
positive × positive = positive
negative × positive = negative
even × even = even
odd × odd = odd
even × odd = even
even + or − even = even
odd + or − odd = even
even + or − odd = odd

If you have these rules memorized, you won't have to try out examples to figure out the problem; you will have the answer in a matter of moments with nary a need to calculate. This is powerful.

Divisibility is another area where you can use shortcuts. You will rarely need to know exactly how many times one number can be divided by another. Often, all you need to know is whether one number can be divided by another.

Rules of Divisibility

A number is divisible by	Rule	Examples
2	It's even (i.e., its last digit is even).	1,57<u>6</u> √
3	Its digits add up to a multiple of 3.	8,532 8 + 5 + 3 + 2 = 18√
4	Its last two digits are divisible by 4.	121,5<u>32</u> 32 ÷ 4 = 8 √
5	Its last digit is 5 or 0.	568,74<u>5</u> √ 32<u>0</u> √
6	Apply the rules of 2 and 3.	55,740 It's even and 5 + 5 + 7 + 4 + 0 = 21√√
8	Its last three digits are divisible by 8.	345,862,<u>120</u> 120 ÷ 8 = 15 √
9	Its digits add up to a multiple of 9.	235,692 2 + 3 + 5 + 6 + 9 + 2 = 27√
10	Its last digit is zero.	11,13<u>0</u> √
12	Apply the rules of 3 and 4.	3,552 3 + 5 + 5 + 2 = 15 and 52 ÷ 4 = 13 √√

Occasionally you will see questions that seem to relate to rules of divisibility, but that involve numbers too big to calculate. For example, try this question.

Which of the following numbers will divide evenly into 12^{11}: 24, 36, 2^{11}, 2^{22}, 3^{11}, 3^{12}, 40, or 48^2 ?

Clearly, you are not going to calculate each of these answer choices. Therefore, when in doubt, expand it out, but do so using prime factors. Think of the question as a fraction that you will reduce. On the top you have $(2 \times 2 \times 3)$ 11 times. The first answer choice, 24, can be broken down into $(2 \times 2 \times 3)$. You can cancel each one of the numbers on the bottom of the fraction with the equivalent numbers on the top, so 24 will divide evenly into 12^{11}. Now try the other 7 answer choices.

36   Yes. You can cancel out two 2's and two 3's. No problem.

2^{11} Yes. You will have more than eleven 2's on the top that you can cancel with the 2's on the bottom. No problem.

2^{22} Yes. There are two 2's in every group on the top of the fraction and you have 11 groups. That means you will have twenty-two 2's on the top and twenty-two 2's on the bottom. They will cancel out.

3^{11} Yes. You will have eleven 3's on the top and eleven 3's on the bottom. They will cancel out.

3^{12} Nope, you will be one 3 short. You will have eleven 3's on the top of the fraction, but twelve on the bottom. It won't work.

40   Nope. 40 breaks down to $2 \times 2 \times 2 \times 5$. The 2's will cancel out, but there's no 5 on the top to cancel with the 5 on the bottom.

48^2 Yes. 48 breaks down to $2^4 \times 3$. When you square that you get $2^8 \times 3^2$. There are enough 2's and 3's on the top to cancel with the 2's and 3's on the bottom.

$$\frac{12^{11}}{48^2} = \frac{2^{22} \times 3^{11}}{2^8 \times 3^2} =$$

$$\frac{\cancel{2} \times \cancel{2} \times \cancel{2} \times \cancel{2} \times \cancel{2} \times \cancel{2} \times \cancel{2} \times \cancel{2} \times 2 \times 2 \times 2 \times 2 \times 2 \times 2 \times 2 \times 2 \times 2 \times 2 \times 2 \times 2 \times 2 \times 2 \times \cancel{3} \times \cancel{3} \times 3 \times 3 \times 3 \times 3 \times 3 \times 3 \times 3 \times 3 \times 3}{\cancel{2} \times \cancel{2} \times \cancel{2} \times \cancel{2} \times \cancel{2} \times \cancel{2} \times \cancel{2} \times \cancel{2} \times \cancel{3} \times \cancel{3}}$$

When you have a division problem with numbers too big to calculate, use prime factors to figure out how many times one number will divide evenly into the other.

ABSOLUTE VALUE

Simply put, Absolute Value is the distance from zero on a number line. It doesn't matter if you are moving in a positive direction or a negative one. Absolute Value tends to show up on Quant Comp questions, because it's easy to confuse positive and negative numbers. Just remember to plug in both positive and negative numbers when you have a variable inside absolute value brackets.

PEMDAS

The GRE will test the order of operations, and there will be a wrong answer choice waiting for you if you get the order wrong.

Here's how it works.

P|E|M D|A S

- P stands for "parentheses." Solve for your parentheses first.
- E stands for "exponents." Solve for your exponents next.
- M stands for "multiplication" and D stands for "division." The arrow is meant to indicate that you do all your multiplication and division together in the same step, going from left to right.
- A stands for "addition" and S stands for "subtraction." Again, as the arrow indicates, you do all your addition and subtraction together in the same step, going from left to right.

For more practice and a more in-depth look at The Princeton Review math techniques, check out our student-friendly guidebook, *Cracking the GRE*.

NUMBER PROPERTIES DRILL

3 and 5 are factors of x.

Column A	Column B
The remainder when x is divided by 10	6

○ The quantity in Column A is greater.
○ The quantity in Column B is greater.
○ The two quantities are equal.
○ The relationship cannot be determined from the information given.

$$\frac{5 \times 5}{5 + 5} + \frac{5 \times 5}{5 + 5} =$$

○ 1

○ $\dfrac{5}{4}$

○ 2

○ $\dfrac{5}{2}$

○ 5

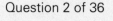

$$\left|1 - 5\right| = \left|5 - m\right|$$

Column A	Column B
m	4

○ The quantity in Column A is greater.
○ The quantity in Column B is greater.
○ The two quantities are equal.
○ The relationship cannot be determined from the information given.

x, y, and z are consecutive even integers.

Column A	Column B
xy	yz

○ The quantity in Column A is greater.
○ The quantity in Column B is greater.
○ The two quantities are equal.
○ The relationship cannot be determined from the information given.

If $bc \neq 0$, and $3b + 2c = 18$, then which of the following is NOT a possible value of c ?

○ $5\dfrac{3}{5}$

○ 6

○ $8\dfrac{2}{5}$

○ 9

○ 12

At the local grocery store, apples normally cost 40 cents each. During a recent sale, the price was reduced to 3 apples for a dollar. How much money would be saved by purchasing 30 apples at the sale price?

○ $1
○ $1.50
○ $2
○ $2.50
○ $3

$$y < 0$$

Column A	Column B
$2y$	$20y$

◯ The quantity in Column A is greater.
◯ The quantity in Column B is greater.
◯ The two quantities are equal.
◯ The relationship cannot be determined
  from the information given.

Which of the following could be the difference between two positive integers whose
product is 28 ?

◯ 1
◯ 3
◯ 4
◯ 7
◯ 14

Set X consists of the positive multiples of 5,
and set Y consists of the odd prime numbers
less than 20. If set Z consists of every distinct integer less than 100 that is the product
of one element from set X and one element
from set Y, then set Z consists of how many
elements?

◯ 12
◯ 14
◯ 15
◯ 16
◯ 18

$$\frac{u}{v}\left(\frac{x}{y + z}\right)$$

If the value of the expression above is to be
doubled by halving exactly one of the five
variables, which variable should be halved?

◯ u
◯ v
◯ x
◯ y
◯ z

$$m > 0, n > 0$$

Column A	Column B
$\dfrac{m}{mn}$	$\dfrac{n}{mn}$

◯ The quantity in Column A is greater.
◯ The quantity in Column B is greater.
◯ The two quantities are equal.
◯ The relationship cannot be determined
  from the information given.

Which of the following is the best

approximation of $\sqrt{\dfrac{(98.763)(0.49)^2}{(0.252)}}$?

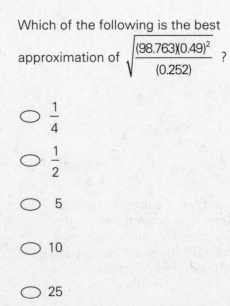

◯ $\dfrac{1}{4}$

◯ $\dfrac{1}{2}$

◯ 5

◯ 10

◯ 25

Column A	Column B
Three times the sum of the prime numbers less than 10	The sum of the prime numbers between 20 and 30

○ The quantity in Column A is greater.
○ The quantity in Column B is greater.
○ The two quantities are equal.
○ The relationship cannot be determined from the information given.

Tasha's favorite number can be written as $3^2 \times 17^2$

Column A	Column B
The number of distinct positive divisors of Tasha's favorite number	9

○ The quantity in Column A is greater.
○ The quantity in Column B is greater.
○ The two quantities are equal.
○ The relationship cannot be determined from the information given.

If x is a positive integer greater than 1, which of the following has the greatest value?

○ $\dfrac{1}{x}$

○ $\dfrac{1}{x+1}$

○ $\dfrac{x}{x+1}$

○ $\dfrac{x}{\left(\dfrac{1}{x+1}\right)}$

○ $\dfrac{x}{\left(\dfrac{x}{x+1}\right)}$

Which of the following CANNOT be the sum of two prime integers?

○ 7
○ 19
○ 23
○ 31
○ 43

If r is an integer multiple of 8, then which of the following could NOT be divisible by r ?

○ 216
○ 384
○ 360
○ 416
○ 420

If x, y, and z are consecutive even integers, such that $x < y < z$ and $xyz = 960$, what is the value of z ?

☐

Which of the following integers has both 12 and 17 as factors?

○ 34
○ 84
○ 120
○ 204
○ 217

f, g, and h are consecutive prime numbers such that $f < g < h$.

Column A	Column B
$f + g + h$	$3g$

- ◯ The quantity in Column A is greater.
- ◯ The quantity in Column B is greater.
- ◯ The two quantities are equal.
- ◯ The relationship cannot be determined from the information given.

How many positive integers less than 20 are factors of 96 ?

- ◯ 5
- ◯ 6
- ◯ 7
- ◯ 8
- ◯ 9

Which of the following sets of numbers has a product that is less than any member of the set?

- I. −6, −3, −2

- II. $-\dfrac{1}{2}, -\dfrac{1}{3}, 6$

- III. $\dfrac{1}{6}, \dfrac{1}{3}, \dfrac{1}{2}$

- ◯ I only
- ◯ II only
- ◯ III only
- ◯ II and III only
- ◯ I and III only

If a and b are integers, $ab = -5$, and $a - b > 0$, which of the following must be true?

- I. $a > -1$
- II. b is odd
- III. $|a| = 5$

- ◯ I only
- ◯ II only
- ◯ I and II only
- ◯ I and III only
- ◯ I, II, and III

$$y = |y|$$
$$y = -|y|$$

Column A	Column B
y	0

- ◯ The quantity in Column A is greater.
- ◯ The quantity in Column B is greater.
- ◯ The two quantities are equal.
- ◯ The relationship cannot be determined from the information given.

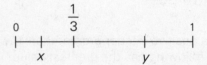

If x and y are letters which correspond to points on the number line shown above, which of the following statements must be true?

- ◯ $x > y$

- ◯ $\dfrac{1}{x} < \dfrac{1}{y}$

- ◯ $\dfrac{1}{x} \times \dfrac{1}{y} > 9$

- ◯ $xy < \dfrac{1}{3}$

- ◯ $x + y > 1$

n is a positive integer.

The remainder when 5n is divided by 4 is 3.

Column A	Column B
The remainder when 10n is divided by 4	2

◯ The quantity in Column A is greater.
◯ The quantity in Column B is greater.
◯ The two quantities are equal.
◯ The relationship cannot be determined from the information given.

$$a < 0 < b$$

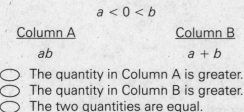

Column A	Column B
ab	a + b

◯ The quantity in Column A is greater.
◯ The quantity in Column B is greater.
◯ The two quantities are equal.
◯ The relationship cannot be determined from the information given.

When the number of people in an office is divided by 12, the remainder is 0. If $\frac{3}{2}$ times the number of people in the office is divided by 12, and the remainder resulting from this operation is greater than 0, the remainder must be

◯ 1
◯ 2
◯ 3
◯ 5
◯ 6

a, b, and c are multiples of 15 and a < b < c

Column A	Column B
The remainder when b is divided by c	The remainder when (b + c) is divided by a

◯ The quantity in Column A is greater.
◯ The quantity in Column B is greater.
◯ The two quantities are equal.
◯ The relationship cannot be determined from the information given.

If $\frac{3 + p}{2q} = 1$, which of the following could be true?

◯ p = −1 and q = 1
◯ p = −1 and q = $\frac{1}{2}$
◯ p = 1 and q = 0
◯ p = 0 and q = 1
◯ p = 0 and q = 0

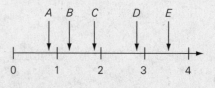

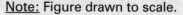

Note: Figure drawn to scale.

If each letter on the number line above is the number that corresponds to the point below it, then which of the following is closest to D ÷ A ?

◯ A
◯ B
◯ C
◯ D
◯ E

Set *X* consists of all the even integers from 1 to 100, inclusive, and set *Y* consists of all the integers divisible by 5 from 1 to 100, exclusive. How many members of set *X* are <u>not</u> members of set *Y* ?

If negative integer *a* is multiplied by *b* and the result is greater than 0 but less than $|a|$, then which of the following must be true of *b* ?

○ $b > 1$

○ $0 < b < 1$

○ $-1 < b < 0$

○ $b < a$

○ $|b| < a$

$$\frac{a+b}{b+c} = 0, \ b > 0$$

Column A	Column B
c^2a	a^2

○ The quantity in Column A is greater.
○ The quantity in Column B is greater.
○ The two quantities are equal.
○ The relationship cannot be determined from the information given.

```
    -1          0          1
 ◄──┼─────┼────┼────┼──►
         f          g
```

If *f* and *g* are numbers on the number line above, which of the following statements must be true?

    I. $-1 < fg < 0$
    II. $-1 < f + g < 0$
    III. $-1 < f - g < 0$

○ I only
○ II only
○ III only
○ I and II only
○ I and III only

A number divisible by a positive even prime number must be

○ prime
○ odd
○ even
○ the square of a prime
○ the square of an odd number

ANSWERS

1. B
2. E
3. D
4. D
5. D
6. C
7. A
8. B
9. B
10. B
11. D
12. D
13. B
14. C
15. D
16. C
17. E
18. 12
19. D
20. D
21. D
22. E
23. C
24. C
25. D
26. C
27. D
28. E
29. A
30. A
31. E
32. 41
33. C
34. B
35. A
36. C

EXPLANATIONS

1. **B** Plug In a value that meets the given requirements; try $x = 15$. The remainder when 15 is divided by 10 is 5; Column B is greater, so eliminate choices (A) and (C). Any acceptable value of x gives the same outcome, so select choice (B).

2. **E** Find the value of each fraction by multiplying the numbers in the numerator and adding the numbers in the denominator. The value of each fraction is $\frac{25}{10} = \frac{5}{2}$. Add the two fractions: $\frac{5}{2} + \frac{5}{2} = \frac{10}{2} = 5$.

3. **D** Solve for m. If $|1 - 5| = |5 - m|$, then $|-4| = |5 - m|$, or $4 = |5 - m|$. When you see absolute values, remember to consider both positive and negative solutions: $5 - m = 4$ or $5 - m = -4$, so m can equal 1 or 9, leaving you with choice (D) for the answer.

4. **D** Try Plugging In; one set of values that could work is $x = -2$, $y = 0$, and $z = 2$. In this case, both Column A and Quantity B have a value of 0. Eliminate choices (A) and (B). However, another set of values that could work is $x = -6$, $y = -4$, and $z = -2$. With this set of values, Column A has a value of 24 and Quantity B has a value of 8. Eliminate choice (C). You are left with choice (D) for the answer.

5. **D** This problem offers a good opportunity to Plug In the answers—for simplicity's sake, start with the integers. If $c = 6$, choice (B), then $3b + 2(6) = 18$, so $3b + 12 = 18$, $3b = 6$, and $b = 2$. The only other requirement given is that $bc \neq 0$, so 6 is, in fact, a possible value of c. If $c = 9$, as in choice (D), then $3b + 2(9) = 18$, so $3b + 18 = 18$, $3b = 0$, and $b = 0$. A value of 0 for b would violate the given requirement, so 9 is NOT a possible value of c.

6. **C** 30 apples at 40 cents apiece cost $12. Buying 30 apples at 3 per dollar would cost $10. Therefore, the sale price is $2 less than the normal price.

7. **A** When $y = -1$, Column A is -2 and Column B is -20. Eliminate choices (B) and (C). Plug In another value for y. When $y = -100$, Column A is -200 and Column B is $-2,000$. Column A is always greater.

8. **B** The two positive integers must have a product of 28, so find the factor pairs of 28: 1 and 28, 2 and 14, and 4 and 7. Only choice (B) gives a possible difference: $7 - 4 = 3$.

9. **B** Solve this problem by brute force, but be systematic about it. Set Y has a finite number of elements, so list them out and start finding the products when those elements are multiplied by positive multiples of 5. Set Y = {3, 5, 7, 11, 13, 17, 19}, so multiplying by 5—the first positive multiple of 5—yields 15, 25, 35, 55, 65, 85, and 95; that's 7 elements for set Z thus far. Multiplying by 10—the next positive integer multiple of 5—yields 3 more products, 30, 50, and 70. Multiplying by 15 yields two new products, 45 and 75; multiplying by 20 yields only one new product, 60. That's a total of 13 elements for set Z so far. You already have 75 as a member of set Z, so multiplying by 25 yields no new products; multiplying by 30 yields the final new product, 90. Set Z thus consists of 14 elements: set Z = {15, 25, 30, 35, 45, 50, 55, 60, 65, 70, 75, 85, 90, 95}. If you got choice (E), you may have mistakenly included 2 as an element of set Y.

10. **B** Plug In values for the variables, such as $u = 2$, $v = 4$, $x = 6$, $y = 8$, and $z = 10$. With these values, the expression equals $\frac{1}{6}$. Try halving each of the values to find which one would change the value of the expression to $\frac{1}{3}$. Halving v to 2 works; the answer is choice (B).

11. **D** Time to Plug In! If you make $m = 2$ and $n = 3$, then Column A becomes $\frac{2}{2 \times 3} = \frac{1}{3}$, and Column B becomes $\frac{3}{2 \times 3} = \frac{1}{2}$. Column B is bigger; eliminate choices (A) and (C). However, if you make and $n = 2$, then the situation is reversed: Column A will be $\frac{1}{2}$, and Column B will be $\frac{1}{3}$. Eliminate choice (B); the answer must be choice (D).

12. **D** Try rounding your values before you calculate. The expression can be estimated as

$$\sqrt{\frac{(100)(\frac{1}{2})^2}{(\frac{1}{4})}} = \sqrt{\frac{100(\frac{1}{4})}{(\frac{1}{4})}} = \sqrt{\frac{25}{(\frac{1}{4})}} = \sqrt{25 \times \frac{4}{1}} = \sqrt{100} = 10.$$

13. **B** The prime numbers less than 10 are 2, 3, 5, and 7—don't forget, 1 is not prime. Their sum is 17, and $3 \times 17 = 51$. The only prime numbers between 20 and 30 are 23 and 29, and their sum is 52. Column B is greater.

14. **C** It is easier to work with the factors of Tasha's favorite number, rather than with the number itself. Write out the number as $3 \times 3 \times 17 \times 17$ and make a list of the divisors—or factors—in pairs. The pairs are: 1 and $3 \times 3 \times 17 \times 17$, 3 and $3 \times 17 \times 17$, 17 and $3 \times 3 \times 17$, 3×3 and 17×17, and 3×17 and 3×17. The final pair contains only one *distinct* factor, giving you a total of 9 factors.

15. **D** Try Plugging In on this one. If $x = 4$, then choice (A) is $\frac{1}{4}$ or 0.25, choice (B) is $\frac{1}{5}$ or 0.2, choice (C) is $\frac{4}{5}$ or 0.8, choice (D) is $\frac{4}{\frac{1}{5}} = 4 \div \frac{1}{5} = 4 \times 5 = 20$, and choice (E) is $\frac{4}{\frac{4}{5}} = 4 \div \frac{4}{5} = 4 \times \frac{5}{4} = 5$. Choice (D) is the greatest.

16. **C** Rather than listing out all of the prime numbers up to 43, stay focused on the unique number, 2, the only even prime number. All of the choices are odd, and two odd numbers would yield an even sum, so you'll only be able to eliminate answers by adding 2 to an odd number. Each of the incorrect answers, therefore, is the sum of 2 and the previous prime number: choice (A) is 2 + 5; choice (B) is 2 + 17; choice (D) is 2 + 29; and choice (E) is 2 + 41. The answer is choice (C).

17. **E** Plug In a value for r: the first integer multiple of 8 is 8 itself. Only choice (E) fails to yield an integer: $\frac{420}{8} = 52.5$.

18. **12** Ballpark that 960 is about 1,000, which is 10 × 10 × 10. Then test a set of consecutive even integers near 10, such as 10 × 12 × 14 = 1,680. This product is too large. Try 8 × 10 × 12 = 960, giving you $z = 12$.

19. **D** Eliminate choices (A) and (E) because they are not divisible by 12. Eliminate choices (B) and (C) because they are not divisible by 17.

20. **D** The intervals between consecutive prime numbers does not follow a consistent, predictable pattern. Prove it by Plugging In: Try $f = 2$, $g = 3$, and $h = 5$. Now $f + g + h = 10$ and $3g = 9$. Column A is greater; eliminate choices (B) and (C). Now try $f = 7$, $g = 11$, and $h = 13$. This time, $f + g + h = 31$, and $3g = 33$. Column B is now greater. Eliminate choice (A), and you're left with choice (D).

21. **D** The factors of 96 are 1, 2, 3, 4, 6, 8, 12, 16, 24, 32, 48, and 96. Eight of these numbers are less than 20.

22. **E** The product of the numbers of the set in (I) is (–6) × (–3) × (–2), or –36; because the product is less than any individual member of the set, the set in (I) meets the requirement in the problem. Before you calculate the product for the set in (II), note that eliminating any choices that don't contain (I) leaves only choices (A) and (E) as possible answers. Neither choice contains (II), so (II) must <u>not</u> meet the requirement—go straight to (III). The product of the members of the set in (III) is $\frac{1}{6} \times \frac{1}{3} \times \frac{1}{2}$, or $\frac{1}{36}$; because the product is less than any individual member of the set, the set in (III) meets the requirement in the problem, giving you choice (E) for the answer.

23. **C** If a and b are integers with a product of –5, then there are only 4 options: $a = 5$ and $b = -1$; $a = -5$ and $b = 1$; $a = 1$ and $b = -5$; and $a = -1$ and $b = 5$. The requirement that $a - b > 0$ eliminates the second and fourth options, leaving only $a = 5$ and $b = -1$ and $a = 1$ and $b = -5$. (I) and (II) are both true for these two cases and (III) is not true if $a = 1$, making choice (C) the answer.

24. **C** The first equation tells you that y cannot be a negative number. The second equation tells you that y cannot be a positive number. Therefore, y must be 0.

25. **D** Plug In values for x and y that fit the figure: try $x = \frac{1}{6}$ and $y = \frac{2}{3}$. Now, plug these numbers into each of the choices and use POE. Only choice (D) is correct: $\frac{1}{6} \times \frac{2}{3} = \frac{2}{18} = \frac{1}{9}$, which is less than $\frac{1}{3}$.

26. **C** If the remainder is 3, then $5n$ must be 3 more than a multiple of 4, such as 4, 8, 12, or 16. Try adding 3 to these multiples to find a possible value for $5n$. $12 + 3$ yields 15 as a value for $5n$; $n = 3$. Column A is the remainder when 30 is divided by 4, or 2. Eliminate choices (A) and (B). Try a different number. If n is 7, then $5n$ is 35, which also has a remainder of 3 when divided by 4. In Column A, 70 divided by 4 has a remainder of 2. For any other numbers you try, choice (C) will be the answer.

27. **D** Plug In values for a and b. If $a = -2$ and $b = 2$, then Column B is greater. Eliminate choices (A) and (C). If $a = -\frac{1}{2}$ and $b = \frac{1}{4}$, then Column A is greater. Eliminate choice (B).

28. **E** Plug In 12 for the number of people in the office, because the remainder is 0 when 12 is divided by 12. Because $\frac{3}{2} \times 12$ is 18, and the remainder when 18 is divided by 12 is 6, choice (E) must be correct.

29. **A** Try Plugging In. If $a = 15$, $b = 30$, and $c = 60$, Column A is 30 because c cannot divide into b even one time. Column B is 0 because 90 divided by 15 has no remainder. Eliminate choices (B) and (C). Try a new set of numbers to further narrow your choices. If $a = 30$, $b = 45$, and $c = 120$, Column A is 45, and Column B is 15. The answer is choice (A).

30. **A** Try Plugging In the answers; you can immediately eliminate choices (C) and (E) because a value of 0 for q would yield a fraction with 0 in the denominator. In choice (A), $\frac{3 + (-1)}{2(1)} = \frac{2}{2} = 1$. This is a "could be true" question, rather than a "must be true" question, so select choice (A) because it works.

31. **E** Estimate that D is approximately 2.8 and A is approximately 0.8. So the answer is $2.8 \div 0.8$, or 3.5, which is closest to choice (E).

32. **41** Half of the integers from 1 to 100—inclusive—are even, so set X has 50 members. Set Y has 19 members, the integers divisible by 5 from 1 to 100 *exclusive*, so don't include 100. Of the 19 members of set Y, 9 are even and therefore, in set X. The 50 members of set X minus the 9 members that <u>are also in set Y</u> yields 50 – 9 = 41 members.

33. **C** To solve this problem, Plug In for a and b, but don't forget your restrictions. If $a = -4$, then a value of $-\dfrac{1}{2}$ for b would yield a product greater than 0 but less than $|a|$. Only choice (C) works.

34. **B** If $\dfrac{a+b}{b+c} = 0$, then $a + b = 0$ (remember that you cannot divide by 0, and thus, $b + c \neq 0$). This means $a = -b$. You are given that b is positive, so a must be negative. Looking at Column A, you don't know what type of number c is, but any number squared is positive, so c^2 is positive. It is multiplied by a, which is negative, giving you a negative product. In Column B, a^2 is positive, making Column B greater.

35. **A** Evaluate the statements by plugging in possible values for f and g; if $g = \dfrac{1}{2}$ and $f = -\dfrac{2}{3}$, then in (I), $fg = -\dfrac{2}{6}$, or $-\dfrac{1}{3}$, so (I) is true for these values. In (II), $f + g = -\dfrac{1}{6}$, so (II) is also true for these values; in (III), though, $f - g = -\dfrac{7}{6}$, so (III) is false for these values. Eliminate choices (C) and (E). Knowing that the figure isn't drawn to scale, try some other values: if $f = -\dfrac{1}{2}$ and $g = \dfrac{1}{2}$, for example, then $f + g = 0$, and (II) can be eliminated—along with choices (B) and (D). Only choice (A) remains.

36. **C** The only number that is positive, even, and prime is 2. Because the number is divisible by 2, it must be even.

Fractions, Decimals, and Percentages

FRACTIONS

You will see plenty of fractions on the GRE, but don't worry; everything you need to know about them you learned in second grade. You must be able to add, subtract, multiply, divide, and compare fractions. Here are the basics, with a couple of neat tricks thrown in.

Adding

In grade school, you learned to find the lowest common denominator. That still works. The Bowtie method is a convenient way to find the common denominator.

It looks like this.

$$10 = \qquad = 12$$
$$\frac{2}{3} + \frac{4}{5} = \frac{10}{15} + \frac{12}{15} = \frac{22}{15}$$

Just multiply across the bottom to get your common denominator. Multiply on the diagonal to figure out your numerators and then add across the top. It works the same way for subtracting.

$$\frac{3}{8} \ \ \frac{1}{5} = \frac{15}{40} - \frac{8}{40} = \frac{7}{40}$$

Here's another helpful tip. If you have a fraction with addition or subtraction in the numerator, and a single number or variable in the denominator, you can split your original fraction into two separate fractions.

$$\frac{25+13}{19} = \frac{25}{19} + \frac{13}{19}$$

Comparing

The Bowtie method is also useful for comparing fractions; this comes in very handy on Quant Comp questions. Just multiply up on the diagonals to compare any two fractions. If you want to compare $\frac{5}{8}$ and $\frac{7}{12}$, for example, multiply 5 by 12 and 8 by 7, then compare. The larger number, 60, belongs to the larger fraction, $\frac{5}{8}$. Make sure you do this work on your scratch paper and not in your head.

$$\frac{5}{8} \text{ vs } \frac{7}{12} \qquad 60 = \frac{5}{8} \diagup\!\!\!\!\!\diagdown \frac{7}{12} = 56$$

Reducing

In general, get in the habit of reducing all fractions to their simplest forms; it will make your life easier. Before you do, however, have a quick look at the answer choices to make sure your fractions need to be reduced. You don't want to do more work than necessary.

Remember the following rules:

- Do not reduce across a +, -, or = sign. You can reduce individual fractions, but you cannot reduce the numerator of one fraction with the denominator of another, if +, - or = signs are involved.
- When multiplying fractions, you can reduce anything, including the numerator of one fraction with the denominator of another.
- You can reduce fractions by common factors. While 20 does not go evenly into 30, if you have the fraction $\frac{20}{36}$, you can take sevens out of both.

$$\frac{20}{36} = \frac{\cancel{2} \times \cancel{2} \times 5}{\cancel{2} \times \cancel{2} \times 3 \times 3} = \frac{5}{3 \times 3} = \frac{5}{9}$$

Dividing a fraction by a fraction is the same thing as multiplying the first fraction by the reciprocal of the second fraction. You may be able to do this in your head, but don't. Take the extra two seconds to lay it out on your scratch paper. It won't take you much more time, and you're less likely to make a careless error.

$$\frac{\frac{1}{2}}{\frac{3}{4}} = \frac{1}{2} \div \frac{3}{4} = \frac{1}{\cancel{2}} \times \frac{\cancel{4}^{2}}{3} = \frac{2}{3}$$

DECIMALS

Occasionally ETS will give you a question in fractions and the answers in decimals, or one side of a quant comp in decimals and the other side in fractions. To convert a fraction to a decimal, use long division.

$$\frac{3}{7} = 7\overline{)3} = 7\overline{)\begin{array}{r} 0.428 \\ 3.000 \\ 2\ 8 \\ \hline 20 \\ 14 \\ \hline 60 \\ 56 \\ \hline 4 \end{array}}$$

Make sure you check your answer choices and eliminate as you go, so you don't waste time doing extra work. You will rarely have to divide a fraction out to more than two decimal places.

Converting

When converting from a decimal to a fraction, think of the decimal point as a 1 that goes on the bottom of your new fraction; then count up the number of digits that come after the decimal point and add the same number of zeros after the 1.

$$0.42 = \frac{42}{100} \qquad\qquad 0.003 = \frac{3}{1000}$$

Multiplying

When you multiply decimals, the answer must have the same number of decimal places as the total decimal places in the numbers you are multiplying. For example, if you multiply .4 by .2, the answer must have two places to the right of the decimal, because .4 and .2 have one decimal place each. The answer is .08. Just remember that when you multiply a decimal by a decimal, the answers will get pretty small pretty quickly.

Dividing

When you divide a decimal into a decimal, write it out as long division and convert the divisor into a whole number.

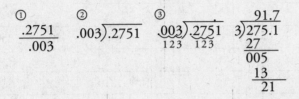

Since 0.003 is a very small number, it makes sense that it will go into 0.2751 (which is close to 0.3) nearly a hundred times. In fact, if you were Ballparking, you would notice that to get from 0.003 to a number close to 0.3 you would have to move your decimal point to the right two spaces. That is the same as multiplying by 100, so you would be looking for an answer choice that's close to 100. Because 0.2751 is a little bit less than 0.3, you want a number that's a little bit less than 100.

PERCENTAGES

How do you express $\frac{1}{2}$ as a percentage? 50 percent, right? How do you express $\frac{1}{2}$ as a decimal? 0.5, right? You may know that 25 percent, $\frac{1}{4}$, and 0.25 are all the same thing. They are all fractions and they all express a $\frac{\text{part}}{\text{whole}}$ relationship. The first tip for mastering percentages is realizing that they are really just fractions.

These are the most common fraction, decimal, and percentage equivalents; learn them, live them, love them.

Decimal	Fraction	Percentage
0.25	¼	25%
0.5	½	50%
0.75	¾	75%
1.0	4/4	100%
3.75	15/4	375%
0.33	1/3	33%
0.66	2/3	66%
1.0	3/3	100%
1.66	5/3	166%
0.2	1/5	20%
0.4	2/5	40%
0.6	3/5	60%
0.8	4/5	80%
1.0	5/5	100%
1.2	6/5	120%
2.4	12/5	240%
0.125	1/8	12.5%
0.250	2/8	25%
0.375	3/8	37.5%
0.5	4/8	50%
0.625	5/8	62.5%
0.75	6/8	75%
0.875	7/8	87.5%
1.0	8/8	100%
1.125	9/8	112.5%
2.5	20/8	250%

Memorize these fractions and be comfortable switching from one format to another, because when a question asks you for 75 percent, it may be easier to think of the percentage as $\frac{3}{4}$. When a Quant Comp asks you whether $\frac{4}{5}$ or $\frac{6}{8}$ is bigger, it may be easier to think of them as 80 percent and 75 percent.

Translating

Complicated percentages are often expressed as word problems rather than math problems. For example, "42 is what percent of 28"? This problem can be translated, word for word, into a single-variable equation.

Here's your translation guide.

Word	Symbol
percent	/100
of	* (times)
what	x, y, or z
is, are, was, were	=

Your translation is $42 = \dfrac{x}{100} \times 28$.

Stress Free Tip Calculating

How often have you used this one? Your bill is $28.50. You want to tip 20 percent. You know that 10% = $2.85. Double it to get $5.70, and you have 20 percent. You only want to leave 15 percent? OK, what is half of 10 percent? Let's call it $1.43. Add that back to the 10 percent, and you have $4.28, or 15 percent. You can do this with any number to quickly calculate exact percentages or to quickly Ballpark answers.

Number	Percentage
1,246	100%
124.6	10%
12.46	1%
62.3	5%
373.8 (10% × 3)	30%
398.72 (10% × 3 + 1% × 2)	32%

Part to Whole

The last, and perhaps most common, method of quickly calculating percentages is to set up a ratio of part to whole. Remember that the word percent simply means of 100, so 42 percent means 42 parts out of a total of 100.

$$\frac{\text{part}}{\text{whole}} = \frac{x}{100}$$

With this set-up, the variable could go anywhere. ETS might give you the percentage and ask you for the whole. For example, "42 is 60 percent of what"?

$$\frac{42}{x} = \frac{60}{100}$$

To solve, simply cross multiply: $4{,}200 = 60x$.

A question might ask you, "42 is what percent of 70"? In this case, the x goes over the 100.

$$\frac{42}{70} = \frac{x}{100}$$

Or a question might ask you, "What is 60 percent of 70"? In this case you know the percentage and the total, but not the part.

$$\frac{x}{70} = \frac{60}{100}$$

Cross multiply and you can solve. You can always put a percentage into this format.

For more practice and a more in-depth look at The Princeton Review math techniques, check out our student-friendly guidebook, *Cracking the GRE*.

FRACTIONS, DECIMALS, AND PERCENTAGES DRILL

$3 \div \dfrac{6}{7} =$

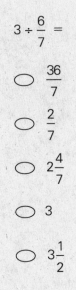

- ○ $\dfrac{36}{7}$

- ○ $\dfrac{2}{7}$

- ○ $2\dfrac{4}{7}$

- ○ 3

- ○ $3\dfrac{1}{2}$

$\dfrac{\dfrac{1}{5} - \dfrac{1}{2}}{\dfrac{1}{5} + \dfrac{1}{2}} =$

- ○ -1

- ○ $-\dfrac{1}{2}$

- ○ $-\dfrac{3}{7}$

- ○ $\dfrac{6}{5}$

- ○ 2

Column A	Column B
$\dfrac{15}{16} + \dfrac{1}{256}$	$1 - \dfrac{1}{64}$

- ○ The quantity in Column A is greater.
- ○ The quantity in Column B is greater.
- ○ The two quantities are equal.
- ○ The relationship cannot be determined from the information given.

A deposit at a local bank earns between 2 percent and 5 percent simple interest in a year. If Shirley makes an initial deposit of $800 at the bank, which of the following could be the amount of money in her account at the end of one year?

- ○ $814
- ○ $820
- ○ $842
- ○ $848
- ○ $860

Column A	Column B
The change in price of a pair of shoes marked down by 50%	The change in price of a pair of shoes marked down by 30%

- ○ The quantity in Column A is greater.
- ○ The quantity in Column B is greater.
- ○ The two quantities are equal.
- ○ The relationship cannot be determined from the information given.

Joey works at a clothing store and receives an employee discount of 10 percent off the regular price of any item. What is the regular price of an item that Joey purchases for $99 ?

- ○ $89.10
- ○ $108.90
- ○ $109.00
- ○ $109.90
- ○ $110.00

Rohan began a savings account with a balance of $200. His current balance is $150.

Column A	Column B
The percent decrease from Rohan's original balance to his current balance	The percent increase that would return Rohan's current balance to his original balance

- ○ The quantity in Column A is greater.
- ○ The quantity in Column B is greater.
- ○ The two quantities are equal.
- ○ The relationship cannot be determined from the information given.

If 20 percent of x is $5y$, and $y = 7$, what is 60 percent of x ?

- ○ 105
- ○ 115
- ○ 125
- ○ 145
- ○ 175

$$\frac{1}{48} + \frac{1}{48} + \frac{1}{12} + \frac{1}{8} + \frac{1}{4} + \frac{1}{2} =$$

- ○ $\frac{49}{48}$
- ○ 1
- ○ $\frac{47}{48}$
- ○ $\frac{3}{4}$
- ○ $\frac{2}{3}$

The Warm Muffin Bakery's cookie sales are always 60 percent of its muffin sales. What would be the increase in The Warm Muffin Bakery's cookie sales if its muffin sales increased from 10,000 to 20,000 ?

- ○ 10,000
- ○ 8,000
- ○ 6,000
- ○ 4,000
- ○ 2,000

Column A	Column B
$\frac{7}{8} - 0.25$	$0.325 + \frac{1}{3}$

- ○ The quantity in Column A is greater.
- ○ The quantity in Column B is greater.
- ○ The two quantities are equal.
- ○ The relationship cannot be determined from the information given.

Which of the following inequalities is true?

○ $\dfrac{1}{11} < 0.08 < \dfrac{1}{9}$

○ $\dfrac{1}{10} < 0.11 < \dfrac{1}{8}$

○ $\dfrac{1}{7} < 0.17 < \dfrac{1}{6}$

○ $\dfrac{1}{5} < 0.26 < \dfrac{1}{4}$

○ $\dfrac{1}{3} < 0.30 < \dfrac{1}{2}$

Company A's output of 245 widgets per week is 35 percent of Company B's weekly widget output.

Column A	Column B
700	Company B's weekly widget output.

○ The quantity in Column A is greater.
○ The quantity in Column B is greater.
○ The two quantities are equal.
○ The relationship cannot be determined from the information given.

If $mn \neq 0$, $\dfrac{2+m}{mn} =$

○ $\dfrac{2}{m} + \dfrac{2}{mn}$

○ $2 + \dfrac{m}{mn}$

○ $\dfrac{2}{mn} + n$

○ $\dfrac{2}{mn} + \dfrac{1}{m}$

○ $\dfrac{2}{mn} + \dfrac{1}{n}$

A car with all available options costs $18,000, an increase of 20% from the base price of the car.

Column A	Column B
The base price of the car	$14,400

○ The quantity in Column A is greater.
○ The quantity in Column B is greater.
○ The two quantities are equal.
○ The relationship cannot be determined from the information given.

What percent is equivalent to 0.0025 ?

○ $\frac{1}{25}$%

○ $\frac{1}{5}$%

○ $\frac{1}{4}$%

○ 4%

○ 5%

Which of the following fractions is closest in value to $\frac{5}{8}$?

○ $\frac{2}{3}$

○ $\frac{3}{4}$

○ $\frac{7}{11}$

○ $\frac{19}{23}$

○ $\frac{23}{30}$

A certain brand of imported cigars costs $30 for a box of 20; when bought individually, the cigars cost $2 each.

Column A	Column B
The percent saved when a box of cigars is purchased, rather than 20 individual cigars	$33\frac{1}{3}$

○ The quantity in Column A is greater.
○ The quantity in Column B is greater.
○ The two quantities are equal.
○ The relationship cannot be determined from the information given.

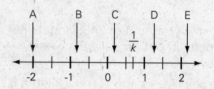

Which of the labeled coordinates on the number line above could represent the value of k ?

○ A
○ B
○ C
○ D
○ E

What is the median of the fractions $\frac{8}{25}$, $\frac{9}{28}$, $\frac{5}{16}$, $\frac{7}{20}$, and $\frac{4}{9}$?

☐

$$\left(\frac{1}{3}\right)a = \left(\frac{1}{4}\right)b = \left(\frac{1}{6}\right)c = d$$

$$c = 20$$

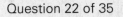

Column A	Column B
$2a$	$b + d$

◯ The quantity in Column A is greater.
◯ The quantity in Column B is greater.
◯ The two quantities are equal.
◯ The relationship cannot be determined from the information given.

$(4 \times 100) + (6 \times 1{,}000) + (2 \times 1) + (3 \times 10) =$

◯ 2,346
◯ 4,632
◯ 4,623
◯ 6,324
◯ 6,432

What is the value of $\dfrac{3}{\left(\frac{3}{4}\right)} - \dfrac{\left(\frac{3}{2}\right)}{3}$?

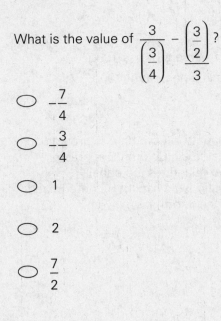

◯ $-\dfrac{7}{4}$

◯ $-\dfrac{3}{4}$

◯ 1

◯ 2

◯ $\dfrac{7}{2}$

a is 40% of 45

18 is b% of 90

Column A	Column B
a	b

◯ The quantity in Column A is greater.
◯ The quantity in Column B is greater.
◯ The two quantities are equal.
◯ The relationship cannot be determined from the information given.

$$\frac{\dfrac{x}{5} + \dfrac{x}{5} + \dfrac{x}{5} + \dfrac{x}{5}}{4} =$$

◯ $16x$

◯ $\dfrac{24x}{5}$

◯ $4x$

◯ $\dfrac{4x}{5}$

◯ $\dfrac{x}{5}$

$$n > 0$$

$$\frac{6n}{15}, \ 0.3n, \ \frac{19n}{50}, \ \frac{n}{4}$$

Column A	Column B
The positive difference between the greatest and least values above	Three times the positive difference between the two least values above

◯ The quantity in Column A is greater.
◯ The quantity in Column B is greater.
◯ The two quantities are equal.
◯ The relationship cannot be determined from the information given.

Halfway through the season, Antonio's scoring average per game was 20% higher than David's. The two scored the same number of points in the second half of the season.

Column A	Column B
90% of Antonio's scoring average for the whole season	David's scoring average for the whole season

○ The quantity in Column A is greater.
○ The quantity in Column B is greater.
○ The two quantities are equal.
○ The relationship cannot be determined from the information given.

The annual interest rate on a certain savings account increases from 1.25% to 1.5%. What percent increase in the annual interest rate does this change represent?

○ 0.2%
○ 0.25%
○ 0.167%
○ 20%
○ 25%

Which of the following is equal to $\frac{1}{5}$ of the reciprocal of 0.004 percent?

○ 0.5
○ 50
○ 500
○ 5,000
○ 50,000

Column A	Column B
The total value of 100 dollars after it is invested for m months at 8 percent simple annual interest	$100\left(1+\dfrac{0.08}{m}\right)$ dollars

○ The quantity in Column A is greater.
○ The quantity in Column B is greater.
○ The two quantities are equal.
○ The relationship cannot be determined from the information given.

27 percent of p is 100.

p is q percent of 100.

Column A	Column B
q	400

○ The quantity in Column A is greater.
○ The quantity in Column B is greater.
○ The two quantities are equal.
○ The relationship cannot be determined from the information given.

Which expression is equivalent to $\dfrac{1}{y - \dfrac{1}{y}} - y$?

○ $\dfrac{y^3 + y - 1}{y^2 - 1}$

○ $\dfrac{2y - y^3}{y^2 - 1}$

○ $\dfrac{-y^3}{y^2 - 1}$

○ $y^3 + y - 1$

○ $-y - 1$

One cup of nuts that contains exactly half peanuts and half cashews is added to a bowl of nuts that is exactly one third peanuts, one third cashews, and one third almonds. This results in a three-cup mixture of nuts. What fraction of the new nut mixture is peanuts?

```
┌──────────┐
│          │
└──────────┘
```

Column A	Column B
16 percent of 83	83 percent of 16

○ The quantity in Column A is greater.
○ The quantity in Column B is greater.
○ The two quantities are equal.
○ The relationship cannot be determined
  from the information given.

Leah wants to shrink her photos to fit a computer screen. Her photos currently have a width of 1,024 pixels and a height of 768 pixels. If she reduces the width to 800 pixels, then to what height, in pixels, must she reduce the photos to preserve the same ratio of width to height?

○ 1,066.7
○ 600
○ 576
○ 544
○ 500

ANSWERS

1. E
2. C
3. B
4. B
5. D
6. E
7. B
8. A
9. B
10. C
11. B
12. B
13. C
14. E
15. A
16. C
17. C
18. B
19. D
20. $\frac{9}{28}$
21. A
22. E

23. E
24. B
25. E
26. C
27. D
28. D
29. D
30. D
31. B
32. B
33. $\frac{7}{18}$
34. C
35. B

EXPLANATIONS

1. **E**   When dividing by a fraction, flip the fraction and multiply: $3 \div \frac{6}{7} = 3 \times \frac{7}{6} = \frac{21}{6} = 3\frac{1}{2}$. Alternatively, you may estimate and realize that 3 divided by something slightly smaller than 1 must be slightly larger than 3.

2. **C**   Use the bowtie when adding or subtracting fractions: $\dfrac{\frac{1}{5} - \frac{1}{2}}{\frac{1}{5} + \frac{1}{2}} = \dfrac{\frac{2-5}{10}}{\frac{2+5}{10}} = \dfrac{-\frac{3}{10}}{\frac{7}{10}}$. Next, divide the fractions by flipping the numerator and denominator and multiplying: $\dfrac{-\frac{3}{10}}{\frac{7}{10}} = (-\frac{3}{10}) \times (\frac{10}{7}) = -\frac{3}{7}$.

3. **B**   In Column A, $\frac{15}{16} + \frac{1}{256} = \frac{241}{256}$, and in Column B, $1 - \frac{1}{64} = \frac{63}{64}$. If you multiply the numerator and denominator of $\frac{63}{64}$ by 4, you obtain a common denominator: $\frac{63}{64} = \frac{252}{256}$. Clearly $\frac{252}{256} > \frac{241}{256}$, so column B is greater.

4. **B**   5% of $800 is $40, thus, the maximum amount of money that could be in the account at the end of one year is $840; eliminate choices (C), (D), and (E). Similarly, the minimum amount that could be in the account at the end of one year is $800 plus 2% of $800, or $816; eliminate choice (A).

5. **D**   Be careful: You're not given the original price of either pair of shoes, and because you can't assume they're the same price, try Plugging In a variety of values. If the shoes in both Columns originally cost 10 dollars, then the change in price of the shoes in Column A is 5 dollars, and the change in price of the shoes in Column B is 3 dollars; Column A is greater, so eliminate choices (B) and (C). If the shoes in Column B originally cost 20 dollars, though, then the change in price is 6 dollars. Column B is now greater, so eliminate choice (A), and you're left with choice (D), the correct answer.

6. **E**   With his employee discount, Joey purchases an item for 90% of its regular price, so 90% of the regular price of this item is equivalent to $99 or $\frac{90}{100}x = 99$. Solve for x to find that the regular price is $110.

7. **B** The percent change formula is $\dfrac{difference}{original} \times 100$. Remember that the "original" is the amount before the change. So, in Column A, the difference is $200 - 150 = 50$, and the original is 200, which yields a 25% change. In Column B, the difference is also 50, but the number changes from 150 to 200, so the "original" is 150, which yields roughly a 33.3% change. Thus, Column B is greater.

8. **A** Begin by Plugging In 7 for y, so 20 percent of x is 35. You could go on to solve for x, but a shortcut would be to say that 60 percent of x is three times 20 percent of x, so multiply 35 by 3 to get 105.

9. **B** You have far too many fractions to add quickly with the bowtie. Instead, convert all of the fractions to the common denominator of 48: $\dfrac{1}{48} + \dfrac{1}{48} + \dfrac{1}{12} + \dfrac{1}{8} + \dfrac{1}{4} + \dfrac{1}{2} = \dfrac{1+1+4+6+12+24}{48} = \dfrac{48}{48} = 1$.

10. **C** If The Warm Muffin Bakery sells 10,000 muffins, it sells 6,000 cookies. If the Warm Muffin Bakery then sold 20,000 muffins, it would sell 12,000 cookies. The cookie sales would thus increase by 6,000.

11. **B** Convert the fractions to decimals. So $\dfrac{7}{8} = 0.875$, making Column A 0.625. In Column B, $\dfrac{1}{3}$ is about 0.333, making Column B about 0.658. Column B is greater.

12. **B** Convert the fractions to decimals to see which inequality is correct. You can divide them out (remember, numerator divided by denominator), but it might help to have some common fraction/decimal equivalents memorized. Starting with choice (A), $\dfrac{1}{11} \approx 0.09$, so this inequality is not true. Convert the fractions in choice (B): $0.1 < 0.11 < 0.125$; this inequality is true.

13. **C** Translate the question into a percent formula. So, "245 widgets per week is 35 percent of Company B's weekly widget output" means $245 = \dfrac{35}{100} \times B$. Try Plugging In Column A into this formula. Does $\dfrac{35}{100} \times 700 = 245$? Yes, so the Columns must be equal.

14. **E** Plug In for the variables. Let $m = 3$ and $n = 5$, and $\dfrac{2+3}{3 \times 5} = \dfrac{5}{15} = \dfrac{1}{3}$. Only choice (E) works. Alternatively, you could manipulate the fractions: $\dfrac{2+m}{mn} = \dfrac{2}{mn} + \dfrac{m}{mn} = \dfrac{2}{mn} + \dfrac{1}{n}$.

15. **A** The question asks for a percent <u>increase</u> from the original price; be careful not to find 20% of $18,000, and reduce the higher total ($18,000) by that amount. Instead, you'll need to find the amount that yields the higher total, when increased by 20%, though, it's much easier to just increase the price in Column B and compare it to the total in the problem: 10% of $14,400 is $1,440, so 20% must be $2,880; adding this to the base price of $14,400 yields a total of $17,280. That's smaller than what you were looking for, so Column A is greater.

16. **C** Convert 0.0025 to a percent by sliding the decimal point two places to the right: 0.25%. Then convert 0.25 to a fraction to get $\frac{1}{4}$%.

17. **C** There are two ways to go about this problem. One is to use the bowtie method to compare fractions. $\frac{2}{3}$ versus $\frac{5}{8}$ yields a 16 versus 15. Pretty close. $\frac{3}{4}$ versus $\frac{5}{8}$ yields 24 versus 20. Not as close, so eliminate it $\frac{7}{11}$ versus $\frac{5}{8}$ yields 56 versus 55, that's really close on a percentage basis because the number are bigger. Eliminate choice (A). $\frac{19}{25}$ versus $\frac{5}{8}$ yields 152 versus 115. Get rid of it. Choice (E) yields 18 versus a50. Get rid of it. Alternatively, you could also use long division, but if you do, there is no need to finish out the math for each answer. 5 divided by 8 = .625. $\frac{2}{3}$ = .66keet it. Wen you start to divide 3 by four, the first number you see is a 7. Don't continue to divide, just eliminate it because .7 is farther from .625 than .66. Choice (C) yields .63, so keep it and eliminate Choice (A). The answer is 19 divided by 23 begins with .8, so get rid of it. The answer to 23 divided by 30 begins with .7 so get rid of that too.

18. **B** Twenty cigars bought individually would cost $40, so apply the percent change formula—$\frac{difference}{original} \times 100$—to determine Column A. In this case, the difference is $10, and the original, because it's a percent decrease, is $40: $\frac{10}{40} \times 100 = 25$, so Column A is 25%. Column B is greater.

19. **D** Try Plugging In a possible value for $\frac{1}{k}$. If $\frac{1}{k} = \frac{3}{4}$, then $k = \frac{4}{3}$, which is closest to coordinate D.

20. $\frac{9}{28}$ Convert each of the fractions to decimals: $\frac{8}{25} = 0.32$, $\frac{9}{28} \approx 0.3214$, $\frac{5}{16} = 0.3125$, $\frac{7}{20} = 0.35$, and $\frac{4}{9} = 0.\overline{4}$. The middle value is $\frac{9}{28} \approx 0.3214$.

21. **A** If $c = 20$, one can quickly calculate that $d = \frac{10}{3}$. If $\left(\frac{1}{4}\right)b = d$, then $b = \frac{40}{3}$ and Column B is $\frac{50}{3}$, or about 17. So $\left(\frac{1}{3}\right)a = d$, thus, you know $a = \frac{30}{3} = 10$; this means the value of Column A is 20, making choice (A) correct.

22. **E** This question is really asking about place value. Start with the greatest place: the thousands. So, $6 \times 1,000$ means a 6 in the thousands place. Eliminate choices (A), (B), and (C). Next, 4×100 means the next digit should be 4. Eliminate choice (D), and select choice (E).

23. **E** To calculate this expression, break it into pieces: $\dfrac{3}{\left(\dfrac{3}{4}\right)} - \dfrac{\left(\dfrac{3}{2}\right)}{3} = 3 \div \dfrac{3}{4} - \dfrac{3}{2} \div 3 = 3 \times \dfrac{4}{3} - \dfrac{3}{2} \times \dfrac{1}{3} = 4$ $-\dfrac{1}{2} = \dfrac{7}{2}$.

24. **B** Solve each equation by translating into algebra. The first is $a = \dfrac{40}{100} \times 45$. Reduce and multiply to find $a = 18$. The second is $18 = \dfrac{b}{100} \times 90$. Multiply both sides by 100 then divide by 90 to find $b = 20$. Column B is greater.

25. **E** Plug In a value for x: if $x = 20$, then the expression $\dfrac{\dfrac{20}{5} + \dfrac{20}{5} + \dfrac{20}{5} + \dfrac{20}{5}}{4}$ becomes

$\dfrac{4+4+4+4}{4} = \dfrac{16}{4} = 4$. Now Plug In 20 for x in the answer choices; only choice (E) hits your target answer of 4. Alternatively, you could factor the expression: $\dfrac{\dfrac{x}{5} + \dfrac{x}{5} + \dfrac{x}{5} + \dfrac{x}{5}}{4} = \dfrac{4 \times \left(\dfrac{x}{5}\right)}{4} = \dfrac{x}{5}$.

26. **C** The first thing you need to do is to clean up these expressions. You have 15th, 50th, and decimals, so it is very difficult to compare values. $\dfrac{6n}{15}$ can be reduced to $\dfrac{2n}{5}$. $0.3n$ is the same as $\dfrac{3n}{10}$.

Change your first expression from $\dfrac{2n}{5}$ to $\dfrac{4n}{10}$. $\dfrac{19n}{50}$ is pretty close to $\dfrac{20n}{50}$ or $\dfrac{2n}{5}$, the first expression,

but a bit smaller. Because $\dfrac{n}{4}$ is clearly the smallest expression and you need only concern yourself

with the smallest, the second smallest, and the biggest, you can ignore $\dfrac{19n}{50}$. Convert $\dfrac{n}{4}$ to $\dfrac{5n}{20}$

, and convert your other expressions to 20ths as well. You now have $\dfrac{8n}{20}, \dfrac{6n}{20}$, and $\dfrac{5n}{20}$. The difference

between the smallest and largest is 3. Three times the difference between the two smallest is also

3. The answer is choice (C).

27. **D** Plug In some real numbers to compare Columns. For example, plug in 10 for the number of games in the season. For the first 5 games of the season, try an average of 10 points for David (for a total of 50 points), which makes an average of 12 points for Antonio (for a total of 60 points). Next, try a total of 0 points for each player for the second half of the season; now Antonio's average for the season is 6 points, and David's is 5. Because 90% of 6 is 5.4, Column A is greater, so eliminate choices (B) and (C). Finally, try a total of 100 points for each player for the second half of the season; now Antonio has scored a total of 160 points in 10 games, for an average of 16 points, and David has scored a total of 150 points in 10 games, for an average of 15 points. Because 90% of 16 is 14.4, Column B is now greater, so eliminate choice (A), and you're left with choice (D).

28. **D** The percent change formula is $\dfrac{difference}{original} \times 100$, so plugging the numbers from the problem into

the formula yields $\dfrac{0.25}{1.25} \times 100 = \dfrac{25}{125} \times 100 = \dfrac{1}{5} \times 100 = 20$. If you selected choice (E), you may

have used the wrong value as the original: remember, in a percent <u>increase</u>, the original number is

the <u>smaller</u> value.

29. **D** Solve this problem in chunks. To find the numerical value for 0.004 percent, divide by 100:

$0.004 \div 100 = 0.00004$. The reciprocal of that is $\dfrac{1}{0.00004} = 25{,}000$. So $\dfrac{1}{5}$ of the result is

$\dfrac{1}{5} \times 25{,}000 = 5{,}000$.

30. **D** Plug In values for m. When $m = 1$, Column B is larger. When $m = 12$, Column A is larger.

31. **B** To find exact values for p and q, apply percent translation: $\dfrac{27}{100} \times p = 100$, so $\dfrac{27p}{100} = 100$,

$27p = 10{,}000$, and $p = 370.37$; p is q percent of 100, so $q = 370.37$ as well. Column B is greater.

Alternatively, you could avoid the calculation altogether and Ballpark this one all the way through:

100 is more than 25% (or $\dfrac{1}{4}$) of p, so p must be less than 400—and so must q.

32. **B** This is a good problem for Plugging In. If $y = 2$, then the expression becomes equal to $-\dfrac{4}{3}$. Choice

(B) is the only choice that gives you $-\dfrac{4}{3}$ when you replace y with 2.

33. $\dfrac{7}{18}$ The total mixture contains three cups, so the second bowl must contain two cups. This 2-cup

bowl of nuts divided into even thirds consists of $\dfrac{2}{3}$ cups peanuts, $\dfrac{2}{3}$ cups cashews, and $\dfrac{2}{3}$ cups

almonds. Combining this with the 1-cup mixture of $\dfrac{1}{2}$ cup peanuts and $\dfrac{1}{2}$ cup cashews results in

$\dfrac{7}{6}$ cups peanuts in a 3-cup mixture. So, $\dfrac{\frac{7}{6}}{3} = \dfrac{7}{18}$ of the new nut mixture is peanuts.

34. **C** To find 16 percent of 83, multiply 83 by 0.16. To find 83 percent of 16, multiply 16 by 0.83. Both expressions yield 13.28, so choice (C) is correct.

35. **B** Set up a proportion so that the original ratio equals the final ratio: $\dfrac{1024}{800} = \dfrac{768}{x}$. Cross-multiply and then divide both sides by 1024 to find $x = 600$.

Ratios and Proportions

RATIOS AND PROPORTIONS

Much like averages, rates, and Quant Comp Plug Ins, ratios are all about organizing your information. That means recognizing when and how to effectively use your scratch paper.

USE A RATIO BOX

A ratio is simply a fraction. Rather than expressing a part-to-whole relationship, it expresses the relationship between two parts. The two parts combined make up the whole. If you have a bag with 5 red marbles and 4 blue marbles, your ratio of red to blue is 5 : 4. Ratios can be expressed as fractions, so you can also express the relationship as $\frac{5}{4}$. Either way your total number of marbles is 9, because 5 plus 4 is 9.

You can keep the same ratio of red to blue marbles as long as you increase your total to a multiple of 9. If you had 27 marbles total, you would have 15 red and 12 blue, but your ratio would still be 5 : 4. To keep it straight, use a ratio box.

> The minute you see the word RATIO, draw a ratio box on your scratch paper.

Here's what the ratio box looks like.

	Red Marbles	Blue Marbles	Total	
	5	4	9	◄——— Ratio Total
	×3	×3	×3	◄——— Multiplier
	15	12	27	◄——— Actual Total

In this case you know that the ratio of red to blue marbles is 5 : 4, but the actual numbers of red and blue marbles are 15 and 12. $\frac{4}{9}$ of the marbles are blue, and approximately 55 percent ($\frac{5}{9}$) of the marbles are red. Unless a question asks for fractions of marbles, the actual total of marbles must be a multiple of nine.

As usual, ETS will give you just enough information to fill out the chart. The question may give you the actual number of marbles, the ratio of red to blue, and then ask you for the actual number of blue marbles. Alternatively, the question may ask you what the new ratio will be if the number of blue or red marbles is increased. A really tricky question may state that some blue ones have been added, give you the new ratio, and then ask you for the actual total of red ones. No matter what is asked, a ratio is still a ratio; the ratio box will organize the information you're given and help you get the information you need.

RATIO AND RATES

Sometimes you will be given a simple ratio in the form of a rate. The question may tell you the number of widgets a factory can produce in an hour, the price of one gallon of gasoline, and the speed with which a silo fills with grain. You will then have to scale this rate up or down, depending on what is asked. Alternatively, you may have to find the number of widgets the factory will produce in ten hours, the price of a 30 gallon tank of gasoline, or the percentage of the silo that will be filled in two hours. To solve these rate problems, set them up as proportions on your scratch paper, check your units, and label everything.

Example

> A digital scanner can scan five lines every second. If each line is one eightieth of an inch, how many minutes will it take to scan a 4½ inch photo?

$$\begin{array}{c} \text{lines} \\ \text{Inches} \end{array} \quad \frac{80}{1} : \frac{x}{4.5} \quad x = 360 \text{ lines total}$$

$$\begin{array}{c} \text{lines} \\ \text{Seconds} \end{array} \quad \frac{360}{x} : \frac{5}{1} \quad x = 72 \text{ seconds}$$

$$\begin{array}{c} \text{Seconds} \\ \text{Minutes} \end{array} \quad \frac{60}{1} : \frac{72}{x} \quad x = 1.2 \text{ minutes}$$

For more practice and a more in-depth look at The Princeton Review math techniques, check out our student-friendly guidebook, *Cracking the GRE*.

RATIOS AND PROPORTIONS DRILL

A certain recipe calls for 2 cups of sugar and $3\frac{1}{2}$ cups of flour. What is the ratio of sugar to flour in this recipe?

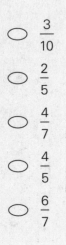

$\bigcirc$ $\dfrac{3}{10}$

$\bigcirc$ $\dfrac{2}{5}$

$\bigcirc$ $\dfrac{4}{7}$

$\bigcirc$ $\dfrac{4}{5}$

$\bigcirc$ $\dfrac{6}{7}$

CHARITABLE ANNUAL DONATIONS TO CHARITY GROUP X

Employees of Company:	Years 1980 – 1990		Years 1980 – 2000	
	Average (mean) annual donation per employee	Greatest Single annual Donation by an employee	Average (mean) annual donation per employee	Greatest Single annual Donation by an employee
A	24.3	1,000	34.6	1,000
B	18.2	500	40.2	500
C	45.5	300	45.5	2,000
D	34.6	2,000	34.6	2,000
E	34.7	1,000	32.4	1,000
F	150.3	2,000	100.8	2,000
G	23.7	500	23.7	500
H	34.7	500	34.7	1,000
I	74.5	5,000	80.2	5,000
J	85.6	3,000	85.6	3,000
K	126.7	5,000	104.4	5,000
L	234.4	3,000	234.4	3,000
M	422.4	400	455.2	2,000

What is the approximate ratio of Company F's average annual donation to charity group X for the period 1980–1990 to that of the period 1980–2000 ?

$\bigcirc$ 1 : 1
$\bigcirc$ 3 : 2
$\bigcirc$ 3 : 5
$\bigcirc$ 3 : 40
$\bigcirc$ 5 : 2

If a certain vitamin pill has 400 milligrams of magnesium, then how many grams of magnesium are in a bottle of 500 vitamin pills? (1 gram = 1,000 milligrams)

○ 20
○ 200
○ 2,000
○ 20,000
○ 200,000

$a = \dfrac{1}{6}$ and $\dfrac{6}{7} = \dfrac{5}{b}$, what is the value of $a + b$?

○ $\dfrac{71}{210}$

○ 3

○ $\dfrac{187}{42}$

○ 6

○ $\dfrac{47}{6}$

James can swim 750 yards in 10 minutes. If he swims at the same constant rate, how many minutes will it take him to swim 4.2 times this distance?

○ 14.2
○ 42
○ 52.8
○ 75
○ 315

b is a multiple of positive integer a

Column A	Column B
The ratio of a to b	$\dfrac{1}{2}$

○ The quantity in Column A is greater.
○ The quantity in Column B is greater.
○ The two quantities are equal.
○ The relationship cannot be determined from the information given.

Keri, Neill, and Rich use toilet paper in their apartment in a ratio of 3:2:2. Rich buys two cases of toilet paper online at 28 rolls per case, an average of $3.50/roll and a $19 delivery charge. If they each contribute to the cost of the toilet paper in direct proportion to the amount they use, how much must Keri contribute?

[ ]

$$36a = 25b$$
$$ab \neq 0$$

Column A	Column B
$\dfrac{5}{6}$	$\dfrac{a}{b}$

○ The quantity in Column A is greater.
○ The quantity in Column B is greater.
○ The two quantities are equal.
○ The relationship cannot be determined from the information given.

By volume, cranberry juice makes up 12.5 percent of Bee's punch and 25 percent of Flo's punch. If 3 liters of Bee's punch are mixed with 6 liters of Flo's punch, approximately what percent of the mixture, by volume, is cranberry juice?

- ⬭ 6.25%
- ⬭ 18.75%
- ⬭ 20.83%
- ⬭ 33.33%
- ⬭ 50.00%

At the beginning of the day, the ratio of cats to dogs at a boarding kennel was 10 to 11. Throughout the day, 4 dogs and 5 cats were admitted to the boarding kennel and no animals were released.

Column A	Column B
The number of cats in the boarding kennel at the end of the day	The number of dogs in the boarding kennel at the end of the day

- ⬭ The quantity in Column A is greater.
- ⬭ The quantity in Column B is greater.
- ⬭ The two quantities are equal.
- ⬭ The relationship cannot be determined from the information given.

If $7(a - 1) = 17(b - 1)$, and a and b are both positive integers with products greater than 1, then what is the least possible sum of a and b ?

- ⬭ 2
- ⬭ 7
- ⬭ 17
- ⬭ 24
- ⬭ 26

A machine works at a constant rate and produces a bolts in 15 minutes and b bolts in c hours.

Column A	Column B
b	$3ac$

- ⬭ The quantity in Column A is greater.
- ⬭ The quantity in Column B is greater.
- ⬭ The two quantities are equal.
- ⬭ The relationship cannot be determined from the information given.

ANSWERS

1. C
2. B
3. B
4. D
5. B
6. D
7. 90
8. A
9. C
10. D
11. E
12. A

EXPLANATIONS

1. **C**   A ratio is a part-to-part relationship, but it can be expressed and manipulated just like a fraction—

   in this case, $\dfrac{3}{3\frac{1}{2}}$. None of the answers have a fractional value in the denominator, so you need to

   find a multiplier that will get rid of the fraction. In this case, just doubling the entire ratio will do

   the trick: $\dfrac{2}{3\frac{1}{2}} \times \dfrac{2}{2} = \dfrac{4}{7}$.

2. **B**   Read the chart carefully and then ballpark. Company F's annual average donation was about 150 for 1980–1990 and about 100 for 1980–2000. Reduce 150 : 100 to 3 : 2.

3. **B**   First, find that 400 milligrams × 500 pills = 200,000 milligrams total. Then, convert to grams by dividing by 1,000 to find the answer: 200 grams. When doing multiple conversions, be sure to label carefully and watch for arithmetic errors.

4. **D**   Layout your ratios on your scratch paper. $\dfrac{g}{ma}\ \dfrac{1}{1000} = \dfrac{x}{200,000}$ then cross multiply: 200,000 = 1000x. Divide by 1000 and you get 200. Cross multiply to find the value of b, $\dfrac{35}{6}$. Then substitute in the values of a and b: $a + b = \dfrac{1}{6} + \dfrac{35}{6} = \dfrac{36}{6} = 6$

5. **B**   To swim 4.2 times the original distance, James needs to swim for 4.2 times as long. So multiply the original time (10 minutes) by 4.2 to get 42 minutes.

6. **D**   Because you have variables, make your set-up on your scratch paper. Plug In different values for a

   and b. First, try 2 and 4: $\dfrac{2}{4}$ reduces to $\dfrac{1}{2}$, making the quantities equal. Eliminate choices (A) and

   (B). Next, try 2 and 6. $\dfrac{2}{6}$ reduces to $\dfrac{1}{3}$, which is less than $\dfrac{1}{2}$. Column B is now greater, so elimi-

   nate choice (C). You're left with choice (D).

7. **1,050**   The three roommates spend a total of $210 on toilet paper. If you make your ratio box you will see that your ratio total is 7 and your actual total is 210, so your multiplier is 30. Keri, therefore needs to contribute $90.00 to the cost of the toilet paper.

8. A   Divide both sides by b, then divide both sides by 36 to find: $\dfrac{a}{b} = \dfrac{25}{36}$. Although $\dfrac{5}{6} \times \dfrac{5}{6} = \dfrac{25}{36}$, this does not mean that $\dfrac{25}{36}$ reduces to $\dfrac{5}{6}$. Use the bowtie to compare the two fractions: 36 times 5 equals 180, while 6 times 25 equals 150. 180 is bigger, so Column A is greater.

9. C   Estimate to solve this one. The answer must be between 12.5 percent and 25 percent because you are mixing two punches with these percentages—eliminate all choices except choices (B) and (C). Because there is more of Flo's punch, the answer must be closer to 25 percent than to 12.5 percent, so choice (C) is correct. You could also try to plug in, but it will take a lot more work.

10. D   Try Plugging In. If there are 10 cats at the beginning of the day, then there are 11 dogs; at the end of the day, there would be 15 cats and 15 dogs. In this case, Column A and Column B are equal. Eliminate choices (A) and (B). However, there could be 20 cats and 22 dogs at the beginning of the day; then there would be 25 cats and 26 dogs at the end of the day. In that situation, Column B is greater; eliminate choice (C). Only choice (D) remains.

11. E   Because 7 and 17 are prime, and have no common factor greater than 1, their least common multiple will be their product: $7 \times 17 = 119$. The least possible value for $(a - 1)$, then, is 17, so $a = 18$; likewise, the least possible value for $(b - 1)$ is 7, so $b = 8$. The least possible sum for a and b, therefore, is $18 + 8 = 26$. Be careful if you selected choice (A): although Plugging In a value of 1 for both a and b would yield 0 on both sides of the equation, the problem specifies that the product of a and b be greater than 1.

12. A   Plug In values. If $a = 5$ and $c = 1$, then $b = 20$. In that situation Column A is larger; eliminate choices (B) and (C). Plug In again to see if this is always the case. If $a = 100$ and $c = 2$, then $b = 800$. Column A is still larger. There isn't anything else you can try that would change the values, so choice (A) is the best answer.

Exponents and Square Roots

EXPONENTS AND SQUARE ROOTS

For some reason, exponents and square roots always look scary; maybe it's the funny little symbols. ETS has a real gift for making them look challenging, but they are all based on the same set of basic rules.

EXPONENTS

If you see a^2, it simply means $a \times a$. If you see a^3, it means $a \times a \times a$, and so on. Hence, the golden rule of exponents is

> When in doubt, expand it out.

x^2 times x^3 equals x^5, because

$$x^2 \cdot x^3 = (x \cdot x) \cdot (x \cdot x \cdot x) = x^{2+3} = x^5$$

When you multiply numbers raised to powers, simply add the exponents.

You can continue this logic when you are dividing exponents.

$\dfrac{x^2}{x^3}$ equals $\dfrac{1}{x}$, because expanding out and canceling leaves you with only one x in the divisor.

$$\frac{x^2}{x^3} = \frac{x \cdot x}{x \cdot x \cdot x} = \frac{\cancel{x} \cdot \cancel{x}}{\cancel{x} \cdot \cancel{x} \cdot x} = \frac{1}{x} = x^{2-3} = x^{-1}$$

When you divide numbers raised to powers, simply subtract the exponents. Thus,

x^{2-3} equals x^{-1} which is the same thing as $\dfrac{1}{x}$.

This same rule applies to exponents and parentheses as well.

$$\left(x^2\right)^3 = (x \cdot x)(x \cdot x)(x \cdot x) = x^{2 \cdot 3} = x^6$$

When you raise a number with a power to another power, simply multiply the exponents.

The one thing to remember with an exponent outside of a parenthesis is that the exponent applies to everything inside the parenthesis. Thus: $\left(\dfrac{2}{5}\right)^2 = \dfrac{4}{25}$, and $(4x)^2 = 16x^2$.

Adding and Subtracting Large Exponents

If you see a problem that asks you to add or subtract large exponents, look for an opportunity to factor. This is particularly true on Quant Comp problems. Often, you don't need to solve; you just need to make the two columns look similar.

Here's an example:

Column A	Column B
$\dfrac{3^{30} - 3^{28}}{2^3}$	3^{28}

Column A involves the subtraction of two large exponents. Column B has a large exponent suspiciously similar to the ones in Column A. When a question like this appears, you know two things right away. First, you will never be asked to figure out the actual value of 3^{30}. The answer to this problem will come from knowledge and manipulation, not from calculation. Second, the number in Column B is a clue: 3^{28} exists in both columns. Your strategy is to isolate the information that is the same in both columns and examine the information that is different.

> When large exponents are added or subtracted, look for opportunities to factor.

Start by trying to isolate the 3^{28} in Column A.

Here's what happens

$$\frac{3^{30} - 3^{28}}{2^3} = \frac{3^{28}(3^2 - 1)}{2^3} = \frac{3^{28}(9-1)}{2^3} = \frac{3^{28}(8)}{8} = 3^{28}$$

When you factor 3^{28} out of the expression on top, you are left with 3^2 minus 1. This you can solve; it equals 8. Low and behold, there is an 8 on the bottom, and now you know you're getting somewhere. The 8's cancel out and you're left with 3^{28} in both columns; thus, the answer is choice (C).

Exponent Rules

Here are some other things to keep in mind about exponents.

- Any number raised to the zero power equals one.
- Any number raised to the first power is itself.
- A negative number raised to an even power is positive.
- A negative number raised to an odd power is negative.
- Fractions less than one raised to higher powers get smaller; the higher the power, the smaller they get.

SQUARE ROOTS

Square Roots are the same thing as exponents, but in reverse. Rather than making things exponentially larger, square roots make them exponentially smaller. There's not much you can do with square roots. You can add them or subtract them only when the roots are the same; thus $\sqrt{3} + \sqrt{3} = 2\sqrt{3}$, because now there are two of them. When the roots are different, though, you can't add or subtract them.

When you are multiplying square roots, you can combine things under a single symbol.

$$\sqrt{4} \times \sqrt{16} = \sqrt{4 \times 16} = \sqrt{64} = 8$$

You can also combine when dividing.

$$\frac{\sqrt{64}}{\sqrt{4}} = \sqrt{\frac{64}{4}} = \sqrt{16} = 4$$

Remember that even if the number under a square root sign is not a perfect square, it doesn't mean that there aren't some perfect squares in there. These you can factor out. For example, there is no even square root of 12, but 12 is a product of three and four. Three has no even square root, so it must stay under the sign. Four is a perfect square, though; you can take it out from under the sign and call it two.

$$\sqrt{12} = \sqrt{3 \times 4} = \sqrt{3} \times \sqrt{4} = \sqrt{3} \times 2 = 2\sqrt{3}$$

Remember that $2\sqrt{3}$ means two times the square root of three.

Negative Squares

There is one tricky thing about square roots: negative numbers. When you square 3, you get 9, but when you square –3, you also get 9. That means that when you're going in the other direction, you have two possible answers. Thus, if you're told that $x^2 = 9$, then $x = \pm 3$. However, on the GRE, the square root of a number is defined as the positive root only, so $\sqrt{9}$ equals 3, <u>not</u> ±3.

> A square root only has a positive solution, but an exponent to the 2nd power has both a positive and a negative solution.

For more practice and a more in-depth look at The Princeton Review math techniques, check out our student-friendly guidebook, *Cracking the GRE*.

EXPONENTS & SQUARE ROOTS DRILL

$$a < 0$$

Column A	Column B
a^2	$2a$

○ The quantity in Column A is greater.
○ The quantity in Column B is greater.
○ The two quantities are equal.
○ The relationship cannot be determined from the information given.

$$8z^4 = 96$$

Column A	Column B
2	z

○ The quantity in Column A is greater.
○ The quantity in Column B is greater.
○ The two quantities are equal.
○ The relationship cannot be determined from the information given.

What is the value of $3^{3a} - 2$ when $a = 2$?
○ 16
○ 52
○ 79
○ 697
○ 727

Column A	Column B
$x + y$	$(x + y)^2$

○ The quantity in Column A is greater.
○ The quantity in Column B is greater.
○ The two quantities are equal.
○ The relationship cannot be determined from the information given.

Column A	Column B
$\dfrac{5^{15}}{5^5}$	$\dfrac{5^{18}}{5^6}$

○ The quantity in Column A is greater.
○ The quantity in Column B is greater.
○ The two quantities are equal.
○ The relationship cannot be determined from the information given.

What is the value of $\sqrt{\sqrt{64}}$?
○ $2\sqrt{2}$
○ 4
○ $4\sqrt{2}$
○ 16
○ 32

Column A	Column B
$(0.5)^3$	$\left(5\right)^3\left(\dfrac{1}{2}\right)^3\left(\dfrac{1}{5}\right)^3$

○ The quantity in Column A is greater.
○ The quantity in Column B is greater.
○ The two quantities are equal.
○ The relationship cannot be determined from the information given.

$$\sqrt{81 + 9} =$$

○ 9
○ 10
○ $3\sqrt{10}$
○ 12
○ 30

$$x > 0$$

Column A	Column B
$\left(\dfrac{1}{3}\right)^x$	$\left(-\dfrac{1}{2}\right)^x$

○ The quantity in Column A is greater.
○ The quantity in Column B is greater.
○ The two quantities are equal.
○ The relationship cannot be determined
  from the information given.

Column A	Column B
$-\sqrt{9}$	$\sqrt[3]{-27}$

○ The quantity in Column A is greater.
○ The quantity in Column B is greater.
○ The two quantities are equal.
○ The relationship cannot be determined
  from the information given.

If $(x - 1)(2x + 3)(x + 5) = 0,$ then which of the following could be the value of x ?

○ $-\dfrac{3}{2}$

○ -1

○ $\dfrac{2}{3}$

○ 5

○ 6

What is the value of $\sqrt[3]{69}$ approximated to the nearest integer?

○ 13
○ 8
○ 5
○ 4
○ 3

$$y > 0$$

Column A	Column B
$\left(\dfrac{2}{y}\right)^3$	$\left(\dfrac{3}{y}\right)^2$

○ The quantity in Column A is greater.
○ The quantity in Column B is greater.
○ The two quantities are equal.
○ The relationship cannot be determined
  from the information given.

$$\left(\dfrac{1}{2}\right)^3 + \left(\dfrac{2}{3}\right)^2 + \left(\dfrac{1}{6}\right)^1 =$$

○ $\dfrac{1}{6}$

○ $\dfrac{1}{18}$

○ $\dfrac{5}{36}$

○ $\dfrac{53}{72}$

○ $\dfrac{8}{6}$

$$\frac{9^2 - 3^2}{6^2} =$$

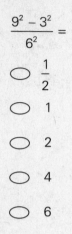

- $\frac{1}{2}$
- 1
- 2
- 4
- 6

Column A	Column B
$\sqrt{\dfrac{1}{4^2}}$	$\dfrac{1}{4}$

- The quantity in Column A is greater.
- The quantity in Column B is greater.
- The two quantities are equal.
- The relationship cannot be determined from the information given.

Column A	Column B
$(x^3 + 1)^2$	x^6

- The quantity in Column A is greater.
- The quantity in Column B is greater.
- The two quantities are equal.
- The relationship cannot be determined from the information given.

$$\left(\sqrt{5} + \sqrt{7}\right)^2 =$$

- 12
- $12 + 2\sqrt{3}$
- $12 + 4\sqrt{3}$
- $12 + \sqrt{35}$
- $12 + 2\sqrt{35}$

If $\sqrt{x} = 4$, then $x^2 =$

- 2
- 4
- 8
- 16
- 256

What is the value of $x^2 - 1$ when $9^{x + 1} = 27^{x - 1}$?

Column A	Column B
$(y - x)^7$	$(y - x)^2$

- The quantity in Column A is greater.
- The quantity in Column B is greater.
- The two quantities are equal.
- The relationship cannot be determined from the information given.

Column A	Column B
$2^2(420)$	$2^5(105)$

- The quantity in Column A is greater.
- The quantity in Column B is greater.
- The two quantities are equal.
- The relationship cannot be determined from the information given.

If $b = \dfrac{c + d^2}{c}$ and $a = \dfrac{c}{d^2}$, what is b in terms of a ?

○ $1 + \dfrac{1}{a}$

○ $1 + a$

○ $\dfrac{1}{1 + a}$

○ $a^2 + 1$

○ $\dfrac{a}{a + 1}$

If $-1 < a < 0$, $q = a - 1$, $r = a^2$, and $s = a^3$, then which of the following is true?

○ $q < r < s$
○ $q < s < r$
○ $r < q < s$
○ $s < q < r$
○ $s < r < q$

$$\sqrt{10y} = 5$$
$$z^4 = 81$$

Column A	Column B
z	y

○ The quantity in Column A is greater.
○ The quantity in Column B is greater.
○ The two quantities are equal.
○ The relationship cannot be determined from the information given.

0.1 is how many times greater than $(0.01)^3$?

○ 10^6
○ 10^5
○ 10^4
○ 10^3
○ 10^2

If $x \geq 0$, then $\sqrt{0.49x^{16}}$ must be equal to

○ $0.07x^8$
○ $0.07x^4$
○ $0.7x^{14}$
○ $0.7x^8$
○ $0.7x^4$

$$0 > d > e$$

Column A	Column B
de	$\sqrt{de}$

○ The quantity in Column A is greater.
○ The quantity in Column B is greater.
○ The two quantities are equal.
○ The relationship cannot be determined from the information given.

If $m > 0$ and $n > 0$, which of the following is equivalent to $\dfrac{nm}{m^2}\sqrt{\dfrac{m^2}{n}}$?

○ $\sqrt{n}$

○ $\dfrac{nm}{\sqrt{n}}$

○ $\dfrac{m^2}{n}$

○ $\dfrac{n^2}{m}$

○ $\dfrac{1}{nm}$

Column A

20^7

Column B

$\left(\dfrac{4^{13}}{4^6}\right)(5^4 \times 5^3)$

◯ The quantity in Column A is greater.
◯ The quantity in Column B is greater.
◯ The two quantities are equal.
◯ The relationship cannot be determined from the information given.

Column A

$0.8^2 + 0.8^2 + 0.8^2 + 0.8^2$

Column B

1.6^2

◯ The quantity in Column A is greater.
◯ The quantity in Column B is greater.
◯ The two quantities are equal.
◯ The relationship cannot be determined from the information given.

Which expression is equivalent to $\dfrac{2 - \sqrt{3}}{2 + \sqrt{3}}$?

◯ $-\dfrac{1}{5}$

◯ -1

◯ $\dfrac{4\sqrt{3} - 1}{7}$

◯ $4\sqrt{3} - 7$

◯ $7 - 4\sqrt{3}$

$5^{50} + 5^{50} + 5^{50} + 5^{50} + 5^{50} =$

◯ 5^{51}
◯ 5^{25}
◯ 25^{50}
◯ 25^{51}
◯ 25^{250}

b is an integer, and $0 \leq b \leq 2$

Column A

$\left(b^2 + \dfrac{1}{2}\right)^b$

Column B

$20 + \dfrac{1}{4}$

◯ The quantity in Column A is greater.
◯ The quantity in Column B is greater.
◯ The two quantities are equal.
◯ The relationship cannot be determined from the information given.

$ab = 12$

$b^2 = 16$

Column A

a

Column B

b

◯ The quantity in Column A is greater.
◯ The quantity in Column B is greater.
◯ The two quantities are equal.
◯ The relationship cannot be determined from the information given.

$(x + y)(x - y) = 0$

$xy \neq 0$

Column A

$6\sqrt{\dfrac{19}{2x^2}}$

Column B

$\sqrt{\dfrac{342}{y^2}}$

◯ The quantity in Column A is greater.
◯ The quantity in Column B is greater.
◯ The two quantities are equal.
◯ The relationship cannot be determined from the information given.

ANSWERS

1. A
2. A
3. E
4. D
5. B
6. A
7. C
8. C
9. D
10. C
11. A
12. D
13. D
14. D
15. C
16. C
17. D
18. E
19. E
20. 24
21. D
22. B
23. A
24. B
25. D
26. B
27. D
28. D
29. A
30. C
31. C
32. E
33. A
34. D
35. D
36. C

EXPLANATIONS

1. **A** Try Plugging In. If $a = -3$, then Column A is $(-3)^2 = 9$ and Column B is $2(-3) = -6$. Notice that Column A must always be positive because anything raised to an even power is positive. Column B must be negative because a positive times a negative is always negative. Thus, Column A must always be greater.

2. **A** Divide both sides by 8 to get $z^4 = 12$. Rather than finding the fourth root of 12, try Plugging In 2 for z: $2^4 = 16$, so z must be less than 2. Of course, z may be negative, but any negative number is also less than 2.

3. **E** Plug In 2 for a to find $3^{3(2)} - 2$ or $3^6 - 2$. When in doubt, expand it out. So, $(3 \times 3 \times 3 \times 3 \times 3 \times 3) - 2 = 729 - 2 = 727$.

4. **D** Plug In! If $x = 2$ and $y = 3$, then Column A is 5 and Column B is 25. Column B is greater, so eliminate choices (A) and (C). Next, make x and y both 0. Both Columns A and B are now 0, thus, they are equal. Eliminate choice (B), and you're left with choice (D).

5. **B** Simplify each of the expressions by subtracting the exponents. You get 5^{10} in Column A and 5^{12} in Column B.

6. **A** First, take the square root of 64, which is 8. $\sqrt{8} = \sqrt{4} \times \sqrt{2} = 2\sqrt{2}$. To simplify $\sqrt{\sqrt{64}} = \sqrt{8}$, divide out the perfect square 4. $\sqrt{8}$, The answer is choice (A).

7. **C** Column A, $(0.5)^3$, equals 0.125. Column B, $(5)^3 \left(\dfrac{1}{2}\right)^3 \left(\dfrac{1}{5}\right)^3$, equals $(125)\left(\dfrac{1}{8}\right)\left(\dfrac{1}{125}\right)$; the first and third terms cancel to leave only $\dfrac{1}{8} = 0.125$. The Columns are equal. Alternatively, if you're comfortable with your exponent rules, you can combine and cancel the terms in Column B, and compare the Columns without calculating either one: $(5)^3 \left(\dfrac{1}{2}\right)^3 \left(\dfrac{1}{5}\right)^3 = \left(5 \times \dfrac{1}{2} \times \dfrac{1}{5}\right)^3$; again, the first and third terms cancel to leave only $\left(\dfrac{1}{2}\right)^3$, which is the same as $(0.5)^3$.

8. **C** First, add the numbers under the root symbol. To simplify $\sqrt{90}$, divide out the perfect square 9. $\sqrt{90} = \sqrt{9} \times \sqrt{10} = 3\sqrt{10}$. The answer is choice (C).

9. **D** Evaluate the relationship between the Columns by Plugging In values for x. If $x = 2$, then Column A is $\dfrac{1}{9}$ and Column B is $\dfrac{1}{4}$; Column B is greater, so eliminate answer choices (A) and (C). Now, if $x = 3$, then Column A is $\dfrac{1}{27}$ and Column B is $-\dfrac{1}{8}$; Column A is now greater, so eliminate choice (B), and you're left with choice (D).

10. **C** In Column A, evaluate the root first, then attach the minus sign: $-\sqrt{9} = -3$; this is equivalent to Column B: $\sqrt[3]{-27} = -3$. Thus, the answer is choice (C).

11. **A** Zero times any number is zero, so the left side of the equation will equal zero when any of the expressions in parentheses equals zero, i.e. when $x - 1 = 0$, $2x + 3 = 0$, or $x + 5 = 0$. Solving these equations yields $x = 1$, $-\dfrac{3}{2}$, and -5, respectively. Of these, only $-\dfrac{3}{2}$ is in the answers, which is choice (A). Alternatively, try Plugging In the answer choices, starting with the easier numbers.

12. **D** $\sqrt[3]{69}$ means "the number that when you cube it, gives you 69". So Plug In the answer choices, cubing each one until you find the value closest to 69. It is easier to start with the smaller values first. $3^3 = 27$; $4^3 = 64$; $5^3 = 125$. Clearly, 4^3 is closest to 69, so the answer is choice (D).

13. **D** Plug In values for y. If $y = 1$, then Column A is 8 and Column B is 9. In this case, Column B is larger, so eliminate choices (A) and (C). If $y = \dfrac{1}{2}$, then Column A is 64 and Column B is 36; eliminate choice (B). You are left with choice (D).

14. **D** First, use the exponent rules to find the values you need to add:

$$\left(\frac{1}{2}\right)^3 + \left(\frac{2}{3}\right)^2 + \left(\frac{1}{6}\right)^1 = \frac{1^3}{2^3} + \frac{2^2}{3^2} + \frac{1^1}{6^1} = \frac{1}{8} + \frac{4}{9} + \frac{1}{6}.$$ Then, because you have so many types of fractions, convert them all to the common denominator of 72: $\dfrac{9}{72} + \dfrac{32}{72} + \dfrac{12}{72} = \dfrac{53}{72}$. The answer is choice (D).

15. **C** Although it may be tempting to try some fancy factoring, this problem is more easily solved by calculating the individual exponential expressions: $\dfrac{9^2 - 3^2}{6^2} = \dfrac{81 - 9}{36} = \dfrac{72}{36} = 2$. Be careful, if you got choice (B): you may have incorrectly subtracted $9^2 - 3^2$ in the numerator and gotten 6^2.

16. **C** Simplify Column A: $\sqrt{\dfrac{1}{4^2}} = \dfrac{\sqrt{1}}{\sqrt{4^2}} = \dfrac{1}{4}$. The answer is choice (C).

17. **D** Plug In a value for x; you're dealing with exponents, so keep your numbers small. If $x = 0$, then Column A is greater, so eliminate choices (B) and (C). If $x = -1$, though, then Column A = 0; Column B is now greater, so eliminate choice (A), and you're left with choice (D).

18. **E** You could use the common quadratic pattern $(x + y)^2 = x^2 + 2xy + y^2$. So, $(\sqrt{5} + \sqrt{7})^2 = \sqrt{5}^2 + 2\sqrt{5 \times 7} + \sqrt{7}^2 = 5 + 2\sqrt{35} + 7 = 12 + 2\sqrt{35}$. The answer is choice (E). Alternatively, you can just FOIL it. So, $(\sqrt{5} + \sqrt{7})^2 = (\sqrt{5} + \sqrt{7})(\sqrt{5} + \sqrt{7}) = 5 + \sqrt{5 \times 7} + \sqrt{5 \times 7} + 7 = 12 + 2\sqrt{35}$.

19. **E** First, square both sides of the equation to get $x = 16$. Then, square both sides of the equation again to get $x^2 = 256$. The answer is choice (E).

20. **24** Start by expressing both terms in the original equation as powers of 3: $9^{x+1} = 27^{x-1}$ becomes $\left(3^2\right)^{x+1} = \left(3^3\right)^{x-1}$. To raise a power to another power, multiply the exponents, so your equation becomes $3^{2x+2} = 3^{3x-3}$. Now that the bases are the same, set the exponents equal to each other and solve for x: $2x + 2 = 3x - 3$, so $x = 5$. Finally, remember to enter the correct value: the problem asks for $x^2 - 1$, so $5^2 - 1 = 25 - 1 = 24$.

21. **D** Try Plugging In values for x and y. If $x = 1$ and $y = 3$, then Column A is 2^7 and Column B is 2^2. Column A is greater, so eliminate choices (B) and (C). Then try $x = 1$ and $y = 1$; now both Columns are equal, so eliminate choice (A) and select choice (D).

22. **B** To make it easier to compare the Columns, rearrange the terms in Column B to get $2^2 \times (2^3 \times 105) = 2^2 \times 840$. Alternatively, you can rearrange Column A to get $2^2 \times (2^2 \times 105)$.

23. **A** Plug In for c and d, in both equations, and solve for a and b. If $c = 8$ and $d = 4$, then $a = \frac{1}{2}$ and $b = 3$, your target answer. Now plug in $\frac{1}{2}$ for a in the answer choices; only choice (A) hits your target answer of 3.

24. **B** Plug In to solve this one, but don't forget your restrictions. If $a = -\frac{1}{2}$, then $q = -\frac{3}{2}$, $r = \frac{1}{4}$, and $s = -\frac{1}{8}$. Only choice (B) lists the values in the correct order.

25. **D** To find y, square both sides of the given equation: if $\sqrt{10y} = 5$, then $\left(\sqrt{10y}\right)^2 = 5^2$, so $10y = 25$, and $y = 2.5$. To find z, do the opposite and take the square root of both sides of the given equation: if $z^4 = 81$, then $\sqrt{z^4} = \sqrt{81}$, so $z^2 = 9$, and $z = 3$ [eliminate choices (B) and (C)] or $z = -3$ [eliminate choice (A)]. The answer is, therefore, choice (D).

26. **B** $0.1 = 10^{-1}$ and $(0.01)^3 = (10^{-2})^3 = 10^{-6}$. Dividing one by the other gives you $\frac{10^{-1}}{10^{-6}} = 10^{(-1)-(-6)} = 10^5$. The answer is choice (B).

27. **D** The term under the radical is a product, so you can separate the number and the variable $\sqrt{0.49x^{16}} = \sqrt{0.49} \times \sqrt{x^{16}}$. Just as the square root of 49 is 7, $\sqrt{0.49} = 0.7$; eliminate choices (A) and (B). Next convert $\sqrt{x^{16}}$ to $\sqrt{\left(x^8\right)^2}$; the radical and the outer exponent cancel out, and you're left with x^8. Select choice (D).

28. **D** To solve this one, Plug In for d and e, but don't forget your restriction: $0 > d > e$. First, make $d = -2$

and $e = -8$; Column A is 16, and Column B is $\sqrt{16} = 4$. Column A is greater, so eliminate answer

choices (B) and (C). Next, make $d = -\dfrac{1}{8}$ and $e = -\dfrac{1}{2}$; now, Column A is $\dfrac{1}{16}$, and Column B is

$\sqrt{\dfrac{1}{16}} = \dfrac{1}{4}$. Column B is now greater, so eliminate choice (A), and you're left with choice (D).

29. **A** Plug In $m = 2$ and $n = 4$, so $\dfrac{2 \times 4}{2^2}\sqrt{\dfrac{2^2}{4}} = \dfrac{8}{4}\sqrt{\dfrac{4}{4}} = 2\sqrt{\dfrac{1}{1}} = 2$, your target answer. When you Plug In

the values you chose for m and n, only choice (A) works. Alternatively, you could do the algebra:

$\dfrac{nm}{m^2}\sqrt{\dfrac{m^2}{n}} = \dfrac{n\sqrt{m^2}}{m\sqrt{n}} = \dfrac{nm}{m\sqrt{n}} = \dfrac{n}{\sqrt{n}}$. To eliminate the radical in the denominator of the fraction,

multiply both the numerator and the denominator by $\sqrt{n}$: $\dfrac{n}{\sqrt{n}} \times \dfrac{\sqrt{n}}{\sqrt{n}} = \dfrac{n\sqrt{n}}{n} = \sqrt{n}$.

30. **C** First, factor Column A into $4^7 \times 5^7$ to make it resemble Column B. Next, simplify the individual terms

in Column B: $\left(\dfrac{4^{13}}{4^6}\right) = 4^7$, and $(5^4 \times 5^3) = 5^7$. The Columns are equal, so the answer is choice (C).

31. **C** Don't get caught up in tricks involving exponent rules—just calculate the Columns. In Column A, $0.8^2 = 0.64$, so $0.8^2 + 0.8^2 + 0.8^2 + 0.8^2$ equals 4×0.64, or 2.56. In Column B, 1.6^2 also equals 2.56 (make sure you put the decimal in the right place), so the Columns are equal.

32. **E** To rationalize (get rid of the root sign in) the denominator, multiply the numerator and denomina-

tor by $2 - \sqrt{3}$: $\dfrac{(2-\sqrt{3})(2-\sqrt{3})}{(2+\sqrt{3})(2-\sqrt{3})} = \dfrac{4-4\sqrt{3}+3}{4-3} = \dfrac{7-4\sqrt{3}}{1}$.

33. **A** Factor 5^{50} out of the original equation to yield $5^{50} \times 5$. To multiply, change the 5 to 5^1 and—because you have two numbers with the same base—add the exponents: $5^{50} \times 5^1 = 5^{51}$.

34. **D** There are only 3 possible values for b: 0, 1, and 2. So just plug those values into Column A. Start

with 0, because it's the easiest: anything raised to the power of 0 is 1. Column B is greater, so

eliminate choices (A) and (C). Next, try 1: $\left(1n+\dfrac{1}{2}\right)^1 = \dfrac{3}{2}$. Column B is still greater, so no new

answers can be eliminated. Finally, try 2: $\left(2n+\dfrac{1}{2}\right)^2 = \left(4\dfrac{1}{2}\right)^2 = \left(\dfrac{9}{2}\right)^2 = \dfrac{9^2}{2^2} = \dfrac{81}{4} = 20\dfrac{1}{4}$. The two

Columns are equal, so eliminate choice (B) and select choice (D).

35. **D** Start by using the second equation to Plug In values for b, and then use the first equation to find the corresponding value for a. In the equation: $b^2 = 16$, b could be 4, then a would be 3; Column B is greater, so eliminate choices (A) and (C). However, b could also be -4, in which case a would be -3; Column A is now greater, so eliminate choice (B), and you're left with choice (D).

36. C If $(x + y)(x - y) = 0$ and $xy \neq 0$, then either $x + y = 0$ or $x - y = 0$; hence, $x = y$ or $x = -y$. Fortunately, the

variables only show up in the Columns as squared values, so all the calculations will work out the

same either way. Plug In values for x and y to simplify the comparison: Try making both x and y

equal to 2. Now Column A is $6\sqrt{\dfrac{19}{2(2)^2}}$, or $6\sqrt{\dfrac{19}{2^3}}$; Column B is $\sqrt{\dfrac{342}{4}}$. At this point, manipu-

late Column B to make it look like Column A: $\sqrt{\dfrac{342}{4}} = \sqrt{\dfrac{19 \times 9 \times 2}{2^2}}$; multiplying by $\dfrac{2}{2}$ under the

radical yields $\sqrt{\dfrac{19 \times 9 \times 2 \times 2}{2^2 \times 2}}$, or $\sqrt{\dfrac{19 \times 36}{2^3}}$. Moving the perfect square 36 outside the radical

yields $6\sqrt{\dfrac{19}{2^3}}$.

Lines and Angles

LINES AND ANGLES

This is geometry 101. Before you get to shapes, such as circles and triangles, you must first have a solid grasp of lines, intersecting lines, parallel lines, and degree measurements.

There are a couple of key concepts you need to know.

- There are 180 degrees in a straight line.
- A perpendicular line forms a right angle.
- When two lines intersect, four angles are formed.
- Opposite angles are equal.

PARALLEL LINES

Line and angle questions will often involve parallel lines. Never assume two lines are parallel, no matter what they show you, unless you are told they are parallel or you can prove it.

> When two parallel lines are intersected by a third line, two kinds of angles are formed, big ones and small ones. All big angles are equal, all small angles are equal, and any big angle plus any small angle will add up to 180 degrees.

On all geometry problems, use your scratch paper and follow these five steps.

Step 1: Draw your shape

In some cases the test will give you a shape, which you may or may not be able to trust, or it will give you a word problem and leave it up to you to envision the shape. As with every other part of the test, getting your hand moving is an important first step to entering the problem. Get your shape down on your scratch paper so that you can begin working with it there. On Quant Comp questions involving geometry, instead of Plugging In more than once, you may have to draw your shape more than once.

Step 2: Fill in what you know

Whether you are given the shape or not, you will be given a certain amount of information regarding the shape, such as the measure of some angles, lengths of some sides, area of some sides, or volume. Fill in what you know.

Step 3: Make deductions

If you are given two angles of a triangle, find the third. If you are given the radius of a circle, find the area. Often this will be the entire problem. Geometry on the GRE is all about finding the missing piece of information. You will be given just enough information to find the piece that is missing.

Step 4: Write down relevant formulas

If step three didn't get you the answer, you must still be missing a piece of information. Writing down the formula is a way to organize your information and to tell you what is missing. When you write your formulas down, fill in the information you have directly underneath the relevant part of the formula. It seems simple, but this way you can't make a mistake, and finding the missing piece of information becomes a simple case of solving for x.

Step 5: Drop heights/draw lines

If you're still stuck, you may need to manipulate or subdivide your shapes. If you have triangles, draw in the height. Have you created a 30-60-90? A 45-45-90? Or a Pythagorean triple? Try subdividing the shape or, if it's a three-dimensional figure, dashing in the hidden lines.

For more practice and a more in-depth look at The Princeton Review math techniques, check out our student-friendly guidebook, *Cracking the GRE*.

LINES AND ANGLES DRILL

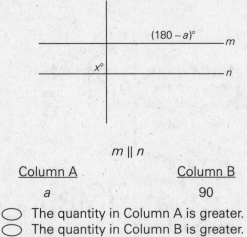

$m \parallel n$

Column A	Column B
a	90

- The quantity in Column A is greater.
- The quantity in Column B is greater.
- The two quantities are equal.
- The relationship cannot be determined from the information given.

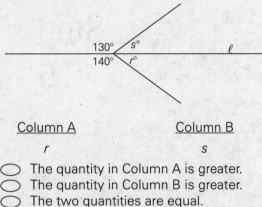

Column A	Column B
r	s

- The quantity in Column A is greater.
- The quantity in Column B is greater.
- The two quantities are equal.
- The relationship cannot be determined from the information given.

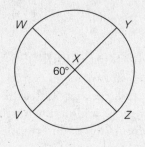

If X is the center of the circle above, then what is the sum of the measures of $\angle WXY$ and $\angle VXZ$?

- 60°
- 120°
- 220°
- 240°
- 280°

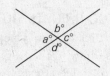

In the figure above, c is $\dfrac{4}{5}$ of d. What is the value of c ?

- 72
- 80
- 100
- 108
- 120

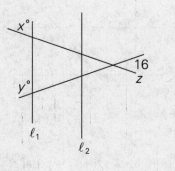

In the figure above, ℓ_1 is parallel to ℓ_2. If $x = 40$ and $y = 70$, what is the value of z ?

- ⭕ 70
- ⭕ 60
- ⭕ 50
- ⭕ 40
- ⭕ 30

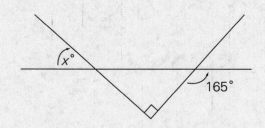

What is the value of x ?

- ⭕ 15
- ⭕ 55
- ⭕ 65
- ⭕ 75
- ⭕ 115

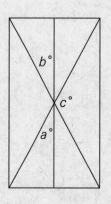

Column A	Column B
$a + b$	$180 - c$

- ⭕ The quantity in Column A is greater.
- ⭕ The quantity in Column B is greater.
- ⭕ The two quantities are equal.
- ⭕ The relationship cannot be determined from the information given.

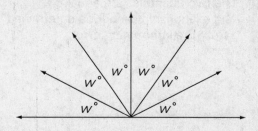

In the figure above, what is the value of w ?

- ⭕ 10
- ⭕ 15
- ⭕ 30
- ⭕ 45
- ⭕ 60

What is the area of a regular hexagon with side length 8 ?

- ⬭ 64
- ⬭ $64\sqrt{3}$
- ⬭ 78
- ⬭ $78\sqrt{3}$
- ⬭ $96\sqrt{3}$

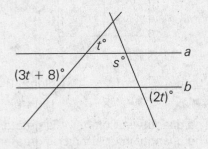

$a \parallel b$

Column A	Column B
95	s

- ⬭ The quantity in Column A is greater.
- ⬭ The quantity in Column B is greater.
- ⬭ The two quantities are equal.
- ⬭ The relationship cannot be determined from the information given.

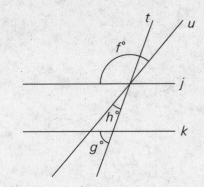

In the figure above, line j is parallel to line k. If $f = 130$ and $g = 70$, then $h =$

- ⬭ 10
- ⬭ 20
- ⬭ 30
- ⬭ 60
- ⬭ 80

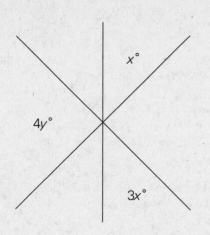

What is the value of y in the figure above, if
5x = 4y ?

- ⬭ 25
- ⬭ 50
- ⬭ 60
- ⬭ 80
- ⬭ 100

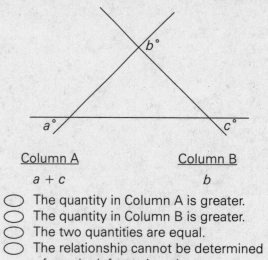

Column A	Column B
a + c	b

- ⬭ The quantity in Column A is greater.
- ⬭ The quantity in Column B is greater.
- ⬭ The two quantities are equal.
- ⬭ The relationship cannot be determined
  from the information given.

ANSWERS

1. D
2. B
3. D
4. B
5. E
6. D
7. C
8. C
9. E
10. A
11. B
12. A
13. C

EXPLANATIONS

1. **D** Two parallel lines—with a line cutting through them—create big angles (bigger than 90°) and small angles (smaller than 90°). Any big angle plus any small angle equals 180°. In the figure, x *appears to be* a big angle and $(180 - a)$ *appears to be* a small angle. So $x + (180° - a) = 180°$, or $x = a$. But in fact, because you can't trust the figure, you don't know whether x (and therefore a) is really a big, small, or 90° angle. The answer is choice (D).

2. **B** Use the Rule of 180 to find $r = 40$ and $s = 50$.

3. **D** Because $\angle WXY$ forms a line with a 60° angle, it must be $180° - 60° = 120°$; $\angle WXY$ and $\angle VXZ$ are vertical angles, so $\angle VXZ$ must be 120° as well. The sum of the measures of $\angle WXY$ and $\angle VXZ$ is $120° + 120° = 240°$.

4. **B** The sum of c and d is 180, so you know that $\frac{4}{5}d + d = 180$. Solve this equation: $d = 100$. If $d = 100$, then $c = 80$. The answer is choice (B).

5. **E** All of the angles are related to the interior angles of the larger triangle in the figure. The interior angle at the upper vertex of this triangle and the angle with measure $x°$ are vertical angles, so each measures 40°. The interior angle at the lower vertex of the triangle and the angle with measure $y°$ must add up to 180° to form a straight line, so the lower vertex angle measures 110°. You've accounted for 150 of the 180° of the triangle, so the remaining angle of the triangle must measure 30°. The angle with measure $z°$ and that angle are vertical angles, so z must also measure 30°. The answer is choice (E).

6. **D** Remember that a straight line measures 180°. Therefore, the angle inside the triangle next to the 165° angle measures $180° - 165° = 15°$. A triangle contains 180° and a right angle measures 90°. The third angle in that triangle must measure $180° - (90° + 15°) = 75°$. Vertical angles are equal, so $x = 75$. The answer is choice (D).

7. **C** Plug In your own numbers, choosing easy values for the angle measures. If $a = 40$, and $b = 60$, then the angle in between them must measure 80° to complete the 180° in a straight line. That angle and the angle measuring $c°$ are vertical, so $c = 80$ as well. Both quantities then equal 100; eliminate choices (A) and (B). Try a new pair of numbers for b and c, and you will realize that plugging in any values yields the same result, making choice (C) the answer.

8. **C** There are 180° in a straight line. The straight line is divided into six equal angles in this figure, so $180° \div 6 = 30°$.

9. E A hexagon has 6 sides. The total number of degrees in the interior of a polygon of n sides is given by $(n-2)180 = (6-2)180 = 720$. A regular polygon is one in which the sides and angles are all equal. Dividing 720° by 6 gives you 120° for each interior angle in the hexagon. Now draw the hexagon and a point in its center. Connecting the center to each vertex divides the hexagon into six equal triangles. These segments from the center to each vertex are all of equal length, so the triangles are isosceles. These segments also bisect each of the interior angles, so the base angles of these triangles each measure 60°. Thus, the remaining angle in each triangle (near the center of the hexagon) also measures 60°, and therefore these triangles are equilateral, with sides of length 8. The area of an equilateral triangle of side x is $\dfrac{x^2\sqrt{3}}{4} = \dfrac{8^2\sqrt{3}}{4} = 16\sqrt{3}$. Multiplying the area of each triangle by 6 gives you $96\sqrt{3}$; the answer is choice (E).

10. A First, solve for t: lines a and b are parallel, so $(3t + 8) + t = 180$; $4t + 8 = 180$; $4t = 172$; $t = 43$. Lines a and b are parallel and you know that $2t + s = 180$, so $2(43) + s = 180$; $86 + s = 180$; $s = 94$. Column A is greater.

11. B If $f = 130$, then both large angles formed by lines t and k also measure 130°. The small angles formed by those two lines therefore measure 50° (notice that one of these angles is the left base angle of the triangle). If $g = 70$, then the angle above it (the other base angle of the triangle) must measure 110° to complete the 180° in a straight line. So far, you have 160° in the triangle. To complete the 180° total in the triangle, h must measure 20°. The answer is choice (B).

12. A The angle between the ones marked $x°$ and $3x°$ is vertical to the one that measures $4y°$. These three angles form a straight line, so $x + 4y + 3x = 180$. Since $4y = 5x$, $x + 5x + 3x = 180$; $9x = 180$; $x = 20$. Therefore $4y = 5x = 100$; $y = 25$.

13. C Plug In values for the unknown angles. When $a = 60$ and $b = 130$, the angle vertical to a also measures 60°, and the angle adjacent to b within the triangle must measure $180° - 130° = 50°$. The sum of the angles in a triangle is 180°. Therefore, the remaining angle measures $180° - 60° - 50° = 70°$. Angle c is vertical to the 70° angle, so $c = 70$. Column A is $60 + 70 = 130$ and Column B is 130; the quantities are equal. Eliminate choices (A) and (B). Plugging In a second set of numbers will show you that any set of numbers yields the same result, so the answer is choice (C). Alternatively, you could use algebra to determine that the three angles in the triangle measure $a°$, $(180 - b)°$, and $c°$. Therefore, $a + (180 - b) + c = 180$. Subtract 180 from each side of this equation and add b to each side; $a + c = b$. The Columns are equal.

Triangles

TRIANGLES

Triangles on the GRE are suspicious. They are suspicious because of their tendency to fall into one of two categories: special right triangles and Pythagorean triples. Luckily, this also makes them suspiciously easy.

Triangles have sides, angles, and heights. The angles of any triangle will always add up to 180°. This means that if you have two angles, you can always figure out the third. If two angles of a triangle are equal (isosceles triangles) then the sides opposite those angles will also be equal. The same is true of the reverse; if the sides are equal, then the angles will be too. The height of a triangle is the line (not necessarily shown) from any point perpendicular to the side opposite that point. The height of a triangle is not necessarily drawn on a figure. Here are some examples.

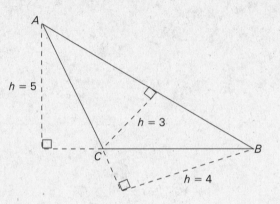

Note: the height is the dashed line.

In this case, if you use side *CB* as your base, your height will be five. If you use side *AC* as your base, your height will be four. You can use any side of a triangle as a base.

RIGHT TRIANGLES

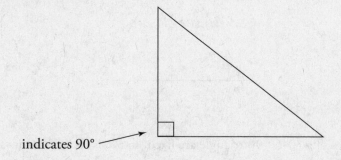

indicates 90°

A right triangle means that one of the angles in a triangle is 90°. This will be noted on the figure. Never assume an angle is 90° unless you're told it is or you can prove it. The side opposite the 90° angle is called the hypotenuse. On right triangles you can apply the Pythagorean theorem, which states that $a^2 + b^2 = c^2$ where c^2 is the hypotenuse. This means that the sum of the squares of the two shorter sides will always be equal to the square of the longest side. If you are given the length of any two sides of a right triangle, you can always find the third. Don't forget to Ballpark and eliminate before you spend time figuring out the square root of one of the sides.

SPECIAL RIGHT TRIANGLES

Remember that the GRE is not a test of your ability to be a calculator. Rarely will you have to actually apply the Pythagorean theorem to find the third side of a triangle. More often, right triangles will turn out to be one of three common types called special right triangles. Because of this, be suspicious. When you see that a triangle has a right angle, start looking for clues that it is a special right triangle. Once you see it, the problem will go much faster.

30-60-90 Triangles

Take an equilateral triangle and fold it in half. The angle at the top has been bisected (cut in half). What was a 60° angle is now a 30° angle. The angles on the sides have not been touched, they are still 60°. The base of your triangle will be cut in half, and the angles where your fold hits the base will be 90°.

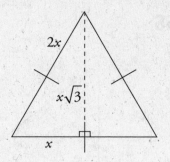

As the angles of a 30-60-90 triangle are fixed, so too is the ratio of its sides. If the short side—the one that was cut in half when you cut the equilateral triangle in half—is x, then the longest side—the untouched one—will be $2x$. The middle side—the height of your equilateral triangle—is $x\sqrt{3}$. It's easy to get lost on a 30-60-90 triangle. Just remember that the longest side, $2x$, is opposite the 90° angle. If you see a right triangle pop up on a question and you see a $\sqrt{3}$ in the answer choices, look for this triangle. It is because of this triangle that you always know the area of an equilateral triangle because you always know the height.

Isosceles Right Triangles

When you cut a square in half on the diagonal, you create an isosceles right triangle. The untouched angles—one corner of the square—remains 90°. The other two angles have been bisected by the hypotenuse and are opposite the equal sides of the square. These angles are both 45°. If the two equal sides of this triangle have a side length of x, then the long side, the diagonal of the square, has a side length of $x\sqrt{2}$. This means that you always know the length of the diagonal of a square. Like the 30-60-90 triangle, if you know the length of one side, you know the length of the other two.

Remember that $\sqrt{2}$ is 1.4 (or Valentine's Day, 2/14) and $\sqrt{3}$ is 1.7 (St. Patrick's Day, 3/17). $\sqrt{2}$ is less than one and a half and $\sqrt{3}$ is less than two. This will help enormously with Ballparking. Also, so that you don't get confused, a 30-60-90 triangle has three different sides and three different angles, and the length of the middle side is $\sqrt{3}$. A right isosceles triangle has only two different side lengths and two different angles; the length of the longest side is the lenth of one of the equal sides times $\sqrt{2}$.

Pythagorean Triples

Some right triangles have whole numbers for all three sides. These are called Pythagorean triples. On a 3-4-5 triangle, for example, three squared is nine and four squared is 16, so they add to 25. If you double this triangle, you get a 6-8-10. The other most common Pythagorean triple is a 5-12-13.

When you see a right triangle, be suspicious

When you see a right triangle, be suspicious. If you see a $\sqrt{3}$ or $\sqrt{2}$ anywhere in the problem, you know what you're looking for. If you see any of the numbers above (3, 4, 5, 6, 8, 10, 12, or 13), be very suspicious. If you see them paired with any of the other numbers, you most likely have your answer. Spotting a Pythagorean triple will save you lots of time—you won't have to do any calculating.

Step 1: Draw your shape

In some cases the test will give you a shape, which you may or may not be able to trust, or it will give you a word problem and leave it up to you to envision the shape. As with every other part of the test, getting your hand moving is an important first step to solving the problem. Get your shape down on your scratch paper so that you can begin working with it there. On Quant Comp questions involving geometry, instead of Plugging In more than once, you may have to draw your shape more than once.

Step 2: Fill in what you know

Whether you are given the shape or not, you will be given a certain amount of information regarding your shape such as the measure of some angles, lengths of some sides, area of some sides, or volume. Fill in what you know.

Step 3: Make deductions

If you are given two angles of a triangle, find the third. You are given the radius of a circle, find the area. Often this will be the entire problem. Geometry on the GRE is all about finding the missing piece of information. You will be given just enough information to find the piece that is missing.

Step 4: Write down relevant formulas

If step three didn't get you the answer, you must still be missing a piece of information. Writing down the formula is a way of both organizing your information and telling you what is missing. When you write your formulas down, fill in the information you have directly underneath the relevant part of the formula. It seems simple, but this way you can't make a mistake and finding the missing piece of information becomes a simple case of solving for x.

Step 5: Drop heights/Draw lines

If you're still stuck, you may need to manipulate or subdivide your shapes. If you have triangles, draw in the height. Have you created a 30-60-90? A 45-45-90? Or a Pythagorean triple? Try subdividing the shape or, if it's a three-dimensional figure, dashing in the hidden lines.

For more practice and a more in-depth look at The Princeton Review math techniques, check out our student-friendly guidebook, *Cracking the GRE*.

TRIANGLES DRILL

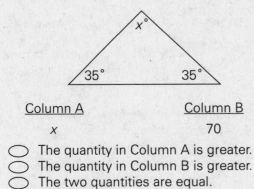

Column A   Column B

    x 70

- ◯ The quantity in Column A is greater.
- ◯ The quantity in Column B is greater.
- ◯ The two quantities are equal.
- ◯ The relationship cannot be determined from the information given.

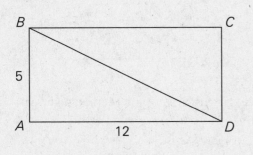

In the figure above, if *ABCD* is a rectangle, then what is the perimeter of △*BCD* ?

- ◯ 30
- ◯ 32
- ◯ 34
- ◯ 40
- ◯ 44

In the figure above, *WX* = *XY* and points *W*, *Y*, and *Z* lie on the same line. What is the value of *q* ?

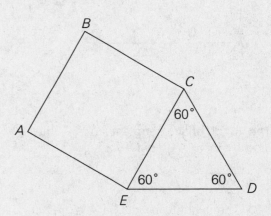

In square *ABCE*, *AB* = 4.

Column A   Column B

   24   The perimeter of polygon *ABCDE*

- ◯ The quantity in Column A is greater.
- ◯ The quantity in Column B is greater.
- ◯ The two quantities are equal.
- ◯ The relationship cannot be determined from the information given.

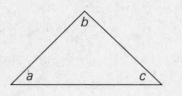

In the figure above, what is the value of

$$\frac{a + b + c}{30}$$?

- ⬭ 4
- ⬭ 6
- ⬭ 8
- ⬭ 10
- ⬭ 16

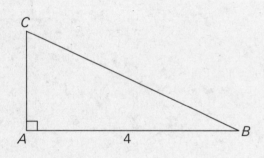

The length of line segment AC is $\frac{3}{4}$ the length of line segment AB.

Column A	Column B
BC	6

- ⬭ The quantity in Column A is greater.
- ⬭ The quantity in Column B is greater.
- ⬭ The two quantities are equal.
- ⬭ The relationship cannot be determined from the information given.

A ship captain sails 500 miles due south and then 1,200 miles due east.

Column A	Column B
1,350 miles	The minimum number of miles the captain must sail to return to his original position

- ⬭ The quantity in Column A is greater.
- ⬭ The quantity in Column B is greater.
- ⬭ The two quantities are equal.
- ⬭ The relationship cannot be determined from the information given.

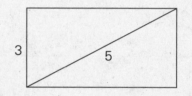

What is the area of the rectangle shown above?

- ⬭ 4
- ⬭ 6
- ⬭ 8
- ⬭ 10
- ⬭ 12

In triangle ABC, side AB has a length of 12, and side BC has a length of 5.

Column A	Column B
The length of side AC	7

- ⬭ The quantity in Column A is greater.
- ⬭ The quantity in Column B is greater.
- ⬭ The two quantities are equal.
- ⬭ The relationship cannot be determined from the information given.

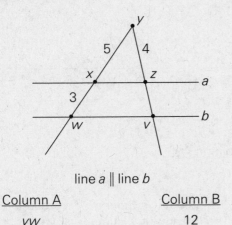

line a ∥ line b

Column A	Column B
vw	12

○ The quantity in Column A is greater.
○ The quantity in Column B is greater.
○ The two quantities are equal.
○ The relationship cannot be determined
from the information given.

A hiker left her tent and traveled due east for
5 miles, then traveled due south for 24 miles,
then due east for 5 miles, arriving at a hut.
What is the straight-line distance from her
tent to the hut?

○ 13
○ 20
○ 26
○ 28
○ 29

The perimeter of triangle A is 24. Which of
the following is NOT a potential side length of
triangle A ?

○ 1
○ 3
○ 8
○ 10
○ 12

Triangle ABC is not equilateral, and angle ABC
= 60 degrees.

Column A	Column B
The angle opposite the shortest side of the triangle	60 degrees

○ The quantity in Column A is greater.
○ The quantity in Column B is greater.
○ The two quantities are equal.
○ The relationship cannot be determined
from the information given.

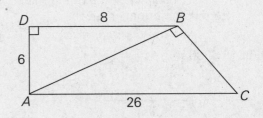

What is the area of triangle ABC, shown
above?

○ 24
○ 48
○ 60
○ 120
○ 240

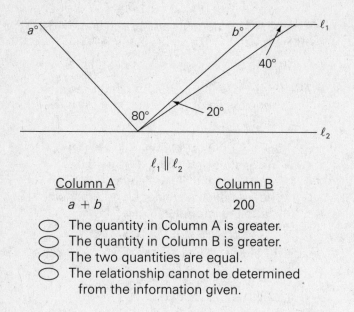

$\ell_1 \parallel \ell_2$

Column A	Column B
$a + b$	200

○ The quantity in Column A is greater.
○ The quantity in Column B is greater.
○ The two quantities are equal.
○ The relationship cannot be determined from the information given.

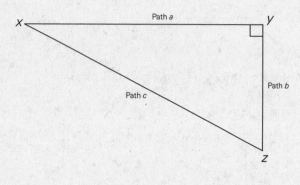

John and James walk from point x to point z (shown in the figure above). John walks directly from x to y on Path a and then directly from y to z on Path b. James walks directly from x to z on Path c. If Path a is 13 miles long and Path b is 5 miles long, John walks about how many miles longer than James?

○ 2
○ 3
○ 4
○ 5
○ 6

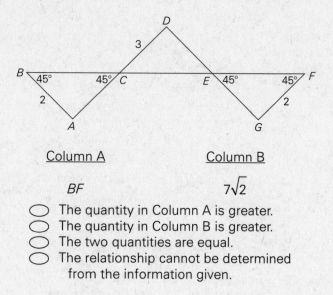

Column A	Column B
BF	$7\sqrt{2}$

○ The quantity in Column A is greater.
○ The quantity in Column B is greater.
○ The two quantities are equal.
○ The relationship cannot be determined from the information given.

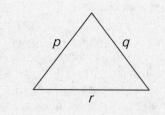

Column A	Column B
r	$p + q - 1$

○ The quantity in Column A is greater.
○ The quantity in Column B is greater.
○ The two quantities are equal.
○ The relationship cannot be determined from the information given.

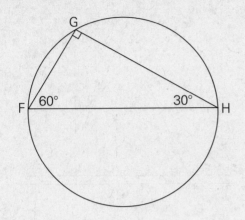

In the figure above, *FG* = 4, and *FH* is a diameter of the circle. What is the area of the circle?

- ○ 4π
- ○ 8π
- ○ 12π
- ○ 16π
- ○ 20π

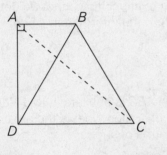

Column A	Column B
$(AB)^2 + (AD)^2$	$(AC)^2$

- ○ The quantity in Column A is greater.
- ○ The quantity in Column B is greater.
- ○ The two quantities are equal.
- ○ The relationship cannot be determined from the information given.

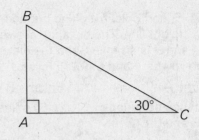

If the area of the above triangle is $8\sqrt{3}$, what is the length of side AB ?

- ○ 3
- ○ 4
- ○ $4\sqrt{3}$
- ○ $6\sqrt{3}$
- ○ $8\sqrt{3}$

Mei is building a garden in the shape of an isosceles triangle with one side of 10. If the perimeter of the garden is 32, which of the following is a possible area of the garden?

- ○ 32
- ○ 48
- ○ 50
- ○ 60
- ○ 64

Column A	Column B
The area of an equilateral triangle with a side length of 4	The area of an isosceles right triangle with a hypotenuse of $4\sqrt{2}$

- ○ The quantity in Column A is greater.
- ○ The quantity in Column B is greater.
- ○ The two quantities are equal.
- ○ The relationship cannot be determined from the information given.

Towns *A*, *B*, and *C* lie in a plane but do not lie on a straight line. The distance between Towns *A* and *B* is 40 miles, and the distance between Towns *A* and *C* is 110 miles.

Column A	Column B
The distance between Towns B and C	60 miles

○ The quantity in Column A is greater.
○ The quantity in Column B is greater.
○ The two quantities are equal.
○ The relationship cannot be determined from the information given.

Point *A* is both in the interior of triangle *B* and on line *C*. If *A*, *B*, and *C* are in the same plane, in how many places does line *C* intersect triangle *B* ?

○ Zero
○ One
○ Two
○ Three
○ Five

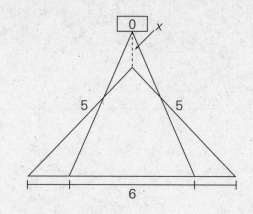

A photographer is using a bipod to steady his camera while taking pictures, as shown in the figure above. The legs of the bipod are 5 feet long and are currently 6 feet apart. If he pulls the legs another 2 feet apart, the top of the bipod drops *x* feet.

Column A	Column B
1	*x*

○ The quantity in Column A is greater.
○ The quantity in Column B is greater.
○ The two quantities are equal.
○ The relationship cannot be determined from the information given.

If triangle *ABC* is equilateral and side *AB* has a length of *s*, then what is the area of triangle *ABC* in terms of *s* ?

○ $\dfrac{s^2}{4}\sqrt{3}$

○ $\dfrac{s^2}{2}\sqrt{3}$

○ $\dfrac{s^2}{2}\sqrt{2}$

○ $s\sqrt{3}$

○ $s\sqrt{2}$

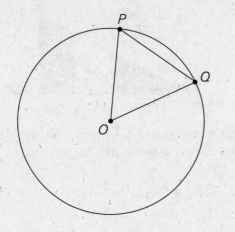

In the figure above, equilateral triangle *OPQ* is inscribed in the central angle of the circle and has perimeter 18. What is the area of circle O ?

- ◯ 6π
- ◯ 12π
- ◯ 18π
- ◯ 36π
- ◯ 72π

Column A	Column B
The length of the side of a square with diagonal $\sqrt{50}$	The height of an equilateral triangle with side 6

- ◯ The quantity in Column A is greater.
- ◯ The quantity in Column B is greater.
- ◯ The two quantities are equal.
- ◯ The relationship cannot be determined from the information given.

In a triangle, one angle is twice as large as the smallest angle, and another angle is three times as large as the smallest angle. What is the measure of the largest angle?

- ◯ 30°
- ◯ 45°
- ◯ 60°
- ◯ 75°
- ◯ 90°

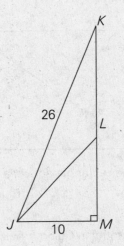

The area of △*JKL* is 65.

Column A	Column B
KL	LM

- ◯ The quantity in Column A is greater.
- ◯ The quantity in Column B is greater.
- ◯ The two quantities are equal.
- ◯ The relationship cannot be determined from the information given.

Given four rods of length 1 meter, 3 meters, 5 meters, and 7 meters, how many different triangles can be made using one rod for each side?

- ◯ 6
- ◯ 4
- ◯ 3
- ◯ 2
- ◯ 1

How much greater, in square inches, is the area of a square with a diagonal of 8 inches than the area of a square with a diagonal of 4 inches?

- ⬭ 4
- ⬭ 24
- ⬭ 32
- ⬭ 48
- ⬭ 96

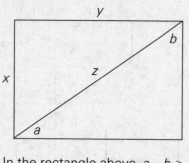

In the rectangle above, $a - b > b - a$.

Column A	Column B
$z^2 - 2x^2$	0

- ⬭ The quantity in Column A is greater.
- ⬭ The quantity in Column B is greater.
- ⬭ The two quantities are equal.
- ⬭ The relationship cannot be determined from the information given.

The image of a star is projected onto a planetarium wall by a projector that sits atop a vertical 4-foot stand. If the projector is directed 30 degrees above the horizontal, and the image appears 16 feet above the level floor of the planetarium, then, in feet, how far is the projector from the wall?

- ⬭ $12\sqrt{2}$
- ⬭ $12\sqrt{3}$
- ⬭ $16\sqrt{2}$
- ⬭ $16\sqrt{3}$
- ⬭ 24

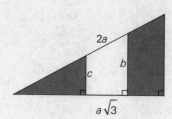

What is the area of the shaded region in the figure above, in terms of a, b, and c ?

- ⬭ $\sqrt{3}\left(a^2 + b^2 + c^2\right)$
- ⬭ $\dfrac{\sqrt{3}}{2}\left(a^2 - b^2 - c^2\right)$
- ⬭ $\dfrac{\sqrt{3}}{2}\left(a^2 - b^2 + c^2\right)$
- ⬭ $\dfrac{\sqrt{3}}{2}\left(a^2 + b^2 - c^2\right)$
- ⬭ $\dfrac{\sqrt{3}}{2}\left(a^2 + b^2 + c^2\right)$

ANSWERS

1. A
2. A
3. 105
4. A
5. B
6. B
7. A
8. E
9. A
10. D
11. C
12. E
13. B
14. D
15. C
16. C
17. C
18. D
19. D
20. D
21. B
22. B
23. B
24. A
25. C
26. C
27. A
28. D
29. B
30. E
31. A
32. E
33. B
34. B
35. B
36. C

EXPLANATIONS

1. **A** The interior angles of a triangle add up to 180°, therefore, $x = 110$.

2. **A** In a rectangle, opposite sides are equal, and each angle measures 90 degrees. Triangle ABD is a 5-12-13 right triangle, so $BD = 13$. Furthermore, $BC = 12$, and $CD = 5$. To find the perimeter of any figure, add the lengths of the sides. In this case, $5 + 12 + 13 = 30$, so the answer is choice (A).

3. **105** There are 180 degrees in both a straight line and a triangle. In the figure, $\angle XWY$ and $\angle XYW$ are congruent and their measures add up to $180° - 30° = 150°$, so each angle measures 75°. A straight line measures 180°, so $q = 180 - 75 = 105$.

4. **A** $\triangle CDE$ has equal angles, so it is equilateral. $ABCE$ is also equilateral, as are all squares. To find the perimeter of any figure, add up all of the side lengths on the outside of the figure. In this case, 5 equal segments of length 4 result in a perimeter of 20, so Column A is greater.

5. **C** First, draw a rectangle and its diagonals, like this:

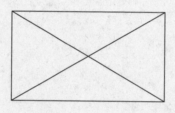

    Now, count the triangles. There are four large right triangles—two formed by each of the diagonals—as well as four smaller triangles with vertices at the center. That's a total of 8, so select answer choice (C).

6. **B** AC has a length of 3, so you can use Pythagorean theorem, or recognize the Pythagorean triple, to find that BC has a length of 5. The answer is choice (B).

7. **A**   Draw a right triangle representing the captain's route so far and the path back to his starting point; it should look something like this:

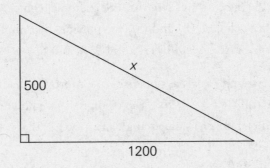

A right triangle with legs of 500 and 1,200 is a multiple of the familiar 5-12-13 triangle, so the hypotenuse—and the number of miles the captain must sail to return to his original position—is 1,300. The answer is choice (A).

8. **E**   Recognize the 3-4-5 triple or use the Pythagorean theorem to find that the missing side length of the rectangle is 4. The area of the rectangle is $bh = 3 \times 4 = 12$, so the answer is choice (E).

9. **A**   The Third Side Rule states that the third side in any triangle must be shorter than the sum of, and longer than the difference between, the other two sides. Hence, the third side of this triangle must be greater than 7, and less than 17. Column A is greater.

10. **D**   Lines a and b are parallel, so you have two similar triangles: xyz and wyv. Set up a proportion to solve for yv: $\dfrac{5}{8} = \dfrac{4}{x}$, so $5x = 32$, and $x = 6.4$. Remember that the third side of any triangle must be less than the sum of the other two sides and greater than the difference between them. $wy = 8$ and side yv is 6.4, so vw must be greater than 1.6 but less than 14.4. Thus, side vw can be less than, greater than, or equal to 12, so select choice (D).

11. **C**   First, draw the picture (see below). Notice that this makes two right triangles, each with legs of 5 and 12. Either recognize the 5-12-13 triple or use the Pythagorean theorem to see that the distance is $13 + 13 = 26$.

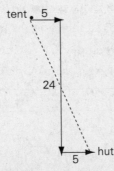

12.   **E**   The Third Side Rule states that the third side of any triangle must be greater than the difference between, and less than the sum of the other two sides. If a triangle has a perimeter of 24, then a side of 12 would <u>equal</u> the sum of the other two sides. Select choice (E). Alternatively, you could eliminate answers by Plugging In side lengths. For example, choice (A) is possible if triangle *A* has sides of 1, 11.5, and 11.5; choices (B) and (D) are possible if triangle *A* has sides of 3, 10, and 11; and choice (C) is possible if triangle *A* has sides of 8, 8, and 8.

13.   **B**   The smallest angle in a triangle is always opposite the shortest side. If angle *ABC* is 60 degrees, the other two angles total 180° − 60° = 120°. The triangle isn't equilateral, the remaining two angles cannot both be 60°. Therefore, the smaller angle must be less than 60°, and Column B is greater.

14.   **D**   Triangle *ABD* is the familiar 6-8-10 triangle, so *AB* = 10. Use the Pythagorean theorem to find *BC*, or recognize the 5-12-13 triangle, multiplied by 2 to give a 10-24-26 triangle. The area of triangle *ABC* is thus $\frac{1}{2} \times 10 \times 24$, or 120.

15.   **C**   Start by finding the remaining angles of the triangle on the right: if the two small angles add up to 20° + 40° = 60°, then the unmarked angle must be 120°, and *b* must be 60. The remaining angle in the triangle on the left must be 40°, and *a* must be 140. So Column A is 140 + 60 = 200; the Columns are equal.

16.   **C**   Use the Pythagorean theorem to find the length of path *C*: $5^2 + 13^2 = c^2$. So path *c* is approximately 14 miles. John walks 18 miles, and James walks 14 miles, so the answer is choice (C).

17.   **C**   Although the figure may look complex, it's really just three 45-45-90 triangles attached end-to-end; *BF* is the sum of the long sides of the three triangles. If *AB* = 2, then *AC* = 2, and *BC* = $2\sqrt{2}$; similarly, *EG* and *FG* are 2, and *EF* = $2\sqrt{2}$. Two of the angles in triangle *DCE* are vertical angles with 45° angles in the other two triangles, so it must be a 45-45-90 triangle also—the legs are each 3, so *CE* = $3\sqrt{2}$. So *BF* = $2\sqrt{2}$ + $2\sqrt{2}$ + $3\sqrt{2}$ = $7\sqrt{2}$; the Columns are equal.

18.   **D**   According to the Third Side Rule, *r* must be less than the sum of *p* and *q*. Plug In to test if *r* is less than *p* + *q* − 1. Let *p* = 5 and *q* = 4. If *r* = 2, Column A is 2 and Column B is 8; Column B is greater, so eliminate choices (A) and (C). However, a value of 8 for *r* would also satisfy the Third Side Rule; now the Columns are equal, so eliminate choice (B) and select choice (D).

19.   **D**   This is a 30-60-90 triangle, so *FH* = 8. If the diameter is 8, then the radius is 4, so the area is 16π.

20.   **D**   Although the Pythagorean theorem dictates that $(AB)^2 + (AD)^2$—the sum of the squares of two sides of a right triangle—is equal to the square of the hypotenuse, or $(BD)^2$, there's no way to determine the relationship between $(BD)^2$ and $(AC)^2$. Remember, figures are not drawn to scale on the GRE: although it looks like *AC* is longer than *BD*, it's possible to redraw the figure so that either segment is longer: try varying the length of *DC*.

21. **B** Plug In the answers, and be sure to note that this is a 30-60-90 triangle. In choice (B), if AB is 4 and AC is $4\sqrt{3}$, then the area is $\frac{1}{2}(4)\left(4\sqrt{3}\right) = 8\sqrt{3}$. So the answer is choice (B).

22. **B** If the triangle is isosceles, it must have two equal sides; thus, the triangle could have sides of 10, 10, and 12 or sides of 10, 11, and 11. To find one of the possible areas, draw out your 10-10-12 triangle. With the height drawn in, it should look like this:

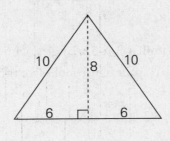

Note that the big triangle divides nicely into two of the familiar 6-8-10 triangles; you now have a triangle with a base of 12 and a height of 8, so the area is $\frac{1}{2} \times 12 \times 8 = 48$. The answer is choice (B).

23. **B** In Column A, an equilateral triangle with a side length of 4 has a base of 4 and a height of $2\sqrt{3}$: remember, an equilateral triangle cut in half yields two 30-60-90 triangles. The triangle, thus, has an area of $\frac{1}{2} \times 4 \times 2\sqrt{3}$, or $4\sqrt{3}$. Remember that $\sqrt{3}$ is approximately 1.7, so $4\sqrt{3}$ is about 6.8. In Column B, "isosceles right triangle" means 45-45-90, so a long side of $4\sqrt{2}$ yields a base and a height both equal to 4, and an area of $\frac{1}{2} \times 4 \times 4$, or 8. Column B is greater.

24. **A** If the towns do not lie on a straight line, they must lie on a triangle; Column A represents the third side of the triangle. According to the Third Side Rule this side must be greater than the difference between, and less than the sum of, of the other two sides. Thus, Column A lies between 110 – 40 = 70 miles and 110 + 40 = 150 miles, but is always greater than 60 miles; the answer is choice (A).

25. **C** Draw a triangle with a point inside. Draw a line through the point to see how many places the line intersects with the triangle. There are many ways to draw the line, but each way intersects the triangle at two points.

26. **C** Split the initial triangle into two right triangles. The figure should look like this:

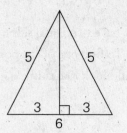

The smaller triangles are the familiar 3-4-5 triangles, with a height of 4. When the photographer pulls the legs another 2 feet apart, your figure looks like this:

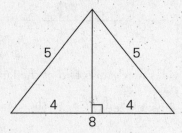

Again, the smaller triangles are 3-4-5 triangles, but now the height is 3. Because x is the change in the triangle's height, $x = 1$, so the Columns are equal.

27. **A** First, draw your figure and write out the area formula for triangles, $A = \frac{1}{2}bh$. Then, Plug In a number for s; try $s = 6$. In order to find the height of an equilateral triangle, you need to draw an altitude from the top vertex down the middle to the opposite base, creating two 30-60-90 right triangles. The height of this equilateral triangle is $3\sqrt{3}$, so the area formula is $\frac{1}{2} \times (6) \times (3\sqrt{3}) = 9\sqrt{3}$. Now plug 6 in for s in the answer choices. Eliminate choices (C) and (E) because they have the wrong root. Of the remaining answers, only choice (A) yields the target answer of $9\sqrt{3} : \frac{s^2}{4}\sqrt{3} = \frac{36}{4}\sqrt{3} = 9\sqrt{3}$.

28. **D** The triangle is equilateral, so dividing the perimeter by 3 gives you the length of 6 for each side. The triangle is inscribed in the central angle of the circle, so sides OP and OQ are also radii of the circle. Thus, the area of the circle is $\pi r^2 = \pi 6^2 = 36\pi$, so the answer is choice (D).

29. **B** A square cut in half from corner to corner yields two 45-45-90 triangles, so a diagonal of $\sqrt{50}$ —also known as $5\sqrt{2}$ —gives a side of 5. The height of an equilateral triangle splits it into two 30-60-90 triangles, so a side of 6 gives a height of $3\sqrt{3}$. To compare, express both sides as square roots: 5 is equal to $\sqrt{25}$, and $3\sqrt{3}$ is equal to $\sqrt{27}$. Column B is greater.

30. **E** If x is the measure of the smallest angle, then the other two angle are $2x$ and $3x$. The sum of the angles is 180°, so $x + 2x + 3x = 180$. Solve the equation to find $x = 30$, which means the largest angle measures 90°.

31. **A** Triangle JKM is the familiar 5-12-13 triple, but doubled, so $KM = 24$. KL may look the same length as LM, but remember that figures on the GRE are not drawn to scale. In any triangle, the height is always measured perpendicular to the base from the opposite vertex. So the height of triangle JKL is the length of JM, 10. You are given the area of triangle JKL, so plug all the information you know into the area formula for triangles: $A = \frac{1}{2}bh; 65 = \frac{1}{2}(KL)(10); KL = 13$. Subtracting KL from KM gives you LM: $24 - 13 = 11$; $LM = 11$. Column A is 13, and Column B is 11, so the answer is choice (A).

32. **E** According to the third side rule for triangles, the longest side of a triangle must be shorter than the sum of the other two sides. Hence, the only possible triangle has sides of lengths 3, 5, and 7.

33. **B** Draw your own figures. The diagonal of a square creates 45-45-90 triangles with sides in the ratio of $x : x : x\sqrt{2}$. So, the larger square has a diagonal of $x\sqrt{2} = 8$. Divide by $\sqrt{2}$ to find the side length, $\frac{8}{\sqrt{2}}$. The area is $\left(\frac{8}{\sqrt{2}}\right)^2 = 32$. The smaller square has a diagonal of $x\sqrt{2} = 4$. Divide by $\sqrt{2}$ to find the side length, $\frac{4}{\sqrt{2}}$. The area is $\left(\frac{4}{\sqrt{2}}\right)^2 = 8$. The area of the larger square is $32 - 8 = 24$ greater than that of the smaller square.

34. **B** Manipulate $a - b > b - a$ to get $a > b$; hence y, which is the same length as the side across from b, is shorter than x, which is the same length as the side across from a. The diagonal divides the rectangle into two right triangles. According to the Pythagorean theorem, $z^2 = x^2 + y^2$, so $z^2 - x^2 - y^2 = 0$. Because $x > y$, $x^2 > y^2$. so in Column A you are subtracting more than $x^2 - y^2$ from z^2. Therefore, $z^2 - 2x^2 < 0$, so the answer is choice (B).

35.   B   Start by drawing your figure as a triangle—with the long side running from the projector to the wall—atop a rectangle, with one side of the rectangle determined by the height of the stand, and the other by the distance from the projector to the wall. With all of the pertinent information, it should look like this:

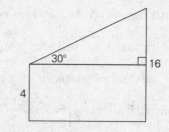

The triangle on top is a 30-60-90 triangle with a short side of 16 − 4 = 12; so the side across from the other leg (the distance from the projector to the wall) is $12\sqrt{3}$, so the answer is choice (B).

36.   C   The ratio of the given leg to the hypotenuse is $\sqrt{3}$ to 2 in the largest right triangle, so it is a 30-60-90 triangle, and the length of the other leg must be a. The smaller two triangles also contain 90 degree angles, and all three triangles share the left vertex angle, so all three triangles are similar, and therefore all of their sides are in the same proportion. So the horizontal leg of the smallest right triangle is $c\sqrt{3}$, and the horizontal leg of the medium-sized right triangle is $b\sqrt{3}$. To find the area of the shaded region, find the area of the largest triangle, subtract the area of the medium-sized one, and then add the area of the smallest one. The area of the largest triangle is $\frac{1}{2}bh = \frac{1}{2}(a)\left(a\sqrt{3}\right) = \frac{a^2\sqrt{3}}{2}$. Similarly, the areas of the medium-sized and smallest triangles are $\frac{b^2\sqrt{3}}{2}$ and $\frac{c^2\sqrt{3}}{2}$, respectively. So the area of the shaded region is $\frac{a^2\sqrt{3}}{2} - \frac{b^2\sqrt{3}}{2} + \frac{c^2\sqrt{3}}{2}$. Factoring out $\frac{\sqrt{3}}{2}$ gives you the expression in choice (C). Alternatively, you could plug in values for the variables, such as $a = 3$, $b = 2$, and $c = 1$.

Circles

CIRCLES

There are only three formulas you will need to solve circle problems.

$$\pi r^2,\ 2\pi r \text{ or } \pi d,\text{ and}$$

$$\frac{\text{angle}}{360} = \frac{\text{arc}}{\text{circumference}} = \frac{\text{area sector}}{\text{area circle}}$$

The radius is involved in all three formulas. Once you have the radius of a circle, you will know almost everything there is to know about that circle.

πr^2 measures the area of a circle. It's easy to remember because area, such as the area of a house or apartment, is always measured in units squared.

πd or $2\pi r$ measures circumference. If you know circumference, you know the radius, and if you know the radius you know the area. Most GRE circle questions ask you to find one or the other or require you to convert from one to the other. You must be able to do these tasks quickly and easily. If you write the formulas down on your scratch paper and fill in the information from the question directly underneath the relevant part of the formula, finding the answer shouldn't be a problem.

$\dfrac{\text{angle}}{360} = \dfrac{\text{arc}}{\text{circumference}} = \dfrac{\text{area sector}}{\text{area circle}}$ is one formula that they don't give you in any of the official GRE literature, but it can comes in handy. It essentially means that angles, arcs, and areas are all proportional. If you were to divide a circle into quarters, the central angle, 90 over 360 reduces to $\dfrac{1}{4}$. The resulting arc is $\dfrac{1}{4}$ of the circumference of the circle and the area of the sector is $\dfrac{1}{4}$ the area of the circle.

Pi, or π, equals 3.14159….or 3 and change. If you are given a circle with a radius of five and asked for the area, set π equal to 3 and ballpark. Eliminate any answer choice which is less than or equal to 75, or greater than or equal to 100. You know that the correct answer will be far closer to 75 than it will be to 100.

The five-step approach to geometry problems applies to circles as well.

Step 1: Draw your shape

In some cases the test will give you a shape, which you may or may not be able to trust, and in others it will give you a word problem and leave it up to you to envision the shape. As with every other part of the test, getting your hand moving is an important first step to entering the problem. Get your shape down on your scratch paper so that you can begin working with it there. On Quant Comp questions involving geometry, instead of Plugging In more than once, you may have to draw your shape more than once.

Step 2: Fill in what you know

Whether you are given the shape or not, you will be given a certain amount of information regarding the shape such as the measure of some angles, lengths of some sides, areas of some sides, or volume. Put that information in the figure.

Step 3: Make deductions

If you are given two angles of a triangle, find the third. If you are given the radius of a cirlce, find the area. Often this will be the entire problem. Geometry on the GRE is all about finding the missing piece of information. You will be given just enough information to find the piece that is missing.

Step 4: Write down relevant formulas

If step three didn't get you the answer, you must still be missing a piece of information. Writing down the formula is a way of both organizing your information and telling you what is missing. When you write your formulas down, fill in the information you have directly underneath the relevant part of the formula. It seems simple, but this way you can't make a mistake. Finding the missing piece of information becomes a simple case of solving for x.

Step 5: Drop heights/draw lines

If you're still stuck, you may need to manipulate or subdivide your circle into smaller shapes. If create triangles, draw in the height. Have you created a 30-60-90? A 45-45-90? Or a Pythagorean triple? Try subdividing the shape or, if it's a three-dimensional figure, dashing in the hidden lines.

Often, you will see circles in combination with other shapes. If you don't immediately see the correct path to the solution, look for the radius. Everything about a circle derives from there. It is possible that you will see a circle inscribed on a coordinate plane. The same rules apply. Use right triangles to find the end points of as many radii as you need to check the answer choices that you can't eliminate through Ballparking.

For more practice and a more in-depth look at The Princeton Review math techniques, check out our student-friendly guidebook, *Cracking the GRE*.

CIRCLES DRILL

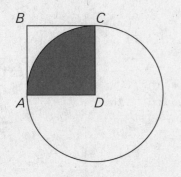

ABCD is a square with side length 2.

Column A	Column B
The area of the shaded region	π

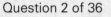

- ○ The quantity in Column A is greater.
- ○ The quantity in Column B is greater.
- ○ The two quantities are equal.
- ○ The relationship cannot be determined from the information given.

What is the degree measure of the smaller angle formed by the two hands of a circular clock at 10:00 a.m.?

- ○ 50°
- ○ 55°
- ○ 60°
- ○ 65°
- ○ 70°

The area of circle C is 9π.

Column A	Column B
The radius of circle C	6

- ○ The quantity in Column A is greater.
- ○ The quantity in Column B is greater.
- ○ The two quantities are equal.
- ○ The relationship cannot be determined from the information given.

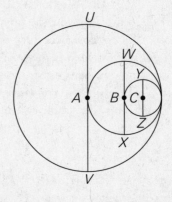

Line segments UV, WX, and YZ are diameters of the circles with centers A, B, and C, respectively. If YZ = 2, then what is the area of the circle with center A ?

- ○ 4π
- ○ 8π
- ○ 9π
- ○ 16π
- ○ 64π

Column A	Column B
The circumference of a circle with a diameter of 6	The circumference of a circle with a radius of 12

- ○ The quantity in Column A is greater.
- ○ The quantity in Column B is greater.
- ○ The two quantities are equal.
- ○ The relationship cannot be determined from the information given.

Column A

Four times the area of a circular region with a circumference of 4π

Column B

The circumference of a circular region with an area of 64π

- ◯ The quantity in Column A is greater.
- ◯ The quantity in Column B is greater.
- ◯ The two quantities are equal.
- ◯ The relationship cannot be determined from the information given.

An office needs to buy circular pizzas for 20 employees. If each pizza is cut into equal slices and equal slice has a central angle of 40°, how many pizzas need to be ordered so that each employee gets at least two slices?

- ◯ 1
- ◯ 2
- ◯ 3
- ◯ 4
- ◯ 5

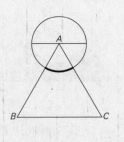

Triangle ABC is equilateral. If the circle with center A has a diameter of 6, what is the length of the darkened arc?

- ◯ $\dfrac{\pi}{2}$
- ◯ π
- ◯ 6
- ◯ 6π
- ◯ $6\sqrt{3}$

A circle with center C has a radius of 6.

Column A

The ratio of the circumference of C to the radius of C

Column B

Half the diameter of C

- ◯ The quantity in Column A is greater.
- ◯ The quantity in Column B is greater.
- ◯ The two quantities are equal.
- ◯ The relationship cannot be determined from the information given.

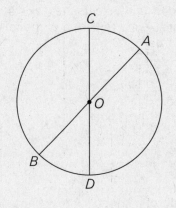

O is the center of the circle above.

Column A

Length of line segment AB

Column B

Length of line segment CD

- ◯ The quantity in Column A is greater.
- ◯ The quantity in Column B is greater.
- ◯ The two quantities are equal.
- ◯ The relationship cannot be determined from the information given.

The circle with center *O* has radius of 3 and is inscribed in a square.

Column A	Column B
The circumference of the circle with center *O*	The perimeter of the square

- ○ The quantity in Column A is greater.
- ○ The quantity in Column B is greater.
- ○ The two quantities are equal.
- ○ The relationship cannot be determined from the information given.

In the standard *xy*-plane, the circle with center *B* and radius 3 intersects the *x*-axis at exactly two points, *A* and *C*. Which of the following must be true?

- ○ $AC \leq 3$
- ○ $AC < 6$
- ○ $AC \leq 6$
- ○ $AC = 6$
- ○ $AC > 6$

The height of a right circular cylinder is increased by *p* percent and the radius is decreased by *p* percent.

Column A	Column B
The volume of the cylinder if $p = 10$.	The volume of the cylinder if $p = 20$.

- ○ The quantity in Column A is greater.
- ○ The quantity in Column B is greater.
- ○ The two quantities are equal.
- ○ The relationship cannot be determined from the information given.

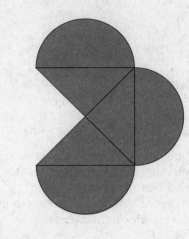

The diameters of the semicircles above are 8, and the diameter of the semicircle on the right is perpendicular to those of the other two semicircles. What is the total area of the shaded region?

- ○ $12\pi + 64$
- ○ $24\pi + 12$
- ○ $24\pi + 48$
- ○ $32\pi + 48$
- ○ $32\pi + 64$

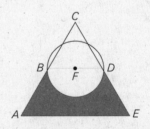

Triangle *ACE* is equilateral with side lengths of 8. Points *B* and *D* are the midpoints of line segments *AC* and *CE* respectively. Line segment *BD* is a diameter of the circle with center *F*. What is the area of the shaded region?

- ○ $8\sqrt{2} - 4\pi$
- ○ $12\sqrt{3} - 2\pi$
- ○ $12\sqrt{3} - 4\pi$
- ○ $16\sqrt{3} - 2\pi$
- ○ $16\sqrt{2} - 4\pi$

An 8″ diameter circular pie is divided equally into 8 slices. After two slices have been removed. If the remaining pizza is divided into three equal slices, what is the area of one of those slices?

- ⭕ π
- ⭕ 2π
- ⭕ 3π
- ⭕ 4π
- ⭕ 5π

Column A	Column B
The area of a square with a perimeter of p	The area of a circle with a circumference of p

- ⭕ The quantity in Column A is greater.
- ⭕ The quantity in Column B is greater.
- ⭕ The two quantities are equal.
- ⭕ The relationship cannot be determined from the information given.

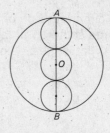

Line AB passes through the center of circle O and through the centers of each of the 3 identical smaller circles. Each circle touches two other circles at exactly one point each.

Column A	Column B
The circumference of circle O	The sum of the circumferences of the 3 smaller circles

- ⭕ The quantity in Column A is greater.
- ⭕ The quantity in Column B is greater.
- ⭕ The two quantities are equal.
- ⭕ The relationship cannot be determined from the information given.

A square has edges of length 12 inches.

Column A	Column B
24π	The area of the largest circle that can fit inside the square

- ⭕ The quantity in Column A is greater.
- ⭕ The quantity in Column B is greater.
- ⭕ The two quantities are equal.
- ⭕ The relationship cannot be determined from the information given.

A circle with a circumference of 12π is divided into three sectors with areas in a ratio of 3:4:5. What is the area of the largest sector?

○   6π
○   9π
○   12π
○   15π
○   18π

A can of paint contains exactly the amount required to paint 20 circles each with a diameter of 5 feet. How many circles with a diameter of 2 feet could be filled with the same can of paint?

○   40
○   50
○   100
○   125
○   150

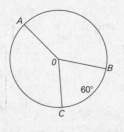

Column A	Column B
The measure of angle *AOB*	The measure of angle *AOC*

○ The quantity in Column A is greater.
○ The quantity in Column B is greater.
○ The two quantities are equal.
○ The relationship cannot be determined from the information given.

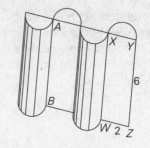

Rectangle *WXYZ* has a length of 6 and a width of 2. Rectangle *AYZB* bisects right cylinders *ABC* and *D*. If all the cylinders have the same radius, what is the combined volume of the four half cylinders?

○   6π
○   9π
○   12π
○   18π
○   21π

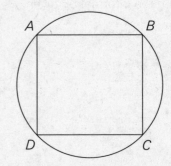

Inscribed square *ABCD* has a side length of 4. What is the area of the circle?

○   2π
○   4π
○   6π
○   8π
○   10π

If the diameter of circle A is eight times that of circle B, what is the ratio of the area of circle A to the area of circle B ?

- 4 : 1
- 8 : 1
- 16 : 1
- 32 : 1
- 64 : 1

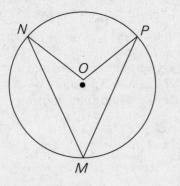

Point O is the center of the circle.

Column A   Column B

The measure of $\angle NOP$ The measure of $\angle NMP$

- The quantity in Column A is greater.
- The quantity in Column B is greater.
- The two quantities are equal.
- The relationship cannot be determined from the information given.

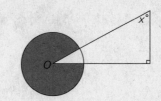

The circle above has a center O and a radius of 4. If the area of the shaded region is 14π, what is the value of x ?

- 30
- 40
- 45
- 50
- 55

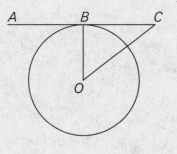

Line segment AC is tangent to the circle with center O and $CO = 5$.

Column A   Column B

Circumference of the 10π
circle

- The quantity in Column A is greater.
- The quantity in Column B is greater.
- The two quantities are equal.
- The relationship cannot be determined from the information given.

The area of Circle *A* is increased by a factor of *x* to create Circle *B*.

The area of Circle *B* is increased by a factor of *x* to create Circle *C*.

Column A	Column B
The ratio of the radius of Circle *A* to the radius of Circle *C*	$\dfrac{1}{x}$

◯ The quantity in Column A is greater.
◯ The quantity in Column B is greater.
◯ The two quantities are equal.
◯ The relationship cannot be determined from the information given.

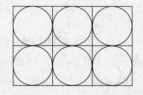

In the figure above, if the area of the smaller circular region is $\dfrac{1}{2}$ the area of the larger circular region, then the diameter of the larger circle is how many inches longer than the diameter of the smaller circle?

◯ $\sqrt{2} - 1$

◯ $\dfrac{1}{2}$

◯ $\dfrac{\sqrt{2}}{2}$

◯ $\dfrac{2 - \sqrt{2}}{2}$

◯ $\sqrt{2}$

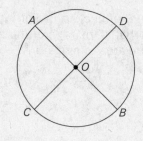

Column A	Column B
$AB + CD$	The circumference of the circle with center *O*

◯ The quantity in Column A is greater.
◯ The quantity in Column B is greater.
◯ The two quantities are equal.
◯ The relationship cannot be determined from the information given.

The figure shows a topical view of a rectangular box with a bottom and dividers, open at the top. The box holds six right circular cylindrical drinking glasses, 4" in diameter and 5" in height, with no extra space between them. What is the least amount of additional cardboard, in square inches, that would be needed to construct a box that could hold six right circular cylindrical glasses 5" in diameter and 6" in height?

◯ 96
◯ 170
◯ 224
◯ 510
◯ 660

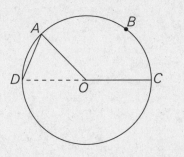

No line segment with endpoints on the circle with center O is longer than line segment DC.

$$OA = AD = 3$$

Column A	Column B
The area of sector	9
$OABC$

○ The quantity in Column A is greater.
○ The quantity in Column B is greater.
○ The two quantities are equal.
○ The relationship cannot be determined
   from the information given.

A lounge manager decides to decorate one wall of the lounge with an evenly spaced row of vinyl records. The wall is 31'6" long and each record has an area of 36π square inches. If the manager wants to leave a space of x inches between each record and at either end of the row, and x is an integer, then what is the greatest possible number of records that the manager can use?

○ 28
○ 29
○ 30
○ 31
○ 32

$\dfrac{1}{r}$ of a circular pizza has been eaten. If the rest of the pizza is divided into m equal slices, then each of these slices is what fraction of the whole pizza?

○ $\dfrac{r}{m}$

○ $\dfrac{r-1}{m}$

○ $\dfrac{1}{m}$

○ $\dfrac{m-1}{m}$

○ $\dfrac{m-r}{m}$

A single slice cut from the center of a circular pizza has an edge length (from the center of the pizza to the edge of the crust) of 5", has an arc length of 1.25π", and weighs 4 ounces. If a serving weighs 8 ounces, then, to the nearest integer, what is the largest number of servings that six 6" diameter pizzas can yield? (Note that servings must weigh 8 ounces, but they do not need to be equal in shape.)

○ 1
○ 4
○ 6
○ 8
○ 9

ANSWERS

1. C
2. C
3. B
4. D
5. B
6. C
7. E
8. B
9. A
10. A
11. B
12. C
13. A
14. C
15. B
16. D
17. B
18. C
19. B
20. D
21. D
22. D
23. C
24. D
25. E
26. A
27. C
28. B
29. C
30. D
31. B
32. C
33. A
34. B
35. B
36. D

EXPLANATIONS

1. **C** The side length of the square is the radius of the circle, so the area of the circle is $\pi r^2 = 4\pi$. Central angle CDA measures 90 degrees because $ABCD$ is a square. 90 degrees represents $\frac{90}{360} = \frac{1}{4}$ of the circle, so the area of the shaded region will be $\frac{1}{4}$ of the area of the circle, π. The quantities are equal.

2. **C** When the hour hand is on the 10, and the minutes hand is on the 12, the angle between the two hands represents $\frac{2}{12}$ of the 360 degrees in a circle, or 60 degrees.

3. **B** The formula for the area of a circle is πr^2, where r is the radius of the circle. If you set this formula equal to the area of circle C, you get $\pi r^2 = 9\pi$. Dividing by π on both sides of the equation yields $r^2 = 9$, and taking the square root of both sides results in $r = 3$. The radius of circle C is 3, giving you choice (B) for the answer.

4. **D** All diameters in a circle are of equal length. Draw a horizontal diameter in the smallest circle; it must be 2 units long. This diameter is also the radius of the circle with center B, whose diameter must therefore be 4 units long. Draw this diameter horizontally, and you realize that it is also the radius of the circle with center A, whose area is $\pi r^2 = 16\pi$.

5. **B** The circumference of a circle with a diameter of 6 is $\pi d = 6\pi$. The circumference of a circle with a radius of 12 is $2\pi r = 24\pi$, so choice (B) is larger.

6. **C** For this problem, use the circle formulas—area $= \pi r^2$ and circumference $= 2\pi r$—and do the problem one step at a time. For Column A, a circle with a circumference of 4π yields $4\pi = 2\pi r$, so $2r = 4$, and $r = 2$; thus, the area of the circle is $2^2\pi$, or 4π, and 4 times that is 16π. For Column B, a circle with an area of 64π yields $64\pi = \pi r^2$, so $r^2 = 64$, and $r = 8$; thus, the circumference of the circle is $2(8)\pi$, or 16π. The Columns are equal.

7. **E** For 20 employees to receive at least two slices, you need at least 40 slices. The total number of degrees in a circle is 360. Dividing 360 by 40 gives you 9—the number of slices in each pizza. 40 slices total divided by 9 slices per pizza gives you 4 with a remainder. To order enough pizzas for 40 slices, you need to order a fifth pizza.

8. **B** Each angle in an equilateral triangle measures 60°. The degree measure of the darkened arc is therefore 60°, which represents $\frac{1}{6}$ of the 360° in the circle. Thus, the length of the darkened arc will be $\frac{1}{6}$ of the circumference of the circle. If the diameter is 6, the radius is 3, so the circumference is $2\pi r = 6\pi$. $\frac{1}{6}$ of 6π is π.

9. **A** For Column A, the circumference of C is $2\pi r = 2\pi(6) = 12\pi$; the radius is 6. So, the ratio is $\frac{12\pi}{6} = 2\pi$. For Column B, half the diameter is the same as the radius, 6. Ballpark that 2π is a little more than 6, making Column A greater.

10. **A** Notice that chord AB goes through the center of the circle. Thus, AB is a diameter; a diameter is the longest chord in a circle. Chord CD does not go through the center of the circle, so AB must be longer than CD.

11. **B** First, draw the figure. The formula for the circumference of a circle is $2\pi r$, or in this case, $2\pi3$, or 6π—a little bigger than 18. The side of the square is equal to the diameter of the circle, or 6, and a square with a side of 6 has a perimeter of $6 \times 4 = 24$. Column B is greater.

12. **C** Draw it. If the circle is bisected by the x-axis, then $AC = 6$; eliminate choices (A), (B), and (E). If the circle is not bisected by the x-axis, then $AC < 6$; eliminate choice (D), leaving you with choice (C).

13. **A** Plug In 10 for the height and radius of the cylinder. So Column A is $\pi r^2 h = \pi 9^2 11 = 891\pi$. Column B is $\pi 8^2 12 = 768\pi$.

14. **C** Draw a fourth triangle and semicircle, and you can see that the figure shown represents $1\frac{1}{2}$ circles and $\frac{3}{4}$ of a square. Because the three diameters are perpendicular and congruent, they represent three sides of a square; the isosceles right triangles shown constitute three of the four triangles in the completed square. The area of a circle with diameter of 8 (and radius of 4) is $\pi r^2 = 16\pi$. $1\frac{1}{2}$ times this area is 24π. Eliminate choices (A), (D), and (E) because they do not contain 24π. The diameter of each semicircle is the length of the side of the square. The area of the entire square would be $s^2 = 8^2 = 64$. $\frac{3}{4}$ of this area is 48. Adding the two areas together gives you the expression in choice (C).

15. **B** To find the shaded region, subtract the unshaded region (the triangle and semicircle) from the entire triangle. The area of an equilateral triangle of side x is $\frac{x^2\sqrt{3}}{4} = \frac{8^2\sqrt{3}}{4} = 16\sqrt{3}$. Triangle BCD is also equilateral, and has sides of length 4, so its area is $\frac{4^2\sqrt{3}}{4} = 4\sqrt{3}$. The radius of the circle is 2, so the area of the semicircle is $\left(\frac{1}{2}\right)\pi r^2 = \left(\frac{1}{2}\right)\pi 2^2 = 2\pi$. So the answer is $16\sqrt{3} - 4\sqrt{3} - 2\pi = 12\sqrt{3} - 2\pi$.

16. **D** First find the area of the entire pie, which is 16π. After two slices have been removed, you are left with $\frac{3}{4}$ of the pie or 12π. One third of 12π is 4π. The answer is D.

17. **B**   Plug In a value for p. If $p = 8$, then the side of the square is 2 and the area is 4. If the circumference of the circle is 8, then the radius is $\dfrac{4}{\pi}$, and the area is $\dfrac{16}{\pi}$—approximately 5. Column B is larger. Plug In another value for p and you will find that Column B remains larger.

18. **C**   Start by Plugging In a radius for the smaller circles; try $r = 2$. The circumference of each circle is $2\pi r = 4\pi$, and the sum of all three circumferences is 12π. Because the diameter of circle O is equal to the sum of the 3 shorter diameters, the diameter of circle O is $4 + 4 + 4 = 12$, its radius is 6, and its circumference is 12π, so the Columns are equal.

19. **B**   For Column B, the side of the square is the same length as the diameter of the circle. The diameter is twice the radius, so the radius is 6. Plug this into the formula for area: $A = \pi r^2$ to find that $A = 36\pi$. Column B is greater.

20. **D**   The diameter of the circle is 12, so the radius is 6, and the area is 36π. The total number of parts in the ratio is $3 + 4 + 5 = 12$, so each part covers an area of $\dfrac{36\pi}{12} = 3\pi$. The largest ratio part is 5 times this amount, or 15π.

21. **D**   The radius of a circle is half the diameter, so the radius of the painted circles is $\dfrac{5}{2}$. The area of the 20 circles is given by $20\pi\left(\dfrac{5}{2}\right)^2 = 125\pi$. The radius of the proposed circles is 1, so the area of each such circle will be $\pi 1^2 = \pi$. Dividing 125π by π gives you 125.

22. **D**   Just because the two angles look equal doesn't mean that they are. Try redrawing the figure to exaggerate how the angles could be different. First, make AB a straight line: Column A is greater, so eliminate choices (B) and (C). Next, make AC a straight line: Column B is now greater, so eliminate choice (A), leaving you with choice (D) for the answer.

23. **C**   The four half-cylinders are equivalent to two cylinders of radius 1, whose total volume will therefore be $2\left(\pi 1^2 6\right) = 12\pi$. The answer is choice (C).

24. **D**   Draw in either diagonal of the square, which also is the diameter of the circle. You have now created two isosceles right triangles, so the length of the diagonal/diameter is $4\sqrt{2}$, and the radius is $2\sqrt{2}$. The area of the circle is $\pi\left(2\sqrt{2}\right)^2 = 8\pi$.

25. **E**   Plug In 4 for circle B's diameter; thus circle A's diameter is 32. The radius of A is 2, and the radius of B is 16; circle B has an area of 4π and circle A has an area of 256π. The ratio is $256\pi : 4\pi$, which reduces to $64 : 1$.

26. **A**   In a circle, an inscribed angle is exactly half the corresponding central angle drawn from the same two endpoints into the same arc of the circle. Column A is greater.

27. **C** The area of the entire circle is $\pi 4^2 = 16\pi$. The shaded region represents $\dfrac{14\pi}{16\pi} = \dfrac{7}{8}$ of the circle, so the central angle of the unshaded region represents $\dfrac{1}{8}$ of the 360° in a circle, or 45°. The triangle is a right triangle, so the 45 degree central angle and the right angle total 135°, leaving 45° for the remaining angle.

28. **B** A tangent to a circle forms a right angle with a radius drawn to the point of tangency. If CO is the hypotenuse of $\triangle OBC$, then you know that the legs of the right triangle must be shorter than 5. Since OB is the radius of the circle, you know that the radius of the circle must be less than 5, so the circumference must be less than 10π.

29. **C** Try Plugging In 5 for x. If circle A has an area of 9π, it has a radius of 3. Circle B then has an area of $9\pi \times 5 = 45\pi$. Circle C has an area of $45\pi \times 5 = 225\pi$, with a radius of 15. Therefore, the ratio of circle A's radius of 3 to circle C's radius of 15 is 1 : 5 or 1 : x. Alternatively, note that circle C's area is the area of circle A times x^2, making the ratio of the areas 1 : x^2. The ratio of the radii should be the square root of this ratio, because area is πr^2, giving you the ratio 1 : x. Both solution methods prove that the Quantities are equal.

30. **D** The diameter of the larger circle, in inches, is 1, so the radius is $\dfrac{1}{2}$. Therefore, the area of the larger circle is $\pi \left(\dfrac{1}{2}\right)^2 = \dfrac{\pi}{4}$, and the area of the smaller circle is half this area, $\dfrac{\pi}{8}$. Setting this amount equal to the area formula allows you to determine the radius of the smaller circle: $\pi r^2 = \dfrac{\pi}{8}; r = \dfrac{\sqrt{2}}{4}$. Therefore, the diameter is $\dfrac{\sqrt{2}}{2}$. Subtract this amount from 1 (the diameter of the larger circle): $1 - \dfrac{\sqrt{2}}{2} = \dfrac{2-\sqrt{2}}{2}$.

31. **B** Plug In a value for the radius of the circle, say $r = 2$, making the diameter 4; $\overline{AB}$ and $\overline{CD}$ are both diameters of the circle, so Column A is 8. The circumference of the circle is $4\pi \approx 12$, so Column B is greater.

32. **C** The diameter of the glasses are the same length as the side of the boxes that surround them, 4". Therefore, the bottom of the original box is constructed of six squares 4" on a side. The area of each square is $4^2 = 16$ square inches, so the total area of the bottom is (6)(16) = 96 square inches. The sides of the box and the dividers that surround the glasses are composed of rectangles that also have 4" sides, and are the same height as the glasses, 5". The area of each of these rectangles is (5)(4) = 20 square inches. In the diagram, you can see the top edges of these rectangles. Counting them, there are 9 horizontal and 8 vertical rectangles, for a total of 17. The total area of these rectangles is therefore 340 square inches. The original amount of material is the bottom of the box plus the dividers, 96 + 340 = 436 square inches. The area of the cardboard needed to compose the proposed box can be calculated similarly. The area of the square bottom pieces totals (6)(5)(5) = 150 square inches, and the area of the dividers and sides of the box totals (5)(6)(17) = 510 square inches, for a grand total of 660 square inches. Subtracting 436 from 660 gives you 224 square inches, the amount of additional cardboard needed to make the proposed box.

33. **A**   Note that *OD* must be a diameter because it is the longest possible line segment crossing the circle. *OA* and *OD* (draw it in) are both radii, and therefore equal in length (3), and both of them are equal to *AD*. Therefore, triangle *OAD* is equilateral, and the measure of $\angle AOD$ is 60°. The central angle for sector *OABC* is 120° (the supplement to 60°), making this sector's area $\frac{1}{3}$ the area of the circle: $\frac{1}{3}3^2\pi = 3\pi$. Because π is slightly greater than 3, 3π is slightly greater than 9, giving you choice (A) for the answer.

34. **B**   Draw a rough sketch of the wall, the records, and the spaces. Notice that the number of spaces is one greater than the number of records (2 records yields 3 spaces, 3 records yields 4 spaces, etc.). The area of each record is $36\pi = \pi r^2$, so $r = 6$, and the diameter of each record is 12," or one foot. Using PITA, try 31 records first. If you try to put 31 records end-to-end, that covers 31 feet, but dividing the remaining 6 inches into 32 pieces does not give you an integer. 30 records leaves 18 inches of space, but this cannot be divided into 31 pieces of integer length either. 29 records leaves 30 inches, which can be divided into 30 pieces of integer length (1 inch).

35. **B**   To solve this one, Plug In for *r* and *m*: try *r* = 2 and *m* = 4. If $\frac{1}{2}$ of the pizza has been eaten, and the remaining $\frac{1}{2}$ is divided into 4 equal slices, then each of those remaining pieces is $\frac{1}{8}$ of the whole pizza. Now Plug In 2 for *r* and 4 for *m* in the answer choices; only choice (B) hits your target answer of $\frac{1}{8}$.

36. **D**   The original slice is cut from a pizza with a diameter of 10, and therefore a circumference of 10π. This slice represents $\frac{1.25\pi}{10\pi} = \frac{1}{8}$ of the circumference and therefore $\frac{1}{8}$ of the area, $\frac{25\pi}{8}$, which weighs 4 ounces. A serving weighs 8 ounces, which covers double the area, $\frac{25\pi}{4}$. The area of the six pizzas is $(6)\pi 3^2 = 45\pi$. Dividing this by the area of one serving gives you the total number of servings that the six pizzas represent: $\frac{54\pi}{\left(\frac{25\pi}{4}\right)} = 8\frac{16}{25} = 8.64$. The six pizzas yield 8 servings.

3D Figures

3D FIGURES

Three-dimensional figures on the GRE involve the same fundamental geometry that you will see elsewhere on the test. They just offer ETS new ways to combine the usual circles, triangles, and quadrilaterals. The five-step approach remains the same.

Step 1: Draw your shape

In some cases the test will give you a shape, which you may or may not be able to trust, and in others it will give you a word problem and leave it up to you to envision the shape. As with every other part of the test, getting your hand moving is an important first step to entering the problem. Get your shape down on your scratch paper so that you can begin working with it there. On quantitative comparison questions involving geometry, instead of plugging in more than once, you may have to draw your shape more than once.

Step 2: Fill in what you know

Whether you are given the shape or not, you will be given a certain amount of information regarding your shape such as the measure of some angles, lengths of some sides, area of some sides, or volume. Put that information in the figure.

Step 3: Make deductions

If you are given two angles of a triangle, find the third. If you are given the radius of a circle, find the area. Often this will be the entire problem. Geometry on the GRE is all about finding the missing piece of information. You will be given just enough information to find the piece that is missing.

Step 4: Write down relevant formulas

If step three didn't get you the answer, you must still be missing a piece of information. Writing down the formula is a way of both organizing your information and telling you what is missing. When you write your formulas down, fill in the information you have directly underneath the relevant part of the formula. It seems simple, but this way you can't make a mistake. Finding the missing piece of information becomes a simple case of solving for x.

Step 5: Drop heights/draw lines

If you're still stuck, you may need to manipulate or subdivide your shapes. If you have triangles, draw in the height. Have you created a 30-60-90? A 45-45-90? Or a Pythagorean triple? Try subdividing the shape or, if it's a three dimensional figure, dashing in the hidden lines.

FORMULAS

There are only three formulas that you need to know for three-dimensional figures. The volume of a rectangular solid is length times width, times height. Remember that it has eight sides should you need to know how to find the surface area. The formula for a right cylinder is easy to remember. Just take the area of the circle and multiply it by the height, pi times radius squared times height. You might occasionally need to know the super Pythagorean theorem, which is $a^2 \times b^2 \times c^2 = d$. This is used to find the diagonal distance between the farthest two vertices of a rectangular solid, but check to see if there is a Pythagorean triple involved before you end up calculating large numbers.

Pythagorean triples show up just as frequently on three-dimensional solids as they do on triangle questions.

For more practice and a more in-depth look at The Princeton Review math techniques, check out our student-friendly guidebook, *Cracking the GRE*.

3D FIGURES DRILL

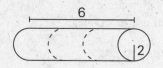

A right circular cylinder with a radius of 2 feet and a length of 6 feet is cut into three equal pieces. What is the volume, in cubic feet, of each of the three pieces?

- ⬭ 2π
- ⬭ 3π
- ⬭ 8π
- ⬭ 12π
- ⬭ 24π

Column A	Column B
Three times the total surface area of a cube with edge length of 1 centimeter	The total surface area of a cube with edge length of 3 centimeters

- ⬭ The quantity in Column A is greater.
- ⬭ The quantity in Column B is greater.
- ⬭ The two quantities are equal.
- ⬭ The relationship cannot be determined from the information given.

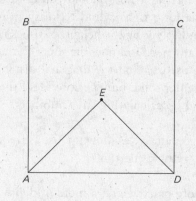

E is the center of square $ABCD$.

$AB = 8$

Column A	Column B
AE	4

- ⬭ The quantity in Column A is greater.
- ⬭ The quantity in Column B is greater.
- ⬭ The two quantities are equal.
- ⬭ The relationship cannot be determined from the information given.

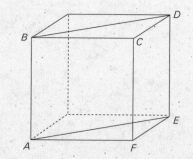

Each edge of the cube shown above has length n. What is the perimeter of quadrilateral $ABDE$?

- ⬭ $2n(1 + \sqrt{2})$
- ⬭ $n\sqrt{2}$
- ⬭ $4n\sqrt{2}$
- ⬭ $4n$
- ⬭ $2n^2$

ABCG and CDEF are squares with the same area
and ∠BCD is a right angle touching at points,
and

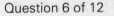

Column A	Column B
3 times the length of AB	The length of AE

○ The quantity in Column A is greater.
○ The quantity in Column B is greater.
○ The two quantities are equal.
○ The relationship cannot be determined
   from the information given.

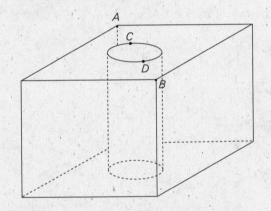

The figure above is a cube with edges of
length 9. Points C and D lie on diagonal AB
such that points A, C, D, and B are equally
spaced. As shown, a right circular cylindrical
hole is cut out of the cube so that segment
CD is a diameter of the top of the hole. What
is the volume of the resulting figure?

○ 729 – 162

○ $729 - \dfrac{81\pi}{2}$

○ 729 – 81π

○ 729 – 9π

○ 729

What is the total surface area of a cube with a
volume of 512 ?

○ 384
○ 320
○ 256
○ 152
○ 48

The total surface area of a cube is 54.

Column A	Column B
The length of a diagonal of one face of the cube	3

○ The quantity in Column A is greater.
○ The quantity in Column B is greater.
○ The two quantities are equal.
○ The relationship cannot be determined
   from the information given.

Cube C has an edge of 4 and cube D has an
edge of 5.

Column A	Column B
The ratio of cube C's total surface area to its volume	The ratio of cube D's total surface area to its volume

○ The quantity in Column A is greater.
○ The quantity in Column B is greater.
○ The two quantities are equal.
○ The relationship cannot be determined
   from the information given.

A certain building is a rectangular solid with a square base of side length 25m and a volume of 13,000m³. What is the volume, in cubic meters, of a building that has a square base with a side of 75m and the same height as the other building?

○   1,444.4
○   4,333.3
○   39,000
○ 117,000
○ 351,000

Marty has a right circular cylindrical pool of diameter 12 feet and his neighbor, Rusty, has a right circular cylindrical pool of diameter 18 feet. If the depths of the pools are equal, then the volume of water in Rusty's pool is how many times that in Marty's pool?

○ 1.5
○ 2.25
○ 2.5
○ 4
○ 4.25

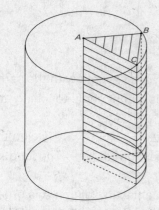

A is the center of the top face of the right circular cylinder in the figure above. If the degree measure of ∠*BAC* is four times that of ∠*ACB* and the height of the cylinder is equal to the diameter of its base, then the volume of the shaded region is what fraction of the volume of the entire cylinder?

○ $\dfrac{1}{12}$

○ $\dfrac{1}{6}$

○ $\dfrac{1}{4}$

○ $\dfrac{1}{3}$

○ It cannot be determined from the information given.

ANSWERS

1. C
2. B
3. A
4. A
5. A
6. B
7. A
8. A
9. A
10. D
11. B
12. D

EXPLANATIONS

1. **C**   The answer asks for $\frac{1}{3}$ of the whole volume, so begin by dividing the height of the trunk by 3 to find the volume of one of the sections of the trunk: $\frac{6 \text{ ft}}{3}$ = 2ft. The volume formula for a cylinder is: $V = \pi r^2 h = \pi \times 2^2 \times 2 = 8\pi$.

2. **B**   Three times the surface area of a cube with edge length of 1 cm is three times the area of each square face times the number of faces: 3 x (1 cm x 1 cm) × 6 faces = 18 cm². The surface area of a cube with edge length of 3 cm is (3 cm x 3 cm) × 6 faces = 54 cm². Column B is greater.

3. **A**   The diagonal of a square is always longer than its side, so half a diagonal—segment AE—must be longer than half a side. Half the length of a side of this square is 4. Therefore, AE is larger than 4.

4. **A**   Plug In a value for n: Try $n = 3$. If each edge of the cube is 3, $AB = DE = 3$, and because the diagonal of a square forms two 45-45-90 triangles, $BD = AE = 3\sqrt{2}$. The total perimeter is $3 + 3 + 3\sqrt{2} + 3\sqrt{2} = 6 + 6\sqrt{2}$. Now Plug In 3 for n in the answer choices; only choice (A) hits your target.

5. **A**   Draw it! You should end up with two squares oriented the same way touching at C. The squares have the same area, so their sides must be the same length. Plug in a side length for the squares to simplify the comparison—try 2. A square cut in half along its diagonal yields a pair of 45-45-90 triangles, so these two squares with sides of 2 each have diagonals of $2\sqrt{2}$. Diagonals AC and CE connect to form segment AE. Column A is 3 × 2 = 6, and Column B is $2\sqrt{2} + 2\sqrt{2} = 4\sqrt{2} \approx 4(1.4) = 5.6$. Column A is greater.

6. **B**   You will be subtracting the volume of the cylinder from that of the cube, so the answer will contain π; eliminate choices (A) and (E). To find the volume of the figure, start with the volume of the cube: $V = s^3 = 9^3 = 729$. The formula for volume of a cylinder is $V = \pi r^2 h$. The cylinder runs the length of the cube, so its height is the same as the length of the cube's edge, 9. Next, find the radius. The length of diagonal AB is $9\sqrt{2}$ (remember your special triangles—this is a 45-45-90 triangle!). The points between A and B are equally spaced, so the length of CD, the circle's diameter, is $\frac{1}{3}$ the length of AB, $3\sqrt{2}$. The radius is 1/2 the diameter, or $\frac{3\sqrt{2}}{2}$. Plug the radius and the height into the formula: $V = \pi r^2 h = \pi \left(\frac{3\sqrt{2}}{2} \right)^2 (9) = \frac{81\pi}{2}$. Subtract this from the cube's volume for a final answer of $729 - \frac{81\pi}{2}$.

7.   **A**   First, write out your formulas and draw a figure. The volume of a cube is $V = s^3 = 512$, giving you $s = 8$. The surface area of a cube is 6 times the area of each square face of the cube ($SA = 6s^2$), therefore, $6 \times 8^2 = 384$.

8.   **A**   The surface area of a cube is 6 times the area of each square face of the cube ($SA = 6s^2$), or $54 = 6s^2$. So each side is 3. The diagonal of the square forms the hypotenuse of a right triangle. Remember that the hypotenuse of a right triangle is always longer than either leg. Therefore, the diagonal is larger than 3.

9.   **A**   A cube has 6 identical faces, each with an area of s^2, so the surface area of a cube is $6s^2$; the volume of a cube is s^3. Column A is $\dfrac{6 \times 4^2}{4^3} = \dfrac{6}{4}$, and Column B is $\dfrac{6 \times 5^2}{5^3} = \dfrac{6}{5}$. Column A is greater.

10. **D**   First, eliminate choices (A) and (B) because the volume must increase when the side of the square base increases. Next, set up a proportion using the square base of the prism: $\dfrac{13,000}{25^2} = \dfrac{x}{75^2}$. Finally, cross-multiply and solve for x to get choice (D).

11. **B**   Try Plugging In a value for the depth, 2 feet. Note that the radii are half the given diameters. Therefore, the volume of water held by Marty's pool is $V = \pi r^2 h = \pi(6)^2(2) = 72\pi$ and the volume of water held by Rusty's pool is $V = \pi r^2 h = \pi(9)^2(2) = 162\pi$. Dividing 162π by 72π yields 2.25.

12. **D**   The center of the circular base is A, and B and C lie on the circle, so segments AB and AC are radii. Triangle ABC is therefore isosceles, and the degree measures of $\angle ACB$ and $\angle ABC$ are equal. Call those degree measures x. The measure of $\angle BAC$ now equals $4x$. The sum of the angles of triangle ABC is therefore $x + x + 4x = 6x = 180$. Solving the equations gives you $x = 30$ and $\angle BAC$ measures 120°. $\dfrac{120}{360} = \dfrac{1}{3}$, so this central angle covers $\dfrac{1}{3}$ of the circular base. The volume of the shaded region is therefore $\dfrac{1}{3}$ of the volume of the cylinder.

Charts and Graphs

CHARTS AND GRAPHS

The first step on a Charts and Graphs question is to get familiar with the data. You will often be given two or occasionally even three charts full of information. Just like in a reading comprehension question, you may have to scroll down to get to the second chart. **Make sure that you always scroll down to see if there is a second chart.** The questions would be pretty confusing if you missed a whole chart.

Pay careful attention to footnotes, parenthesis, and small print. They almost always include information you will need to read the chart or to answer a question. Take note of the units as well. You won't need them when you calculate, but you will almost certainly see wrong answer choices that provide the right numbers with the wrong decimal points. If the chart gives you information in thousands or in millions make sure to count your zeros.

THE MATH

The math involved in chart questions is pretty fundamental. Typically it involves fractions, percentages, addition, multiplication, and subtraction. The addition, subtraction, and multiplication will be made more difficult by including large numbers with lots of zeros (information given in thousands etc.), answer choices expressed in scientific notation, or information taken from multiple charts.

Ballpark Before You Calculate

Remember that the answer choices are part of the question. As you go through these drills, note the range in numbers given in your answer choices. The highest answer choices could be double or even five times the size of the smallest answer choice. These questions are ripe for Ballparking. In fact, they are even designed for it. While you will have to do more actual calculating on charts questions than anywhere else on the test, you should never have to calculate all five answer choices; in fact, rarely will you have to calculate more than two. When ETS asks you to find approximately some piece of information, what they're really saying is, "It's OK to Ballpark." If there is a large value range in the answer choices, you should be able to eliminate at least two if not three answer choices by Ballparking, leaving you with only two close answer choices to calculate.

Percent Change

There is one formula to keep in mind for Chart questions. That is the percentage change formula. If a question asks you to find the percentage increase, or percentage decrease, the formula is difference/original x 100. For example, a question may give you the sales figures for company X for the years 1972 through 1986. The question may then ask you which period had the greatest percentage increase in sales. The answer choices will say 1979 to 1980, 1982 to 1983, etc. At least one answer choice will have a percentage decrease. You can eliminate that. One or two others will have very small increases, so you can eliminate those. The remaining answer choices may have the exact, or very close, numerical increases, but differing totals. You should realize that the same numerical increase on a smaller total will yield a greater percentage increase (if you increase the total by one, from five to six, that is a 20 percent increase, but if you increase the total by one from ten to eleven, that is only a 10 percent increase). If you have to calculate, use the percentage change formula. If the sales total in 1982 was 5.4 million and the sales total in 1983 was 6.8 million, then the difference was 1.4 million. Divide that by the original of 5.4 million and you get approximately .26. Multiply this by one hundred and you're left with a percentage increase of 26 percent. If you don't want to do the long division, reduce your fraction to +/- ¼ and look for answer choices about 25 percent.

SCRATCH PAPER

As always, scratch paper is key. **Label everything.** Not only will you be dealing with multiple pieces of information, but you may be able to use information you found for one question on another question based upon the same chart. Because you will be doing some calculating, that scratch paper can get messy and confusing. Block out some clean space to do your work and label every number you put down. This becomes especially important if you need to check your units. Wrong answers on Charts problems can often be directly traced to sloppy scratch paper and unlabeled information. Don't be messy.

For more practice and a more in-depth look at The Princeton Review math techniques, check out our student-friendly guidebook, *Cracking the GRE*.

CHARTS AND GRAPHS DRILL

Questions 1–3 refer to the following data.

NEW AND REFURBISHED YACHT
SALES OF COMPANY J, 1994 TO
2004 AND MEDIAN SALE PRICE
FOR SELECTED YEARS

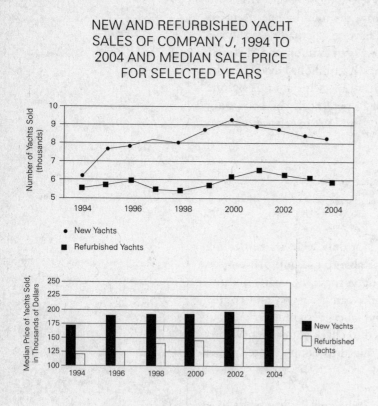

- ● New Yachts
- ■ Refurbished Yachts

In which of the following years did Company J sell more refurbished yachts than in the previous year, but fewer new yachts than in the previous year?

○ 1995
○ 1997
○ 1999
○ 2001
○ 2003

In the year when the median price of new yachts sold by Company J was closest to the median price of refurbished yachts sold by Company J, how many thousand refurbished yachts did the company sell?

○ 6.3
○ 6.7
○ 7.9
○ 8.3
○ 8.7

According to the graph, which of the following could be the number of refurbished yachts sold in 1996 ?

○ 7,750
○ 5,900
○ 5,590
○ 5,400
○ 5,390

Questions 4–6 refer to the following data.

TOTAL BUDGET FOR THE CITY OF SPRINGFIELD
1992 AND 1998

INCOME SOURCES (IN THOUSANDS OF DOLLARS)　　EXPENDITURES (IN THOUSANDS OF DOLLARS)

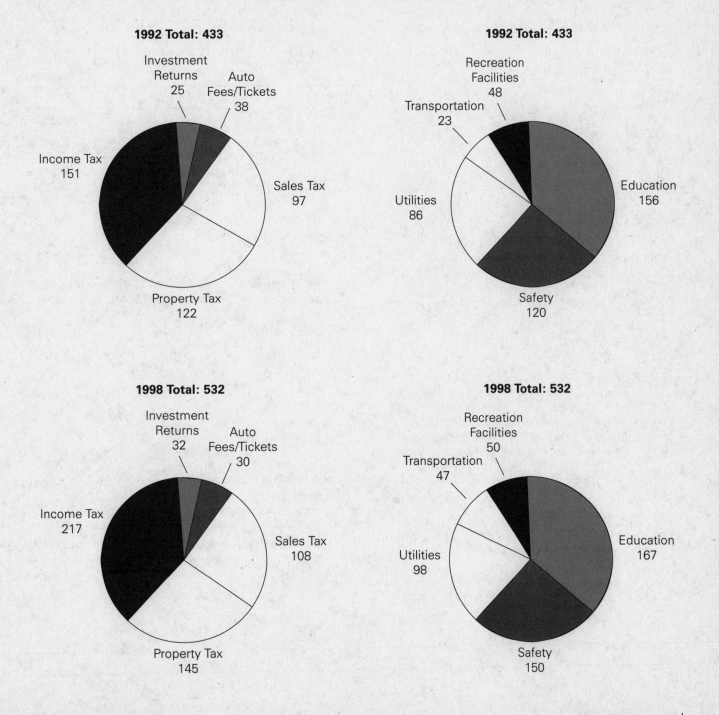

1992 Total: 433

Investment Returns 25
Auto Fees/Tickets 38
Income Tax 151
Sales Tax 97
Property Tax 122

1992 Total: 433

Recreation Facilities 48
Transportation 23
Utilities 86
Education 156
Safety 120

1998 Total: 532

Investment Returns 32
Auto Fees/Tickets 30
Income Tax 217
Sales Tax 108
Property Tax 145

1998 Total: 532

Recreation Facilities 50
Transportation 47
Utilities 98
Education 167
Safety 150

In 1998, the amount that the city of Springfield spent on safety was how many times the amount the city spent on recreation facilities?

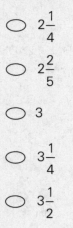

- ○ $2\frac{1}{4}$
- ○ $2\frac{2}{5}$
- ○ 3
- ○ $3\frac{1}{4}$
- ○ $3\frac{1}{2}$

In 1992, approximately what percent of Springfield's income came from income tax?

- ○ 50%
- ○ 45%
- ○ 40%
- ○ 35%
- ○ 30%

What was the approximate percent increase in Springfield's total income from 1992 to 1998 ?

- ○ 19%
- ○ 23%
- ○ 36%
- ○ 42%
- ○ 48%

Questions 7–8 refer to the following data.

AIRLINE DEPARTURES BY COUNTRY
IN 1990 AND 2001

Country	1990 (percent)	2001 (percent)
United States	24.2	31.1
United Kingdom	10.8	9.5
France	9.1	5.0
Germany	5.5	6.2
Japan	4.3	3.1
Brazil	3.1	4.0
China	2.0	7.7
Spain	1.2	0.3
Australia	0.8	0.6
All Others	39.0	32.5
Total Number of Departures	12,050,205	18,205,301

By approximately what percent did the total number of departures increase from 1990 to 2001 ?

- ○ 33%
- ○ 50%
- ○ 66%
- ○ 133%
- ○ 150%

If the nine individually listed countries (excluding those categorized as "All Others") are ranked from highest to lowest by number of departures in both 1990 and 2001, how many countries ranked lower in 2001 than in 1990 ?

- ○ 2
- ○ 3
- ○ 4
- ○ 5
- ○ 6

Questions 9–12 refer to the following data.

By approximately what percent did total cat sales change from 2002 to 2003 ?

- ⬭ 0%
- ⬭ 1%
- ⬭ 2%
- ⬭ 5%
- ⬭ 9%

The total sales at Happy Puppy Pet Depot is calculated by adding the sales from Store A to those from Store B. Both stores sold an equal number of pets in 2002. If the sales of pets in Store A increased by 34% in 2003, by approximately what percent did sales decrease in Store B during the same year?

- ⬭ 12%
- ⬭ 34%
- ⬭ 42%
- ⬭ 66%
- ⬭ 97%

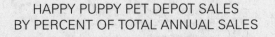

HAPPY PUPPY PET DEPOT SALES
BY PERCENT OF TOTAL ANNUAL SALES

- ■ 100% sales in 2003 = 10,000 animals
- □ 100% sales in 2002 = 9,000 animals

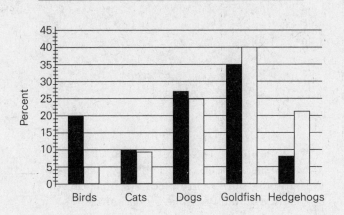

In 2002, how many categories of animals individually accounted for more than 20% of the depot's annual sales?

- ⬭ 1
- ⬭ 2
- ⬭ 3
- ⬭ 4
- ⬭ 5

From 2002 to 2003, what was the increase in the total number of goldfish sold?

- ⬭ 5
- ⬭ 70
- ⬭ 225
- ⬭ 850
- ⬭ 1,380

Questions 13–15 refer to the following data.

MEMBERSHIP OF THE NORTH COUNTY AUTO MECHANICS AND AUTO SALES ASSOCIATIONS IN 1998

Auto Mechanics Association		Auto Sales Association
	Gender	
345	Male	500
464	Female	400
809	Total	900
	Age	
23	Youngest	25
68	Oldest	72
34	Average	44
	Number of Children	
125	0	209
223	1	126
204	2	98
117	3	85
54	4	132
52	5	128
34	6 or more	122
	Highest Education Level	
129	Some High School	185
286	High School Graduate	419
307	College Graduate	202
87	Advanced Degrees	94

If 50 of the male members of the Auto Sales Association were replaced by 50 female members, what would be the ratio of male to female members in the Auto Sales Association ?

- ◯ 1 to 1
- ◯ 1 to 2
- ◯ 1 to 3
- ◯ 2 to 1
- ◯ 3 to 1

If 92 members of the Auto Sales Association were females with 5 children, how many members of the Auto Sales Association were males who did not have 5 children?

- ◯ 122
- ◯ 228
- ◯ 308
- ◯ 436
- ◯ 464

If all the members of the Auto Mechanics Association who held advanced degrees and all the members of the Auto Mechanics Association who had at least 5 children voted for a measure, how many more votes were needed to gain a majority?

- ◯ 173
- ◯ 344
- ◯ 556
- ◯ 636
- ◯ It cannot be determined from the information given.

Questions 16–18 refer to the following data.

NUMBER OF BOOKS SOLD BY BOOK STORE X IN 2005 LISTED BY MAJOR CATEGORY AND TARGET AUDIENCE

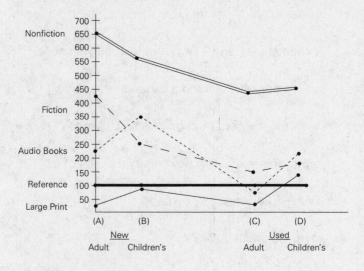

	New Adult (A)	New Children's (B)	Used Adult (C)	Used Children's (D)
Nonfiction	650	540	380	420
Fiction	430	250	120	170
Audio Books	220	330	50	200
Reference	100	120	90	80
Large Print	20	90	10	140

	New Adult (A)	New Children's (B)	Used Adult (C)	Used Children's (D)
Textbooks	210	240	80	40
Science/Nature	150	120	70	120
Biographical	60	80	30	90
History/Cultural Studies	50	90	20	70
Other	180	10	180	100

NUMBER OF NONFICTION BOOKS SOLD BY BOOK STORE X IN 2005

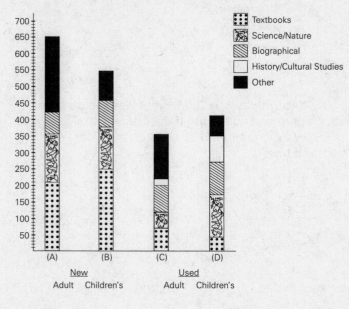

For which major category of books was the number sold most nearly the same for each of the four groups?

- ◯ Nonfiction
- ◯ Fiction
- ◯ Audio Books
- ◯ Reference
- ◯ Large Print

Approximately how many Used Adult Science/Nature books did Book Store X sell in 2005 ?

- ◯ 70
- ◯ 90
- ◯ 110
- ◯ 150
- ◯ 180

Which of the following correctly lists the number of audio books sold for each of the four groups from greatest to least?

○ B, D, A, C
○ B, A, D, C
○ A, D, B, C
○ A, C, B, D
○ D, A, C, B

Questions 19–21 refer to the following data.

INCOME AND EXPENDITURES AT UNIVERSITY F IN 2004

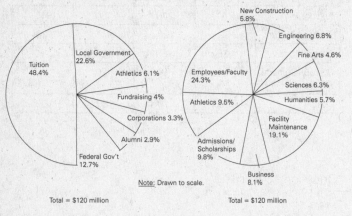

Note: Drawn to scale.

Total = $120 million   Total = $120 million

University F's expenditures in which of the following categories were most nearly equal to $5.4 million in 2004 ?

○ Fine Arts
○ Facility Maintenance
○ Humanities
○ Athletics
○ Business

In 2004, $\frac{1}{2}$ of University F's new construction expenditures, $\frac{1}{4}$ of its facility maintenance expenditures, and $\frac{3}{5}$ of both the athletics and admissions/scholarships expenditures went towards the construction of a new gymnasium. Approximately how many millions of dollars did University F spend on the new gymnasium in 2004 ?

○ $13 million
○ $18 million
○ $20 million
○ $24 million
○ $30 million

At University F in 2004, what was the closest approximation to the percentage of athletics expenditures NOT covered by athletics income?

○ 32%
○ 36%
○ 42%
○ 56%
○ 64%

Questions 22–23 refer to the following data.

AVERAGE TEMPERATURE HIGHS AND LOWS FOR CITY X

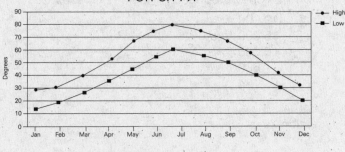

AVERAGE MONTHLY RAINFALL FOR CITIES X AND Y

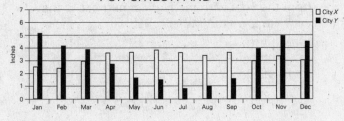

The "monthly midpoint" is calculated by taking the average (arithmetic mean) of a month's average high and low. Which of the following is the average monthly midpoint in City X for the 3-month period from July to September?

- ⬭ 55.3
- ⬭ 60.0
- ⬭ 64.7
- ⬭ 69.3
- ⬭ 74.0

During how many of the months in which City Y's average rainfall exceeded 3 inches was City X's average low temperature greater than or equal to 30 degrees?

- ⬭ One
- ⬭ Two
- ⬭ Three
- ⬭ Four
- ⬭ All

Questions 24–25 refer to the following data.

HONEY PRODUCTION IN REGION *Z*:
1980 TO 1986

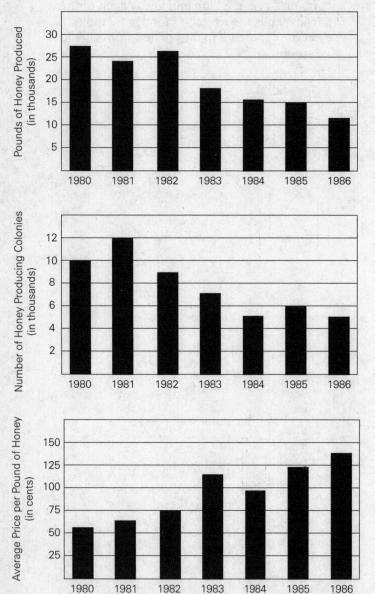

What was the approximate value, in dollars, of the honey produced in Region *Z* in 1985 ?

- ⭘ 19,000
- ⭘ 15,000
- ⭘ 6,000
- ⭘ 580
- ⭘ 124

Question 25 of 36

By approximately what percentage did the number of colonies in Region *Z* decrease from the year with the highest number to that with the lowest number?

- ⭘ 140%
- ⭘ 60%
- ⭘ 40%
- ⭘ 30%
- ⭘ 7%

Questions 26–28 refer to the following data.

PRODUCTION OF GOLF EQUIPMENT AND SUPPLIES
WORLD PRODUCTION 1994-1998
(values are in millions of dollars)

Country	1994 Value	1994 Percent of Total	1995 Value	1995 Percent of Total	1996 Value	1996 Percent of Total	1997 Value	1997 Percent of Total	1998 Value	1998 Percent of Total
United States	2,691	62.3	2,975	63.7	3,248	65.1	3,424	65.1	3,438	63.2
Japan	678	15.7	752	16.1	793	15.9	831	15.8	876	16.1
South Korea	376	8.7	383	8.2	384	7.7	426	8.1	457	8.4
Germany	177	4.1	159	3.4	180	3.6	179	3.4	201	3.7
Great Britain	125	2.9	140	3.0	135	2.7	153	2.9	169	3.1
Canada	125	2.9	103	2.2	105	2.1	100	1.9	125	2.3
Argentina	99	2.3	103	2.2	95	1.9	100	1.9	114	2.1
Other Countries	49	1.1	55	1.2	50	1.0	47	0.9	60	1.1
Total	4,320	100	4,670	100	4,990	100	5,260	100	5,440	100

UNITED STATES PRODUCTION

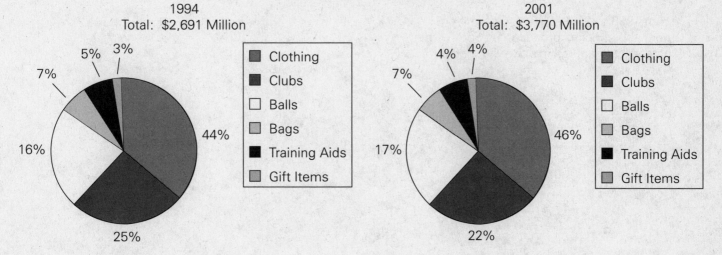

1994
Total: $2,691 Million

2001
Total: $3,770 Million

Legend: Clothing, Clubs, Balls, Bags, Training Aids, Gift Items

1994: 44%, 25%, 16%, 7%, 5%, 3%

2001: 46%, 22%, 17%, 7%, 4%, 4%

In 1994, the value of clubs produced in the United States was approximately what percent of the value of golf equipment and supplies produced in the world?

- ⬭ 33%
- ⬭ 25%
- ⬭ 16%
- ⬭ 13%
- ⬭ 9%

In 1994, the total production for golf equipment and supplies from which country was nearest in value to the combined production of balls, bags, and gift items in the United States in the same year?

- ⬭ Japan
- ⬭ North Korea
- ⬭ Germany
- ⬭ Great Britain
- ⬭ Canada

From 1996 to 1998, the value of golf equipment and supplies produced by South Korea increased by approximately what percent?

- ⬭ 1%
- ⬭ 7%
- ⬭ 16%
- ⬭ 19%
- ⬭ 27%

Questions 29–30 refer to the following data.

U.S. ENERGY SOURCES, 1979 AND 2004

What is the approximate ratio of energy used from oil in 1979 to energy used from oil in 2004 ?

- ⬭ $\dfrac{55}{1}$
- ⬭ $\dfrac{35}{1}$
- ⬭ $\dfrac{11}{7}$
- ⬭ $\dfrac{25}{18}$
- ⬭ $\dfrac{9}{10}$

Which of the following can be inferred from
the graphs?

I. The number of power plants
constructed in the United States
between 1979 and 2004.

II. The amount of energy used from natural gas sources was greater in 1979
than the amount used from natural
gas sources in 2004.

III. The amount of energy used from hydroelectric sources in 2004 was less than
half the amount of energy used from
hydroelectric sources in 1979.

- ◯ II only
- ◯ III only
- ◯ I and II only
- ◯ II and III only
- ◯ None of the above

Questions 31–33 refer to the following data.

2002 AIRPLANE INVENTORY FOR AIRLINES *A* AND *B*
BY YEAR OF PURCHASE
(as a percent of the 2002 inventory)

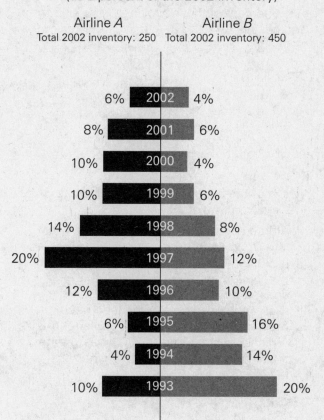

What was the total number of inventoried airplanes purchased by both airlines from 1997
to 1999 ?

- ◯ 110
- ◯ 117
- ◯ 175
- ◯ 227
- ◯ 315

In 1994, Airline *A* bought 25 airplanes. All of these airplanes either remained in Airline *A*'s inventory or were sold to another airline. What percent of these airplanes were sold to another airline?

○ 4%
○ 10%
○ 40%
○ 60%
○ 90%

Which of the following statements can be inferred from the graph?

I. Airline *A* had fewer customers than Airline *B* over the period shown.
II. In 2002, Airline *B*'s inventory of planes purchased in 1993 was twice that purchased by Airline *A* in 1993.
III. If all airplanes were purchased new, then the median age of an airplane in Airline *B*'s inventory in 2002 was greater than that of an airplane in Airline *A*'s inventory in 2002.

○ None
○ II only
○ III only
○ I and II only
○ I, II, and III

Questions 34–36 refer to the following data.

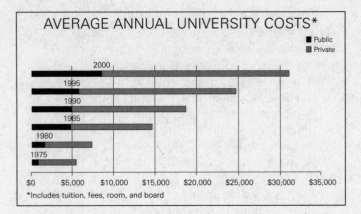

AVERAGE ANNUAL UNIVERSITY COSTS*

*Includes tuition, fees, room, and board

In 2005, the ratio of the average annual cost to attend a private university to the average annual cost to attend a public university was the same as it was in 1990. If the average annual cost to attend a public university in 2005 was $11,000, what was the average annual cost to attend private university in that year, to the nearest $1,000 ?

○ $18,000
○ $24,000
○ $29,000
○ $32,000
○ $34,000

By approximately what percent did the average annual cost to attend a private university increase from 1980 to 2000 ?

○ 27%
○ 73%
○ 138%
○ 267%
○ 367%

The average annual cost to attend a private university increased at a constant rate from 1995 to 2000, and 2.5 million students attended private universities in 1998. If 2 million students attended private universities in 1990, then by approximately what percent did the total dollar amount spent on private universities increase from 1990 to 1998?

- ◯ 25%
- ◯ 30%
- ◯ 55%
- ◯ 70%
- ◯ 90%

ANSWERS

1. B
2. D
3. A
4. C
5. D
6. B
7. B
8. B
9. B
10. D
11. A
12. A
13. A
14. E
15. E
16. D
17. A
18. B
19. A
20. D
21. B
22. B
23. C
24. A
25. B
26. C
27. A
28. D
29. D
30. E
31. D
32. D
33. C
34. C
35. D
36. E

EXPLANATIONS

1. **B**   Be sure you've identified the correct chart, the correct year, and the correct data line: Use the chart showing the number of yachts sold, the data line showing refurbished yachts, and the information for 1996. The data point for 1996 lies just below 6,000, so select choice (B). If you selected choice (A), you may have used the data line showing information for new yachts; if you selected choice (C), (D), or (E), you may have used information from the wrong year.

2. **D**   Because the number of new yachts sold by Company *J* was always greater than the number of refurbished yachts it sold, a decrease in the former and an increase in the latter results in the two data lines coming closer together. Only the year 2001 shows the correct pattern and both of the proper changes: the number of refurbished yachts sold increased from about 6,200 to about 6,500, and the number of new yachts sold decreased from about 9,300 to about 8,800. The answer is choice (D).

3. **A**   First, use the median price chart to determine that 2002 was the year when the median prices of new and refurbished yachts were most similar. Next, use the data line for refurbished yachts in the other chart to determine that the number of yachts sold by Company *J* that year was less than halfway from 6,000 to 7,000; only choice (A) falls in the acceptable range.

4. **C**   In 1998, Springfield spent $150,000 on safety and $50,000 on recreation facilities; hence, the city spent three times as much on safety as on recreation facilities. If you selected choice (B), you may have used the wrong chart.

5. **D**   In 1992, Springfield collected $151,000 from income tax out of its total income of $433,000; $\dfrac{\$151,000}{\$433,000}$ is slightly greater than $\dfrac{1}{3}$, so select choice (D).

6. **B**   The percent change formula is $\dfrac{\textit{difference}}{\textit{original}} \times 100$, so, $\dfrac{532 - 433}{433} \times 100 = \dfrac{99}{433} \times 100$, or slightly less than a quarter (25%). The answer is choice (B).

7. **B**   Round the values and use the percent change formula to approximate the answer; ignore the millions, because they are in both numbers. The percent change formula is $\dfrac{\textit{difference}}{\textit{original}} \times 100$, so $\dfrac{18 - 12}{12} \times 100 = 50\%$.

8. **B**   The chart has already ranked the countries in order in 1990. In 2001, the rankings were as follows: United States—1st; United Kingdom—2nd; France—5th; Germany—4th; Japan—7th; Brazil—6th; China—3rd; Spain—9th; and Australia—8th. Thus, 3 countries—France, Japan, and Spain—ranked lower in 2001; the answer is choice (B).

9. **B** For the year 2002, only dogs and goldfish accounted for more than 20% of the store's total sales.

10. **D** The number of goldfish sold in 2002 was 35% of 9,000, or 3,150 goldfish. The number of goldfish in 2003 was 40% of 10,000, or 4,000. To find the difference, simply subtract: 4,000 − 3,150 = 850.

11. **A** Total cat sales in 2002 can be calculated as 10% of 9,000, or 900 total cats. In 2003, the figure is 9% of 10,000, or 900 total cats. Therefore, the same number of cats was sold in both years. The answer is choice (A).

12. **A** Store *A* and Store *B* both sold an equal number of pets in 2002, meaning both sold 4,500 animals.

    If the total number of pets sold by Store *A* then increases by 34%, Store *A* sold 6,030 animals in

    2003. The total number of animals sold in 2003 was 10,000, meaning store *B* sold only 3,970 pets.

    Use the percent change formula: $\frac{4500 - 3970}{4500} \times 100$ to get choice (A).

13. **A** If 50 male members were replaced by 50 female members, there would be 450 male members and 450 female members. The ratio would be 1 to 1.

14. **E** Use the equation: Group1 + Group2 − Both + Neither = Total. In this case, using the second column of values, you have Females + Members with 5 children − Females with 5 children + Males without 5 children = Total. Substituting the values given in the table and question, 400 + 128 − 92 + Males without 5 children = 900. Solving this equation gives Males without 5 children = 464.

15. **E** There is not enough information given to answer this question since all, some, or none of the members who hold advanced degrees could also have 5 or more children.

16. **D** Use the first graph. Find the line that is the straightest across the four groups, thus, the line with the smallest range. Notice that the Reference line shows about 100, 120, 90, and 80 for the four groups. These numbers are more similar than any other category. For example, the numbers for Large Print are approximately 20, 90, 10, and 140. The range for Large Print (140 − 10 = 130) is much greater than the range for Reference (120 − 80 = 40). The answer is choice (D).

17. **A** Use the second graph. The section of the Used Adult bar for Science/Nature (grey portion) starts at approximately 80 and ends at approximately 150. So, the number of Science/Nature books is approximately 150 − 80 = 70, choice (A).

18. **B** Use the first chart. There were approximately 220 New Adult (A) audio books, 330 New Children's (B) audio books, 50 Used Adult (C), and 200 Used Children's (D) audio books. Putting these in order from greatest to least gives you: (B) 330, (A) 220, (D) 200, (C) 50, choice (B).

19. **A** Be sure to Ballpark this one: 10% of $120 million is $12 million, so 5% would be $6 million. Hence, we're looking for something just less than 5%. Of the options given, Fine Arts comes closest.

20. D   Ballpark this one: $\frac{1}{2}$ of the university's New Construction expenditures is about 3%, $\frac{1}{4}$ of the Facility Maintenance expenditures is about 5%, and $\frac{3}{5}$ of the Athletics and Admissions/Scholarships expenditures is about 12%. That's a total of 3% + 5% + 12% = 20%, and 20% of $120 million is $24 million, so the answer is choice (D).

21. B   Athletic expenditures were 9.5%, while income was 6.1%; the difference is 3.4%, and $\frac{3.4}{9.5}$ can be Ballparked to about $\frac{3.5}{10}$, or about 35%.

22. B   First, look on the bar chart to figure out which months had an average rainfall greater than 3 inches and then apply that information to the temperature chart. According to the bar chart, the only months that had an average rainfall exceeding 3 inches were January, February, March, October, November, and December. According to the line chart, only two of those months had average lows exceeding 30 degrees: October and November.

23. C   This is a multi-step problem, so you should take it one step at a time. First, determine the monthly midpoint for each month. The high in July is 78, and the low is 59, so the monthly midpoint is: 78 + 59 = 137 ÷ 2 = 68.5. Similarly, the midpoint for August is: 76 + 57 = 133 ÷ 2 = 66.5. September's midpoint is: 68 + 50 = 118 ÷2 = 59. The average of the three midpoints is: 59 + 66.5 + 68.5 = 194 ÷ 3 = 64.7, choice (C).

24. A   Since the problem asks for the approximate value of Region Z's honey production in 1985, you'll need to use the first and third graphs. The first graph tells you that there were about 15,000 pounds of honey produced that year, and the third graph tells you that each pound was worth just less than 125 cents, so try 120 cents—or, since the answer needs to be in dollars, $1.20: 15,000 pounds × $1.20 per pound = $18,000. The closest answer is choice (A).

25. B   Use the graph to estimate your starting values and then use the percent change formula, which is $\frac{\text{difference}}{\text{original}} \times 100$. The largest number of colonies—about 12,000—was in 1981, while 1984 and 1986 appear to be tied for lowest at about 5,000 colonies. Since all values are in the thousands, simplify by calling your values 12 and 5: $\frac{12-5}{12} \times 100 = \frac{7}{12} \times 100$, which is approximately 60%. As always, watch out for trap answers: if you selected choice (A), you may have set the original value to 5 instead of 12.

26. **C** Avoid the temptation to work this problem in dollars—you can save considerable effort by dealing directly with the percentages. The pie chart for 1994 shows that clubs made up 25% of the total U.S. production, and the table shows that the United States accounted for 62.3% of the total world production; 25% (or $\frac{1}{4}$) of 62.3% is 15.575%, which is closest to choice (C), 16%.

27. **A** Start by adding the appropriate percentages from the pie chart for 1994: 16% (balls) + 7% (bags) + 3% (gift items) = 26%. Next, find the percentage for the United States total for that year: 26% of $2,691 million is $699.66 million. Finally, find the value in the chart that is nearest $699.66 million—Japan, at $678 million, is the closest.

28. **D** For this problem, be sure to get the correct dollar values from the chart and to use the percent change formula: $\frac{difference}{original} \times 100$. Because the increase was from $384 million in 1996 to $457 million in 1998, the difference is $73 million; $\frac{73}{384} \times 100$ reduces to 19.01%. The answer is choice (D). If you got choice (C), you may have mistakenly used the ending value, $457 million, in place of the original value.

29. **D** For 1979, find 27.5% of 18,509, which is approximately 5,090. For 2004, find 17.5% of 20,623, which is approximately 3,609. Round the numbers and reduce the ratio: $\frac{5000}{3600} = \frac{25}{18}$, choice (D).

30. **E** The chart gives information only about energy use. It does not give any information about the number of power plants constructed. Statement I cannot be inferred from the chart, so eliminate choice (C). While the percent of natural gas use is higher in 1979 than in 2004, the actual amount is lower. Statement II cannot be inferred from the chart, so eliminate choices (A) and (D). The amount of energy used from hydroelectric sources in 2004 is similar to the amount of energy used from hydroelectric sources in 1979. Statement III cannot be inferred from the chart, so eliminate choice (B), leaving you with choice (E) for the answer.

31. **D** From 1997 to 1999, Airline *A* bought 44% of its 250 airplanes, or 110 airplanes. In the same time period, Airline *B* bought 26% of its 450 airplanes, or 117 airplanes. The sum of 110 and 117 is 227 airplanes, choice (D).

32. **D** Looking at the 2002 inventory at Airline *A*, 4% was purchased in 1994. The actual number in inventory is 4% of 250, or 10 airplanes. Of the 25 airplanes purchased, 15 must have been sold. Use percent translation to translate the question into algebra: "15 is what percent of 25" becomes $15 = \frac{x}{100} \times 25$. Solving for x gives you 60, choice (D).

33.   C   Although Airline *A* has fewer airplanes than Airline *B*, you have no information about the number of customers served by each airline. Statement I cannot be inferred, so eliminate choices (D) and (E). While the percent of airplanes purchased by Airline *B* is twice as large as the percent of airplanes purchased by Airline *A*, the actual number is not twice as large. In fact, 20% of 450 is almost four times as large as 10% of 250. Statement II cannot be inferred, so eliminate choice (B). To evaluate Statement III, you need to add the percents in each column year by year until you get to 50%. The airplane with the median age for Airline *A* was purchased in 1997. For Airline *B*, the median is between 1995 and 1996, which makes the median age for the airplanes in Airline *B*'s inventory older. Statement III can be inferred, giving you choice (C) for the answer.

34.   C   The private : public ratio in 1990 was about $\frac{13}{5}$. Setting the ratios equal for the two years (setting up a proportion) gives you: $\frac{13}{5} = \frac{x}{11,000}$. The private cost is approximately $29,000, so the answer is choice (C).

35.   D   The cost increases from about $6,000 to $22,000. Use the percent change formula to find the percent increase: $\frac{16,000}{6,000} \times 100 \approx 267\%$, so the answer is (D).

36.   E   The average cost of a private university in 1995 was $17,000, and the cost in 2000 was $22,000, as you discovered in the previous question. The increase over the 5-year period was $5,000. If the average cost increased at a constant rate, then the increase was $1,000 per year. The 3-year increase from 1995 to 1998 was therefore $3,000, putting the average cost for a private university at $20,000 in 1998. To find the total cost for that year, multiply the average cost per student times the number of students: ($20,000)(2.5 million) = $50 billion. Similarly, in 1990, the total dollar amount spent on private universities was ($13,000)(2 million) = $26 billion. The billions cancel out of the percent change formula, giving you $\frac{24}{26} \times 100 \approx 92\%$, choice (E).

Linear Equations
and Inequalities

LINEAR EQUATIONS AND INEQUALITIES

Linear equations are simply problems that require manipulating the equations and solving for x. In a general sense, your job is to get all the numbers on one side and all the letters on the other. Whatever you do to one side, you must do to the other so that they remain equal. You can subtract a number from both sides. You can divide both sides by a variable so that it disappears from one side and its reciprocal shows up on the other.

As you are manipulating your equations, make sure that you aren't doing more work than you have to. If the question asks for the value of $3x$, you don't need to know the value of x, only $3x$. If you are asked for the value of $2x + 2y$, you may not need to know the actual value of either x or y—just manipulate the equation into a $2x + 2y$ format.

If you have a >, <, ≥, or ≤ sign, the processes remain exactly the same with one exception: If you multiply or divide by a negative number, you must reverse the sign.

USE PLUGGING IN

Don't forget that you can always Plug In if you're given the right conditions. If you have variables in the answer choices, Plug In. If it is a Quant Comp, this means making your set up. If it is a problem solving question, you must write down your answer choices, label your terms, circle your target number, and check all of your answer choices.

If you see the phrase "how much," "how many," or "what is the value of," you can plug in the answer choices. Label your first column—assume choice (C) to be the correct answer choice—and work though the problem in bite-sized pieces making a new answer choice for every step.

SIMULTANEOUS EQUATIONS

You may also see simultaneous equations. This means that you have two equations with two variables or three equations with three variables. To get rid of one variable, you simply stack the equations, line up the variables and either add or subtract the equations. Your goal is to nullify one variable so that you can solve for the other.

Example

$$
\begin{array}{r}
2x + 3y = 12 \\
+ \quad x - 3y = 3 \\
\hline
3x = 15 \\
x = 5
\end{array}
$$

When you add these two equations, the y's cancel out and you're left with only x's. If you're not sure whether to add or subtract, don't worry, just try one. If it doesn't work, try the other. Sometimes you may have to manipulate an equation a bit in order to make sure that one variable cancels out. For example, if you were to add

$$2x + 3y = 12$$

$$x - y = 3$$

. . . you wouldn't get very far. However, if you multiply the second equation by three (remember that whatever you do on one side of the equal sign you must do on the other) you can get the y's to cancel out.

$$
\begin{array}{r}
2x + 3y = 12 \qquad 2x + 3y = 12 \\
3(x - y = 3) = + \quad 3x - 3y = 9 \\
\hline
5x = 21 \\
x = \dfrac{21}{5}
\end{array}
$$

For more practice and a more in-depth look at The Princeton Review math techniques, check out our student-friendly guidebook, *Cracking the GRE*.

LINEAR EQUATIONS AND INEQUALITIES DRILL

$4c + 6 = 26$. What is the value of $3c - 2$?

○ $-\dfrac{1}{2}$

○ 4

○ 5

○ 13

○ 22

$$-3 < a < 2$$
$$2 < b < 4$$

Column A	Column B
$a - b$	1

○ The quantity in Column A is greater.
○ The quantity in Column B is greater.
○ The two quantities are equal.
○ The relationship cannot be determined
   from the information given.

Column A	Column B
$\dfrac{3k - 12j}{9}$	$\dfrac{k - 4j}{3}$

○ The quantity in Column A is greater.
○ The quantity in Column B is greater.
○ The two quantities are equal.
○ The relationship cannot be determined
   from the information given.

What is the value of $(n - 5)(m + 5)$ when
$n = -5$ and $m = 5$?

○ -100

○ -10

○ 0

○ 10

○ 100

$$\frac{2}{3}y = \frac{1}{8}$$

Column A	Column B
y	$\dfrac{1}{12}$

○ The quantity in Column A is greater.
○ The quantity in Column B is greater.
○ The two quantities are equal.
○ The relationship cannot be determined
   from the information given.

$$7a + 8 = 8a - 24$$

Column A	Column B
a	24

○ The quantity in Column A is greater.
○ The quantity in Column B is greater.
○ The two quantities are equal.
○ The relationship cannot be determined
   from the information given.

If x does not equal 0 or 1, the expression

$$\dfrac{\dfrac{1}{x} - 1}{\dfrac{1}{x}}$$ is equivalent to which of the following?

○ $\dfrac{x}{x-1}$

○ $x - 1$

○ -1

○ $1 - x$

○ 1

$$0 < a < b < 1$$

Column A	Column B
0	$2(a - b)$

○ The quantity in Column A is greater.
○ The quantity in Column B is greater.
○ The two quantities are equal.
○ The relationship cannot be determined
   from the information given.

If $a \geq 30$ and $b \leq 15$, then which of the following must also be true?

○ $a - b \leq 45$
○ $a - b \leq 15$
○ $a - b \geq 15$
○ $a + b \leq 45$
○ $a + b \geq 45$

Lyle bought used CDs at a store where all the CDs cost either $8 or $12. If Lyle bought an equal number of CDs at each price, and he spent a total of $200, what was the total number of CDs that Lyle bought?

○ 10
○ 14
○ 20
○ 24
○ 30

What is the greatest integer that does NOT satisfy $3(x - 9) < 5x - 2(1 - 3x)$?

○ −4
○ −3
○ 0
○ 3
○ 4

If $y = 4$ is a solution of the equation $y^2 + ay + 8 = 36$, then what is the value of a ?

○ −7
○ −4
○ −3
○ 3
○ 7

$$a = 4$$
$$6 < b < 8$$

Column A	Column B
0.6	$\dfrac{a}{b}$

○ The quantity in Column A is greater.
○ The quantity in Column B is greater.
○ The two quantities are equal.
○ The relationship cannot be determined from the information given.

If $a = 3b + 2$, then, in terms of a, what is the value of b ?

○ $b = \dfrac{a}{3} - \dfrac{2}{3}$

○ $b = \dfrac{a}{3} + \dfrac{2}{3}$

○ $b = \dfrac{a}{3} - 2$

○ $b = a - \dfrac{2}{3}$

○ $b = a + \dfrac{2}{3}$

$b = \dfrac{4a}{c}$. If a is halved and c is doubled, by what percentage will b decrease?

○ 4%
○ 25%
○ 50%
○ 75%
○ 100%

If $\dfrac{1}{2x} + \dfrac{2}{x} = \dfrac{5}{8}$, what is the value of x ?

○ 2
○ 3
○ 4
○ 7
○ 8

Every box of cookies contains exactly 6 cookies.

Column A	Column B
The total number of cookies purchased if Sally purchased 3 more than twice as many boxes of oatmeal cookies as boxes of chocolate chip cookies	The total number of cookies purchased if Sally purchased 2 fewer than 3 times as many boxes of oatmeal cookies as boxes of chocolate chip cookies

○ The quantity in Column A is greater.
○ The quantity in Column B is greater.
○ The two quantities are equal.
○ The relationship cannot be determined from the information given.

What is the value of $\dfrac{xy}{z^2}$ when $z = 3x$, $y = 4z$, and $xy \neq 0$?

○ 12

○ $\dfrac{4}{3}$

○ 1

○ $\dfrac{3}{4}$

○ $\dfrac{1}{12}$

The sum of two integers is 27. The larger integer is 25% greater than the smaller integer. What is the positive difference between the two integers?

○ 3
○ 6
○ 9
○ 12
○ 15

If $3a + 8b = 2$ and $5a + 15b = 10$, then what is the value of $a + b$?

○ -14
○ -6
○ -4
○ 6
○ 14

If a is a positive even integer, and ab is a negative even integer, then b must be which of the following?

○ A negative number
○ A negative even integer
○ A negative integer
○ A positive even integer
○ A positive integer

$-1 < a - b < 10$, with b an integer such that $-3 \leq b \leq 1$. What most accurately describes the range of a^2 ?

○ $-16 < a^2 < 11$
○ $-4 < a^2 < 11$
○ $0 < a^2 < 16$
○ $0 < a^2 < 121$
○ $16 < a^2 < 121$

If $0.5(y - x) = -1$ and $x^2 - y^2 = 24$, what is the sum of x and y ?

○ -48
○ -12
○ 6
○ 12
○ 48

The quotient of x and y is 2. If x is 75% of z, which is $\dfrac{3}{4}$ larger than w, what is w in terms of y ?

○ $\dfrac{21}{32}y$

○ $\dfrac{20}{21}y$

○ $\dfrac{32}{21}y$

○ $\dfrac{32}{9}y$

○ $\dfrac{21}{8}y$

The sum of x and y is at least 2 but no more than 5. If the total of twice x and three times y is nonnegative and no more than 40, which of the following expresses all possible values of y ?

○ $-4 \leq y \leq 36$
○ $-10 \leq y \leq 30$
○ $-10 \leq y \leq 36$
○ $0 \leq y \leq 40$
○ $2 \leq y \leq 5$

$$\left(\frac{1}{x}\right) + \left(\frac{1}{y}\right) = 6$$

$$-\frac{1}{3} = -2\left(\frac{zy}{z+y}\right)$$

Column A	Column B
z	x

○ The quantity in Column A is greater.
○ The quantity in Column B is greater.
○ The two quantities are equal.
○ The relationship cannot be determined
from the information given.

a, b, and c are integers such that $ab + c = 7$, $ac + b = 5$, and $a + b + c = 6$. What is the value of abc ?

○ 2
○ 6
○ 9
○ 12
○ 18

ANSWERS

1. D
2. B
3. C
4. A
5. A
6. A
7. D
8. A
9. C
10. C
11. A
12. D
13. D
14. A
15. D
16. C
17. D
18. B
19. A
20. B
21. A
22. D
23. D
24. C
25. C
26. C
27. B

EXPLANATIONS

1. **D** When solving algebraically, be careful to perform the same operation on both sides of the equation: $4c + 6 = 26$, so subtract 6 from both sides to find $4c = 20$ and $c = 5$. Therefore, $3c - 2 = (3 \times 5) - 2 = 13$.

2. **B** Try Plugging In values for a and b. If $a = 0$ and $b = 3$, then $a - b = -3$; Column B is greater, so eliminate choices (A) and (C). Any set of values gives the same outcome of Column B being greater, so select choice (B).

3. **C** You can find the two Columns to be equal by Plugging In values for k and j: if $k = 2$ and $j = 3$, then Column A is $\dfrac{3(2) - 12(3)}{9}$, or $-\dfrac{30}{9}$, which can be reduced to $-\dfrac{10}{3}$; Column B is $\dfrac{2 - 4(3)}{3}$, or $-\dfrac{10}{3}$. Algebraically, try factoring and canceling a 3 out of the numerator of Column A: $\dfrac{3k - 12j}{9} = \dfrac{3(k - 4j)}{3 \times 3} = \dfrac{k - 4j}{3}$.

4. **A** Start by substituting the given values for the variables in the equation. You'll be left with $(-5 - 5)(5 + 5)$, which simplifies to $(-10)(10)$, or -100.

5. **A** Solve the given equation by multiplying both sides of the equation by $\dfrac{3}{2}$. You get a value of $\dfrac{3}{16}$ for y. Then use the bowtie method to compare the fractions in the Columns; the fraction in Column A is greater.

6. **A** To solve this single-variable equation, you'll just need to isolate the variable. First, add 24 to both sides to yield $7a + 32 = 8a$. Then subtract $7a$ from both sides to yield $32 = a$. Column A is greater.

7. **D** You are told that $\dfrac{\frac{1}{x} - 1}{\frac{1}{x}}$, which you can manipulate to $(\frac{1}{x} - 1)(\frac{x}{1}) = \frac{x}{x} - \frac{x}{1} = 1 - x$, so the answer is choice (D). Alternatively, you can solve this "must be" problem by Plugging In values for x: if $x = 2$, then $\dfrac{\frac{1}{x} - 1}{\frac{1}{x}} = \dfrac{\frac{1}{2} - 1}{\frac{1}{2}} = \dfrac{-\frac{1}{2}}{\frac{1}{2}} = -\frac{1}{2} \times \frac{2}{1} = -1$. Eliminate choices (A), (B), and (E), because none of them hit your target of -1. Next, try $x = 3$: now $\dfrac{\frac{1}{x} - 1}{\frac{1}{x}} = \dfrac{\frac{1}{3} - 1}{\frac{1}{3}} = -\frac{2}{3} \times \frac{3}{1} = -2$; eliminate choice (C). Choice (D) gives the target answer of -2, so it is the correct answer.

8. **A** You know that b is greater than a, so $(a - b)$ will always be negative, and Column A will always be greater. Alternatively, you can solve this one by Plugging In values for a and b. Try making $a = \dfrac{1}{4}$ and $b = \dfrac{1}{2}$: the value in Column B is now $2\left(\dfrac{1}{4} - \dfrac{1}{2}\right) = 2\left(-\dfrac{1}{4}\right) = -\dfrac{1}{2}$. Column A is greater, so eliminate choices (B) and (C).

9. **C** Solve this "must be" problem by Plugging In values for a and b. Starting with the simplest allowable values, $a = 30$ and $b = 15$, does not eliminate any answer choices. Next, try $a = 100$ and $b = 0$; now choices (A), (B), and (D) can be eliminated. Finally, try $a = 30$ and $b = -30$; now choice (E) can be eliminated, leaving only choice (C), which is the correct answer.

10. **C** Rather than writing equations to reflect the given information, just Plug In the answers to see whether they yield the desired total. Start with the middle answer choice: if Lyle bought a total of 20 CDs, then he must have bought 10 at each price. That's a total of 10 × $8, or $80, on the less expensive CDs, and a total of 10 × $12, or $120, on the more expensive CDs; $80 + $120 is $200, so select choice (C).

11. **A** The given inequality is equivalent to $3x - 27 < 11x - 2$, which becomes $-8x < 25$. Dividing both sides by -8 (and flipping the inequality sign), you get $x > -3\dfrac{1}{8}$. Therefore, any number that is greater than $-3\dfrac{1}{8}$ *will* satisfy the inequality, so the greatest integer that does *not* satisfy it is $x = -4$, choice (A).

12. **D** Replace y with 4 to get $16 + 4a + 8 = 36$. Then solve the equation to find that a equals 3.

13. **D** Start by combining the 2 given equations: if $a = 4$ and $6 < b < 8$, then the acceptable range for $\dfrac{a}{b}$ is $\dfrac{4}{6} > \dfrac{a}{b} > \dfrac{4}{8}$, which can be reduced to $\dfrac{2}{3} > \dfrac{a}{b} > \dfrac{1}{2}$ or, in decimal form, $0.5 < \dfrac{a}{b} < 0.67$. Select choice (D) because $\dfrac{a}{b}$ can be either larger or smaller than 0.6.

14. **A** The problem has variables in the answer choices so Plug In. Because the problem says, "in terms of a," a is the variable that you want to Plug In for. If $a = 8$, then $b = 2$, and that is now your target. When you Plug In your value for a into choice (B), you get $\dfrac{8}{3} - \dfrac{2}{3} = \dfrac{6}{3} = 2$, thus, the correct answer.

15. **D** Try Plugging In values for a and c. Let $a = 6$ and $c = 2$. Then $b = \dfrac{4(6)}{2} = 12$. If a is halved, equal it will 3. If c is doubled, it will equal 4. So now, $b = \dfrac{4(3)}{4} = 3$. Because the question is looking for a percentage decrease, apply the percentage change formula: $\dfrac{12 - 3}{12} \times 100 = \dfrac{9}{12} \times 100 = \dfrac{3}{4} \times 100 = 75\%$.

16. **C**   Plug In The Answers starting with choice (C). Choice (C) yields $\frac{1}{8}+\frac{2}{4}=\frac{1}{8}+\frac{4}{8}=\frac{5}{8}$, so it's the correct answer.

17. **D**   First, Plug In 1 for the number of boxes of chocolate chip cookies. In Column A, if Sally buys 1 box of chocolate chip cookies, then she buys 2(1) + 3 = 5 boxes of oatmeal cookies, for a total of 6 boxes, or 36 cookies. In Column B, if Sally buys 1 box of chocolate chip cookies, then she buys 3(1) − 2 = 1 box of oatmeal cookies, for a total of 2 boxes, or 12 cookies. Column A is greater, so eliminate choices (B) and (C). Now Plug In 10 boxes of chocolate chip cookies: Column A is now 2(10) + 3 = 23 boxes of oatmeal cookies, for a total of 33 boxes, or 198 cookies, and Column B is now 3(10) − 2 = 28 boxes of oatmeal cookies, for a total of 38 boxes, or 228 cookies. Column B is now greater, so eliminate choice (A), and you're left with choice (D).

18. **B**   You know that $\frac{xy}{z^2}$, so solve this one by Plugging In values for z, x, and y. If $x = 12$, then $z = 36$ and $y = 144$; $\frac{xy}{z^2}=\frac{12\times144}{36^2}=\frac{4}{3}$. The correct answer is choice (B).

19. **A**   Use the information in the problem to write the equations $x + y = 27$ and $\frac{x}{4}+x=y$. You can combine these two equations to say that $\frac{x}{4}+x+x=27$. When you solve this new equation you find that $x = 12$. You can then go back to your first equation and find that $y = 15$. The positive difference between 15 and 12 is 3, so select choice (A).

20. **B**   First, you should look for a way you can stack the equations and end up with them in a + b form. If you multiply the first equation by 2 to get $6a + 16b = 4$, you can stack the equations and subtract the second equation from $6a + 16b = 4$. This gives the result of $a + b = −6$.

21. **A**   The problem contains the phrase "must be," so try to find numbers to Plug In that disprove four of the five answer choices. If $a = 4$ and $ab = −12$, then $b = −3$; eliminate choices (B), (D), and (E). Now determine whether b must be an integer. If $a = 4$ and $ab = −2$, then $b = −\frac{1}{2}$; eliminate choice (C), and you're left with choice (A), the correct answer.

22. **D**   If a range of values for a can be found, then the range of values for a^2 can be found. Start by testing the end values of b, −3 and 1. Plug In −3 for b in the first given inequality then solve for a. You find that $−4 < a < 7$. If $b = 1$, $0 < a < 11$; b could be any integer in the range $−3 \le b \le 1$, this means $−4 < a < 11$ overall. Remember to take the last step, though! The question is looking for the range of a^2, not a; a^2 is always positive, i.e. $0 < a^2$. Because $a < 11$, $a^2 < 121$. This means $0 < a^2 < 121$; the answer is choice (D).

23. D Know your common quadratics. You are asked for the value of $x + y$. Because $x^2 - y^2 = (x + y)(x - y)$ $= 24$, if the value of $(x - y)$ is found, $(x + y)$ can be figured out. Manipulate the equation $0.5(y - x)$ $= -1$ to get $(y - x) = -2$. Multiplying both sides by -1, you get $x - y = 2$. Substitute this value into the equation $(x + y)(x - y) = 24$ and then divide both sides of the equation by 2 to get $(x + y) = 12$. The answer is choice (D).

24. C Translate what you are told into algebra: $\dfrac{x}{y} = 2$ and $x = \dfrac{75}{100} \times z = \dfrac{3}{4}z$. Notice that the problem then tells you that z is $\dfrac{3}{4}$ larger than w, not z is $\dfrac{3}{4}$ of w. That means $z = w + \left(\dfrac{3}{4}w\right) = \left(1 + \dfrac{3}{4}\right)w = \dfrac{7}{4}w$.

At this point, you can either Plug In or do algebra. To Plug In, choose 4 for w, so $z = 7$, and $x = \dfrac{3}{4} \times 7 = \dfrac{21}{4}$. If $\dfrac{x}{y} = 2$, then $x = 2y$, so $\dfrac{21}{4} = 2y$; $y = \dfrac{21}{8}$. Now plug $\dfrac{21}{8}$ into the answer choices for y to see which hits your target number, $w = 4$. Only choice (C) does. Alternatively, to do algebra, combine the first two equations you translated into algebra: $2y = \dfrac{3}{4}z$; $z = \dfrac{8}{3}y$. Combining this equation with the one you derived above, it follows that $\dfrac{8}{3}y = \dfrac{7}{4}w$, and $w = \dfrac{32}{21}y$; the answer is choice (C).

25. C Translate what you are told into algebra: $2 \le x + y \le 5$ and $0 \le 2x + 3y \le 40$. By manipulating the inequalities, you find that $2 - y \le x \le 5 - y$ and $-2x \le 3y \le 40 - 2x$. Substitute the endpoints of the values of x into the second inequality: $-2(2 - y) \le 3y \le 40 - 2(2 - y)$ and $-2(5 - y) \le 3y \le 40 - 2(5 - y)$. By solving for y, the first range yields $-4 \le y \le 36$, and the second yields $-10 \le y \le 30$, meaning $-10 \le y \le 36$ overall.

26. C Using the Bowtie method, you find that $\dfrac{y + x}{xy} = 6$. By multiplying both sides of the second equation by $-\dfrac{1}{2}$, you find that $\dfrac{1}{6} = \dfrac{zy}{z + y}$. Flipping both fractions yields $\dfrac{z + y}{zy} = 6$, and thus, $\dfrac{y + x}{xy} = \dfrac{z + y}{zy}$. Inspecting the two fractions, you may realize that z must equal x. Alternatively, by applying the Bowtie again, you obtain $(y + x)(zy) = (z + y)(xy)$, and thus $zy^2 + xyz = xyz + xy^2$, meaning $zy^2 = xy^2$, or $z = x$, so the answer is choice (C).

27. B By rearranging the first two equations, you obtain $c = 7 - ab$ and $b = 5 - ac$. By substituting these relationships into the third equation, $a + (5 - ac) + (7 - ab) = 6$ is obtained. Manipulating the equation yields $a - ac - ab + 12 = 6$, or $a - a(c + b) + 6 = 0$. Since $a + b + c = 6$, $b + c = 6 - a$. Substituting this into the previous equation yields $a - a(6 - a) + 6 = a - 6a + a^2 + 6 = 0$, or $a^2 - 5a + 6 = 0$. Factoring and finding the roots gives you $a = 2$ or $a = 3$. If $a = 2$—by substituting the value back into the equations—then $b = 2$ and $c = 1$. If $a = 3$, then $b = 3$ and $c = 1$. You are looking for abc, and either way, the value is $3 \times 2 \times 1 = 6$. The answer is choice (B).

Quadratic Equations

QUADRATIC EQUATIONS

You probably remember FOIL (First Outer Inner Last) from high school and you may also remember how to find the roots of an equation. On the GRE, there are really only three quadric equation formats that you will see.

Memorize these equations:

$(x + y)^2 = x^2 + 2xy + y^2$

$(x - y)^2 = x^2 - 2xy + y^2$

$(x + y)(x - y) = x^2 - y^2$

Each of the above expressions has two states—the factored state and the squared state. When you see an expression in one state, rewrite it in the other state. Typically these questions will be about manipulating equations, not about solving for x. If the equations don't match one of these three formats, see if you can factor numbers or variables out of them until they do.

Naturally, the minute you see a quadratic equation, either on a quantitative comparison or a problem-solving question, if you see variables in the question and variables in the answer choices, you can always Plug In. Use your Plug In set-up for Quant Comp and plug in more than once. On problem solving questions make sure you have labeled the terms, circled a target number, and checked all of the answer choices.

For more practice and a more in-depth look at The Princeton Review math techniques, check out our student-friendly guidebook, *Cracking the GRE*.

QUADRATIC EQUATIONS DRILL

Column A	Column B
$(3p + 1)(3p - 1)$	$9p^2$

○ The quantity in Column A is greater.
○ The quantity in Column B is greater.
○ The two quantities are equal.
○ The relationship cannot be determined from the information given.

$$a > 0$$

Column A	Column B
$(a + 2)(3a + 6)$	$(3a + 2)(a + 6)$

○ The quantity in Column A is greater.
○ The quantity in Column B is greater.
○ The two quantities are equal.
○ The relationship cannot be determined from the information given.

Column A	Column B
$3^2 - 2^2$	$(3 - 2)(3 + 2)$

○ The quantity in Column A is greater.
○ The quantity in Column B is greater.
○ The two quantities are equal.
○ The relationship cannot be determined from the information given.

If $(4x + 2)^2 = 0$, then $x =$

○ -4

○ -2

○ $-\dfrac{1}{2}$

○ $\dfrac{1}{2}$

○ 2

$$a > 0$$

Column A	Column B
$(-a - 10)(10 + a)$	10

○ The quantity in Column A is greater.
○ The quantity in Column B is greater.
○ The two quantities are equal.
○ The relationship cannot be determined from the information given.

$$(y - 1)(y + 5) = 0$$

Column A	Column B
y	3

○ The quantity in Column A is greater.
○ The quantity in Column B is greater.
○ The two quantities are equal.
○ The relationship cannot be determined from the information given.

$$8^2 + 10^2 - \left[2(8)(10)\left(\frac{8}{10}\right) \right] =$$

- ○ 2
- ○ 36
- ○ 100
- ○ 164
- ○ 196

If the difference between two numbers is 4, then which of the following would NOT be sufficient to determine the value of each of the numbers?

- ○ The sum of the numbers is 4.
- ○ The difference between the squares of the numbers is 16.
- ○ The square of the difference between the numbers is 16.
- ○ The product of the two numbers is 0, and neither of the numbers is negative.
- ○ Twice the greater number is 8.

A rectangle is formed by increasing two opposite sides of a square of side length x by y units, and decreasing the two remaining sides of the square by y units. What is the area of the rectangle?

- ○ $4x$
- ○ $4x - 2y$
- ○ $x^2 - 2y$
- ○ $x^2 + 2y$
- ○ $x^2 - y^2$

The net profit that Ann makes from selling x pillows is given by the expression $x^2 - 2x - 288$.

Column A	Column B
The number of pillows that Ann must sell for her net profit to be zero	20

- ○ The quantity in Column A is greater.
- ○ The quantity in Column B is greater.
- ○ The two quantities are equal.
- ○ The relationship cannot be determined from the information given.

If $6x^2 - 5x - 6 = 0$, then x could equal

- ○ $-\dfrac{2}{3}$ or $\dfrac{6}{11}$
- ○ $-\dfrac{2}{3}$ or $\dfrac{3}{2}$
- ○ $\dfrac{3}{2}$ or $\dfrac{6}{11}$
- ○ $-\dfrac{3}{2}$ or $\dfrac{2}{3}$
- ○ $-\dfrac{6}{11}$ or $-\dfrac{2}{3}$

What is the greatest value of x for which $(3x - 2)(x + 1) = 0$?

- ○ -1
- ○ $-\dfrac{2}{3}$
- ○ $\dfrac{2}{3}$
- ○ 1
- ○ 2

$$x^2 = y^2 + 1 \text{ and } y \neq 0.$$

Column A	Column B
x^4	$y^4 + 1$

- The quantity in Column A is greater.
- The quantity in Column B is greater.
- The two quantities are equal.
- The relationship cannot be determined from the information given.

The solutions of $x^2 + x - 20 = 0$ are

- 4 and –5
- 5 and –4
- 10 and –2
- 20 and –1
- none of the above

If x is positive and y is 1 more than the square of x, then what is the value of x in terms of y ?

- $y^2 - 1$
- $y^2 + 1$
- $\sqrt{y} - 1$
- $\sqrt{y - 1}$
- $\sqrt{y + 1}$

$$x^2 - 49 = 0$$

Column A	Column B
$x^2 - 7x$	$-7x + 49$

- The quantity in Column A is greater.
- The quantity in Column B is greater.
- The two quantities are equal.
- The relationship cannot be determined from the information given.

For $x \neq -2$ and $x \neq -4$, $\dfrac{x}{x + 4} + \dfrac{-3}{x + 2} =$

- $\dfrac{x^2 - x - 12}{(x + 4)(x + 2)}$

- $\dfrac{-3x}{(x + 4)(x + 2)}$

- $\dfrac{x - 3}{2x + 6}$

- $\dfrac{1}{x + 4}$

- -2

$$a \neq -b$$

Column A	Column B
$\dfrac{6a^2 + 12ab + 6b^2}{a + b}$	$6(a + b)$

- The quantity in Column A is greater.
- The quantity in Column B is greater.
- The two quantities are equal.
- The relationship cannot be determined from the information given.

Column A	Column B
$(141)^2 - (28)^2$	$(141 - 28)^2$

- The quantity in Column A is greater.
- The quantity in Column B is greater.
- The two quantities are equal.
- The relationship cannot be determined from the information given.

$(-x + y)(-y + x) =$

- ⬭ $x^2 - y^2$
- ⬭ $y^2 - x^2$
- ⬭ 0
- ⬭ $-(x - y)^2$
- ⬭ $(y - x)^2$

$$x \geq 0$$
$$y \geq 0$$

Column A	Column B
$\sqrt{x^{12}} - y$	$\left(x^3 + \sqrt{y}\right)\left(x^3 - \sqrt{y}\right)$

- ⬭ The quantity in Column A is greater.
- ⬭ The quantity in Column B is greater.
- ⬭ The two quantities are equal.
- ⬭ The relationship cannot be determined from the information given.

Column A	Column B
$(s + t)^2$	$s^2 + t^2$

- ⬭ The quantity in Column A is greater.
- ⬭ The quantity in Column B is greater.
- ⬭ The two quantities are equal.
- ⬭ The relationship cannot be determined from the information given.

$$x^2 - 2xy + y^2 = 0 \text{ and } y = \frac{9}{x}$$

Column A	Column B
y	3

- ⬭ The quantity in Column A is greater.
- ⬭ The quantity in Column B is greater.
- ⬭ The two quantities are equal.
- ⬭ The relationship cannot be determined from the information given.

If the average (arithmetic mean) of two numbers is 9 and the difference between their squares is 144, what is the result when the smaller number is subtracted from the larger number?

- ⬭ 169
- ⬭ 144
- ⬭ 25
- ⬭ 9
- ⬭ 8

If $y = x^2 - 32x + 256$, then what is the least possible value of y ?

- ⬭ 256
- ⬭ 32
- ⬭ 16
- ⬭ 8
- ⬭ 0

ANSWERS

1. B
2. B
3. C
4. C
5. B
6. B
7. B
8. C
9. E
10. B
11. B
12. C
13. A
14. A
15. D
16. C
17. A
18. C
19. A
20. D
21. C
22. D
23. D
24. E
25. E

EXPLANATIONS

1. **B**   Evaluate the relationship between the Columns by Plugging In values for p: try $p = 2$. Column A is $7 \times 5 = 35$, and Column B is $9 \times 4 = 36$; Column B is greater, so eliminate choices (A) and (C). Any value gives the same outcome, so select answer choice (B). Algebraically, you could either FOIL Column A or recognize the common quadratics—either way, Column A simplifies to $9p^2 - 1$, which is always exactly 1 less than Column B.

2. **B**   Try FOILing. For Column A, you get $3a^2 + 6a + 6a + 12$, or $3a^2 + 12a + 12$. For Column B, you get $3a^2 + 18a + 2a + 12$, or $3a^2 + 20a + 12$. Remember to compare, not calculate. Notice that the only difference between the Columns is that between $20a$ and $12a$. Because a is positive, $20a$ must be greater than $12a$, thus, Column B will always be greater.

3. **C**   This is one of the common quadratic equations: $(3 - 2)(3 + 2) = 3^2 - 2^2$. The answer is choice (C). If you don't recognize the common quadratic, you can just do the arithmetic and discover that $9 - 4 = (1)(5)$.

4. **C**   For the left side of the equation to be zero, the expression in parentheses must also be zero. So solve $4x + 2 = 0$; $x = -\dfrac{1}{2}$. The answer is choice (C).

5. **B**   FOIL out Column A to find $-10a - a^2 - 100 - 10a$, or $-a^2 - 20a - 100$. Anything other than zero to an even power is positive, so $-a^2$ is negative. A negative number minus a positive number ($20a$) will remain negative. A negative minus 100 will be even more negative. So, Column A must be negative, and it must be less than Column B. The answer is choice (B). Alternatively, Plugging In a few positive values for a will give you, in the parentheses: (negative) times (positive) = negative for Column A, except if $a = 10$, which yields 0 for Column A. But Column A is still less than Column B.

6. **B**   If $(y - 1)(y + 5) = 0$, $(y - 1) = 0$ or $(y + 5) = 0$. So, y could be 1 or –5. Thus, Column B is greater.

7. **B**   Simply use the order of operations to solve this problem. First, deal with the numbers inside the parentheses. The 10s cancel out, so you're left with 2(8)(8), which is 128. Next, square the first two terms to get 64 and 100. Now, add 64 and 100 and subtract 128. The answer is 36, choice (B).

8. **C** Translate the question and answer choices into algebra. You are given that $x - y = 4$. Choice (A) further tells you that $x + y = 4$. You can solve two different linear equations in two variables simultaneously (if you do so, you find that $x = 4$ and $y = 0$). Choice (B) tells you that $x^2 - y^2 = 16$. You can factor this into $(x + y)(x - y) = 16$. You are given that $x - y = 4$, so $x + y$ must also equal 4 (for the product to be 16), which is what you discovered in choice (A). Choice (C) tells you that $(x - y)^2 = 16$, but this is simply the result of squaring what you are given, and so you have gained no additional information. The answer is choice (C). If you aren't sure, you can analyze choice (D): if their product is zero, one of the two numbers must be zero. You are given that their difference is 4, so the other number must be either 4 or -4. However, you are also told that neither number is negative, so the numbers must be 4 and 0. Choice (E) tells you that the greater number is 4. The difference between the two is 4, so the smaller number must be 0.

9. **E** The dimensions of the new rectangle will be $x + y$ and $x - y$. To find the area of the rectangle, multiply the length by the width: $(x + y)(x - y) = x^2 - y^2$. The answer is choice (E). Or, you can just Plug In values for x and y.

10. **B** Set the expression equal to zero and then factor it. You are looking for factors of 288 that have a difference of 2. So find the integer factor pairs, starting with 1 : 1 and 288; 2 and 144; 3 and 96; 4 and 72; 6 and 48; 8 and 36; 9 and 32; 12 and 24; 16 and 18. The last pair you found works, so the factored form of your equation is: $(x - 18)(x + 16) = 0$. The solutions are 18 and -16, but obviously Ann cannot sell a negative number of pillows. The answer is choice (B).

11. **B** Try Plugging In the answers. Start with $-\dfrac{2}{3}$, because it's in 3 of your answer choices. When you Plug In $-\dfrac{2}{3}$ into the equation, you get:

$$6\left(-\frac{2}{3}\right)^2 - 5\left(-\frac{2}{3}\right) - 6 = 6\left(\frac{4}{9}\right) + \frac{10}{3} - 6 = \frac{24}{9} + \frac{30}{9} - 6 = \frac{54}{9} - 6 = 6 - 6 = 0.$$ Because $-\dfrac{2}{3}$ works,

eliminate choices (C) and (D). Of the fractions in the remaining answer choices, the only other one that works is $\dfrac{3}{2}$, so select choice (B). Alternatively, you can factor the quadratic: $6x^2 - 5x - 6 = 0$ factors into $(3x + 2)(2x - 3)$, and setting each root equal to 0 yields $x = -\dfrac{2}{3}$ and $\dfrac{3}{2}$. If factoring, be wary of choice (D), which makes the wrong root negative.

12. **C** The expression on the left side of the equation will equal zero when either $(3x - 2) = 0$ or $(x + 1) = 0$. Solving these equations yields $x = \dfrac{2}{3}$ or $x = -1$. The question asks you for the greatest value of x, so the answer is choice (C).

13.　A　Plugging In 2 for y gives you $x^2 = 5$ in the given equation and 17 for Column B. Squaring this gives you $x^4 = 25$ for Column A, which is therefore larger. Plugging In any other number gives the same result. Alternatively, doing algebra by squaring both sides of the given equation reveals Column A: $x^4 = (y^2 + 1)(y^2 + 1) = y^4 + 2y^2 + 1$. The only difference between Columns A and B is the $2y^2$ in Column A. You are told that $y \neq 0$, so $2y^2$ is always positive, and Column A will always therefore be larger. The answer is choice (A).

14.　A　Factoring the given equation gives you $(x + 5)(x - 4) = 0$. This equation will be true when $(x + 5) = 0$ or $(x - 4) = 0$. Solving these equations gives you $x = -5$ or $x = 4$. The answer is choice (A). Alternatively, you can PITA to determine which pair of x-values will satisfy the equation.

15.　D　Plug In $x = 4$, so $y = 17$. Now Plug In 17 into the answers to see which gives you 4. Only choice (D) does.

16.　C　Remember that when a variable is squared, it yields a positive and a negative solution; hence, $x^2 - 49 = 0$ means that $x^2 = 49$ and $x = \pm 7$. If $x = 7$, then both Columns are equal to zero. If $x = -7$, then both Columns are equal to 98. The answer is choice (C).

17.　A　Plug In $x = 2$, and the original expression turns into $\dfrac{2}{6} + \dfrac{-3}{4} = \dfrac{1}{3} - \dfrac{3}{4} = -\dfrac{5}{12}$, using the Bowtie. Now Plug In 2 to the answer choices for x to see which equals $-\dfrac{5}{12}$. Only choice (A) does.

18.　C　Whenever you see exponents, think common quadratics. If you factor the 6 out of the numerator in Column A, you get $6(a^2 + 2ab + b^2)$, which includes a common quadratic $(a + b)^2$. Then you can cancel $(a + b)$ from both the numerator and the denominator; Column A is really just $6(a + b)$. The Columns are equal.

19.　A　Don't do the arithmetic! These are common quadratic patterns. It's not important that $x = 141$ and $y = 28$; Column A is $x^2 - y^2 = (x + y)(x - y)$, and Column B is $(x - y)(x - y)$. Since $(x - y)$ is a positive number, you can simply compare the remaining factors after it is removed from both Columns. Since x and y are positive, $(x + y)$ is greater than the remaining $(x - y)$ in Column B, and the answer is choice (A).

20.　D　Factor out -1 from the parentheses on the left and rearrange the expression in the parentheses on the right to get $-1(x - y)(x - y) = -(x - y)^2$. The answer is choice (D).

21.　C　In Column A, $\sqrt{x^{12}} - y = \sqrt{(x^6)^2} - y = x^6 - y$. In Column B, you may recognize one of the common quadratics: $(a + b)(a - b) = a^2 - b^2$. If not, FOIL; either way, Column B is $x^6 - y$. Thus, the two quantities are equal.

22.　D　The best approach here is to Plug In. First, try $s = 2$ and $t = 3$: Column A is $(2 + 3)^2 = 5^2 = 25$, and Column B is $2^2 + 3^2 = 4 + 9 = 13$. Column A is greater, so eliminate choices (B) and (C). Next, make s and t both 0: Now Column A is $(0)^2 = 0$, and Column B is $0^2 + 0^2 = 0$. Now the two quantities are equal, so eliminate choice (A), and you're left with choice (D).

23. **D** Factor the quadratic expression to get $(x-y)(x-y) = 0$; $x-y$ must equal 0, so you know that $x = y$. Thus, $y = \dfrac{9}{y}$, $y^2 = 9$, and $y = 3$—eliminate choices (A) and (B)—or -3—eliminate choice (C). The answer is choice (D).

24. **E** Translate what you are given into algebra: $\dfrac{x+y}{2} = 9$; $x + y = 18$. $x^2 - y^2 = 144$. The question is asking you for $x - y$, where x is the larger number. Recognizing that the common quadratic can be factored, you find that $(x + y)(x - y) = 144$. Substituting 18 for $(x + y)$ and then dividing both sides by 18 yields $(x - y) = 8$. The answer is choice (E). If you aren't sure which is the larger number, then solve the linear equations $x - y = 18$ and $x - y = 8$ simultaneously to find $x = 13$ and $y = 5$.

25. **E** First, factor the quadratic equation: $x^2 - 32x + 256 = (x - 16)^2$. Any quantity squared is either positive or zero. To minimize the expression $(x - 16)^2$ and the value of y, let $x = 16$, so that $y = 0$. The answer is choice (E).

Probability, Rates, and Statistics

PROBABILITY, RATES, AND STATISTICS

These kinds of arithmetic problems are all about having simple, effective ways to organize your information. ETS will always give you just enough information to figure out the one piece that is missing. A good set-up will help you fill in the missing pieces quickly and easily.

Once you understand how the set-ups work, you need only train yourself to recognize the opportunity and use them. Think of words such as average and probability as triggers that provoke a very specific action. Sensitize yourself to these words and once you see them, before you've even finished reading the question, start making your set up.

MEAN

Known to ETS as "arithmetic mean" and to the rest of us as "average," these problems can be time consuming if you don't know what you're doing, but will unravel easily when you do. To find the average of five, seven, and nine, add the three numbers together and divide by three. Thus, averages consist of three parts, the average, the number of things, and the total. The minute you see the word average in a problem, draw your pie.

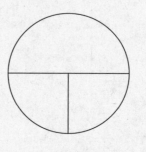

> When you see the word **AVERAGE** make a pie on your scratch paper. If you see the word **AVERAGE** again, make another pie.

If ETS were to give a list of numbers and ask for the average, it would be too easy. They will always give you two out of the three pieces. They may give you the average and the total and ask for the number of things, or they may give the average and the number of things and ask for the total.

Fill in the information you have.

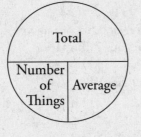

If you have the number of things and the total, you will divide to get the average. If you have the average and the total, you will divide to get the number of things. If you have the number of things and the average, simply multiply to get the total.

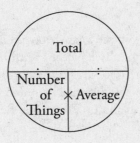

If asked to find the average of five, seven, and nine, your scratch paper would look like the image shown below.

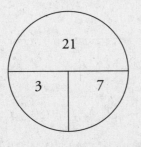

Of course, it's not usually quite that simple. ETS may give you the average of one group, the total of a second, and then ask for the average of both combined. Just make sure that you draw a new pie every time you see the word average. Work the problem through in bite-sized pieces, read with your finger, and make sure your hand is moving on the scratch paper.

RATE

Rate problems work the same way that average problems do. In fact, you can use the same method to organize your information.

This is what a Rate Pie looks like.

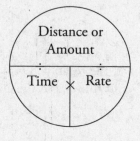

The first thing you do when you see a rate problem is to make your Rate Pie. ETS will always give you two of the three pieces of information. You will have to find the third. If you're asked for time, divide the distance or amount by the rate. If you're asked for rate, divide the distance or amount by the time, and if you're asked for distance or amount, multiply the time by the rate. Make sure to keep an eye on your units. You may be given a rate in miles per hour but asked for a number of minutes.

> The way to prevent units errors is to use your scratch paper and label everything.

MEDIAN

When you see the word average, before you've even finished reading the problem, make a pie on your scratch paper. When you see the word median, find a group of numbers and put them in order. Median, like the median on a highway, simply means the number in the middle. It's not a difficult concept, so there are only two ways ETS can try to mess you up. The most common trick is to give you numbers out of order. Your first step must always be to put the numbers in order on your scratch paper.

> When you see the word **MEDIAN**, find a group of numbers and put them in order.

The second trick they may try is to give you an even number of numbers. In this case, the median will be the average of the two numbers in the middle. In the case of 2, 2, 3, 4, 5, 5, 5, 6, 7, 7, 120, 345, 607, the median is 5. In the case of 2, 2, 3, 4, 5, 5, 5, 6, 7, 7, 120, 345, 607, 1250, the median is 5.5.

MODE AND RANGE

Mode means the number that comes up most often. The mode of the set {4, 6, 6, 13, 14, 21} is six. The Range is the difference between the highest number and the lowest. In this case it is 17, or 21 − 4. Rarely will you see a problem testing mode by itself. It is more likely to come up in connection with Mean, Median, and/or Standard Deviation.

STANDARD DEVIATION

There are not a lot of standard deviation questions in the question pool, so they don't come up that often. However, because they might come up, you need to know how to handle them. But don't worry, on the GRE, they stick to the basics. You will never need to know how to calculate standard deviation. You will only be asked about percentages of people or things that fall a few standard deviations from the norm.

Imagine you measured the weight of all apples picked at Orchard X. Suppose the average weight of an apple is 6 ounces. As you can imagine, the vast majority of those apples will weigh somewhere close to 6 ounces. A much smaller number will be about 7.5 ounces, and you may even get a few that are heavier than eight ounces. The weight of these apples is likely to follow a *normal distribution*, which means that if you graphed the number of apples at each weight on a bar graph, you would end up with a *bell curve*.

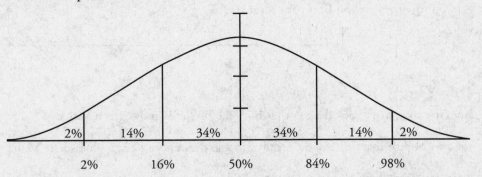

This chart is the bell curve. It will never change. Memorize the numbers 34, 14, and 2.

The minute you see the words **STANDARD DEVIATION**, or **NORMAL DISTRIBUTION**, draw your bell curve and fill in the percentages.

On this curve, the mean, the median, and the mode are all the same. It makes sense, right? The average weight of our apples is also the most common weight and falls in the middle of the pack. If the apples have a standard deviation of 1.25 ounces, 34 percent of the apples picked in the orchard weigh between 6 and 7.25 ounces, 14 percent weigh between 7.25 and 8.5, and only 2 percent weigh more than 8.5 ounces. As you move from one percentage group to another you are moving one standard deviation from the norm. If you're asked, "What percentage of apples weighs more or less than two standard deviations from the norm?" the answer will be 4 percent.

PROBABILITY

Probability, on the GRE, can be defined as $\dfrac{\text{the \# of things you want}}{\text{the \# of things you could get}}$. It's a fraction with the total on the bottom. The minute you see the word probability, make your divisor line and find your total. Once you've done this, you are already half way to the answer.

The minute you see the word **PROBABILITY**, on your scratch paper make your divisor line and find your total.

One Event

Imagine you have a sock drawer that has 12 blue socks and 8 green socks. What is the probability that, when you reach into the drawer, you get a blue sock? Make your divisor and find your total. On the bottom you have 20 because there 20 socks you could get. On top you have 12 because there are twelve socks (blue) that you want. The probability is $\dfrac{3}{5}$. The probability of getting a blue sock is $\dfrac{8}{20}$ or $\dfrac{2}{5}$. The probability of getting any sock is 20 things you want over 20 things you could

get, or 1. The probability of getting a ham and cheese sandwich is, we hope, 0
($\dfrac{0 \text{ things you want}}{20 \text{ things you could get}}$). It is important to note that probability is always between 1 and 0. The chance that something will happen added to the chance that it won't happen will always add up to 1.

Two Events

If two events are to occur, the probability of them both happening is equal to the probability of the first happening multiplied by the probability of the second happening. This makes sense because a fraction times a fraction equals a much smaller fraction. If you have a very low probability of one event occurring and a very low probability of a second event happening, the odds of them both happening will be even lower. The probability of getting a green sock in the drawer above is $\dfrac{2}{5}$. The probability of getting a green sock the second time is $\dfrac{7}{19}$, because there are seven green socks left, after you've removed the first one, and 19 socks left in the drawer. The probability of getting a green sock both times is $\dfrac{2}{5} \times \dfrac{7}{19}$, or $\dfrac{14}{95}$.

One of Two Events

Imagine you now have five purple socks in your drawer. If you are asked to find the probability of getting a purple **OR** a green sock, you have to add the probabilities. With 12 blue socks, eight green socks, and five purple socks, your new total is 25. You have an $\dfrac{8}{25}$ chance of getting a green sock and a $\dfrac{5}{25}$ chance of getting a purple one. The chance of getting one or the other is $\dfrac{5}{25} + \dfrac{8}{25}$ or $\dfrac{13}{25}$.

At Least One Event

The one last wrinkle to look at is what happens if you are asked to find the probability of *at least* one event happening. When rolling dice, for example, what is the probability that you roll 1 *at least* once out of three rolls? This will get complicated because at least one means that the event could occur once, twice, or even three times. That's more calculating than you want to do. Instead, when asked to find at least one, find the probability that none will occur and subtract it from 1. This will leave you with at least one. In this case, the chances of not rolling a one on the first roll are $\frac{5}{6}$. The chances on the second and third rolls are the same. Therefore the chances of not rolling a one go down with each additional roll, but only by a little bit because you have a very strong possibility that it will not happen. The chances that you will not roll a 1 in your first three rolls are $\frac{5}{6} \times \frac{5}{6} \times \frac{5}{6}$, or $\frac{125}{216}$. The chances that you will roll at least one 1, therefore are $\frac{91}{216}$ (216 − 125 = 91).

For more practice and a more in-depth look at math techniques, check out our student-friendly guidebook, *Cracking the GRE*.

PROBABILITY, RATES, AND STATISTICS DRILL

In terms of y, what is the average (arithmetic mean) of $4y$ and 22 ?

○ $4y + 22$
○ $4y + 11$
○ $4y - 22$
○ $2y + 11$
○ $2y + 22$

Column A	Column B
The average (arithmetic mean) of 14, 22, and 48	The average (arithmetic mean) of 12, 22, and 50

○ The quantity in Column A is greater.
○ The quantity in Column B is greater.
○ The two quantities are equal.
○ The relationship cannot be determined from the information given.

2, 3, 5, 7

Column A	Column B
The average (arithmetic mean) of the numbers above	The median of the numbers above

○ The quantity in Column A is greater.
○ The quantity in Column B is greater.
○ The two quantities are equal.
○ The relationship cannot be determined from the information given.

Susan travels by car at an average speed of 50 miles per hour for 4 hours and then at an average speed of 20 miles per hour for 2 hours. What is her average speed, in miles per hour, for the entire 6 hour trip?

○ 25
○ 30
○ 35
○ 40
○ 45

Liz owns 2 green t-shirts, 4 blue t-shirts, and 5 red t-shirts.

Column A	Column B
The probability that Liz randomly selects a blue t-shirt	$\dfrac{2}{5}$

○ The quantity in Column A is greater.
○ The quantity in Column B is greater.
○ The two quantities are equal.
○ The relationship cannot be determined from the information given.

Column A	Column B
The area of the average (arithmetic mean) of 4 numbers, each less than 6 and greater than the smaller square	The median of 6 numbers, each less than 5 and greater than 4

○ The quantity in Column A is greater.
○ The quantity in Column B is greater.
○ The two quantities are equal.
○ The relationship cannot be determined from the information given.

For which of the following values of x is the mode of $2x$, $x + 5$, $3x - 2$, $5x - 7$, and $4x$ equal to 4 ?

- ○ 2
- ○ 3
- ○ 4
- ○ 5
- ○ 7

A hat contains 18 raffle tickets, numbered 1 through 18. If two raffle tickets are chosen at random from the hat, what is the probability that both tickets are even numbers?

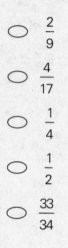

- ○ $\dfrac{2}{9}$
- ○ $\dfrac{4}{17}$
- ○ $\dfrac{1}{4}$
- ○ $\dfrac{1}{2}$
- ○ $\dfrac{33}{34}$

$$k > j > 0$$

Column A	Column B
The time it takes to read k words at j words per minute	The time it takes to read $(k + 10)$ words at $(j + 10)$ words per minute

- ○ The quantity in Column A is greater.
- ○ The quantity in Column B is greater.
- ○ The two quantities are equal.
- ○ The relationship cannot be determined from the information given.

How many committees of 5 members can be chosen from a group of 8 people?

- ○ 28
- ○ 56
- ○ 118
- ○ 336
- ○ 6,720

The average (arithmetic mean) number of passengers on a subway car is 60. If the number of passengers on a car has a normal distribution with a standard deviation of 20, approximately what percent of subway cars carry more than 80 passengers?

- ○ 16%
- ○ 48%
- ○ 68%
- ○ 88%
- ○ 98%

If the average of 10, 12, n, and n is greater than 25, what is the least possible value of integer n ?

- ○ 38
- ○ 39
- ○ 40
- ○ 41
- ○ 42

$$x, x^2, x^y, x^{y-1}, x^4, x^6$$

$$x > 1$$

Column A	Column B
The mode of the numbers above when $y = 4$	The median of the numbers above when $y = 5$

- ○ The quantity in Column A is greater.
- ○ The quantity in Column B is greater.
- ○ The two quantities are equal.
- ○ The relationship cannot be determined from the information given.

Trip A is $6x$ miles long and takes $5y$ hours. Trip B is $5x$ miles long and takes $4y$ hours.

Column A	Column B
The rate of trip A in miles per hour	The rate of trip B in miles per hour

- ○ The quantity in Column A is greater.
- ○ The quantity in Column B is greater.
- ○ The two quantities are equal.
- ○ The relationship cannot be determined from the information given.

If the probability that the first event will occur is $\dfrac{1}{4}$, and the probability that the second event will occur is $\dfrac{1}{\sqrt{x+2}}$, then what is the probability that both events will occur?

- ○ $\dfrac{\sqrt{x+2}}{4x+8}$
- ○ $\dfrac{\sqrt{x+2}}{4}$
- ○ $\dfrac{\sqrt{x+2}}{16x+32}$
- ○ $\dfrac{4}{\sqrt{x+2}}$
- ○ $4\sqrt{x+2}$

Five numbers in a set are arranged from least to greatest. If the median of the first two numbers is 13 and the average (arithmetic mean) of the remaining numbers is 23, what is the average (arithmetic mean) of the entire set?

- ○ 14.6
- ○ 16.4
- ○ 17.0
- ○ 18.0
- ○ 19.0

A bag contains 12 marbles: 5 of the marbles are red, 3 are green, and the rest are blue.

Column A	Column B
The probability of consecutively choosing two red marbles and a green marble without replacement	The probability of consecutively choosing a red and two blue marbles with replacement

○ The quantity in Column A is greater.
○ The quantity in Column B is greater.
○ The two quantities are equal.
○ The relationship cannot be determined from the information given.

If the average (arithmetic mean) of twelve numbers is 25 and the average (arithmetic mean) of eleven of the numbers is 20, then what is the remaining number?

○ 5
○ 55
○ 60
○ 70
○ 80

Water flows into a 25-liter bucket through a hose and out through a hole in the bottom of the bucket. The rate of flow through the hose is 1 liter per minute. If the bucket is filled to capacity in 40 minutes, at what rate, in liters per minute, was water flowing out of the bucket through the hole?

○ $\frac{3}{8}$

○ $\frac{3}{5}$

○ $\frac{5}{8}$

○ $\frac{8}{5}$

○ $\frac{13}{8}$

A pair of dice is tossed twice. What is the probability that the first toss gives a total of either 7 or 11 and the second toss gives a total of 7 ?

○ $\frac{1}{27}$

○ $\frac{1}{18}$

○ $\frac{1}{9}$

○ $\frac{1}{6}$

○ $\frac{7}{18}$

A photocopier can copy r pages per hour. How many pages can it copy in s seconds?

○ $\frac{rs}{60}$

○ $\frac{r}{60s}$

○ $\frac{s}{3,600r}$

○ $\frac{rs}{3,600}$

○ 3,600rs

Column A	Column B
The average (arithmetic mean) cost per hinge for 16 hinges that cost a total of $2p$ cents	The average (arithmetic mean) cost per hinge for 4 hinges that cost a total of $\frac{p}{2}$ cents

○ The quantity in Column A is greater.
○ The quantity in Column B is greater.
○ The two quantities are equal.
○ The relationship cannot be determined from the information given.

In both rural and urban areas of country G, the average annual number of holidays taken by citizens is 8, and the annual number of holidays follows a normal distribution. In rural areas, 2% of the citizens take more than 12 holidays per year. In urban areas, 2% of the citizens take more than 16 holidays per year. How much greater is the standard deviation of the annual number of holidays taken by urban citizens than that of rural citizens?

- ○ 1
- ○ 2
- ○ 3
- ○ 4
- ○ 8

Three dice are rolled simultaneously. What is the probability that two of the dice will come up as the same number?

- ○ $\dfrac{5}{12}$
- ○ $\dfrac{11}{24}$
- ○ $\dfrac{25}{54}$
- ○ $\dfrac{13}{27}$
- ○ $\dfrac{1}{2}$

There are 32 students in Jamie's eighth-grade class. Each student took a 50-point test; the class average (arithmetic mean) was 82% correct. The teacher has assigned one 4-point, extra-credit question. How many students will need to answer the extra-credit question correctly in order to bring the class average to 86% correct?

- ○ 15
- ○ 16
- ○ 17
- ○ All of the students
- ○ It will not be possible for the class to reach an average of 86% correct.

The residents of Phillipstown consume a median of 2,750 calories per day. If their calorie consumption has a normal distribution with a standard deviation of 300, what percent of residents consume either more than 3,350 calories or fewer than 2,150 calories per day?

- ○ 2%
- ○ 4%
- ○ 12%
- ○ 16%
- ○ 34%

Vinay and Phil are driving in separate cars to Los Angeles, both leaving from the same place and traveling along the same route. If Vinay leaves at 1 a.m. and travels at 40 miles per hour, and Phil leaves at 5 a.m. and travels at 50 miles per hour, at what time does Phil catch up to Vinay?

- ○ 1 p. m.
- ○ 5 p.m.
- ○ 7 p.m.
- ○ 9 p.m.
- ○ 11 p.m.

ANSWERS

1. D
2. C
3. A
4. D
5. B
6. A
7. A
8. B
9. A
10. B
11. A
12. C
13. C
14. B
15. A
16. E
17. B
18. E
19. A
20. A
21. D
22. C
23. B
24. A
25. B
26. B
27. D

EXPLANATIONS

1. **D** To find the average, add up the values and divide by 2: $\dfrac{4y+22}{2}=\dfrac{2(2y+11)}{2}=2y+11$. You can also Plug In on this one. If $y = 3$, then $\dfrac{4(3)+22}{2}=17$, your target number. Only choice (D) hits the target.

2. **C** The average is the sum divided by the number of items. Both Columns ask for the average of three numbers. The sum of the three numbers in both Columns is 84, so their averages must be equal.

3. **A** The mean is found by dividing the sum of the elements by the number of elements. In this case: $2 + 3 + 5 + 7 = 17$, and $17 \div 4 = 4.25$, the mean. The median is the middle number, or, if the list contains an even number of elements, the average of the middle two elements (when they are arranged in increasing order). In this case, the average of 3 and 5 is 4. Column A is greater than Column B.

4. **D** Use the given averages to figure out Susan's total distance: 4 hours at an average speed of 50 miles per hour is a total of 200 miles, and 2 hours at an average speed of 20 miles per hour is a total of 40 miles. Susan goes a total of 240 miles in 6 hours, thus, her average speed is $\dfrac{240\ \text{miles}}{6\ \text{hours}}$, or 40 miles per hour. The answer is choice (D).

5. **B** To calculate the probability, divide the part by the whole: $\dfrac{\text{blue shirts}}{\text{total shirts}}=\dfrac{4}{11}$. Choice (B) is correct because $\dfrac{4}{11}<\dfrac{4}{10}$ (which is simply $\dfrac{2}{5}$ multiplied by 2).

6. **A** Although you can't find an exact value for either Column, you can find a possible range for each. In Column A, if all 4 numbers are between 5 and 6, then their average is, too. Similarly, in Column B, if all 6 numbers are between 4 and 5, then so is their median. Any number between 5 and 6 is greater than any number between 4 and 5, so Column A is greater.

7. **A** Remember that mode means the number that appears "most often." Plug In the answers. For choice (C), if $x = 4$, then the numbers become: 8, 9, 10, 13, 16. For a list of numbers to have a mode, there has to be at least two of one of the numbers. So this list has no mode; eliminate choice (C). For choice (A), if $x = 2$, then the numbers become: 4, 7, 4, 3, 8. Because 4 appears twice, 4 is the mode—the answer is choice (A).

8. **B** Think of this problem as if you're pulling out an even ticket and then another even ticket. So, for the first ticket there are 9 possible evens out of 18 total, so the probability that the first ticket is even is $\dfrac{9}{18}$. Now you have one fewer even ticket in the hat. So there are 8 evens out of 17 total tickets for the second ticket, thus, the probability is $\dfrac{8}{17}$. You want an even AND an even, so multiply: $\dfrac{9}{18}\times\dfrac{8}{17}=\dfrac{4}{17}$. The answer is choice (B).

9. **A** Plug In numbers and use the rate formula—*amount = rate × time*—to check the Columns. If $j = 1$ and $k = 2$, then Column A is 2 minutes and Column B is $\frac{20}{11}$ minutes. Column A is greater, so eliminate choices (B) and (C). Any acceptable set of values gives the same outcome; select choice (A).

10. **B** This is the number of combinations of 8 items taken 5 at a time (because the order does not matter). This number is equal to $\frac{8 \times 7 \times 6 \times 5 \times 4}{5 \times 4 \times 3 \times 2 \times 1} = 8 \times 7 = 56$.

11. **A** Adding the standard deviation (20) to the mean (60) gives you the number of passengers in a car that carries exactly one standard deviation above the mean number of passengers (80). The first standard deviation above the mean represents 34% of the population in a normal distribution, and a further 50% falls below the mean, so 84% of the cars will carry 80 people or fewer. Subtracting this from the entire population (100%) gives you the percent of cars that carry greater than 80: 100% – 84% = 16%. The answer is choice (A).

12. **C** To find the average, divide the total by the number of values. So, $\frac{10 + 12 + n + n}{4} > 25$. Multiply both sides of the inequality by 4 and then subtract 22 (10 + 12) to find $2n > 78$. Divide by 2 to find $n > 39$. So, n is NOT 39; it is the least integer greater than 39, which is 40. Alternatively, you could Plug In the answers starting with choice (A) because the question asks for the least possible value. If $n = 38$ or 39, then the average is not greater than 25. If $n = 40$, the average is greater than 25. The answer is choice (C).

13. **C** In Column A, if $y = 4$, then the numbers (arranged in increasing order) become $x, x^2, x^3, x^4, x^4, x^6$; the mode is x^4. In Column B, if $y = 5$, then the numbers become $x, x^2, x^4, x^4, x^5, x^6$. Usually, you'd need to take the average of the middle two numbers to find the median because there is an even number of values, but in this case they're both x^4. The median, then, is x^4, so the Columns are equal. Because $x > 1$, you don't have to worry about special cases such as 0, 1, negatives, or fractions, and the correct answer is choice (C).

14. **B** Rate is calculated by dividing the distance traveled by the time elapsed. Plug In to compare the two rates. If you Plug In $x = 4$ and $y = 2$, the rate for trip A will be: $\frac{6(4)}{5(2)} = \frac{24}{10} = 2.4$ mph and the rate for trip B will be: $\frac{5(4)}{4(2)} = \frac{20}{8} = 2.5$ mph; eliminate choices (A) and (C). Any set of values will have a greater rate for trip B, so select choice (B).

15. **A**   Plug In to make this problem much simpler. If you Plug In $x = 2$, then the probability for the second event is: $\frac{1}{\sqrt{4}} = \frac{1}{2}$. Now, because this is an "and" probability problem, you multiply the two probabilities together to find the target answer: $\frac{1}{4} \times \frac{1}{2} = \frac{1}{8}$. Choice (A) is the only one that works: $\frac{\sqrt{2+2}}{4(2)+8} = \frac{2}{16} = \frac{1}{8}$.

16. **E**   If you are asked for the median of a set with an even number of elements, you must take the middle two numbers and average them. Here, you are given the median for only two numbers, so you can treat it just as you would an average. If the median of two numbers is 13, their total is $13 \times 2 =$ 26. You are given the average of the rest of the numbers, so you know they must add up to $23 \times 3 =$ 69. Add these two to find the total of all the elements, then divide by the total number of elements in the set to find the average: $69 + 26 = 95$; $95 \div 5 = 19$. The answer is choice (E).

17. **B**   Column A asks for the probability "without replacement," so that means you have to take into account that there will be one marble less in the total after each draw. The probability of first choosing a red marble is $\frac{5}{12}$, a second red marble is $\frac{4}{11}$, and then a green marble is $\frac{3}{10}$. This is an "and" probability problem, so you have to multiply the probability of each event together: $\frac{5}{12} \times \frac{4}{11} \times \frac{3}{10} = \frac{60}{1320} = \frac{1}{22}$. For Column B, you do the same thing, but the total stays the same for each draw: $\frac{5}{12} \times \frac{4}{12} \times \frac{4}{12} = \frac{80}{1728} = \frac{5}{108}$. Column B is greater.

18. **E**   Use the average pie to find that the total of the eleven numbers is $11 \times 20 = 220$. The total for all twelve numbers is $12 \times 25 = 300$. Thus, the remaining number is $300 - 220 = 80$. The answer is choice (E).

19. **A**   Remember that amount = rate × time. So, 25 liters = rate × 40 minutes. The rate was $\frac{25\,\text{liters}}{40\,\text{minutes}} = \frac{5}{8}$ liters/min. The net rate at which the bucket is filling is the difference between the hose's rate and the leaking rate. So, (1 liter/min) − (leaking rate) = $\frac{5}{8}$. Solve for the leaking rate to find the leaking rate is $\frac{3}{8}$ liters/min; the answer is choice (A).

20. **A** There are a total of $6^2 = 36$ possibilities for each toss. There are a total of 8 ways we can get a total of 7 or 11 on the first toss: 6 ways to get a total of 7—(1, 6), (2, 5), (3, 4), (4, 3), (5, 2), or (6, 1)—plus 2 ways to get a total of 11—(5, 6) or (6, 5). Therefore, the probability of getting a total of either 7 or 11 on the first toss is $\frac{8}{36} = \frac{2}{9}$. The probability of getting a total of 7 on the second toss is $\frac{6}{36} = \frac{1}{6}$, so the probability that both of these independent events occur is the product $\frac{2}{9} \times \frac{1}{6} = \frac{1}{27}$, choice (A).

21. **D** Try Plugging In a number for s that divides easily by 60, such as 7,200. So, if $s = 7,200$ seconds, that's 120 minutes or 2 hours. Plug In a nice number for r such as 5. So, if the copier makes 5 pages per hour for 2 hours, your target is 10 pages. Plug $s = 7,200$ and $r = 5$ into the answers. Ballpark: choice (A) is too large, choice (B) too small, choice (C) too small, and choice (E) far too large. Only choice (D) yields your target of 10.

22. **C** Plug In a value for p. Try $p = 16$: in Column A, then 16 hinges cost a total of 32 cents, for an average cost of 2 cents per hinge; in Column B, 4 hinges cost a total of 8 cents, for, again, an average cost of 2 cents per hinge. The Columns are equal, so eliminate choices (A) and (B). Any value for p will yield the same results: the Columns will always equal; the answer is choice (C).

23. **B** In a normal distribution, the first two standard deviations above the mean represent 34% + 14% = 48% of the population, so the top half of the bell curve contains 50% − 48% = 2% of the population. In rural areas, 12 is two standard deviations above 8, the mean, so the standard deviation is the difference divided by 2, i.e. 2. In urban areas, similarly, the standard deviation is 16 − 8 divided by 2, i.e. 4. The difference between the two standard deviations is thus 4 − 2 = 2, and the answer is choice (B).

24. **A** There are a total of $6^3 = 216$ total possible rolls for the three dice. First figure out the probability of getting exactly two 1's. There are $5 \times 3 = 15$ ways this could happen: 112, 113, 114, 115, 116; 121, 131, 141, 151, 161; or 211, 311, 411, 511, 611. You could repeat this list of 15 possibilities in the obvious way for exactly two 2's, exactly two 3's, and so on. Thus, the total number of favorable rolls is $6 \times 15 = 90$. Because there are 216 possible rolls, 90 of which are favorable, the probability of getting exactly two of the three dice to show the same number is $\frac{90}{216} = \frac{5}{12}$, choice (A).

25. **B** If the class average is 82% on a 50-point test, the average score was 41 points out of 50. Use the average pie to find the sum of the class's scores: (41)(32) = 1,312. To reach a class average of 86%, each student will need to average 43 points out of 50 points. Use the average pie to find the desired sum of the class's scores: (43)(32) = 1,376. The difference is 1,376 − 1,312 = 64, so the class needs to make up 64 points; $\frac{64}{4} = 16$, so 16 students need to answer the extra credit question correctly. The answer is (B). Alternatively, notice that the class's average needs to increase by 4%, or 2 points on average for a 50-question test. But the extra credit is worth 4 points, so to average half of a 4-point increase, only half the students (16) need to get the extra credit correct.

26. **B** Subtracting 2,750 − 2,150 = 600 = 2(300), so 2,150 is two standard deviations below the mean. Similarly, 3,350 − 2,750 = 600 = 2(300), so 3,350 is two standard deviations above the mean. The first standard deviation above and below the mean contains 68% of the populations, and the second contains an additional 28%. Together, these are 96% of the population, so the remaining population is 100% − 96% = 4%, and the answer is choice (B).

27. **D** Before Phil leaves, Vinay has traveled for 4 hours; the rate formula is *distance = rate × time*, so Vinay has gone 40 miles per hour × 4 hours = 160 miles. Upon leaving, Phil is gaining on Vinay at a rate of 10 miles per hour, because he travels 10 more miles per hour than Vinay. Now your equation is 160 miles = 10 miles per hour × *time*, so *time* = 16 hours. Phil left at 5 a.m., so he'll catch up to Vinay at 9 p.m., so the answer is choice (D).

Groups, Sequences, and Functions

GROUPS, SEQUENCES, AND FUNCTIONS

None of these concepts show up very frequently on the test. Therefore, if you have only a limited amount of time to prepare, spend it on Plugging In, geometry, exponents and square roots, and other concepts that you are guaranteed to see. As a general rule, the more questions on a particular subject that are in this book, the more likely those questions are to show up on your test.

GROUPS

There are two kinds of group problems on the GRE. Both include overlapping groups. Because of this, it will be difficult to think your way through. As usual, once you recognize the type, use the appropriate set-up on your scratch paper, and organize your information, the solutions end up being a matter of simple arithmetic.

The first type of group problem you will recognize because it will include the words NEITHER and BOTH.

Example

> Of the 60 employees of company X, 22 have laptops, and 52 have desktop computers. If 12 of the employees have neither laptops nor desk tops, how many employees have both?

Once you recognize the type of problem, use the formula

$$\text{Total} = \text{Group 1} + \text{Group 2} + \text{Neither} - \text{Both}$$

So, $60 = 22 + 52 + 12 - x$. $x = 26$.

The first type includes two overlapping groups and a population that might belong to one, the other, neither, or both. The second type actually involves four overlapping groups and a population that can belong to any two of the groups at one time. There is no option for NEITHER in this type of group problem.

Example

> Of the 60 employees at company X 25 use Macs and 35 use PCs. Four fifths of the Mac users are in the graphics department and there are forty people in the graphics department total, how many of the non-graphics employees use a PC?

To solve these problems, just get your pencil on your scratch paper and organize your information in a grid.

	Mac	PC	Total
Graphics	20	20	40
Non-Graphics	5	(15)	20
Total	25	35	60

SEQUENCES

Sequence questions are really all about pattern recognition. You will recognize them because they will ask you specifically about a sequence of numbers, as in, "Each term in the sequence above is twice the previous term minus one. What is the value of the sixth term in the sequence?" or because they will involve a number that is too big to calculate, as in, "What is the value of the tens digit of $5^{26} - 6$?"

In both cases you will find the phrase, "What is the value of?" This is a sure tip off that you can Plug In the answer choices. As always, when you see this phrase, label your first column, assume choice (C) to be the correct answer, and work though the problem in bite-sized pieces making a new answer choice for every step.

It may be the case that this problem is really a simple matter of following directions. If that is the case, you will have to go through multiple steps to get to the correct answer. Make sure you work slowly, carefully, methodically, and, above all, do your work on your scratch paper.

In the second case, you will never be asked to calculate 5^{26}. The question contains the phrase, "What is the value of...," but there is still no way to calculate a number of that size, even with the answer choices. Therefore, there must be a pattern. Begin to calculate the sequence, starting from the lowest term and working up. When the pattern emerges, figure out how often it repeats itself (Every third term? Every fourth term? Every fifth?). If the pattern repeats itself every fourth term, then the value of the ones digit on the eighth term will be the same as the one on the forth term. It will be the same, as well, on the twelfth, the sixteenth, the twentieth, the fortieth, and the forty-fourth. To find the value on the twenty-sixth term, just find the value on the twenty-fourth term and count up two.

FUNCTIONS

If you see a strange symbol on the GRE, (it could be a star, a clover, a letter of the Greek alphabet) it doesn't mean that math has changed since you left high school and they've rewritten all of the text books. It just means that you are seeing a rare functions question. The symbol will be attached to a variable and an equal sign. It acts like a series of instructions and tells you what to do in generic terms.

Example

If $x \heartsuit y = \left(\dfrac{x + y}{4} \right)^2$ for all integers x and y, then $10 \heartsuit 6 =$

As crazy as it looks, all this problem is telling you to do is plug in a 10 every time you see an x and a 6 every time you see a y in the equation, $(\dfrac{x + y}{4})^2$. Use your scratch paper, be meticulous, and follow directions. It's not upper-level math, just basic arithmetic with weird looking symbols.

For more practice and a more in-depth look at The Princeton Review math techniques, check out our student-friendly guidebook, *Cracking the GRE*.

GROUPS, SEQUENCES, & FUNCTIONS: DRILL 1

If the function f is defined by $f(x) = 2x + 5$, what is the value of $f(4)$?

- ⟶ 17
- ⟶ 15
- ⟶ 13
- ⟶ 11
- ⟶ 9

Let the "par" of a rectangle be defined as one half the area of that rectangle.

Column A	Column B
The par of a rectangle with a perimeter of 24 and a width of 2	11

- ⟶ The quantity in Column A is greater.
- ⟶ The quantity in Column B is greater.
- ⟶ The two quantities are equal.
- ⟶ The relationship cannot be determined from the information given.

$$3, 4.5, 6, 7.5, \ldots$$

Each term in the sequence above is formed by adding the positive number k to the preceding term.

Column A	Column B
The eighth term in the sequence above	14

- ⟶ The quantity in Column A is greater.
- ⟶ The quantity in Column B is greater.
- ⟶ The two quantities are equal.
- ⟶ The relationship cannot be determined from the information given.

The operation denoted by the symbol

$\rightarrow$ is defined for all real numbers a and

b as $a \rightarrow b = a\sqrt{b}$. What is the value of

$3 \rightarrow \left(2 \rightarrow 4\right)$?

- ⟶ $\dfrac{1}{4}$
- ⟶ 4
- ⟶ 6
- ⟶ $6\sqrt{2}$
- ⟶ 12

Each of the even-numbered terms in a certain sequence are formed by multiplying the preceding term by −1. Each of the odd-numbered terms in the sequence are formed by adding 3 to the preceding term. If the first term in the sequence is 3, then what is the 168th term?

- ⟶ −3
- ⟶ −1
- ⟶ 0
- ⟶ 1
- ⟶ 3

Column A	Column B
The sum of all the even integers from 18 to 36 inclusive	The sum of all the even integers from 22 to 38 inclusive

- ⟶ The quantity in Column A is greater.
- ⟶ The quantity in Column B is greater.
- ⟶ The two quantities are equal.
- ⟶ The relationship cannot be determined from the information given.

A club of 65 people includes only standard members and gold members. Of the club's 30 gold members, 18 are men. Exactly 20 women are standard members.

Column A	Column B
The number of standard members who are men	13

○ The quantity in Column A is greater.
○ The quantity in Column B is greater.
○ The two quantities are equal.
○ The relationship cannot be determined from the information given.

$$x\# = x^2 + 3x$$
$$x\S = x^2 + 2x$$

Column A	Column B
$(x\S)\#$	$(x\#)\S$

○ The quantity in Column A is greater.
○ The quantity in Column B is greater.
○ The two quantities are equal.
○ The relationship cannot be determined from the information given.

For positive integers n, which of the following could NOT be the units digit of 7^n ?

○ 1
○ 3
○ 5
○ 7
○ 9

Mary is building a pyramid out of stacked rows of soup cans. When completed, the top row of the pyramid contains a single soup can, and each row below the top row contains 6 more cans than the one above it. If the completed pyramid contains 16 rows, then how many soup cans did Mary use to build it?

○ 91
○ 96
○ 728
○ 732
○ 736

The sequence of numbers $S = \left\{ s_1, s_2, s_3, \cdots \right\}$ is defined by $s_1 = 2$, $s_2 = 10$, and $s_n = s_{n-1}^{\,s_{n-2}}$ for each positive integer n greater than or equal to 3. For example, $s_3 = 10^2$ What is the greatest value of n for which s_n has 2,000 or fewer digits?

○ 100
○ 20
○ 5
○ 4
○ 3

$$f(x) = x^2 + 1$$
$$g(x) = x - 2$$

Column A	Column B
$f(g(-1))$	$g(f(-1))$

○ The quantity in Column A is greater.
○ The quantity in Column B is greater.
○ The two quantities are equal.
○ The relationship cannot be determined from the information given.

GROUPS, SEQUENCES, & FUNCTIONS: DRILL 2

The "pluck" of a circle is defined as its area divided by π. What is the pluck of a circle with radius 5 ?

- ○ 5
- ○ 10
- ○ 15
- ○ 20
- ○ 25

$\underline{a}$ is the sum of the second and third positive integer multiples of a.

Column A	Column B
$\underline{5}$	15

- ○ The quantity in Column A is greater.
- ○ The quantity in Column B is greater.
- ○ The two quantities are equal.
- ○ The relationship cannot be determined from the information given.

A certain vent releases steam every 20 minutes. If the vent releases steam at 6:25 p.m., which of the following could be a time at which the vent releases steam?

- ○ 9:15 p.m.
- ○ 10:40 p.m.
- ○ 11:00 p.m.
- ○ 12:20 p.m.
- ○ 1:05 a.m.

For all nonzero integers l and m, let the operation § be defined by $l \,§\, m = -\left|\dfrac{l+m}{lm}\right|$.

Column A	Column B
$3\,§\,\dfrac{3}{2}$	-1

- ○ The quantity in Column A is greater.
- ○ The quantity in Column B is greater.
- ○ The two quantities are equal.
- ○ The relationship cannot be determined from the information given.

There are 30 students in Mr. Peterson's gym class. 14 of them play basketball, 13 play baseball, and 9 play neither basketball nor baseball.

Column A	Column B
The number of students who play both basketball and baseball	6

- ○ The quantity in Column A is greater.
- ○ The quantity in Column B is greater.
- ○ The two quantities are equal.
- ○ The relationship cannot be determined from the information given.

In a regular n-sided polygon the measure of a single angle is $\dfrac{(n-2)180°}{n}$. The measure of an angle in a regular 10-sided polygon is how much greater than the measure of an angle in a regular 6-sided polygon?

- ○ 144°
- ○ 120°
- ○ 90°
- ○ 24°
- ○ 4°

For all real numbers a and b, the operation $\oplus$ is defined by $a \oplus b = 2a - b$. What is the absolute value of the difference between $(3 \oplus 1) \oplus 2$ and $6 \oplus 3$?

- ○ −1
- ○ 1
- ○ 6
- ○ 12
- ○ 18

Starting with the third term, each term in Sequence S is one-half the sum of the previous 2 terms. If the first 2 terms of Sequence S are 64 and 32, respectively, and the nth term is the first non-integer term of Sequence S, then $n =$

Column A	Column B
The units digit of 7^{29}	The units digit of 3^{27}

- ○ The quantity in Column A is greater.
- ○ The quantity in Column B is greater.
- ○ The two quantities are equal.
- ○ The relationship cannot be determined from the information given.

Of the employees at a company, 60 percent were men and, of these, $\dfrac{1}{10}$ were still employed after a recent corporate restructuring. If the number of women who were still employed after the restructuring was five times the number of men who were employed after it, what percent of the women were still employed after the restructuring?

- ○ 6%
- ○ 20%
- ○ 30%
- ○ 50%
- ○ 75%

If q is even, then $\#q = -2$;
If q is odd, then $\#q = -4$.
a and b are integers such that $b - 3$ is odd.

Column A	Column B
$\#(6a)$	$\#b$

- ○ The quantity in Column A is greater.
- ○ The quantity in Column B is greater.
- ○ The two quantities are equal.
- ○ The relationship cannot be determined from the information given.

$$f(x) = 3x^2$$
$$g(x) = x + 1$$

x is an integer such that $-10 \leq x \leq -1$.

Column A	Column B
$f(g(x))$	$g(f(x))$

○ The quantity in Column A is greater.
○ The quantity in Column B is greater.
○ The two quantities are equal.
○ The relationship cannot be determined from the information given.

Three digits have been removed from each of the following numbers. If $n = 25$, which of the numbers is equal to $3 \times 2^{n-1}$?

○ 47, __ __6, __23
○ 47, __ __6, __32
○ 49, __ __2, __64
○ 49, __ __2, __36
○ 50, __ __1, __48

ANSWERS

Drill 1

1. C
2. B
3. B
4. C
5. C
6. C
7. A
8. D
9. C
10. E
11. D
12. A

Drill 2

1. E
2. A
3. E
4. C
5. C
6. D
7. B
8. 8
9. C
10. E
11. C
12. B
13. E

EXPLANATIONS
Drill 1

1. **C**   If $f(x) = 2x + 5$, then $f(4) = 2(4) + 5 = 13$.

2. **B**   Draw it. The rectangle in Column A has two sides of 2, for a total of 4. The remaining 20 units in the perimeter are divided evenly into two sides of length 10; the area of this rectangle is $lw = (2)(10) = 20$, and the "par" is one half that, or 10. Column B is greater.

3. **B**   Notice that each term in the sequence is 1.5 greater than the last, i.e. $k = 1.5$. So the second term is $3 + 1.5 = 4.5$, the third term is $4.5 + 1.5 = 6$, and so forth. So the fifth term is $7.5 + 1.5 = 9$, the sixth term is $9 + 1.5 = 10.5$, the seventh term is $10.5 + 1.5 = 12$, and finally, the eighth term is $12 + 1.5 = 13.5$. So, Column A is 13.5, and the answer is choice (B). Another way to attack this problem is to use the sequence formula of $3 + 1.5(n - 1)$, where the 3 is the first term, the 1.5 is the increase, and you are looking for the nth term. So, the 8th term is $3 + 1.5(8 - 1) = 13.5$.

4. **C**   To follow the order of operations, first evaluate the expression in parentheses.
    $3 \rightarrow (2 \rightarrow 4) = 3 \rightarrow 2\sqrt{4} = 3 \rightarrow 4 = 3\sqrt{4} = 6$. The answer is choice (C).

5. **C**   Write out sequences until you see the pattern. The second term in the sequence is $3(-1) = -3$. Adding 3 gives you the third term, 0. Multiplying by -1 gives you the fourth term, also 0. Adding 3 gives you 3, the fifth term. So the sequence repeats every four terms: 3, -3, 0, 0, 3, -3, 0, 0, and so forth. Dividing 168 by 4 gives you a remainder of zero, and the fourth, eighth, twelfth, and every other nth term where n is a multiple of 4 (including the 168th term) will all be the same value, 0. The answer is choice (C).

6. **C**   Even if you know the summation formula, you can avoid a lot of time-consuming calculation by disregarding the numbers that are common to both sums—the even integers from 22 to 36, inclusive. That leaves $18 + 20 = 38$ as the sum of the unique terms in Column A, and 38 as the only unique term in Column B. The Columns are equal.

7. **A**   Set up a group grid and fill in what you have:

	Men	Women	Total
Standard		20	
Gold	18		30
Total			65

Use this to find that there are $65 - 30 = 35$ total standard members. So there are $35 - 20 = 15$ standard male members, thus, Column A is 15. The answer is Choice (A).

8. **D**   Whenever you have a function within another function, you have to first calculate the value of the function on the inside, and then plug that value into the function on the outside. Plug in to test the values. If you Plug In 2 for x, then, in Column A, $2\S = 2^2 + 2(2) = 8$ and $8\# = 8^2 + 3(8) = 88$; in Column B, $2\# = 2^2 + 3(2) = 10$ and $10\S = 10^2 + 2(10) = 120$; eliminate choices (A) and (C). However, if you Plug In 0 for x, then both Columns are 0; eliminate choice (B), and you're left with choice (D), the correct answer.

9. **C**   Write out the powers of 7 until you see the pattern in the last digit. You really only need to calculate the last digit: $7^1 = 7; 7^2 = 49; 7^3 = 343; 7^4 = ...1; 7^5 = ...7; 7^6 = ...9; 7^7 = ...3; 7^8 = ...1$, and so forth. The units digits 7, 9, 3, and 1 repeat, but 5 does not appear as a units digit, so the answer is choice (C).

10. **E**   The top row contains 1 can, the second row contains $1 + 1(6) = 7$ cans, the third row contains $1 + 2(6) = 13$ cans, and so forth, so that the sixteenth row contains $1 + 15(6) = 91$ cans. But you need to find the total number of cans, which is $1 + 7 + 13 + ... + 79 + 85 + 91$. Notice that adding the first and last term in the sequence gives you 92. Adding the second and second to last term also gives you 92: as you move to the next term at the beginning of the sequence, you are adding 6, while as you move to the previous term at the end of the sequence, you are subtracting 6, so the sum will remain constant. Thus, for each pair of rows, the sum is 92. Sixteen rows represents eight pairs of rows, so the total number of cans is $(8)(92) = 736$. The answer is choice (E).

11. **D**   Decoding the definition of the sequence tells you that, to find the value of each term, you take the previous term, and raise it to the power of the term before it. You know $s_3 = 10^2 = 100$, $s_4 = \left(10^2\right)^{10} = 10^{20}$, and $s_5 = \left(10^{20}\right)^{100} = 10^{2000}$. So s_4 is the digit 1 followed by twenty zeroes, which is a total of 21 digits, and s_5 is the digit 1 followed by 2,000 zeroes, for a total of 2,001 digits. So the fourth term is the one that meets the condition set forth in the question, and the answer is choice (D).

12. **A**   For Column A, start with the innermost parentheses: $g(-1) = (-1) - 2 = -3$. So $f(-3) = (-3)^2 + 1 = 9 + 1 = 10$. For Column B, $f(-1) = (-1)^2 + 1 = 1 + 1 = 2$. So, $g(2) = 2 - 2 = 0$. Thus, Column A is greater.

Drill 2

1. **E** The area of a circle with radius 5 is $\pi r^2 = 5^2 \pi = 25\pi$. Dividing the area by π gives you 25. The answer is choice (E).

2. **A** The second positive integer multiple of 5 is 10. The third positive integer multiple of 5 is 15. The sum of 10 and 15 is 25, so Column A is larger.

3. **E** Rather than listing out the actual times, figure out the pattern. The vent releases steam at 25, 45, and then 5 minutes after 6 p.m., and repeats this pattern every hour thereafter. Only choice (E) fits the pattern.

4. **C** When a problem gives you a relationship signified by an unfamiliar symbol: just Plug In the given values into the given "function" and solve. If $l \, \S \, m = -\left| \dfrac{l+m}{lm} \right|$, then $3 \S \dfrac{3}{2} = -\left| \dfrac{3 + \dfrac{3}{2}}{3\left(\dfrac{3}{2}\right)} \right| = -\left| \dfrac{\dfrac{9}{2}}{\dfrac{9}{2}} \right| = -|1| = -1$.

   The Columns are equal, so select choice (C).

5. **C** Use the group formula and fill in what you know. So *Total = Group*1 + *Group*2 − *Both* + *Neither* becomes 30 = 14 + 13 − *Both* + 9. So *Both* = 6, and the answer is choice (C).

6. **D** Find the measure of an angle in a regular 10-sided polygon by Plugging In 10 into the formula $\dfrac{(10-2)180°}{10} = 144°$. Then find the measure of an angle in a regular 6-sided polygon by Plugging In 6 into the formula $\dfrac{(6-2)180°}{6} = 120°$. The difference between 144° and 120° is 24°, so the answer is choice (D).

7. **B** To follow the order of operations, first evaluate the expression in parentheses: $3 \oplus 1 = 2(3) - 1 = 5$. Now evaluate the two expressions: $5 \oplus 2 = 2(5) - 2 = 8$ and $6 \oplus 3 = 2(6) - 3 = 9$. The absolute value of the difference between these is $|8 - 9| = |-1| = 1$, so the answer is choice (B).

8. **8** Use brute force to solve this one: Write down the 2 given terms, find half the sum of the previous 2 terms, and repeat the process until you have a non-integer. When you work it out, Sequence *S* should begin 64, 32, 48, 40, 44, 42, 43, 42.5; the first non-integer term is the 8th term, so *n* = 8.

9. **C** To find the pattern in each sequence, write out the units digit of the first few terms in the sequence. The pattern for the units digit of powers of 7 is: 7, 9, 3, 1. The pattern for the units digit of powers of 3 is: 3, 9, 7, 1. For both numbers, 1 repeats as the units digit every 4 powers, so the 4th power will have a units digit of 1, as will the 8th, the 12th, and so on. Because 28 is a multiple of 4, you know that 7^{28} will have a units digit of 1. So moving forward one in the pattern, 7^{29} will have a units digit of 7. Similarly, 3^{28} will have a units digit of 1, so moving backward one in the pattern, 3^{27} must have a units digit of 7. The Columns are equal, so the answer is choice (C).

10. E Set up a group grid and, because you are dealing with percents and fractions, plug in 100 for the total number of employees at the company. There will be 60 men, of whom 6 are still employed after the restructuring. Subtracting 60 from 100 gives you 40, the total number of women. Five times the 6 men who are still employed gives you 30, the number of women still employed. After filling in this information, the group grid looks like the figure below.

	Still employed	No longer employed	Total
Men	6		60
Women	30		40
Total			100

There are 30 women, but the question asks you what percent this represents of the total number of women. 30 out of 40 is 75 percent, so the answer is choice (E).

11. C Rather than trying to remember a bunch of rules about even and odd numbers, Plug In for a and b. If a is 2, then $6a$ is 12, and #12 = –2. Because $b - 3$ is odd, make $b = 6$, and #b = –2 as well. The two Columns are equal, so eliminate choices (A) and (B). Any set of values gives the same outcome, so select choice (C).

12. B Plugging 10 values into two compound functions is going to involve lots of arithmetic and will take a long time, so it is better to do this one algebraically. Working from the inside out, find Column A: $f\big(g(x)\big) = f\big(x+1\big) = 3\big(x+1\big)^2 = 3x^2 + 6x + 3$; remember to FOIL the $(x + 1)$ when you square it. Similarly, find Column B: $g(f(x)) = g(3x^2) = 3x^2 + 1$. You can add or subtract the same value from both Columns without affecting which is bigger; doing so with $3x^2 + 1$ leaves you with $6x + 3$ in Column A and 0 in Column B. Because $6x + 3$ is a linear function whose graph is a line with positive slope, you know that the values of the function will increase as the values of x increase. So you only need to plug in the endpoints of the given range of x-values to see what happens to the function: $6(-10) + 3 = -57$ and $6(-1) + 3 = -3$. So all possible values of Column A are still less than 0, and the answer is choice (B).

13. E The equation $3 \times 2^{n-1}$ follows a pattern. When $n = 1$, the result is 3. When $n = 2$, the result is 6. When $n = 3$, the result is 12. When $n = 4$, the result is 24. When $n = 5$, the result is 48. When $n = 6$, the result is 96. Beginning with the second term, the final digit in each result follows the pattern: 6, 2, 4, 8, 6, 2, 4, 8, etc. The 25th term will thus end in the same digit as all the other kth terms, where k is one greater than a multiple of 4. Thus, the (4 + 1)th, (8+1)th, (12+1)th….(24+1)th terms all have a final digit of 8, and the only answer in which that is true is choice (E).

Combinations and Permutations

COMBINATIONS AND PERMUTATIONS

You will recognize these problems because they will ask you about the number of possible combinations, arrangements, groups, or ways to order a number of things or people. You may be asked about toppings on a salad, members in a group or on a committee, children in a line, or runners in a race.

When doing these problems there are only two possible numbers you can generate, a big one and a small one. The big one happens when order matters, the small one happens when order does not matter.

EXAMPLE 1

Supposed you are asked for the number of different ways eight runners come in first, second, or third in a race. The first step is to make slots on your scratch paper. You are looking at the runners in first, second, or third place, therefore you need three slots.

_ _ _

Before the race starts, everyone is a winner, or at least a potential winner, so there are eight possible runners who could come in first place. Once one runner comes in first, there are seven potential runners left who could come in second place, and six left for third place.

<u>8</u> <u>7</u> <u>6</u>

To figure out the number of ways eight runners could finish first, second, and third in a race, simply multiply all three numbers. Order, in the case of runners in a race, is highly significant. If Tom comes in first place, Jenny in second, and Alicia in third, that is one arrangement, but if Alicia comes in first, Tom in second, and Jenny in third, it counts as a new arrangement. There are 336 possible arrangements.

EXAMPLE 2

Now imagine that you are asked to find the number of different ways eight senators can be arranged on a three-person committee. There are three seats on the committee so you need three slots. The problem begins the same way. There are eight potential senators for the first slot, seven for the second, and six left for the third.

<u>8</u> <u>7</u> <u>6</u>

As opposed to the situation of the runners in a race, however, order, in this case, does not matter. A committee made up of Ross, LB, and Shirley or a committee made up of LB, Shirley, and Ross is the same committee. The larger number counts each of these committees separately. You need a way to get rid of all of these committees of the same three people that you've counted just because they are in a different order. The way to do this is to divide by the factorial of the number of slots. It sounds complicated, but in reality, all you have to do is count down the number of slots in the divisor.

$$\frac{8 \ 7 \ 6}{3 \ 2 \ 1}$$

Before you multiply, reduce your fractions. You will always be able to reduce all of the numbers in the denominator. The three and the two each go evenly into the six once, so you are simply left with 56 (8 × 7). There are 56 different committees that can be made from a group of eight senators.

SUMMARY

That's it. It doesn't have to be anymore complicated than that. There are two numbers you can produce, a bigger one and a smaller one. The bigger number happens when order matters. In this case, just figure out the number of slots, fill in the numbers, and multiply across the top. The smaller number happens when order doesn't matter. In this case, figure out the number of slots, fill in the numbers on the top and count down the number of slots on the bottom, then reduce and multiply whatever remains.

Occasionally, if you are doing really well, they will give you some rules for your slots. For example, you might have three boys and four girls lining up for gym class. The question may ask you how many different ways they can be arranged in a line, but might stipulate that there must be a girl in first and last place. In this case, the approach is the same, just start with the slots that have the rules—we call these the restricted slots.

There are seven slots total because there will be seven children in the line. The first slot must be a girl, so there are four potential girls for that slot. The last slot must be a girl too, so there are three girls left who can stand last in line. The second slot is wide open. There are six children—four boys and two remaining girls—who are available for the second slot, five for the third, four for the forth, and so on.

Your scratch paper will look like this.

$$\underline{4 \ 6 \ 5 \ 4 \ 3 \ 2 \ 3}$$

Because order matters and every different arrangement of students must be counted separately, you want the bigger number. Simply multiply across the top, and you are done. There are 1,080 different ways three boys and four girls can be arranged in a line with a girl at the head of the line and the back.

For more practice and a more in-depth look at The Princeton Review math techniques, check out our student-friendly guidebook, *Cracking the GRE*.

COMBINATIONS AND PERMUTATIONS DRILL

A club consists of 8 women and 8 men.

The club has a president and a vice-president.

No club member can hold more than one position.

Column A	Column B
The number of possible assignments such that a woman is president and a man is vice- president	The number of possible assignments such that both the president and vice-president positions are filled by women

- ◯ The quantity in Column A is greater.
- ◯ The quantity in Column B is greater.
- ◯ The two quantities are equal.
- ◯ The relationship cannot be determined from the information given.

Given an alphabet of 26 letters, with 21 consonants and 5 vowels, approximately how many three-letter words can be formed with a vowel as the middle letter and a consonant as the last letter?

- ◯ 1000
- ◯ 1500
- ◯ 2500
- ◯ 3500
- ◯ 4000

Of the 100 eighth-graders at Easton Junior High, 60 students take gym, 40 take a foreign language, and 30 take both gym and a foreign language.

Column A	Column B
30	The number of students taking neither gym nor a foreign language

- ◯ The quantity in Column A is greater.
- ◯ The quantity in Column B is greater.
- ◯ The two quantities are equal.
- ◯ The relationship cannot be determined from the information given.

Graham's Catering Service currently employs three chefs and offers three different meals. For an upcoming event, the catering service must provide three meals, with each chef cooking one of the meals.

Column A	Column B
The number of assignments of chefs to meals if each chef must cook a different meal	The number of assignments of chefs to meals if each chef may cook any of the three meals

- ◯ The quantity in Column A is greater.
- ◯ The quantity in Column B is greater.
- ◯ The two quantities are equal.
- ◯ The relationship cannot be determined from the information given.

A certain password must contain 3 distinct digits followed by 2 distinct capital letters. Given ten digits and 26 capital letters, how many different passwords are possible?

◻

190 students go to a school bake sale. 95 buy a chocolate chip cookie, 75 buy a peanut butter cookie, and at least 12 buy both. What is the least number of students who could have bought neither type of cookie?

- ◯ 10
- ◯ 24
- ◯ 30
- ◯ 32
- ◯ 45

Geoff is setting up an aquarium and must choose 4 of 6 different fish and 2 of 3 different plants. How many different combinations of fish and plants can Geoff choose?

- ◯ 8
- ◯ 12
- ◯ 18
- ◯ 45
- ◯ 90

If the current day and time is 9:30 PM on Tuesday, what time will it be (to the nearest minute) 100,000 seconds from now?

- ◯ 1:17 AM, Wednesday
- ◯ 3:47 PM, Wednesday
- ◯ 1:10 AM, Thursday
- ◯ 1:17 AM, Thursday
- ◯ 2:17 AM, Thursday

What is the difference between the number of three-member committees that can be formed from a group of nine members and the total number of ways there are to arrange the members of such a committee?

- ◯ 0
- ◯ 84
- ◯ 252
- ◯ 420
- ◯ 504

Before starting a game, a teacher must divide her 10 students into three teams of three students (where order does not matter) and then assign the remaining student the role of referee. How many different assignments can she make for the 10 students?

- ◯ 10
- ◯ 16,800
- ◯ 604,800
- ◯ 1,209,600
- ◯ 3,628,800

Six students compete in a table tennis tournament. Each student plays each of the other students four times. What is the total number of games played in the tournament?

A four-person leadership committee is to be chosen from a student council that consists of seven juniors and five seniors. Q is the total number of different leadership committees that include three seniors and one junior.

Column A	Column B
Q	75

○ The quantity in Column A is greater.
○ The quantity in Column B is greater.
○ The two quantities are equal.
○ The relationship cannot be determined from the information given.

Contestants at a baking contest must use between 5 and 8 of 10 possible ingredients.

Column A	Column B
The number of ingredients that must be used to get the smallest possible number of different combinations	The number of ingredients that must be used to get the largest possible number of different combinations

○ The quantity in Column A is greater.
○ The quantity in Column B is greater.
○ The two quantities are equal.
○ The relationship cannot be determined from the information given.

ANSWERS

1. A
2. C
3. C
4. B
5. 468,000
6. D
7. D
8. D
9. D
10. B
11. 60
12. B
13. A

EXPLANATIONS

1. **A** For Column A, there are 8 options for president and 8 options for vice-president, giving you 8 × 8 = 64 total assignments. For Column B, once you pick a woman to be president, there are only 7 women left to be vice-president, giving you 8 × 7 = 56 assignments. The answer is choice (A).

2. **C** When you see the phrase "approximately," you are being told to Ballpark. In this case, you have 26 possibile letters for that slot, 5 for the second slot, and 21 for the third slot. Estimate and call this 25 × 20 × 5. The total is 2,500. (C).

3. **C** Substitute the given values into the groups equation: Total = Group 1 + Group 2 – Both + Neither. 100 = 60 + 40 – 30 + N, giving you N = 30, choice (C).

4. **B** Column A places a restriction on which meals a chef can cook because each chef must cook a distinct meal. In this case, there would be 3 × 2 × 1 = 6 different assignments. Column B does not place a restriction on which meals a chef can cook. In this case, there would be 3 × 3 × 3 = 27 different assignments, choice (B).

5. **468,000** List the number of possible options for each character in the password. There are 10 possibilities for the first digit, 9 left for the second, and 8 left for the third. There are 26 possibilities for the first letter and 25 for the second. There are 10 × 9 × 8 × 26 × 25 = 468,000 possible passwords.

6. **D** Substitute the given values into the groups equation: Total = Group 1 + Group 2 – Both + Neither. So 190 = 95 + 75 – 12 + N. N = 32. If you pick a number larger than 12 to represent the number of students who buy both cookies, the number that buy neither cookie also increases. The question asks for the least number that bought neither cookie, so the answer is choice (D).

7. **D** First find the number of groups of fish he can select. This is your number of slots _ _ _ _ _. There are six fish he can choose for the first slot, 5 for the second and so on: $\underline{6}\ \underline{5}\ \underline{4}\ \underline{3}$. Since order doesn't matter, you need to divide by the factorial of the number of slots: $\dfrac{6213}{4321}$. Reduce your number to get $3 \times 5 = 15$. For plants you have two slots so $\dfrac{3}{2} \times \dfrac{2}{1} = 3$. $3 \times 15 = 45$. (D).

8. **D** Dividing 100,000 seconds by 3,600 seconds per hour, you get 27 hours plus $\dfrac{7}{9}$ hr. Multiplying $\dfrac{7}{9}$ hr by 60 minutes per hour, you get $46\dfrac{2}{3}$ minutes. Therefore, to the nearest minute, 100,000 seconds is equal to 27 hours, 47 minutes. After 24 hours, the time will be 9:30 PM Wednesday; 3 hours, 47 minutes after that, it will be 1:17 AM, Thursday, choice (D).

9. D To find the number of different committees. Make your slots and divide by the factorial $\frac{9\ 8\ 7}{3\ 2\ 1} = 84$; eliminate answer choice (B). To find the number of ways to arrange the committee members, just multiply $9 \times 8 \times 7 = 504$, and eliminate partial choice (E). The difference is $504 - 84 = 420$, choice (D).

10. B This is a combinations problem. The order within each group does not matter. Think of each group individually. First, the teacher must choose 3 students from 10. Because the order doesn't matter you will have to divide by the factorial: $\frac{10\ 9\ 8}{3\ 2\ 1} = 120$. For the second team you have $\frac{7\ 6\ 5}{3\ 2\ 1} = 35$. and for the last team you have $\frac{4\ 3\ 2}{3\ 2\ 1} = 4$. The teacher must choose the remaining student as referee (exactly 1 choice). The total number of assignments is $120 \times 35 \times 4 \times 1 = 16,800$, choice (B).

11. 60 When calculating the number of games, order does not matter. There are two students in each game, so two slots: $\frac{6\ 5}{2\ 1}$ —because order does not matter you will divide by the factoral for 15 combinations. Each student plays 4 games against each of the other students, so $4(15) = 60$ games are played.

12. B Start by finding out how many groups of three seniors can be chosen from the five seniors: $\frac{5\ 4\ 3}{3\ 2\ 1} = 10$. Next, multiply that total by the number of individual juniors with which those groups can be paired (7) to form the full committee: $10 \times 7 = 70$. Column B is greater.

13. A You are forming groups where order doesn't matter, so use the combination formula. If you use 5 ingredients, then there are: $\frac{10\ 9\ 8\ 7\ 6}{5\ 4\ 3\ 2\ 1} = 252$ different combinations. If you use 6 ingredients there are $\frac{10\ 9\ 8\ 7\ 6\ 5}{6\ 5\ 4\ 3\ 2\ 1} = 210$ combinations, if you use 7 there are $\frac{10\ 9\ 8\ 7\ 6\ 5\ 4}{7\ 6\ 5\ 4\ 3\ 2\ 1} = 120$, and if you use 8 there are $\frac{10\ 9\ 8\ 7\ 6\ 5\ 4\ 3}{8\ 7\ 6\ 5\ 4\ 3\ 2\ 1} = 45$. Thus, Column A is 8, and Column B is 5, choice (A).

Coordinate Geometry

POINTS AND AREAS

A coordinate plane is simply any flat surface (a piece of paper, a chalkboard) that has been divided up into coordinates. The quadrants are as shown below.

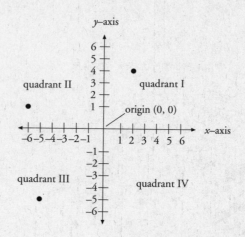

Some coordinate geometry problems will ask you to find the distance between points or the area of the shapes you make when you connect points. When plotting points on a graph, it is helpful to write the coordinates along the axis. This will turn the axis into number lines and make it easier to find the distances between points.

Here is an example.

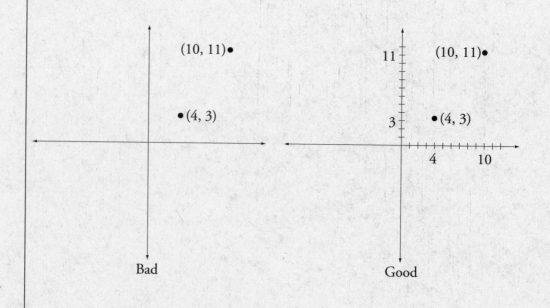

When you are asked to find the distance between these two points, you can use the distance formula or you can simply draw in a right triangle and use the Pythagorean theorem.

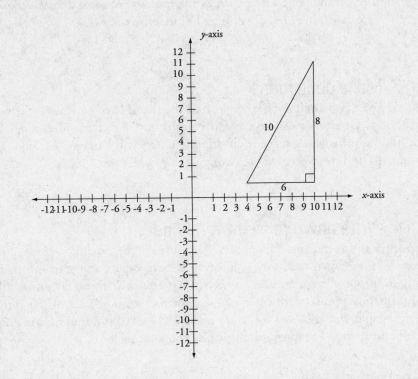

What would normally involve a long formula and some calculations with the distance formula, becomes a simple process with a triangle, especially if it is a special right triangle. If you are finding the areas of shapes, they are the same old triangles, circles, and rectangles you find elsewhere on the test. The same rules apply. No matter what you are asked to find, it is still a geometry question, and you should still use your five steps.

Step 1: Draw your shape

In some cases the test will give you a shape, which you may or may not be able to trust, or it will give you a word problem and leave it up to you to envision the shape. As with every other part of the test, getting your hand moving is an important first step to beginning the problem. Get your shape down on your scratch paper so that you can begin working with it there. On Quant Comp questions involving geometry, instead of Plugging In more than once, you may have to draw your shape more than once.

Step 2: Fill in what you know

Whether you are given the shape or not, you will be given a certain amount of information regarding your shape such as the measure of some angles, lengths of some sides, area of some sides, or volume. Fill in what you know.

Step 3: Make deductions

If you are given two angles of a triangle, find the third. If you are given the radius, find the area. Often this will be the entire problem. Geometry on the GRE is all about finding the missing piece of information. You will be given just enough information to find the piece that is missing.

Step 4: Write down relevant formulas

If step three didn't get you the answer, you must still be missing a piece of information. Writing down the formula is a way of both organizing your information and figuring out what is missing. When you write your formulas down, fill in the information you have directly underneath the relevant part of the formula. It seems simple, but this way you can't make a mistake, and finding the missing piece of information becomes a simple case of solving for *x*.

Step 5: Drop heights/draw lines

If you're still stuck, you may need to manipulate or subdivide your shapes. If you have triangles, draw in the height. Have you created a 30-60-90? A 45-45-90? Or a Pythagorean triple? Try subdividing the shape or, if it's a three-dimensional figure, dashing in the hidden lines.

LINES AND SLOPES

You might see a question that asks about slope or gives the formula for a line. Questions about slope are terrific for Ballparking. Sometimes you can eliminate two or even three answer choices just by knowing the difference between a positive and negative slope.

Here's the difference.

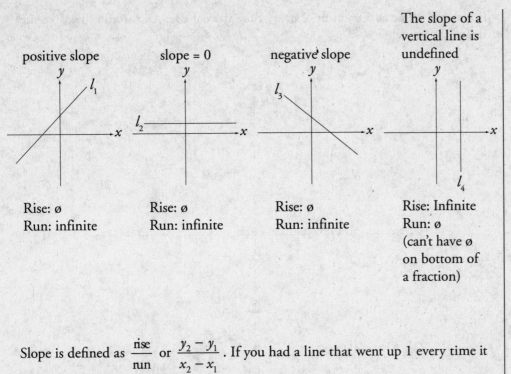

positive slope

Rise: ø
Run: infinite

slope = 0

Rise: ø
Run: infinite

negative slope

Rise: ø
Run: infinite

The slope of a vertical line is undefined

Rise: Infinite
Run: ø
(can't have ø on bottom of a fraction)

Slope is defined as $\dfrac{\text{rise}}{\text{run}}$ or $\dfrac{y_2 - y_1}{x_2 - x_1}$. If you had a line that went up 1 every time it went over 1, it would look the image shown below.

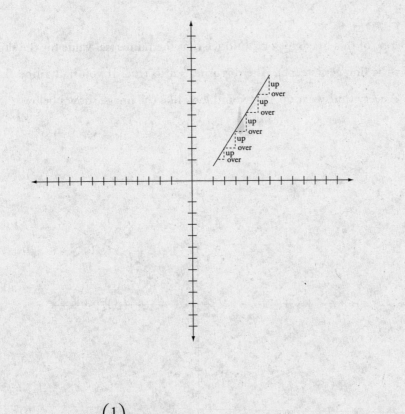

The slope is equal to one $\left(\dfrac{1}{1}\right)$, and the line lies at a 45 degree angle to the x-axis.

If you had a line that went up 2 every time it went over 1, it would look like the image shown below.

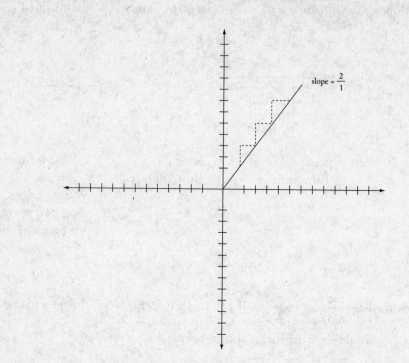

The slope of this line is $\frac{2}{1}$ or 2. Notice that the numerical value for the slope goes up as the line gets steeper. The opposite is also true. If you had a line that went over 2 every time went up 1, it would look like the image shown below.

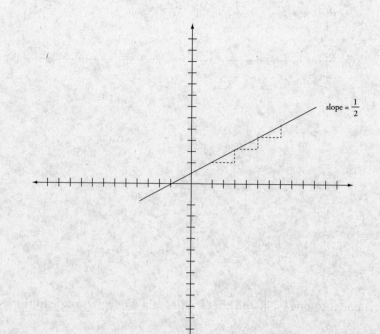

In this case, the slope is $\frac{1}{2}$ and you have shallower angle.

> A line at less than a 45 degree angle will have a slope between 0 and 1. A line that intersects the x-axis at greater than 45 degrees will have a slope greater than 1.

The formula for a line is $y = mx + b$; x and y are the coordinates of a single point, b tells you where the line intersects the y-axis and m (sometimes they use a on the GRE) tells you the slope of the line. With this information, you can accurately draw any line on a graph. ETS is likely to give you some of the information in this equation, sometimes as a picture, sometimes as a pair of points, or sometimes as an equation, and ask you to find the rest.

Remember three things.

1. With any two points you can find the slope.
2. The coordinates of the origin are (0, 0). This is a point like any other and often the second point you need to find slope.
3. If you are given information as an equation, put it in the $y = mx + b$ format.

For example, you might be told that line l passes through the origin, and the coordinates of point A are (7, 4).

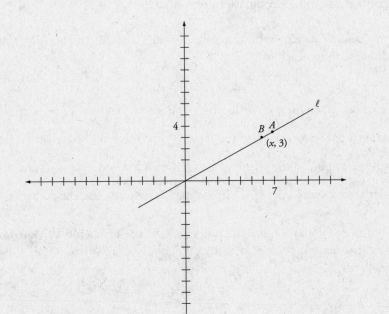

If you are asked to find the value of x at point B, draw it on your scratch paper like this.

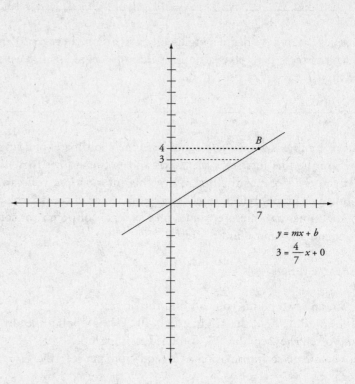

When you take the time to draw your shape carefully and accurately, usually you can immediately eliminate some answer choices just by Ballparking; you'll get some sense of the range of the correct answer. In this case, anything more than 7 is certainly going to be wrong, as is anything less than 4.

On your scratch paper, write out your formula and fill in the information you have directly underneath it.

You have been given the y-coordinate, 3. You know that the line goes up four times every time it goes over seven, so the slope is $\frac{4}{7}$. You also know that the line passes through the origin, so the y-intercept is 0. From here on out, you have a basic formula with one variable $3 = \frac{4}{7}x + 0$. Simply solve for x. The answer is $5\frac{1}{7}$.

For more practice and a more in-depth look at The Princeton Review math techniques, check out our student-friendly guidebook, *Cracking the GRE*.

COORDINATE GEOMETRY DRILL

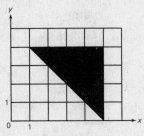 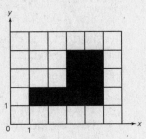

Column A
The area of the shaded region in Figure A

Column B
The area of the shaded region in Figure B

○ The quantity in Column A is greater.
○ The quantity in Column B is greater.
○ The two quantities are equal.
○ The relationship cannot be determined from the information given.

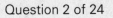

On the number line shown above, the coordinates of points P and Q are $-\dfrac{4}{3}$ and 2, respectively.

Column A
$\dfrac{1}{2}$

Column B
The coordinate of the midpoint of line segment PQ

○ The quantity in Column A is greater.
○ The quantity in Column B is greater.
○ The two quantities are equal.
○ The relationship cannot be determined from the information given.

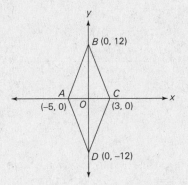

Column A
The perimeter of quadrilateral $ABCD$

Column B
The area of the shaded region

○ The quantity in Column A is greater.
○ The quantity in Column B is greater.
○ The two quantities are equal.
○ The relationship cannot be determined from the information given.

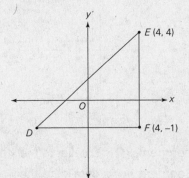

In the rectangular coordinate system above, if the area of right triangle DEF is 15, then which of the following are the coordinates of point D ?

○ $(-4, -1)$
○ $(-2, -1)$
○ $(-2, 4)$
○ $(1, -1)$
○ It cannot be determined from the information given.

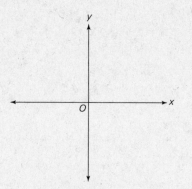

On the coordinate axes shown above, the graph of $y = 4x + 20$ would cross the x-axis at the point where

- ○ $x = -5$ and $y = 0$
- ○ $x = 0$ and $y = -5$
- ○ $x = 0$ and $y = 5$
- ○ $x = 0$ and $y = 20$
- ○ $x = 5$ and $y = 0$

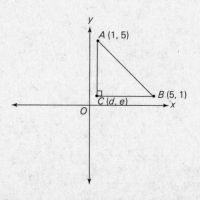

Line segment BC is parallel to the x-axis.

Line segment AC is parallel to the y-axis.

Column A	Column B
d	e

- ○ The quantity in Column A is greater.
- ○ The quantity in Column B is greater.
- ○ The two quantities are equal.
- ○ The relationship cannot be determined from the information given.

Cam's home is 2 miles east and 3 miles north of Atlanta. He drives to town B, which is 3 miles east and 9 miles north of his home.

Column A	Column B
The shortest distance between town B and Atlanta	17 miles

- ○ The quantity in Column A is greater.
- ○ The quantity in Column B is greater.
- ○ The two quantities are equal.
- ○ The relationship cannot be determined from the information given.

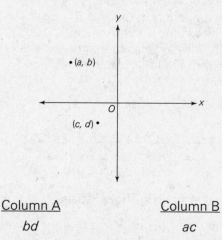

Column A	Column B
bd	ac

- ○ The quantity in Column A is greater.
- ○ The quantity in Column B is greater.
- ○ The two quantities are equal.
- ○ The relationship cannot be determined from the information given.

Which of the following is the graph of the equation $y = -|-x|$?

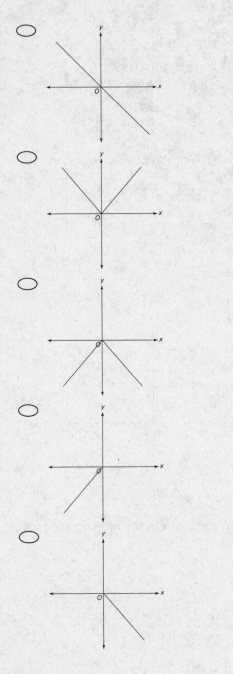

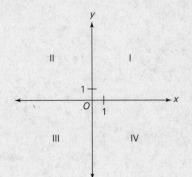

Points (a, b) and (c, d), not shown in the figure above, are in quadrants I and III, respectively. If $abcd \neq 0$, then the point $(-bd, bc)$ must be in which quadrant?

○ I
○ II
○ III
○ IV
○ It cannot be determined from the information given.

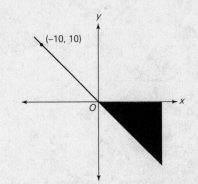

Which of the following pairs of coordinates corresponds to a point in the shaded region of the graph shown above?

○ $(9, -7)$
○ $(-9, -7)$
○ $(9, 7)$
○ $(7, -9)$
○ $(-7, -9)$

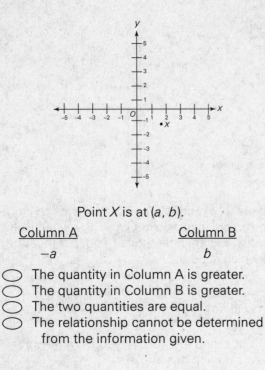

Point X is at (a, b).

Column A	Column B
−a	b

◯ The quantity in Column A is greater.
◯ The quantity in Column B is greater.
◯ The two quantities are equal.
◯ The relationship cannot be determined from the information given.

Question 13 of 24

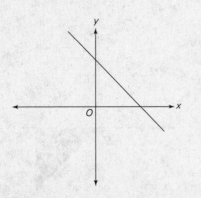

The equation of the line graphed on the rectangular coordinate system above is given by:

$$y = -\frac{13}{12}x + 8$$

Column A	Column B
AO	BO

◯ The quantity in Column A is greater.
◯ The quantity in Column B is greater.
◯ The two quantities are equal.
◯ The relationship cannot be determined from the information given.

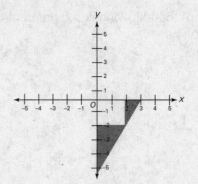

What is the area of the shaded region in the figure above?

◯ 1
◯ 2
◯ 4
◯ 5
◯ 9

Question 15 of 24

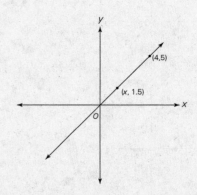

What is the value of x in the rectangular coordinate system above?

◯ 1.0
◯ 1.2
◯ 1.4
◯ 1.6
◯ 1.8

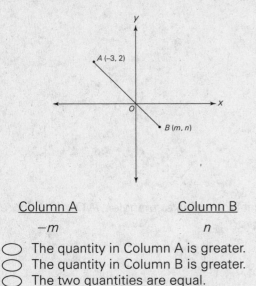

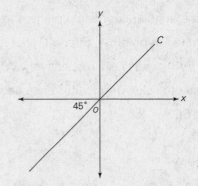

Column A | Column B
$-m$ | n

- ⬭ The quantity in Column A is greater.
- ⬭ The quantity in Column B is greater.
- ⬭ The two quantities are equal.
- ⬭ The relationship cannot be determined from the information given.

If the x-coordinates of the two x-intercepts of a parabola are $3 - \sqrt{2}$ and $5 + \sqrt{2}$, then what is the distance between them?

- ⬭ $2 - 2\sqrt{2}$
- ⬭ $2 + 2\sqrt{2}$
- ⬭ $8 + 2\sqrt{2}$
- ⬭ 2
- ⬭ 8

Point D (not shown) lies below line C in the rectangular coordinate system above.

Column A | Column B
The x-coordinate of point D | The y-coordinate of point D

- ⬭ The quantity in Column A is greater.
- ⬭ The quantity in Column B is greater.
- ⬭ The two quantities are equal.
- ⬭ The relationship cannot be determined from the information given.

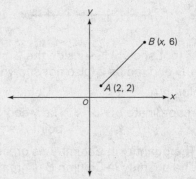

In the coordinate system above, the slope of line segment AB is $\dfrac{4}{3}$.

Column A | Column B
The length of line segment AB | x

- ⬭ The quantity in Column A is greater.
- ⬭ The quantity in Column B is greater.
- ⬭ The two quantities are equal.
- ⬭ The relationship cannot be determined from the information given.

In the rectangular coordinate plane, the coordinates of points A, B, and C are (1, 4), $\left(7, 4 + 6\sqrt{3}\right)$, and (7, 4), respectively. What is the absolute value of the difference between AB and BC ?

○ 6

○ $4 + \sqrt{3}$

○ $6 - 6\sqrt{3}$

○ $6\sqrt{3} - 12$

○ $12 - 6\sqrt{3}$

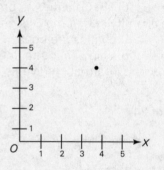

Point Z (not shown) lies inside the circle with center O and radius 2 (also not shown).

Column A	Column B
The x-coordinate of point Z	The y-coordinate of point Z

○ The quantity in Column A is greater.
○ The quantity in Column B is greater.
○ The two quantities are equal.
○ The relationship cannot be determined from the information given.

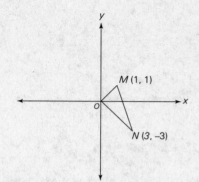

What is the area of triangle MNO in the figure above?

○ 3

○ 6

○ $4\sqrt{2} + 2\sqrt{5}$

○ $2\sqrt{10}$

○ $6\sqrt{10}$

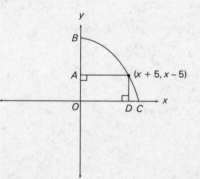

In the figure above, if BC is an arc in the circle with center O, then $AB - DC =$

○ -10

○ 10

○ $2x$

○ $x^2 - 25$

○ $\sqrt{2x^2 + 50}$

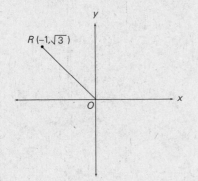

In the coordinate system above, line segment *OR* is rotated clockwise through an angle of 120° to position *OS* (not shown).

<u>Column A</u>	<u>Column B</u>
The *x*-coordinate of point *S*	$\sqrt{3}$

◯ The quantity in Column A is greater.
◯ The quantity in Column B is greater.
◯ The two quantities are equal.
◯ The relationship cannot be determined from the information given.

ANSWERS

1. C
2. A
3. B
4. B
5. A
6. C
7. B
8. B
9. C
10. D
11. A
12. B
13. A
14. D
15. B
16. B
17. B
18. A
19. C
20. E
21. D
22. A
23. B
24. A

EXPLANATIONS

1. **C** Figure A contains 6 whole boxes plus 4 half-boxes, for a total of 8. Figure B contains 8 whole boxes. The answer is choice (C). Alternatively, the area of the right triangle in Figure A is $\frac{1}{2}bh = \frac{1}{2}(4)(4) = 8$ and Figure B contains a rectangle plus two units whose total area is $bh = (3)(2) = 6; 6 + 2 = 8$.

2. **A** The distance between P and Q is 10 ticks, so the midpoint will be 5 ticks from either endpoint, which is the first tick to the right of 0, at $\frac{1}{3}$. To find the coordinate of the midpoint, simply average the coordinates of the endpoints: $\frac{-\frac{4}{3}+2}{2} = \frac{\frac{2}{3}}{2} = \frac{1}{3}$, so Column A is greater. Alternatively, because the smaller ticks divide each unit into 3 equal parts, they represent lengths of $\frac{1}{3}$.

3. **B** The axes split the quadrilateral into four equal 5-12-13 right triangles (note the highly suspicious numbers on the drawing). So the perimeter is 4(13) = 52, and Column B is therefore greater.

4. **B** Subtracting the y-coordinates of the given points gives you the length of leg EF: 4 – (–1) = 5. The area formula for a triangle will give you the length of the other leg, DF: $\frac{1}{2}bh = \frac{1}{2}(b)(5); b = 6$. Subtracting 6 from the x-coordinate of F gives you the x-coordinate of D, and D has the same y-coordinate as F. So the coordinates of D are (–2, –1); the answer is choice (B).

5. **A** On the x-axis, $y = 0$; eliminate choices (B), (C), and (D). Then Plug In 0 for y in the given equation. Solve for x: 0 = 4x + 20, so x = –5, and the answer is choice (A).

6. **C** Point C has the same x-coordinate as point A and the same y-coordinate as point B. The coordinates of C are therefore (1, 1), so the Columns are equal.

7. **B** Draw a rectangular coordinate system with Atlanta as the origin, i.e. the point (0, 0). So Cam's home is at (2, 3). Going 3 miles east and 9 miles north puts town B at (5, 12). Column A is the straight line distance from (0, 0) to (5, 12). Connecting these two points creates the hypotenuse of a 5-12-13 right triangle, so Column A is 13, and the answer is choice (B).

8. **B** Point (a, b) is in the second quadrant where points have signs of (–, +); thus, a is negative and b is positive. Point (c, d) is in the third quadrant where points have signs of (–, –); thus, c is negative and d is negative. So, Column A is a positive times a negative, which is negative. Column B is a negative times a negative, which is positive. Column B must be greater.

9. **C** Plug values into the equation and eliminate graphs that do not include those values. If x = 1, then y = –1, eliminate choices (B) and (D). If x = –1, then y = –1, eliminate choices (A) and (E). Only choice (C) remains.

10. **D** Plug In points in the appropriate quadrants. If $(a, b) = (1, 2)$ and $(c, d) = (-3, -4)$, then the point in question is $(-bd, bc) = [-(2)(-4), (2)(-3)] = (8, -6)$, which is in quadrant IV; the answer is choice (D).

11. **A** Use Process of Elimination to solve this one. First, only coordinate pairs with a positive x-value and a negative y-value will fall in the proper quadrant, so eliminate answer choices (B), (C), and (E). The line that divides the correct quadrant into shaded and unshaded regions has a slope of -1 because it goes through the origin and the point $(-10, 10)$. On this line, the absolute value of the x-coordinate equals the absolute value of the y-coordinate. In the shaded region, then, $|x| > |y|$, so choice (D) can be eliminated. Only choice (A) remains. Alternatively, realize that this figure is drawn accurately, because of the placement of $(10, -10)$, and plot all 5 points, eliminating all of those that fall outside the shaded region.

12. **B** Point X is at approximately $(2, -1.5)$. So Column A is about -2 and Column B is about -1.5, thus, Column B is greater.

13. **A** Although you have enough information to find the exact values of AO and BO, it's not necessary to do so to compare the Columns. The slope of the line is $-\dfrac{13}{12}$, which means that the vertical distance, or rise, is greater than the horizontal distance, or run, by a ratio of 13 to 12 (you're dealing with distances on a coordinate plane, so disregard the negative sign). Because AO and BO are equal to, respectively, the rise and the run of the same segment of the line, Column A is greater.

14. **D** To find the area of a shaded region, subtract the area of the unshaded region from the whole area. In this case, the area of the whole triangle is given by $\dfrac{1}{2}bh = \dfrac{1}{2}(3)(6) = 9$. The area of the unshaded square is given by $s^2 = 2^2 = 4$. Subtracting 4 from 9 gives you 5, so the answer is choice (D).

15. **B** Note that the line contains three points: $(0, 0)$, $(4, 5)$, and $(x, 1.5)$. The slope between any two of these points is the same. Remember that slope is change in y over change in x. Thus, $\dfrac{5-0}{4-0} = \dfrac{1.5-0}{x-0}$, or $\dfrac{5}{4} = \dfrac{1.5}{x}$. Cross multiply to find $5x = 6.0$. Divide by 5 to find $x = 1.2$. The answer is choice (B).

16. **B** Just because you don't know the values of $-m$ and n doesn't mean you can't determine which is greater. Using point A and the origin, you can find the slope of segment AB: $\dfrac{\text{rise}}{\text{run}} = \dfrac{-2}{3} = -\dfrac{2}{3}$. Now Plug In coordinates for point B that will give you the same slope; the easiest way to pick them would be to simply rise -2 and run 3, bringing you to the point $(m, n) = (3, -2)$. So $-m = -3$, and $n = -2$, and Column B is greater.

17. **B** You don't need to use the distance formula, because the distance between the points $\left(3-\sqrt{2},0\right)$ and $\left(5+\sqrt{2},0\right)$ can be measured horizontally. Distance is positive, so subtract the smaller x-coordinate from the larger: $\left(5+\sqrt{2}\right)-\left(3-\sqrt{2}\right)=2+2\sqrt{2}$; the answer is choice (B).

18. **A** Plug In a few points that lie below line c, such as (1, 0), (0, –1), (–3, –4), (1, 0). In each case, the x-coordinate is greater than the y-coordinate, so Column A is greater. Alternatively, realize that the 45 degree angle and the fact that the line passes through the origin tells us that the equation of line c is $y = x$. So the region below the line is the graph of $y < x$. The coordinates of all points in that region must satisfy the inequality.

19. **C** Break this one into bite-sized pieces: You need x in order to find the length of AB, so find x first. If you insert the given values into the slope formula, $\dfrac{y_2-y_1}{x_2-x_1}$, you get $\dfrac{6-2}{x-2}=\dfrac{4}{3}$, so $x = 5$. Now you need to find the length of AB. Rather than using the distance formula, turn AB into the hypotenuse of a right triangle and find the lengths of the other sides. To make the triangle, add a new vertex at coordinate (5, 2): the length of the horizontal leg is $5 - 2 = 3$, and that of the vertical leg is $6 - 2 = 4$, yielding the familiar 3-4-5 triangle. The length of segment $AB = 5$, so the two Columns are equal.

20. **E** Draw the points and connect the points to form a right triangle. Subtract the x-coordinate of A from that of C to find the length of AC: $7 - 1 = 6$. Subtract the y-coordinate of C from that of B to find the length of BC: $4+6\sqrt{3}-4=6\sqrt{3}$. Notice that the ratio of AC to BC is 1 to $\sqrt{3}$. Therefore, ABC is a 30–60–90 triangle, and the length of AB, the hypotenuse, will be double the length of the shorter side (6), so $AB = 12$. The absolute value of the difference will be the positive value, obtained by subtracting the smaller value (BC) from the larger value (the length of the hypotenuse, AB): $AB - BC = 12-6\sqrt{3}$, which is choice (E).

21. **D** Plug In points. Points (3, 4) and (5, 4) both lie inside the circle, so different values give different outcomes.

22. **A** The slope of MO is 1, so it makes a 45 degree angle with the positive x-axis. Similarly, the slope of NO is –1, so it makes another 45 degree angle with the positive x-axis. The sum of the degree measures of these angles is 90, so MNO is a right triangle. Therefore, MO and NO are the base and height of triangle MNO. To find the area of the triangle, you need to find the length of MO and NO. Drop a perpendicular from point M to the x-axis, to form an isosceles right triangle whose hypotenuse is MO. Each leg of this triangle has length 1 so, $MO = \sqrt{2}$. Similarly, dropping a perpendicular line from the x-axis to point N creates another isosceles right triangle, whose legs have length 3, and whose hypotenuse is NO. Therefore, $NO = 3\sqrt{2}$. So the area of triangle MNO is $\frac{1}{2}bh = \frac{1}{2}\left(\sqrt{2}\right)\left(3\sqrt{2}\right) = 3$, and the answer is choice (A).

23. **B** To find AB, find the radius of the circle and then subtract OA. If the radius is r, then $AB = r - (x - 5) = r - x + 5$. Similarly, $DC = r - (x + 5) = r - x - 5$. So $AB - DC = [r - x + 5] - [r - x - 5] = 10$, so the answer is choice (B). If you use POE, you can eliminate choice (A) because you know the answer has to be positive. If you selected choice (E), you selected the radius.

24. **A** Drawing a horizontal line from point R to the positive y-axis forms a right triangle. The length of the leg that sits on the y-axis is $\sqrt{3}$, and the horizontal leg you just drew has length 1. The ratio of the legs is 1 to $\sqrt{3}$, so you have a 30-60-90 right triangle. Therefore, the hypotenuse (OR) has length 2, and the angle between OR and the positive y-axis is 30 degrees. The first quadrant includes 90 degrees total, so rotating OR 120 degrees clockwise puts OS on the positive x-axis, with a length of 2. Therefore, the x-coordinate of OS is 2, which is slightly larger than $\sqrt{3}$, which is approximately 1.7. The answer is choice (A).

Writing

Analytical Writing

ANALYTICAL WRITING

Unfortunately, the essays are unavoidable; they are the first thing you will see on the GRE. Very few programs care about your essay score. Before you spend time preparing for the essays, call the programs to which you plan to apply, and ask them if they plan to use or look at your essay score. If they don't, skip this chapter. If your program is highly competitive, however, then all numbers count, and you should keep reading.

ESSAY TOPICS

There are two essays on the GRE. The first is the issue essay. On this essay you will be given two topics (or prompts) to choose from and 45 minutes to craft and write your essay. Your job is to formulate an opinion on one of those prompts and to support that opinion with well chosen examples. The issue essay is really more like a debate team exercise than a writing exercise. You need to craft the strongest argument you can in the 45 minutes you are given.

On the second essay, you are the judge. You will be presented with someone else's argument, and it is your job to evaluate its strengths. On this essay, your opinion of the author's conclusion doesn't matter; the only thing that matters is whether the argument is logically sound.

SCORING

Both of your essays will be scored on a six-point scale in half-point increments; the two scores will then be averaged and rounded to the nearest half point. If you score a five on one essay and a six on another, you will end up with a 5.5. A 5.5, by the way, puts you in the 87th percentile. You must score a 4.5 to put yourself above the 50th percentile.

Here is the breakdown of percentiles by score.

Score	Analytical Writing Percentile
6	96
5.5	87
5	71
4.5	52
4	32
3.5	17
3	7
2.5	2
2	1
1.5	0
1	0
0.5	0

For both essays, it is critically important to consider the reader. ETS says that each reader will spend two minutes on your essay, but really, it's more like one. ETS calls the grading style "holistic grading" and claims that readers consider the overall impact of the essay, not every little detail. You have a very short time to grab the reader's attention, make a few strong points, and then wrap up. Your job is not to write the best essay ever. Not only do you not have enough time to do that, but a beautifully written essay that takes a long time to develop and is full of subtle points may miss the mark. Your job is to give the readers what they're looking for as efficiently as possible, so that they can give you the score you want.

Because this is a standardized test, it is not about opinion. It is not the reader's job to respond personally to your arguments or your opinions. In fact, the readers have a very specifically defined scoring rubric.

They are looking at three things:

1. The quality of your thinking
2. The quality of your organization
3. The quality of your writing

Each area counts equally. All three criteria must be present—to some degree—in order for you to score in the top half. An essay in the bottom half, which scores a one, two, or three, will be missing one or more of these three components. The essay may be well structured, but it is too narrow or obvious in its thinking. Alternatively, the thinking may be great and the writing pretty good, but the organization may be a disaster.

Because each of these three factors is so important, you need an approach that gives all three their due. No matter which essay you are working on, you must devote time to thinking, organizing, and writing.

THE ISSUE ESSAY

You will have your choice of two different prompts. Each prompt will give a strongly worded point of view on some subject accessible to all. This means that prompts won't ask about Hamlet, but they may ask about education, society, or personal growth. Other topics could include anything from law, society, or trust, to art, change, or technology. ETS lists all of the possible topics on its website, www.ets.org. Go to GRE → General Test → Test Preparation → Writing Topics.

Step 1: Thinking

The essay topics are fairly general in nature. Education, for example, means different things to different people, and you could take your essay in a number of different directions. One of the most common mistakes test takers make is to write the essay on the first three examples that come to mind while sitting in the test center. These examples are not necessarily the best, the most interesting, or even within the writer's area of expertise. They also tend to be simplistic, similar, and often, really obvious.

To avoid this trap, force yourself to spend time thinking. Specifically, use your scratch paper to make a chart. On one side write, "I agree" and summarize the prompt. On the other side write, "I disagree" and summarize the opposing argument. Now force yourself to brainstorm four examples for each column. It's likely that you will have no trouble filling up one column, but you may struggle on the other. Push yourself to complete it. It is when you really push your thinking that your essay gets interesting.

If you run out of ideas during your brainstorm, use this simple checklist. Ask yourself, "How is this true for me, my family, my children, the elderly, my school, my community, my employer, my state, my country, my species, nature, science, or history?" By using this checklist to generate examples, you will automatically begin to see the issue from multiple perspectives. This will add richness and depth to your thinking.

Of course, the examples you choose need to be good ones. The best place to start is with things you know. Think about your job, your life, or your major in school. Work from your areas of strength or expertise, and the ideas will come more easily and be more powerful. You might think that the Holocaust or Gandhi's march to the sea are perfect examples, but if you don't know much more than the basics about either topic, you run the risk of sounding trite and simplistic. No one wants to sound trite when talking about the Holocaust.

When you come up with a general example, make sure you always attach it to a specific situation. If the topic is education, and your point is that it is necessary so that history does not repeat itself, get specific. Which history, whose education? General essays tend to be short and get average scores. Essays that rest upon clearly defined examples are longer and far more convincing.

Step 1

By the way, it is okay to write the essay in the first person. It is your job to have an opinion on the subject and to express it.

Step 2: Organizing

Now that you have this great list of ideas and examples, it's time to craft your essay. At this point, do NOT pick a point of view. Pick your three best examples. The point of view is irrelevant; it is your examples that make your essay powerful. It doesn't matter if you pick examples from both sides of the agree/disagree divide. If you have examples from both sides, it simply means that you will disagree with the prompt and that your thesis statement will be some variation of: "This is often true but not always." Once you pick your examples, craft a thesis statement to accommodate those three examples.

You will rarely see a topic for which you can't come up with a few powerful exceptions. In fact, an essay that acknowledges that there are two sides to an issue will be far more powerful. Instead of saying, "You are wrong. I disagree," you are saying, "I understand your point of view, but here's why I think my point of view is better." Which position gives your argument more authority?

Your three best examples will be the ones about which you know the most, about which you are the most excited, and which can be linked together in a common thread. You may choose three examples that can sit on either side of the agree/disagree divide, depending upon the point of view. You may pick three different levels and show how the topic affects a child, a family, and a country. You may want examples from wildly different fields such as software development, literature, and psychology. If you have done your brainstorm well, you will have plenty of interesting things from which to choose.

Once you have three good examples, you can craft your thesis statement to accommodate them. That way your examples will appear to be perfectly selected to support your thesis. Isn't it nice to have the perfect examples ready just when you need them? Now, write your thesis statement on your scratch paper. Another common mistake is for essay writers to lose the thread of their arguments halfway through their essays, or to stray from their thesis statements. This happens when they fail to make a plan and stick to it. Most people are actively thinking about what they're going to say next while they're still writing. This causes meandering essays and all kinds of errors and oversights. Don't do it.

Do not think about what you're going to write next when you're still writing. Make a plan before you start, and stick to it.

When you write out your thesis statement, you don't have to go into detail. You've got four more paragraphs in which to do that. Just tell the reader what you intend to prove and give him or her some sense of how you're going to prove it. Your first paragraph will be short, to the point, and no more than three sentences. If your topic is censorship and your examples are spam, parental controls on internet portals, and access to free press in China, then that is all you need to say in your intro. You have plenty of time to get into the specifics in your body paragraphs.

On your scratch paper, write out your thesis statement, your examples, and then a few words to remind yourself why each example is proof of your thesis statement. You don't need a whole sentence, just a few words such as "children, internet, some censorship—good" or "children, internet—children too sheltered, don't learn to censor selves."

When you begin to write your essay, these little guidelines will become the topic sentences of each of your supporting paragraphs. They will ensure that your essay stays on track and that the point of each example is clear to the reader.

Writing

Now that you have three beautifully chosen examples, a point of view that is perfectly supported by those examples, an outline, and even your topic sentences, you are ready to write. In fact, at this point, your essay is 80 percent written. All you need to do is flesh out your paragraphs, come up with a conclusion, and you're done. The great thing about this is that it leaves you free to really focus on your writing.

There are two things that every essay must have and a short list of things that your essay could have to dress up the writing.

Topic Sentences

Your reader will spend a minute on your essay. That's not much time. Don't make your reader work to figure out your point. Topic sentences make it easier for the reader to get your point and see how it fits. To some extent, you can't be too obvious with your topic sentences. Here's an example: "Parental controls on internet filters are an example of censorship that employs both personal choice and social responsibility." The job of the topic sentence is to announce the point of the paragraph and to connect the example to the thesis statement. A good topic sentence will add clarity and power to your argument. You are not trying to be Tolstoy; you're trying to give the reader the things he or she needs to give you the score you want.

Transitions

Transitions give your essay flow. They connect each paragraph to the greater fabric of the essay. They also help make connections between widely varying examples. If you are talking about children text messaging their friends during class in one paragraph and Hitler covering up the existence of concentration camps in another, you will need a transition. If your essay changes direction, you will need a transition. For example, "While censorship leads almost inevitably to abuse, it can be used responsibly. Take the example of…" These linguistic highway signs will help your speeding reader change lanes without slamming on the brakes.

In addition to the quality of your thinking and the organization of your argument, your readers will also be looking at your skill with the written word. Give them a few things that will get them excited.

Specifics

To say that Gandhi stood for non-violent protest is good. To describe how he and 79 of his followers made a 20 day trek to the sea to protest the 1930 salt tax and in so doing invented a method of civil disobedience that would eventually bring down the British Empire, is much, much better. Specifics make you sound like an expert. They give your essay authority, and they draw the reader in by making the essay come alive. You can't get specific enough. Use names, dates, and facts to make it sound like you're knowledgeable.

Quotes

In many ways, quotes are the ultimate specific. If you can drop a relevant quote into your essay, you will sound like a literary rock star. Very few people can do it, so it's impressive when it happens.

Commands

"Take Gandhi's march to the sea, for example." A command will grab your reader's attention. It is a bold and sophisticated style of writing that very few people use. It is sure to garner you a few points.

Rhetorical Questions

"Are there some things that the citizens of a country are better off not knowing?" Again, you are reaching off the page to speak directly to your reader. This a rhetorical flourish that is particularly effective for this type of essay.

Length

No matter what, length counts. Statistically speaking, longer essays score higher, so get your typing skills in order. Don't be afraid to use four examples—if you have time—or to add a few more specifics to each example. Size does matter.

Metaphors

To say that censorship is a double-edged sword may be a bit clichéd, but it's also a very effective way to set up an argument that has two sides. Using a good metaphor is like tucking a snazzy silk handkerchief in your breast pocket. It's not necessary, or even common, but if you can pull it off, it raises the whole ensemble to another level.

Big Words

Big words used correctly are impressive and grab a reader's attention. You can even prepare a few in advance and find a way to work them in on test day.

For a more in depth look at the techniques for the issue essay and some sample essays, check our student-friendly guidebook, *Cracking the GRE* book.

ANALYSIS OF AN ARGUMENT

On the issue essay, your job is to craft your own argument. On the argument essay, your job is the opposite. You will be given someone else's argument, and you must break it down and assess it. In some ways, this is not difficult. The argument you're given will be filled with some pretty obvious flaws.

Breaking Down the Argument

There are three basic parts to any argument:

1. The Conclusion

The conclusion is the main point of the argument. It is the statement the author is trying to prove and may be an opinion, recommendation, or prediction.

2. The Premises

The premises are the facts or reasons the author uses to back up his or her conclusion. Identify the conclusion and then ask yourself, "Why is that true"? The statements in the argument that provide the answer to that question are the premises.

3. Assumptions

You can't point to the assumptions because they're not there. The assumptions link the conclusion to the premises and are unstated facts the author is relying on to support his conclusion. There are hundreds of assumptions.

When you begin to break down an argument, you will want to use the formal language of arguments. First, identify the conclusion, then the premises, and finally the assumptions.

Types of Arguments

There are some types of arguments that you will see frequently. Once you identify the type of argument being made, spotting the assumption is easy.

Causal

A causal argument assumes a cause and effect relationship between two events. For example, sales are down because of a change in demographics. To weaken a causal argument, you need to point out other potential causes for a particular event. Perhaps sales are down because the overall economy is down, or because the product suddenly has competition. To strengthen a causal argument, you need to show that other potential causes are unlikely.

Sampling or Statistical

In these arguments the author assumes that a particular group represents an entire population. For example, all the people in a survey say that they prefer light beer, because it is less filling. To weaken this argument, you need to show that the people in the group surveyed don't represent the whole population. Perhaps they surveyed beer drinkers at a restaurant, where they were also eating dinner, rather than beer drinkers at a bar. Perhaps they surveyed at a liquor store right after lunch. To strengthen this argument, you need to show that the sample population is, in fact, representative of the whole.

Analogy

Analogy arguments claim that what is true for one group is also true for another. For example, voters in Cleveland prefer one candidate; therefore voters in Detroit will too. To weaken analogy arguments you need to show that the two groups are not at all analogous. Perhaps Detroit is the hometown of the rival candidate or perhaps one candidate favors the auto industry and one does not. To strengthen these arguments you must show that the two groups are quite similar indeed.

Crafting Your Argument Essay

The overall process for crafting your essay will be the same as it is for the issue essay. Invariably, you will end up criticizing the argument you have been given, although it is often a good strategy to use the conclusion of your essay to point out ways in which the argument could be improved. Throughout your essay you want to use the language of arguments. That means naming conclusions as conclusions, sampling arguments as sampling arguments, premises as premises, and assumptions as assumptions.

Thinking

Begin by identifying your conclusion, and then identify the major premises upon which it rests. For each premise, note the type of reasoning used (sampling, casual, etc.), and the flaws associated with that type of reasoning. This is as much brainstorming as you will need.

Organizing

Rank the premises by the size of their flaws. Start with the most egregious and work your way down. The outline of your essay will look something like this.

> The author's conclusion is *z*. It is faulty and more research/information is needed before the suggested action is taken.
>
> The first and biggest flaw is premise *y*. It's possible that it is true, but it rests upon the following assumptions. Can we really make these assumptions? What about these alternative assumptions?
>
> Even if we assume *y* to be the case, there is premise *x*. Premise *x* draws an analogy between these two groups and assumes that they are interchangeable. Can we really make this assumption? What about these alternative assumptions?
>
> Even if we assume *x* to be true, there is also *w*; *w* is a sampling argument, but the author not only has not proved the sample to be representative, but he/she also points out that this may not be the case! Perhaps, as noted, blah, blah, blah.
>
> In conclusion, this argument is incomplete and rests upon too many questionable assumptions. To improve this argument, the author needs to show *a*, *b*, and *c* before the building is to be torn down (or the company is to change tactics or the school is to reorganize its curriculum).

Writing

Feel free to have fun with this essay. Reading essays can get pretty boring and a smart, funny critique of a faulty argument can be a welcome break for your reader. You might say, "If I were the president of company *x*, I would fire my marketing director for wasting my time with such a poorly researched plan." It is OK to have personality as long as you get the analysis of the argument done at the same time.

For a more in depth look at the techniques for the argument essay and some sample essays, check our student-friendly guidebook, *Cracking the GRE* book.

ISSUE ESSAY DRILL

Here are some examples of the types of prompts you will see for your issue essay.

"One should not expect respect for disregarding the opinions of others. Only when every point of view is taken into consideration should people take action in the world."

"An increased number of laws or rules, ironically leads to a diminished sense of morality and impoverished relations among people."

"An idea alone, no matter how great, is meaningless unless it is put into practice."

"The value of ancient works, no matter how great, cannot be accurately judged because modern standards are not relevant and ancient standards cannot be known."

"When something is judged as ugly or lacking in style, it is only because it is being perceived by someone other than its target audience."

"Truly innovative ideas tend to come from individuals, because groups tend to work towards consensus and the status quo."

"It is far more important to define what you are for than what you are against."

"Education consists of making errors."

"The unknown is necessary."

"Skill alone, no matter how great, does not guarantee a masterpiece."

"To respect a symbol is to contribute power to a cultural institution, to worship a symbol is to bring about its eventual end."

"Success means a greater ability to communicate one's essence."

"A student who wishes to succeed in business should study anything but business while in school, he or she will learn skills of business. However, the value of adding the additional perspectives gained by studying other fields of knowledge is too valuable to pass up."

"Unexamined conservatism is far more dangerous than reckless change."

"If a student can return home comfortably, a school has not done its job."

ARGUMENT ESSAY DRILL

Here are some examples of the types of prompts you will see for your argument essay.

The following appeared in a memorandum from the regional manager of the Taste of Italy restaurant chain:

> *"After the first month of service, the new restaurant in the Flatplains Mall, which uses the Chipless brand of wine glasses, has reported a far lower rate of breakage than our other restaurants that use the Elegance brand. Since servers and bartenders at all of our restaurants frequently report that breakage is a result of the type of wineglass, and the customers at the Flatplains Mall restaurant seem to like the Chipless style of glasses, we should switch all of our restaurants to the Chipless brand."*

The following appeared in an internal memo circulated amongst the partners of a small graphic design firm:

> *"When the economy was growing, there were more graphics jobs than there were designers and many designers could make more money working as independent contractors, than they could as salaried employees. As we too were growing and needed more designers, we were forced to pay higher salaries to recent design graduates than we had paid in the past. Now that the market is shrinking, we can save lots of money by cutting back the salaries of all designers on staff to match current market rates. Service sector companies and manufacturing companies have both been able to successfully cut wages in a down economy without harming production. We should too."*

The following appeared in a report to the board of a company that produces men's sporting apparel:

> *"While national television advertising is increasingly expensive, it would cost roughly the same amount to reach the same number of people by buying print advertising space in various magazines. Since launching our newest TV ad campaign, sales have gone up significantly, but not in those markets which are served only by print ads. We should, therefore, increase our investment in TV ads and should not renew our magazine contracts once they are up."*

The following appeared in an internal memo circulated amongst the partners of a small design firm:

> "We, the four partners of Max Design, have made the company what it is. When we are hired by a client, it is our taste and style that the client is paying for. In the last two years we have grown significantly and now have project managers handling many of our recent contracts. In my opinion, the work put forth by the teams led by the product managers is not as good as the work put forth when it was just the four of us. At other design firms of a similar size, the principals remain personally involved in all projects. Therefore, from now on, all decisions for all projects, no matter how minute, should be signed off by one of us."

The following appeared in an email written by the head of market research division to the president of a major candy company:

> "In the last four years the gross sales in the candy market have remained static, but ice cream, another confectionary product, has experienced huge increases in gross sales. Specifically, the growth of boutique ice cream brands specializing in unusual savory ice cream flavors such as pink peppercorn, basil, and ginger, has exploded. In response, we have tested some savory flavored candy chews at a number of national gourmet food fairs. The response to our free samples has been extremely enthusiastic. Therefore we should jump to the forefront of this trend and launch our savory candy chews nationally at all retail outlets."

The following was a memorandum by the campaign manger for a state senate candidate:

> "Contributers to nearly every major blog in the state, both democratic and republican, agree that a proposal to increase tolls on the major highways going through our state is a good thing. They don't all agree that the increased revenue should go towards the same thing Some say we need more technology in the schools, others favor subsidizing insurance for the unemployed and independent contractors, and some say it should just be used to cut income tax. However, they all agree that the tolls should go up. Certainly this will cause more commuters to take public transportation, encourage businesses to ship by rail rather than truck, and save on road maintenance fees. Our chief competitor, who accepts major contributions from the trucking companies, opposes the toll increase. We should, therefore, come out strongly in favor of it."

The following appeared on the op-ed page of a local newspaper:

"As violent crime rates have slowly inched up in our city, it is time for city officials to take a stand to protect citizens from harm. The first step is to gate and lock downtown parks after dark. Keys can be passed out to apartment owners and other local residents to ensure that they have continued access to these public spaces while protecting against people who are using the park for things other than the recreational activities for which these public spaces were designed. This approach has been taken in three of the five suburbs that surround this city and polls of both homeowners and police departments in all three report higher property values and lower crime rates. The city needs to act now before we reach a tipping point."

About the Author

Neill Seltzer has been coaching GRE test takers since 1992. He has helped hundreds of students in places as diverse as Hong Kong, Dubai, Miami, New York, Westport, and Vail master both the pencil and paper and the CAT GRE. In addition to teaching, Neill has written or contributed to many Princeton Review books and course materials including *The 500 Best Ways for Teens to Spend the Summer, 11 Fake SATS*, and the 2009 edition of *Cracking the GRE*. In 2008 Neill earned his Masters of Architecture, giving him a first-hand look at the process of applying to and succeeding at grad school. As the National Content Director for the GRE for The Princeton Review, Neill spends a good part of each day thinking of better ways to crack this exam. The 2009 GRE Essentials course reflect Neill's vision for a new and better way to approach the GRE. Many of those methods are contained in this book. He currently lives in New York City and, when he is not working on the GRE in the R&D department, he designs restaurants and runs supper club.

NOTES

NOTES

NOTES

NOTES

NOTES

NOTES

More expert advice from
The Princeton Review

Give yourself the best chances for getting into the graduate school of your choice with **The Princeton Review**. We can help you get higher test scores, make the most informed choices, and make the most of your experience once you get there. We can also help you make the career move that will let you use your skills and education to their best advantage.

Cracking the GRE, 2009 Edition
978-0-375-42863-0 • $21.00/C$23.00

Cracking the GRE with DVD, 2009 Edition
978-0-375-42864-7 • $33.95/C$37.95

Cracking the GRE Biology Test, 5th Edition
978-0-375-76488-2 • $18.00/C$26.00

Cracking the GRE Chemistry Test, 3rd Edition
978-0-375-76489-9 • $18.00/C$26.00

Cracking the GRE Literature Test, 5th Edition
978-0-375-76490-5 • $18.00/C$26.00

Cracking the GRE Math Test, 3rd Edition
978-0-375-76491-2 • $18.00/C$26.00

Cracking the GRE Psychology Test, 7th Edition
978-0-375-76492-9 • $18.00/C$26.00

Verbal Workout for the GRE, 3rd Edition
978-0-375-76573-5 • $19.00/C$25.00

Graduate School Companion
978-0-375-76574-2 • $14.95/C$19.95

Best Entry-Level Jobs, 2008 Edition
978-0-375-76599-5 • $16.95/C$21.95

Guide to Your Career, 6th Edition
978-0-375-76561-2 • $19.95/C$26.95

Available at Bookstores Everywhere
www.PrincetonReview.com